DOWNERS GROVE PUBLIC LIBRARY

3 1191 00709 8312

W9-AUM-469

WITHDRAWN
DOWNERS GROVE PUBLIC LIBRARY

IN SF SUPERMAN

Superman

Downers Grove Public Library
1050 Curtiss St.
Downers Grove, IL 60515

OUR
WORLDS
AT WAR

WRITERS

JEPH LOEB
PHIL JIMENEZ
JOE KELLY
JOE CASEY
PETER DAVID
TODD DEZAGO
MARK SCHULTZ

PENCILLERS

PHIL JIMENEZ
MIKE WIERINGO
DOUG MAHNKE
ED McGUINNESS
PASCUAL FERRY
CARLO BARBERI
KANO
TODD NAUCK
MARK BUCKINGHAM
DUNCAN ROULEAU
YVEL GUICHET
BILL SIENKIEWICZ

INKERS

MARLO ALQUIZA
ANDY LANNING
JOSÉ MARZÁN, JR.
CAM SMITH
KEITH CHAMPAGNE
TOM NGUYEN
JUAN VLASCO
WAYNE FAUCHER
WALDEN WONG
DUNCAN ROULEAU
MARK MORALES
LARY STUCKER
BILL SIENKIEWICZ
DEXTER VINES

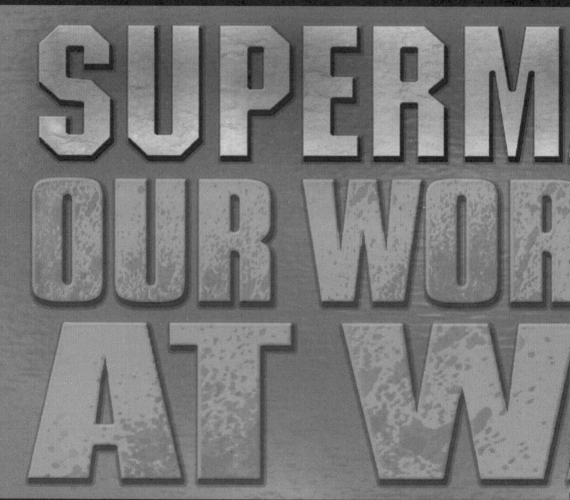

SUPERMAN: OUR WORLDS AT WAR

SUPERMAN CREATED BY JERRY SIEGEL AND JOE SHUSTER
WONDER WOMAN CREATED BY WILLIAM MOULTON MARSTON.
IMPULSE CREATED BY MARK WAID AND MIKE WIERINGO.
BATMAN CREATED BY BOB KANE.

COLORISTS

WILDSTORM FX
PATRICIA MULVIHILL
JASON WRIGHT
ZYLONOL STUDIO
TANYA AND
RICHARD HORIE
TOM McCRAW

LETTERERS

RICHARD STARKINGS
COMICRAFT
KEN LOPEZ
JANICE CHIANG
BILL OAKLEY

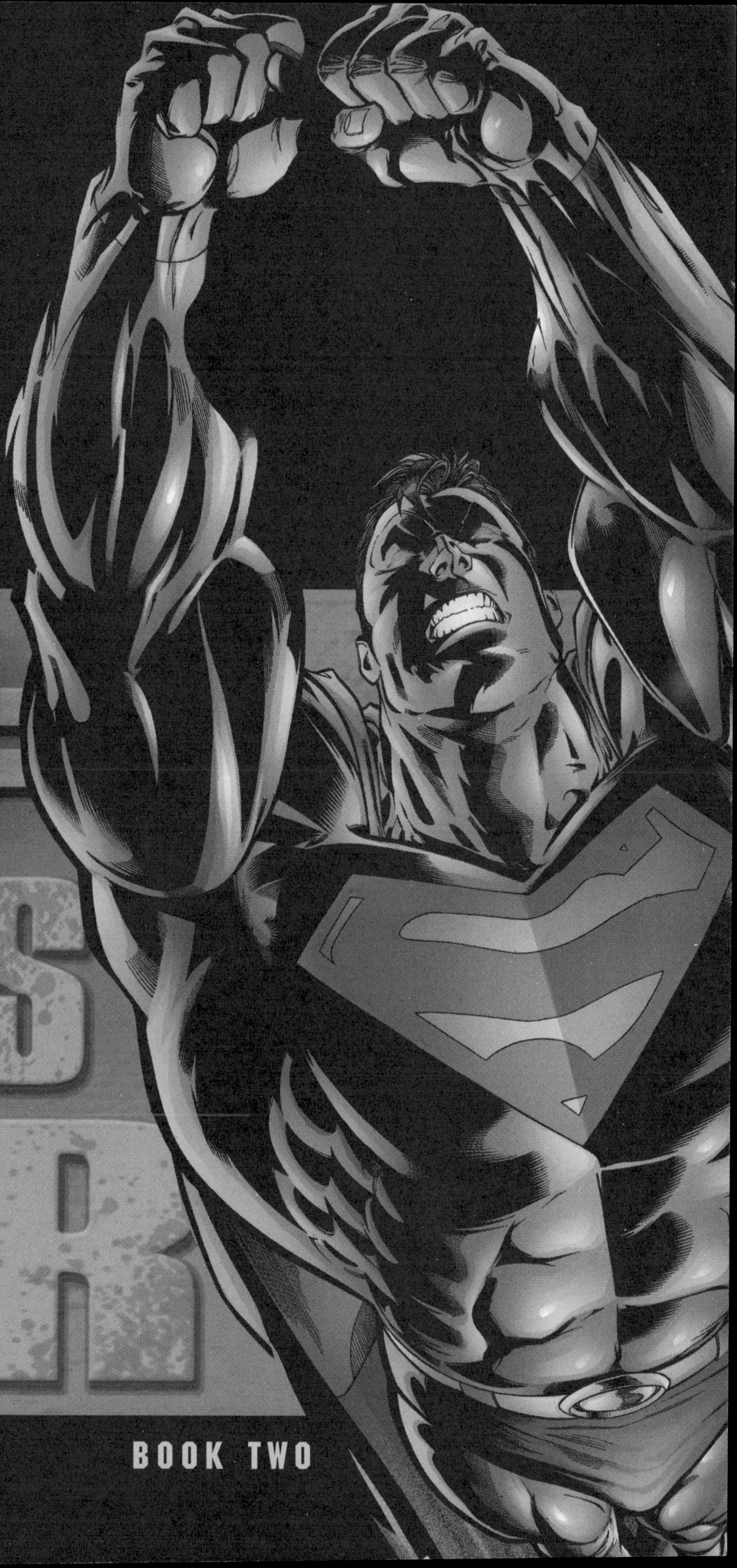

BOOK TWO

VP-EXECUTIVE EDITOR

VP-EDITORIAL

Eddie Berganza
Mike McAvennie
EDITORS-ORIGINAL SERIES

Nick J. Napolitano
EDITOR-COLLECTED EDITION

Tom Palmer
ASSISTANT EDITOR-ORIGINAL SERIES

Scott Nybakken
ASSOCIATE EDITOR-COLLECTED EDITION

Amie Brockway-Metcalf
ART DIRECTOR

Georg Brewer
VP-DESIGN & RETAIL PRODUCT DEVELOPMENT

Richard Bruning
VP-CREATIVE DIRECTOR

Joel Ehrlich
SENIOR VP-ADVERTISING & PROMOTIONS

Alison Gill
VP-MANUFACTURING

Lillian Laserson
VP & GENERAL COUNSEL

Jim Lee
EDITORIAL DIRECTOR-WILDSTORM

David McKillips
VP-ADVERTISING

John Nee
VP-BUSINESS DEVELOPMENT

Cheryl Rubin
VP-LICENSING & MERCHANDISING

Bob Wayne
VP-SALES & MARKETING

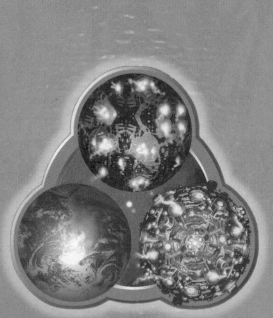

SUPERMAN: OUR WORLDS AT WAR BOOK TWO
PUBLISHED BY DC COMICS. COVER AND COMPILATION COPYRIGHT © 2002 DC COMICS. ALL RIGHTS RESERVED.

ORIGINALLY PUBLISHED IN SINGLE MAGAZINE FORM AS WONDER WOMAN 172, SUPERMAN 173, YOUNG JUSTICE 36,
ADVENTURES OF SUPERMAN 595, IMPULSE 77, SUPERBOY 91, SUPERMAN: THE MAN OF STEEL 117, WONDER WOMAN 173,
ACTION COMICS 782, WORLD'S FINEST: OUR WORLDS AT WAR 1. COPYRIGHT © 2001 DC COMICS. ALL RIGHTS RESERVED.
ALL CHARACTERS, THEIR DISTINCTIVE LIKENESSES AND RELATED INDICIA FEATURED IN THIS PUBLICATION ARE TRADEMARKS OF DC COMICS.
THE STORIES, CHARACTERS, AND INCIDENTS FEATURED IN THIS PUBLICATION ARE ENTIRELY FICTIONAL.
DC COMICS DOES NOT READ OR ACCEPT UNSOLICITED SUBMISSIONS OF IDEAS, STORIES OR ARTWORK.

DC COMICS, 1700 BROADWAY, NEW YORK, NY 10019. A DIVISION OF WARNER BROS. — AN AOL TIME WARNER COMPANY
PRINTED IN CANADA. FIRST PRINTING.
ISBN: 1-56389-916-7
COVER ILLUSTRATION BY MIKE WIERINGO & JOSÉ MARZÁN, JR. - COVER COLOR BY RICHARD & TANYA HORIE.

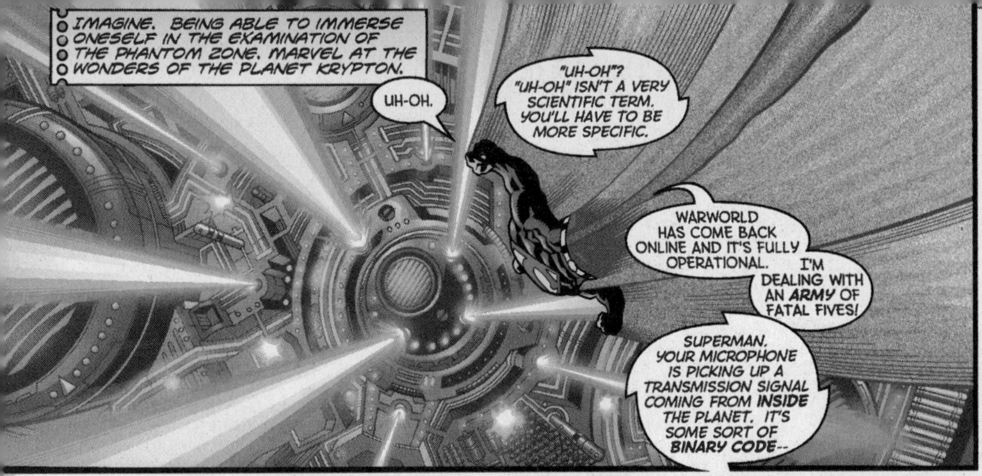
IMAGINE. BEING ABLE TO IMMERSE ONESELF IN THE EXAMINATION OF THE PHANTOM ZONE. MARVEL AT THE WONDERS OF THE PLANET KRYPTON.
UH-OH.
"UH-OH"? "UH-OH" ISN'T A VERY SCIENTIFIC TERM. YOU'LL HAVE TO BE MORE SPECIFIC.
WARWORLD HAS COME BACK ONLINE AND IT'S FULLY OPERATIONAL.
I'M DEALING WITH AN ARMY OF FATAL FIVES!
SUPERMAN, YOUR MICROPHONE IS PICKING UP A TRANSMISSION SIGNAL COMING FROM INSIDE THE PLANET. IT'S SOME SORT OF BINARY CODE--

THE WAR SO FAR...

Investigating the mysterious disappearance of Pluto, Superman discovers that the farthest planet from the sun has been replaced — by the Warworld! After defeating holographic images of the Fatal Five, Superman destroys Warworld's power source, apparently causing its destruction. But Brainiac 13 has simply allowed Superman to believe that Warworld was destroyed so that it can proceed undetected into the coming conflict.

Meanwhile, in anticipation of that conflict, the population of Metropolis has been transplanted to the orbital space ark Paradocs (an outer space M.A.S.H. unit) to keep them out of the line of fire, clearing the way for the city's alien technology to be used as a weapon in the coming war. Superman is then called to Berlin to combat the dictator of Pokolistan, known as the General. In the midst of a heated battle with the General — now revealed to be General Zod — Superman watches helplessly as the invader, Imperiex, launches its first strike at Earth, utterly destroying Topeka, Kansas.

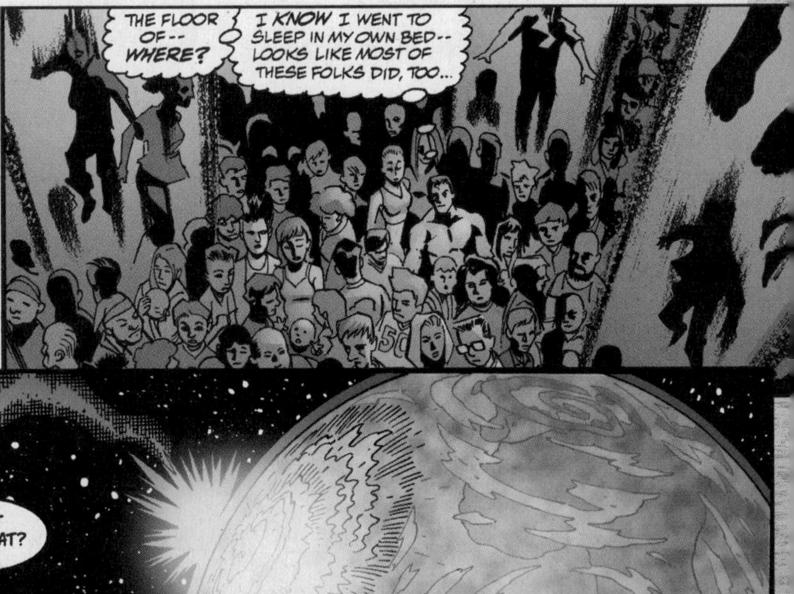
THE FLOOR OF-- WHERE?
I KNOW I WENT TO SLEEP IN MY OWN BED-- LOOKS LIKE MOST OF THESE FOLKS DID, TOO...

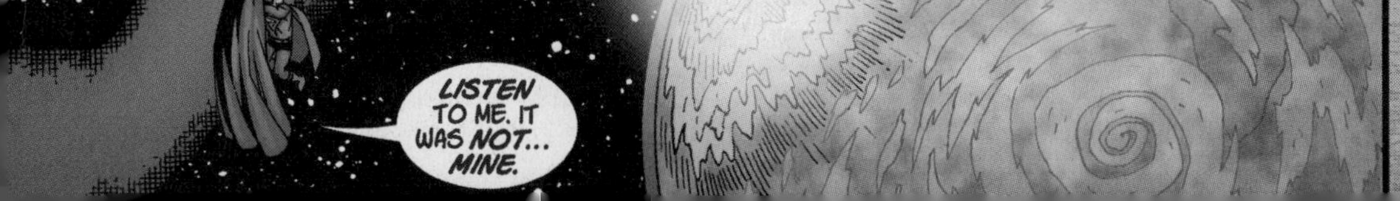
WHAT WAS THAT?
LISTEN TO ME. IT WAS NOT... MINE.

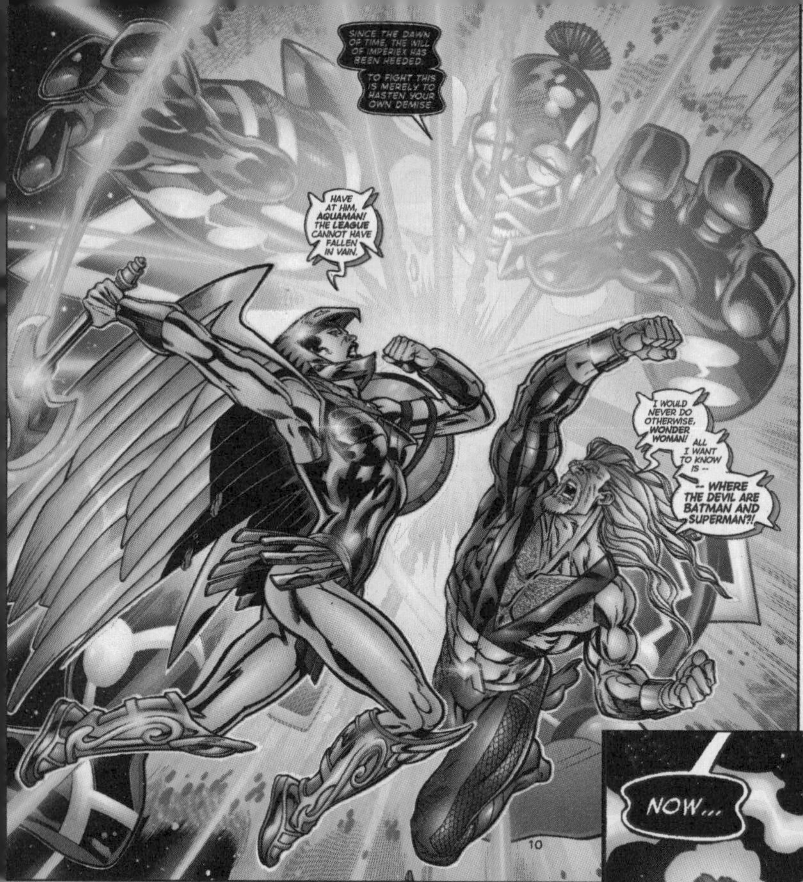
SINCE THE DAWN OF TIME, THE WILL OF IMPERIEX HAS BEEN HEEDED.
TO FIGHT THIS IS MERELY TO HASTEN YOUR OWN DEMISE.
HAVE AT HIM, AQUAMAN! THE LEAGUE CANNOT HAVE FALLEN IN VAIN.
I WOULD NEVER DO OTHERWISE, WONDER WOMAN!
ALL I WANT TO KNOW IS --
-- WHERE THE DEVIL ARE BATMAN AND SUPERMAN?!
10

With all-out war now raging, the JLA intercepts a swarm of Imperiex probes that are attempting to rain destruction down onto the Earth. But the probes are too powerful and too numerous even for the World's Greatest Heroes. One by one, the JLA falls to the onslaught — Wonder Woman is mortally wounded, and Aquaman is lost defending Atlantis.

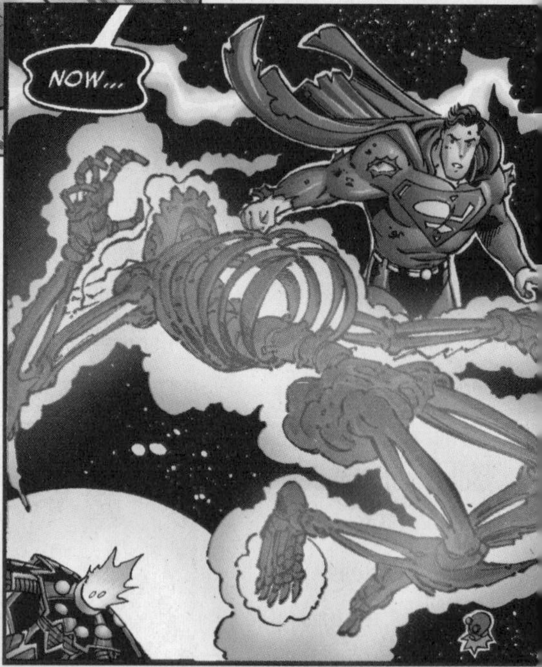
NOW...

In a last-ditch effort, the new Suicide Squad, accompanied by John Henry Irons (Steel), embarks to launch the "Doomsday Project" — releasing the implacable power of Doomsday and sending him against Imperiex. Their mission is a success, but Doomsday slaughters the entire Squad, including Steel, upon his release. Doomsday then confronts Imperiex, but even this seemingly unstoppable force is easily disposed of by the invader's overwhelming might.

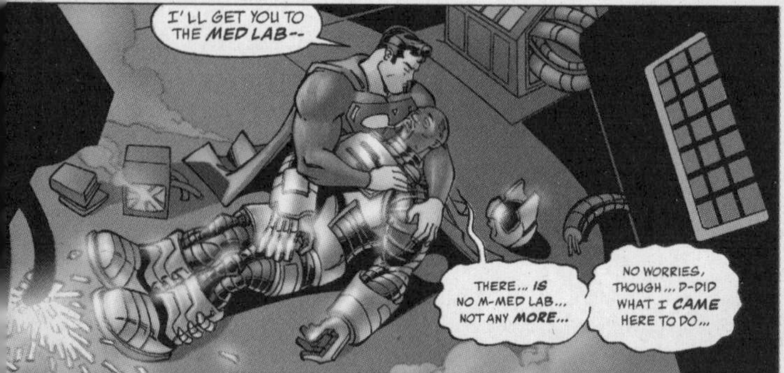
I'LL GET YOU TO THE MED LAB--
THERE... IS NO M-MED LAB... NOT ANY MORE...
NO WORRIES, THOUGH... D-DID WHAT I CAME HERE TO DO...

Finally, a covert mission involving the JSA manages to destroy the Imperiex mother ship, preventing it from producing more probes. But the probes that remain have set their eyes on two targets: Washington, D.C. and the orbiting Paradocs...

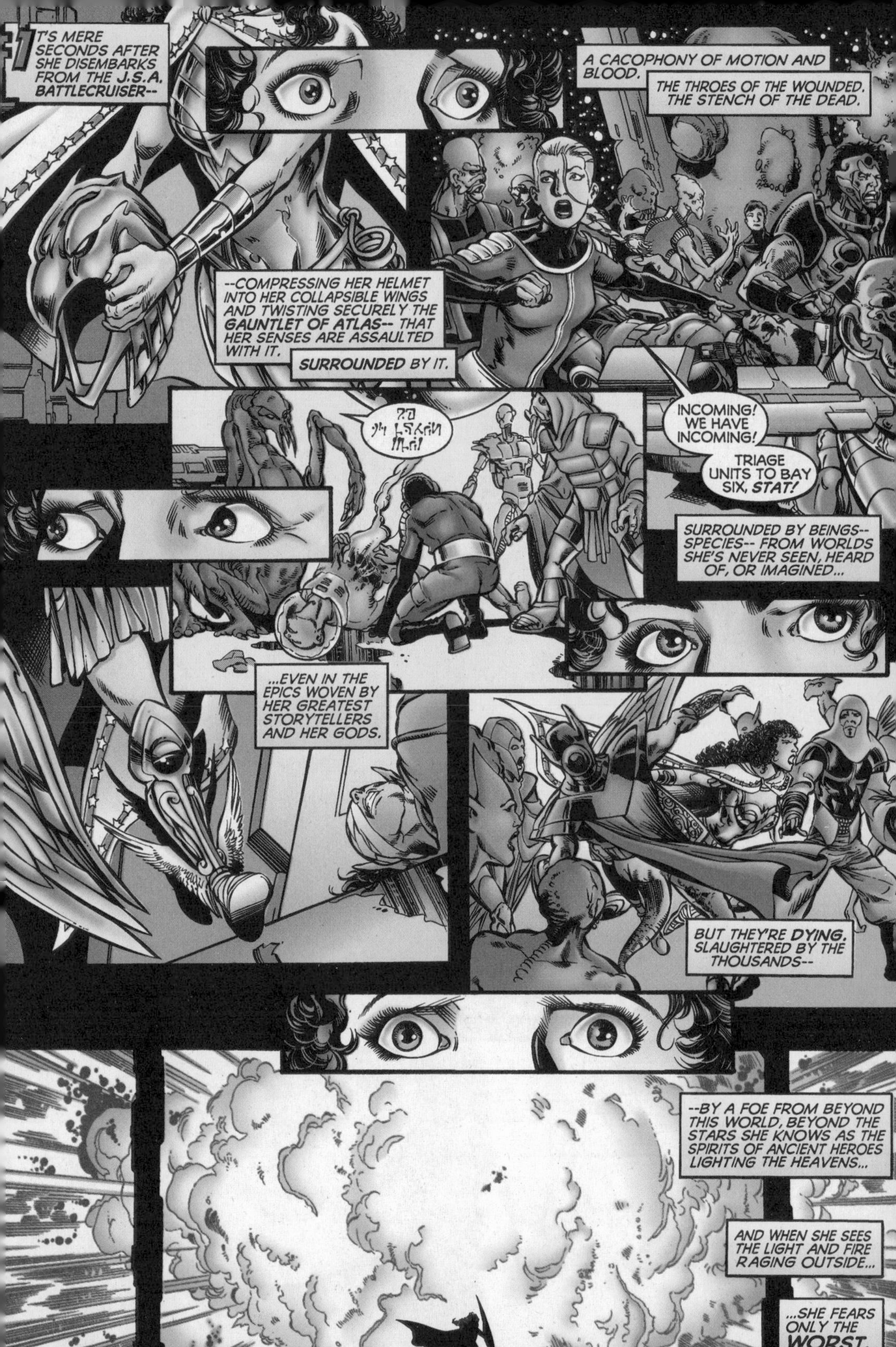
IT'S MERE SECONDS AFTER SHE DISEMBARKS FROM THE J.S.A. BATTLECRUISER--
A CACOPHONY OF MOTION AND BLOOD.
THE THROES OF THE WOUNDED. THE STENCH OF THE DEAD.
--COMPRESSING HER HELMET INTO HER COLLAPSIBLE WINGS AND TWISTING SECURELY THE GAUNTLET OF ATLAS-- THAT HER SENSES ARE ASSAULTED WITH IT.
SURROUNDED BY IT.
INCOMING! WE HAVE INCOMING!
TRIAGE UNITS TO BAY SIX, STAT!
SURROUNDED BY BEINGS-- SPECIES-- FROM WORLDS SHE'S NEVER SEEN, HEARD OF, OR IMAGINED...
...EVEN IN THE EPICS WOVEN BY HER GREATEST STORYTELLERS AND HER GODS.
BUT THEY'RE DYING. SLAUGHTERED BY THE THOUSANDS--
--BY A FOE FROM BEYOND THIS WORLD, BEYOND THE STARS SHE KNOWS AS THE SPIRITS OF ANCIENT HEROES LIGHTING THE HEAVENS...
AND WHEN SHE SEES THE LIGHT AND FIRE RAGING OUTSIDE...
...SHE FEARS ONLY THE WORST.

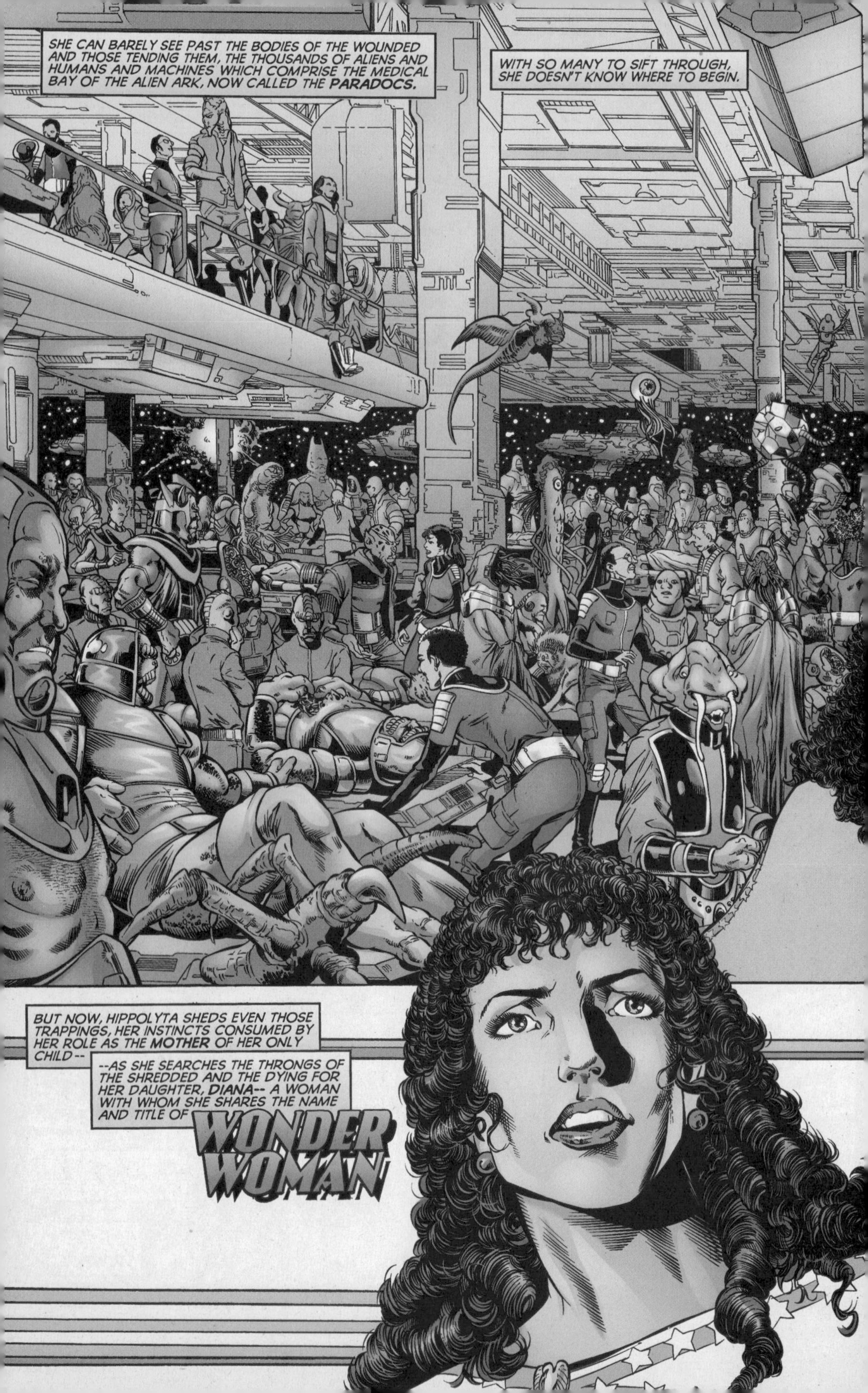
SHE CAN BARELY SEE PAST THE BODIES OF THE WOUNDED AND THOSE TENDING THEM, THE THOUSANDS OF ALIENS AND HUMANS AND MACHINES WHICH COMPRISE THE MEDICAL BAY OF THE ALIEN ARK, NOW CALLED THE PARADOCS.
WITH SO MANY TO SIFT THROUGH, SHE DOESN'T KNOW WHERE TO BEGIN.
BUT NOW, HIPPOLYTA SHEDS EVEN THOSE TRAPPINGS, HER INSTINCTS CONSUMED BY HER ROLE AS THE MOTHER OF HER ONLY CHILD --
--AS SHE SEARCHES THE THRONGS OF THE SHREDDED AND THE DYING FOR HER DAUGHTER, DIANA-- A WOMAN WITH WHOM SHE SHARES THE NAME AND TITLE OF
WONDER WOMAN

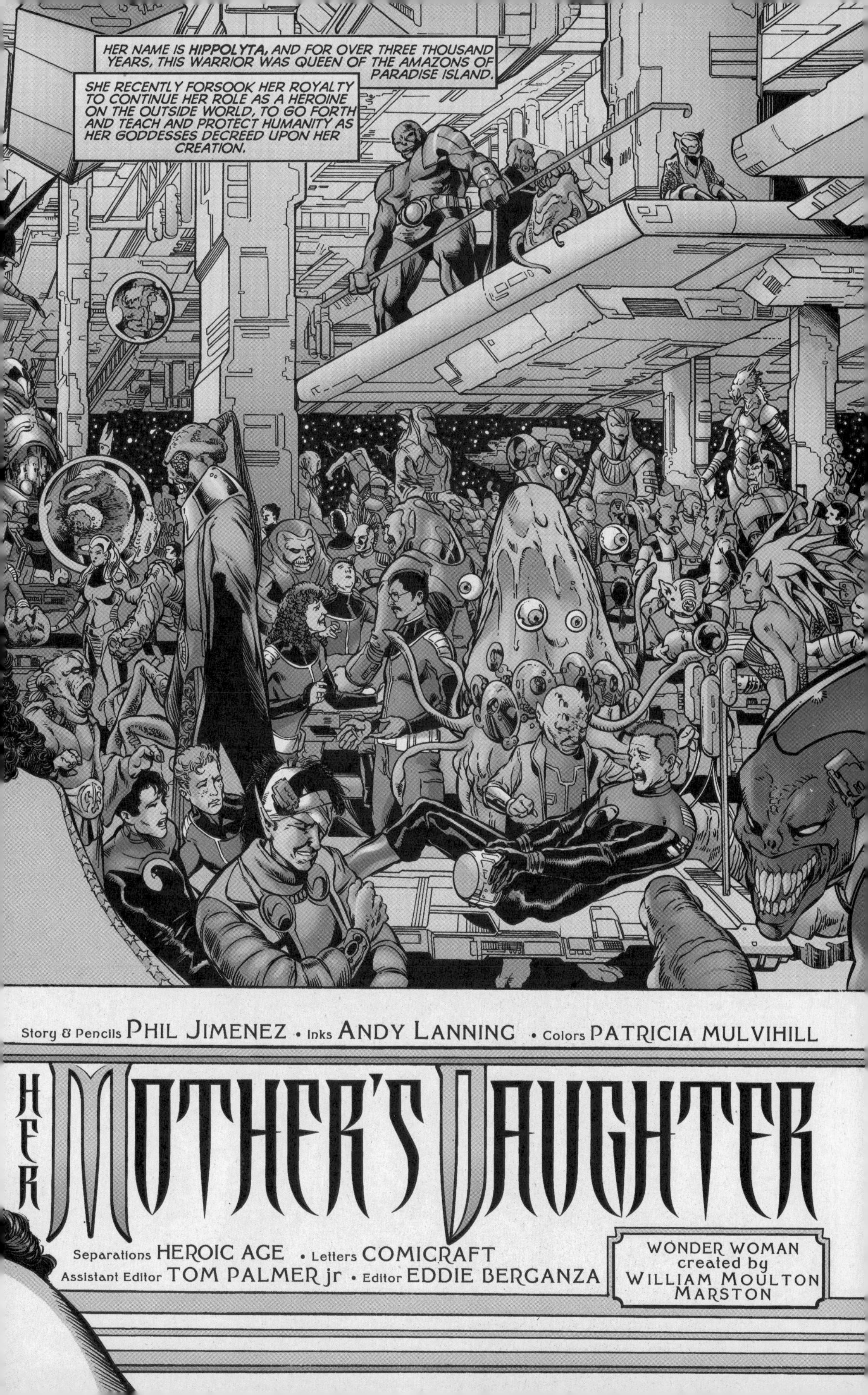
HER NAME IS HIPPOLYTA, AND FOR OVER THREE THOUSAND YEARS, THIS WARRIOR WAS QUEEN OF THE AMAZONS OF PARADISE ISLAND.
SHE RECENTLY FORSOOK HER ROYALTY TO CONTINUE HER ROLE AS A HEROINE ON THE OUTSIDE WORLD, TO GO FORTH AND TEACH AND PROTECT HUMANITY AS HER GODDESSES DECREED UPON HER CREATION.
Story & Pencils PHIL JIMENEZ • Inks ANDY LANNING • Colors PATRICIA MULVIHILL
HER MOTHER'S DAUGHTER
Separations HEROIC AGE • Letters COMICRAFT
Assistant Editor TOM PALMER jr • Editor EDDIE BERGANZA
WONDER WOMAN created by WILLIAM MOULTON MARSTON

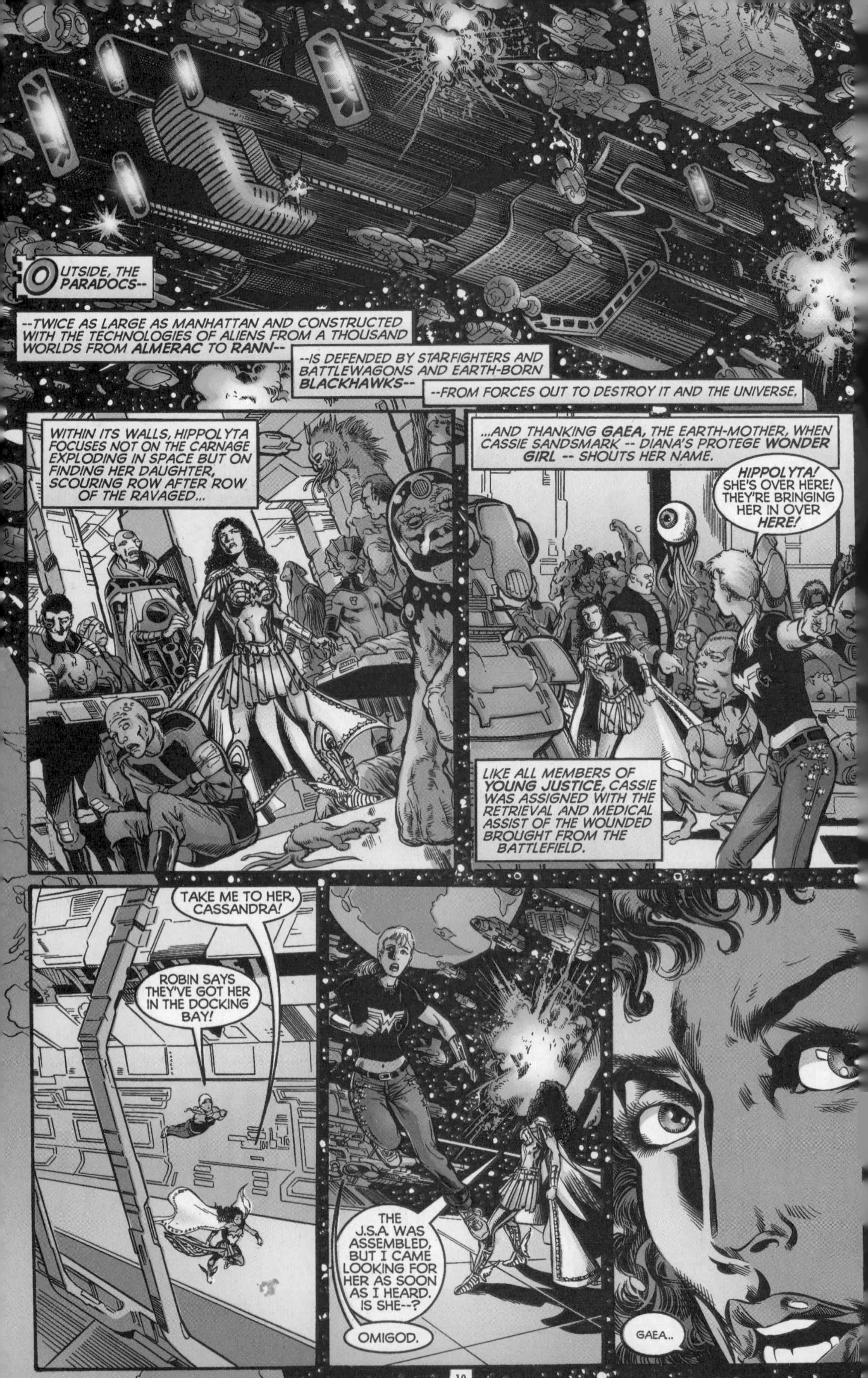
OUTSIDE, THE PARADOCS--
--TWICE AS LARGE AS MANHATTAN AND CONSTRUCTED WITH THE TECHNOLOGIES OF ALIENS FROM A THOUSAND WORLDS FROM ALMERAC TO RANN--
--IS DEFENDED BY STARFIGHTERS AND BATTLEWAGONS AND EARTH-BORN BLACKHAWKS--
--FROM FORCES OUT TO DESTROY IT AND THE UNIVERSE.
WITHIN ITS WALLS, HIPPOLYTA FOCUSES NOT ON THE CARNAGE EXPLODING IN SPACE BUT ON FINDING HER DAUGHTER, SCOURING ROW AFTER ROW OF THE RAVAGED...
...AND THANKING GAEA, THE EARTH-MOTHER, WHEN CASSIE SANDSMARK -- DIANA'S PROTEGE WONDER GIRL -- SHOUTS HER NAME.
HIPPOLYTA! SHE'S OVER HERE! THEY'RE BRINGING HER IN OVER HERE!
LIKE ALL MEMBERS OF YOUNG JUSTICE, CASSIE WAS ASSIGNED WITH THE RETRIEVAL AND MEDICAL ASSIST OF THE WOUNDED BROUGHT FROM THE BATTLEFIELD.
TAKE ME TO HER, CASSANDRA!
ROBIN SAYS THEY'VE GOT HER IN THE DOCKING BAY!
THE J.S.A. WAS ASSEMBLED, BUT I CAME LOOKING FOR HER AS SOON AS I HEARD. IS SHE--?
OMIGOD.
GAEA..

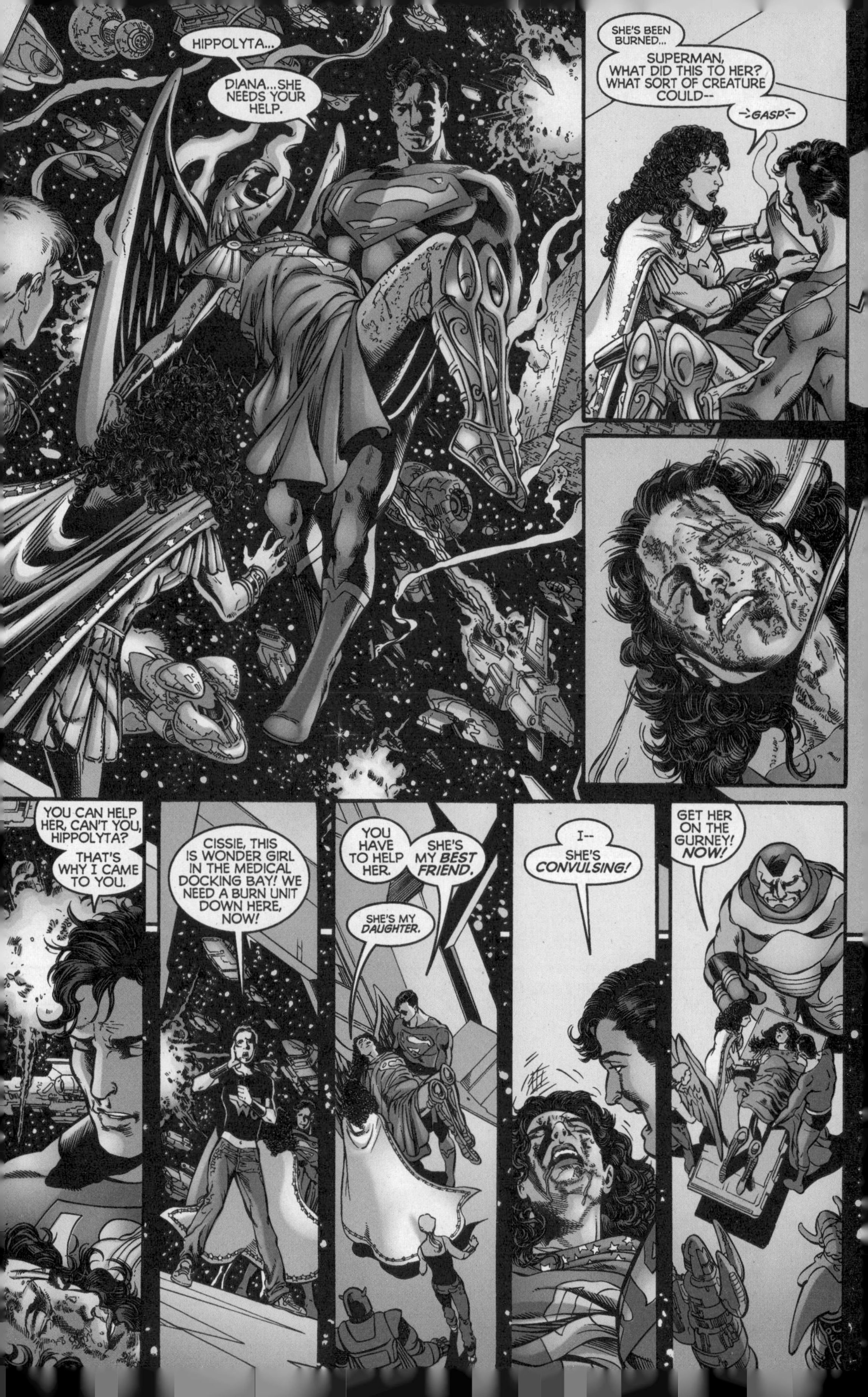
HIPPOLYTA...
DIANA...SHE NEEDS YOUR HELP.
SHE'S BEEN BURNED...
SUPERMAN, WHAT DID THIS TO HER? WHAT SORT OF CREATURE COULD--
GASP
YOU CAN HELP HER, CAN'T YOU, HIPPOLYTA?
THAT'S WHY I CAME TO YOU.
CISSIE, THIS IS WONDER GIRL IN THE MEDICAL DOCKING BAY! WE NEED A BURN UNIT DOWN HERE, NOW!
YOU HAVE TO HELP HER.
SHE'S MY BEST FRIEND.
SHE'S MY DAUGHTER.
I--
SHE'S CONVULSING!
GET HER ON THE GURNEY! NOW!

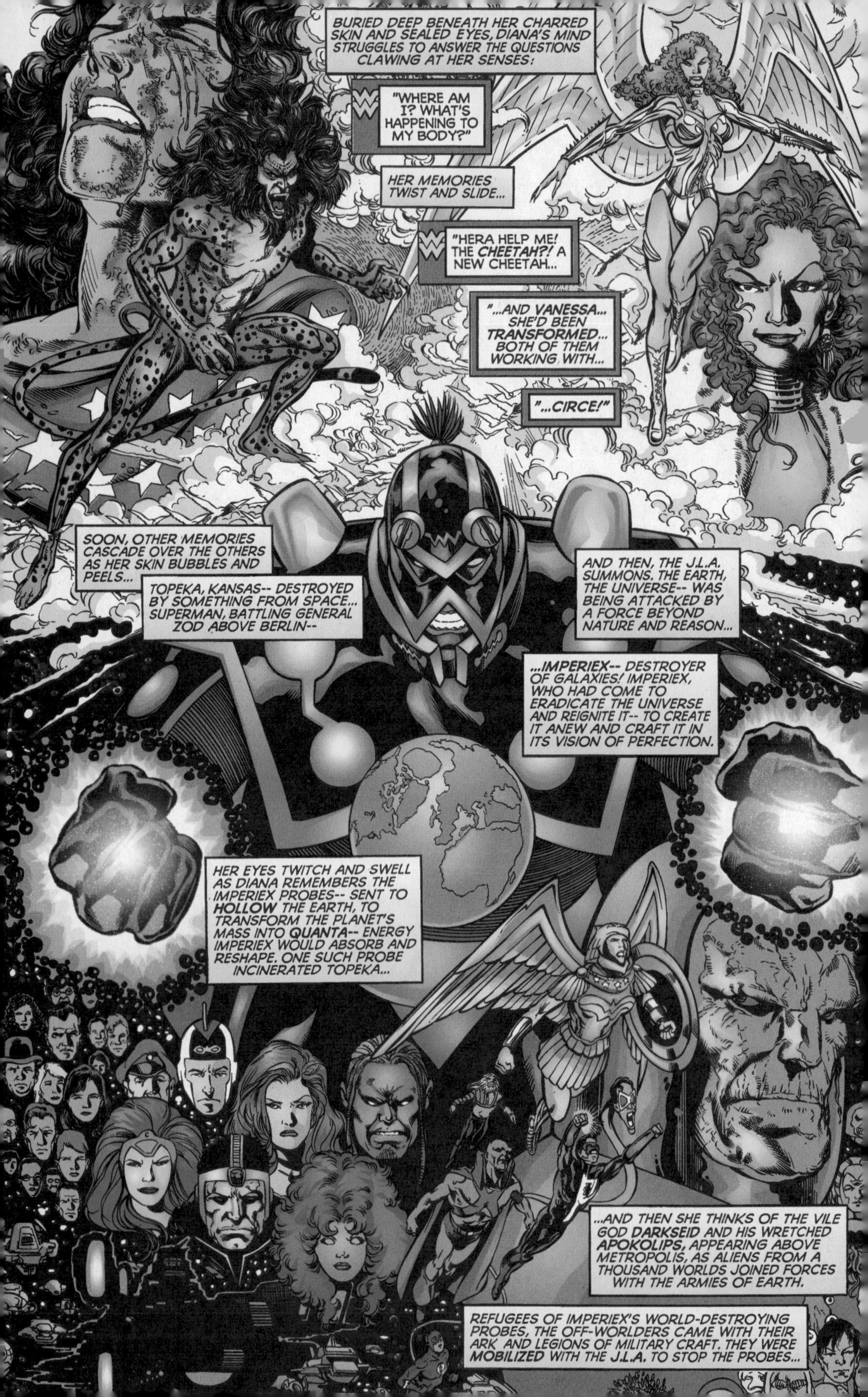
BURIED DEEP BENEATH HER CHARRED SKIN AND SEALED EYES, DIANA'S MIND STRUGGLES TO ANSWER THE QUESTIONS CLAWING AT HER SENSES:
"WHERE AM I? WHAT'S HAPPENING TO MY BODY?"
HER MEMORIES TWIST AND SLIDE...
"HERA HELP ME! THE CHEETAH?! A NEW CHEETAH...
"...AND VANESSA... SHE'D BEEN TRANSFORMED... BOTH OF THEM WORKING WITH...
"...CIRCE!"
SOON, OTHER MEMORIES CASCADE OVER THE OTHERS AS HER SKIN BUBBLES AND PEELS...
TOPEKA, KANSAS-- DESTROYED BY SOMETHING FROM SPACE... SUPERMAN, BATTLING GENERAL ZOD ABOVE BERLIN--
AND THEN, THE J.L.A. SUMMONS. THE EARTH, THE UNIVERSE-- WAS BEING ATTACKED BY A FORCE BEYOND NATURE AND REASON...
...IMPERIEX-- DESTROYER OF GALAXIES! IMPERIEX, WHO HAD COME TO ERADICATE THE UNIVERSE AND REIGNITE IT-- TO CREATE IT ANEW AND CRAFT IT IN ITS VISION OF PERFECTION.
HER EYES TWITCH AND SWELL AS DIANA REMEMBERS THE IMPERIEX PROBES-- SENT TO HOLLOW THE EARTH, TO TRANSFORM THE PLANET'S MASS INTO QUANTA-- ENERGY IMPERIEX WOULD ABSORB AND RESHAPE. ONE SUCH PROBE INCINERATED TOPEKA...
...AND THEN SHE THINKS OF THE VILE GOD DARKSEID AND HIS WRETCHED APOKOLIPS, APPEARING ABOVE METROPOLIS, AS ALIENS FROM A THOUSAND WORLDS JOINED FORCES WITH THE ARMIES OF EARTH.
REFUGEES OF IMPERIEX'S WORLD-DESTROYING PROBES, THE OFF-WORLDERS CAME WITH THEIR ARK AND LEGIONS OF MILITARY CRAFT. THEY WERE MOBILIZED WITH THE J.L.A. TO STOP THE PROBES...

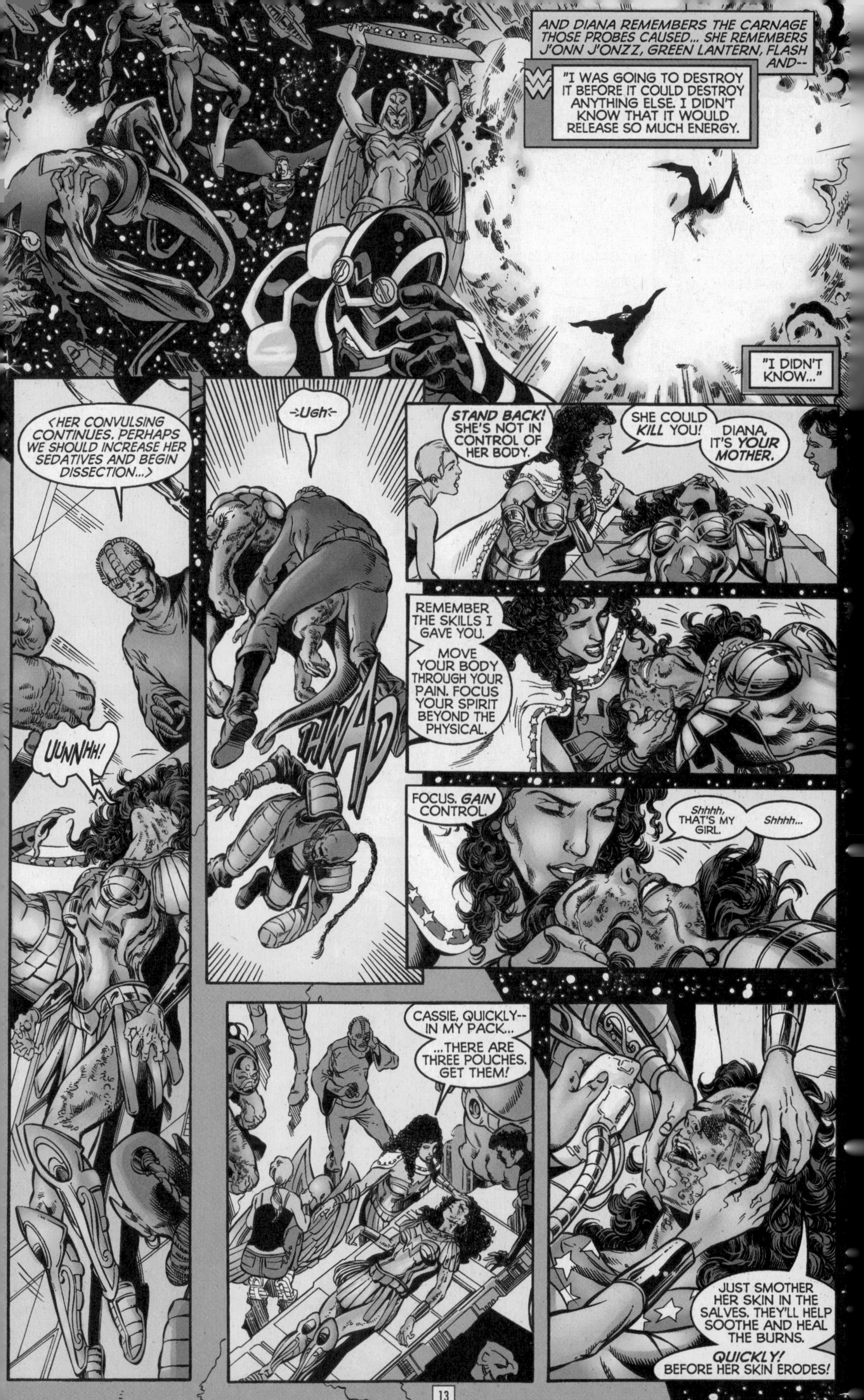

AND DIANA REMEMBERS THE CARNAGE THOSE PROBES CAUSED... SHE REMEMBERS J'ONN J'ONZZ, GREEN LANTERN, FLASH AND--
"I WAS GOING TO DESTROY IT BEFORE IT COULD DESTROY ANYTHING ELSE. I DIDN'T KNOW THAT IT WOULD RELEASE SO MUCH ENERGY.
"I DIDN'T KNOW..."
<HER CONVULSING CONTINUES. PERHAPS WE SHOULD INCREASE HER SEDATIVES AND BEGIN DISSECTION...>
UUNNHH!
-Ugh-
THWAP
STAND BACK! SHE'S NOT IN CONTROL OF HER BODY.
SHE COULD KILL YOU!
DIANA, IT'S YOUR MOTHER.
REMEMBER THE SKILLS I GAVE YOU.
MOVE YOUR BODY THROUGH YOUR PAIN. FOCUS YOUR SPIRIT BEYOND THE PHYSICAL.
FOCUS. GAIN CONTROL.
Shhhh, THAT'S MY GIRL.
Shhhh...
CASSIE, QUICKLY-- IN MY PACK...
...THERE ARE THREE POUCHES. GET THEM!
JUST SMOTHER HER SKIN IN THE SALVES. THEY'LL HELP SOOTHE AND HEAL THE BURNS.
QUICKLY! BEFORE HER SKIN ERODES!

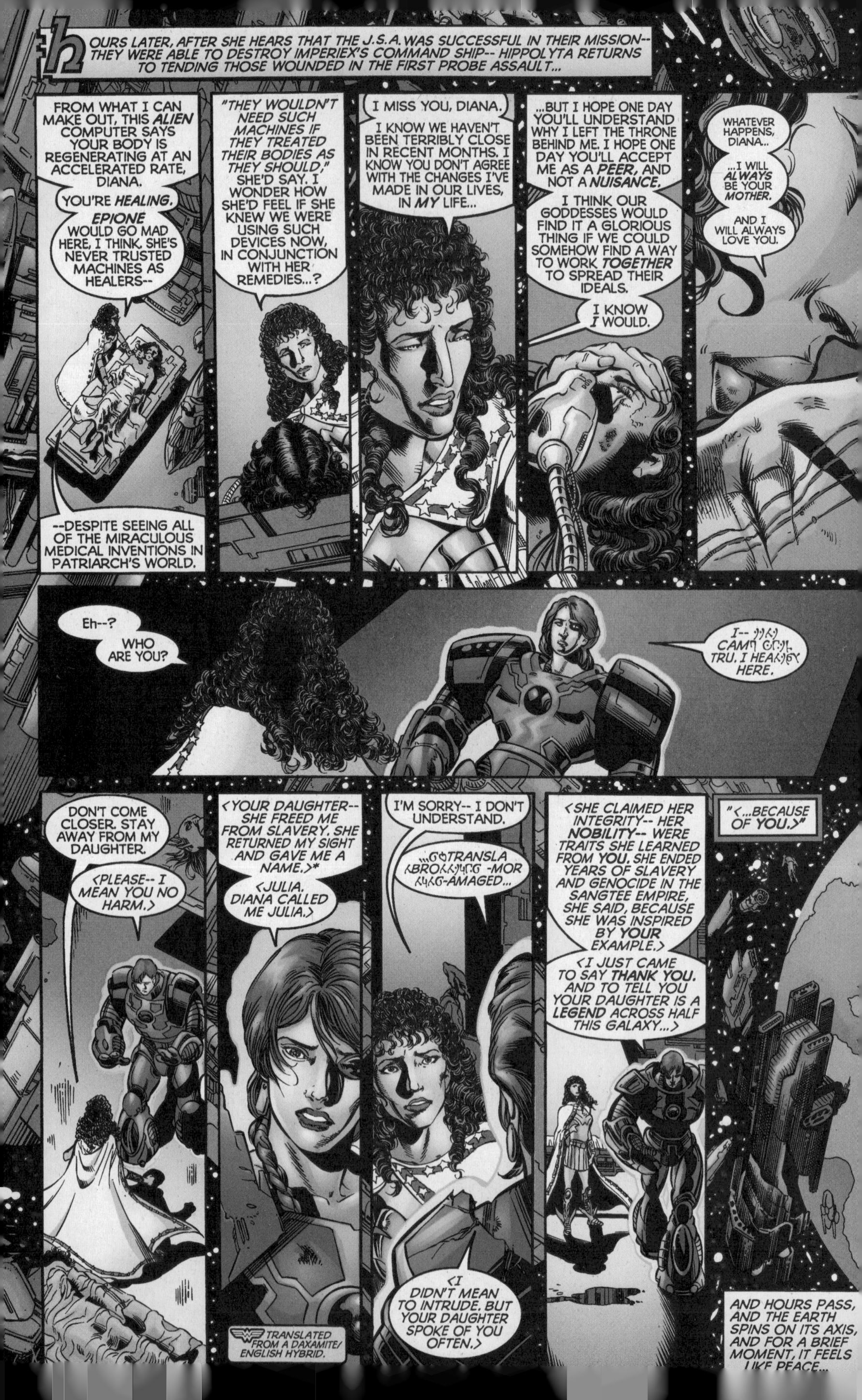
HOURS LATER, AFTER SHE HEARS THAT THE J.S.A. WAS SUCCESSFUL IN THEIR MISSION-- THEY WERE ABLE TO DESTROY IMPERIEX'S COMMAND SHIP-- HIPPOLYTA RETURNS TO TENDING THOSE WOUNDED IN THE FIRST PROBE ASSAULT...
FROM WHAT I CAN MAKE OUT, THIS ALIEN COMPUTER SAYS YOUR BODY IS REGENERATING AT AN ACCELERATED RATE, DIANA.
YOU'RE HEALING.
EPIONE WOULD GO MAD HERE, I THINK. SHE'S NEVER TRUSTED MACHINES AS HEALERS--
--DESPITE SEEING ALL OF THE MIRACULOUS MEDICAL INVENTIONS IN PATRIARCH'S WORLD.
"THEY WOULDN'T NEED SUCH MACHINES IF THEY TREATED THEIR BODIES AS THEY SHOULD," SHE'D SAY. I WONDER HOW SHE'D FEEL IF SHE KNEW WE WERE USING SUCH DEVICES NOW, IN CONJUNCTION WITH HER REMEDIES...?
I MISS YOU, DIANA.
I KNOW WE HAVEN'T BEEN TERRIBLY CLOSE IN RECENT MONTHS. I KNOW YOU DON'T AGREE WITH THE CHANGES I'VE MADE IN OUR LIVES, IN MY LIFE...
...BUT I HOPE ONE DAY YOU'LL UNDERSTAND WHY I LEFT THE THRONE BEHIND ME. I HOPE ONE DAY YOU'LL ACCEPT ME AS A PEER, AND NOT A NUISANCE.
I THINK OUR GODDESSES WOULD FIND IT A GLORIOUS THING IF WE COULD SOMEHOW FIND A WAY TO WORK TOGETHER TO SPREAD THEIR IDEALS.
I KNOW I WOULD.
WHATEVER HAPPENS, DIANA...
...I WILL ALWAYS BE YOUR MOTHER.
AND I WILL ALWAYS LOVE YOU.
Eh--? WHO ARE YOU?
DON'T COME CLOSER. STAY AWAY FROM MY DAUGHTER.
<PLEASE-- I MEAN YOU NO HARM.>
<YOUR DAUGHTER-- SHE FREED ME FROM SLAVERY. SHE RETURNED MY SIGHT AND GAVE ME A NAME.>*
<JULIA. DIANA CALLED ME JULIA.>
*TRANSLATED FROM A DAXAMITE/ ENGLISH HYBRID.
I'M SORRY-- I DON'T UNDERSTAND.
<I DIDN'T MEAN TO INTRUDE. BUT YOUR DAUGHTER SPOKE OF YOU OFTEN.>
<SHE CLAIMED HER INTEGRITY-- HER NOBILITY-- WERE TRAITS SHE LEARNED FROM YOU. SHE ENDED YEARS OF SLAVERY AND GENOCIDE IN THE SANGTEE EMPIRE, SHE SAID, BECAUSE SHE WAS INSPIRED BY YOUR EXAMPLE.>
<I JUST CAME TO SAY THANK YOU. AND TO TELL YOU YOUR DAUGHTER IS A LEGEND ACROSS HALF THIS GALAXY...>
"<...BECAUSE OF YOU.>"
AND HOURS PASS, AND THE EARTH SPINS ON ITS AXIS, AND FOR A BRIEF MOMENT, IT FEELS LIKE PEACE...

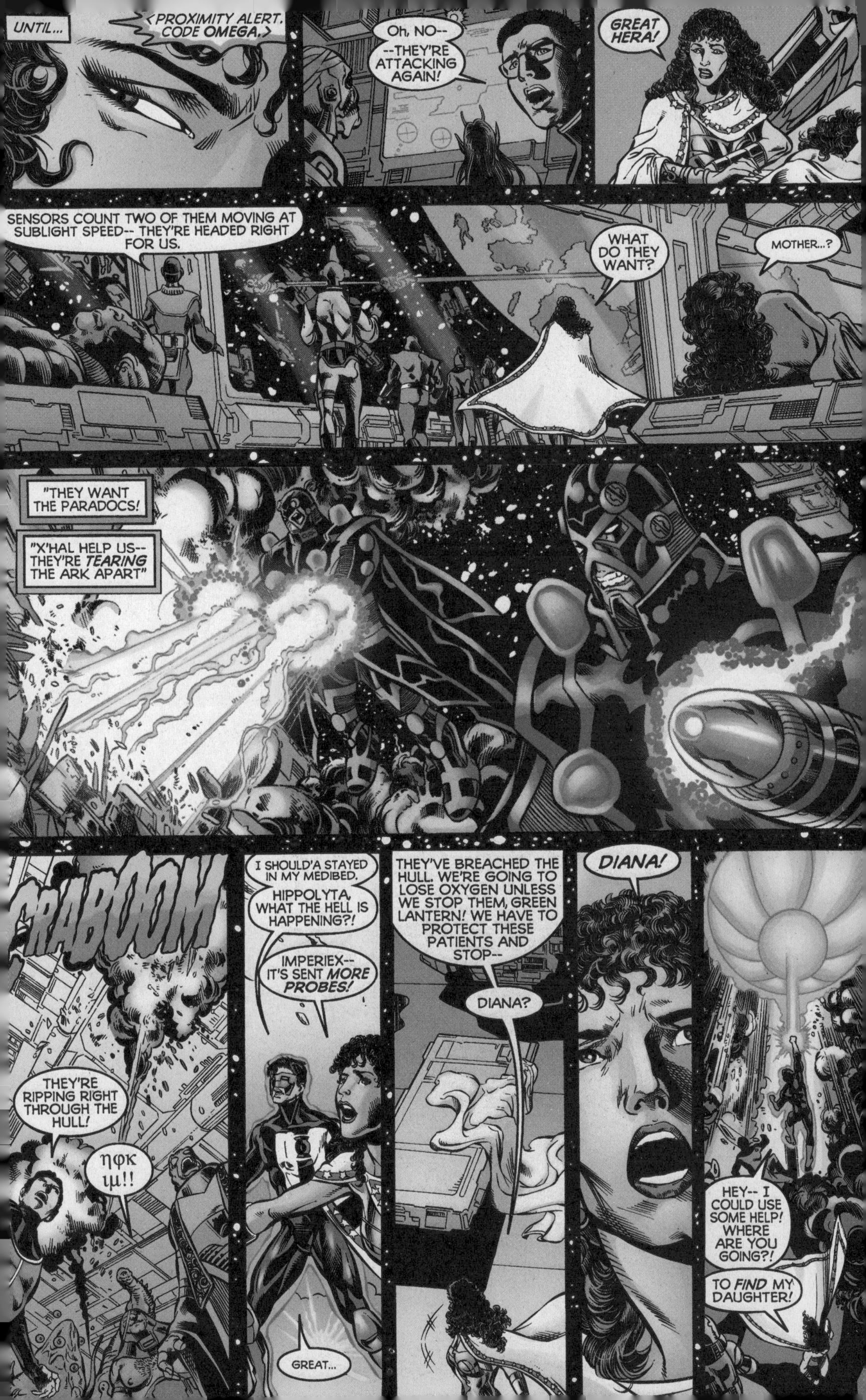
UNTIL...
<PROXIMITY ALERT. CODE OMEGA.>
Oh, NO--
--THEY'RE ATTACKING AGAIN!
GREAT HERA!
SENSORS COUNT TWO OF THEM MOVING AT SUBLIGHT SPEED-- THEY'RE HEADED RIGHT FOR US.
WHAT DO THEY WANT?
MOTHER...?
"THEY WANT THE PARADOCS!
"X'HAL HELP US-- THEY'RE TEARING THE ARK APART"
CRABOOM
THEY'RE RIPPING RIGHT THROUGH THE HULL!
ηφκ ιμ!!
I SHOULD'A STAYED IN MY MEDIBED.
HIPPOLYTA, WHAT THE HELL IS HAPPENING?!
IMPERIEX-- IT'S SENT MORE PROBES!
GREAT...
THEY'VE BREACHED THE HULL. WE'RE GOING TO LOSE OXYGEN UNLESS WE STOP THEM, GREEN LANTERN! WE HAVE TO PROTECT THESE PATIENTS AND STOP--
DIANA?
DIANA!
HEY-- I COULD USE SOME HELP! WHERE ARE YOU GOING?!
TO FIND MY DAUGHTER!

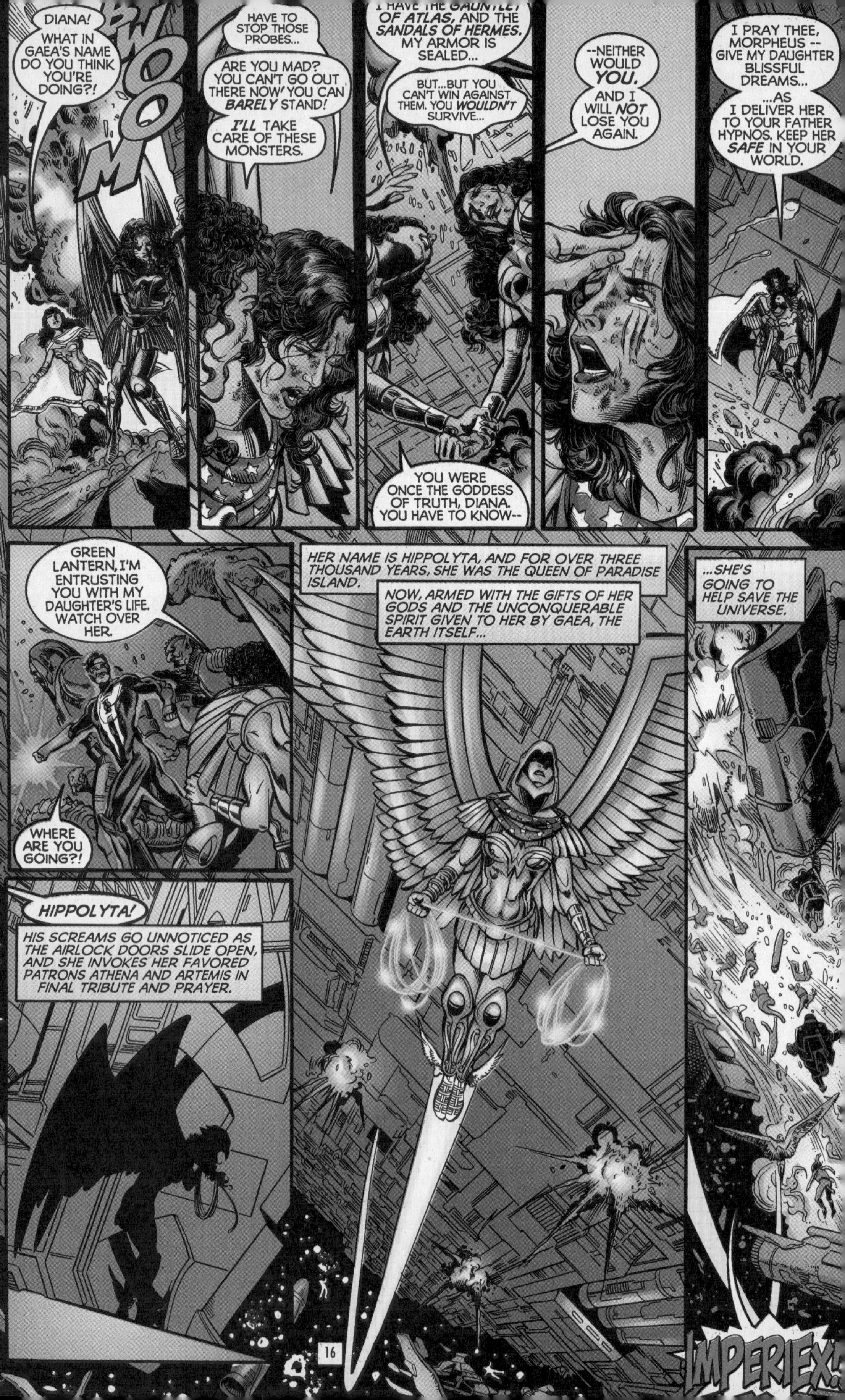

DIANA! WHAT IN GAEA'S NAME DO YOU THINK YOU'RE DOING?!
BWOOOM
HAVE TO STOP THOSE PROBES...
ARE YOU MAD? YOU CAN'T GO OUT THERE NOW! YOU CAN BARELY STAND!
I'LL TAKE CARE OF THESE MONSTERS.
I HAVE THE GAUNTLET OF ATLAS, AND THE SANDALS OF HERMES. MY ARMOR IS SEALED...
BUT...BUT YOU CAN'T WIN AGAINST THEM. YOU WOULDN'T SURVIVE...
--NEITHER WOULD YOU.
AND I WILL NOT LOSE YOU AGAIN.
YOU WERE ONCE THE GODDESS OF TRUTH, DIANA. YOU HAVE TO KNOW--
I PRAY THEE, MORPHEUS -- GIVE MY DAUGHTER BLISSFUL DREAMS...
...AS I DELIVER HER TO YOUR FATHER HYPNOS. KEEP HER SAFE IN YOUR WORLD.
GREEN LANTERN, I'M ENTRUSTING YOU WITH MY DAUGHTER'S LIFE. WATCH OVER HER.
WHERE ARE YOU GOING?!
HER NAME IS HIPPOLYTA, AND FOR OVER THREE THOUSAND YEARS, SHE WAS THE QUEEN OF PARADISE ISLAND.
NOW, ARMED WITH THE GIFTS OF HER GODS AND THE UNCONQUERABLE SPIRIT GIVEN TO HER BY GAEA, THE EARTH ITSELF...
...SHE'S GOING TO HELP SAVE THE UNIVERSE.
HIPPOLYTA!
HIS SCREAMS GO UNNOTICED AS THE AIRLOCK DOORS SLIDE OPEN, AND SHE INVOKES HER FAVORED PATRONS ATHENA AND ARTEMIS IN FINAL TRIBUTE AND PRAYER.
IMPERIEX!

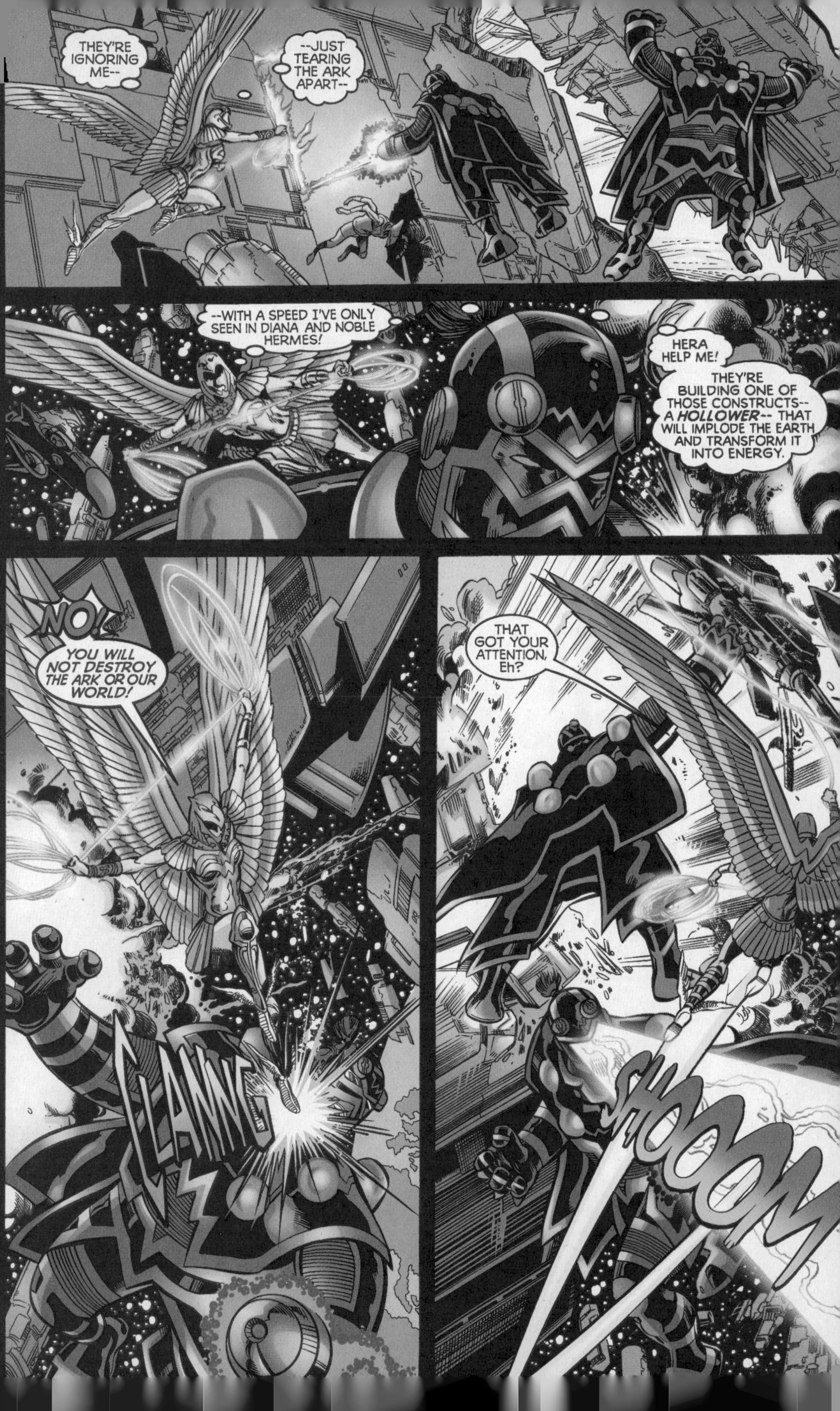
THEY'RE IGNORING ME--
--JUST TEARING THE ARK APART--
--WITH A SPEED I'VE ONLY SEEN IN DIANA AND NOBLE HERMES!
HERA HELP ME!
THEY'RE BUILDING ONE OF THOSE CONSTRUCTS-- A HOLLOWER-- THAT WILL IMPLODE THE EARTH AND TRANSFORM IT INTO ENERGY.
NO!
YOU WILL NOT DESTROY THE ARK OR OUR WORLD!
CLANNG
THAT GOT YOUR ATTENTION, Eh?
SHOOOM

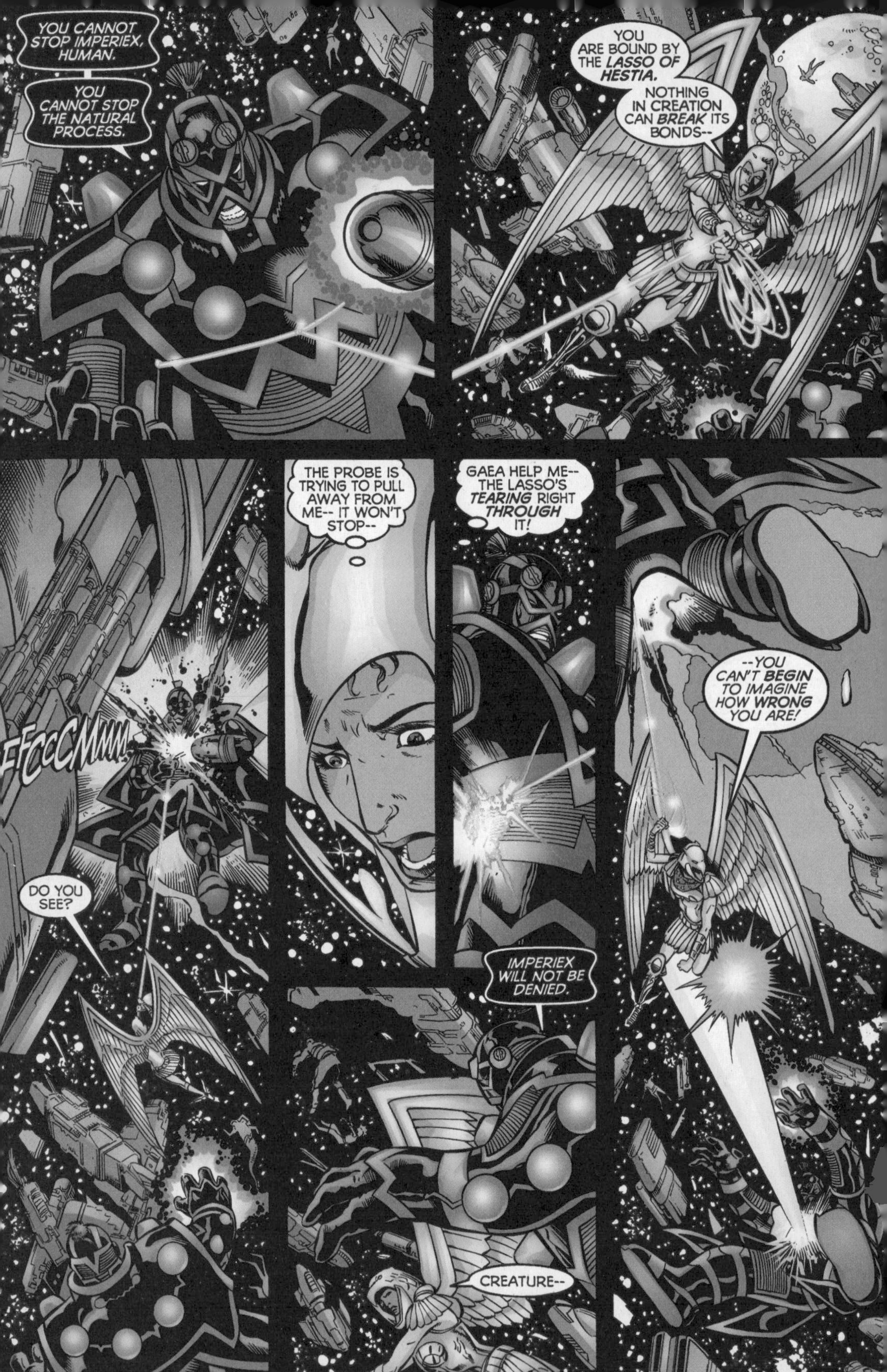
YOU CANNOT STOP IMPERIEX, HUMAN.
YOU CANNOT STOP THE NATURAL PROCESS.
YOU ARE BOUND BY THE LASSO OF HESTIA.
NOTHING IN CREATION CAN BREAK ITS BONDS--
FCcCMMMM
DO YOU SEE?
THE PROBE IS TRYING TO PULL AWAY FROM ME-- IT WON'T STOP--
GAEA HELP ME-- THE LASSO'S TEARING RIGHT THROUGH IT!
IMPERIEX WILL NOT BE DENIED.
CREATURE--
--YOU CAN'T BEGIN TO IMAGINE HOW WRONG YOU ARE!

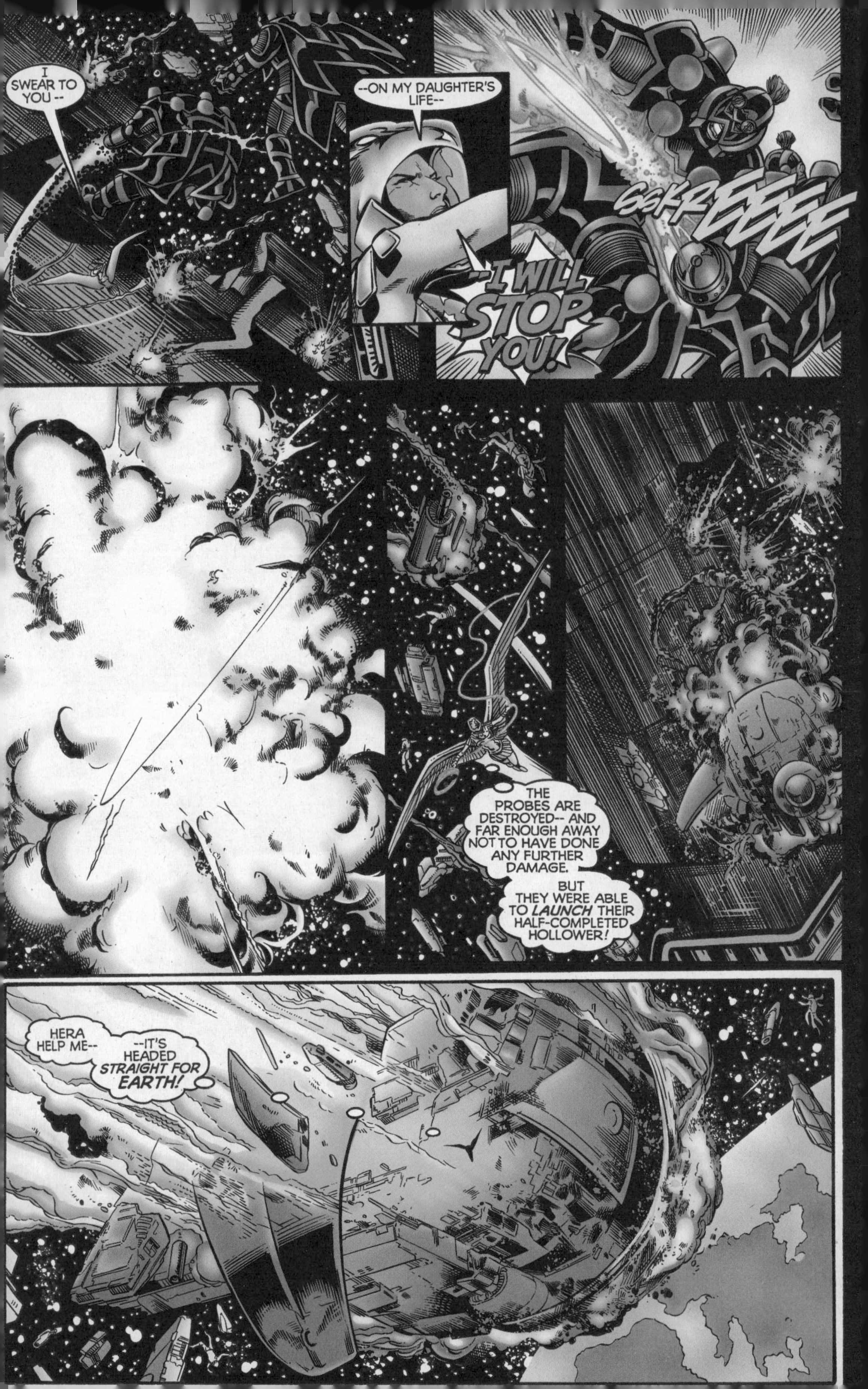
I SWEAR TO YOU --
--ON MY DAUGHTER'S LIFE--
--I WILL STOP YOU!
GGKREEEE
THE PROBES ARE DESTROYED-- AND FAR ENOUGH AWAY NOT TO HAVE DONE ANY FURTHER DAMAGE.
BUT THEY WERE ABLE TO LAUNCH THEIR HALF-COMPLETED HOLLOWER!
HERA HELP ME--
--IT'S HEADED STRAIGHT FOR EARTH!

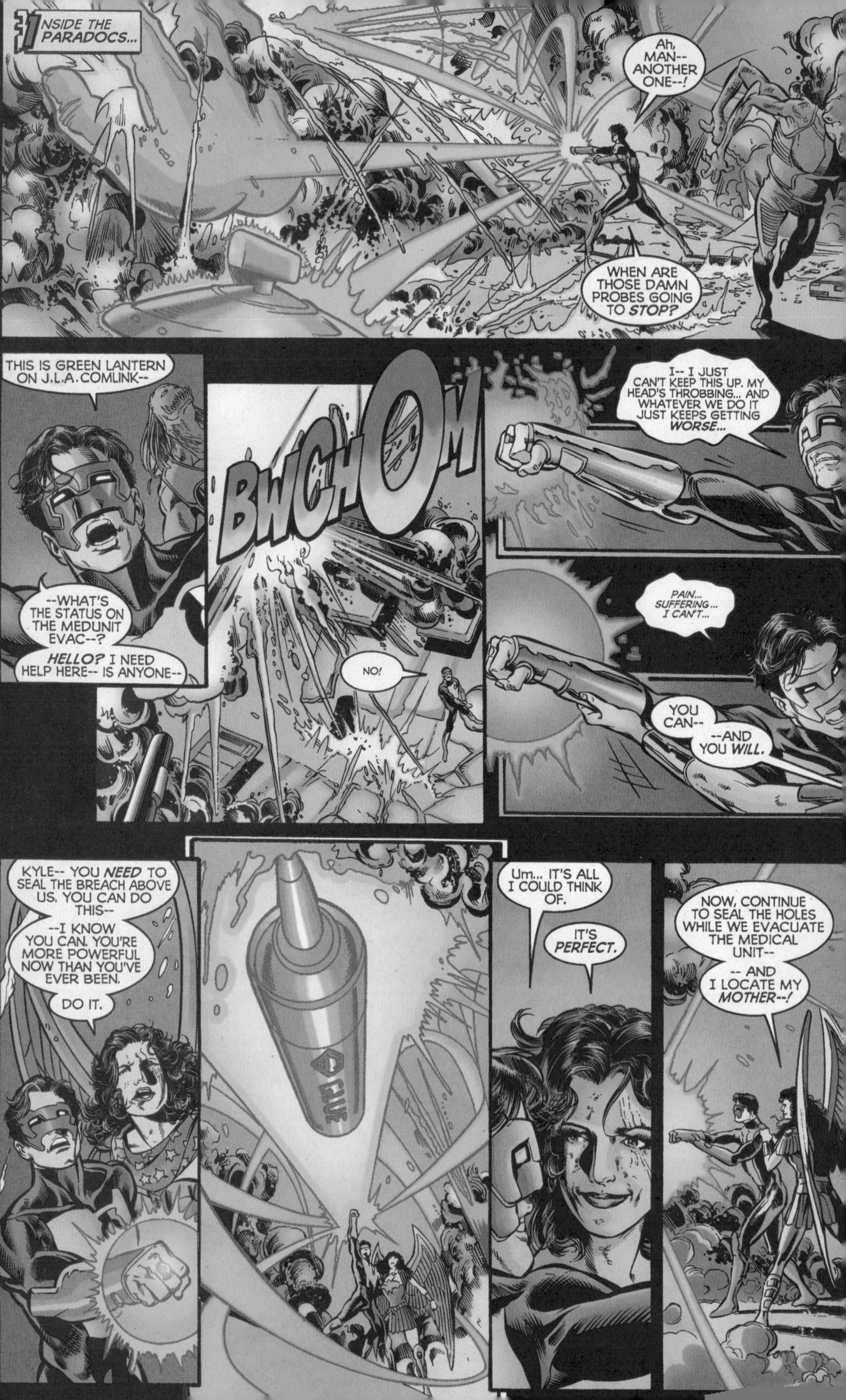
INSIDE THE PARADOCS...
Ah, MAN-- ANOTHER ONE--!
WHEN ARE THOSE DAMN PROBES GOING TO STOP?
THIS IS GREEN LANTERN ON J.L.A. COMLINK--
--WHAT'S THE STATUS ON THE MEDUNIT EVAC--?
HELLO? I NEED HELP HERE-- IS ANYONE--
BWCHOM
NO!
I-- I JUST CAN'T KEEP THIS UP. MY HEAD'S THROBBING... AND WHATEVER WE DO IT JUST KEEPS GETTING WORSE...
PAIN... SUFFERING... I CAN'T...
YOU CAN--
--AND YOU WILL.
KYLE-- YOU NEED TO SEAL THE BREACH ABOVE US. YOU CAN DO THIS--
--I KNOW YOU CAN. YOU'RE MORE POWERFUL NOW THAN YOU'VE EVER BEEN.
DO IT.
GLUE
Um... IT'S ALL I COULD THINK OF.
IT'S PERFECT.
NOW, CONTINUE TO SEAL THE HOLES WHILE WE EVACUATE THE MEDICAL UNIT--
-- AND I LOCATE MY MOTHER--!

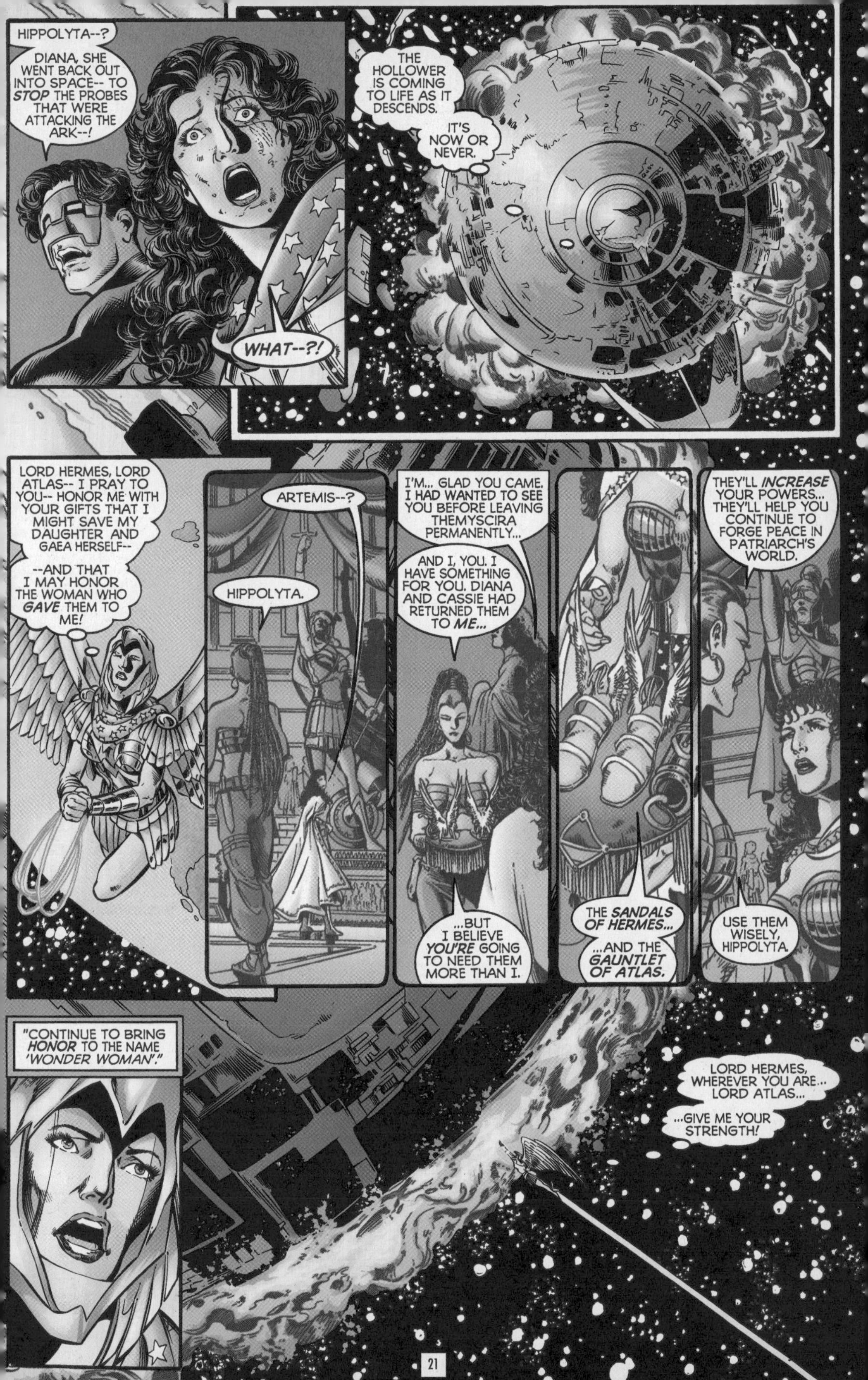

HIPPOLYTA--?
DIANA, SHE WENT BACK OUT INTO SPACE-- TO STOP THE PROBES THAT WERE ATTACKING THE ARK--!
WHAT--?!
THE HOLLOWER IS COMING TO LIFE AS IT DESCENDS.
IT'S NOW OR NEVER.
LORD HERMES, LORD ATLAS-- I PRAY TO YOU-- HONOR ME WITH YOUR GIFTS THAT I MIGHT SAVE MY DAUGHTER AND GAEA HERSELF--
--AND THAT I MAY HONOR THE WOMAN WHO GAVE THEM TO ME!
ARTEMIS--?
HIPPOLYTA.
I'M... GLAD YOU CAME. I HAD WANTED TO SEE YOU BEFORE LEAVING THEMYSCIRA PERMANENTLY...
AND I, YOU. I HAVE SOMETHING FOR YOU. DIANA AND CASSIE HAD RETURNED THEM TO ME...
...BUT I BELIEVE YOU'RE GOING TO NEED THEM MORE THAN I.
THE SANDALS OF HERMES...
...AND THE GAUNTLET OF ATLAS.
THEY'LL INCREASE YOUR POWERS... THEY'LL HELP YOU CONTINUE TO FORGE PEACE IN PATRIARCH'S WORLD.
USE THEM WISELY, HIPPOLYTA.
"CONTINUE TO BRING HONOR TO THE NAME 'WONDER WOMAN'."
LORD HERMES, WHEREVER YOU ARE... LORD ATLAS...
...GIVE ME YOUR STRENGTH!

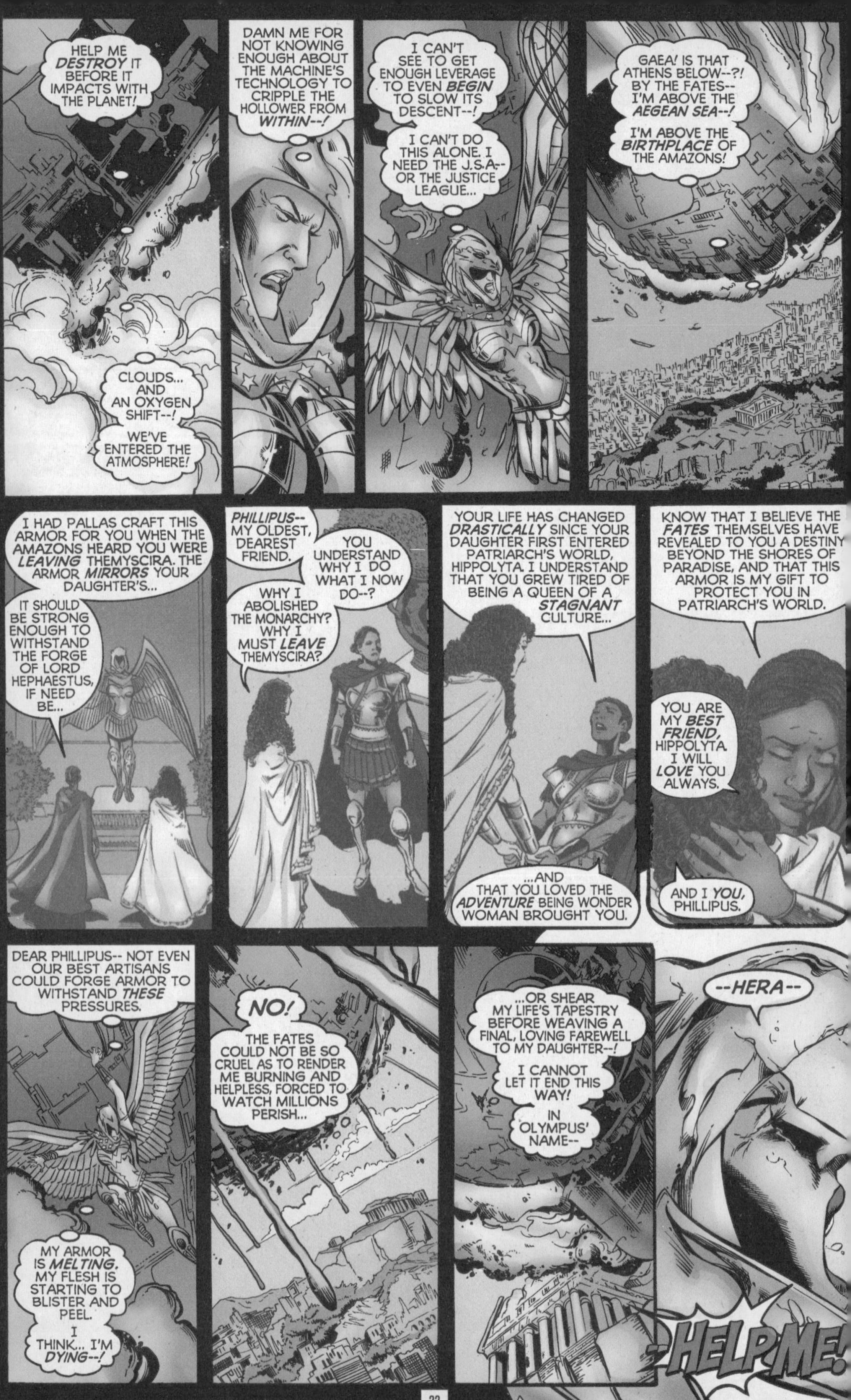
HELP ME DESTROY IT BEFORE IT IMPACTS WITH THE PLANET!
CLOUDS... AND AN OXYGEN SHIFT--!
WE'VE ENTERED THE ATMOSPHERE!
DAMN ME FOR NOT KNOWING ENOUGH ABOUT THE MACHINE'S TECHNOLOGY TO CRIPPLE THE HOLLOWER FROM WITHIN--!
I CAN'T SEE TO GET ENOUGH LEVERAGE TO EVEN BEGIN TO SLOW ITS DESCENT--!
I CAN'T DO THIS ALONE. I NEED THE J.S.A.-- OR THE JUSTICE LEAGUE...
GAEA! IS THAT ATHENS BELOW--?! BY THE FATES-- I'M ABOVE THE AEGEAN SEA--!
I'M ABOVE THE BIRTHPLACE OF THE AMAZONS!
I HAD PALLAS CRAFT THIS ARMOR FOR YOU WHEN THE AMAZONS HEARD YOU WERE LEAVING THEMYSCIRA. THE ARMOR MIRRORS YOUR DAUGHTER'S...
IT SHOULD BE STRONG ENOUGH TO WITHSTAND THE FORGE OF LORD HEPHAESTUS, IF NEED BE...
PHILLIPUS-- MY OLDEST, DEAREST FRIEND.
YOU UNDERSTAND WHY I DO WHAT I NOW DO--?
WHY I ABOLISHED THE MONARCHY? WHY I MUST LEAVE THEMYSCIRA?
YOUR LIFE HAS CHANGED DRASTICALLY SINCE YOUR DAUGHTER FIRST ENTERED PATRIARCH'S WORLD, HIPPOLYTA. I UNDERSTAND THAT YOU GREW TIRED OF BEING A QUEEN OF A STAGNANT CULTURE...
...AND THAT YOU LOVED THE ADVENTURE BEING WONDER WOMAN BROUGHT YOU.
KNOW THAT I BELIEVE THE FATES THEMSELVES HAVE REVEALED TO YOU A DESTINY BEYOND THE SHORES OF PARADISE, AND THAT THIS ARMOR IS MY GIFT TO PROTECT YOU IN PATRIARCH'S WORLD.
YOU ARE MY BEST FRIEND, HIPPOLYTA. I WILL LOVE YOU ALWAYS.
AND I YOU, PHILLIPUS.
DEAR PHILLIPUS-- NOT EVEN OUR BEST ARTISANS COULD FORGE ARMOR TO WITHSTAND THESE PRESSURES.
MY ARMOR IS MELTING. MY FLESH IS STARTING TO BLISTER AND PEEL.
I THINK... I'M DYING--!
NO!
THE FATES COULD NOT BE SO CRUEL AS TO RENDER ME BURNING AND HELPLESS, FORCED TO WATCH MILLIONS PERISH...
...OR SHEAR MY LIFE'S TAPESTRY BEFORE WEAVING A FINAL, LOVING FAREWELL TO MY DAUGHTER--!
I CANNOT LET IT END THIS WAY!
IN OLYMPUS' NAME--
--HERA--
--HELP ME!

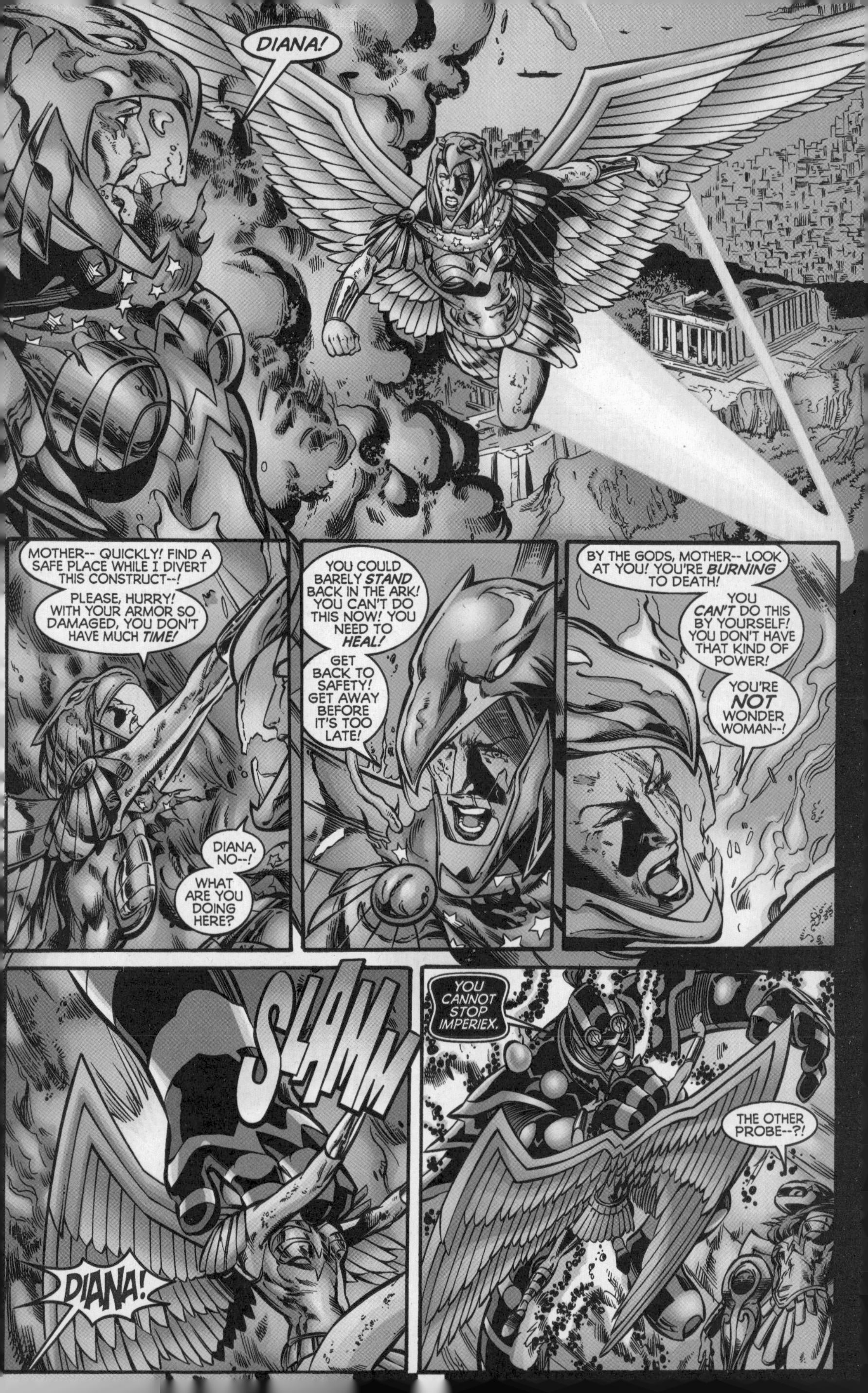
DIANA!
MOTHER-- QUICKLY! FIND A SAFE PLACE WHILE I DIVERT THIS CONSTRUCT--!
PLEASE, HURRY! WITH YOUR ARMOR SO DAMAGED, YOU DON'T HAVE MUCH TIME!
DIANA, NO--!
WHAT ARE YOU DOING HERE?
YOU COULD BARELY STAND BACK IN THE ARK! YOU CAN'T DO THIS NOW! YOU NEED TO HEAL!
GET BACK TO SAFETY! GET AWAY BEFORE IT'S TOO LATE!
BY THE GODS, MOTHER-- LOOK AT YOU! YOU'RE BURNING TO DEATH!
YOU CAN'T DO THIS BY YOURSELF! YOU DON'T HAVE THAT KIND OF POWER!
YOU'RE NOT WONDER WOMAN--!
SLAMM
DIANA!
YOU CANNOT STOP IMPERIEX.
THE OTHER PROBE--?!

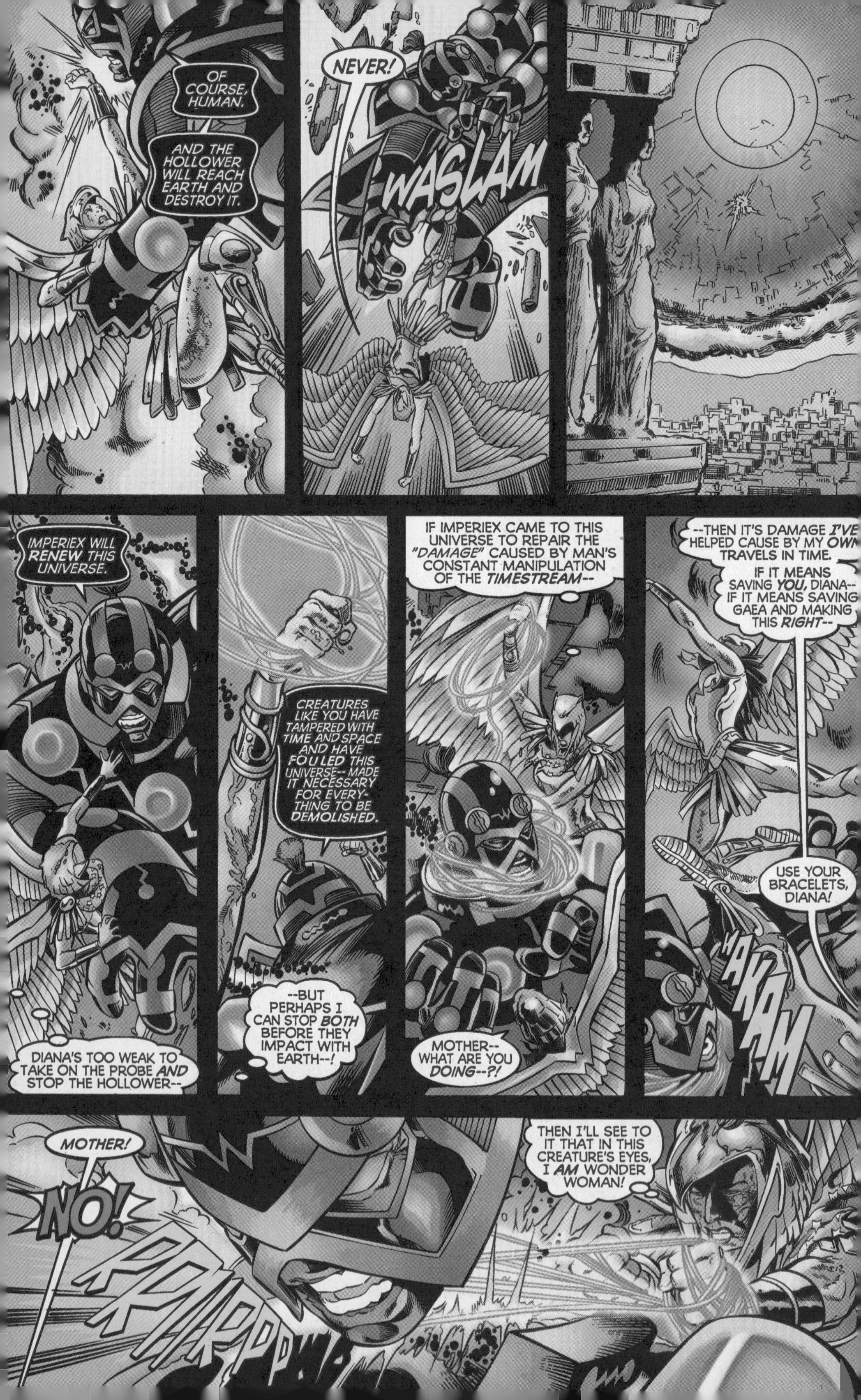
OF COURSE, HUMAN.
AND THE HOLLOWER WILL REACH EARTH AND DESTROY IT.
NEVER!
WASLAM
IMPERIEX WILL RENEW THIS UNIVERSE.
CREATURES LIKE YOU HAVE TAMPERED WITH TIME AND SPACE AND HAVE FOULED THIS UNIVERSE-- MADE IT NECESSARY FOR EVERYTHING TO BE DEMOLISHED.
DIANA'S TOO WEAK TO TAKE ON THE PROBE AND STOP THE HOLLOWER--
--BUT PERHAPS I CAN STOP BOTH BEFORE THEY IMPACT WITH EARTH--!
IF IMPERIEX CAME TO THIS UNIVERSE TO REPAIR THE "DAMAGE" CAUSED BY MAN'S CONSTANT MANIPULATION OF THE TIMESTREAM--
MOTHER-- WHAT ARE YOU DOING--?!
--THEN IT'S DAMAGE I'VE HELPED CAUSE BY MY OWN TRAVELS IN TIME.
IF IT MEANS SAVING YOU, DIANA-- IF IT MEANS SAVING GAEA AND MAKING THIS RIGHT--
USE YOUR BRACELETS, DIANA!
MOTHER!
NO!
THEN I'LL SEE TO IT THAT IN THIS CREATURE'S EYES, I AM WONDER WOMAN!

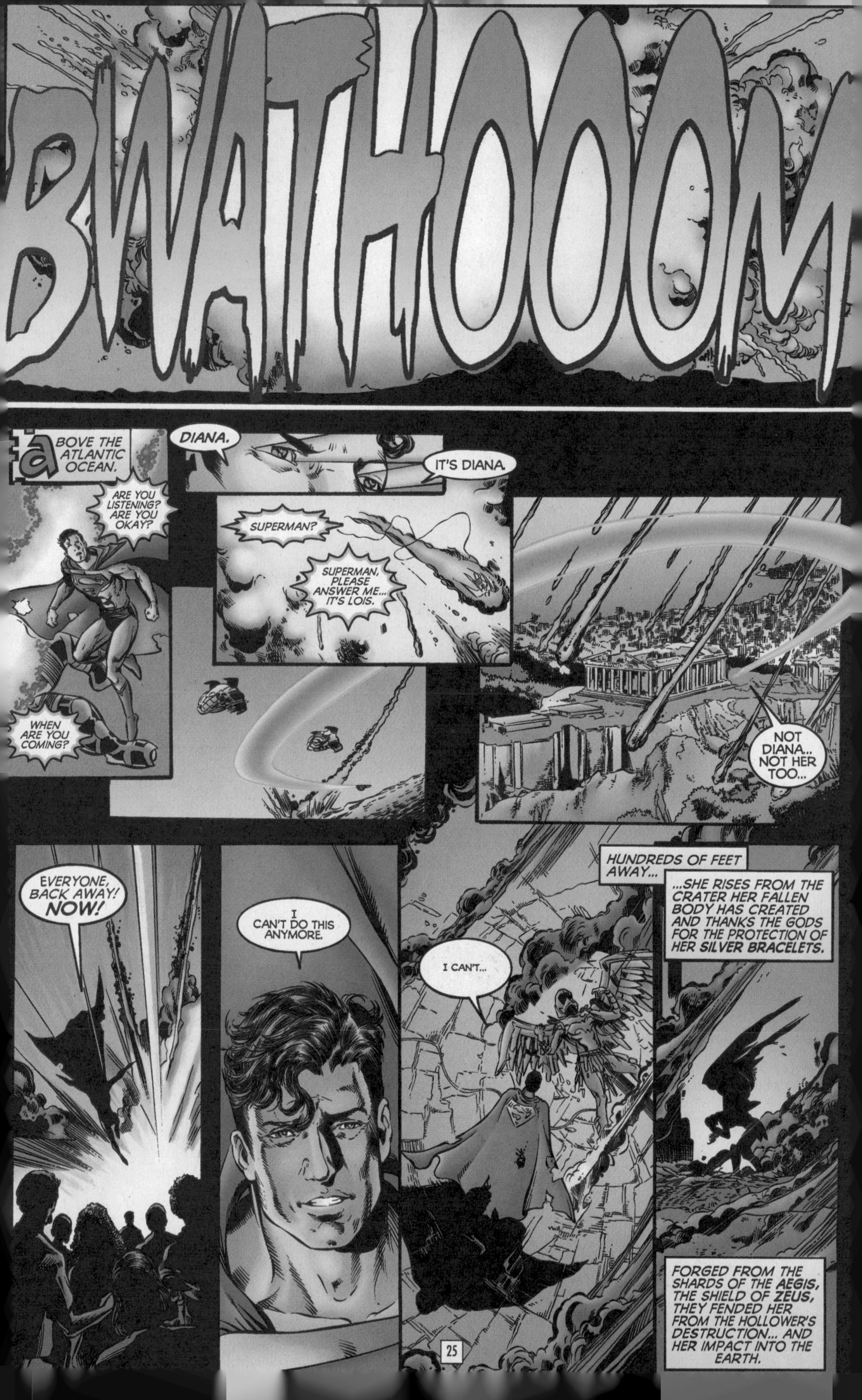
BWATHOOOM
ABOVE THE ATLANTIC OCEAN.
DIANA.
IT'S DIANA.
ARE YOU LISTENING? ARE YOU OKAY?
SUPERMAN?
SUPERMAN, PLEASE ANSWER ME... IT'S LOIS.
WHEN ARE YOU COMING?
NOT DIANA... NOT HER TOO...
EVERYONE, BACK AWAY! NOW!
I CAN'T DO THIS ANYMORE.
HUNDREDS OF FEET AWAY...
I CAN'T...
...SHE RISES FROM THE CRATER HER FALLEN BODY HAS CREATED AND THANKS THE GODS FOR THE PROTECTION OF HER SILVER BRACELETS.
FORGED FROM THE SHARDS OF THE AEGIS, THE SHIELD OF ZEUS, THEY FENDED HER FROM THE HOLLOWER'S DESTRUCTION... AND HER IMPACT INTO THE EARTH.

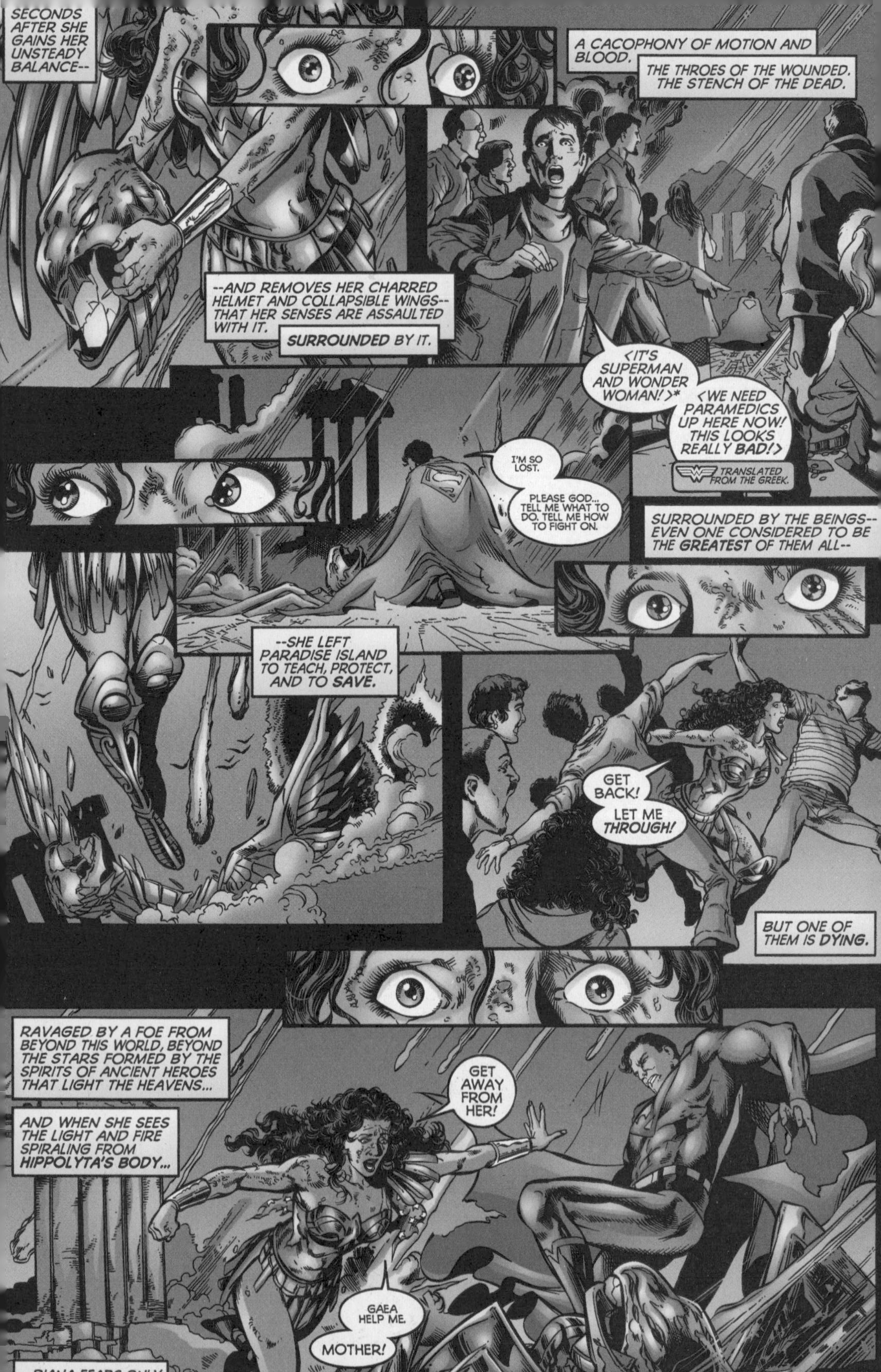
SECONDS AFTER SHE GAINS HER UNSTEADY BALANCE--
A CACOPHONY OF MOTION AND BLOOD.
THE THROES OF THE WOUNDED. THE STENCH OF THE DEAD.
--AND REMOVES HER CHARRED HELMET AND COLLAPSIBLE WINGS-- THAT HER SENSES ARE ASSAULTED WITH IT.
SURROUNDED BY IT.
<IT'S SUPERMAN AND WONDER WOMAN!>*
<WE NEED PARAMEDICS UP HERE NOW! THIS LOOKS REALLY BAD!>
*TRANSLATED FROM THE GREEK.
I'M SO LOST.
PLEASE GOD... TELL ME WHAT TO DO. TELL ME HOW TO FIGHT ON.
SURROUNDED BY THE BEINGS-- EVEN ONE CONSIDERED TO BE THE GREATEST OF THEM ALL--
--SHE LEFT PARADISE ISLAND TO TEACH, PROTECT, AND TO SAVE.
GET BACK!
LET ME THROUGH!
BUT ONE OF THEM IS DYING.
RAVAGED BY A FOE FROM BEYOND THIS WORLD, BEYOND THE STARS FORMED BY THE SPIRITS OF ANCIENT HEROES THAT LIGHT THE HEAVENS...
AND WHEN SHE SEES THE LIGHT AND FIRE SPIRALING FROM HIPPOLYTA'S BODY...
GET AWAY FROM HER!
GAEA HELP ME.
MOTHER!
...DIANA FEARS ONLY THE WORST.

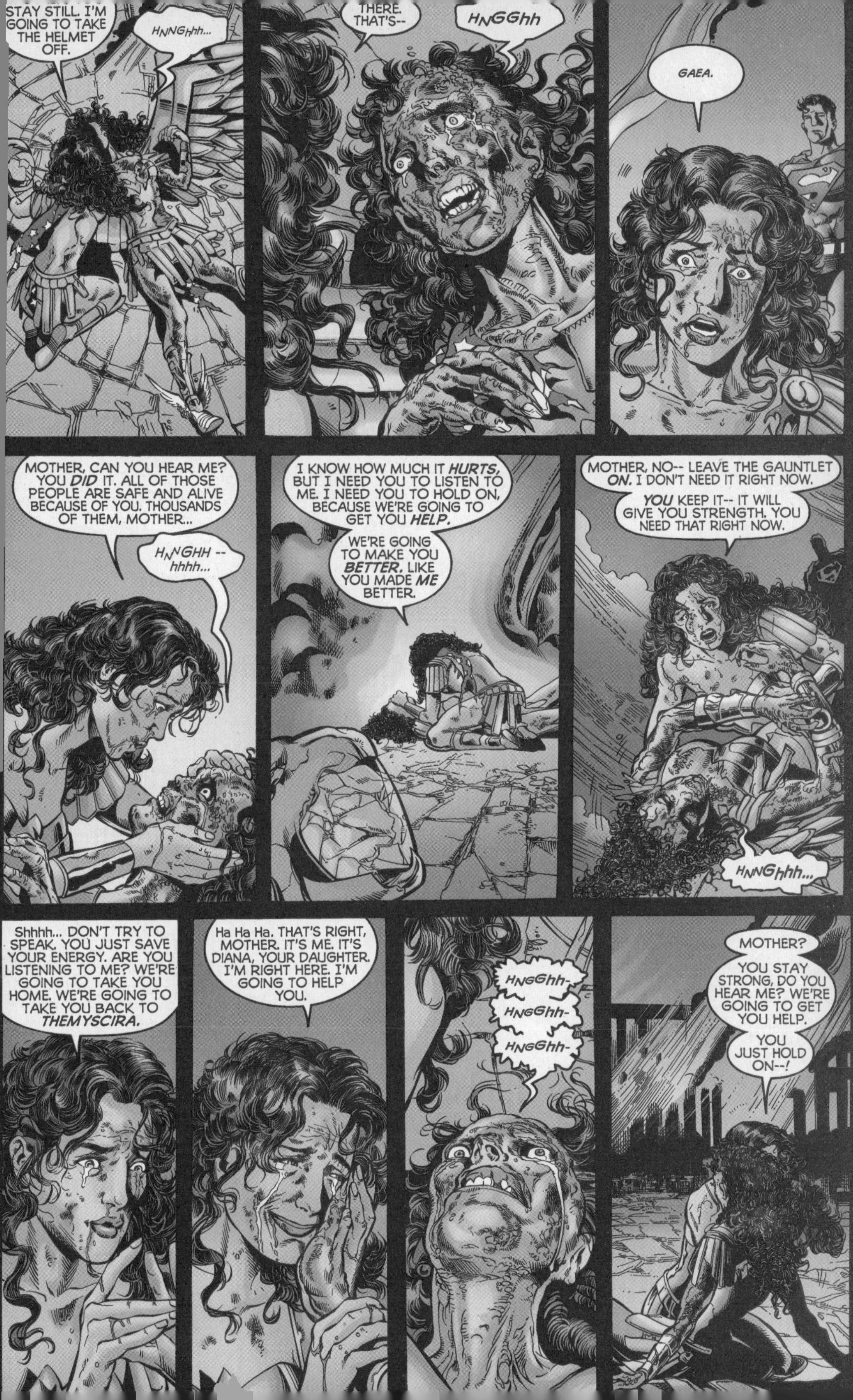
STAY STILL. I'M GOING TO TAKE THE HELMET OFF.
HNNGhhh...
THERE. THAT'S--
HNGGhh
GAEA.
MOTHER, CAN YOU HEAR ME? YOU DID IT. ALL OF THOSE PEOPLE ARE SAFE AND ALIVE BECAUSE OF YOU. THOUSANDS OF THEM, MOTHER...
HNNGHH -- hhhh...
I KNOW HOW MUCH IT HURTS, BUT I NEED YOU TO LISTEN TO ME. I NEED YOU TO HOLD ON, BECAUSE WE'RE GOING TO GET YOU HELP.
WE'RE GOING TO MAKE YOU BETTER. LIKE YOU MADE ME BETTER.
MOTHER, NO-- LEAVE THE GAUNTLET ON. I DON'T NEED IT RIGHT NOW.
YOU KEEP IT-- IT WILL GIVE YOU STRENGTH. YOU NEED THAT RIGHT NOW.
HNNGhhh...
Shhhh... DON'T TRY TO SPEAK. YOU JUST SAVE YOUR ENERGY. ARE YOU LISTENING TO ME? WE'RE GOING TO TAKE YOU HOME. WE'RE GOING TO TAKE YOU BACK TO THEMYSCIRA.
Ha Ha Ha. THAT'S RIGHT, MOTHER. IT'S ME. IT'S DIANA, YOUR DAUGHTER. I'M RIGHT HERE. I'M GOING TO HELP YOU.
HNGGhh-
HNGGhh-
HNGGhh-
MOTHER?
YOU STAY STRONG, DO YOU HEAR ME? WE'RE GOING TO GET YOU HELP.
YOU JUST HOLD ON--!

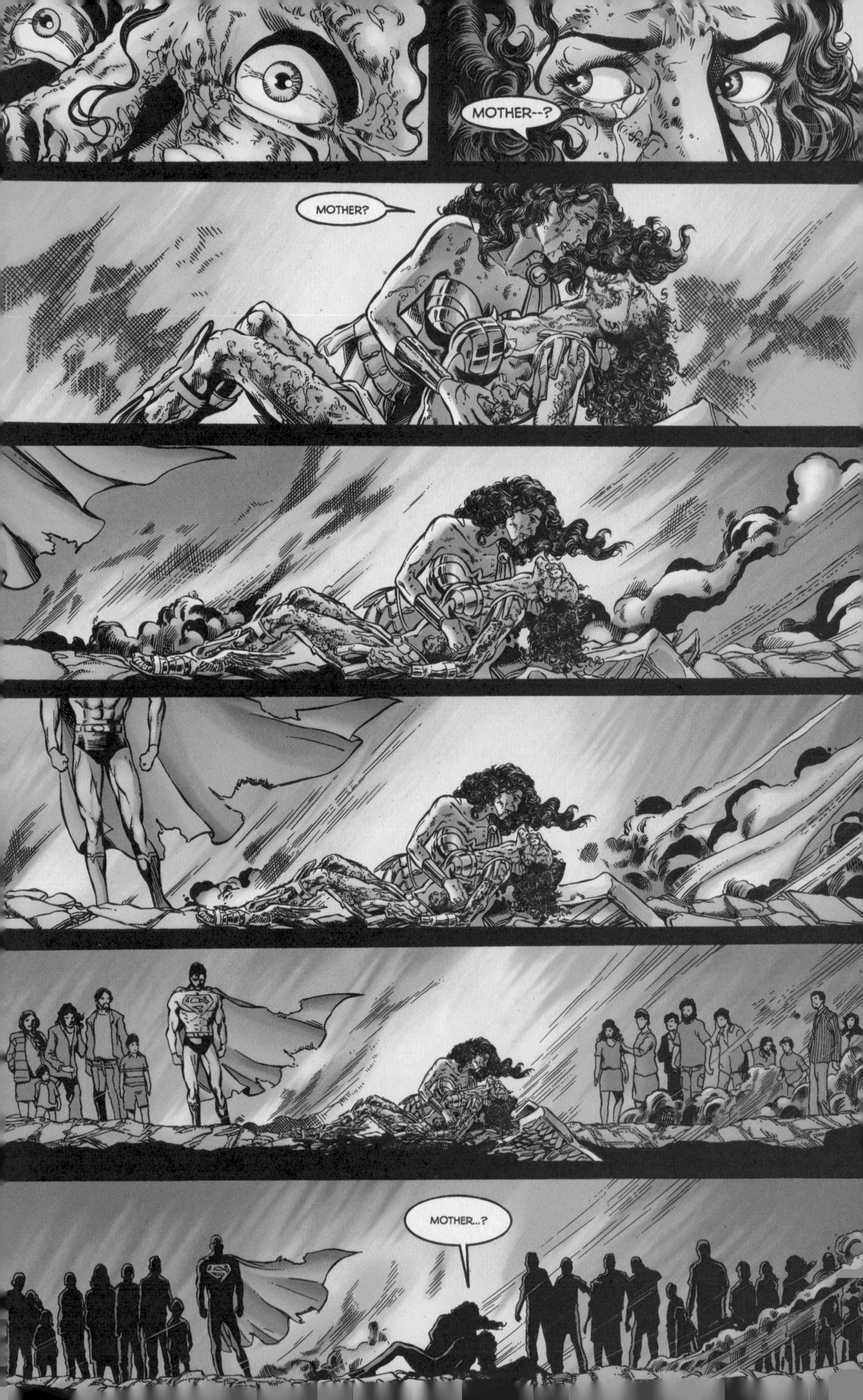
MOTHER--?
MOTHER?
MOTHER...?

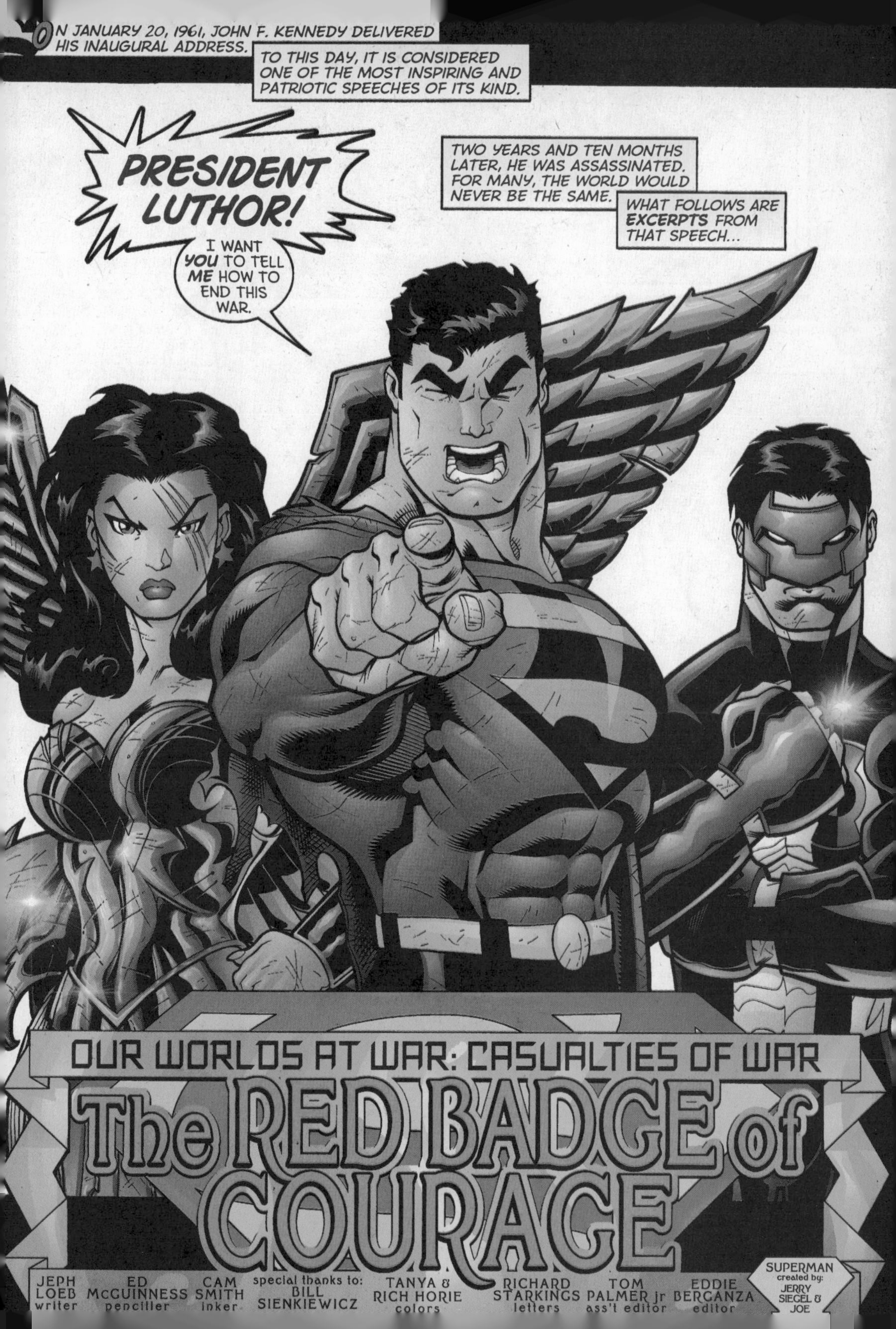
ON JANUARY 20, 1961, JOHN F. KENNEDY DELIVERED HIS INAUGURAL ADDRESS.
TO THIS DAY, IT IS CONSIDERED ONE OF THE MOST INSPIRING AND PATRIOTIC SPEECHES OF ITS KIND.
TWO YEARS AND TEN MONTHS LATER, HE WAS ASSASSINATED. FOR MANY, THE WORLD WOULD NEVER BE THE SAME.
WHAT FOLLOWS ARE EXCERPTS FROM THAT SPEECH...
PRESIDENT LUTHOR!
I WANT YOU TO TELL ME HOW TO END THIS WAR.
OUR WORLDS AT WAR: CASUALTIES OF WAR
The RED BADGE of COURAGE
JEPH LOEB writer
ED McGUINNESS penciller
CAM SMITH inker
special thanks to: BILL SIENKIEWICZ
TANYA & RICH HORIE colors
RICHARD STARKINGS letters
TOM PALMER jr ass't editor
EDDIE BERGANZA editor
SUPERMAN created by: JERRY SIEGEL & JOE

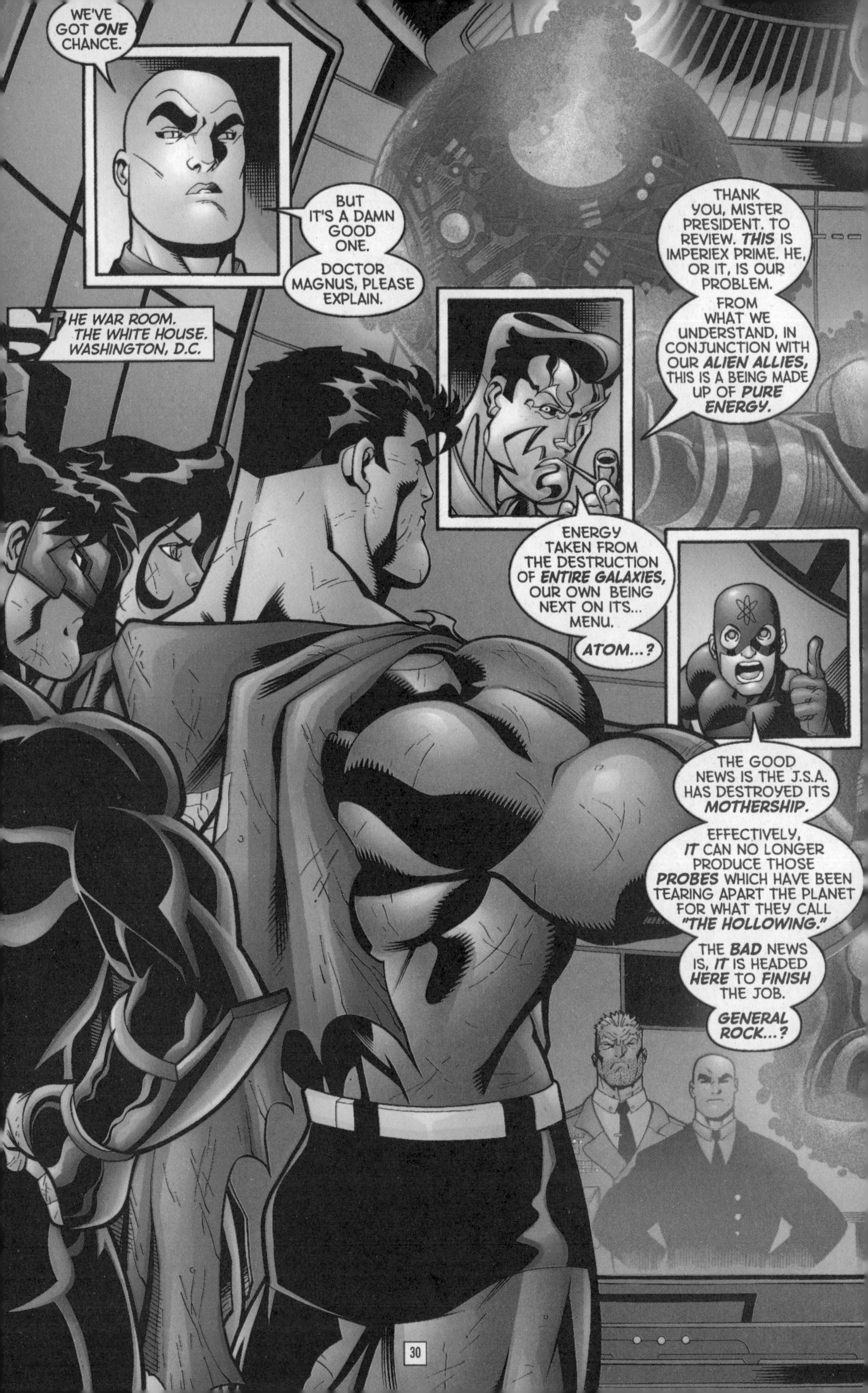

WE'VE GOT ONE CHANCE.
BUT IT'S A DAMN GOOD ONE.
DOCTOR MAGNUS, PLEASE EXPLAIN.
THE WAR ROOM. THE WHITE HOUSE. WASHINGTON, D.C.
THANK YOU, MISTER PRESIDENT. TO REVIEW. THIS IS IMPERIEX PRIME. HE, OR IT, IS OUR PROBLEM.
FROM WHAT WE UNDERSTAND, IN CONJUNCTION WITH OUR ALIEN ALLIES, THIS IS A BEING MADE UP OF PURE ENERGY.
ENERGY TAKEN FROM THE DESTRUCTION OF ENTIRE GALAXIES, OUR OWN BEING NEXT ON ITS... MENU.
ATOM...?
THE GOOD NEWS IS THE J.S.A. HAS DESTROYED ITS MOTHERSHIP.
EFFECTIVELY, IT CAN NO LONGER PRODUCE THOSE PROBES WHICH HAVE BEEN TEARING APART THE PLANET FOR WHAT THEY CALL "THE HOLLOWING."
THE BAD NEWS IS, IT IS HEADED HERE TO FINISH THE JOB.
GENERAL ROCK...?

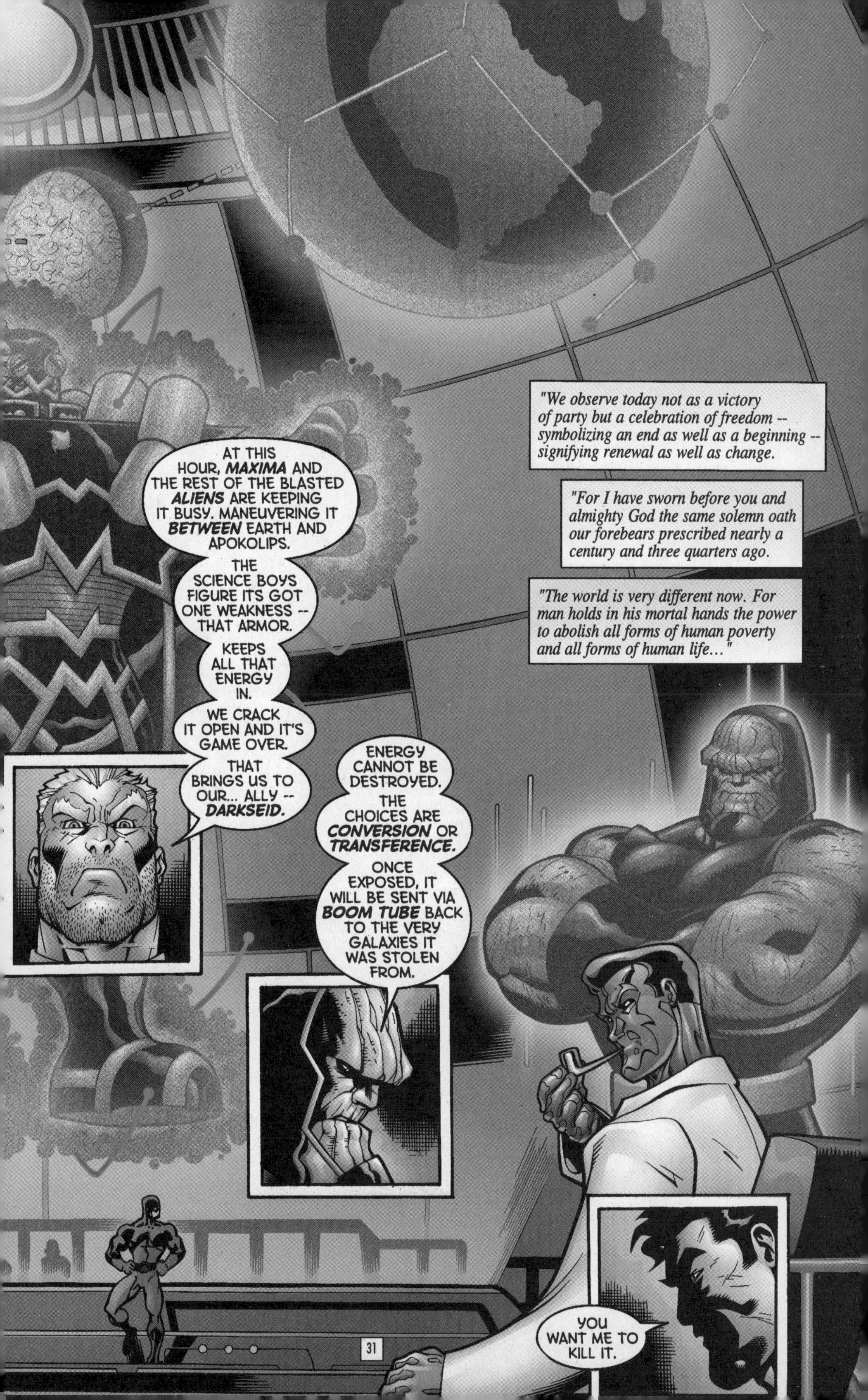
"We observe today not as a victory of party but a celebration of freedom -- symbolizing an end as well as a beginning -- signifying renewal as well as change.
"For I have sworn before you and almighty God the same solemn oath our forebears prescribed nearly a century and three quarters ago.
"The world is very different now. For man holds in his mortal hands the power to abolish all forms of human poverty and all forms of human life..."
AT THIS HOUR, MAXIMA AND THE REST OF THE BLASTED ALIENS ARE KEEPING IT BUSY. MANEUVERING IT BETWEEN EARTH AND APOKOLIPS.
THE SCIENCE BOYS FIGURE ITS GOT ONE WEAKNESS -- THAT ARMOR.
KEEPS ALL THAT ENERGY IN.
WE CRACK IT OPEN AND IT'S GAME OVER.
THAT BRINGS US TO OUR... ALLY -- DARKSEID.
ENERGY CANNOT BE DESTROYED.
THE CHOICES ARE CONVERSION OR TRANSFERENCE.
ONCE EXPOSED, IT WILL BE SENT VIA BOOM TUBE BACK TO THE VERY GALAXIES IT WAS STOLEN FROM.
YOU WANT ME TO KILL IT.

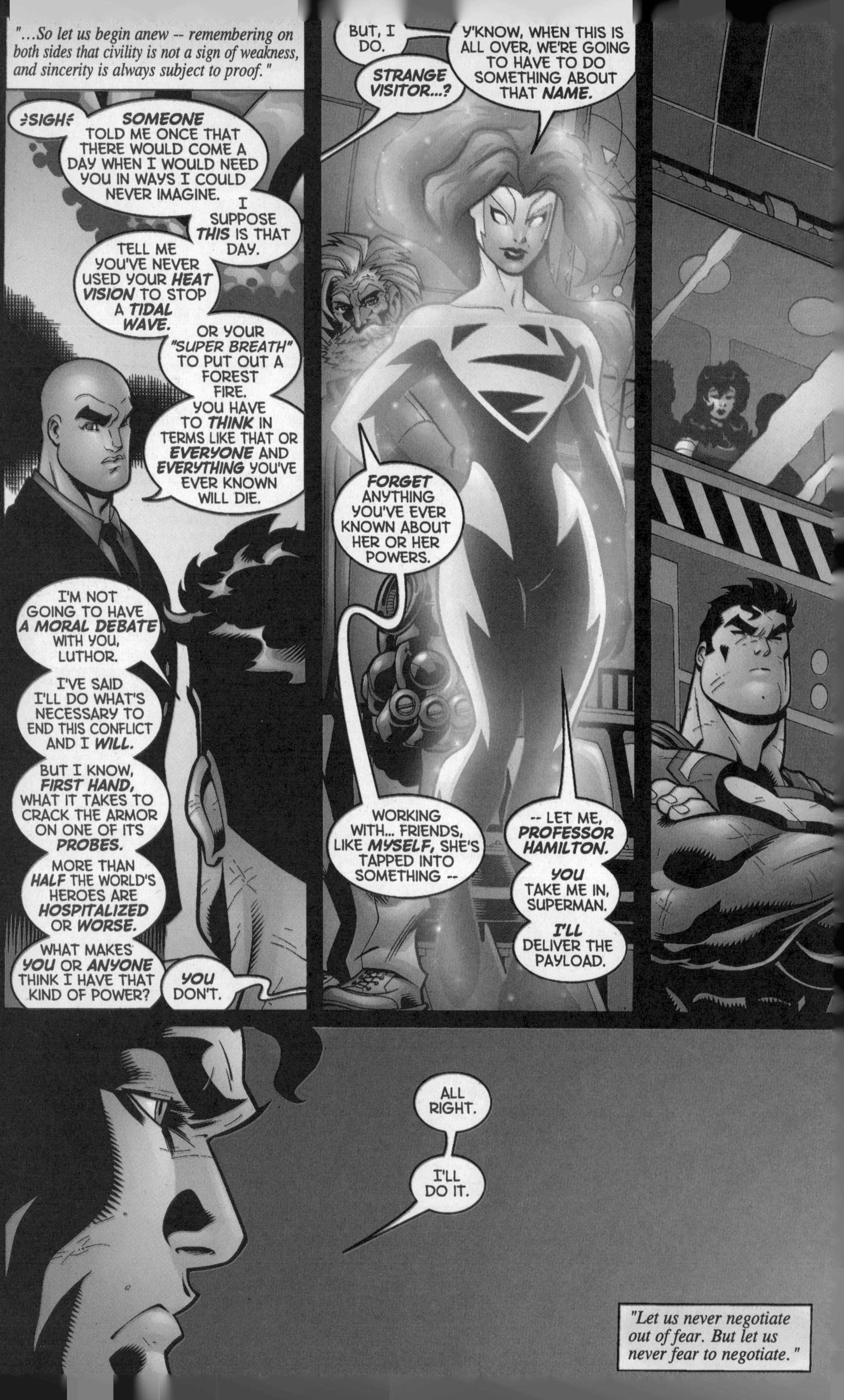
"...So let us begin anew -- remembering on both sides that civility is not a sign of weakness, and sincerity is always subject to proof."
SIGH SOMEONE TOLD ME ONCE THAT THERE WOULD COME A DAY WHEN I WOULD NEED YOU IN WAYS I COULD NEVER IMAGINE.
I SUPPOSE THIS IS THAT DAY.
TELL ME YOU'VE NEVER USED YOUR HEAT VISION TO STOP A TIDAL WAVE.
OR YOUR "SUPER BREATH" TO PUT OUT A FOREST FIRE.
YOU HAVE TO THINK IN TERMS LIKE THAT OR EVERYONE AND EVERYTHING YOU'VE EVER KNOWN WILL DIE.
I'M NOT GOING TO HAVE A MORAL DEBATE WITH YOU, LUTHOR.
I'VE SAID I'LL DO WHAT'S NECESSARY TO END THIS CONFLICT AND I WILL.
BUT I KNOW, FIRST HAND, WHAT IT TAKES TO CRACK THE ARMOR ON ONE OF ITS PROBES.
MORE THAN HALF THE WORLD'S HEROES ARE HOSPITALIZED OR WORSE.
WHAT MAKES YOU OR ANYONE THINK I HAVE THAT KIND OF POWER?
YOU DON'T.
BUT, I DO.
STRANGE VISITOR...?
Y'KNOW, WHEN THIS IS ALL OVER, WE'RE GOING TO HAVE TO DO SOMETHING ABOUT THAT NAME.
FORGET ANYTHING YOU'VE EVER KNOWN ABOUT HER OR HER POWERS.
WORKING WITH... FRIENDS, LIKE MYSELF, SHE'S TAPPED INTO SOMETHING --
-- LET ME, PROFESSOR HAMILTON.
YOU TAKE ME IN, SUPERMAN.
I'LL DELIVER THE PAYLOAD.
ALL RIGHT.
I'LL DO IT.
"Let us never negotiate out of fear. But let us never fear to negotiate."

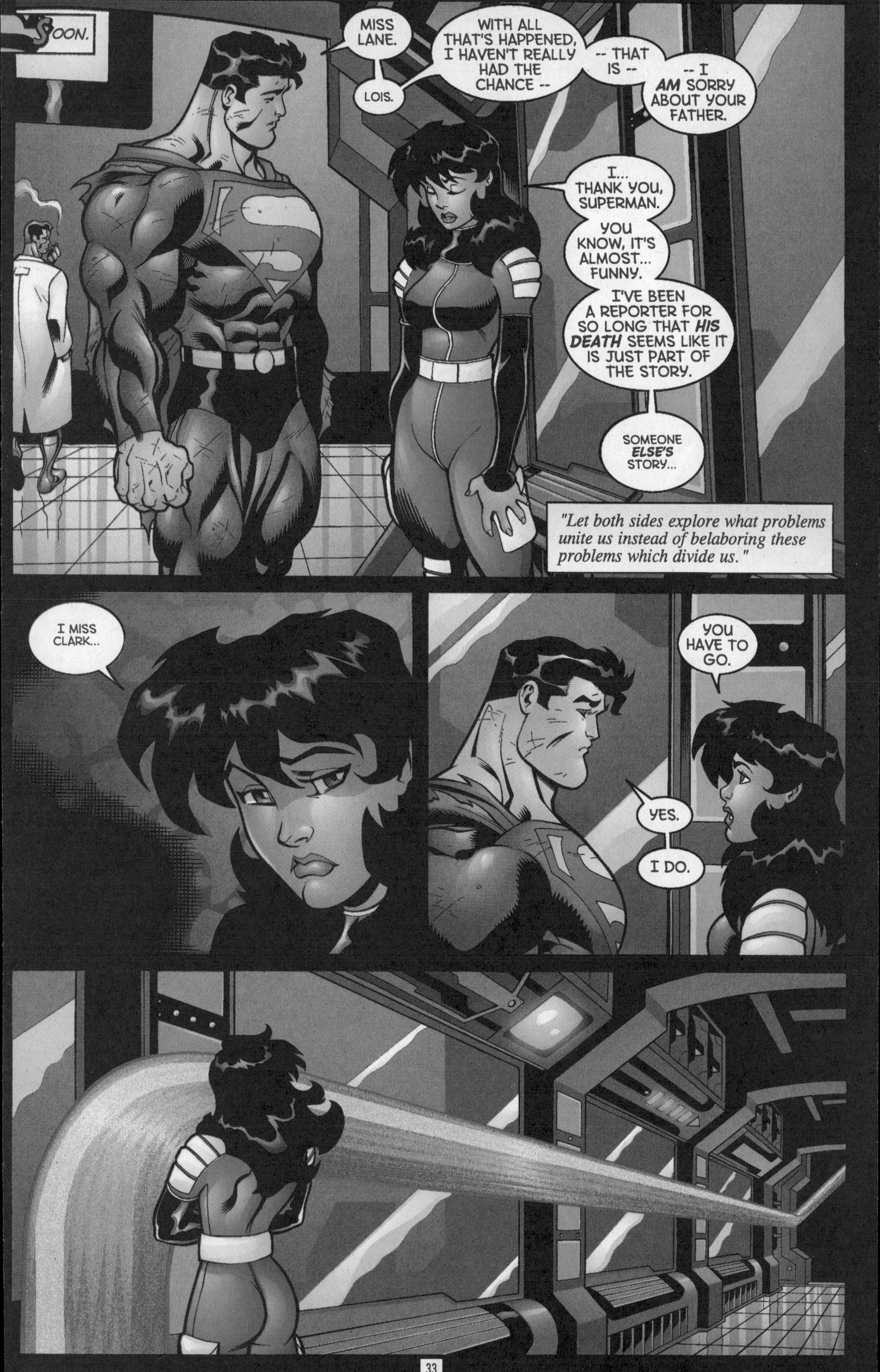
SOON.
MISS LANE.
LOIS.
WITH ALL THAT'S HAPPENED, I HAVEN'T REALLY HAD THE CHANCE --
-- THAT IS --
-- I AM SORRY ABOUT YOUR FATHER.
I... THANK YOU, SUPERMAN.
YOU KNOW, IT'S ALMOST... FUNNY.
I'VE BEEN A REPORTER FOR SO LONG THAT HIS DEATH SEEMS LIKE IT IS JUST PART OF THE STORY.
SOMEONE ELSE'S STORY...
"Let both sides explore what problems unite us instead of belaboring these problems which divide us."
I MISS CLARK...
YOU HAVE TO GO.
YES.
I DO.

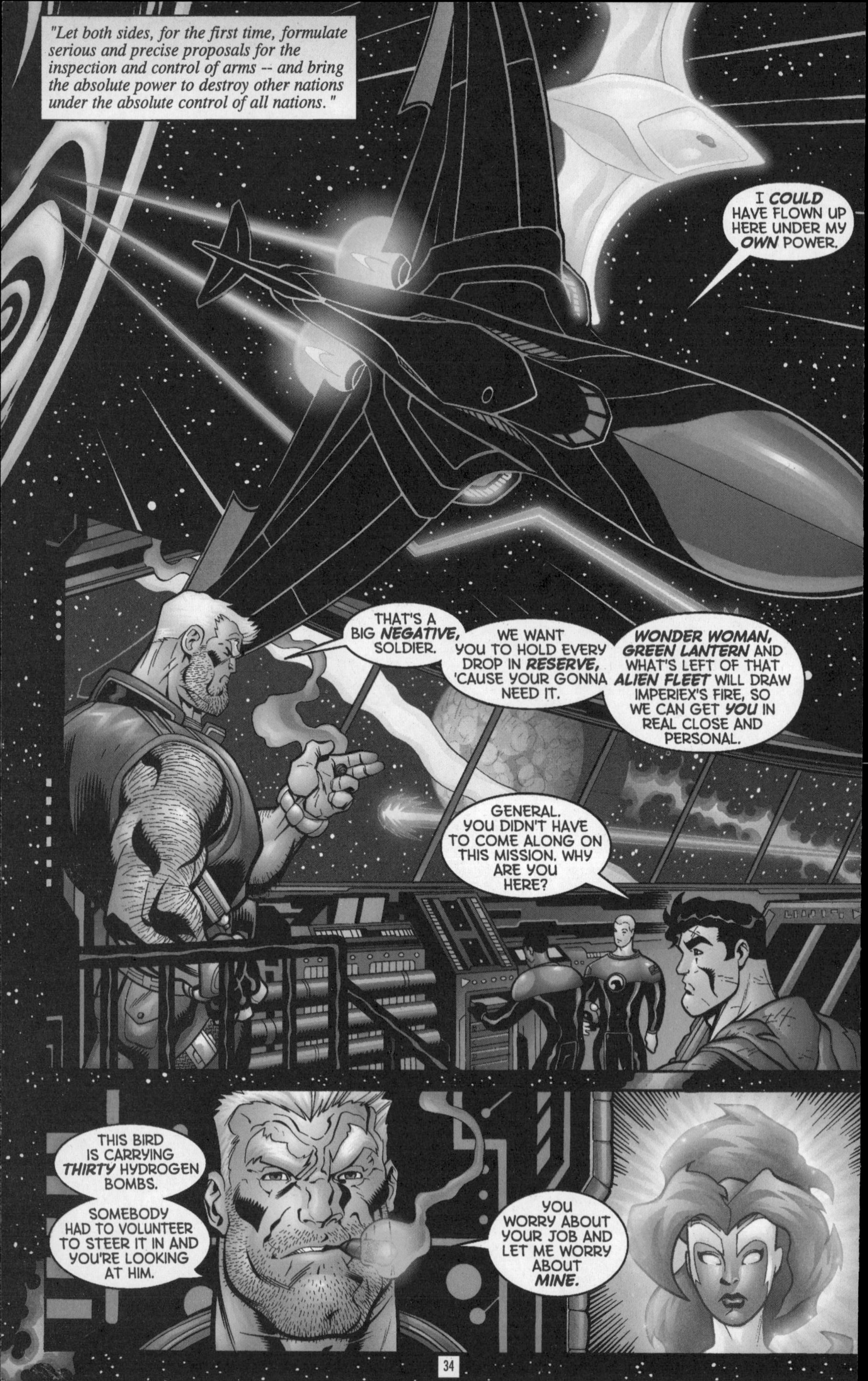
"Let both sides, for the first time, formulate serious and precise proposals for the inspection and control of arms -- and bring the absolute power to destroy other nations under the absolute control of all nations."
I COULD HAVE FLOWN UP HERE UNDER MY OWN POWER.
THAT'S A BIG NEGATIVE, SOLDIER.
WE WANT YOU TO HOLD EVERY DROP IN RESERVE, 'CAUSE YOUR GONNA NEED IT.
WONDER WOMAN, GREEN LANTERN AND WHAT'S LEFT OF THAT ALIEN FLEET WILL DRAW IMPERIEX'S FIRE, SO WE CAN GET YOU IN REAL CLOSE AND PERSONAL.
GENERAL. YOU DIDN'T HAVE TO COME ALONG ON THIS MISSION. WHY ARE YOU HERE?
THIS BIRD IS CARRYING THIRTY HYDROGEN BOMBS.
SOMEBODY HAD TO VOLUNTEER TO STEER IT IN AND YOU'RE LOOKING AT HIM.
YOU WORRY ABOUT YOUR JOB AND LET ME WORRY ABOUT MINE.

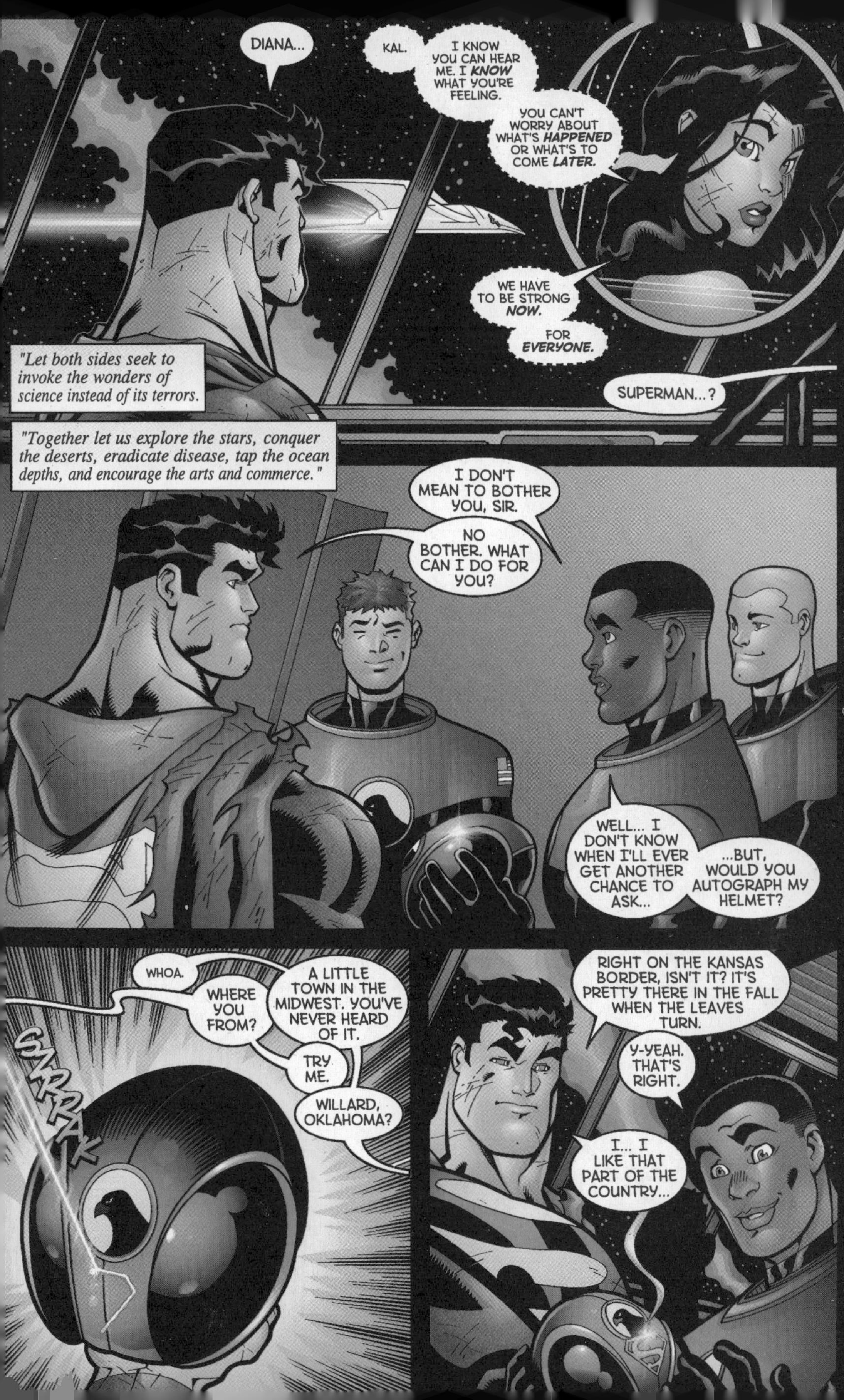

DIANA...
KAL.
I KNOW YOU CAN HEAR ME. I *KNOW* WHAT YOU'RE FEELING.
YOU CAN'T WORRY ABOUT WHAT'S *HAPPENED* OR WHAT'S TO COME *LATER.*
WE HAVE TO BE STRONG *NOW.*
FOR *EVERYONE.*
"Let both sides seek to invoke the wonders of science instead of its terrors.
SUPERMAN...?
"Together let us explore the stars, conquer the deserts, eradicate disease, tap the ocean depths, and encourage the arts and commerce."
I DON'T MEAN TO BOTHER YOU, SIR.
NO BOTHER. WHAT CAN I DO FOR YOU?
WELL... I DON'T KNOW WHEN I'LL EVER GET ANOTHER CHANCE TO ASK...
...BUT, WOULD YOU AUTOGRAPH MY HELMET?
SKRRAK
WHOA.
WHERE YOU FROM?
A LITTLE TOWN IN THE MIDWEST. YOU'VE NEVER HEARD OF IT.
TRY ME.
WILLARD, OKLAHOMA?
RIGHT ON THE KANSAS BORDER, ISN'T IT? IT'S PRETTY THERE IN THE FALL WHEN THE LEAVES TURN.
Y-YEAH. THAT'S RIGHT.
I... I LIKE THAT PART OF THE COUNTRY...

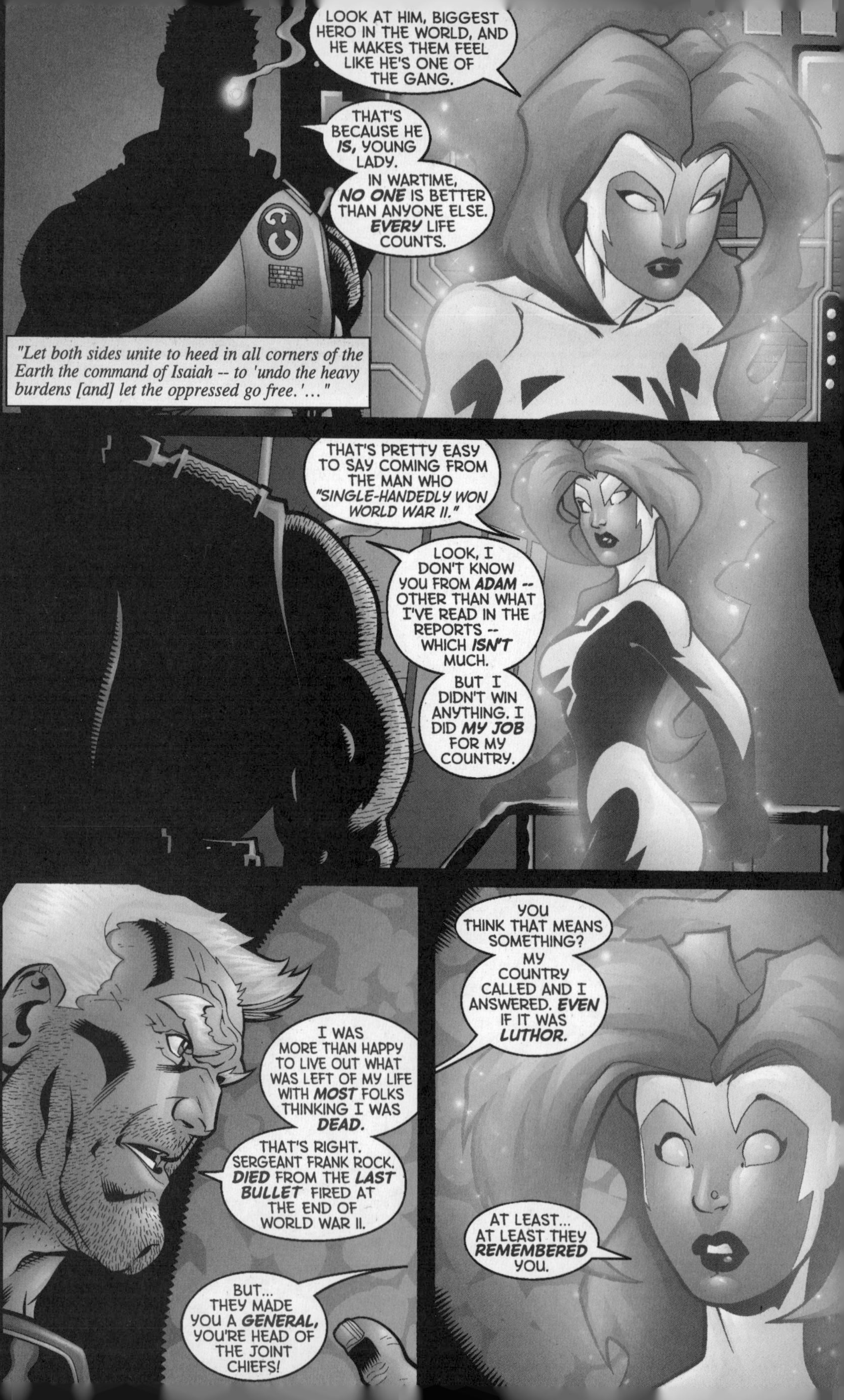
LOOK AT HIM, BIGGEST HERO IN THE WORLD, AND HE MAKES THEM FEEL LIKE HE'S ONE OF THE GANG.
THAT'S BECAUSE HE IS, YOUNG LADY.
IN WARTIME, NO ONE IS BETTER THAN ANYONE ELSE. EVERY LIFE COUNTS.
"Let both sides unite to heed in all corners of the Earth the command of Isaiah -- to 'undo the heavy burdens [and] let the oppressed go free.'..."
THAT'S PRETTY EASY TO SAY COMING FROM THE MAN WHO "SINGLE-HANDEDLY WON WORLD WAR II."
LOOK, I DON'T KNOW YOU FROM ADAM -- OTHER THAN WHAT I'VE READ IN THE REPORTS -- WHICH ISN'T MUCH.
BUT I DIDN'T WIN ANYTHING. I DID MY JOB FOR MY COUNTRY.
I WAS MORE THAN HAPPY TO LIVE OUT WHAT WAS LEFT OF MY LIFE WITH MOST FOLKS THINKING I WAS DEAD.
THAT'S RIGHT. SERGEANT FRANK ROCK. DIED FROM THE LAST BULLET FIRED AT THE END OF WORLD WAR II.
BUT... THEY MADE YOU A GENERAL, YOU'RE HEAD OF THE JOINT CHIEFS!
YOU THINK THAT MEANS SOMETHING?
MY COUNTRY CALLED AND I ANSWERED. EVEN IF IT WAS LUTHOR.
AT LEAST... AT LEAST THEY REMEMBERED YOU.

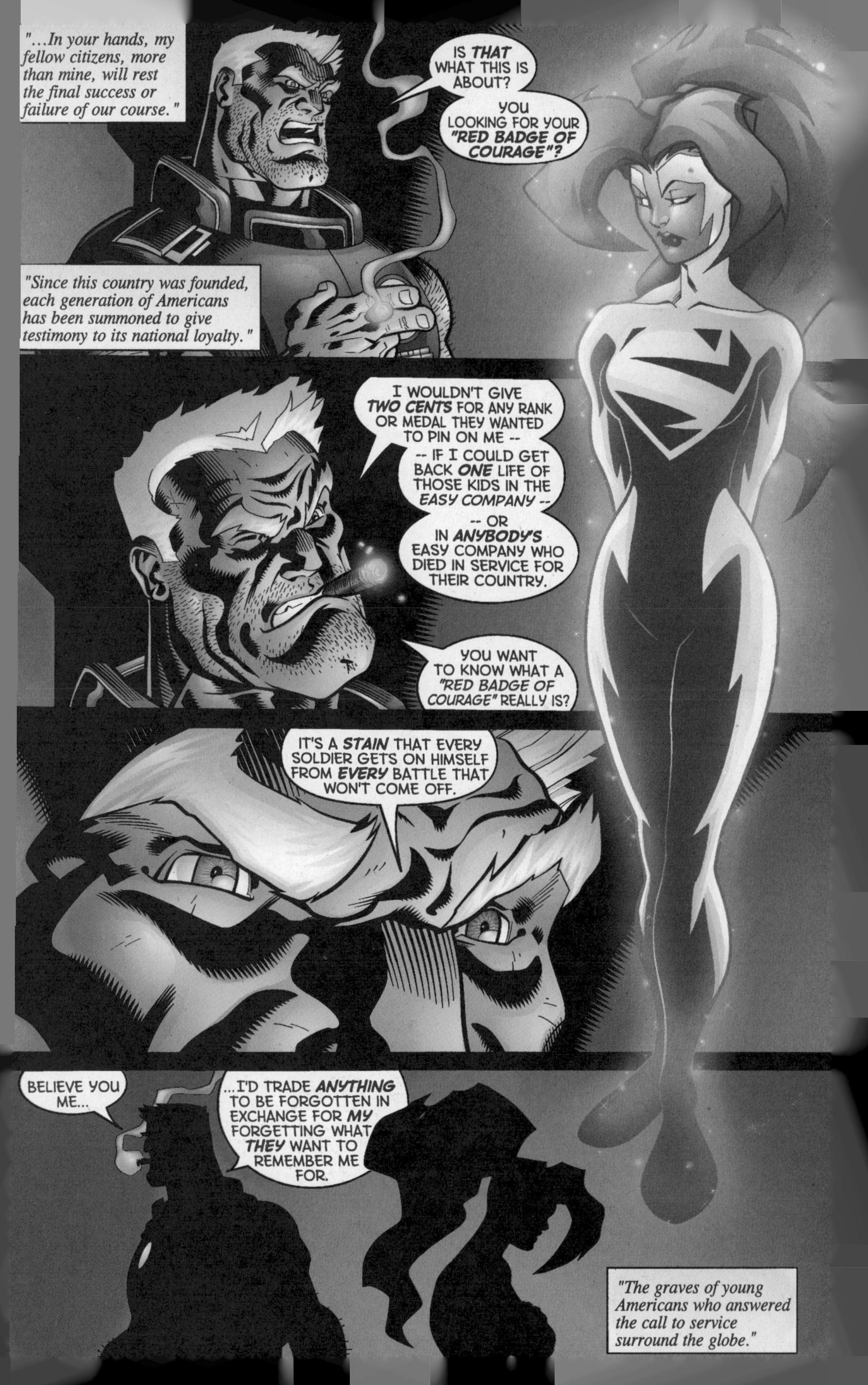
"...In your hands, my fellow citizens, more than mine, will rest the final success or failure of our course."
IS THAT WHAT THIS IS ABOUT?
YOU LOOKING FOR YOUR "RED BADGE OF COURAGE"?
"Since this country was founded, each generation of Americans has been summoned to give testimony to its national loyalty."
I WOULDN'T GIVE TWO CENTS FOR ANY RANK OR MEDAL THEY WANTED TO PIN ON ME --
-- IF I COULD GET BACK ONE LIFE OF THOSE KIDS IN THE EASY COMPANY --
-- OR IN ANYBODY'S EASY COMPANY WHO DIED IN SERVICE FOR THEIR COUNTRY.
YOU WANT TO KNOW WHAT A "RED BADGE OF COURAGE" REALLY IS?
IT'S A STAIN THAT EVERY SOLDIER GETS ON HIMSELF FROM EVERY BATTLE THAT WON'T COME OFF.
BELIEVE YOU ME...
...I'D TRADE ANYTHING TO BE FORGOTTEN IN EXCHANGE FOR MY FORGETTING WHAT THEY WANT TO REMEMBER ME FOR.
"The graves of young Americans who answered the call to service surround the globe."

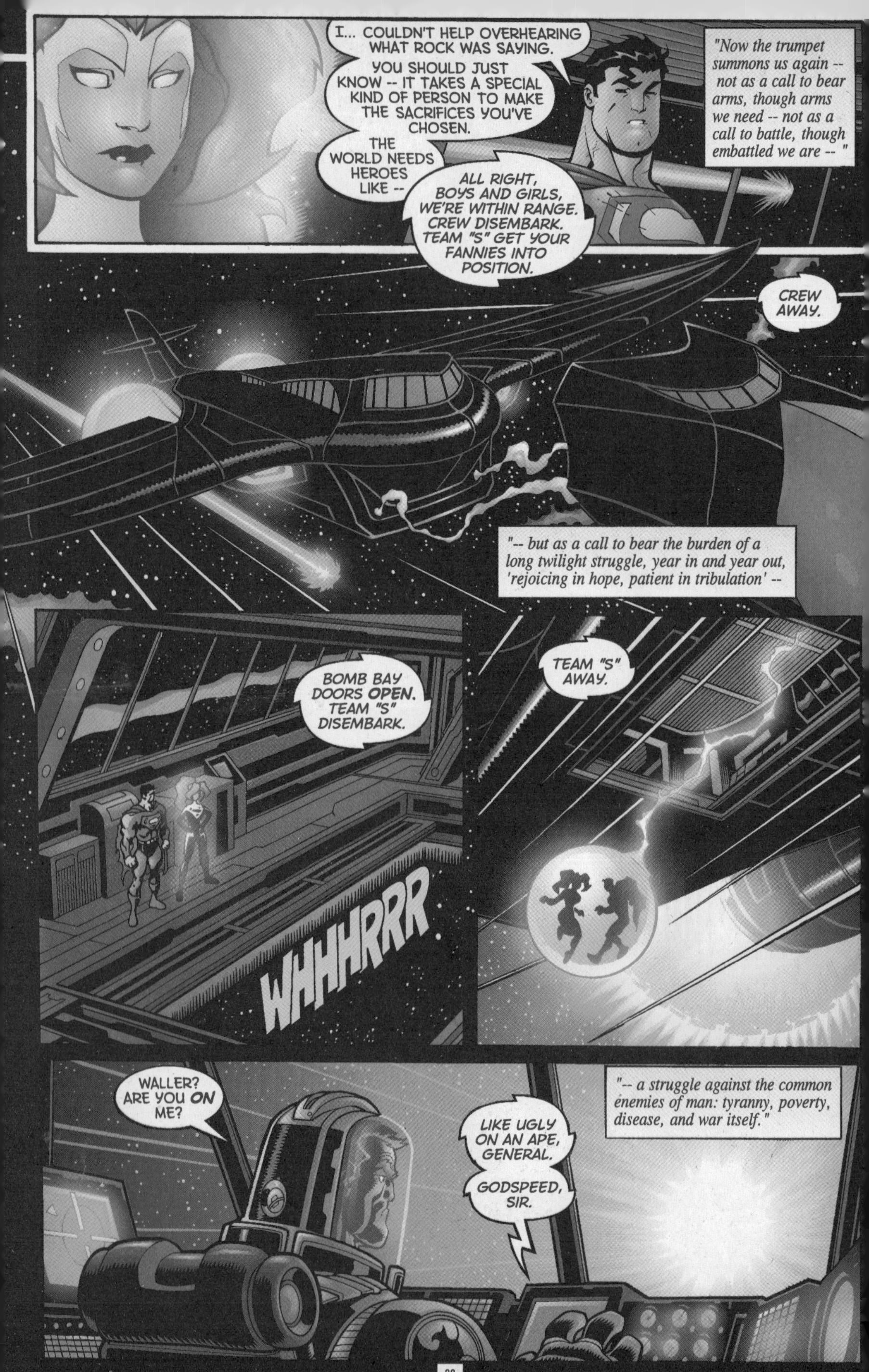
I... COULDN'T HELP OVERHEARING WHAT ROCK WAS SAYING.
YOU SHOULD JUST KNOW -- IT TAKES A SPECIAL KIND OF PERSON TO MAKE THE SACRIFICES YOU'VE CHOSEN.
THE WORLD NEEDS HEROES LIKE --
"Now the trumpet summons us again -- not as a call to bear arms, though arms we need -- not as a call to battle, though embattled we are -- "
ALL RIGHT, BOYS AND GIRLS, WE'RE WITHIN RANGE. CREW DISEMBARK. TEAM "S" GET YOUR FANNIES INTO POSITION.
CREW AWAY.
"-- but as a call to bear the burden of a long twilight struggle, year in and year out, 'rejoicing in hope, patient in tribulation' --
BOMB BAY DOORS OPEN. TEAM "S" DISEMBARK.
WHHHRRR
TEAM "S" AWAY.
WALLER? ARE YOU ON ME?
LIKE UGLY ON AN APE, GENERAL.
GODSPEED, SIR.
"-- a struggle against the common enemies of man: tyranny, poverty, disease, and war itself."

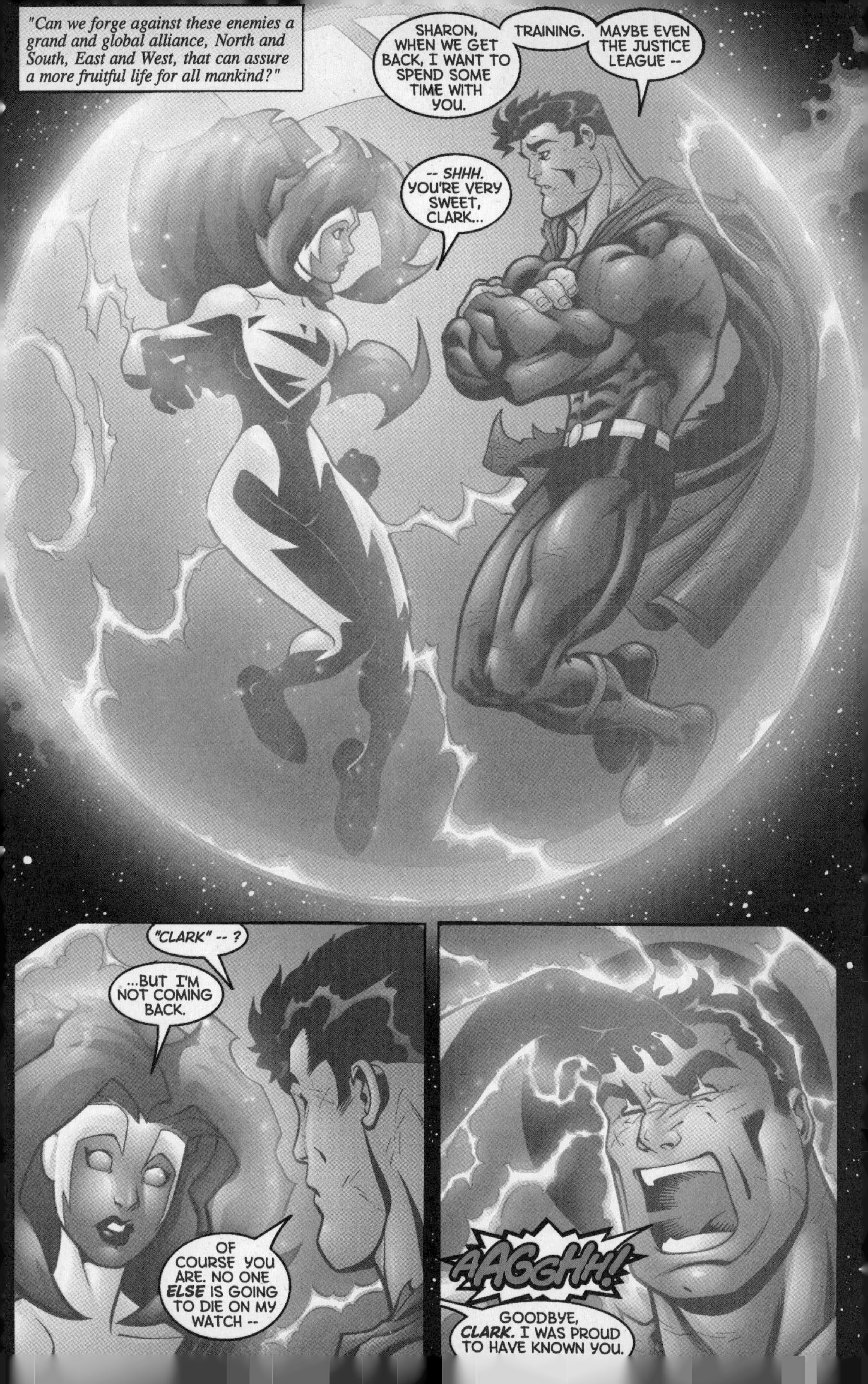
"Can we forge against these enemies a grand and global alliance, North and South, East and West, that can assure a more fruitful life for all mankind?"
SHARON, WHEN WE GET BACK, I WANT TO SPEND SOME TIME WITH YOU.
TRAINING.
MAYBE EVEN THE JUSTICE LEAGUE --
-- SHHH. YOU'RE VERY SWEET, CLARK...
"CLARK" -- ?
...BUT I'M NOT COMING BACK.
OF COURSE YOU ARE. NO ONE ELSE IS GOING TO DIE ON MY WATCH --
AAGGHH!
GOODBYE, CLARK. I WAS PROUD TO HAVE KNOWN YOU.

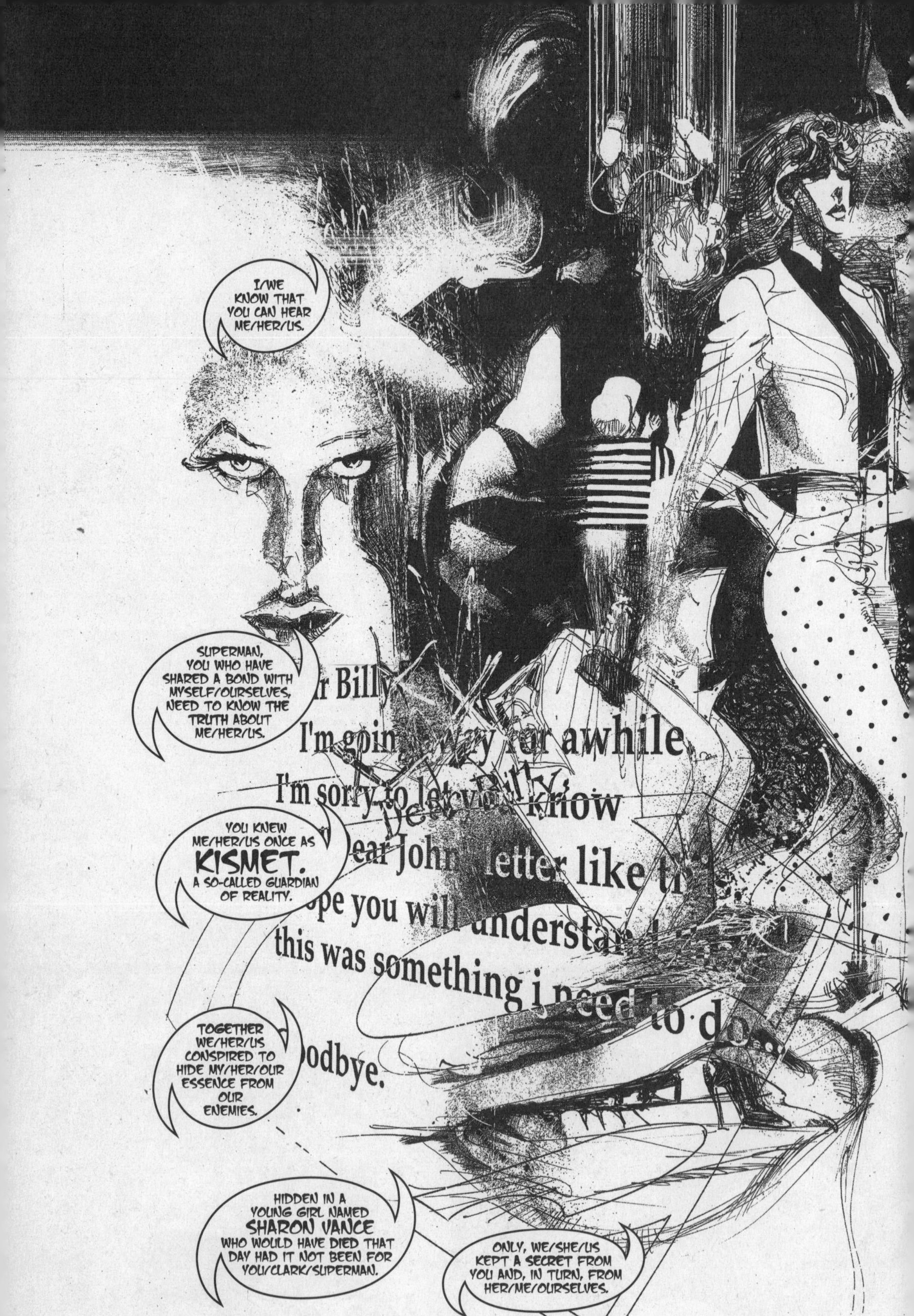
I/WE KNOW THAT YOU CAN HEAR ME/HER/US.
SUPERMAN, YOU WHO HAVE SHARED A BOND WITH MYSELF/OURSELVES, NEED TO KNOW THE TRUTH ABOUT ME/HER/US.
YOU KNEW ME/HER/US ONCE AS KISMET. A SO-CALLED GUARDIAN OF REALITY.
TOGETHER WE/HER/US CONSPIRED TO HIDE MY/HER/OUR ESSENCE FROM OUR ENEMIES.
HIDDEN IN A YOUNG GIRL NAMED SHARON VANCE WHO WOULD HAVE DIED THAT DAY HAD IT NOT BEEN FOR YOU/CLARK/SUPERMAN.
ONLY, WE/SHE/US KEPT A SECRET FROM YOU AND, IN TURN, FROM HER/ME/OURSELVES.

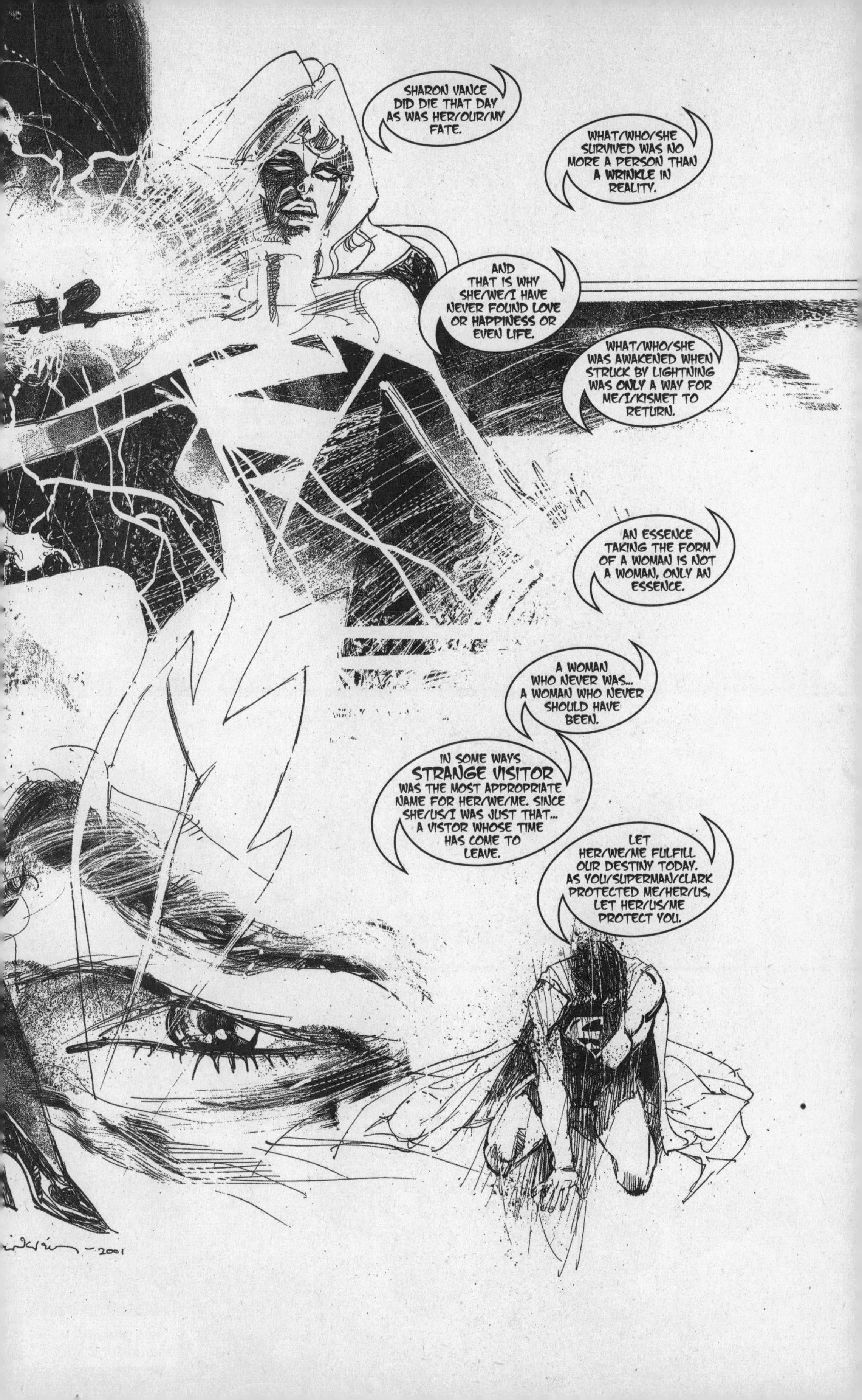
SHARON VANCE DID DIE THAT DAY AS WAS HER/OUR/MY FATE.
WHAT/WHO/SHE SURVIVED WAS NO MORE A PERSON THAN A WRINKLE IN REALITY.
AND THAT IS WHY SHE/WE/I HAVE NEVER FOUND LOVE OR HAPPINESS OR EVEN LIFE.
WHAT/WHO/SHE WAS AWAKENED WHEN STRUCK BY LIGHTNING WAS ONLY A WAY FOR ME/I/KISMET TO RETURN.
AN ESSENCE TAKING THE FORM OF A WOMAN IS NOT A WOMAN, ONLY AN ESSENCE.
A WOMAN WHO NEVER WAS... A WOMAN WHO NEVER SHOULD HAVE BEEN.
IN SOME WAYS STRANGE VISITOR WAS THE MOST APPROPRIATE NAME FOR HER/WE/ME. SINCE SHE/US/I WAS JUST THAT... A VISTOR WHOSE TIME HAS COME TO LEAVE.
LET HER/WE/ME FULFILL OUR DESTINY TODAY. AS YOU/SUPERMAN/CLARK PROTECTED ME/HER/US, LET HER/US/ME PROTECT YOU.
2001

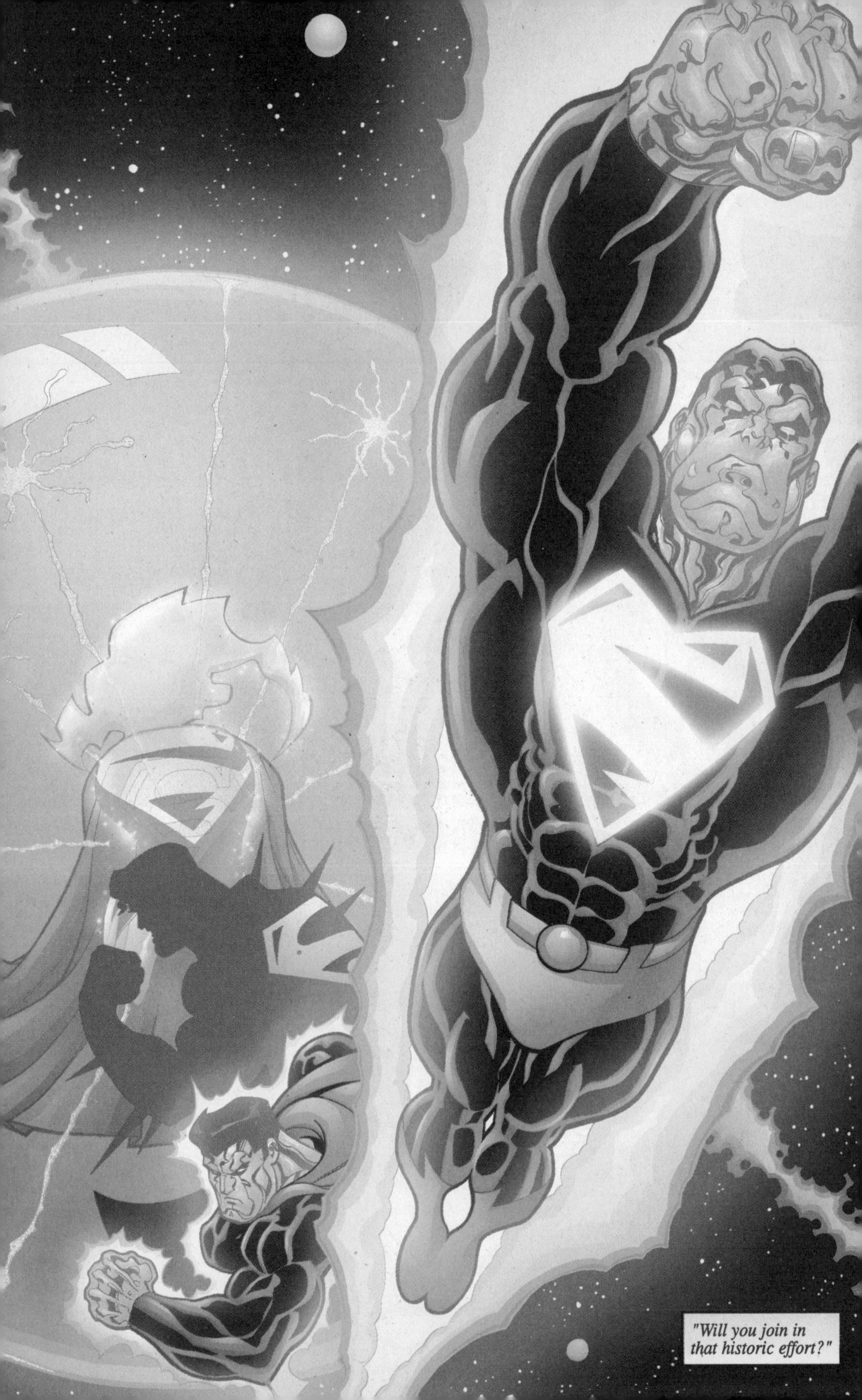
"Will you join in
that historic effort?"

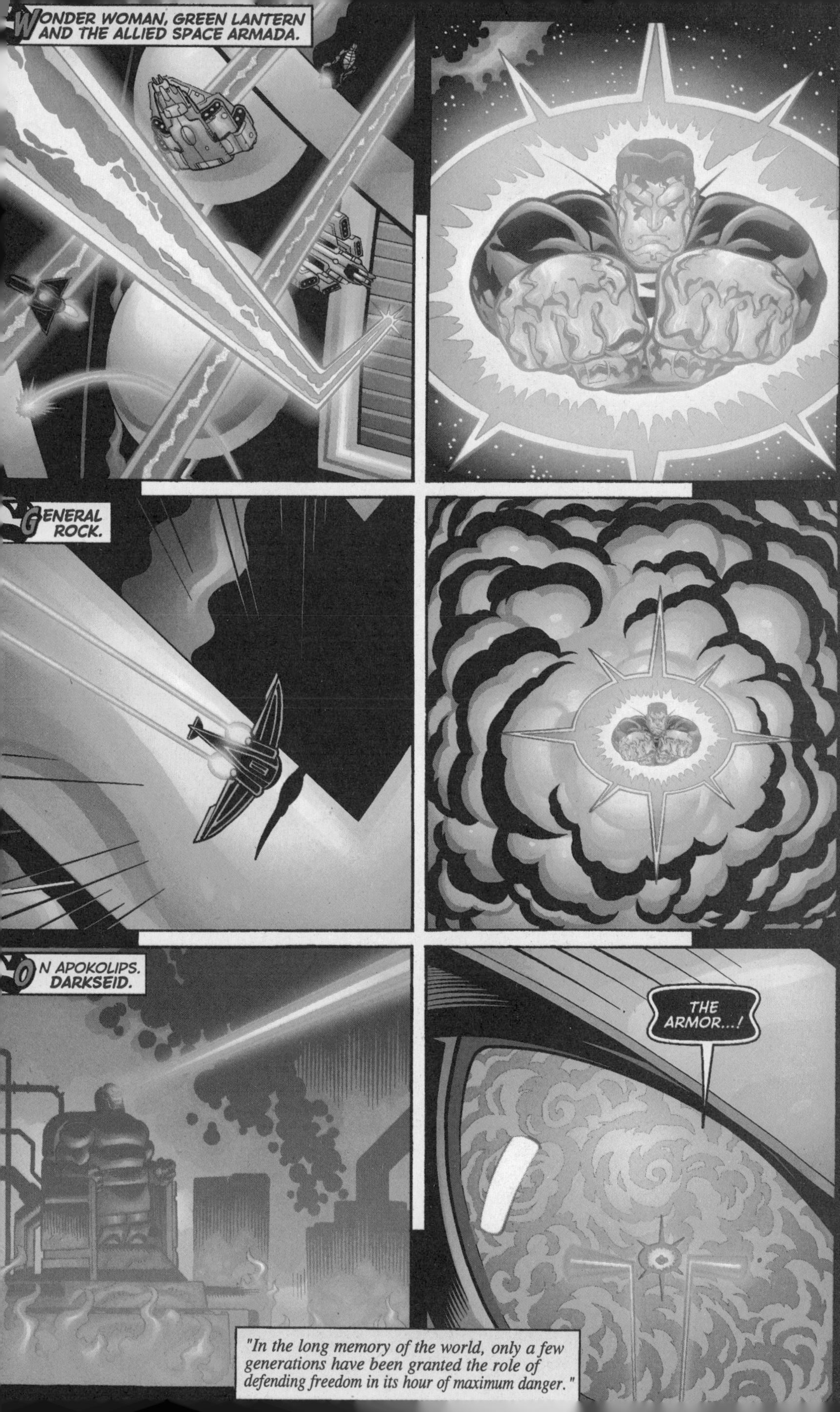
WONDER WOMAN, GREEN LANTERN AND THE ALLIED SPACE ARMADA.
GENERAL ROCK.
ON APOKOLIPS. DARKSEID.
THE ARMOR...!
"In the long memory of the world, only a few generations have been granted the role of defending freedom in its hour of maximum danger."

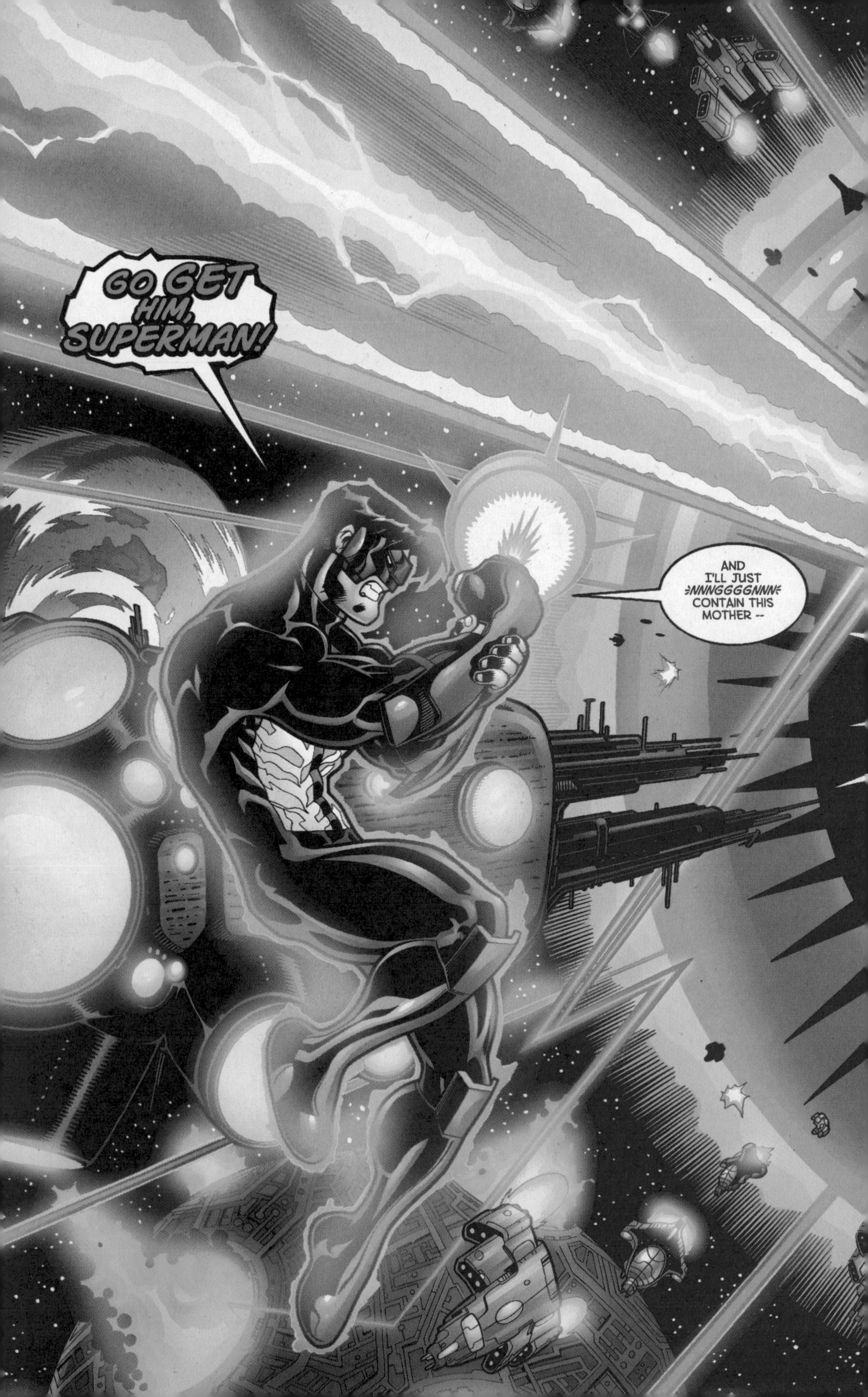
GO GET HIM, SUPERMAN!
AND I'LL JUST NNNGGGGNNN CONTAIN THIS MOTHER --

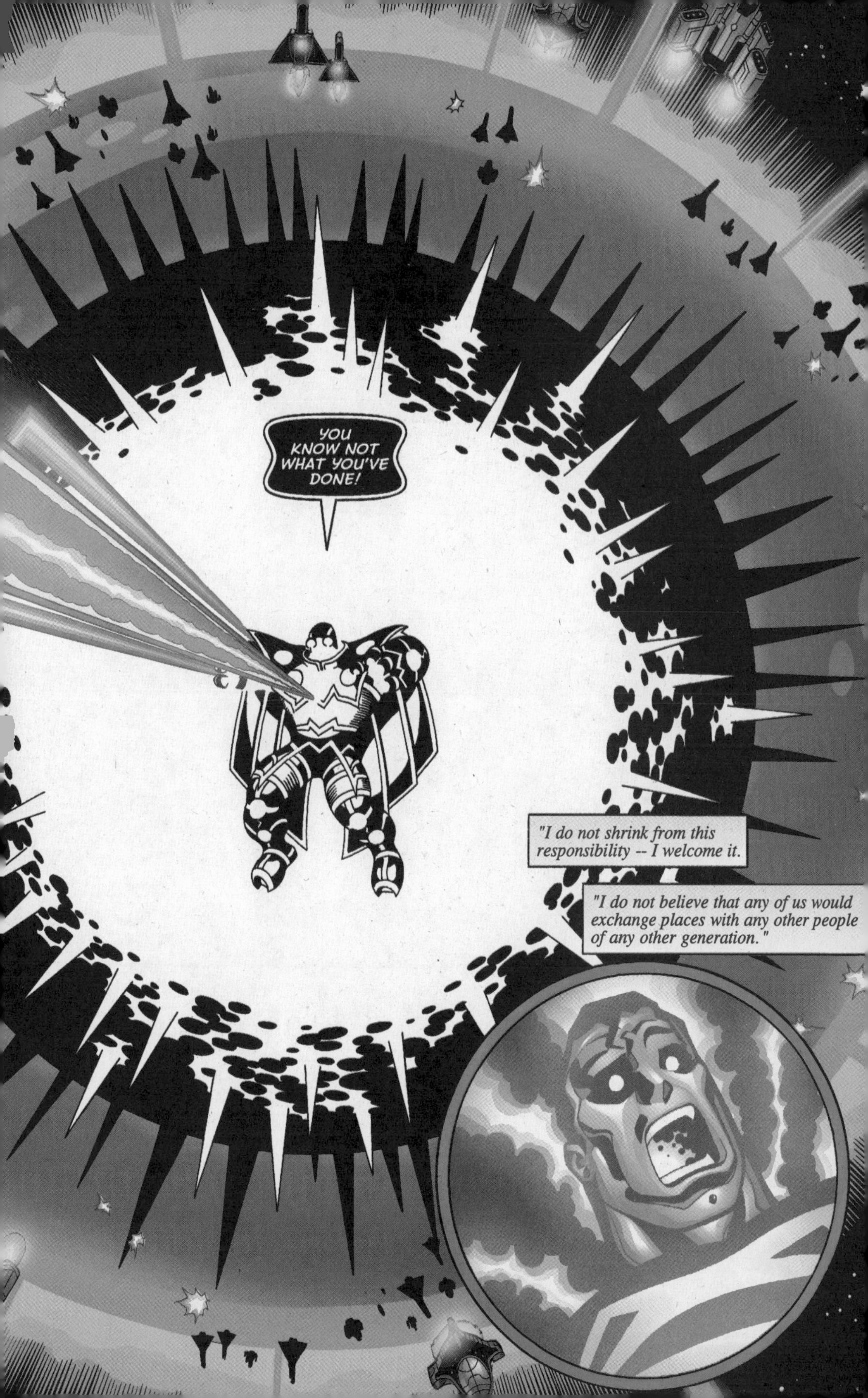
YOU KNOW NOT WHAT YOU'VE DONE!
"I do not shrink from this responsibility -- I welcome it.
"I do not believe that any of us would exchange places with any other people of any other generation."

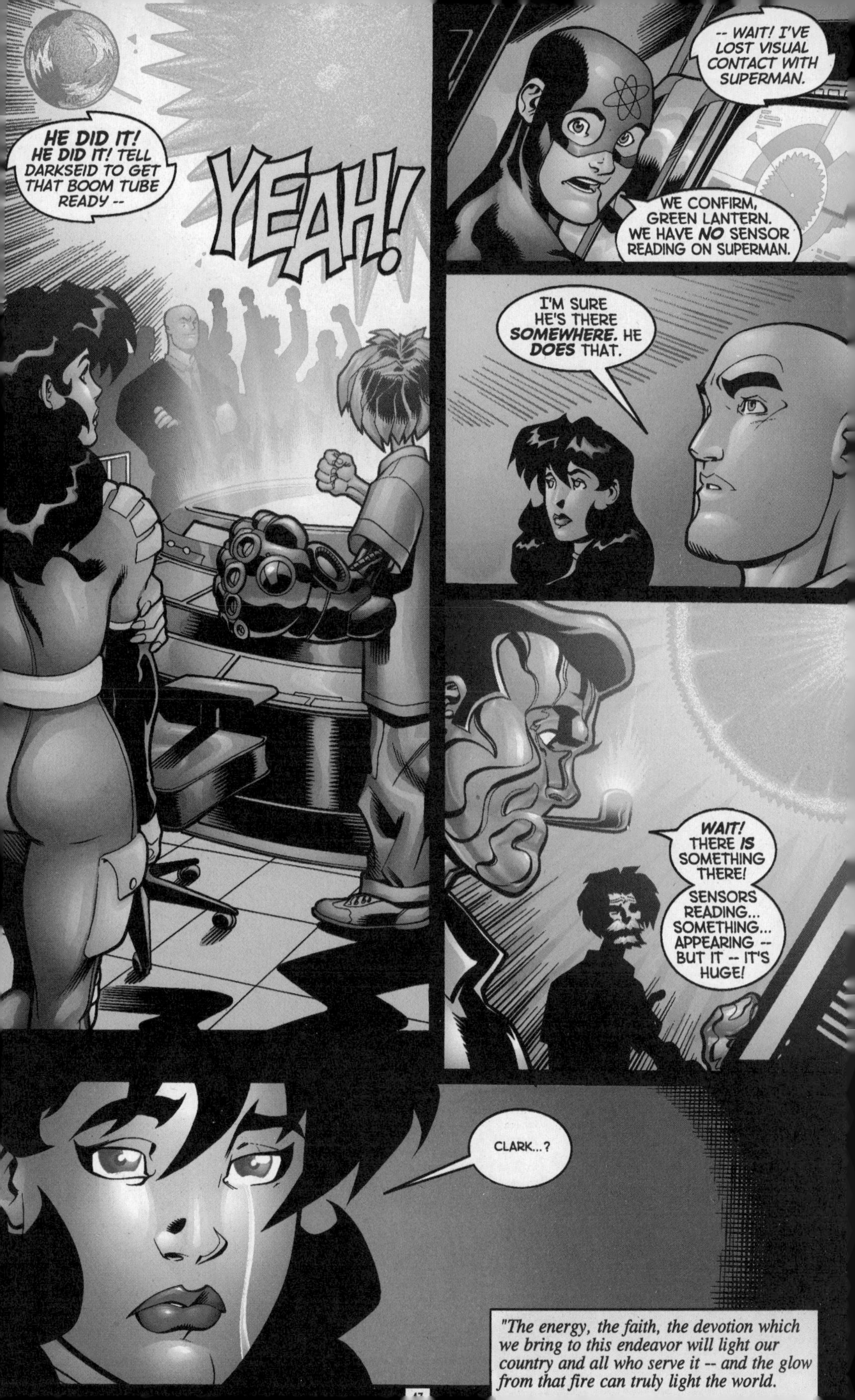
HE DID IT! HE DID IT! TELL DARKSEID TO GET THAT BOOM TUBE READY --
YEAH!
-- WAIT! I'VE LOST VISUAL CONTACT WITH SUPERMAN.
WE CONFIRM, GREEN LANTERN. WE HAVE NO SENSOR READING ON SUPERMAN.
I'M SURE HE'S THERE SOMEWHERE. HE DOES THAT.
WAIT! THERE IS SOMETHING THERE!
SENSORS READING... SOMETHING... APPEARING -- BUT IT -- IT'S HUGE!
CLARK...?
"The energy, the faith, the devotion which we bring to this endeavor will light our country and all who serve it -- and the glow from that fire can truly light the world.

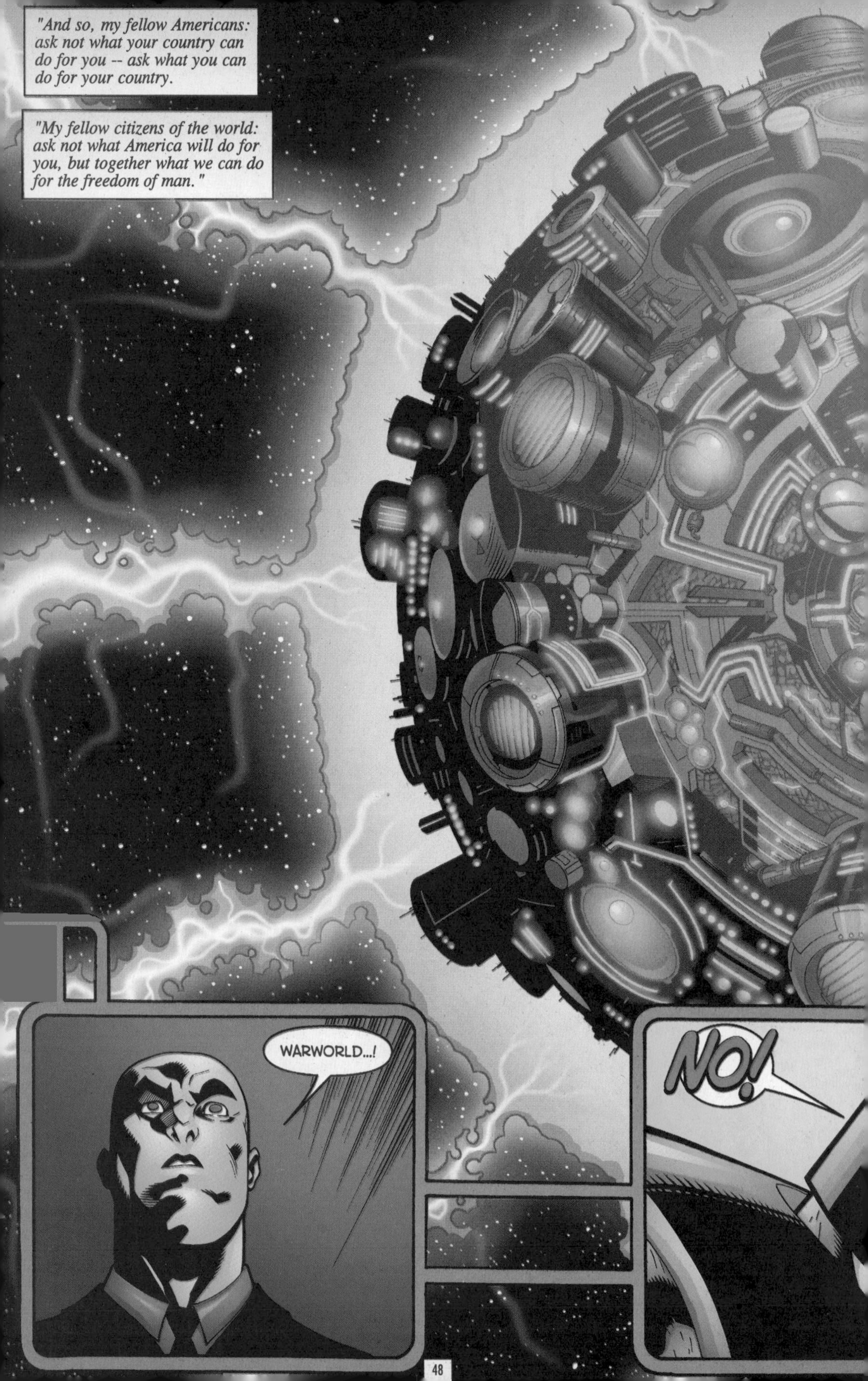
"And so, my fellow Americans: ask not what your country can do for you -- ask what you can do for your country.
"My fellow citizens of the world: ask not what America will do for you, but together what we can do for the freedom of man."
WARWORLD...!
NO!

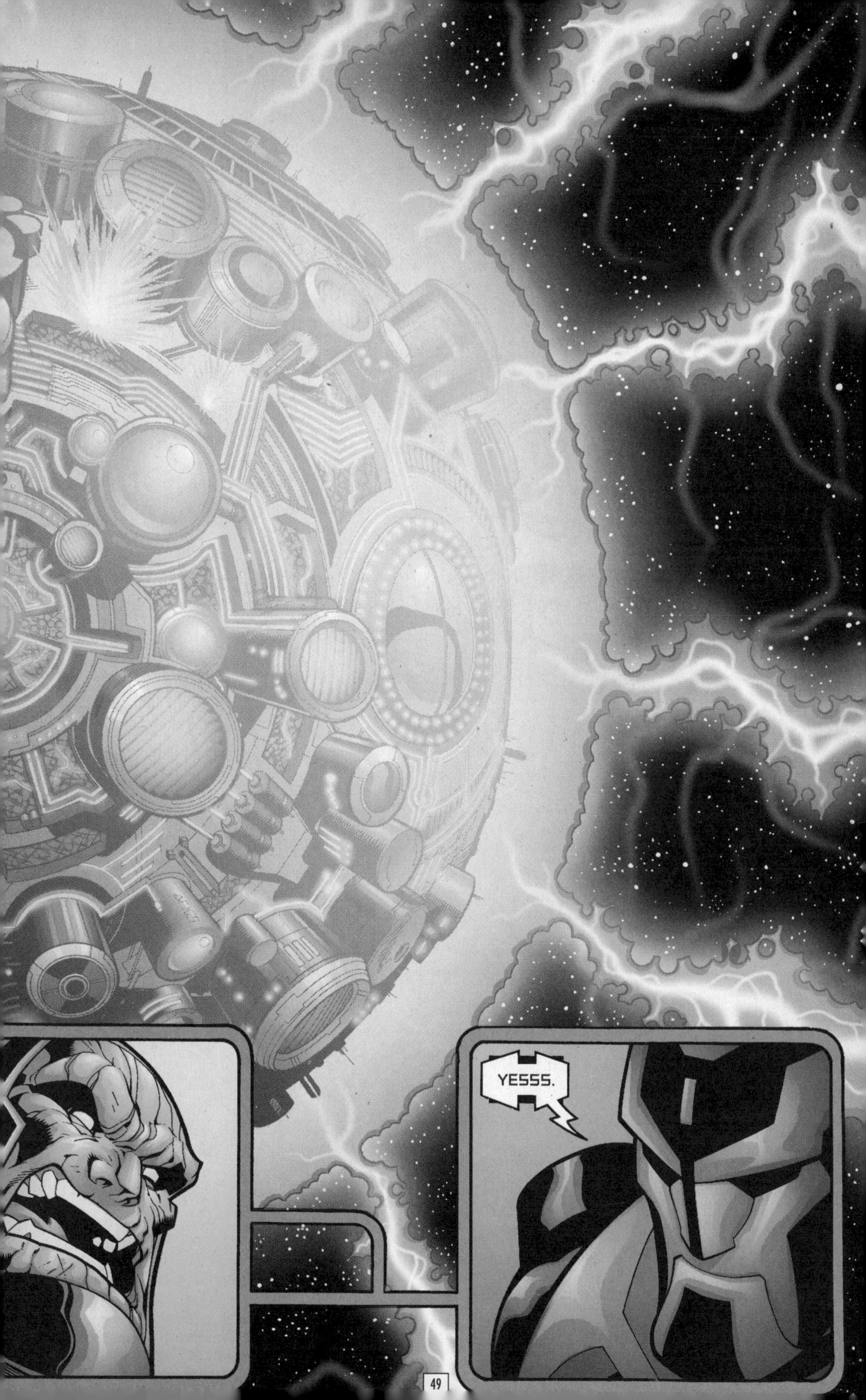
YESSS.

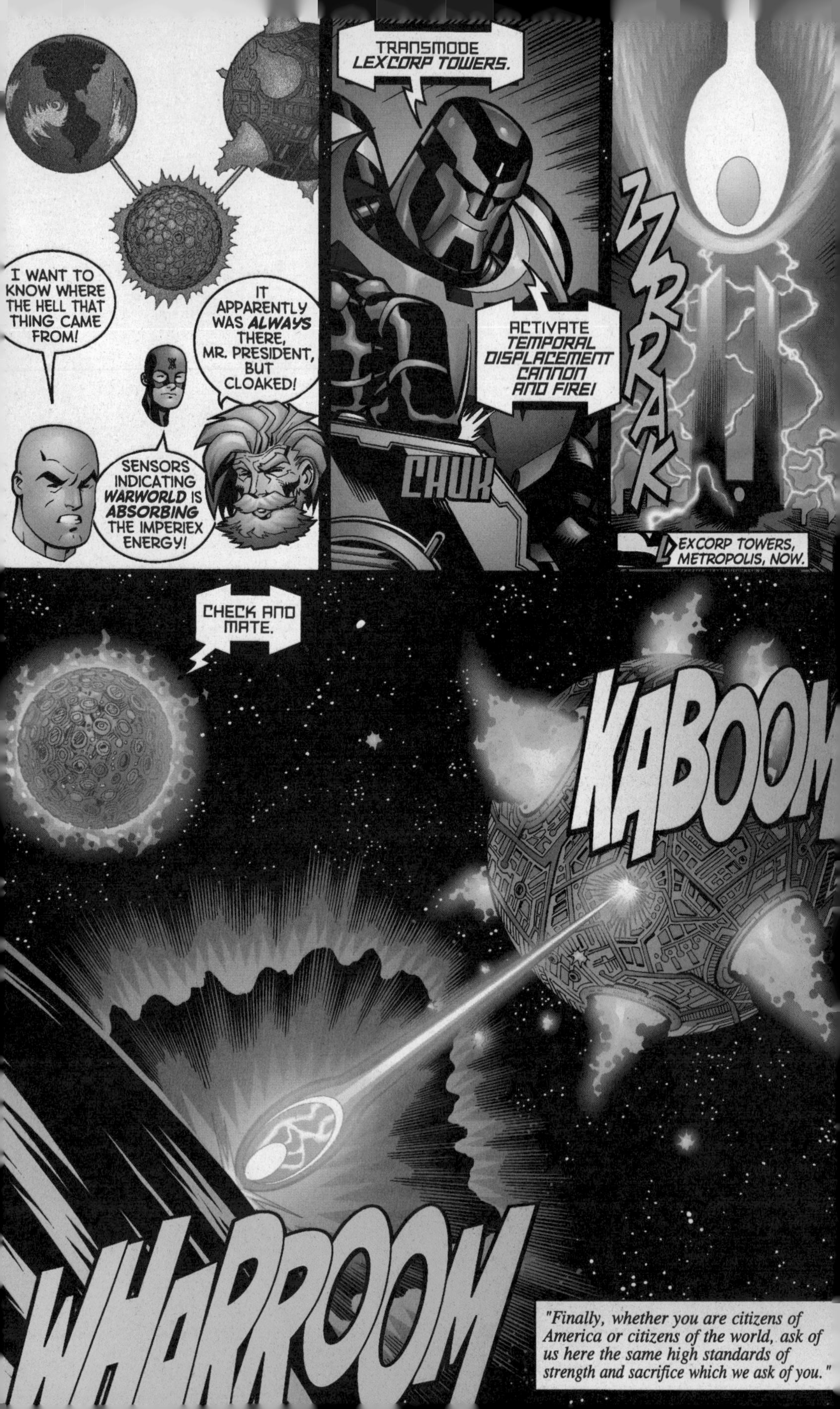

I WANT TO KNOW WHERE THE HELL THAT THING CAME FROM!
IT APPARENTLY WAS ALWAYS THERE, MR. PRESIDENT, BUT CLOAKED!
SENSORS INDICATING WARWORLD IS ABSORBING THE IMPERIEX ENERGY!
TRANSMODE LEXCORP TOWERS.
ACTIVATE TEMPORAL DISPLACEMENT CANNON AND FIRE!
CHUK
ZZZRRRAK
LEXCORP TOWERS, METROPOLIS, NOW.
CHECK AND MATE.
KABOOM
WHARROOM
"Finally, whether you are citizens of America or citizens of the world, ask of us here the same high standards of strength and sacrifice which we ask of you."

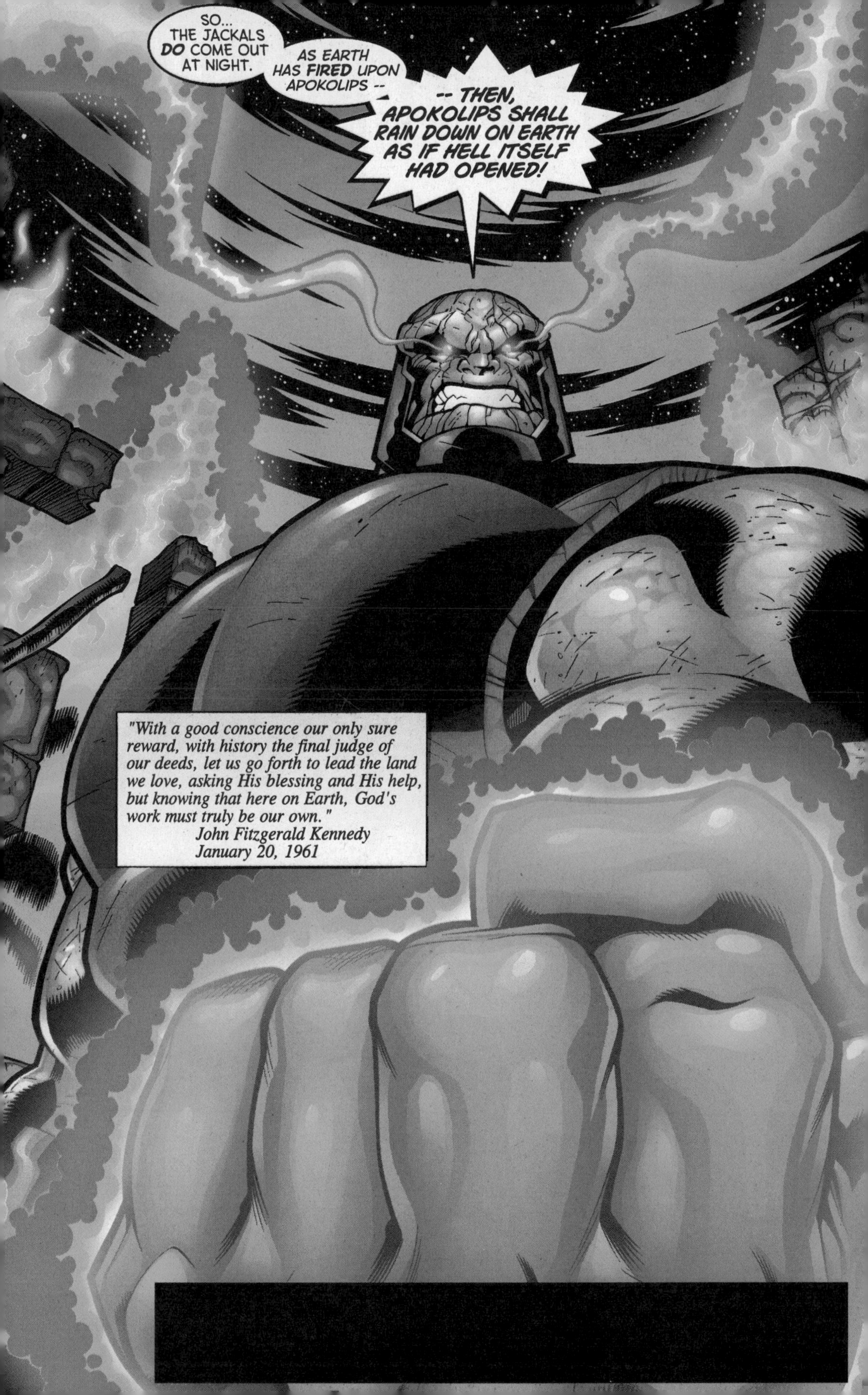
SO... THE JACKALS DO COME OUT AT NIGHT.
AS EARTH HAS FIRED UPON APOKOLIPS --
-- THEN, APOKOLIPS SHALL RAIN DOWN ON EARTH AS IF HELL ITSELF HAD OPENED!
"With a good conscience our only sure reward, with history the final judge of our deeds, let us go forth to lead the land we love, asking His blessing and His help, but knowing that here on Earth, God's work must truly be our own."
John Fitzgerald Kennedy
January 20, 1961
[redacted]

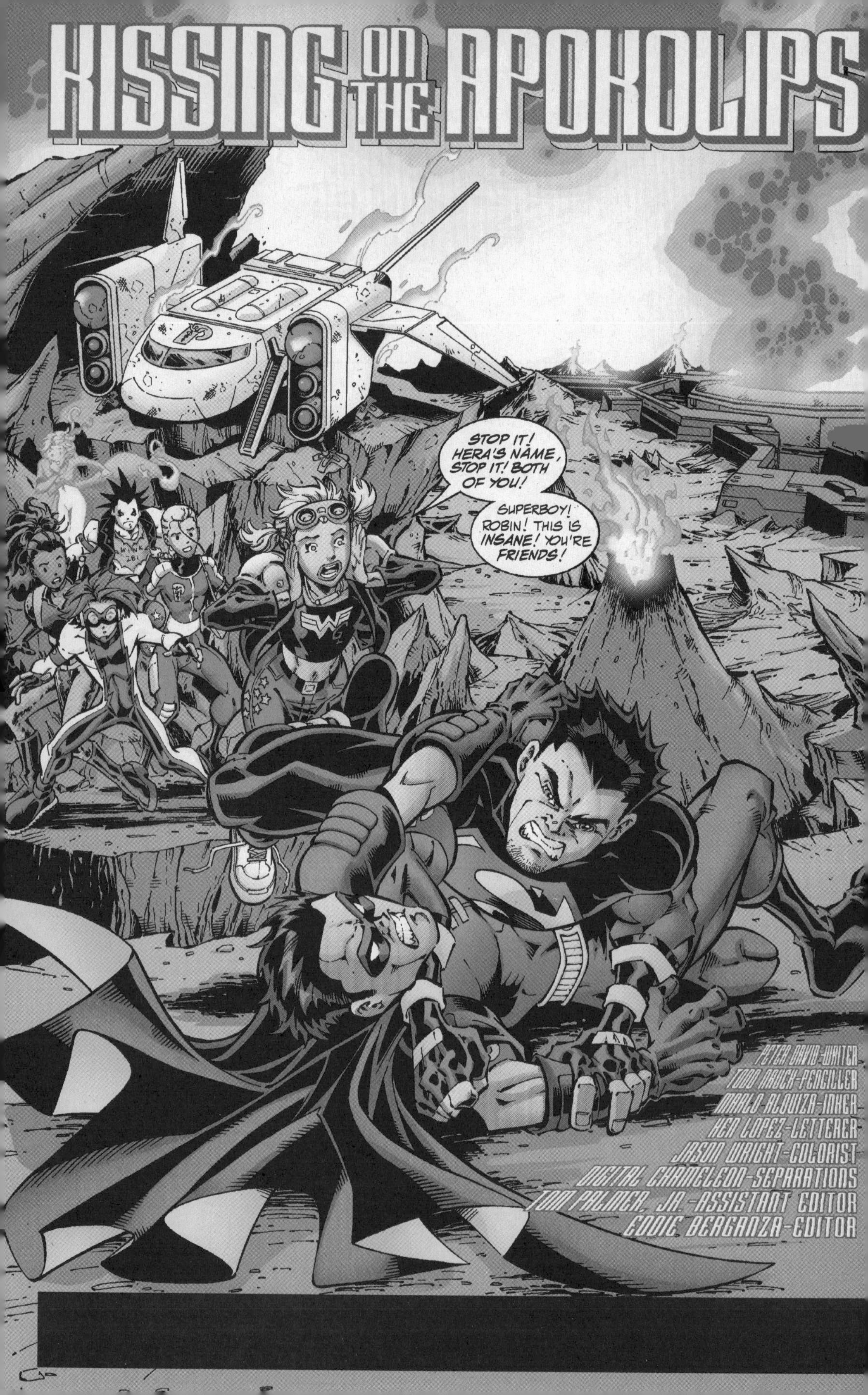
KISSING ON THE APOKOLIPS
STOP IT! HERA'S NAME, STOP IT! BOTH OF YOU!
SUPERBOY! ROBIN! THIS IS INSANE! YOU'RE FRIENDS!
PETER DAVID-WRITER
TODD NAUCK-PENCILLER
MARLO ALQUIZA-INKER
KEN LOPEZ-LETTERER
JASON WRIGHT-COLORIST
DIGITAL CHAMELEON-SEPARATIONS
TOM PALMER, JR.-ASSISTANT EDITOR
EDDIE BERGANZA-EDITOR

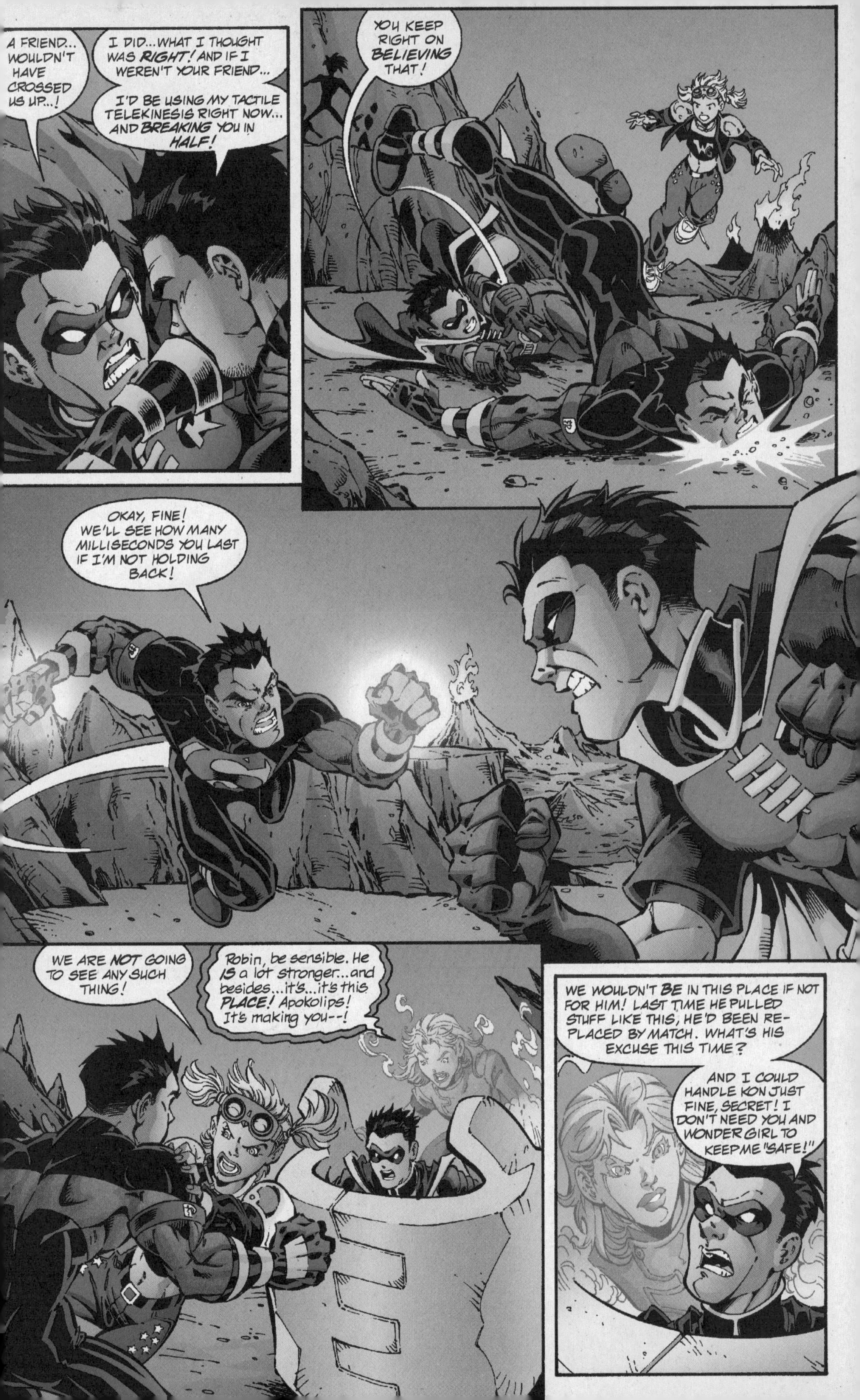
A FRIEND... WOULDN'T HAVE CROSSED US UP...!
I DID...WHAT I THOUGHT WAS RIGHT! AND IF I WEREN'T YOUR FRIEND...
I'D BE USING MY TACTILE TELEKINESIS RIGHT NOW... AND BREAKING YOU IN HALF!
YOU KEEP RIGHT ON BELIEVING THAT!
OKAY, FINE! WE'LL SEE HOW MANY MILLISECONDS YOU LAST IF I'M NOT HOLDING BACK!
WE ARE NOT GOING TO SEE ANY SUCH THING!
Robin, be sensible. He IS a lot stronger...and besides...it's...it's this PLACE! Apokolips! It's making you--!
WE WOULDN'T BE IN THIS PLACE IF NOT FOR HIM! LAST TIME HE PULLED STUFF LIKE THIS, HE'D BEEN RE-PLACED BY MATCH. WHAT'S HIS EXCUSE THIS TIME?
AND I COULD HANDLE KON JUST FINE, SECRET! I DON'T NEED YOU AND WONDER GIRL TO KEEP ME "SAFE!"

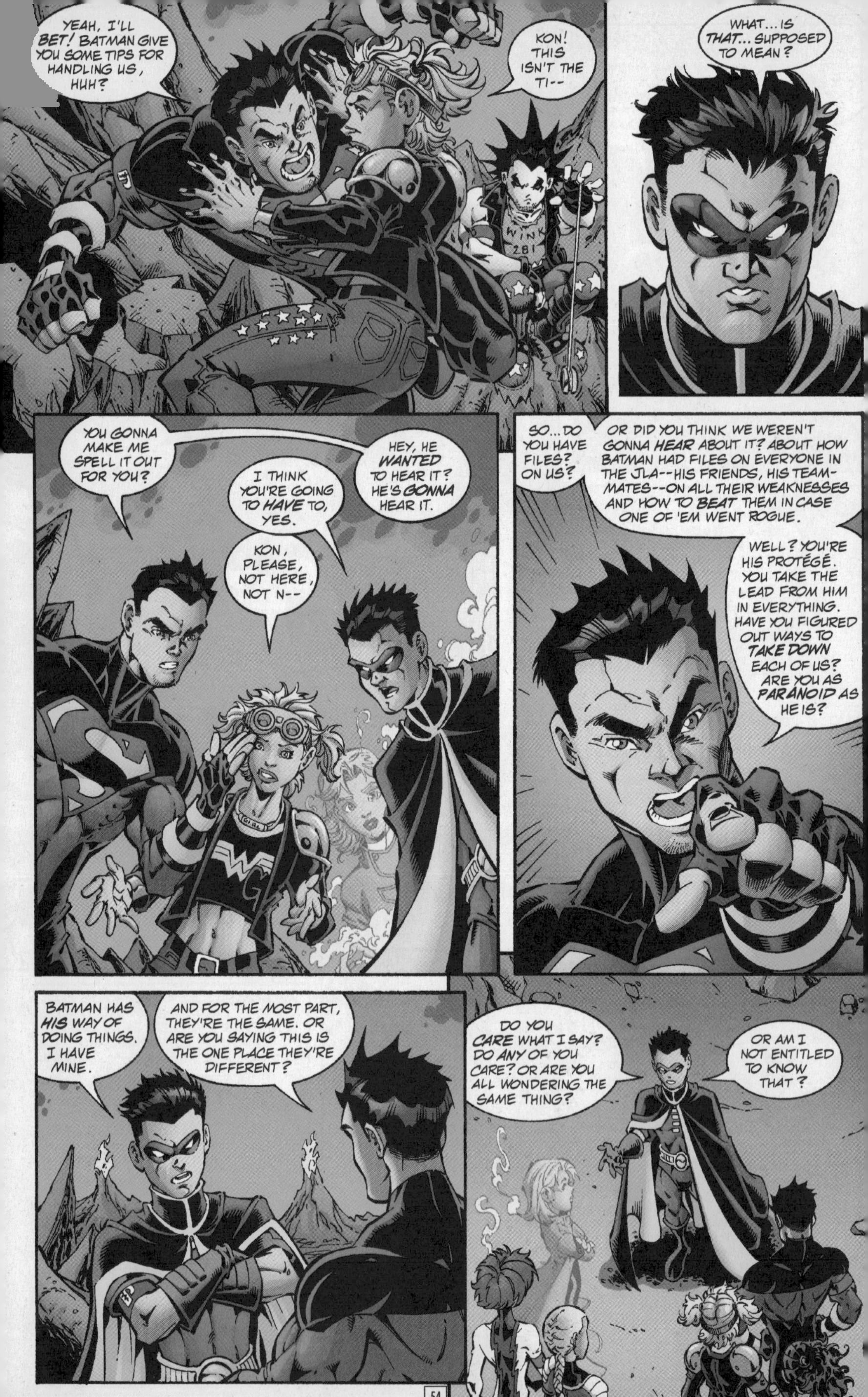
YEAH, I'LL BET! BATMAN GIVE YOU SOME TIPS FOR HANDLING US, HUH?
KON! THIS ISN'T THE TI--
WHAT... IS THAT... SUPPOSED TO MEAN?
YOU GONNA MAKE ME SPELL IT OUT FOR YOU?
I THINK YOU'RE GOING TO HAVE TO, YES.
HEY, HE WANTED TO HEAR IT? HE'S GONNA HEAR IT.
KON, PLEASE, NOT HERE, NOT N--
SO...DO YOU HAVE FILES? ON US?
OR DID YOU THINK WE WEREN'T GONNA HEAR ABOUT IT? ABOUT HOW BATMAN HAD FILES ON EVERYONE IN THE JLA--HIS FRIENDS, HIS TEAM-MATES--ON ALL THEIR WEAKNESSES AND HOW TO BEAT THEM IN CASE ONE OF 'EM WENT ROGUE.
WELL? YOU'RE HIS PROTÉGÉ. YOU TAKE THE LEAD FROM HIM IN EVERYTHING. HAVE YOU FIGURED OUT WAYS TO TAKE DOWN EACH OF US? ARE YOU AS PARANOID AS HE IS?
BATMAN HAS HIS WAY OF DOING THINGS. I HAVE MINE.
AND FOR THE MOST PART, THEY'RE THE SAME. OR ARE YOU SAYING THIS IS THE ONE PLACE THEY'RE DIFFERENT?
DO YOU CARE WHAT I SAY? DO ANY OF YOU CARE? OR ARE YOU ALL WONDERING THE SAME THING?
OR AM I NOT ENTITLED TO KNOW THAT?
WINK
281

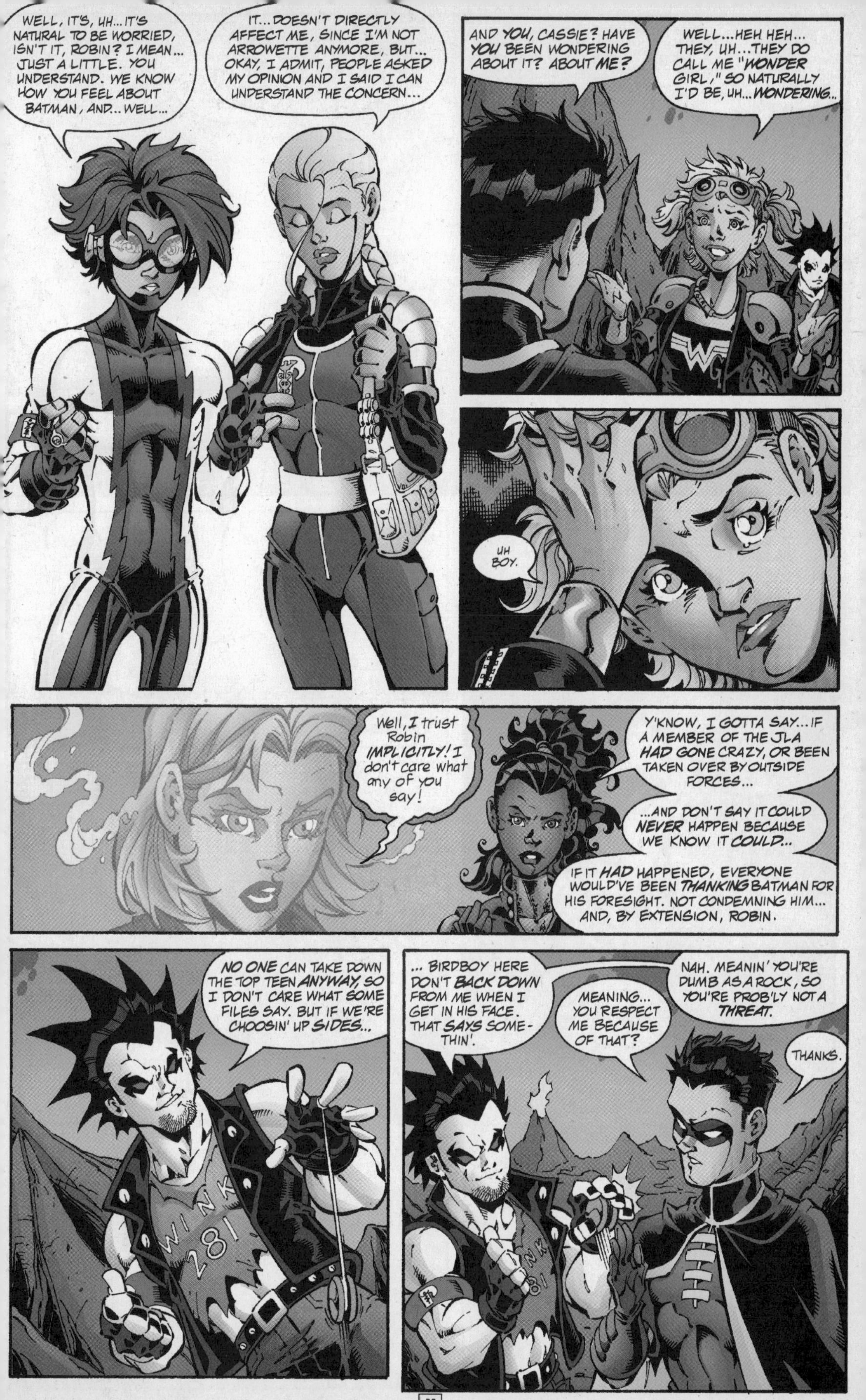
WELL, IT'S, UH... IT'S NATURAL TO BE WORRIED, ISN'T IT, ROBIN? I MEAN... JUST A LITTLE. YOU UNDERSTAND. WE KNOW HOW YOU FEEL ABOUT BATMAN, AND... WELL...
IT... DOESN'T DIRECTLY AFFECT ME, SINCE I'M NOT ARROWETTE ANYMORE, BUT... OKAY, I ADMIT, PEOPLE ASKED MY OPINION AND I SAID I CAN UNDERSTAND THE CONCERN...
AND YOU, CASSIE? HAVE YOU BEEN WONDERING ABOUT IT? ABOUT ME?
WELL... HEH HEH... THEY, UH... THEY DO CALL ME "WONDER GIRL," SO NATURALLY I'D BE, UH... WONDERING...
UH BOY.
Well, I trust Robin IMPLICITLY! I don't care what any of you say!
Y'KNOW, I GOTTA SAY... IF A MEMBER OF THE JLA HAD GONE CRAZY, OR BEEN TAKEN OVER BY OUTSIDE FORCES...
...AND DON'T SAY IT COULD NEVER HAPPEN BECAUSE WE KNOW IT COULD...
IF IT HAD HAPPENED, EVERYONE WOULD'VE BEEN THANKING BATMAN FOR HIS FORESIGHT. NOT CONDEMNING HIM... AND, BY EXTENSION, ROBIN.
NO ONE CAN TAKE DOWN THE TOP TEEN ANYWAY, SO I DON'T CARE WHAT SOME FILES SAY. BUT IF WE'RE CHOOSIN' UP SIDES...
... BIRDBOY HERE DON'T BACK DOWN FROM ME WHEN I GET IN HIS FACE. THAT SAYS SOMETHIN'.
MEANING... YOU RESPECT ME BECAUSE OF THAT?
NAH. MEANIN' YOU'RE DUMB AS A ROCK, SO YOU'RE PROB'LY NOT A THREAT.
THANKS.
WINK 281

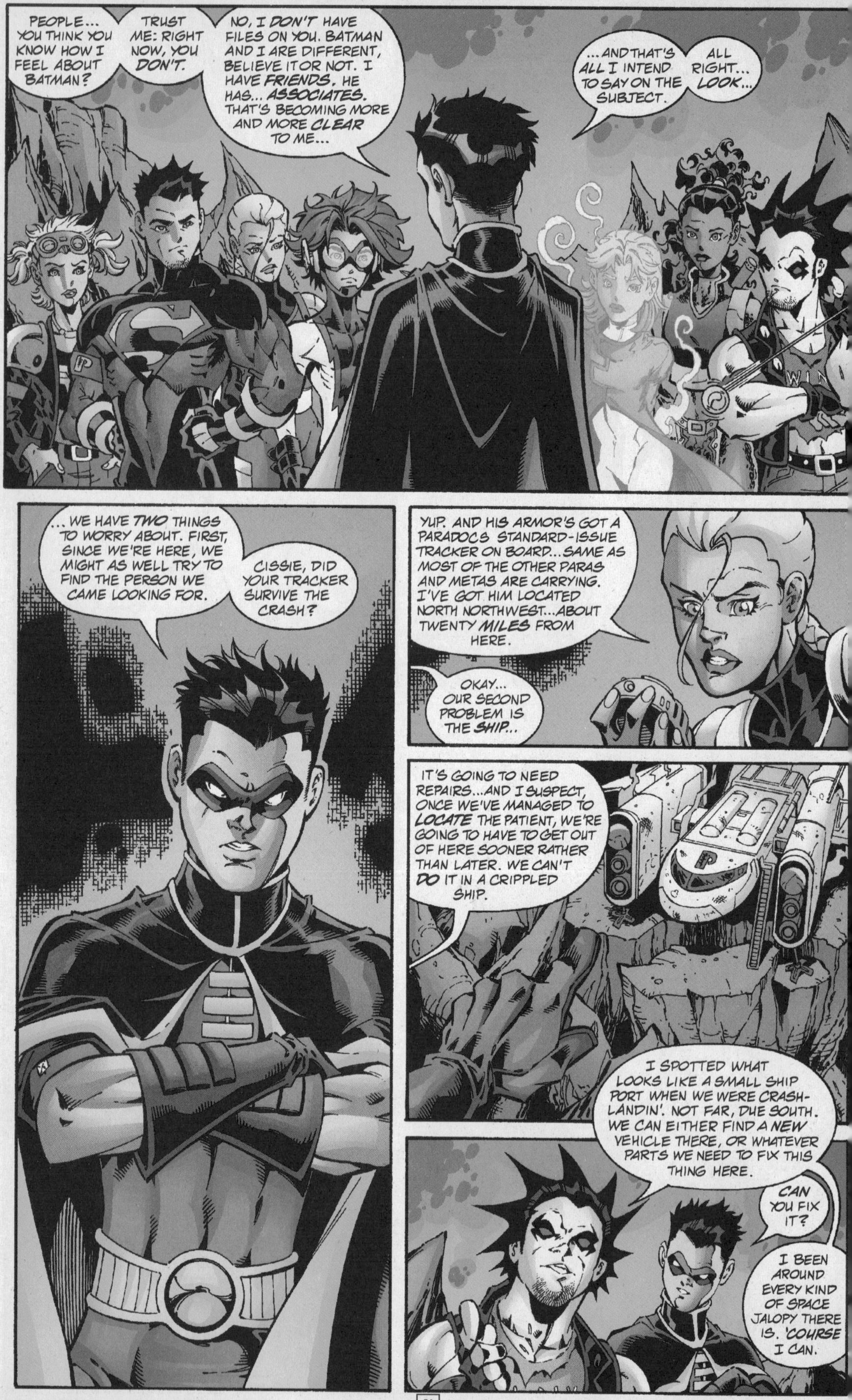

PEOPLE... YOU THINK YOU KNOW HOW I FEEL ABOUT BATMAN?
TRUST ME: RIGHT NOW, YOU DON'T.
NO, I DON'T HAVE FILES ON YOU. BATMAN AND I ARE DIFFERENT, BELIEVE IT OR NOT. I HAVE FRIENDS. HE HAS... ASSOCIATES. THAT'S BECOMING MORE AND MORE CLEAR TO ME...
...AND THAT'S ALL I INTEND TO SAY ON THE SUBJECT.
ALL RIGHT... LOOK...
...WE HAVE TWO THINGS TO WORRY ABOUT. FIRST, SINCE WE'RE HERE, WE MIGHT AS WELL TRY TO FIND THE PERSON WE CAME LOOKING FOR.
CISSIE, DID YOUR TRACKER SURVIVE THE CRASH?
YUP. AND HIS ARMOR'S GOT A PARADOCS STANDARD-ISSUE TRACKER ON BOARD... SAME AS MOST OF THE OTHER PARAS AND METAS ARE CARRYING. I'VE GOT HIM LOCATED NORTH NORTHWEST... ABOUT TWENTY MILES FROM HERE.
OKAY... OUR SECOND PROBLEM IS THE SHIP...
IT'S GOING TO NEED REPAIRS... AND I SUSPECT, ONCE WE'VE MANAGED TO LOCATE THE PATIENT, WE'RE GOING TO HAVE TO GET OUT OF HERE SOONER RATHER THAN LATER. WE CAN'T DO IT IN A CRIPPLED SHIP.
I SPOTTED WHAT LOOKS LIKE A SMALL SHIP PORT WHEN WE WERE CRASH-LANDIN'. NOT FAR, DUE SOUTH. WE CAN EITHER FIND A NEW VEHICLE THERE, OR WHATEVER PARTS WE NEED TO FIX THIS THING HERE.
CAN YOU FIX IT?
I BEEN AROUND EVERY KIND OF SPACE JALOPY THERE IS. 'COURSE I CAN.

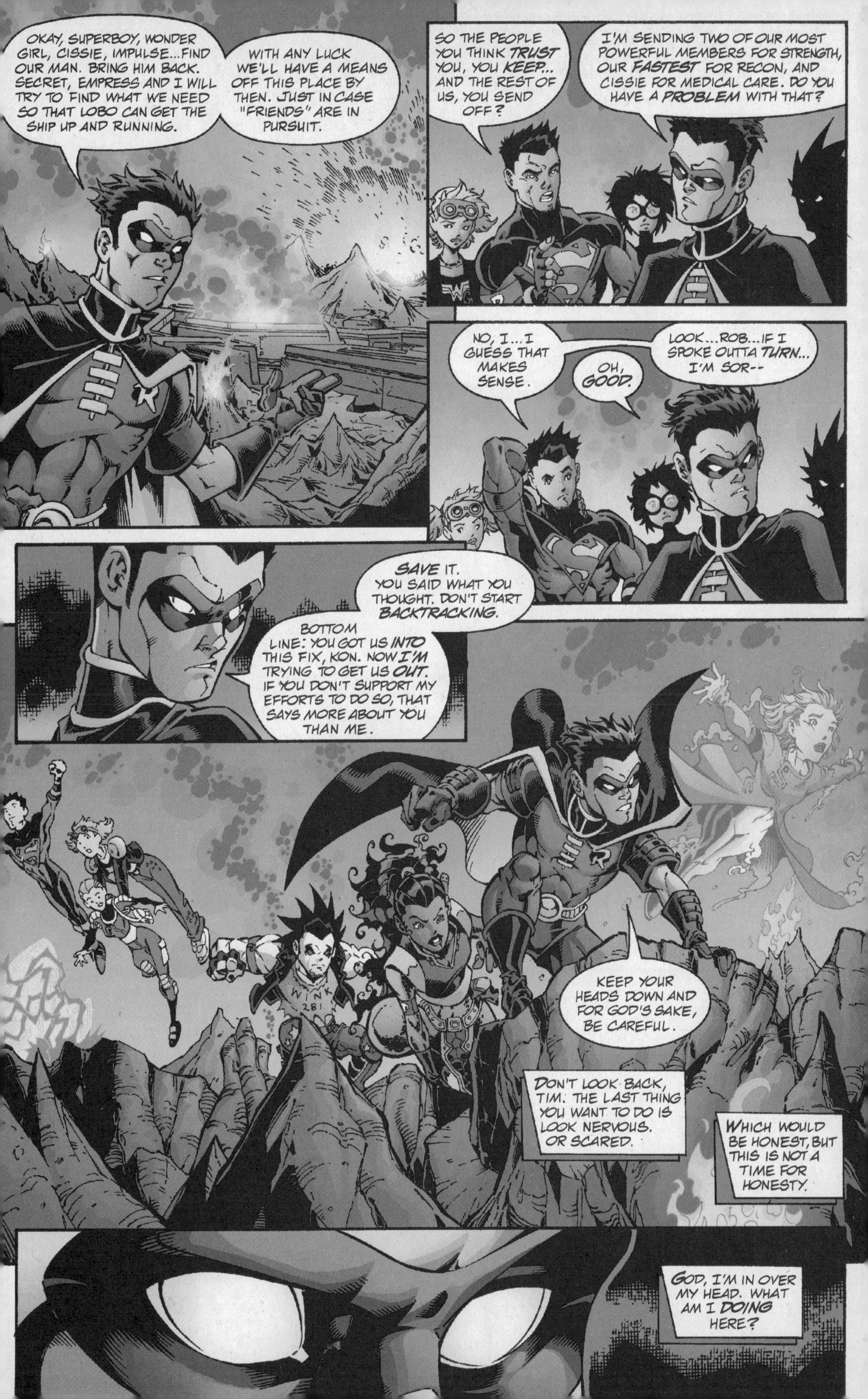
OKAY, SUPERBOY, WONDER GIRL, CISSIE, IMPULSE...FIND OUR MAN. BRING HIM BACK. SECRET, EMPRESS AND I WILL TRY TO FIND WHAT WE NEED SO THAT LOBO CAN GET THE SHIP UP AND RUNNING.
WITH ANY LUCK WE'LL HAVE A MEANS OFF THIS PLACE BY THEN. JUST IN CASE "FRIENDS" ARE IN PURSUIT.
SO THE PEOPLE YOU THINK TRUST YOU, YOU KEEP... AND THE REST OF US, YOU SEND OFF?
I'M SENDING TWO OF OUR MOST POWERFUL MEMBERS FOR STRENGTH, OUR FASTEST FOR RECON, AND CISSIE FOR MEDICAL CARE. DO YOU HAVE A PROBLEM WITH THAT?
NO, I...I GUESS THAT MAKES SENSE.
OH, GOOD.
LOOK...ROB...IF I SPOKE OUTTA TURN... I'M SOR--
SAVE IT. YOU SAID WHAT YOU THOUGHT. DON'T START BACKTRACKING.
BOTTOM LINE: YOU GOT US INTO THIS FIX, KON. NOW I'M TRYING TO GET US OUT. IF YOU DON'T SUPPORT MY EFFORTS TO DO SO, THAT SAYS MORE ABOUT YOU THAN ME.
KEEP YOUR HEADS DOWN AND FOR GOD'S SAKE, BE CAREFUL.
DON'T LOOK BACK, TIM. THE LAST THING YOU WANT TO DO IS LOOK NERVOUS. OR SCARED.
WHICH WOULD BE HONEST, BUT THIS IS NOT A TIME FOR HONESTY.
GOD, I'M IN OVER MY HEAD. WHAT AM I DOING HERE?

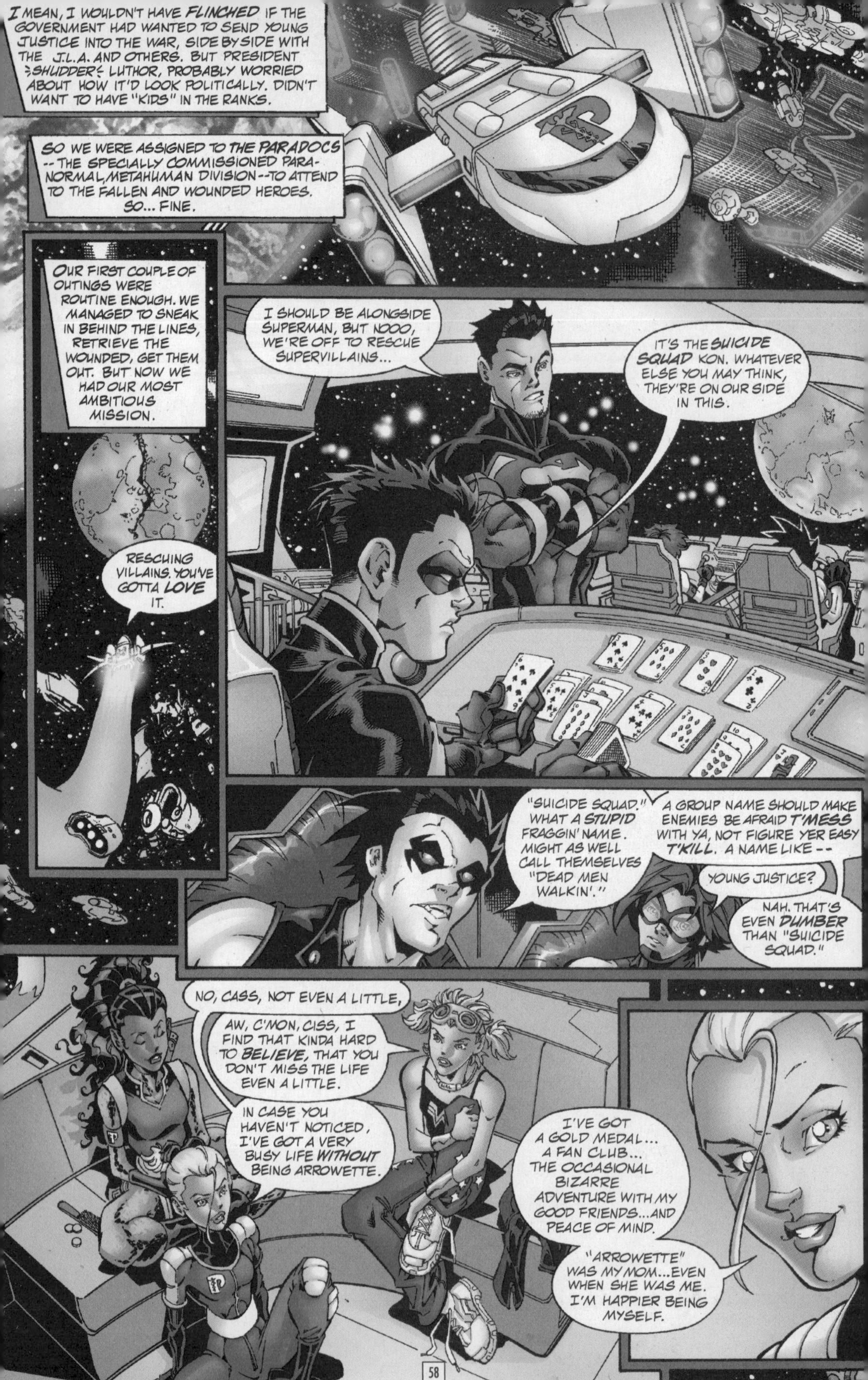
I MEAN, I WOULDN'T HAVE FLINCHED IF THE GOVERNMENT HAD WANTED TO SEND YOUNG JUSTICE INTO THE WAR, SIDE BY SIDE WITH THE J.L.A. AND OTHERS. BUT PRESIDENT >SHUDDER< LUTHOR, PROBABLY WORRIED ABOUT HOW IT'D LOOK POLITICALLY. DIDN'T WANT TO HAVE "KIDS" IN THE RANKS.
SO WE WERE ASSIGNED TO THE PARADOCS -- THE SPECIALLY COMMISSIONED PARA-NORMAL, METAHUMAN DIVISION -- TO ATTEND TO THE FALLEN AND WOUNDED HEROES. SO... FINE.
OUR FIRST COUPLE OF OUTINGS WERE ROUTINE ENOUGH. WE MANAGED TO SNEAK IN BEHIND THE LINES, RETRIEVE THE WOUNDED, GET THEM OUT. BUT NOW WE HAD OUR MOST AMBITIOUS MISSION.
RESCUING VILLAINS. YOU'VE GOTTA LOVE IT.
I SHOULD BE ALONGSIDE SUPERMAN, BUT NOOO, WE'RE OFF TO RESCUE SUPERVILLAINS...
IT'S THE SUICIDE SQUAD KON. WHATEVER ELSE YOU MAY THINK, THEY'RE ON OUR SIDE IN THIS.
"SUICIDE SQUAD." WHAT A STUPID FRAGGIN' NAME. MIGHT AS WELL CALL THEMSELVES "DEAD MEN WALKIN'."
A GROUP NAME SHOULD MAKE ENEMIES BE AFRAID T'MESS WITH YA, NOT FIGURE YER EASY T'KILL. A NAME LIKE --
YOUNG JUSTICE?
NAH. THAT'S EVEN DUMBER THAN "SUICIDE SQUAD."
NO, CASS, NOT EVEN A LITTLE.
AW, C'MON, CISS, I FIND THAT KINDA HARD TO BELIEVE, THAT YOU DON'T MISS THE LIFE EVEN A LITTLE.
IN CASE YOU HAVEN'T NOTICED, I'VE GOT A VERY BUSY LIFE WITHOUT BEING ARROWETTE.
I'VE GOT A GOLD MEDAL... A FAN CLUB... THE OCCASIONAL BIZARRE ADVENTURE WITH MY GOOD FRIENDS... AND PEACE OF MIND.
"ARROWETTE" WAS MY MOM... EVEN WHEN SHE WAS ME. I'M HAPPIER BEING MYSELF.

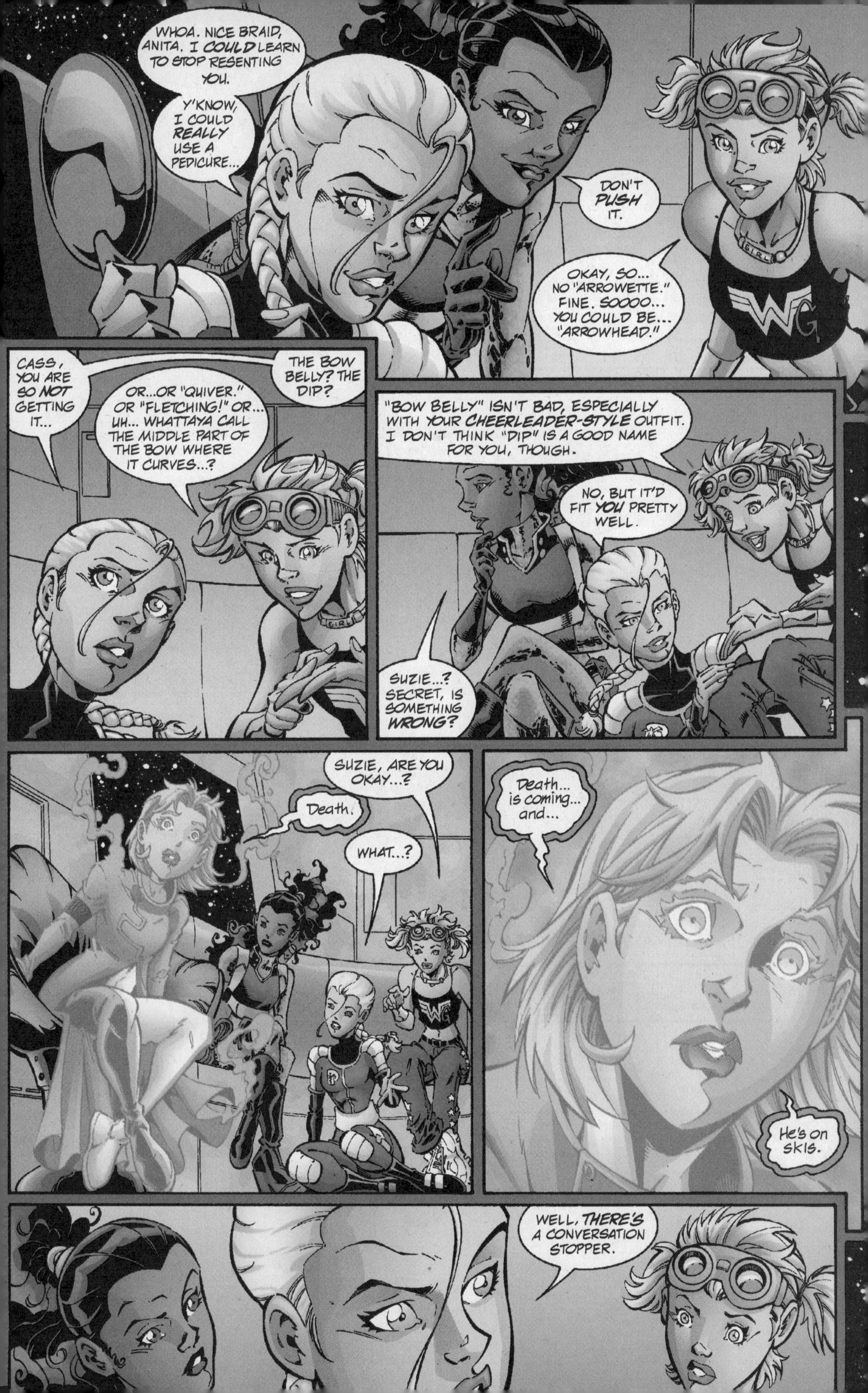
WHOA. NICE BRAID, ANITA. I COULD LEARN TO STOP RESENTING YOU.
Y'KNOW, I COULD REALLY USE A PEDICURE...
DON'T PUSH IT.
OKAY, SO... NO "ARROWETTE." FINE. SOOOO... YOU COULD BE... "ARROWHEAD."
CASS, YOU ARE SO NOT GETTING IT...
OR...OR "QUIVER." OR "FLETCHING!" OR... UH... WHATTAYA CALL THE MIDDLE PART OF THE BOW WHERE IT CURVES...?
THE BOW BELLY? THE DIP?
"BOW BELLY" ISN'T BAD, ESPECIALLY WITH YOUR CHEERLEADER-STYLE OUTFIT. I DON'T THINK "DIP" IS A GOOD NAME FOR YOU, THOUGH.
NO, BUT IT'D FIT YOU PRETTY WELL.
SUZIE...? SECRET, IS SOMETHING WRONG?
SUZIE, ARE YOU OKAY...?
Death.
WHAT...?
Death... is coming... and...
He's on skis.
WELL, THERE'S A CONVERSATION STOPPER.

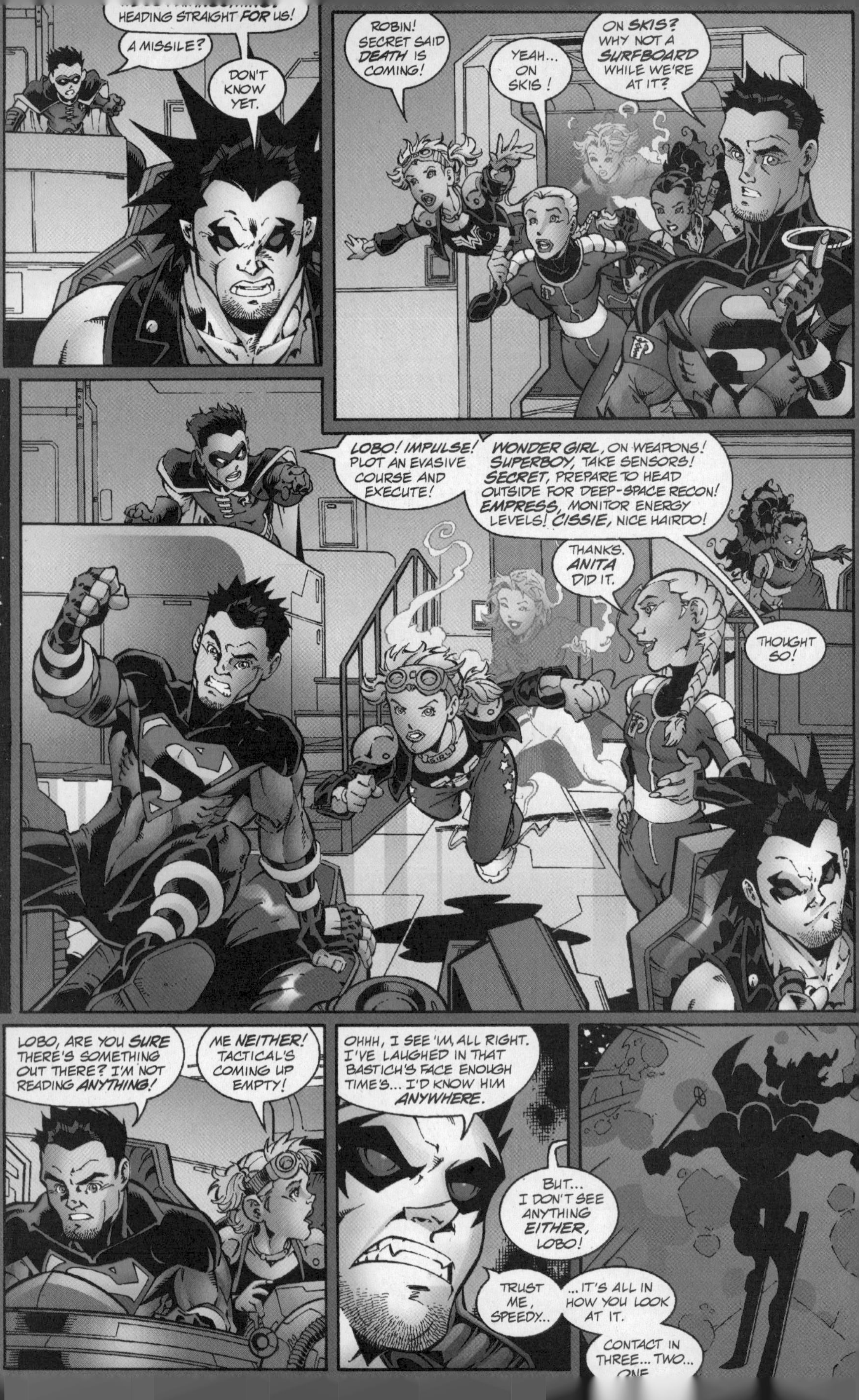
HEADING STRAIGHT FOR US!
A MISSILE?
DON'T KNOW YET.
ROBIN! SECRET SAID DEATH IS COMING!
YEAH... ON SKIS!
ON SKIS? WHY NOT A SURFBOARD WHILE WE'RE AT IT?
LOBO! IMPULSE! PLOT AN EVASIVE COURSE AND EXECUTE!
WONDER GIRL, ON WEAPONS! SUPERBOY, TAKE SENSORS! SECRET, PREPARE TO HEAD OUTSIDE FOR DEEP-SPACE RECON! EMPRESS, MONITOR ENERGY LEVELS! CISSIE, NICE HAIRDO!
THANKS. ANITA DID IT.
THOUGHT SO!
LOBO, ARE YOU SURE THERE'S SOMETHING OUT THERE? I'M NOT READING ANYTHING!
ME NEITHER! TACTICAL'S COMING UP EMPTY!
OHHH, I SEE 'IM, ALL RIGHT. I'VE LAUGHED IN THAT BASTICH'S FACE ENOUGH TIME'S... I'D KNOW HIM ANYWHERE.
BUT... I DON'T SEE ANYTHING EITHER, LOBO!
TRUST ME, SPEEDY...
...IT'S ALL IN HOW YOU LOOK AT IT.
CONTACT IN THREE... TWO...

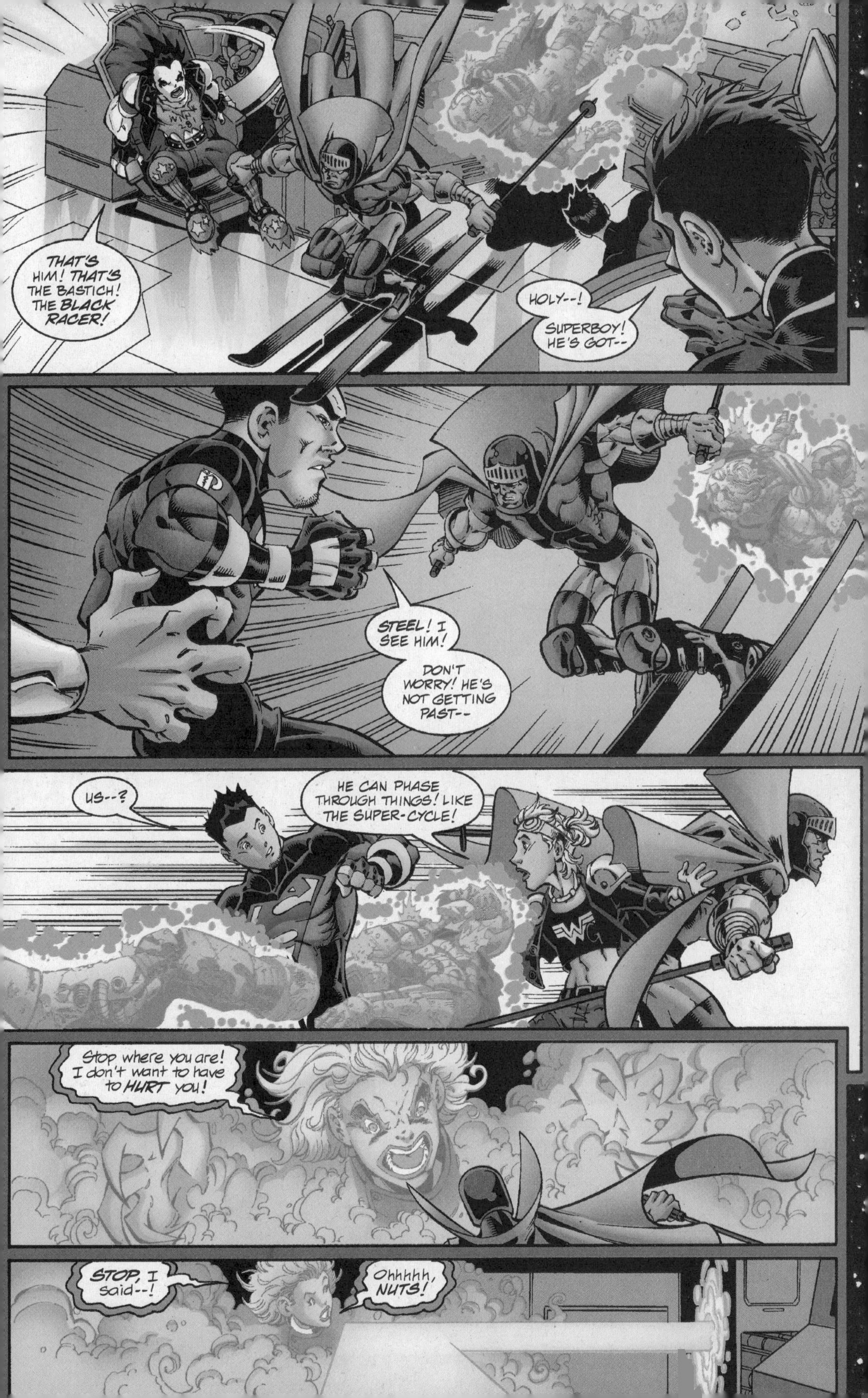
THAT'S HIM! THAT'S THE BASTICH! THE BLACK RACER!
HOLY--!
SUPERBOY! HE'S GOT--
STEEL! I SEE HIM!
DON'T WORRY! HE'S NOT GETTING PAST--
US--?
HE CAN PHASE THROUGH THINGS! LIKE THE SUPER-CYCLE!
Stop where you are! I don't want to have to HURT you!
STOP, I said--!
Ohhhhh, NUTS!

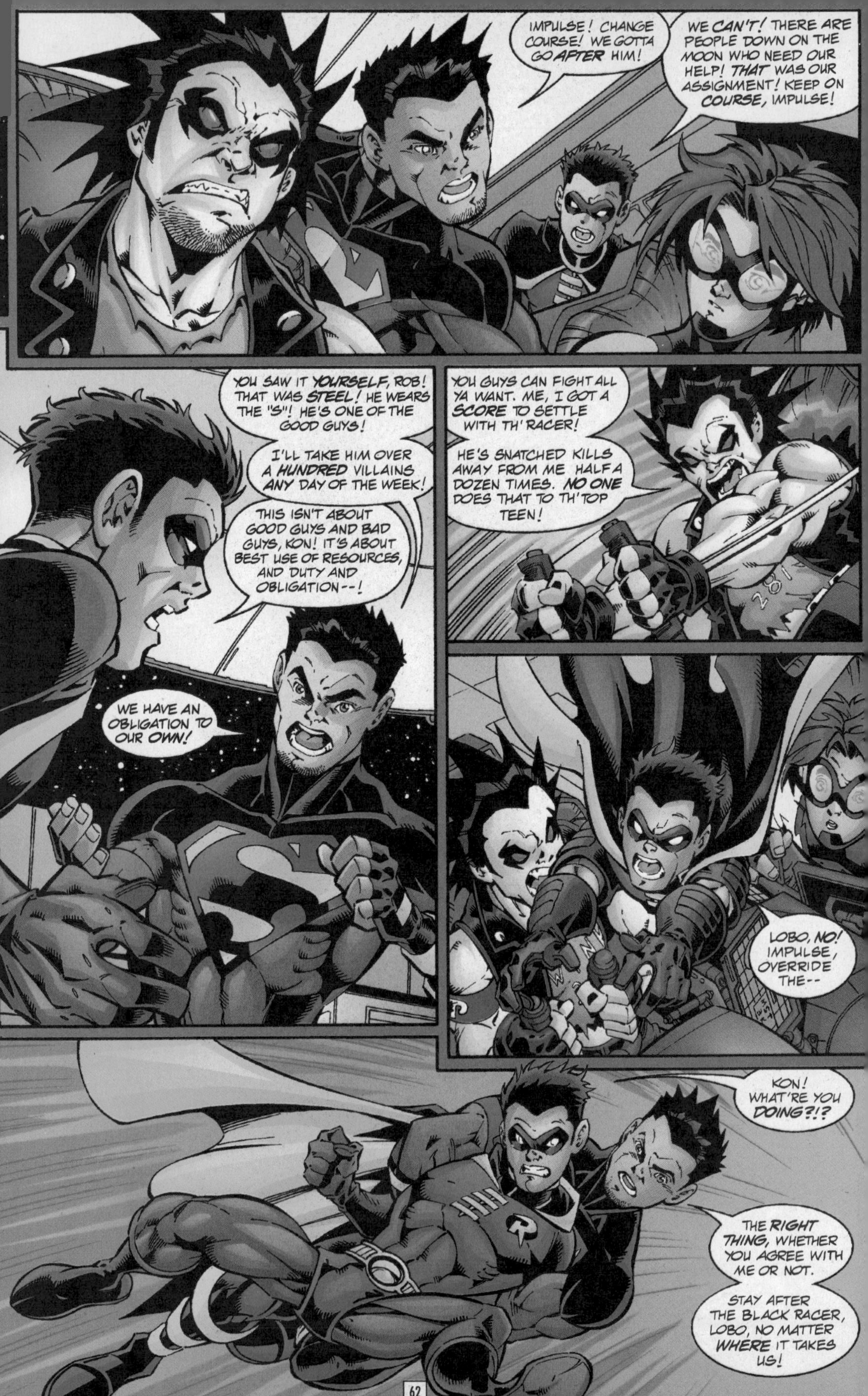
IMPULSE! CHANGE COURSE! WE GOTTA GO AFTER HIM!
WE CAN'T! THERE ARE PEOPLE DOWN ON THE MOON WHO NEED OUR HELP! THAT WAS OUR ASSIGNMENT! KEEP ON COURSE, IMPULSE!
YOU SAW IT YOURSELF, ROB! THAT WAS STEEL! HE WEARS THE "S"! HE'S ONE OF THE GOOD GUYS!
I'LL TAKE HIM OVER A HUNDRED VILLAINS ANY DAY OF THE WEEK!
THIS ISN'T ABOUT GOOD GUYS AND BAD GUYS, KON! IT'S ABOUT BEST USE OF RESOURCES, AND DUTY AND OBLIGATION--!
WE HAVE AN OBLIGATION TO OUR OWN!
YOU GUYS CAN FIGHT ALL YA WANT. ME, I GOT A SCORE TO SETTLE WITH TH' RACER!
HE'S SNATCHED KILLS AWAY FROM ME HALF A DOZEN TIMES. NO ONE DOES THAT TO TH' TOP TEEN!
LOBO, NO! IMPULSE, OVERRIDE THE--
KON! WHAT'RE YOU DOING?!?
THE RIGHT THING, WHETHER YOU AGREE WITH ME OR NOT.
STAY AFTER THE BLACK RACER, LOBO, NO MATTER WHERE IT TAKES US!

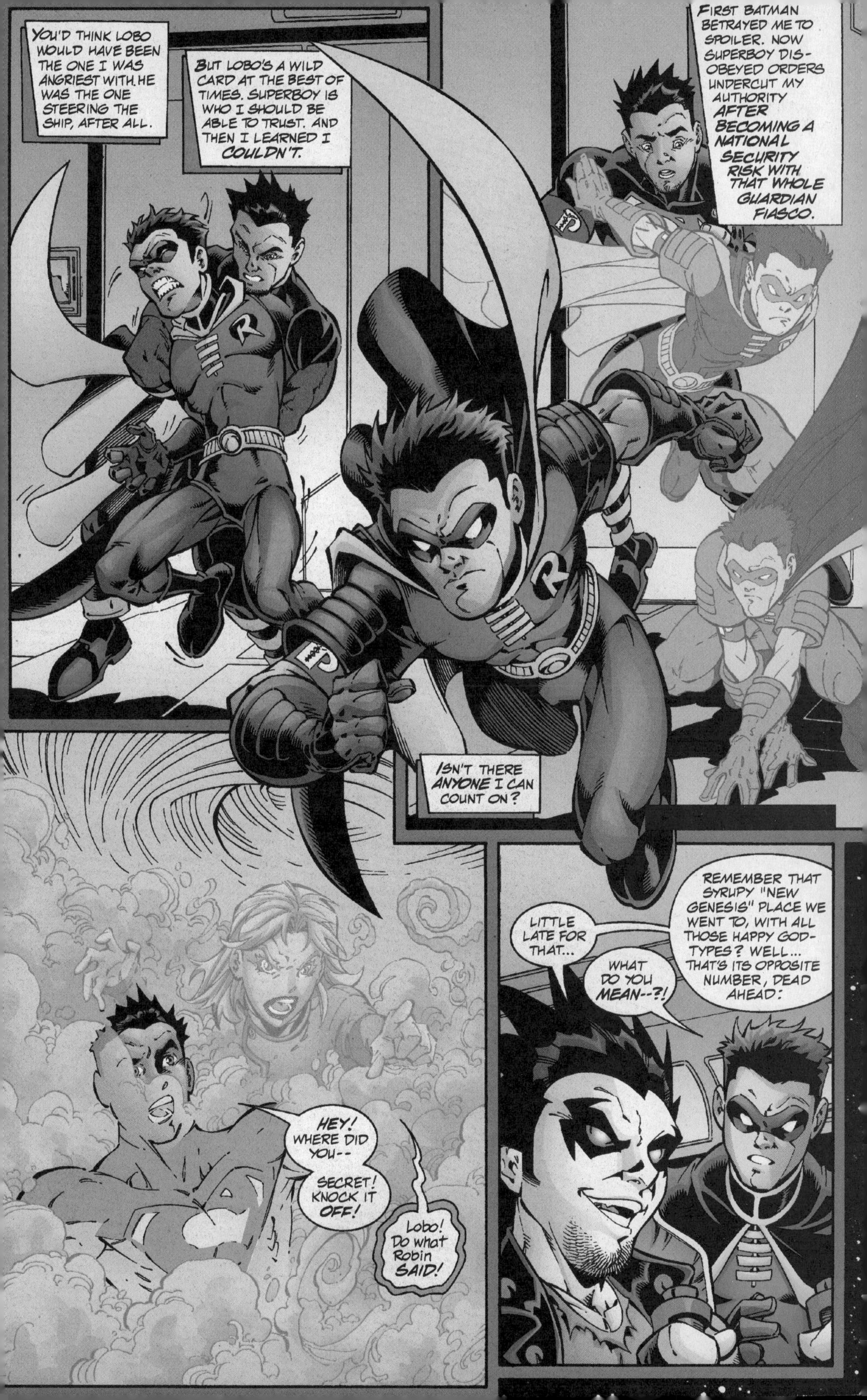
YOU'D THINK LOBO WOULD HAVE BEEN THE ONE I WAS ANGRIEST WITH. HE WAS THE ONE STEERING THE SHIP, AFTER ALL.
BUT LOBO'S A WILD CARD AT THE BEST OF TIMES. SUPERBOY IS WHO I SHOULD BE ABLE TO TRUST. AND THEN I LEARNED I COULDN'T.
FIRST BATMAN BETRAYED ME TO SPOILER. NOW SUPERBOY DIS-OBEYED ORDERS UNDERCUT MY AUTHORITY AFTER BECOMING A NATIONAL SECURITY RISK WITH THAT WHOLE GUARDIAN FIASCO.
ISN'T THERE ANYONE I CAN COUNT ON?
HEY! WHERE DID YOU--
SECRET! KNOCK IT OFF!
Lobo! Do what Robin SAID!
LITTLE LATE FOR THAT...
WHAT DO YOU MEAN--?!
REMEMBER THAT SYRUPY "NEW GENESIS" PLACE WE WENT TO, WITH ALL THOSE HAPPY GOD-TYPES? WELL... THAT'S ITS OPPOSITE NUMBER, DEAD AHEAD:

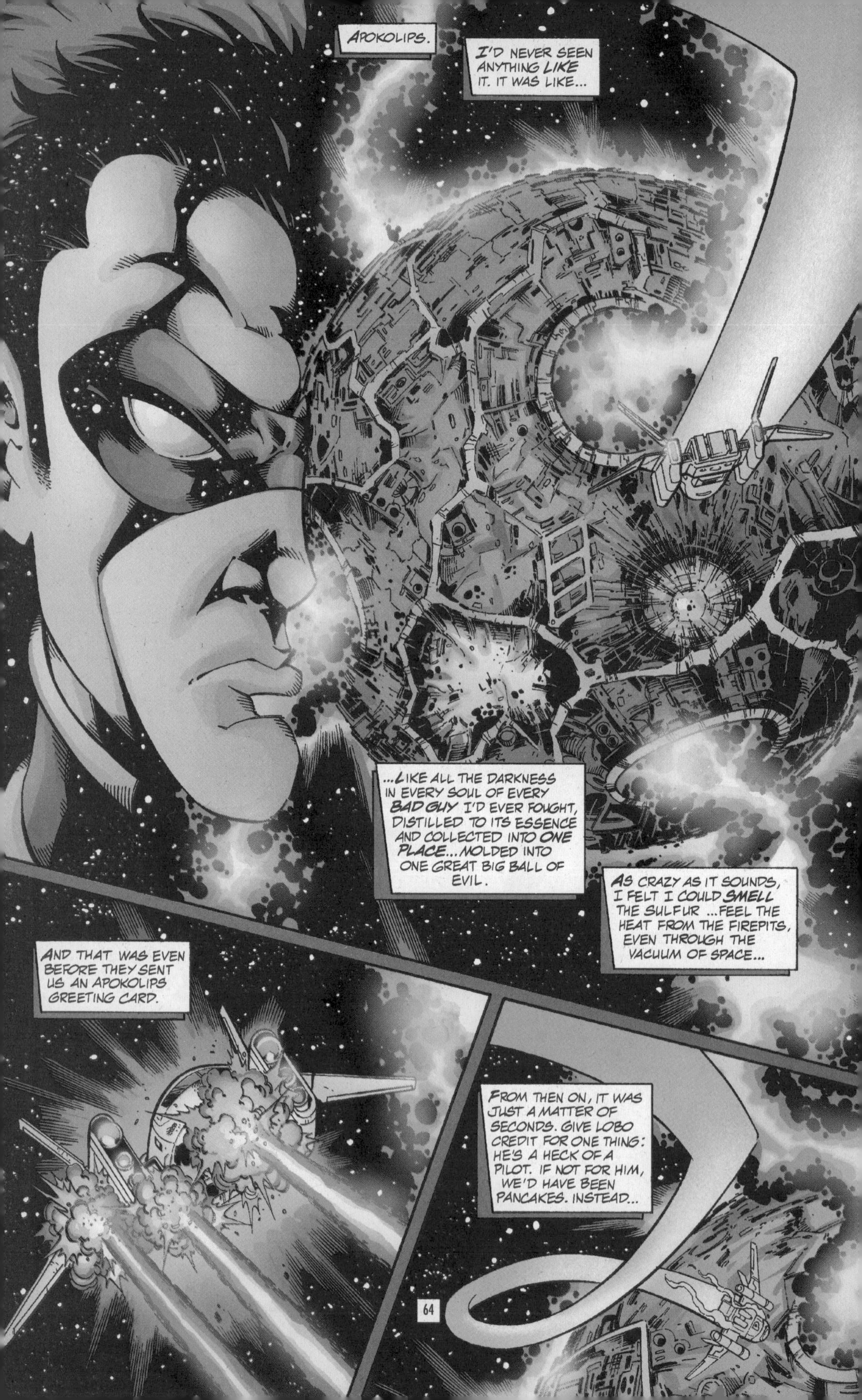
APOKOLIPS.
I'D NEVER SEEN ANYTHING LIKE IT. IT WAS LIKE...
...LIKE ALL THE DARKNESS IN EVERY SOUL OF EVERY BAD GUY I'D EVER FOUGHT, DISTILLED TO ITS ESSENCE AND COLLECTED INTO ONE PLACE... MOLDED INTO ONE GREAT BIG BALL OF EVIL.
AS CRAZY AS IT SOUNDS, I FELT I COULD SMELL THE SULFUR ...FEEL THE HEAT FROM THE FIREPITS, EVEN THROUGH THE VACUUM OF SPACE...
AND THAT WAS EVEN BEFORE THEY SENT US AN APOKOLIPS GREETING CARD.
FROM THEN ON, IT WAS JUST A MATTER OF SECONDS. GIVE LOBO CREDIT FOR ONE THING: HE'S A HECK OF A PILOT. IF NOT FOR HIM, WE'D HAVE BEEN PANCAKES. INSTEAD...

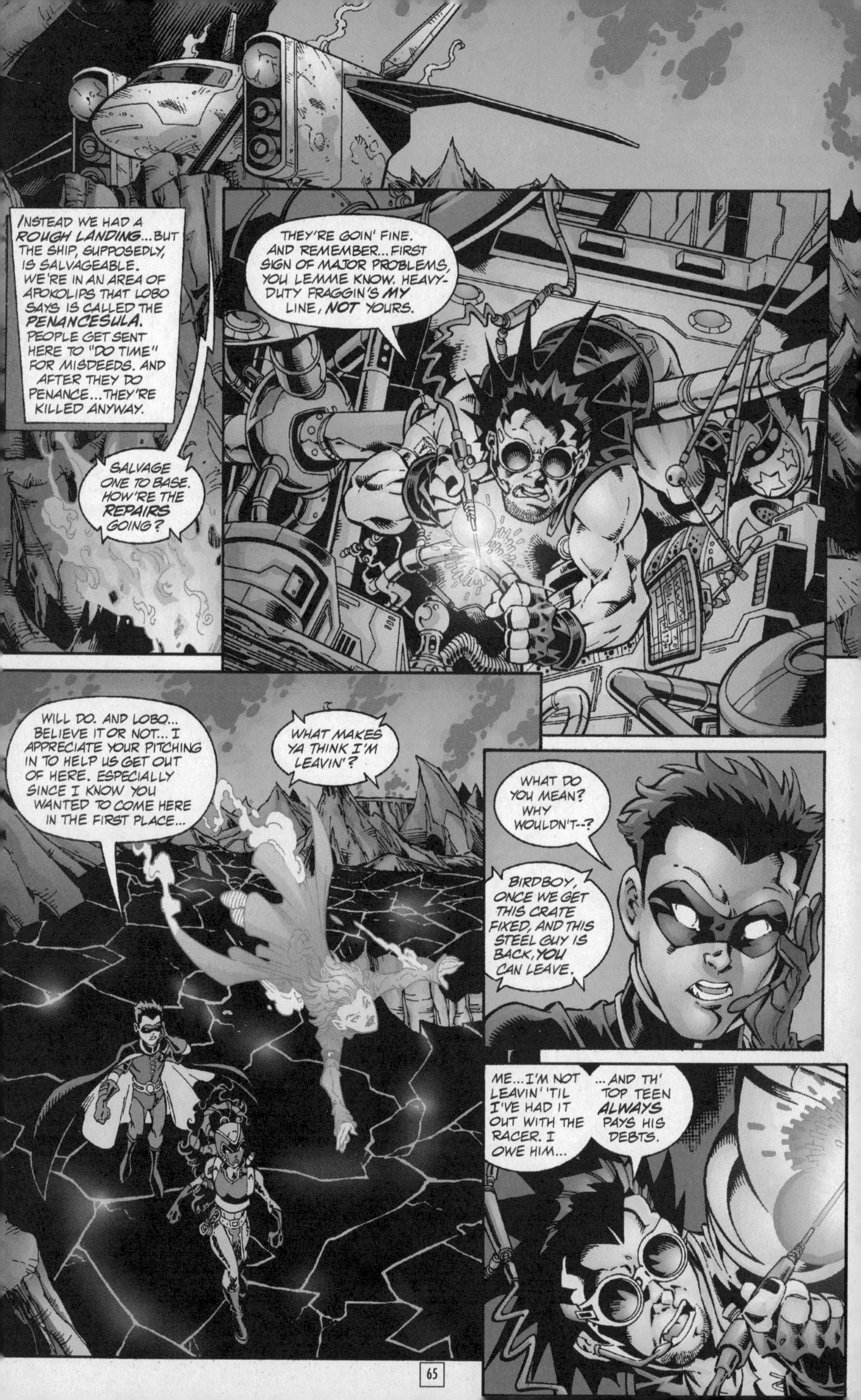
INSTEAD WE HAD A ROUGH LANDING... BUT THE SHIP, SUPPOSEDLY, IS SALVAGEABLE. WE'RE IN AN AREA OF APOKOLIPS THAT LOBO SAYS IS CALLED THE PENANCESULA. PEOPLE GET SENT HERE TO "DO TIME" FOR MISDEEDS. AND AFTER THEY DO PENANCE... THEY'RE KILLED ANYWAY.
SALVAGE ONE TO BASE. HOW'RE THE REPAIRS GOING?
THEY'RE GOIN' FINE. AND REMEMBER... FIRST SIGN OF MAJOR PROBLEMS, YOU LEMME KNOW. HEAVY-DUTY FRAGGIN'S MY LINE, NOT YOURS.
WILL DO. AND LOBO... BELIEVE IT OR NOT... I APPRECIATE YOUR PITCHING IN TO HELP US GET OUT OF HERE. ESPECIALLY SINCE I KNOW YOU WANTED TO COME HERE IN THE FIRST PLACE...
WHAT MAKES YA THINK I'M LEAVIN'?
WHAT DO YOU MEAN? WHY WOULDN'T--?
BIRDBOY, ONCE WE GET THIS CRATE FIXED, AND THIS STEEL GUY IS BACK, YOU CAN LEAVE.
ME... I'M NOT LEAVIN' 'TIL I'VE HAD IT OUT WITH THE RACER. I OWE HIM...
...AND TH' TOP TEEN ALWAYS PAYS HIS DEBTS.

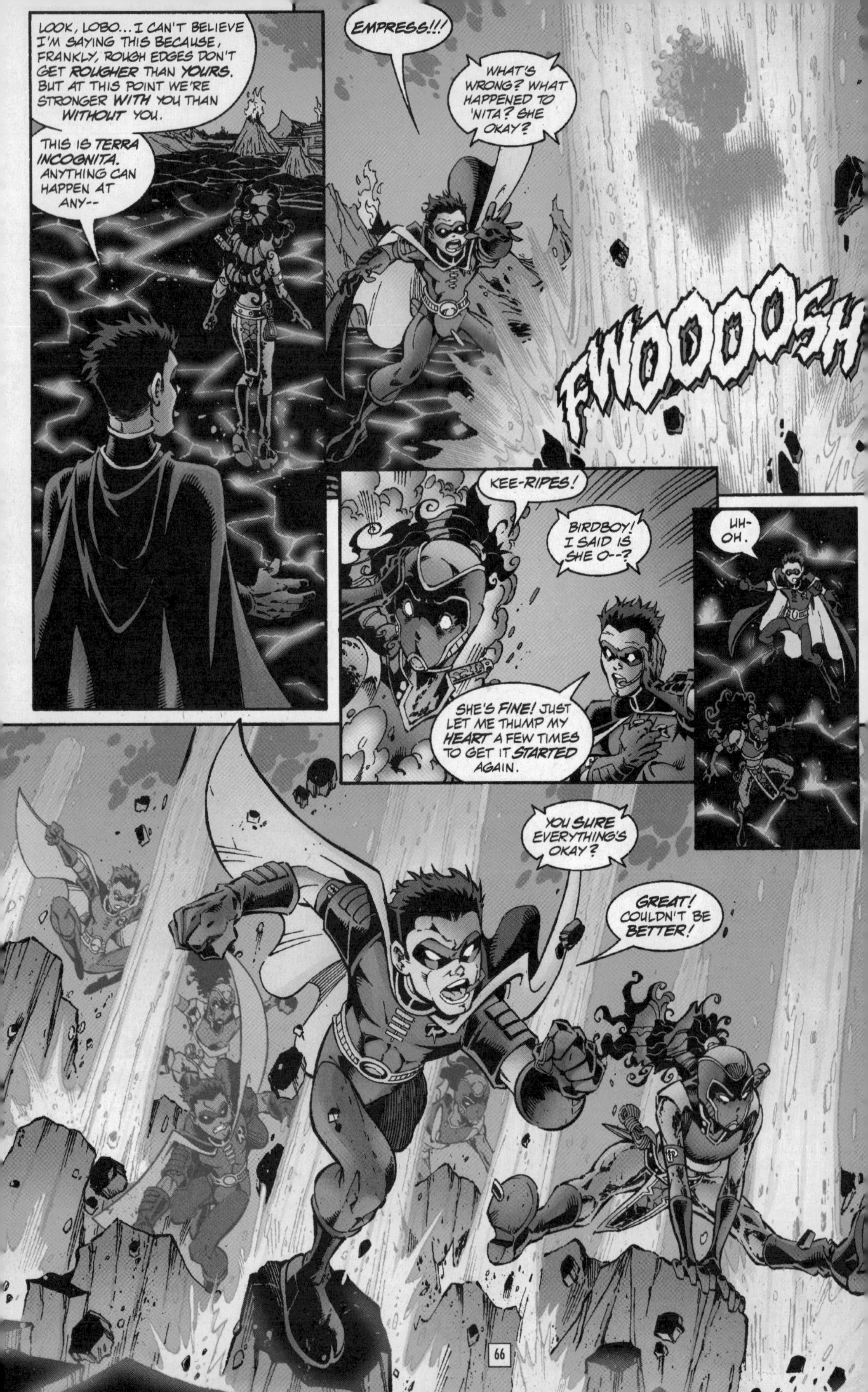
LOOK, LOBO... I CAN'T BELIEVE I'M SAYING THIS BECAUSE, FRANKLY, ROUGH EDGES DON'T GET ROUGHER THAN YOURS. BUT AT THIS POINT WE'RE STRONGER WITH YOU THAN WITHOUT YOU.
THIS IS TERRA INCOGNITA. ANYTHING CAN HAPPEN AT ANY--
EMPRESS!!!
WHAT'S WRONG? WHAT HAPPENED TO 'NITA? SHE OKAY?
FWOOOOSH
KEE-RIPES!
BIRDBOY! I SAID IS SHE O--?
SHE'S FINE! JUST LET ME THUMP MY HEART A FEW TIMES TO GET IT STARTED AGAIN.
UH-OH.
YOU SURE EVERYTHING'S OKAY?
GREAT! COULDN'T BE BETTER!

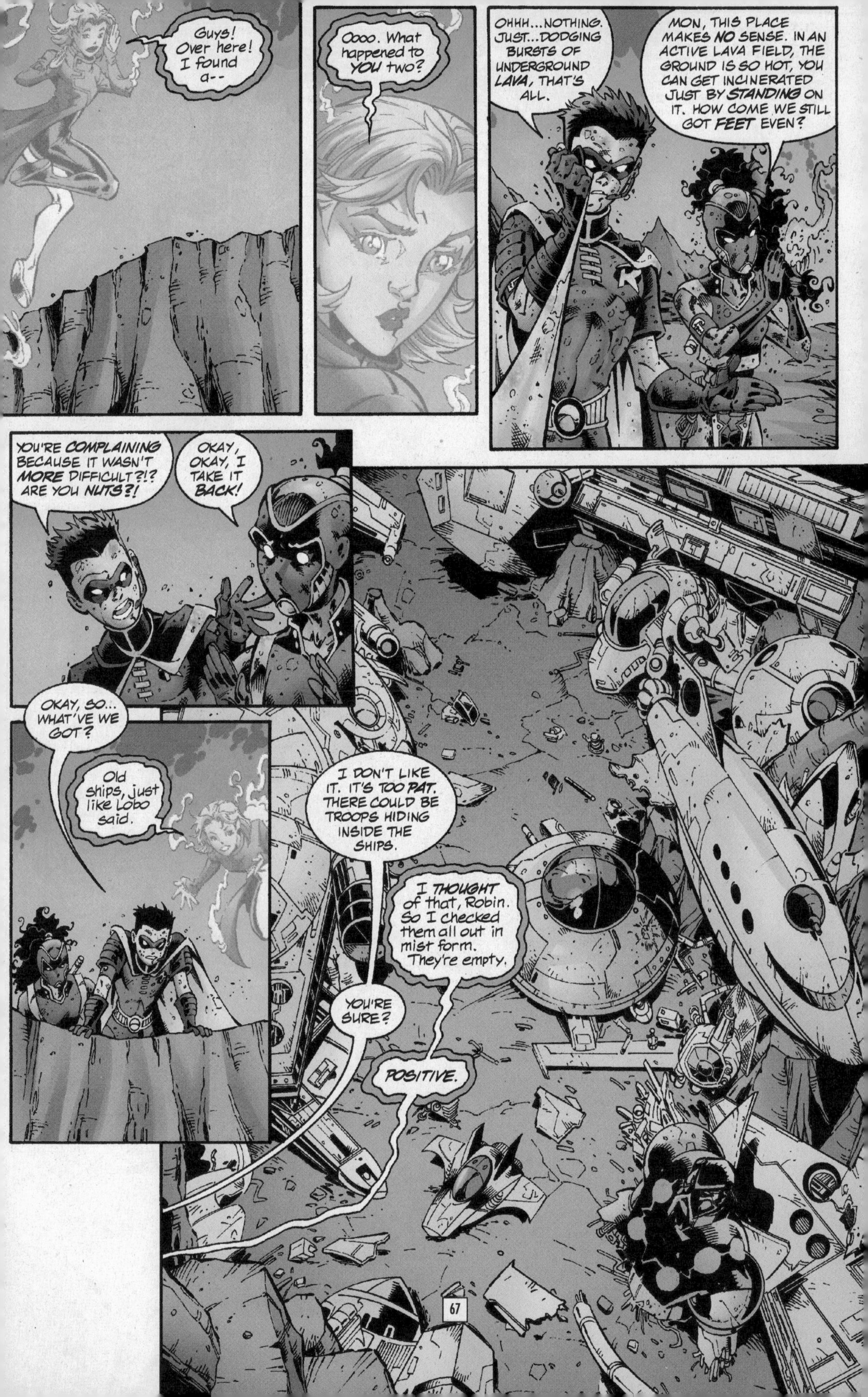
Guys! Over here! I found a--
Oooo. What happened to YOU two?
OHHH...NOTHING. JUST...DODGING BURSTS OF UNDERGROUND LAVA, THAT'S ALL.
MON, THIS PLACE MAKES NO SENSE. IN AN ACTIVE LAVA FIELD, THE GROUND IS SO HOT, YOU CAN GET INCINERATED JUST BY STANDING ON IT. HOW COME WE STILL GOT FEET EVEN?
YOU'RE COMPLAINING BECAUSE IT WASN'T MORE DIFFICULT?!? ARE YOU NUTS?!
OKAY, OKAY, I TAKE IT BACK!
OKAY, SO... WHAT'VE WE GOT?
Old ships, just like Lobo said.
I DON'T LIKE IT. IT'S TOO PAT. THERE COULD BE TROOPS HIDING INSIDE THE SHIPS.
I THOUGHT of that, Robin. So I checked them all out in mist form. They're empty.
YOU'RE SURE?
POSITIVE.

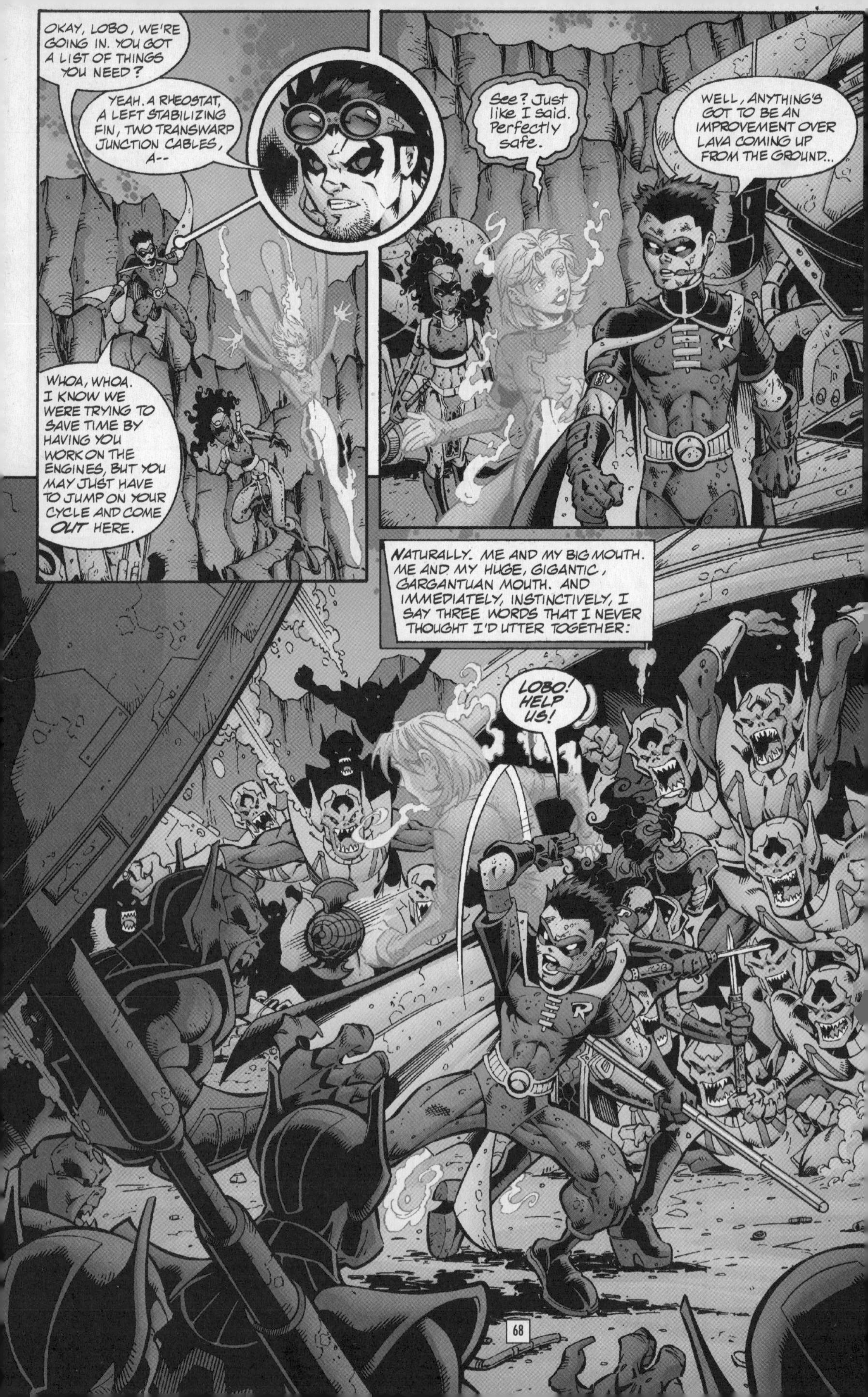
OKAY, LOBO, WE'RE GOING IN. YOU GOT A LIST OF THINGS YOU NEED?
YEAH. A RHEOSTAT, A LEFT STABILIZING FIN, TWO TRANSWARP JUNCTION CABLES, A--
WHOA, WHOA. I KNOW WE WERE TRYING TO SAVE TIME BY HAVING YOU WORK ON THE ENGINES, BUT YOU MAY JUST HAVE TO JUMP ON YOUR CYCLE AND COME OUT HERE.
See? Just like I said. Perfectly safe.
WELL, ANYTHING'S GOT TO BE AN IMPROVEMENT OVER LAVA COMING UP FROM THE GROUND...
NATURALLY. ME AND MY BIG MOUTH. ME AND MY HUGE, GIGANTIC, GARGANTUAN MOUTH. AND IMMEDIATELY, INSTINCTIVELY, I SAY THREE WORDS THAT I NEVER THOUGHT I'D UTTER TOGETHER:
LOBO! HELP US!

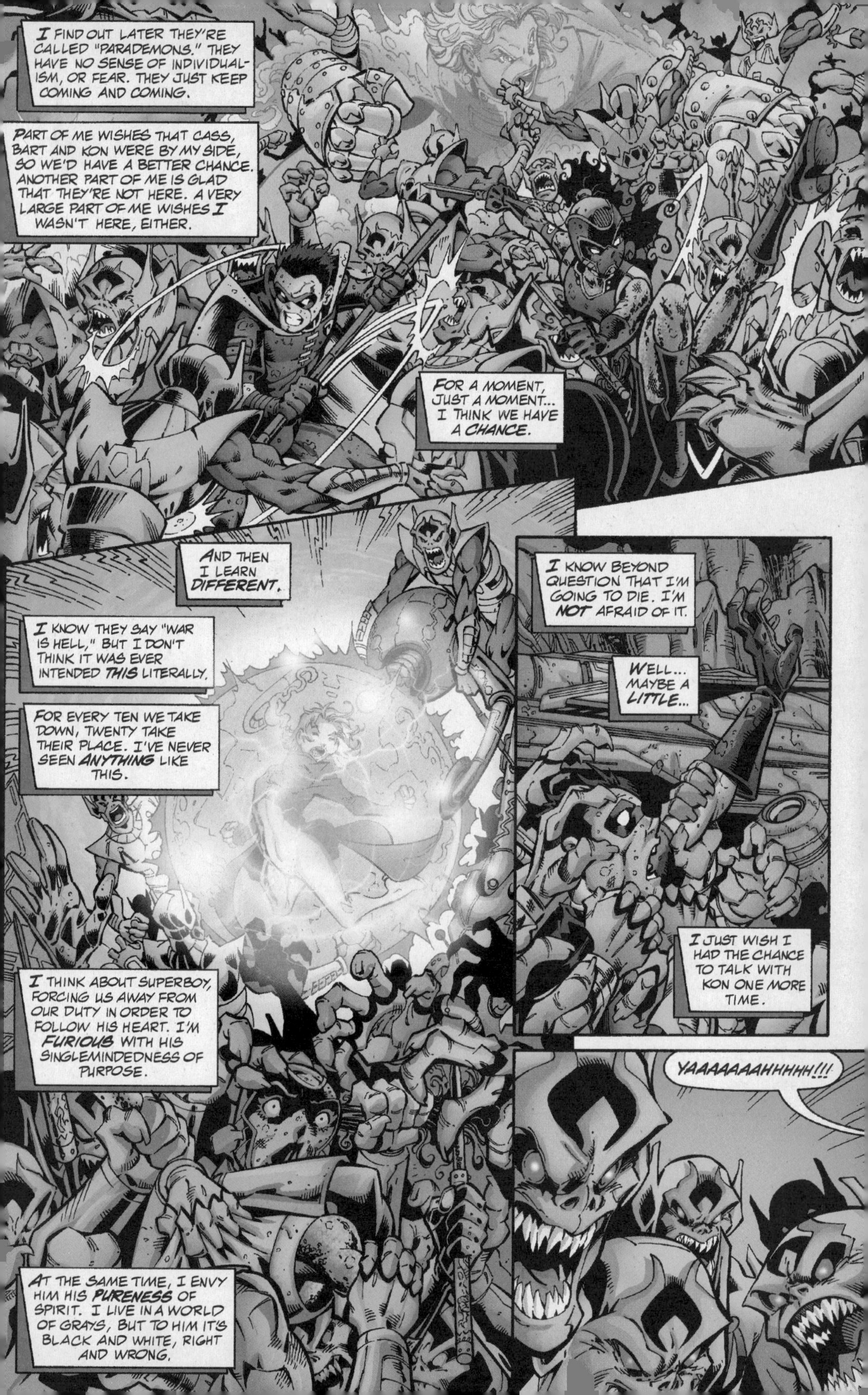

I FIND OUT LATER THEY'RE CALLED "PARADEMONS." THEY HAVE NO SENSE OF INDIVIDUALISM, OR FEAR. THEY JUST KEEP COMING AND COMING.
PART OF ME WISHES THAT CASS, BART AND KON WERE BY MY SIDE, SO WE'D HAVE A BETTER CHANCE. ANOTHER PART OF ME IS GLAD THAT THEY'RE NOT HERE. A VERY LARGE PART OF ME WISHES I WASN'T HERE, EITHER.
FOR A MOMENT, JUST A MOMENT... I THINK WE HAVE A CHANCE.
AND THEN I LEARN DIFFERENT.
I KNOW THEY SAY "WAR IS HELL," BUT I DON'T THINK IT WAS EVER INTENDED THIS LITERALLY.
FOR EVERY TEN WE TAKE DOWN, TWENTY TAKE THEIR PLACE. I'VE NEVER SEEN ANYTHING LIKE THIS.
I KNOW BEYOND QUESTION THAT I'M GOING TO DIE. I'M NOT AFRAID OF IT.
WELL... MAYBE A LITTLE...
I JUST WISH I HAD THE CHANCE TO TALK WITH KON ONE MORE TIME.
I THINK ABOUT SUPERBOY, FORCING US AWAY FROM OUR DUTY IN ORDER TO FOLLOW HIS HEART. I'M FURIOUS WITH HIS SINGLEMINDEDNESS OF PURPOSE.
YAAAAAAAHHHHH!!!
AT THE SAME TIME, I ENVY HIM HIS PURENESS OF SPIRIT. I LIVE IN A WORLD OF GRAYS, BUT TO HIM IT'S BLACK AND WHITE, RIGHT AND WRONG.

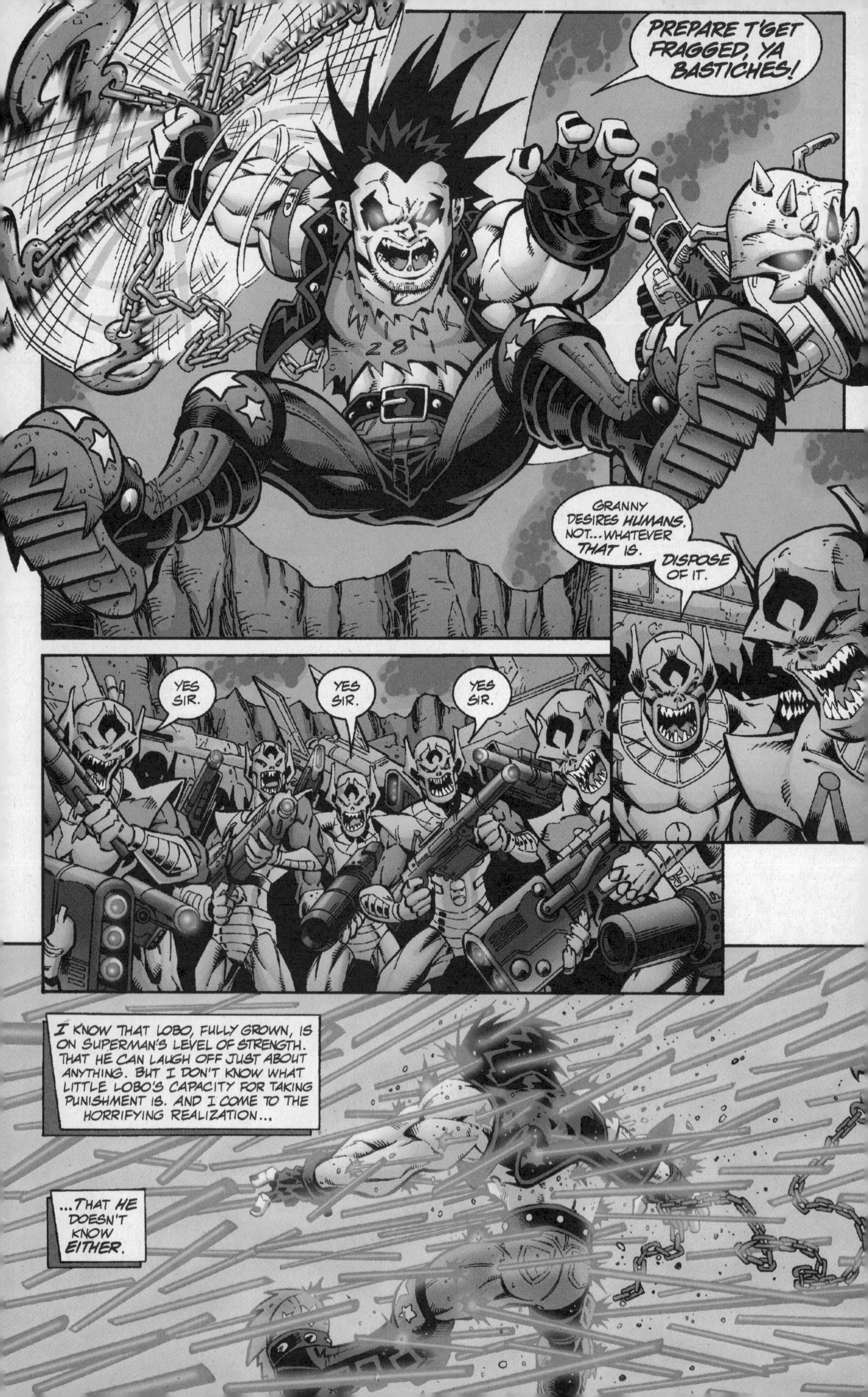
PREPARE T'GET FRAGGED, YA BASTICHES!
GRANNY DESIRES HUMANS. NOT...WHATEVER THAT IS.
DISPOSE OF IT.
YES SIR.
YES SIR.
YES SIR.
I KNOW THAT LOBO, FULLY GROWN, IS ON SUPERMAN'S LEVEL OF STRENGTH. THAT HE CAN LAUGH OFF JUST ABOUT ANYTHING. BUT I DON'T KNOW WHAT LITTLE LOBO'S CAPACITY FOR TAKING PUNISHMENT IS. AND I COME TO THE HORRIFYING REALIZATION...
...THAT HE DOESN'T KNOW EITHER.

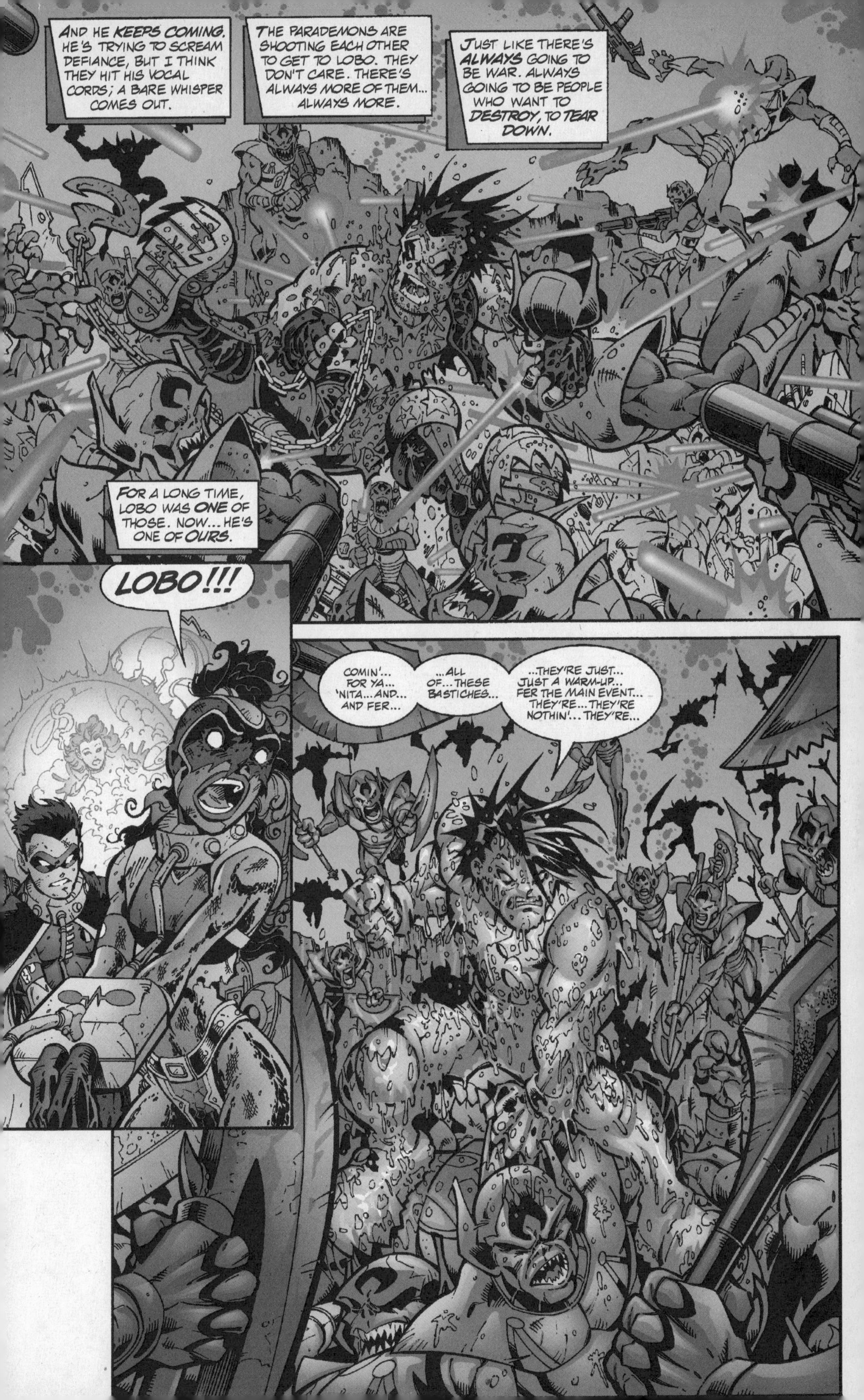

AND HE KEEPS COMING. HE'S TRYING TO SCREAM DEFIANCE, BUT I THINK THEY HIT HIS VOCAL CORDS; A BARE WHISPER COMES OUT.
THE PARADEMONS ARE SHOOTING EACH OTHER TO GET TO LOBO. THEY DON'T CARE. THERE'S ALWAYS MORE OF THEM... ALWAYS MORE.
JUST LIKE THERE'S ALWAYS GOING TO BE WAR. ALWAYS GOING TO BE PEOPLE WHO WANT TO DESTROY, TO TEAR DOWN.
FOR A LONG TIME, LOBO WAS ONE OF THOSE. NOW... HE'S ONE OF OURS.
LOBO!!!
COMIN'... FOR YA... 'NITA...AND... AND FER...
...ALL OF...THESE BASTICHES...
...THEY'RE JUST... JUST A WARM-UP... FER THE MAIN EVENT... THEY'RE...THEY'RE NOTHIN'...THEY'RE...

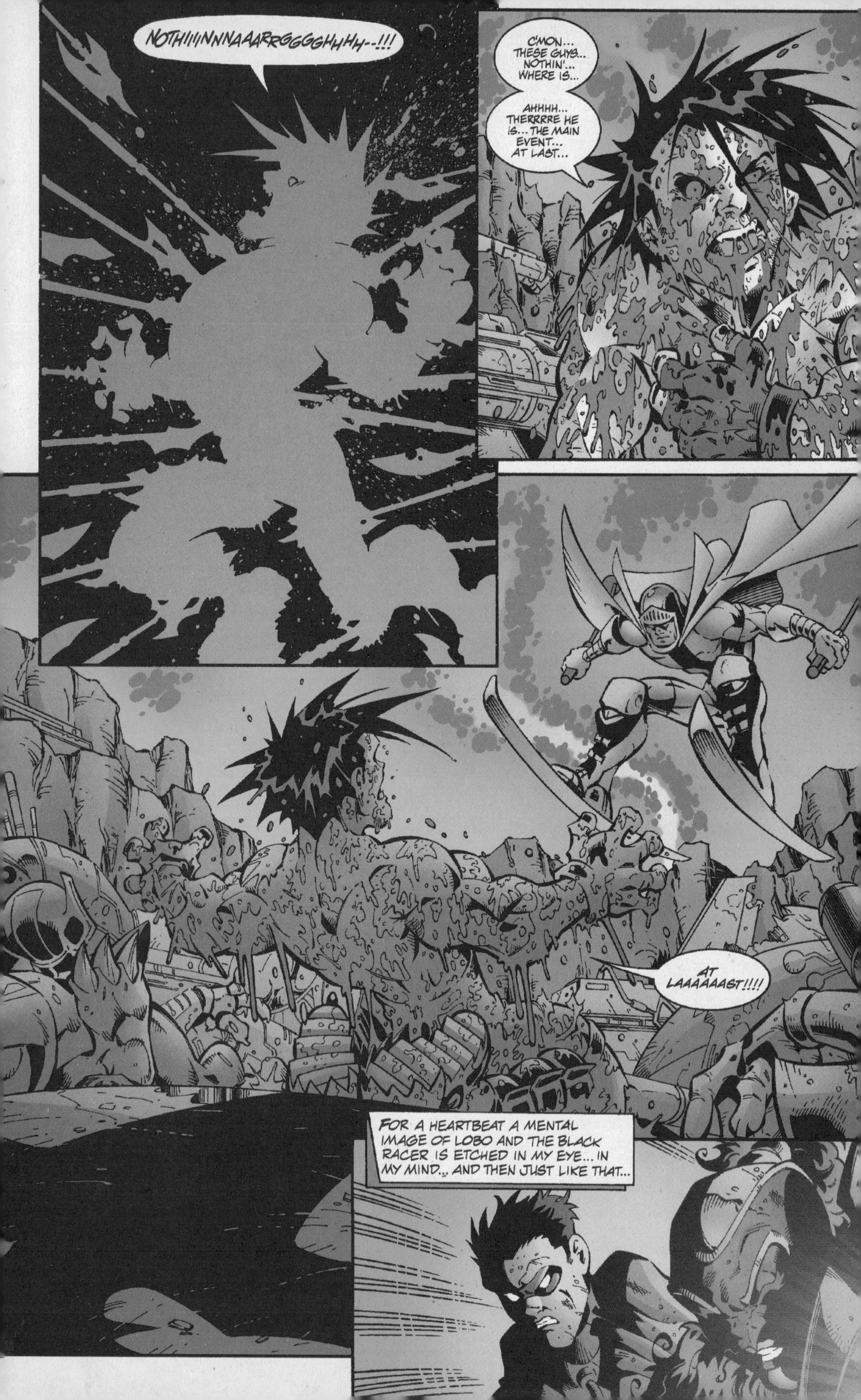
NOTHIIIINNNAAARRGGGGHHHH--!!!
C'MON... THESE GUYS... NOTHIN'... WHERE IS...
AHHHH... THERRRRE HE IS... THE MAIN EVENT... AT LAST...
AT LAAAAAAST!!!!
FOR A HEARTBEAT A MENTAL IMAGE OF LOBO AND THE BLACK RACER IS ETCHED IN MY EYE... IN MY MIND... AND THEN JUST LIKE THAT...

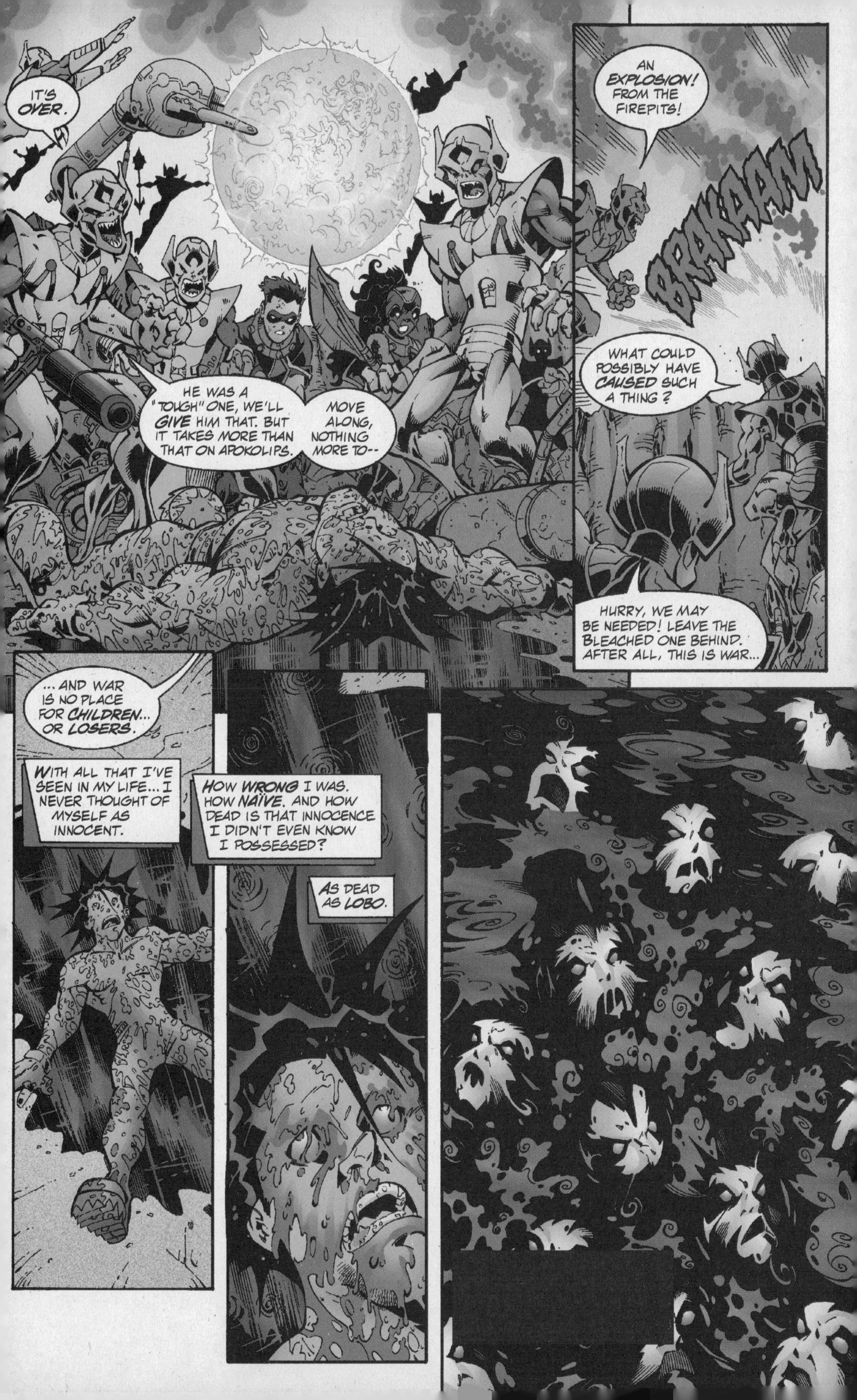
IT'S OVER.
HE WAS A "TOUGH" ONE, WE'LL GIVE HIM THAT. BUT IT TAKES MORE THAN THAT ON APOKOLIPS.
MOVE ALONG, NOTHING MORE TO--
AN EXPLOSION! FROM THE FIREPITS!
BRAKAAM
WHAT COULD POSSIBLY HAVE CAUSED SUCH A THING?
HURRY, WE MAY BE NEEDED! LEAVE THE BLEACHED ONE BEHIND. AFTER ALL, THIS IS WAR...
...AND WAR IS NO PLACE FOR CHILDREN... OR LOSERS.
WITH ALL THAT I'VE SEEN IN MY LIFE... I NEVER THOUGHT OF MYSELF AS INNOCENT.
HOW WRONG I WAS. HOW NAÏVE. AND HOW DEAD IS THAT INNOCENCE I DIDN'T EVEN KNOW I POSSESSED?
AS DEAD AS LOBO.
[redacted]

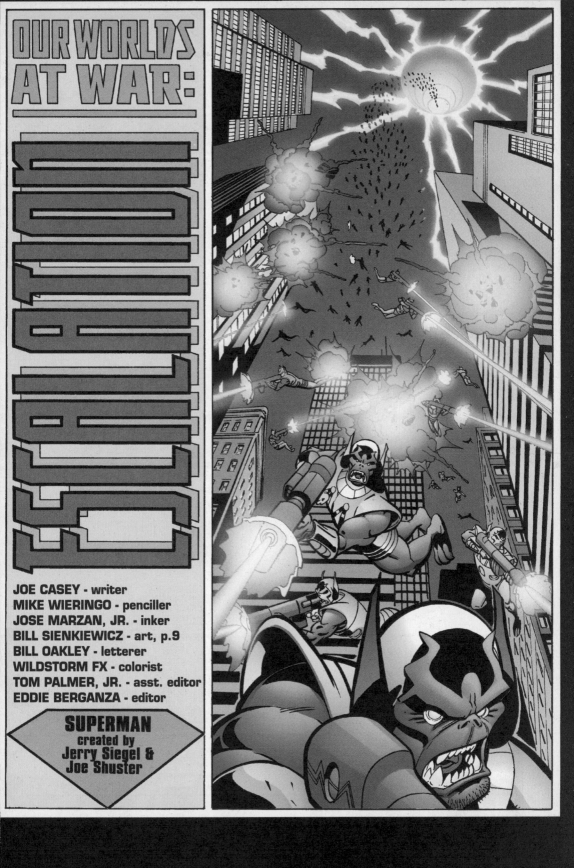

OUR WORLDS AT WAR: ESCALATION

JOE CASEY - writer
MIKE WIERINGO - penciller
JOSE MARZAN, JR. - inker
BILL SIENKIEWICZ - art, p.9
BILL OAKLEY - letterer
WILDSTORM FX - colorist
TOM PALMER, JR. - asst. editor
EDDIE BERGANZA - editor

SUPERMAN
created by
Jerry Siegel &
Joe Shuster

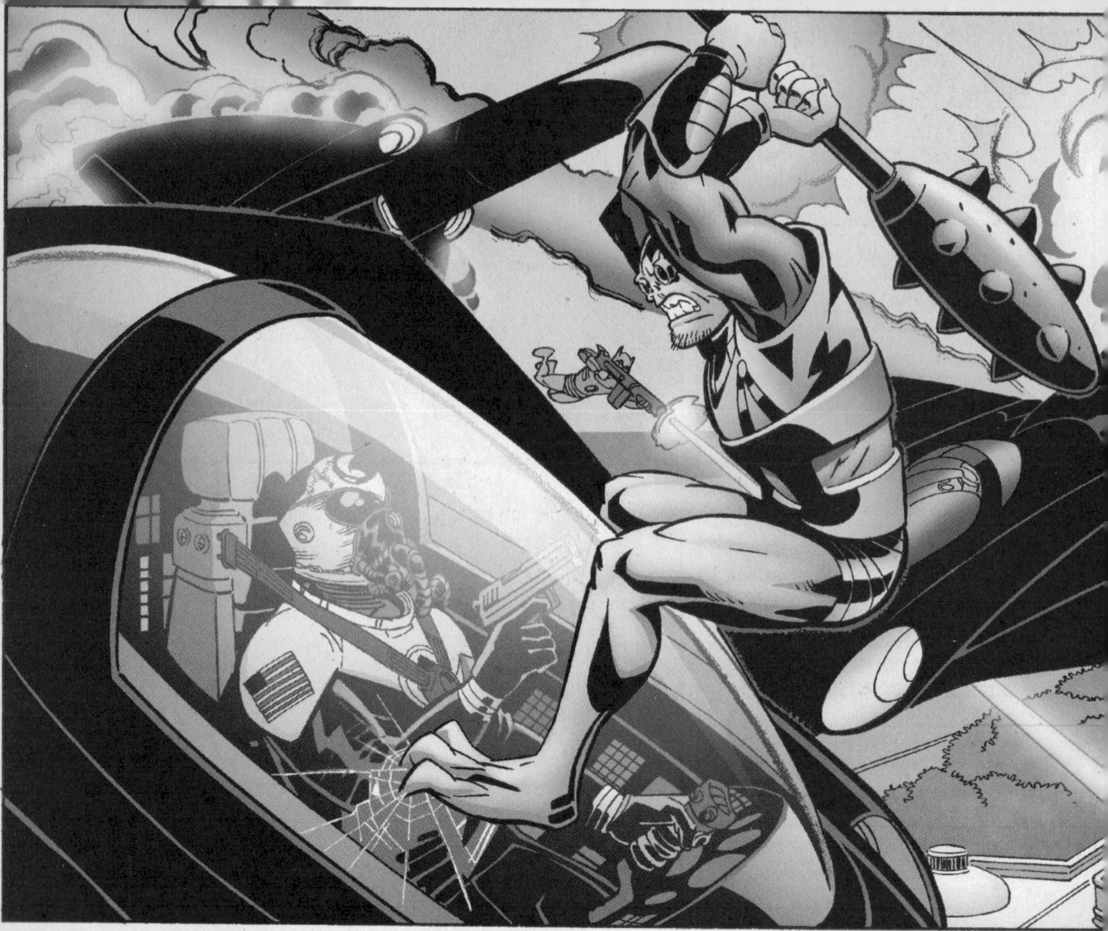

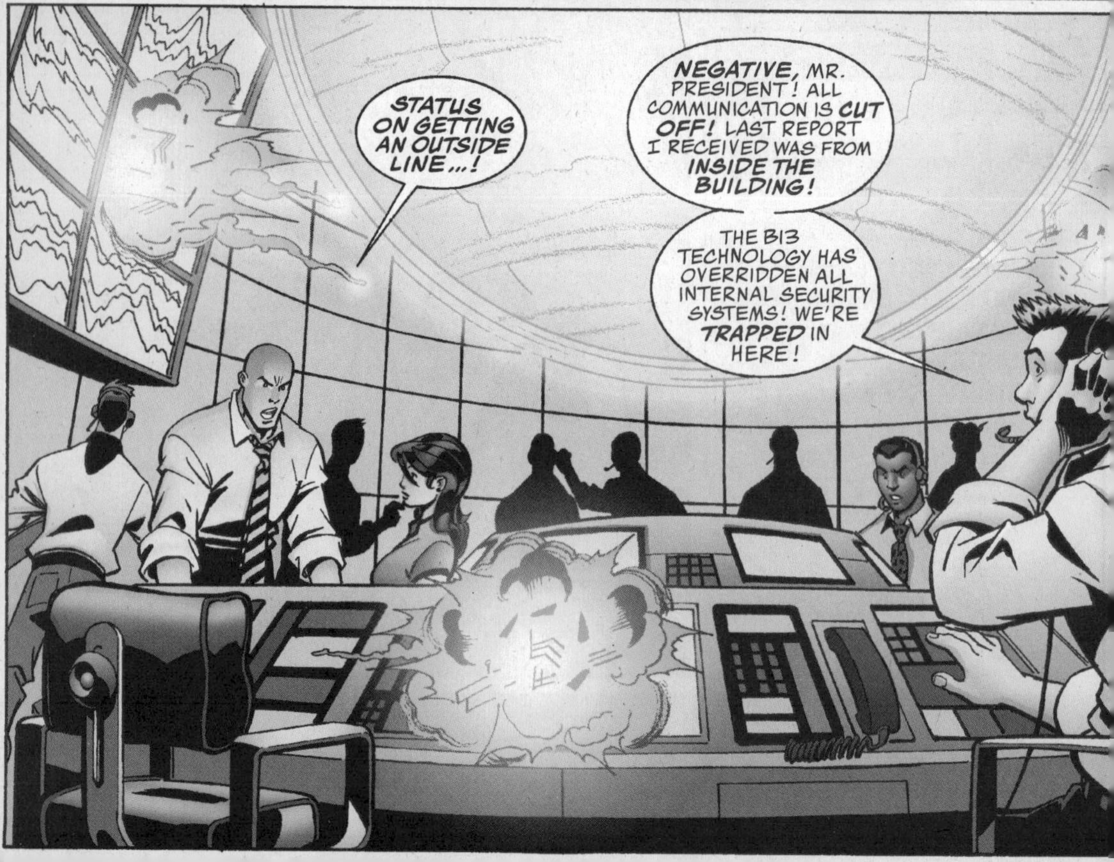
STATUS ON GETTING AN OUTSIDE LINE...!
NEGATIVE, MR. PRESIDENT! ALL COMMUNICATION IS CUT OFF! LAST REPORT I RECEIVED WAS FROM INSIDE THE BUILDING!
THE B13 TECHNOLOGY HAS OVERRIDDEN ALL INTERNAL SECURITY SYSTEMS! WE'RE TRAPPED IN HERE!

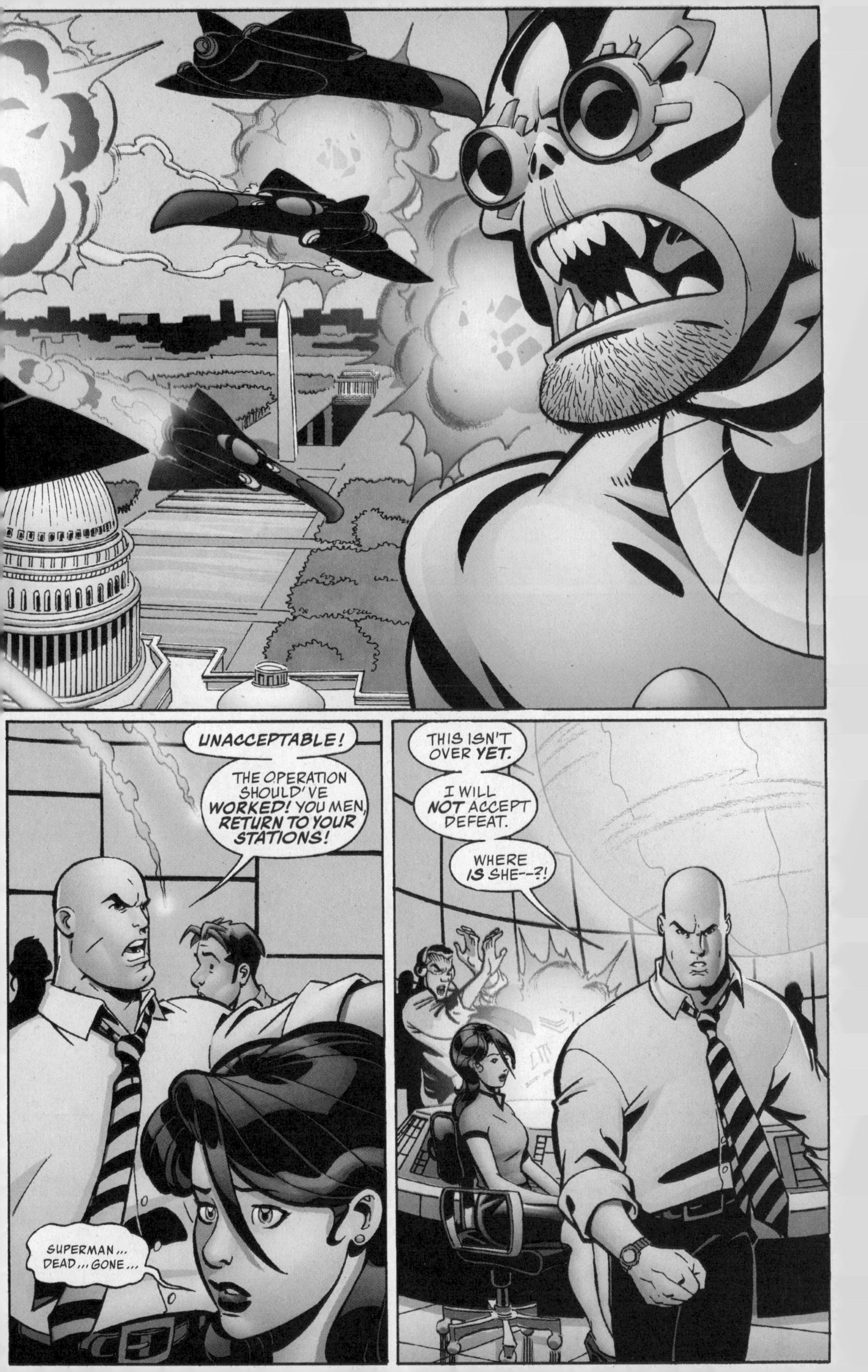
UNACCEPTABLE!
THE OPERATION SHOULD'VE WORKED! YOU MEN, RETURN TO YOUR STATIONS!
SUPERMAN... DEAD... GONE...
THIS ISN'T OVER YET.
I WILL NOT ACCEPT DEFEAT.
WHERE IS SHE--?!

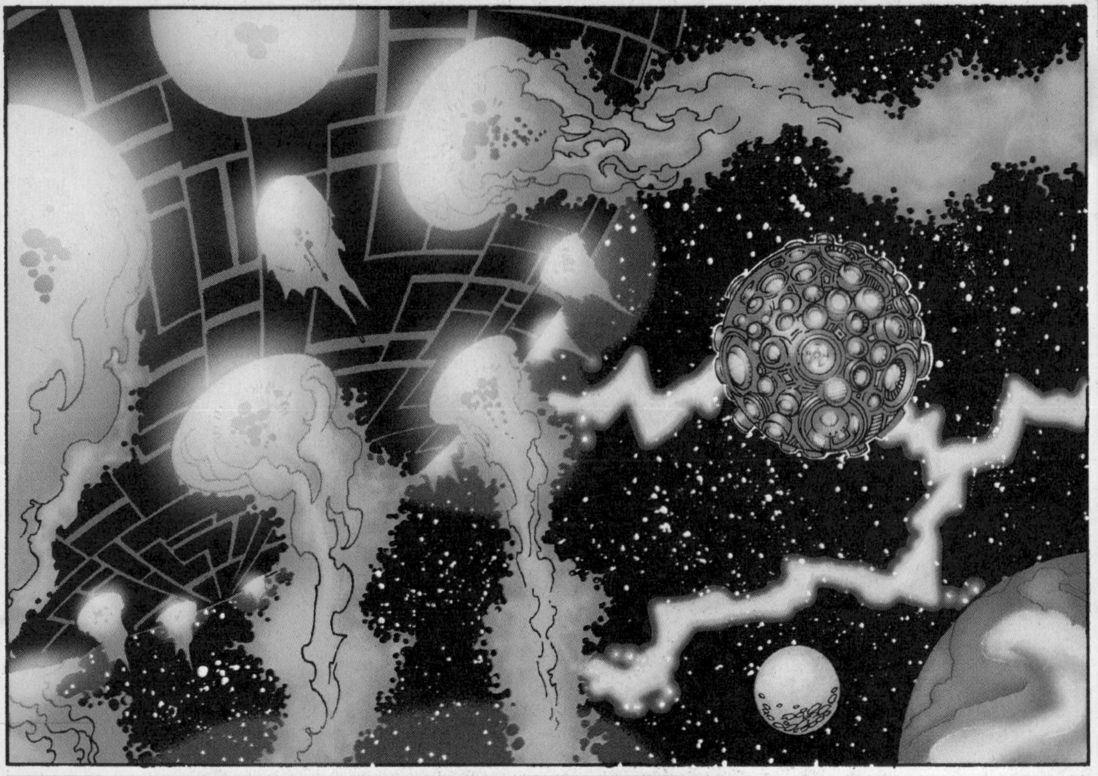

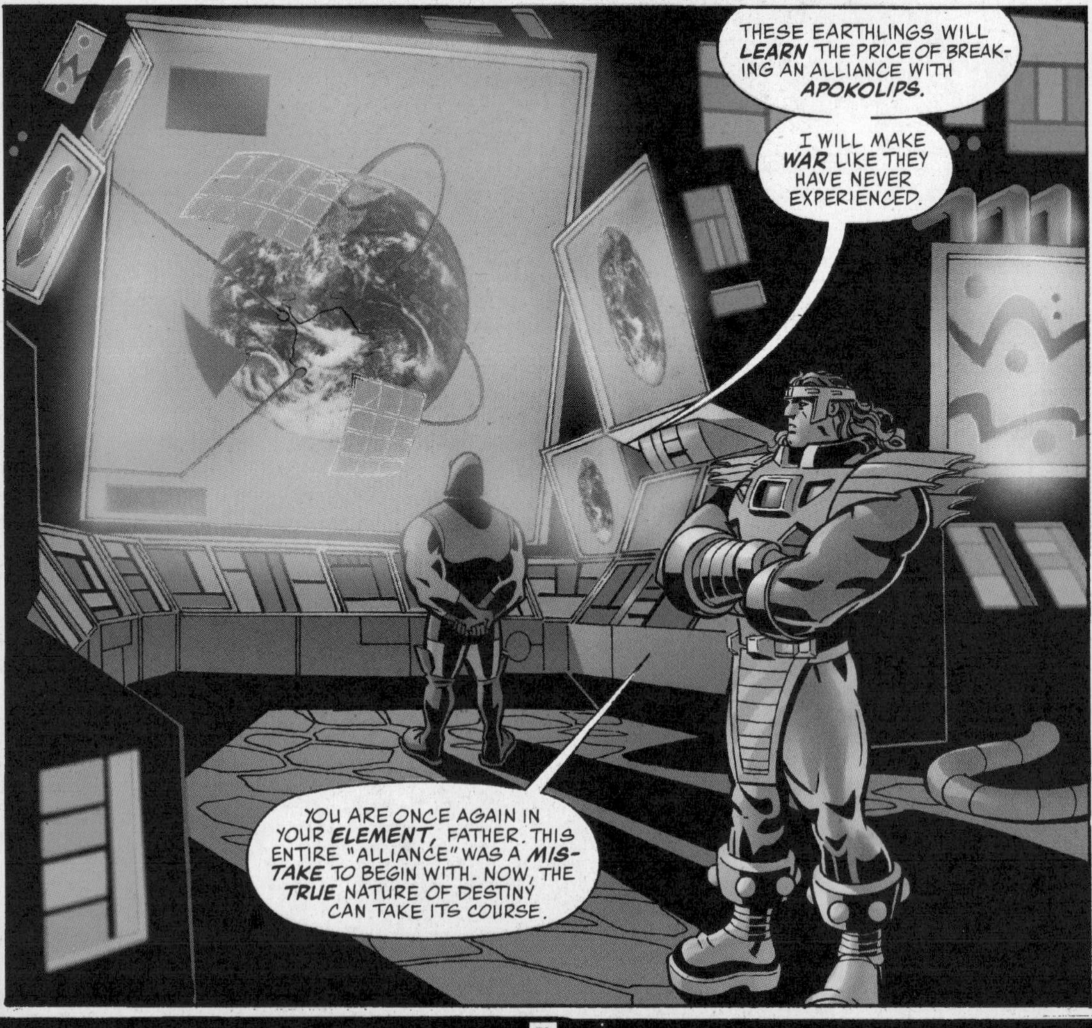
THESE EARTHLINGS WILL LEARN THE PRICE OF BREAKING AN ALLIANCE WITH APOKOLIPS.
I WILL MAKE WAR LIKE THEY HAVE NEVER EXPERIENCED.
YOU ARE ONCE AGAIN IN YOUR ELEMENT, FATHER. THIS ENTIRE "ALLIANCE" WAS A MISTAKE TO BEGIN WITH. NOW, THE TRUE NATURE OF DESTINY CAN TAKE ITS COURSE.

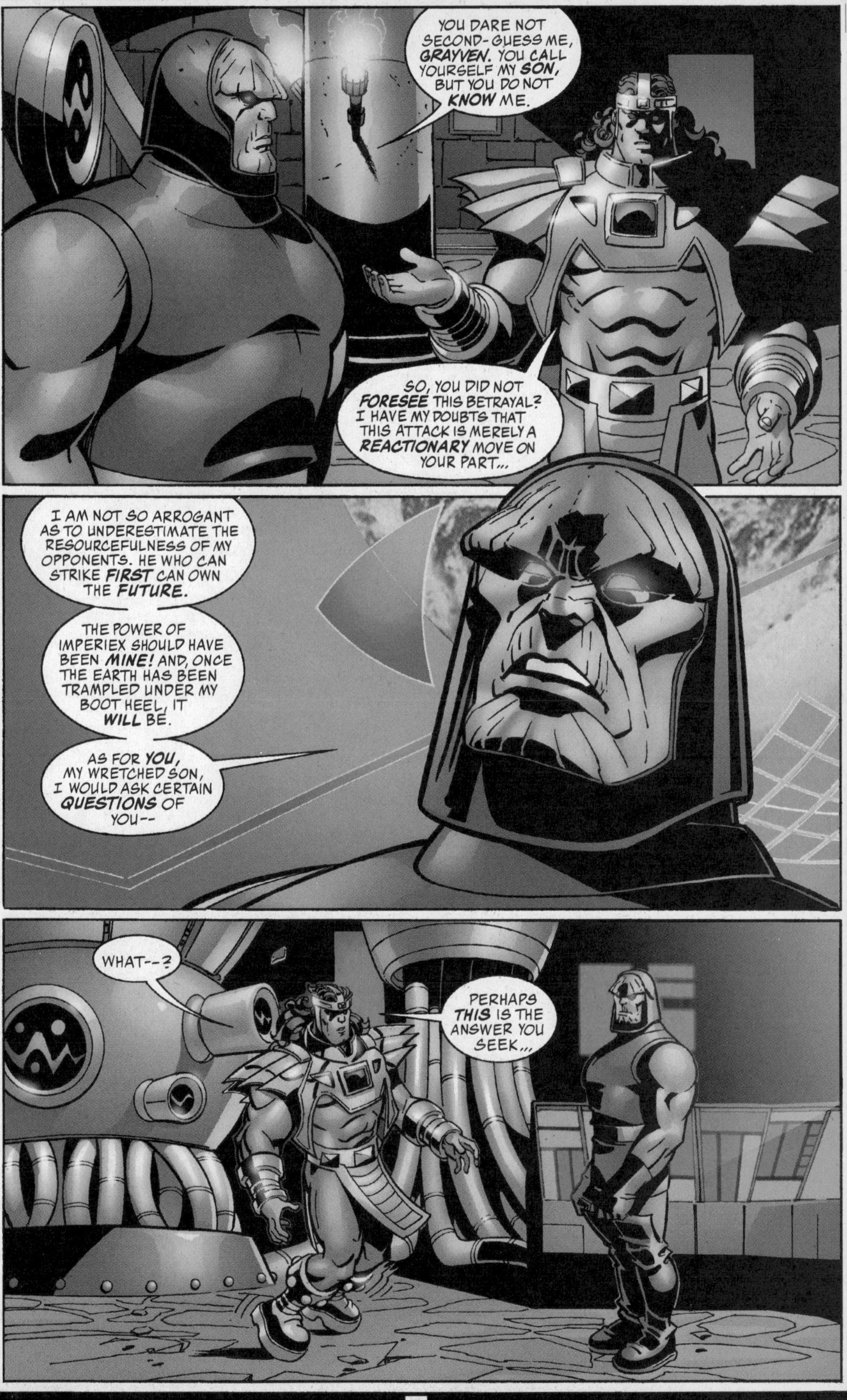

YOU DARE NOT SECOND-GUESS ME, GRAYVEN. YOU CALL YOURSELF MY SON, BUT YOU DO NOT KNOW ME.
SO, YOU DID NOT FORESEE THIS BETRAYAL? I HAVE MY DOUBTS THAT THIS ATTACK IS MERELY A REACTIONARY MOVE ON YOUR PART...
I AM NOT SO ARROGANT AS TO UNDERESTIMATE THE RESOURCEFULNESS OF MY OPPONENTS. HE WHO CAN STRIKE FIRST CAN OWN THE FUTURE.
THE POWER OF IMPERIEX SHOULD HAVE BEEN MINE! AND, ONCE THE EARTH HAS BEEN TRAMPLED UNDER MY BOOT HEEL, IT WILL BE.
AS FOR YOU, MY WRETCHED SON, I WOULD ASK CERTAIN QUESTIONS OF YOU--
WHAT--?
PERHAPS THIS IS THE ANSWER YOU SEEK...

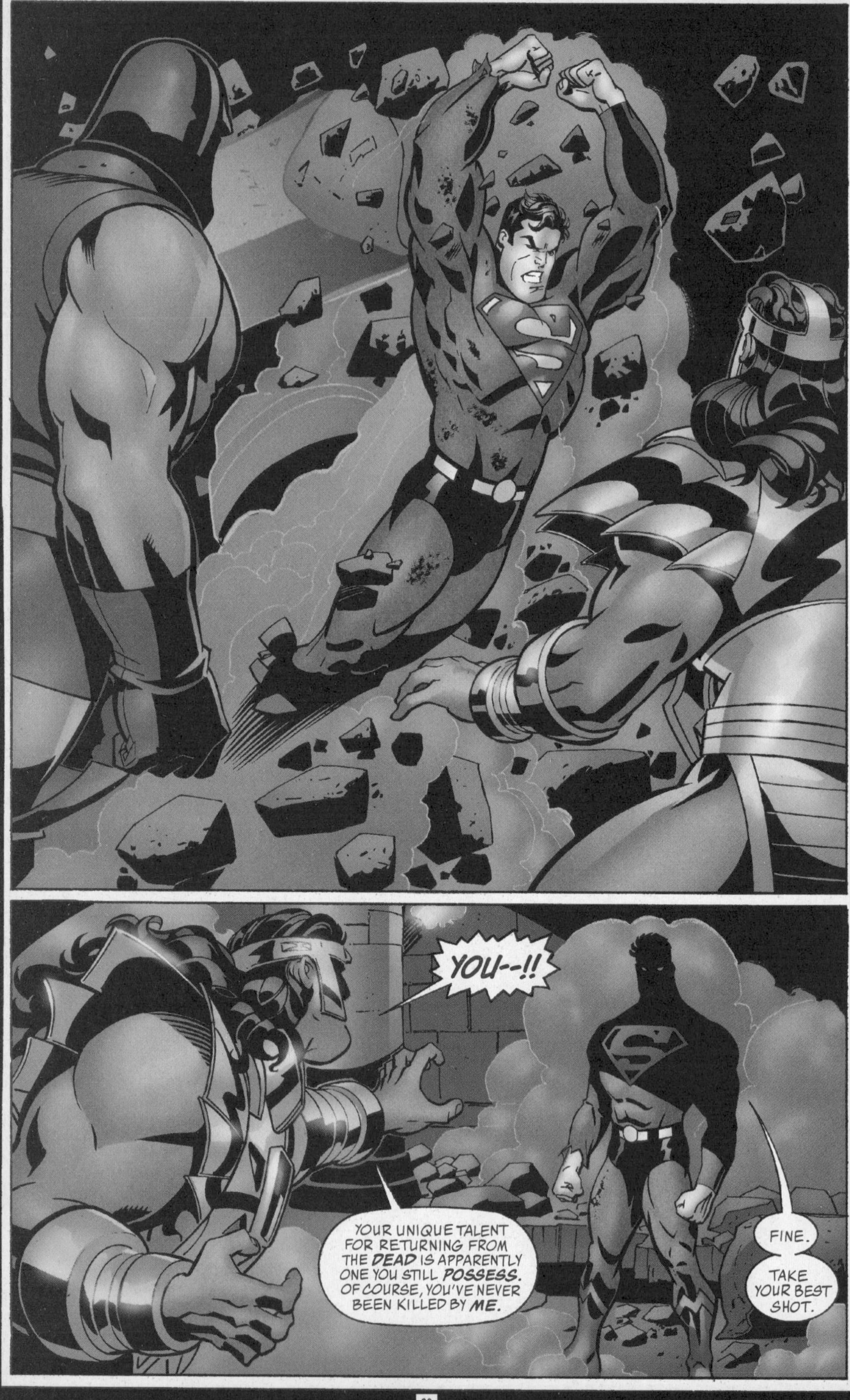
YOU--!!
YOUR UNIQUE TALENT FOR RETURNING FROM THE DEAD IS APPARENTLY ONE YOU STILL POSSESS. OF COURSE, YOU'VE NEVER BEEN KILLED BY ME.
FINE.
TAKE YOUR BEST SHOT.

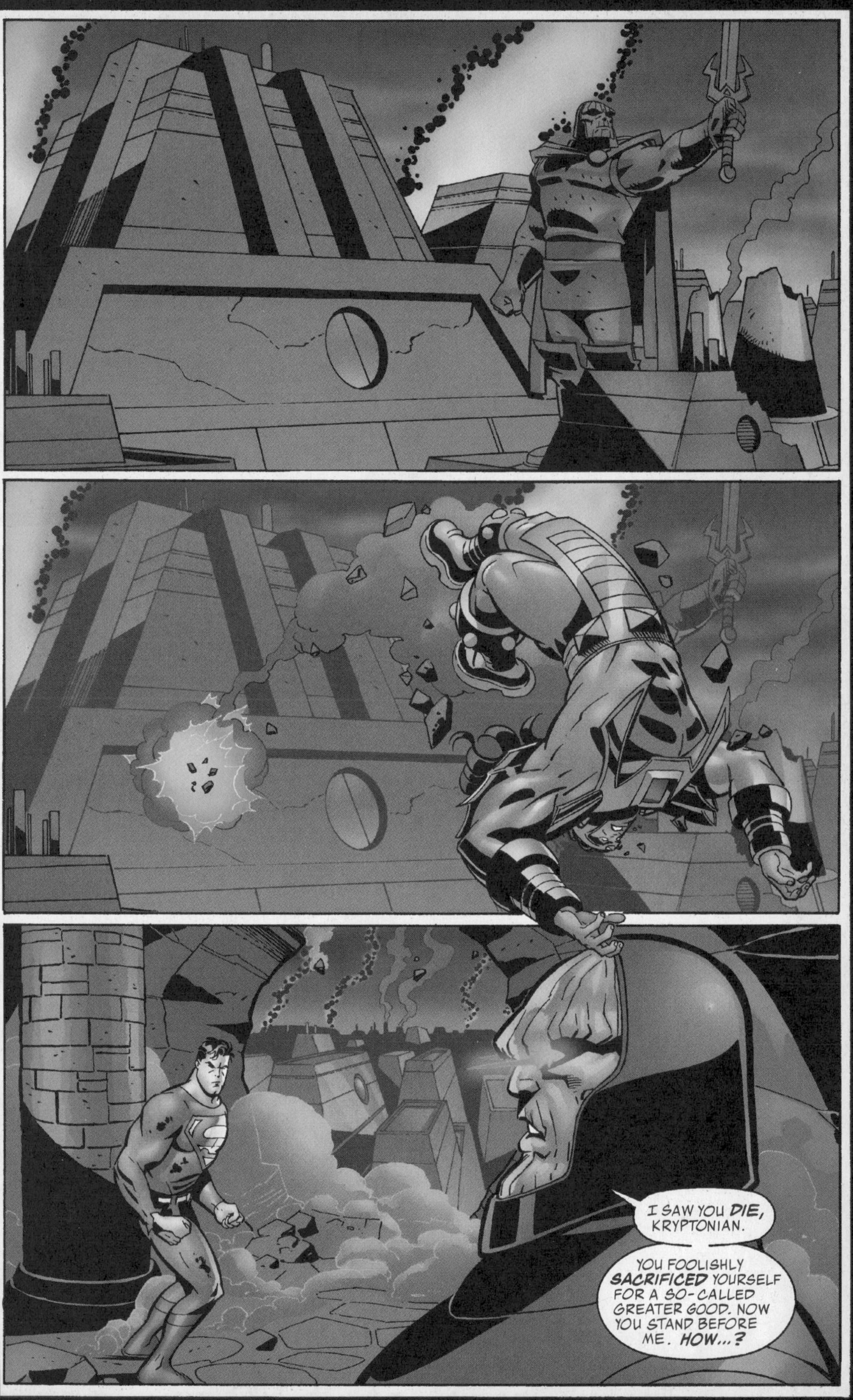
I SAW YOU DIE, KRYPTONIAN.
YOU FOOLISHLY SACRIFICED YOURSELF FOR A SO-CALLED GREATER GOOD. NOW YOU STAND BEFORE ME. HOW...?

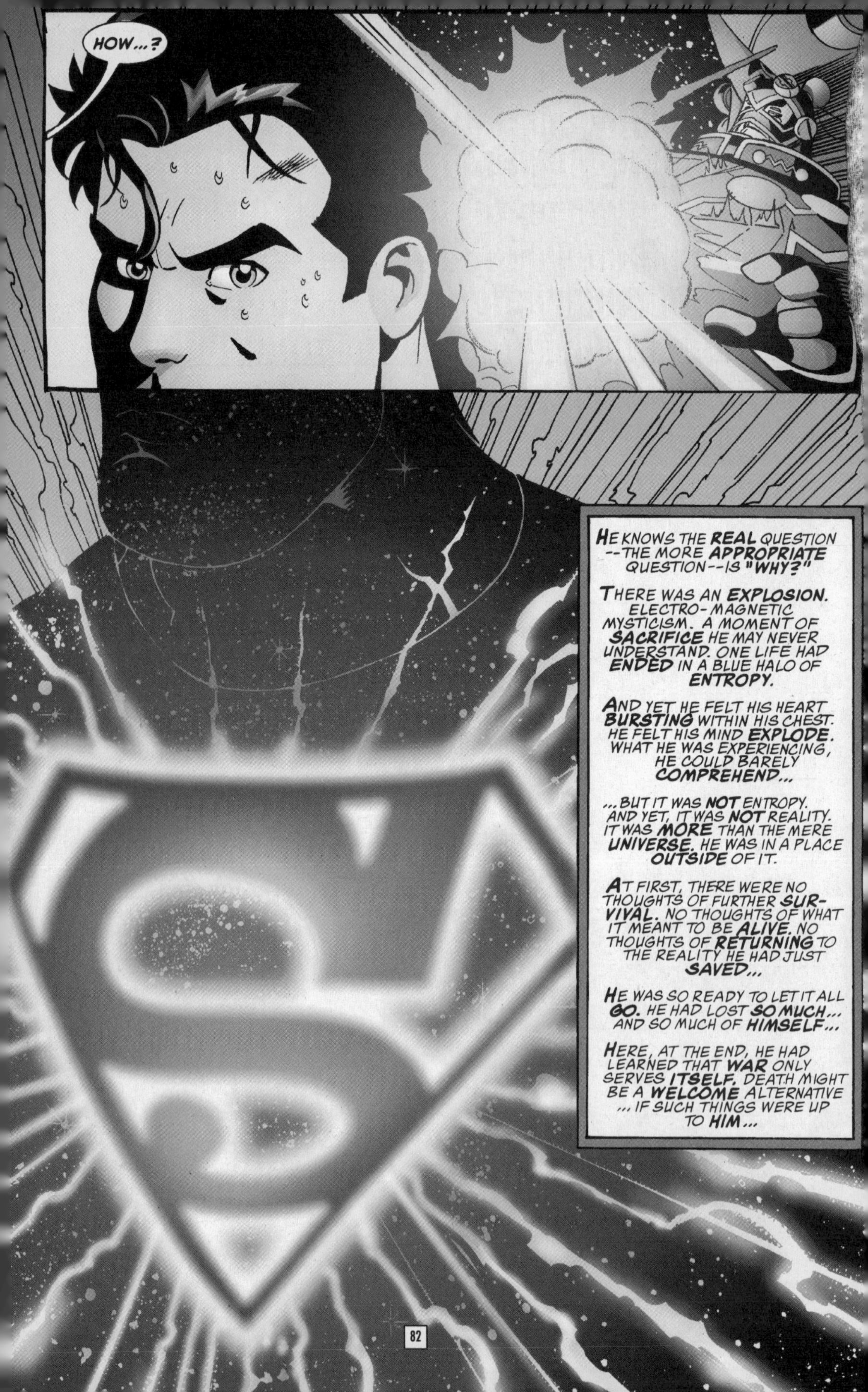
HOW...?
HE KNOWS THE REAL QUESTION --THE MORE APPROPRIATE QUESTION--IS "WHY?"
THERE WAS AN EXPLOSION. ELECTRO-MAGNETIC MYSTICISM. A MOMENT OF SACRIFICE HE MAY NEVER UNDERSTAND. ONE LIFE HAD ENDED IN A BLUE HALO OF ENTROPY.
AND YET HE FELT HIS HEART BURSTING WITHIN HIS CHEST. HE FELT HIS MIND EXPLODE. WHAT HE WAS EXPERIENCING, HE COULD BARELY COMPREHEND...
...BUT IT WAS NOT ENTROPY. AND YET, IT WAS NOT REALITY. IT WAS MORE THAN THE MERE UNIVERSE. HE WAS IN A PLACE OUTSIDE OF IT.
AT FIRST, THERE WERE NO THOUGHTS OF FURTHER SUR-VIVAL. NO THOUGHTS OF WHAT IT MEANT TO BE ALIVE. NO THOUGHTS OF RETURNING TO THE REALITY HE HAD JUST SAVED...
HE WAS SO READY TO LET IT ALL GO. HE HAD LOST SO MUCH... AND SO MUCH OF HIMSELF...
HERE, AT THE END, HE HAD LEARNED THAT WAR ONLY SERVES ITSELF. DEATH MIGHT BE A WELCOME ALTERNATIVE ... IF SUCH THINGS WERE UP TO HIM...

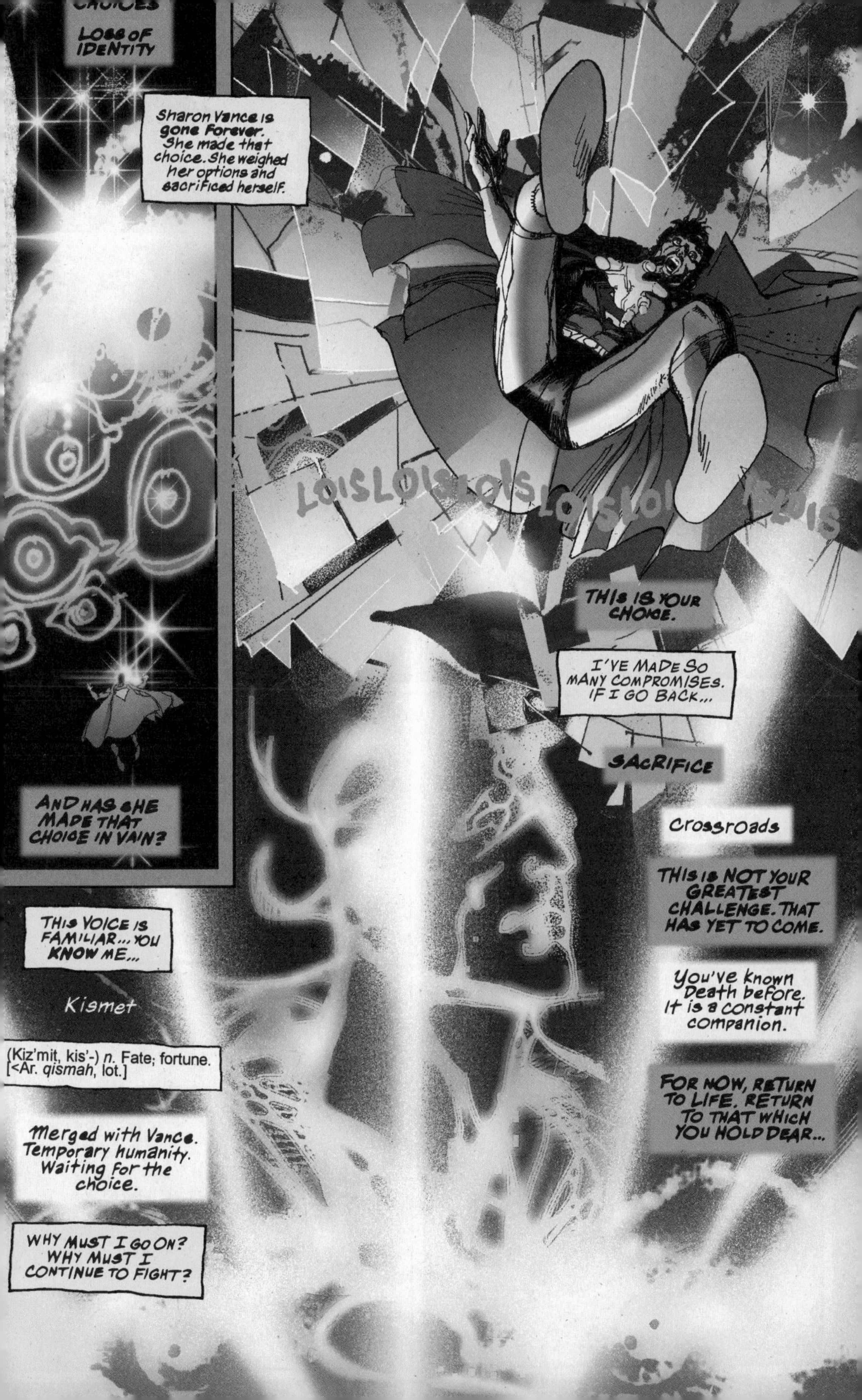

LOSS OF IDENTITY
Sharon Vance is gone forever. She made that choice. She weighed her options and sacrificed herself.
LOISLOISLOIS
THIS IS YOUR CHOICE.
I'VE MADE SO MANY COMPROMISES. IF I GO BACK...
SACRIFICE
AND HAS SHE MADE THAT CHOICE IN VAIN?
Crossroads
THIS IS NOT YOUR GREATEST CHALLENGE. THAT HAS YET TO COME.
THIS VOICE IS FAMILIAR... YOU KNOW ME...
Kismet
(Kiz'mit, kis'-) n. Fate; fortune. [<Ar. qismah, lot.]
You've known Death before. It is a constant companion.
FOR NOW, RETURN TO LIFE. RETURN TO THAT WHICH YOU HOLD DEAR...
Merged with Vance. Temporary humanity. Waiting for the choice.
WHY MUST I GO ON? WHY MUST I CONTINUE TO FIGHT?

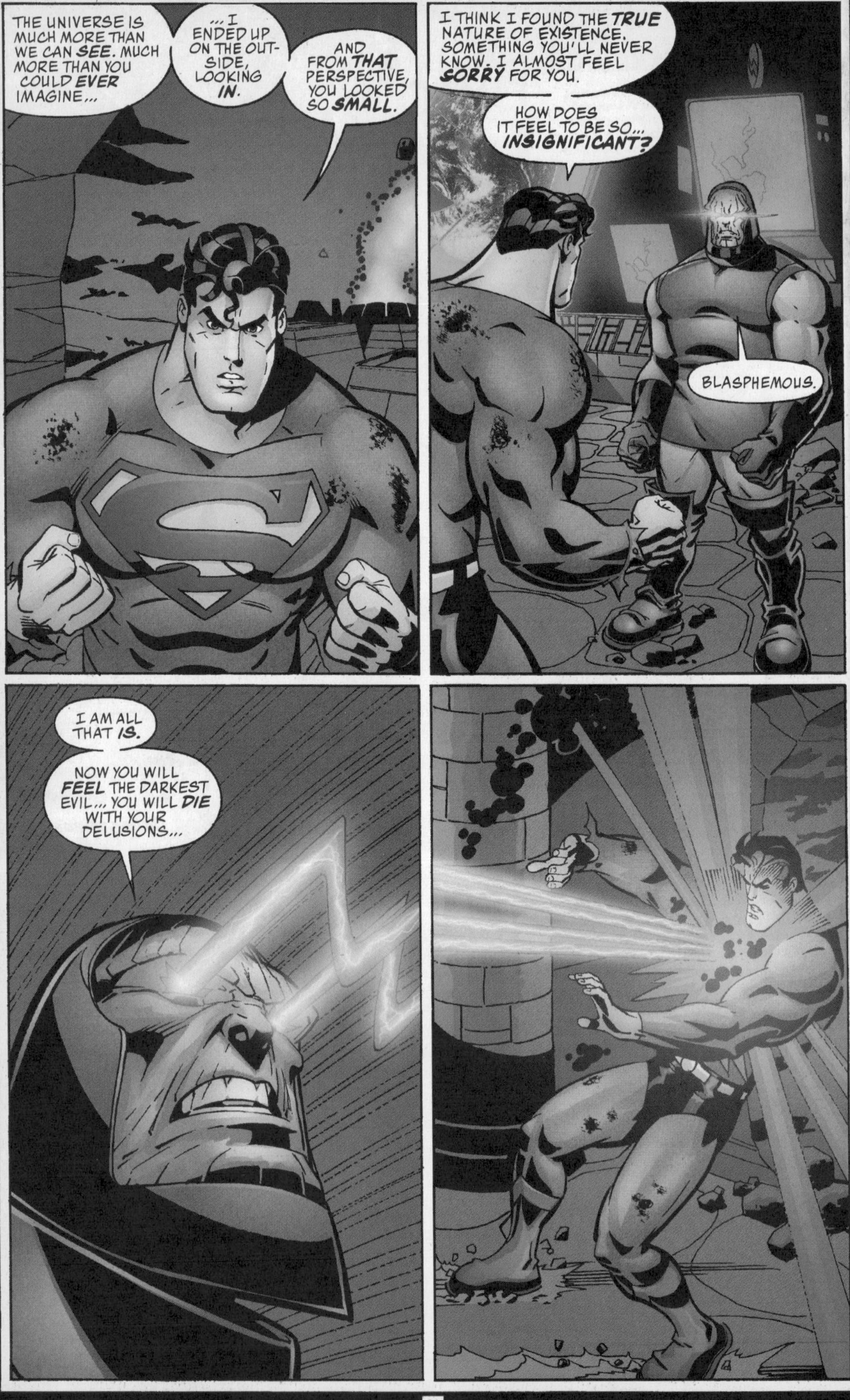

THE UNIVERSE IS MUCH MORE THAN WE CAN SEE. MUCH MORE THAN YOU COULD EVER IMAGINE...
...I ENDED UP ON THE OUT-SIDE, LOOKING IN.
AND FROM THAT PERSPECTIVE, YOU LOOKED SO SMALL.
I THINK I FOUND THE TRUE NATURE OF EXISTENCE. SOMETHING YOU'LL NEVER KNOW. I ALMOST FEEL SORRY FOR YOU.
HOW DOES IT FEEL TO BE SO... INSIGNIFICANT?
BLASPHEMOUS.
I AM ALL THAT IS.
NOW YOU WILL FEEL THE DARKEST EVIL... YOU WILL DIE WITH YOUR DELUSIONS...

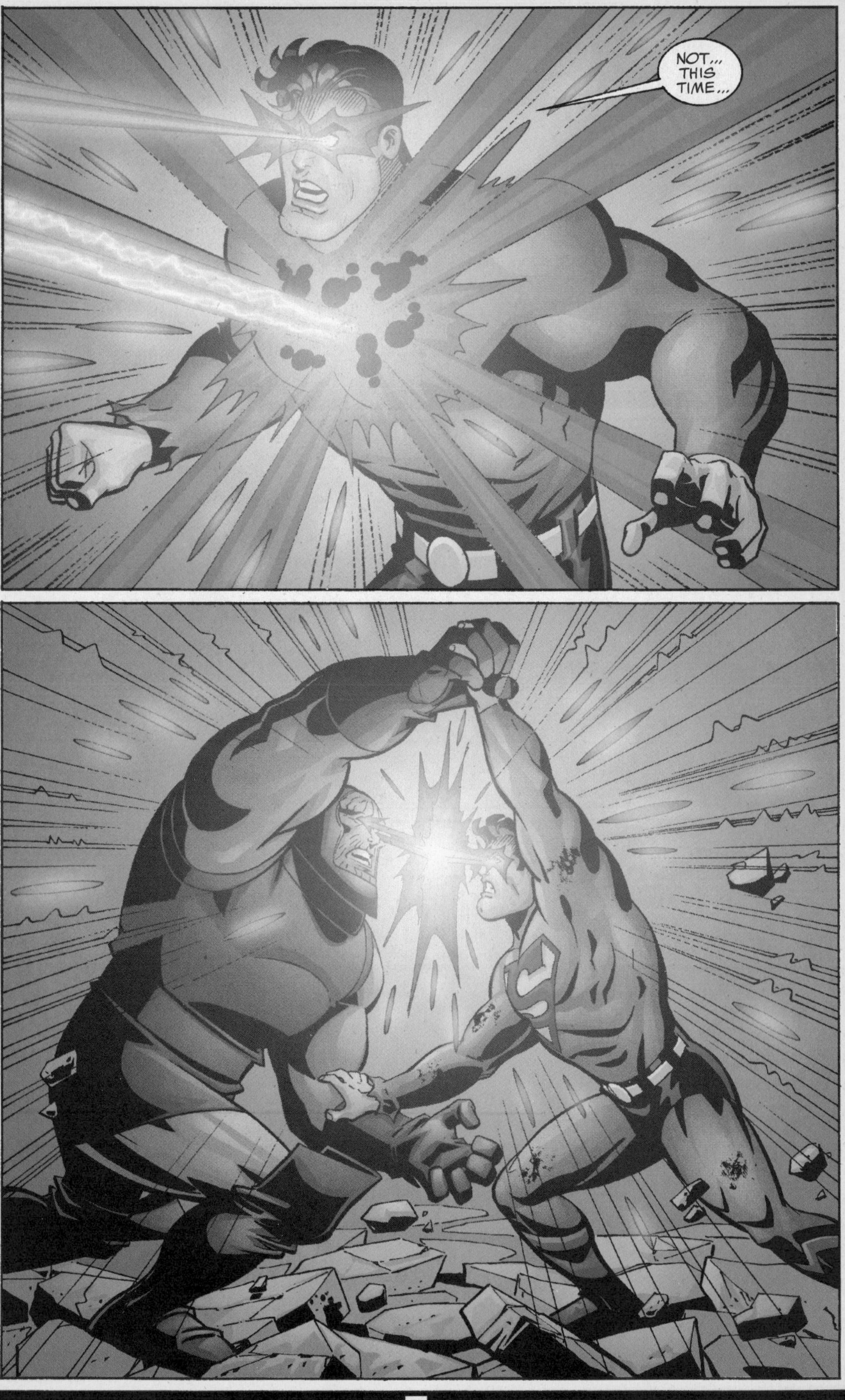
NOT... THIS TIME...

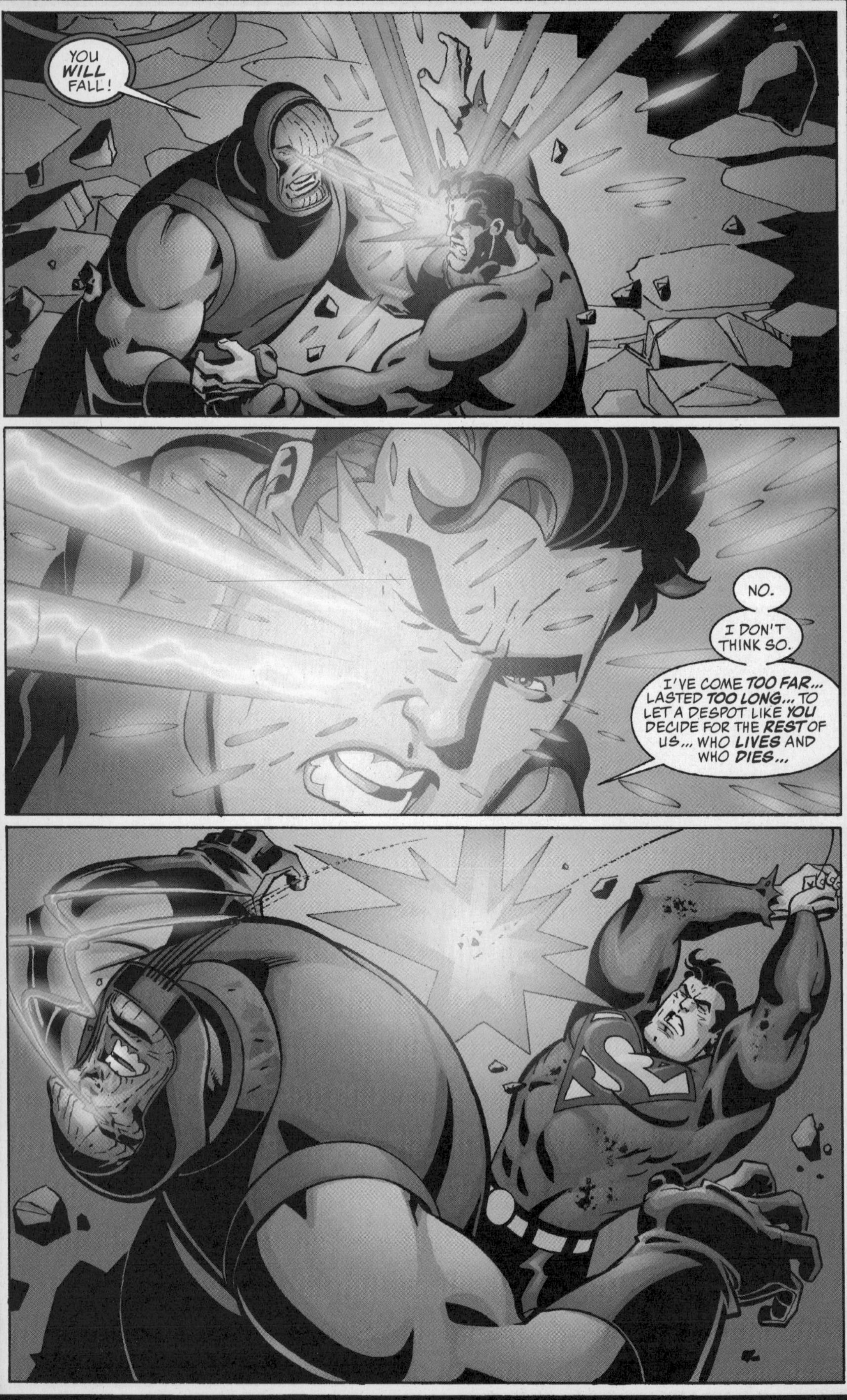
YOU WILL FALL!
NO.
I DON'T THINK SO.
I'VE COME TOO FAR... LASTED TOO LONG... TO LET A DESPOT LIKE YOU DECIDE FOR THE REST OF US... WHO LIVES AND WHO DIES...

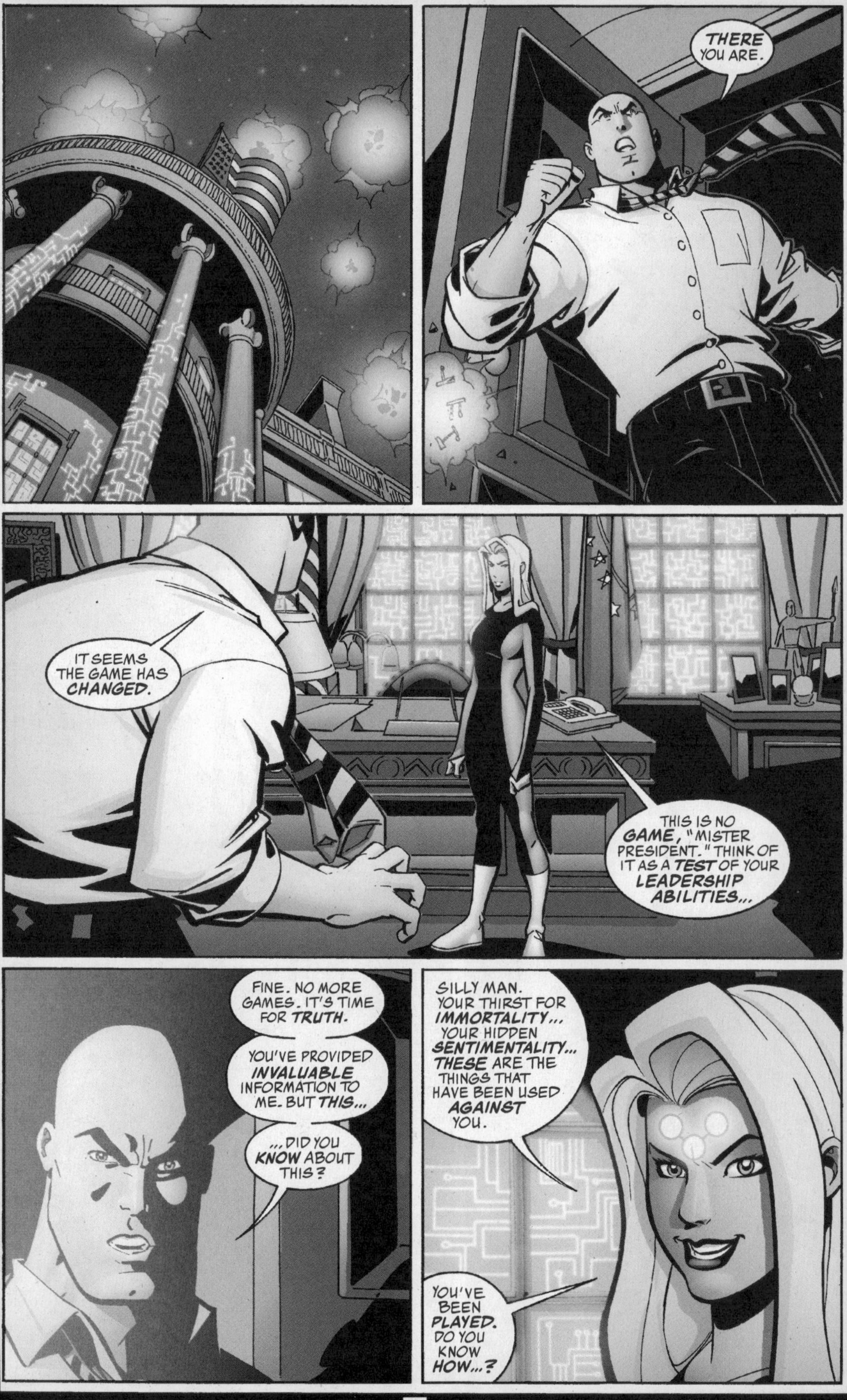
THERE YOU ARE.
IT SEEMS THE GAME HAS CHANGED.
THIS IS NO GAME, "MISTER PRESIDENT." THINK OF IT AS A TEST OF YOUR LEADERSHIP ABILITIES...
FINE. NO MORE GAMES. IT'S TIME FOR TRUTH.
YOU'VE PROVIDED INVALUABLE INFORMATION TO ME. BUT THIS...
...DID YOU KNOW ABOUT THIS?
SILLY MAN. YOUR THIRST FOR IMMORTALITY... YOUR HIDDEN SENTIMENTALITY... THESE ARE THE THINGS THAT HAVE BEEN USED AGAINST YOU.
YOU'VE BEEN PLAYED. DO YOU KNOW HOW...?

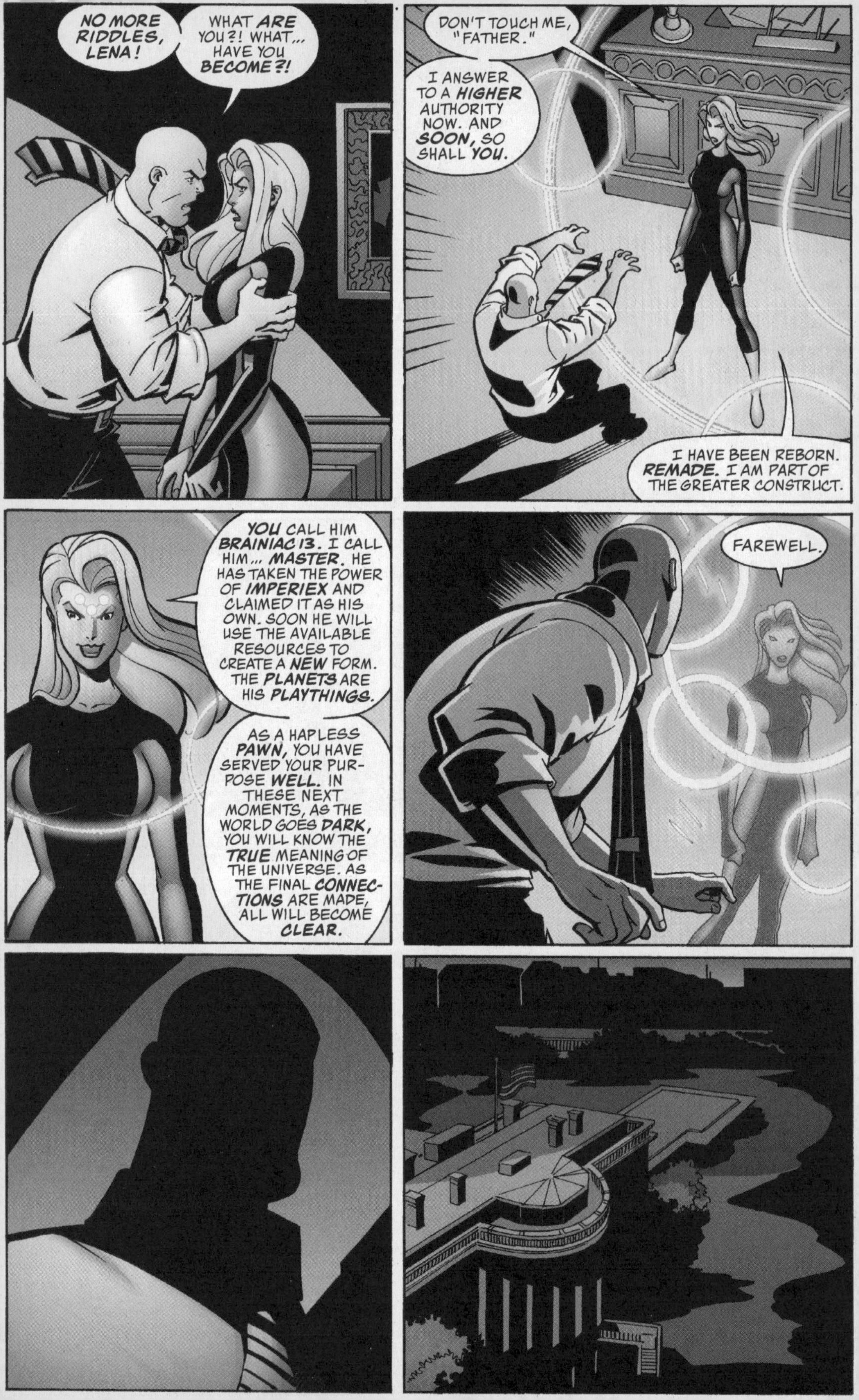
NO MORE RIDDLES, LENA!
WHAT ARE YOU?! WHAT... HAVE YOU BECOME?!
DON'T TOUCH ME, "FATHER."
I ANSWER TO A HIGHER AUTHORITY NOW. AND SOON, SO SHALL YOU.
I HAVE BEEN REBORN. REMADE. I AM PART OF THE GREATER CONSTRUCT.
YOU CALL HIM BRAINIAC 13. I CALL HIM... MASTER. HE HAS TAKEN THE POWER OF IMPERIEX AND CLAIMED IT AS HIS OWN. SOON HE WILL USE THE AVAILABLE RESOURCES TO CREATE A NEW FORM. THE PLANETS ARE HIS PLAYTHINGS.
AS A HAPLESS PAWN, YOU HAVE SERVED YOUR PURPOSE WELL. IN THESE NEXT MOMENTS, AS THE WORLD GOES DARK, YOU WILL KNOW THE TRUE MEANING OF THE UNIVERSE. AS THE FINAL CONNECTIONS ARE MADE, ALL WILL BECOME CLEAR.
FAREWELL.

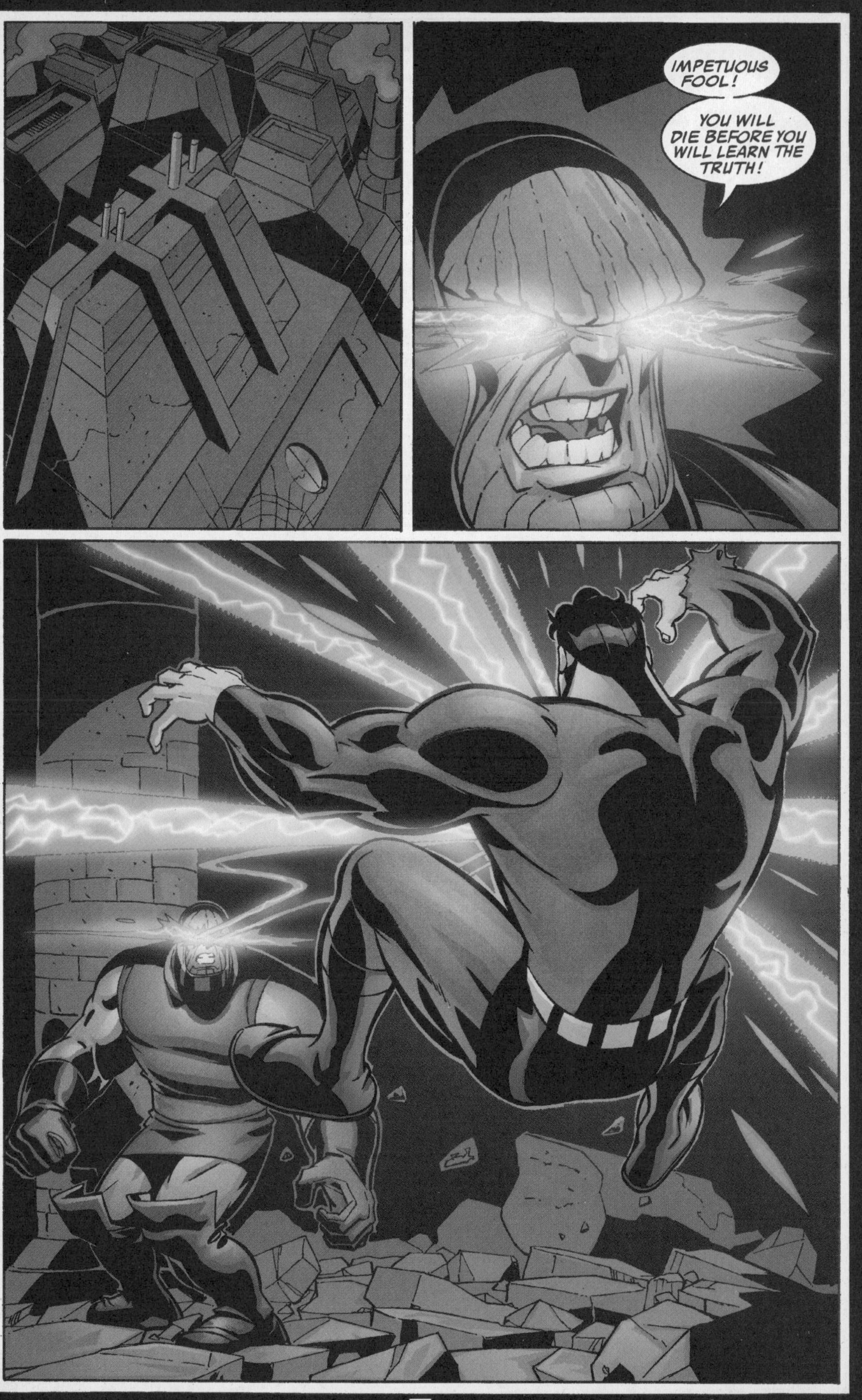
IMPETUOUS FOOL!
YOU WILL DIE BEFORE YOU WILL LEARN THE TRUTH!

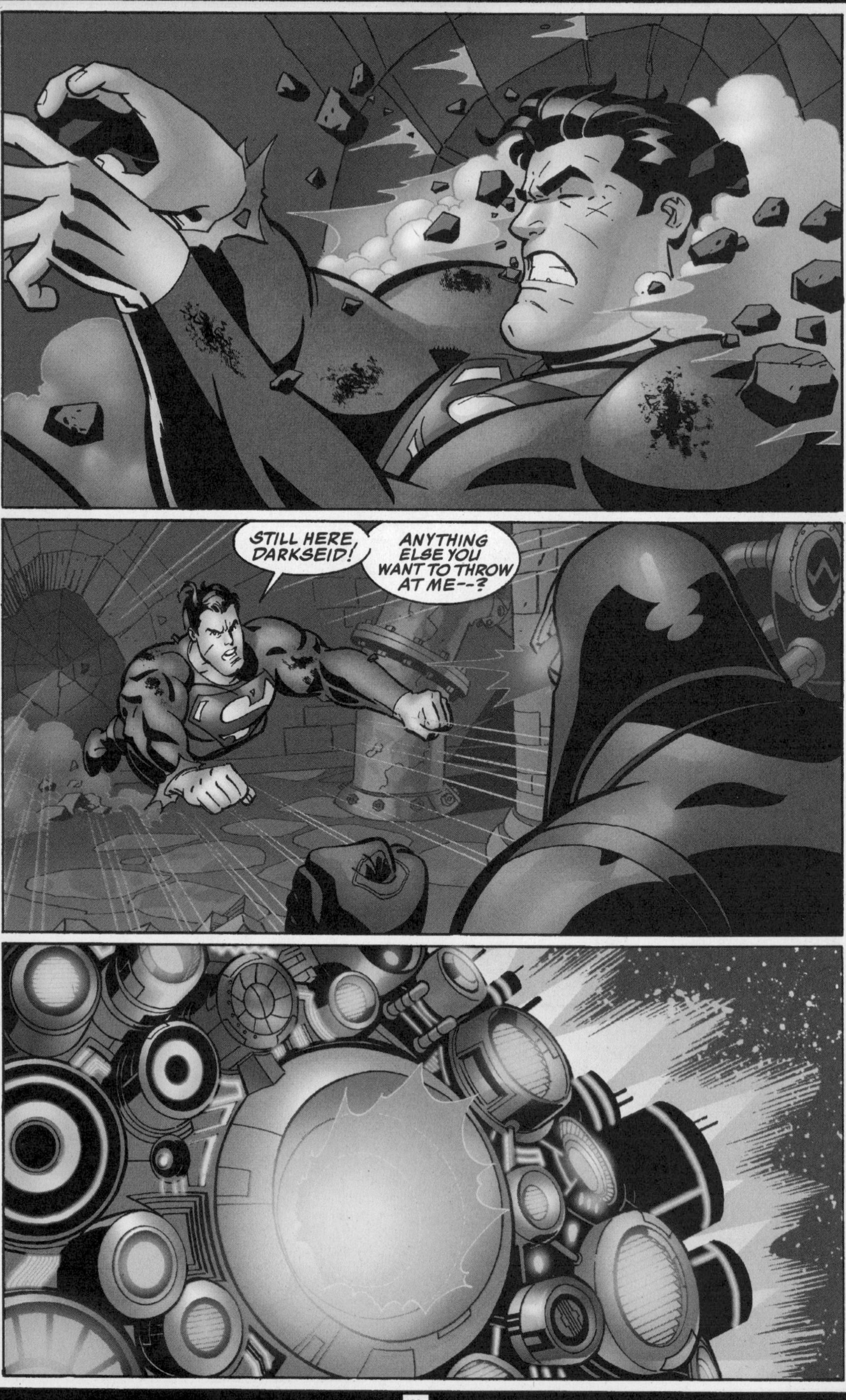
STILL HERE, DARKSEID!
ANYTHING ELSE YOU WANT TO THROW AT ME--?

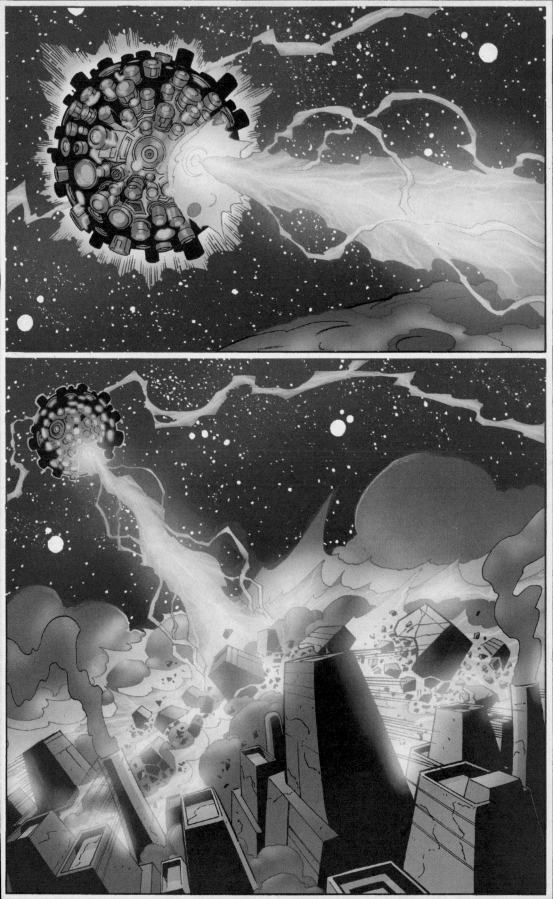

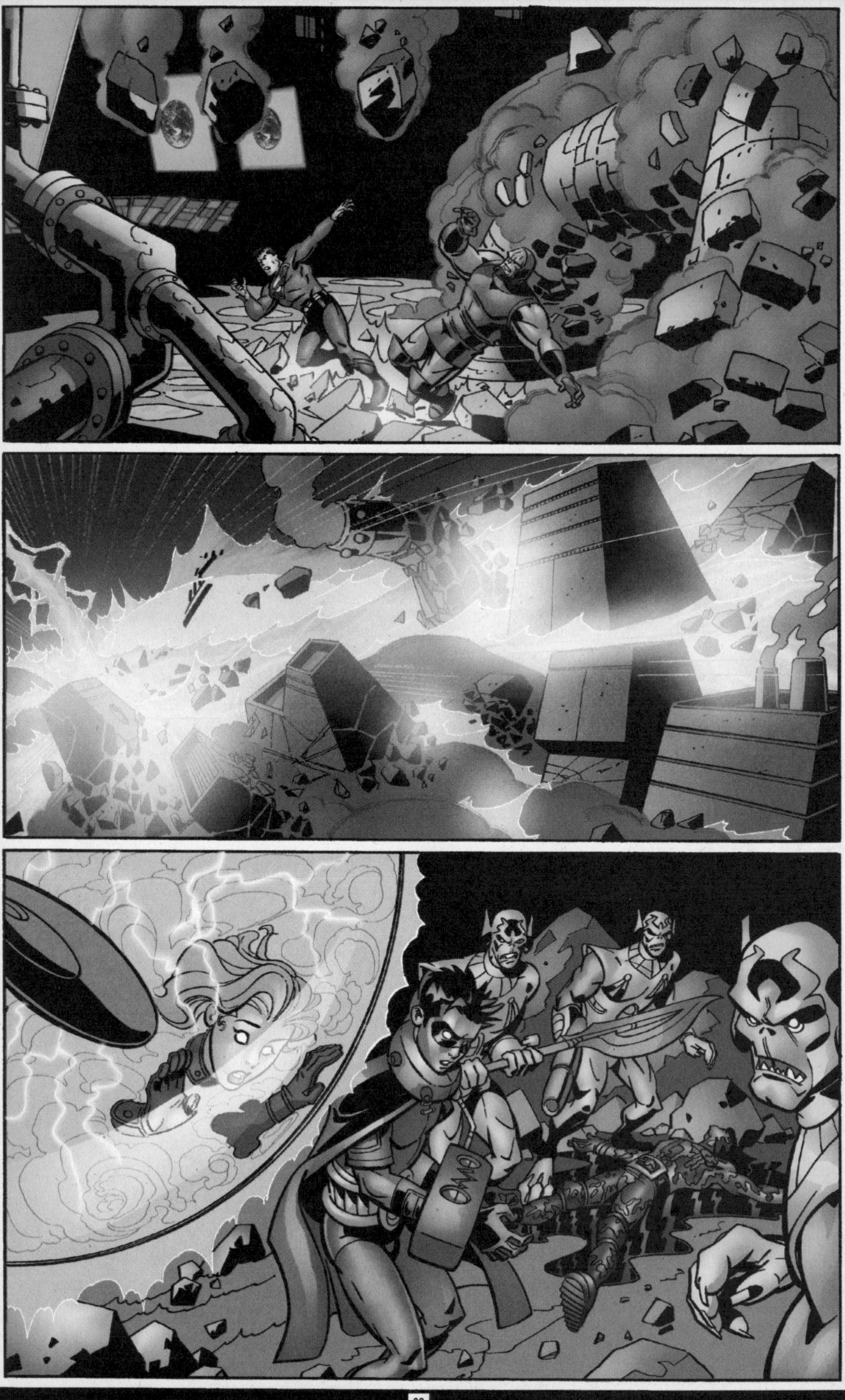

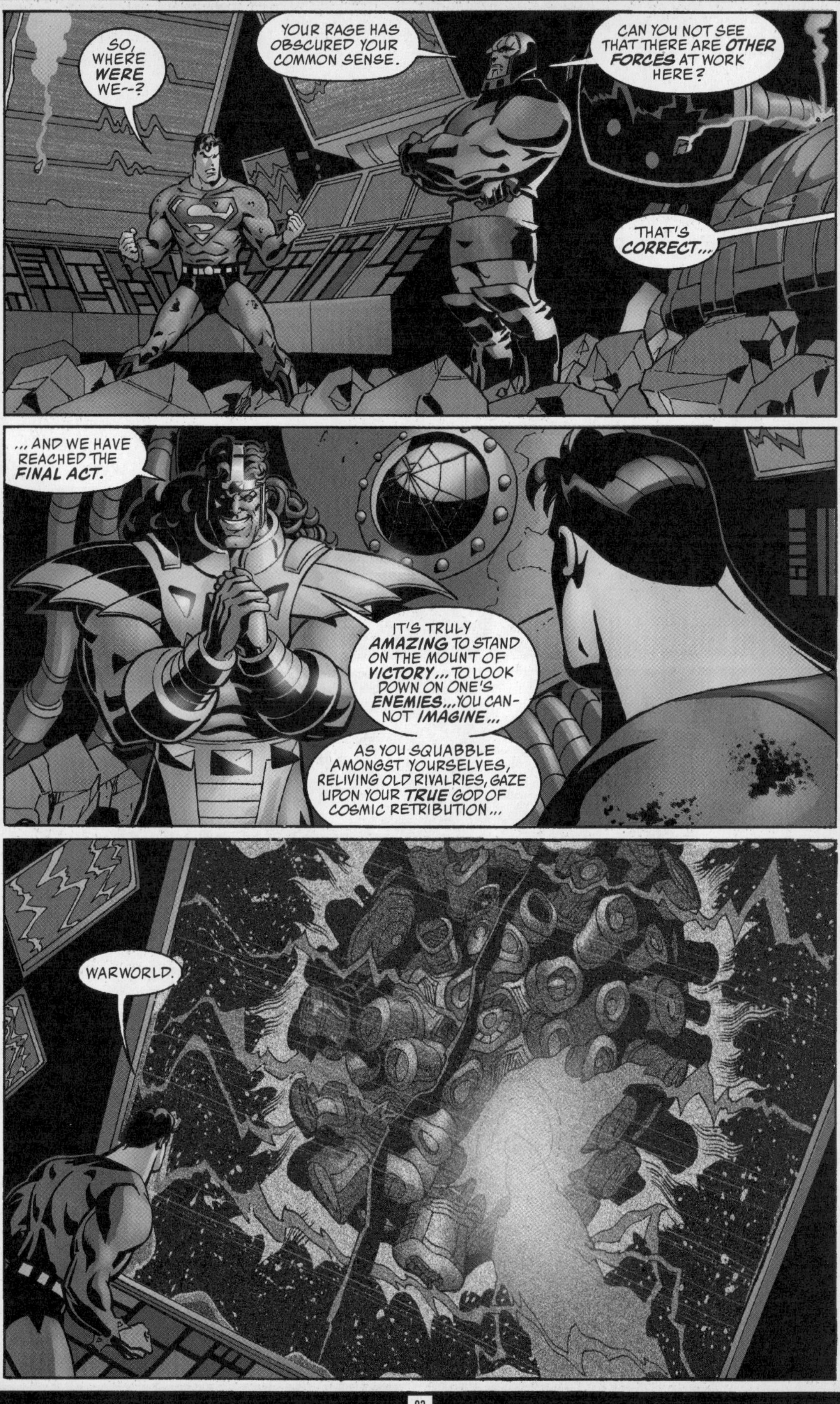
SO, WHERE WERE WE--?
YOUR RAGE HAS OBSCURED YOUR COMMON SENSE.
CAN YOU NOT SEE THAT THERE ARE OTHER FORCES AT WORK HERE?
THAT'S CORRECT...
...AND WE HAVE REACHED THE FINAL ACT.
IT'S TRULY AMAZING TO STAND ON THE MOUNT OF VICTORY... TO LOOK DOWN ON ONE'S ENEMIES... YOU CAN-NOT IMAGINE...
AS YOU SQUABBLE AMONGST YOURSELVES, RELIVING OLD RIVALRIES, GAZE UPON YOUR TRUE GOD OF COSMIC RETRIBUTION...
WARWORLD.

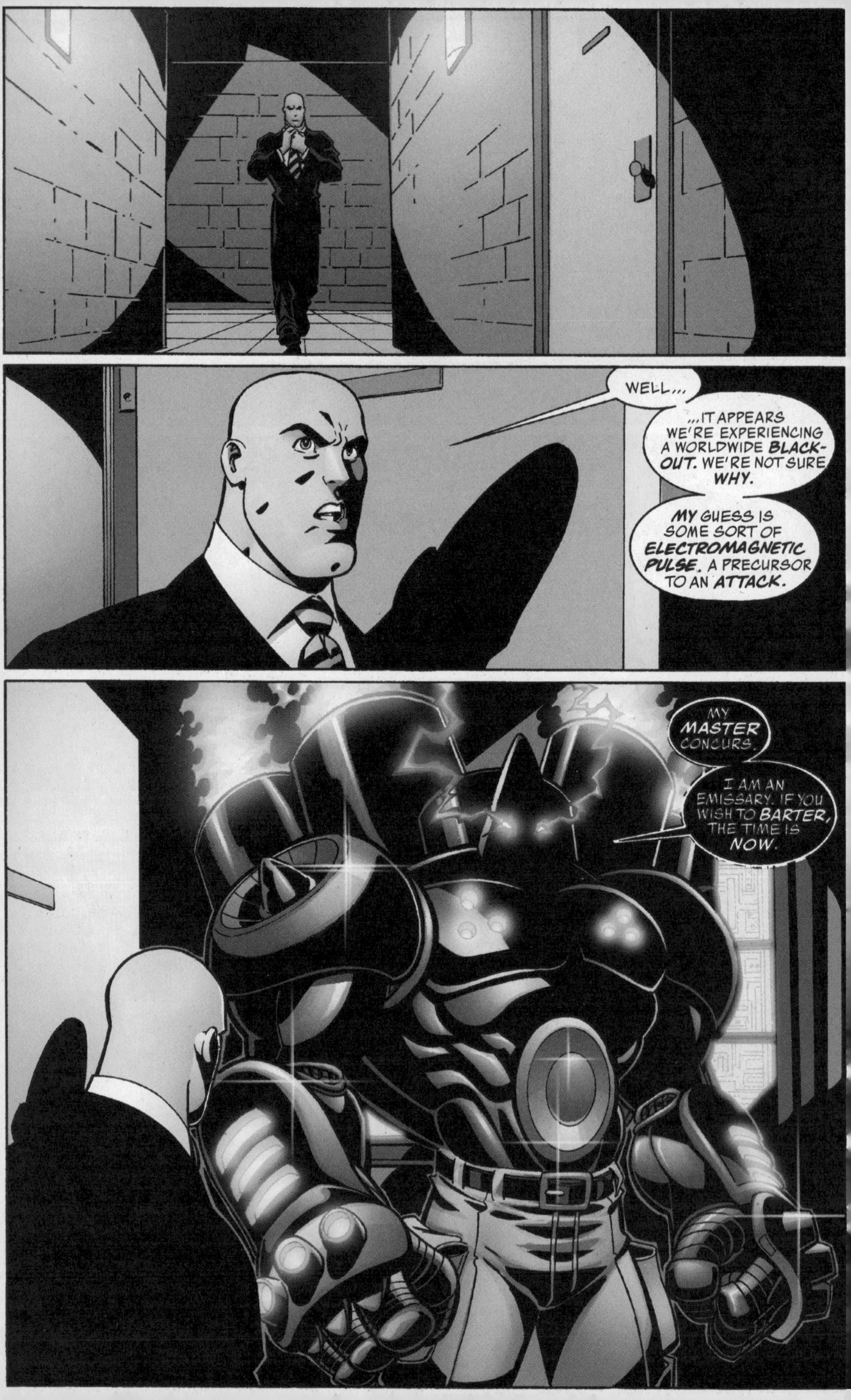

WELL...
...IT APPEARS WE'RE EXPERIENCING A WORLDWIDE BLACK-OUT. WE'RE NOT SURE WHY.
MY GUESS IS SOME SORT OF ELECTROMAGNETIC PULSE. A PRECURSOR TO AN ATTACK.
MY MASTER CONCURS.
I AM AN EMISSARY. IF YOU WISH TO BARTER, THE TIME IS NOW.

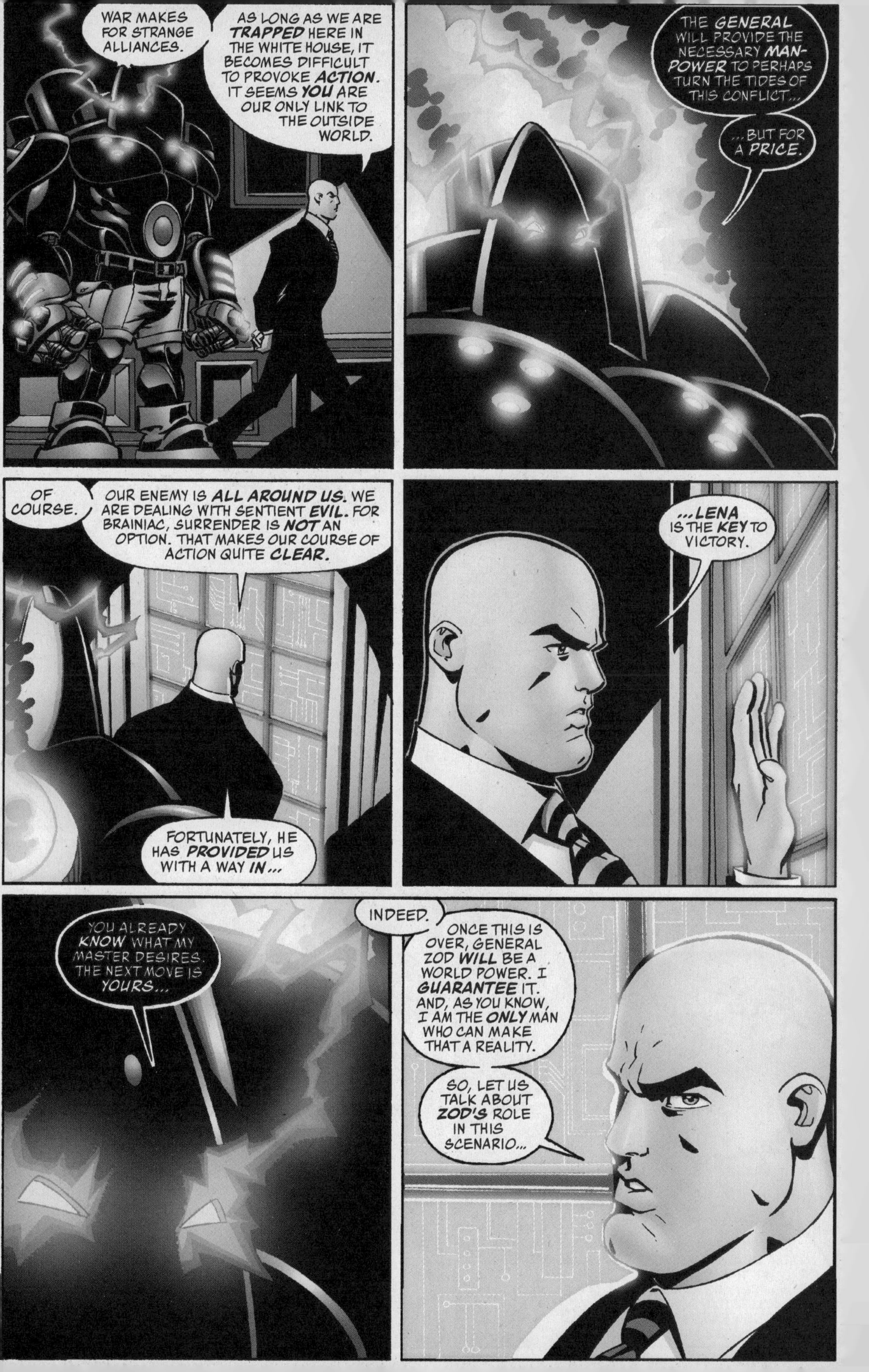
WAR MAKES FOR STRANGE ALLIANCES.
AS LONG AS WE ARE TRAPPED HERE IN THE WHITE HOUSE, IT BECOMES DIFFICULT TO PROVOKE ACTION. IT SEEMS YOU ARE OUR ONLY LINK TO THE OUTSIDE WORLD.
THE GENERAL WILL PROVIDE THE NECESSARY MAN-POWER TO PERHAPS TURN THE TIDES OF THIS CONFLICT...
...BUT FOR A PRICE.
OF COURSE.
OUR ENEMY IS ALL AROUND US. WE ARE DEALING WITH SENTIENT EVIL. FOR BRAINIAC, SURRENDER IS NOT AN OPTION. THAT MAKES OUR COURSE OF ACTION QUITE CLEAR.
FORTUNATELY, HE HAS PROVIDED US WITH A WAY IN...
...LENA IS THE KEY TO VICTORY.
YOU ALREADY KNOW WHAT MY MASTER DESIRES. THE NEXT MOVE IS YOURS...
INDEED.
ONCE THIS IS OVER, GENERAL ZOD WILL BE A WORLD POWER. I GUARANTEE IT. AND, AS YOU KNOW, I AM THE ONLY MAN WHO CAN MAKE THAT A REALITY.
SO, LET US TALK ABOUT ZOD'S ROLE IN THIS SCENARIO...

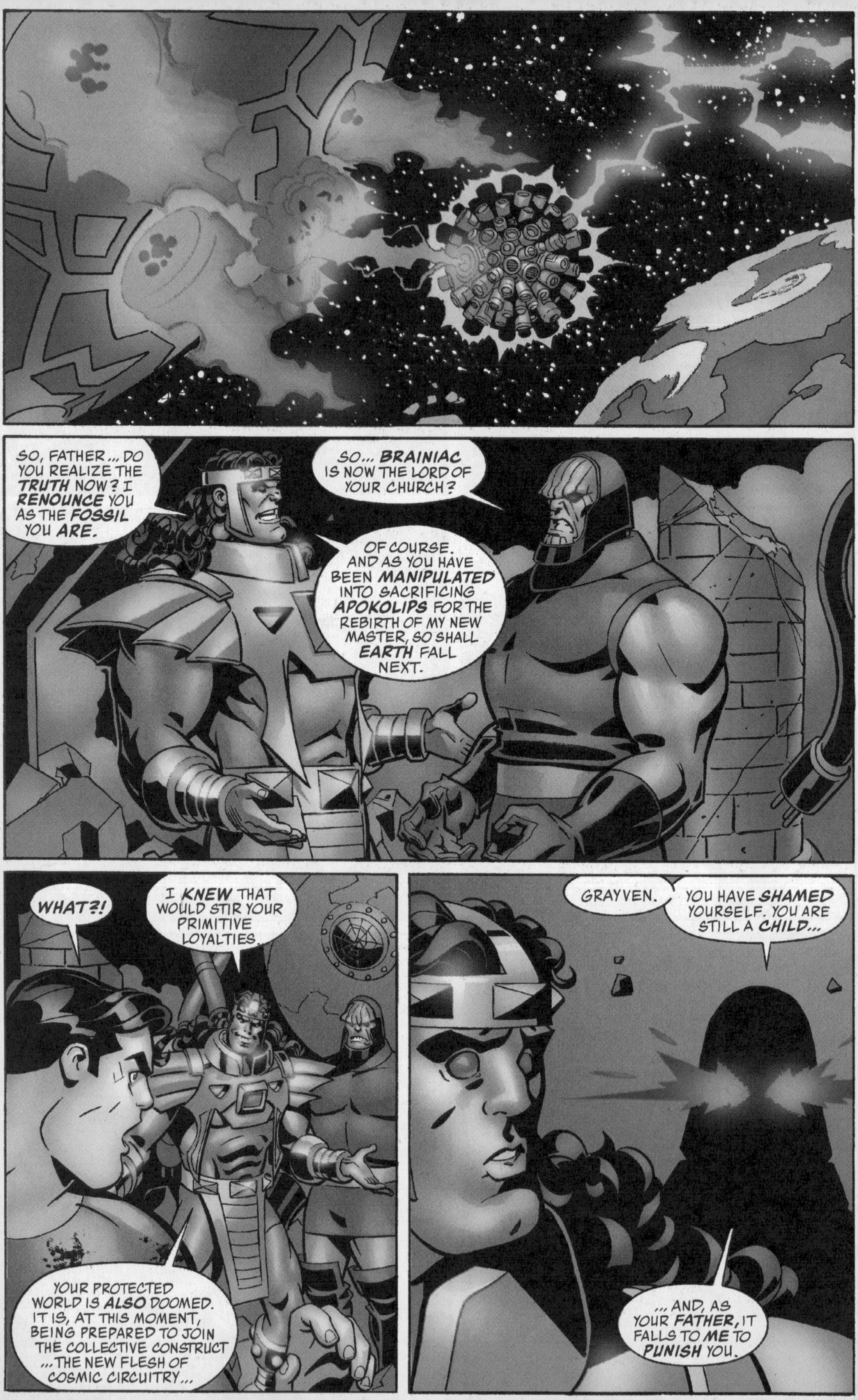
SO, FATHER... DO YOU REALIZE THE TRUTH NOW? I RENOUNCE YOU AS THE FOSSIL YOU ARE.
SO... BRAINIAC IS NOW THE LORD OF YOUR CHURCH?
OF COURSE. AND AS YOU HAVE BEEN MANIPULATED INTO SACRIFICING APOKOLIPS FOR THE REBIRTH OF MY NEW MASTER, SO SHALL EARTH FALL NEXT.
WHAT?!
I KNEW THAT WOULD STIR YOUR PRIMITIVE LOYALTIES.
YOUR PROTECTED WORLD IS ALSO DOOMED. IT IS, AT THIS MOMENT, BEING PREPARED TO JOIN THE COLLECTIVE CONSTRUCT ...THE NEW FLESH OF COSMIC CIRCUITRY...
GRAYVEN.
YOU HAVE SHAMED YOURSELF. YOU ARE STILL A CHILD...
...AND, AS YOUR FATHER, IT FALLS TO ME TO PUNISH YOU.

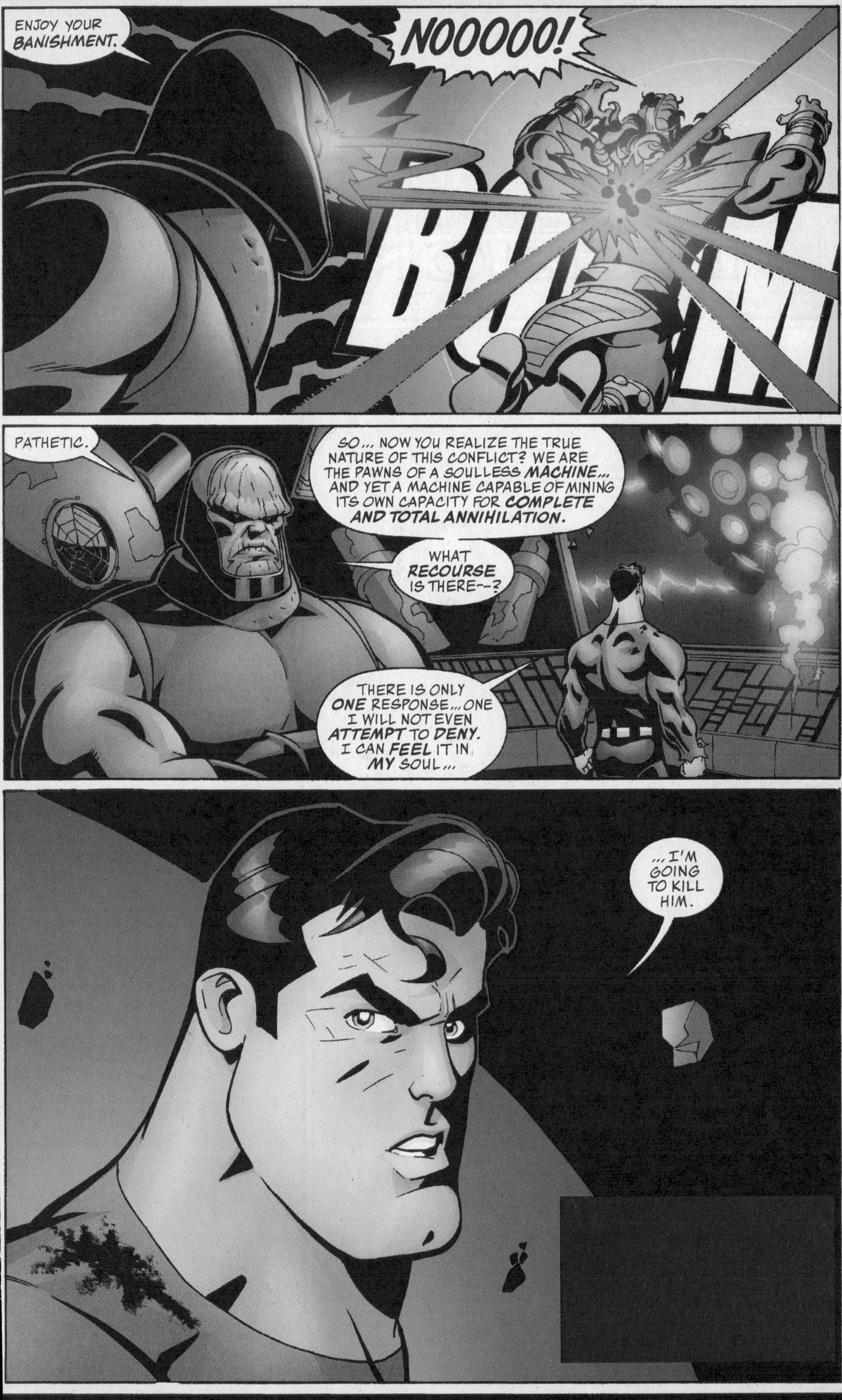
ENJOY YOUR **BANISHMENT**.
NOOOOO!
PATHETIC.
SO... NOW YOU REALIZE THE TRUE NATURE OF THIS CONFLICT? WE ARE THE PAWNS OF A SOULLESS **MACHINE**... AND YET A MACHINE CAPABLE OF MINING ITS OWN CAPACITY FOR **COMPLETE AND TOTAL ANNIHILATION**.
WHAT **RECOURSE** IS THERE--?
THERE IS ONLY **ONE** RESPONSE... ONE I WILL NOT EVEN **ATTEMPT** TO **DENY**. I CAN **FEEL** IT IN **MY** SOUL...
...I'M GOING TO KILL HIM.

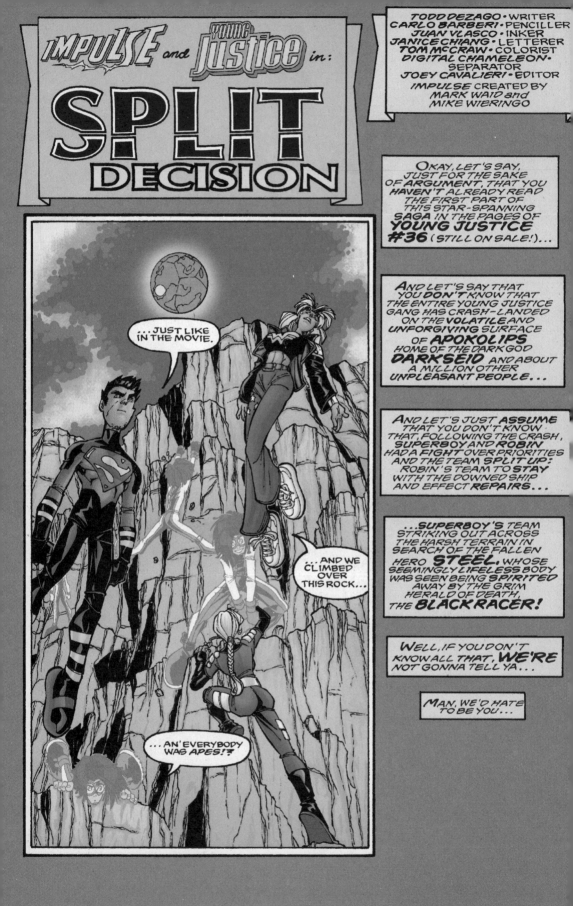

IMPULSE and YOUNG JUSTICE in:

SPLIT DECISION

TODD DEZAGO • WRITER
CARLO BARBERI • PENCILLER
JUAN VLASCO • INKER
JANICE CHIANG • LETTERER
TOM McCRAW • COLORIST
DIGITAL CHAMELEON • SEPARATOR
JOEY CAVALIERI • EDITOR
IMPULSE CREATED BY MARK WAID and MIKE WIERINGO

OKAY, LET'S SAY, JUST FOR THE SAKE OF ARGUMENT, THAT YOU HAVEN'T ALREADY READ THE FIRST PART OF THIS STAR-SPANNING SAGA IN THE PAGES OF YOUNG JUSTICE #36 (STILL ON SALE!)...

AND LET'S SAY THAT YOU DON'T KNOW THAT THE ENTIRE YOUNG JUSTICE GANG HAS CRASH-LANDED ON THE VOLATILE AND UNFORGIVING SURFACE OF APOKOLIPS, HOME OF THE DARK GOD DARKSEID AND ABOUT A MILLION OTHER UNPLEASANT PEOPLE...

AND LET'S JUST ASSUME THAT YOU DON'T KNOW THAT, FOLLOWING THE CRASH, SUPERBOY AND ROBIN HAD A FIGHT OVER PRIORITIES AND THE TEAM SPLIT UP: ROBIN'S TEAM TO STAY WITH THE DOWNED SHIP AND EFFECT REPAIRS...

...SUPERBOY'S TEAM STRIKING OUT ACROSS THE HARSH TERRAIN IN SEARCH OF THE FALLEN HERO STEEL, WHOSE SEEMINGLY LIFELESS BODY WAS SEEN BEING SPIRITED AWAY BY THE GRIM HERALD OF DEATH, THE BLACK RACER!

WELL, IF YOU DON'T KNOW ALL THAT, WE'RE NOT GONNA TELL YA...

MAN, WE'D HATE TO BE YOU...

...JUST LIKE IN THE MOVIE.

...AND WE CLIMBED OVER THIS ROCK...

...AN' EVERYBODY WAS APES!?

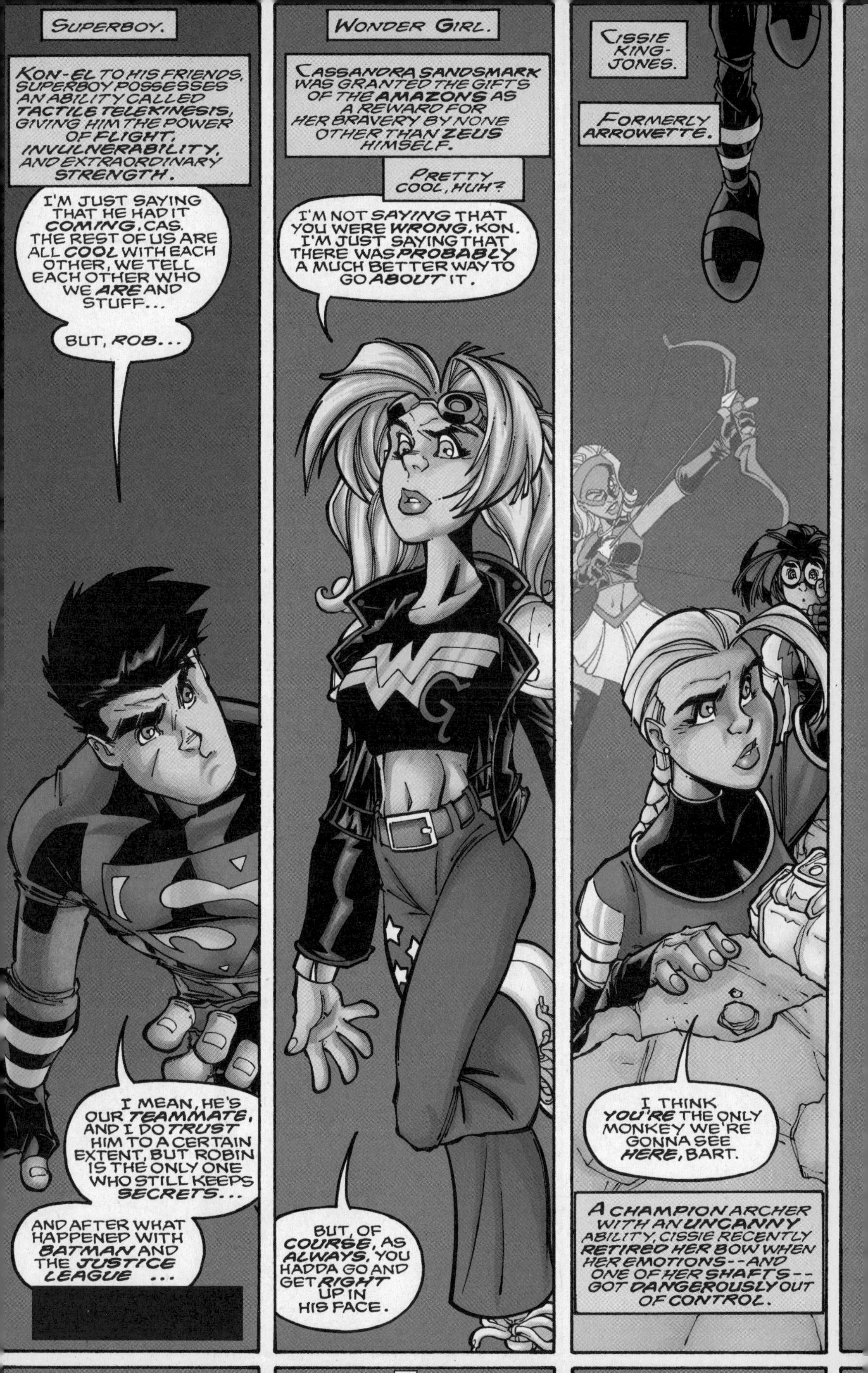
SUPERBOY.
KON-EL TO HIS FRIENDS, SUPERBOY POSSESSES AN ABILITY CALLED TACTILE TELEKINESIS, GIVING HIM THE POWER OF FLIGHT, INVULNERABILITY, AND EXTRAORDINARY STRENGTH.
I'M JUST SAYING THAT HE HAD IT COMING, CAS. THE REST OF US ARE ALL COOL WITH EACH OTHER, WE TELL EACH OTHER WHO WE ARE AND STUFF...
BUT, ROB...
I MEAN, HE'S OUR TEAMMATE, AND I DO TRUST HIM TO A CERTAIN EXTENT, BUT ROBIN IS THE ONLY ONE WHO STILL KEEPS SECRETS...
AND AFTER WHAT HAPPENED WITH BATMAN AND THE JUSTICE LEAGUE ...
[redacted]
WONDER GIRL.
CASSANDRA SANDSMARK WAS GRANTED THE GIFTS OF THE AMAZONS AS A REWARD FOR HER BRAVERY BY NONE OTHER THAN ZEUS HIMSELF.
PRETTY COOL, HUH?
I'M NOT SAYING THAT YOU WERE WRONG, KON. I'M JUST SAYING THAT THERE WAS PROBABLY A MUCH BETTER WAY TO GO ABOUT IT.
BUT, OF COURSE, AS ALWAYS, YOU HADDA GO AND GET RIGHT UP IN HIS FACE.
CISSIE KING-JONES.
FORMERLY ARROWETTE.
I THINK YOU'RE THE ONLY MONKEY WE'RE GONNA SEE HERE, BART.
A CHAMPION ARCHER WITH AN UNCANNY ABILITY, CISSIE RECENTLY RETIRED HER BOW WHEN HER EMOTIONS--AND ONE OF HER SHAFTS--GOT DANGEROUSLY OUT OF CONTROL.

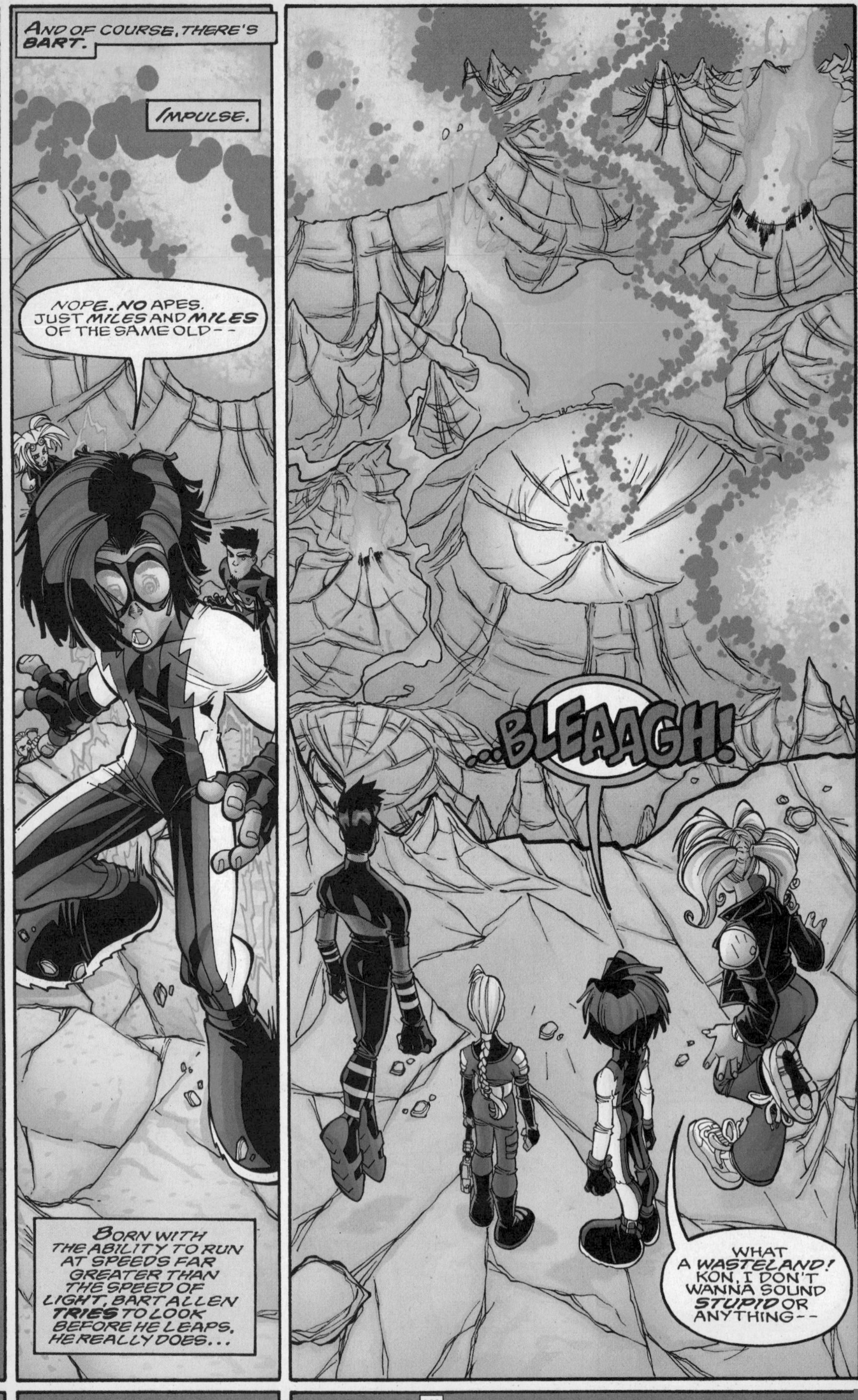
AND OF COURSE, THERE'S BART.
IMPULSE.
NOPE. NO APES. JUST MILES AND MILES OF THE SAME OLD--
BORN WITH THE ABILITY TO RUN AT SPEEDS FAR GREATER THAN THE SPEED OF LIGHT, BART ALLEN TRIES TO LOOK BEFORE HE LEAPS. HE REALLY DOES...
...BLEAAGH!
WHAT A WASTELAND! KON, I DON'T WANNA SOUND STUPID OR ANYTHING--

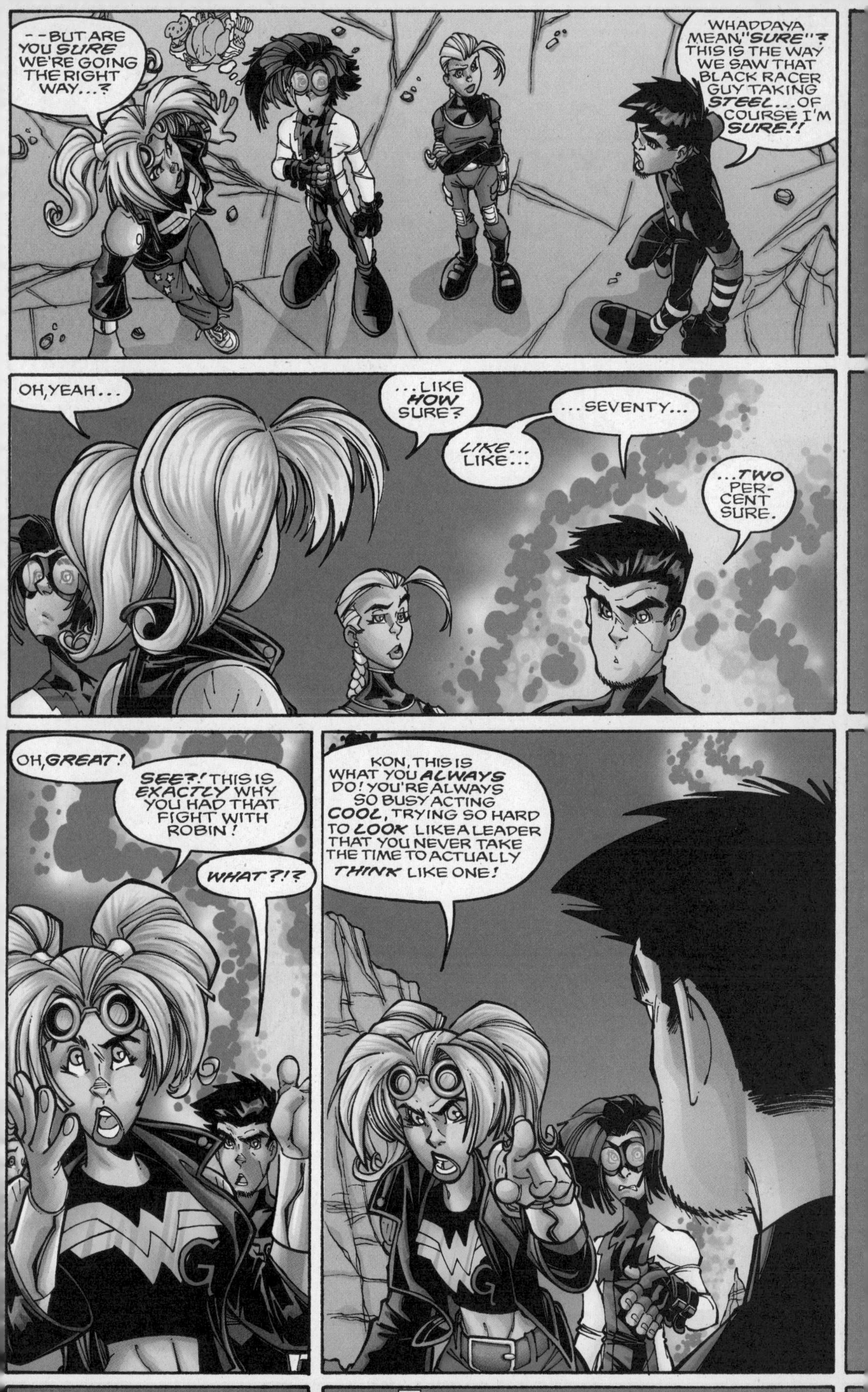
--BUT ARE YOU SURE WE'RE GOING THE RIGHT WAY...?
WHADDAYA MEAN, "SURE"? THIS IS THE WAY WE SAW THAT BLACK RACER GUY TAKING STEEL... OF COURSE I'M SURE!!
OH, YEAH...
...LIKE HOW SURE?
...SEVENTY...
LIKE... LIKE...
...TWO PER-CENT SURE.
OH, GREAT!
SEE?! THIS IS EXACTLY WHY YOU HAD THAT FIGHT WITH ROBIN!
WHAT?!?
KON, THIS IS WHAT YOU ALWAYS DO! YOU'RE ALWAYS SO BUSY ACTING COOL, TRYING SO HARD TO LOOK LIKE A LEADER THAT YOU NEVER TAKE THE TIME TO ACTUALLY THINK LIKE ONE!

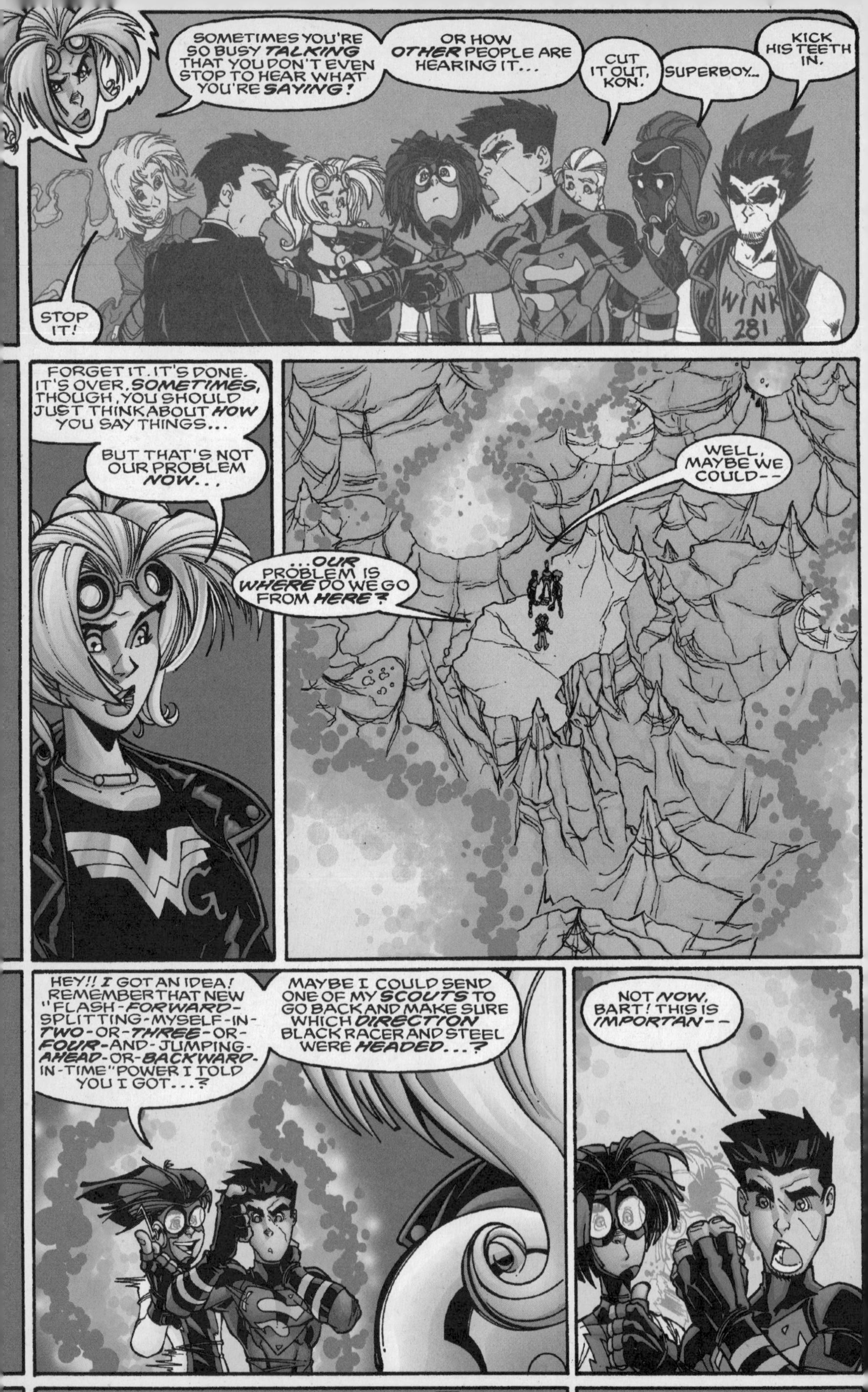
SOMETIMES YOU'RE SO BUSY *TALKING* THAT YOU DON'T EVEN STOP TO HEAR WHAT YOU'RE *SAYING*!
OR HOW *OTHER* PEOPLE ARE HEARING IT...
CUT IT OUT, KON.
SUPERBOY...
KICK HIS TEETH IN.
STOP IT!
WINK
281
FORGET IT. IT'S DONE. IT'S OVER. *SOMETIMES*, THOUGH, YOU SHOULD JUST THINK ABOUT *HOW* YOU SAY THINGS...
BUT THAT'S NOT OUR PROBLEM *NOW*...
WELL, MAYBE WE COULD--
...*OUR* PROBLEM IS *WHERE* DO WE GO FROM *HERE*?
HEY!! *I* GOT AN IDEA! REMEMBER THAT NEW "FLASH-*FORWARD*-SPLITTING-MYSELF-IN-*TWO*-OR-*THREE*-OR-*FOUR*-AND-JUMPING-*AHEAD*-OR-*BACKWARD*-IN-TIME" POWER I TOLD YOU I GOT...?
MAYBE I COULD SEND ONE OF MY *SCOUTS* TO GO BACK AND MAKE SURE WHICH *DIRECTION* BLACK RACER AND STEEL WERE *HEADED*...?
NOT *NOW*, BART! THIS IS *IMPORTAN*--

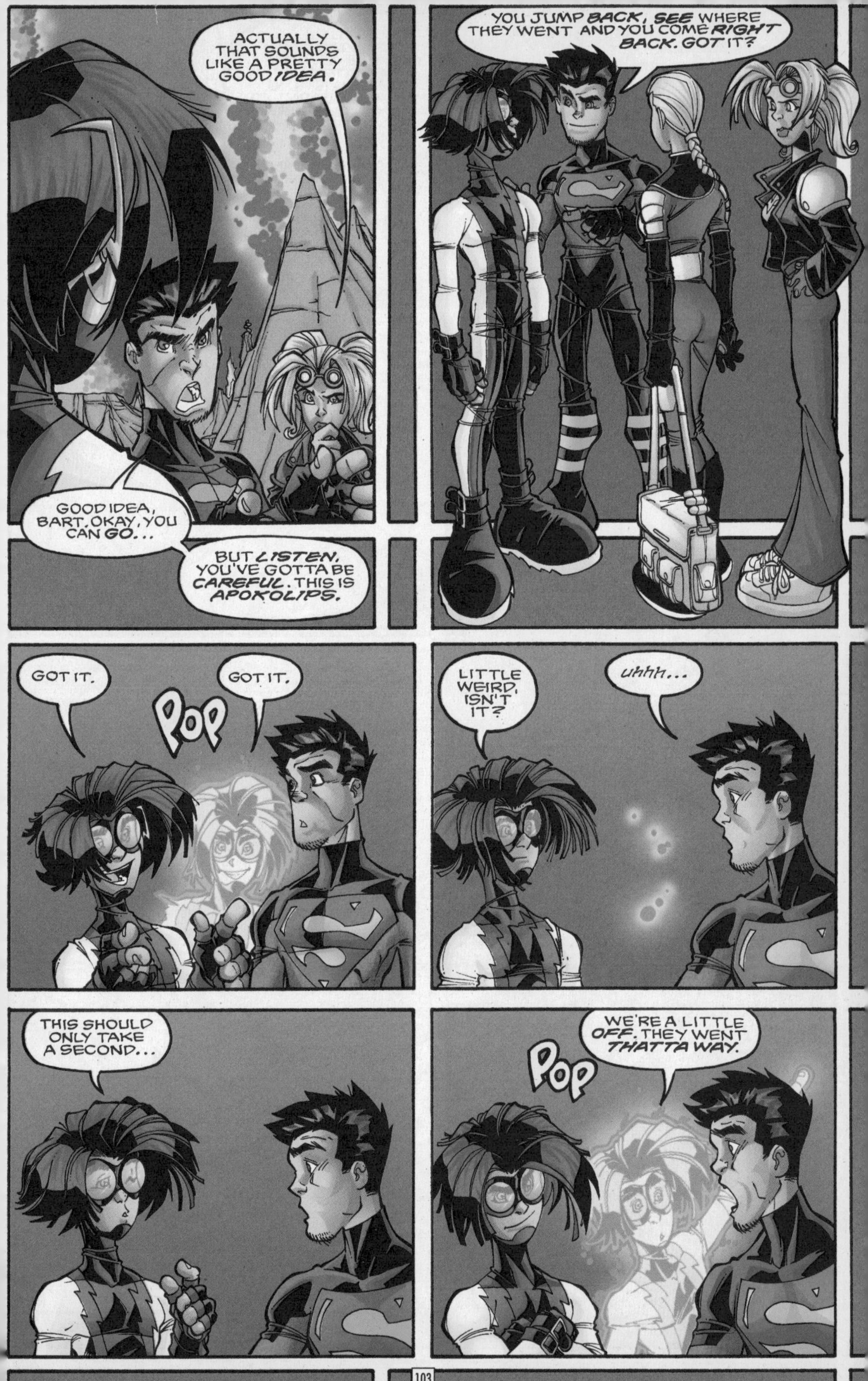

ACTUALLY THAT SOUNDS LIKE A PRETTY GOOD IDEA.
GOOD IDEA, BART. OKAY, YOU CAN GO...
BUT LISTEN. YOU'VE GOTTA BE CAREFUL. THIS IS APOKOLIPS.
YOU JUMP BACK, SEE WHERE THEY WENT AND YOU COME RIGHT BACK. GOT IT?
GOT IT.
POP
GOT IT.
LITTLE WEIRD, ISN'T IT?
uhhh...
THIS SHOULD ONLY TAKE A SECOND...
POP
WE'RE A LITTLE OFF. THEY WENT THATTA WAY.

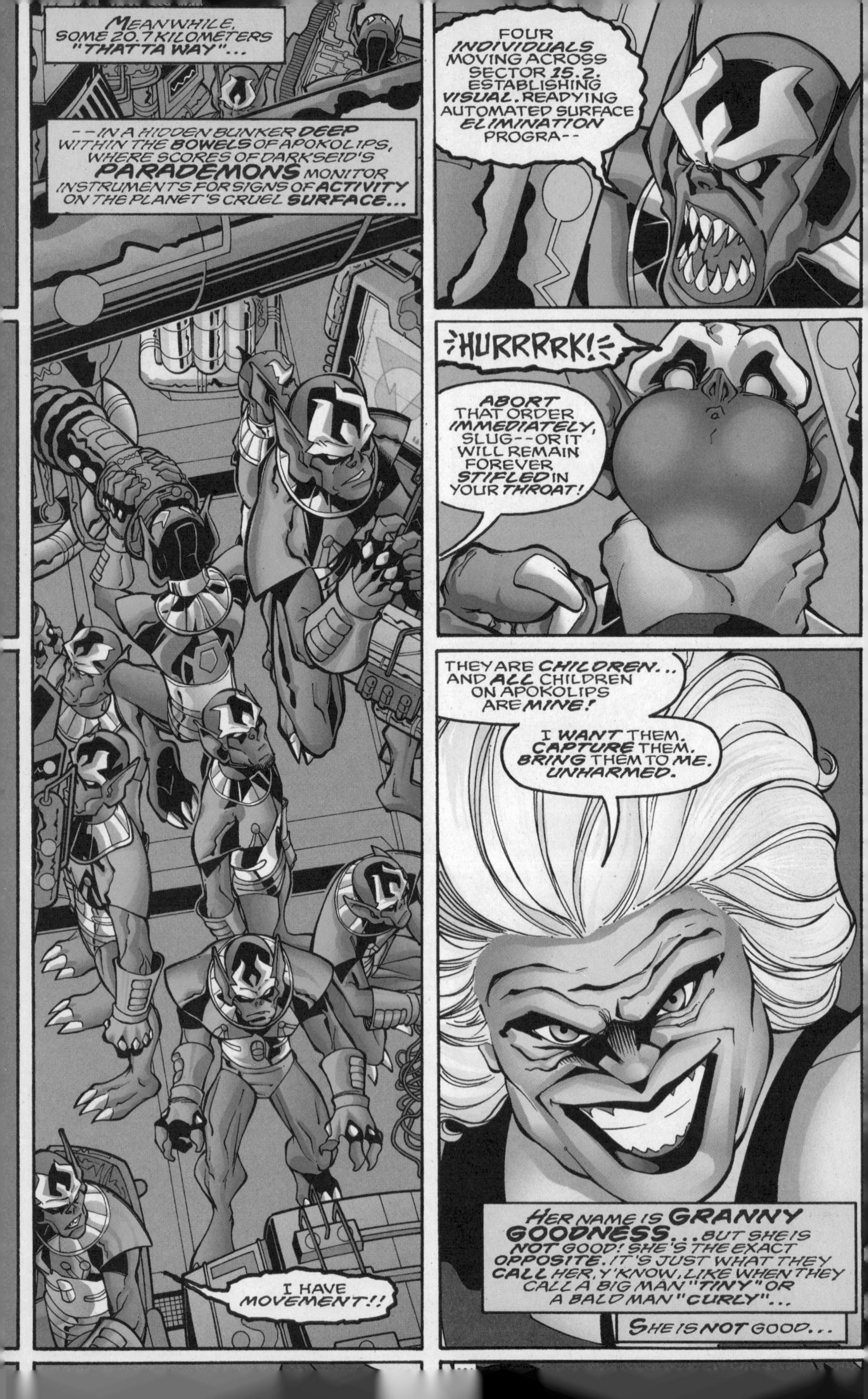
MEANWHILE, SOME 20.7 KILOMETERS "THATTA WAY"...
--IN A HIDDEN BUNKER DEEP WITHIN THE BOWELS OF APOKOLIPS, WHERE SCORES OF DARKSEID'S PARADEMONS MONITOR INSTRUMENTS FOR SIGNS OF ACTIVITY ON THE PLANET'S CRUEL SURFACE...
I HAVE MOVEMENT!!
FOUR INDIVIDUALS MOVING ACROSS SECTOR 15.2. ESTABLISHING VISUAL. READYING AUTOMATED SURFACE ELIMINATION PROGRA--
HURRRRK!
ABORT THAT ORDER IMMEDIATELY, SLUG--OR IT WILL REMAIN FOREVER STIFLED IN YOUR THROAT!
THEY ARE CHILDREN... AND ALL CHILDREN ON APOKOLIPS ARE MINE!
I WANT THEM. CAPTURE THEM. BRING THEM TO ME. UNHARMED.
HER NAME IS GRANNY GOODNESS... BUT SHE IS NOT GOOD! SHE'S THE EXACT OPPOSITE. IT'S JUST WHAT THEY CALL HER, Y'KNOW, LIKE WHEN THEY CALL A BIG MAN "TINY" OR A BALD MAN "CURLY"...
SHE IS NOT GOOD...

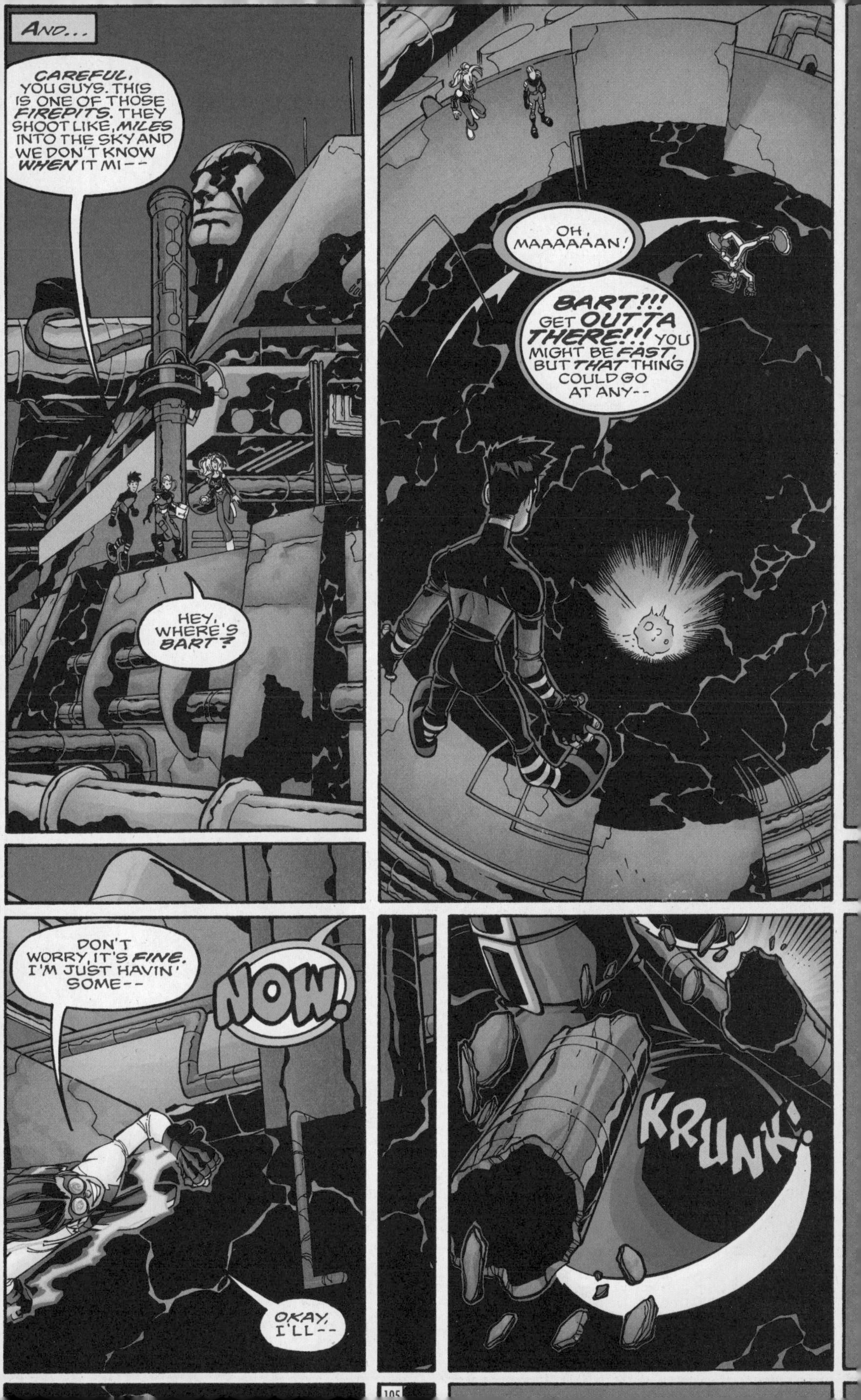
AND...
CAREFUL, YOU GUYS. THIS IS ONE OF THOSE FIREPITS. THEY SHOOT LIKE, MILES INTO THE SKY AND WE DON'T KNOW WHEN IT MI--
HEY, WHERE'S BART?
OH, MAAAAAAN!
BART!!! GET OUTTA THERE!!! YOU MIGHT BE FAST, BUT THAT THING COULD GO AT ANY--
DON'T WORRY, IT'S FINE. I'M JUST HAVIN' SOME--
NOW!
OKAY, I'LL--
KRUNK!

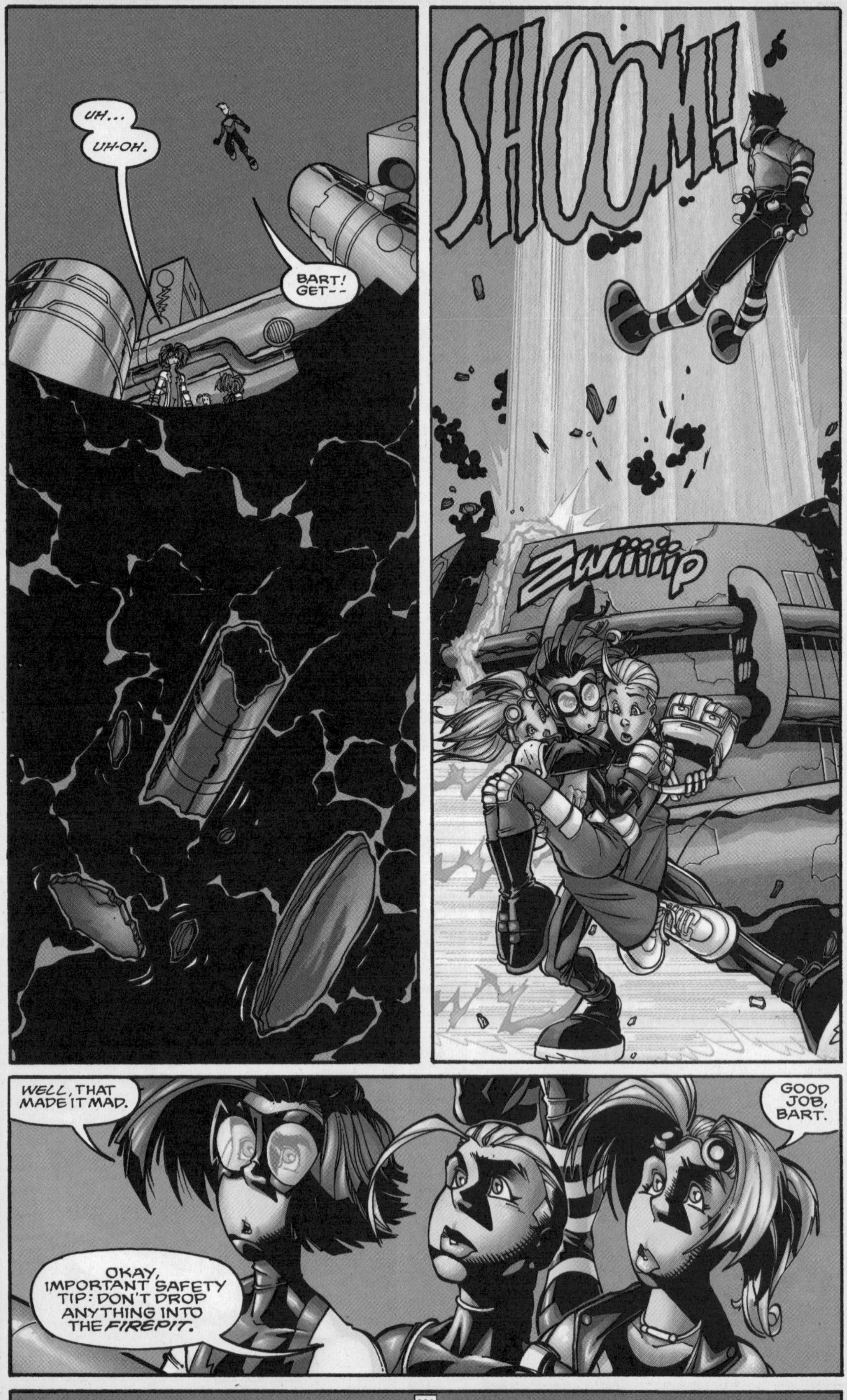
UH...
UH-OH.
BART! GET--
SHOOM!
ZWIIIIIP
WELL, THAT MADE IT MAD.
GOOD JOB, BART.
OKAY, IMPORTANT SAFETY TIP: DON'T DROP ANYTHING INTO THE FIREPIT.

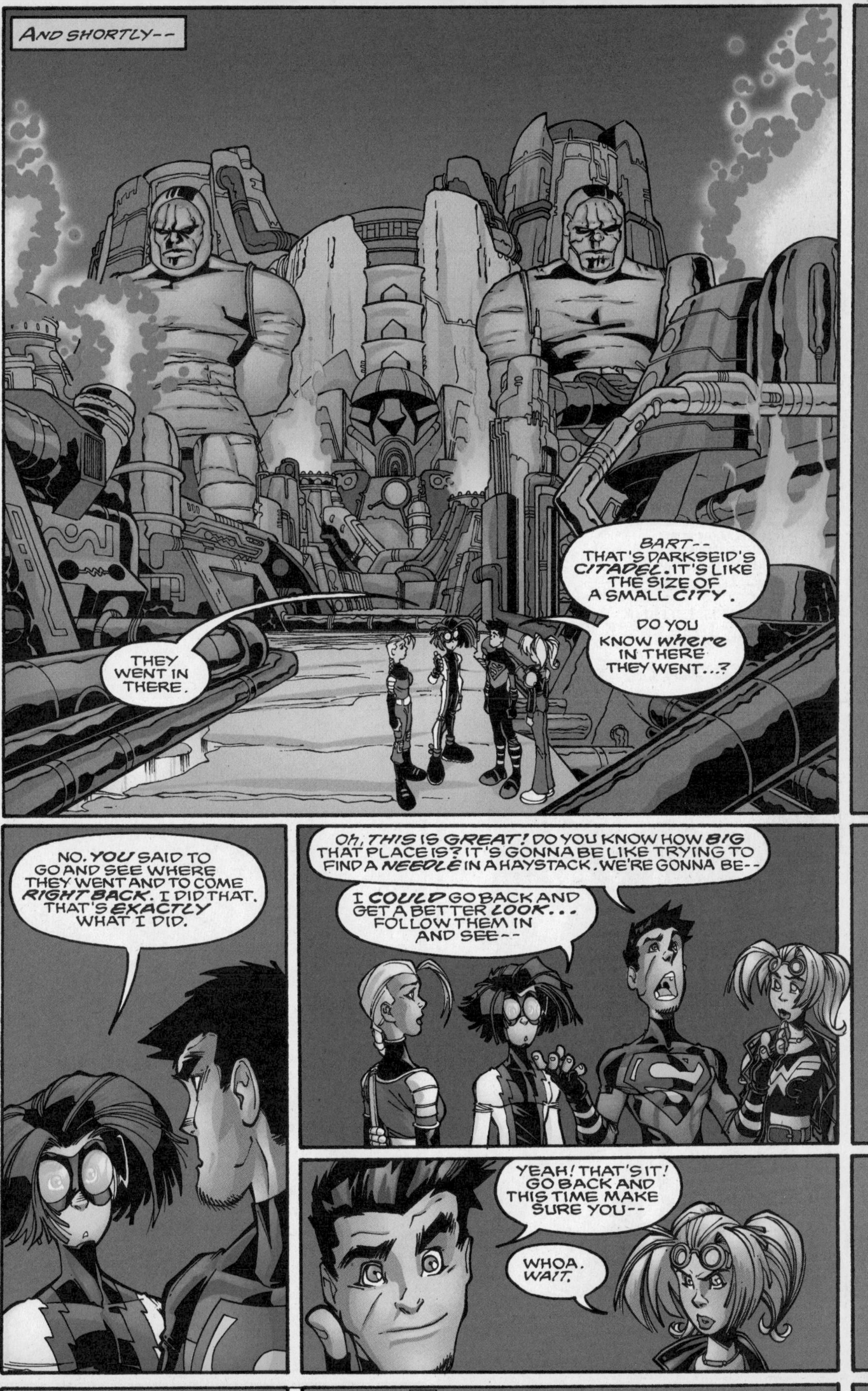
AND SHORTLY--
THEY WENT IN THERE.
BART-- THAT'S DARKSEID'S CITADEL. IT'S LIKE THE SIZE OF A SMALL CITY.
DO YOU KNOW WHERE IN THERE THEY WENT...?
NO. YOU SAID TO GO AND SEE WHERE THEY WENT AND TO COME RIGHT BACK. I DID THAT. THAT'S EXACTLY WHAT I DID.
OH, THIS IS GREAT! DO YOU KNOW HOW BIG THAT PLACE IS? IT'S GONNA BE LIKE TRYING TO FIND A NEEDLE IN A HAYSTACK. WE'RE GONNA BE--
I COULD GO BACK AND GET A BETTER LOOK... FOLLOW THEM IN AND SEE--
YEAH! THAT'S IT! GO BACK AND THIS TIME MAKE SURE YOU--
WHOA. WAIT.

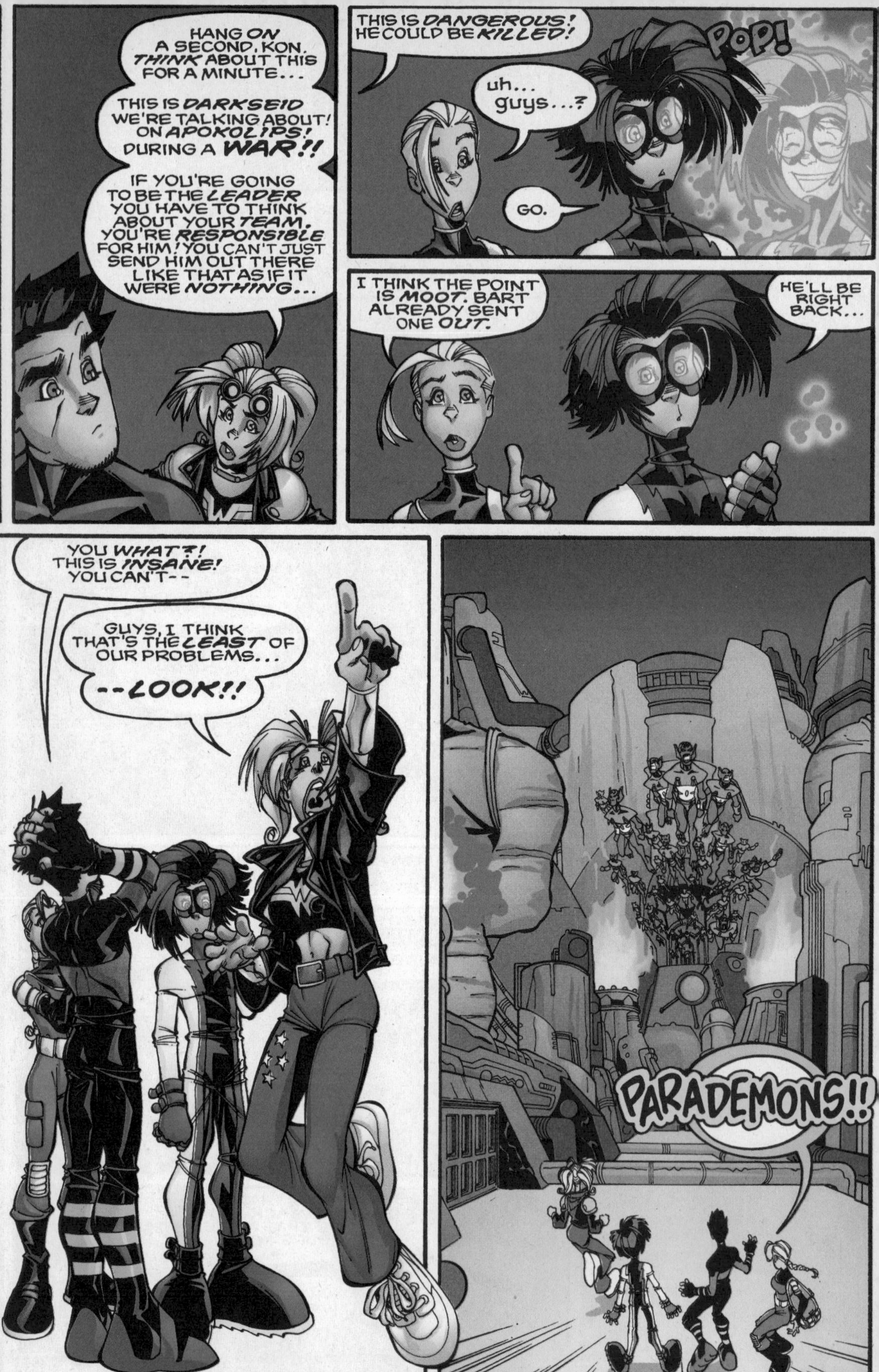
HANG ON A SECOND, KON. THINK ABOUT THIS FOR A MINUTE...
THIS IS DARKSEID WE'RE TALKING ABOUT! ON APOKOLIPS! DURING A WAR!!
IF YOU'RE GOING TO BE THE LEADER YOU HAVE TO THINK ABOUT YOUR TEAM. YOU'RE RESPONSIBLE FOR HIM! YOU CAN'T JUST SEND HIM OUT THERE LIKE THAT AS IF IT WERE NOTHING...
THIS IS DANGEROUS! HE COULD BE KILLED!
POP!
uh... guys...?
GO.
I THINK THE POINT IS MOOT. BART ALREADY SENT ONE OUT.
HE'LL BE RIGHT BACK...
YOU WHAT?! THIS IS INSANE! YOU CAN'T--
GUYS, I THINK THAT'S THE LEAST OF OUR PROBLEMS...
--LOOK!!
PARADEMONS!!

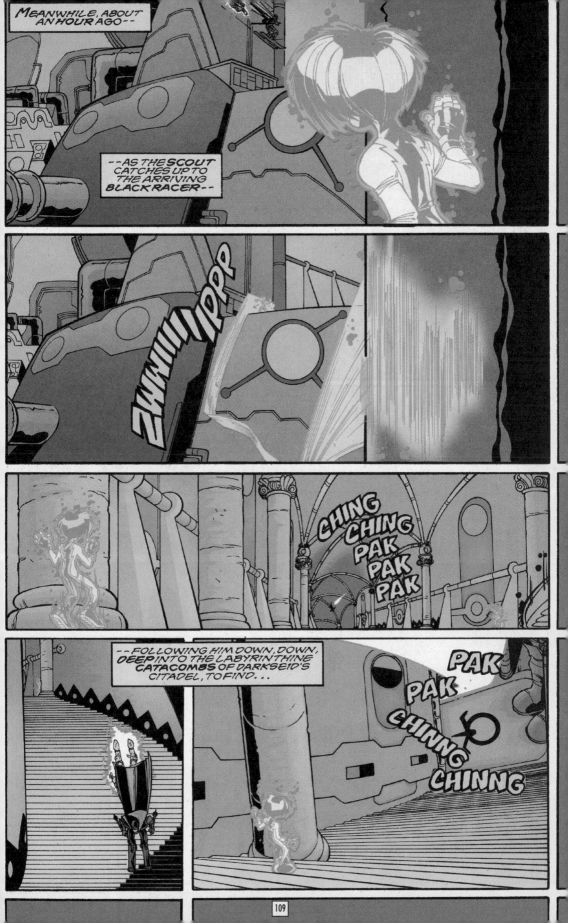

MEANWHILE, ABOUT AN HOUR AGO--

--AS THE SCOUT CATCHES UP TO THE ARRIVING BLACK RACER--

ZHHHHHPPPP

CHING CHING PAK PAK PAK

--FOLLOWING HIM DOWN, DOWN, DEEP INTO THE LABYRINTHINE CATACOMBS OF DARKSEID'S CITADEL, TO FIND...

PAK PAK CHINNG CHINNG

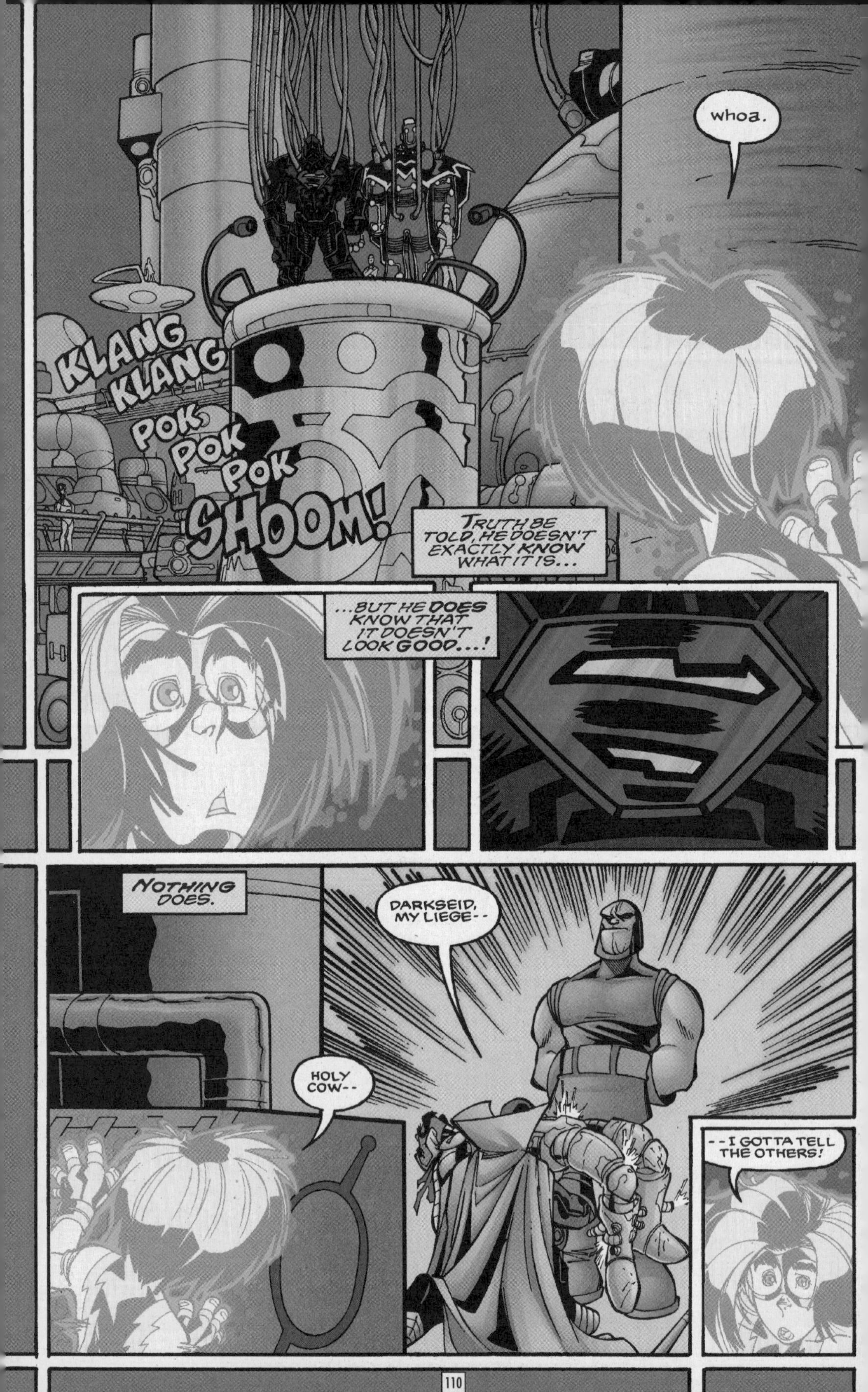
whoa.
KLANG KLANG POK POK POK SHOOM!
TRUTH BE TOLD, HE DOESN'T EXACTLY KNOW WHAT IT IS...
...BUT HE DOES KNOW THAT IT DOESN'T LOOK GOOD...!
NOTHING DOES.
DARKSEID, MY LIEGE--
HOLY COW--
--I GOTTA TELL THE OTHERS!

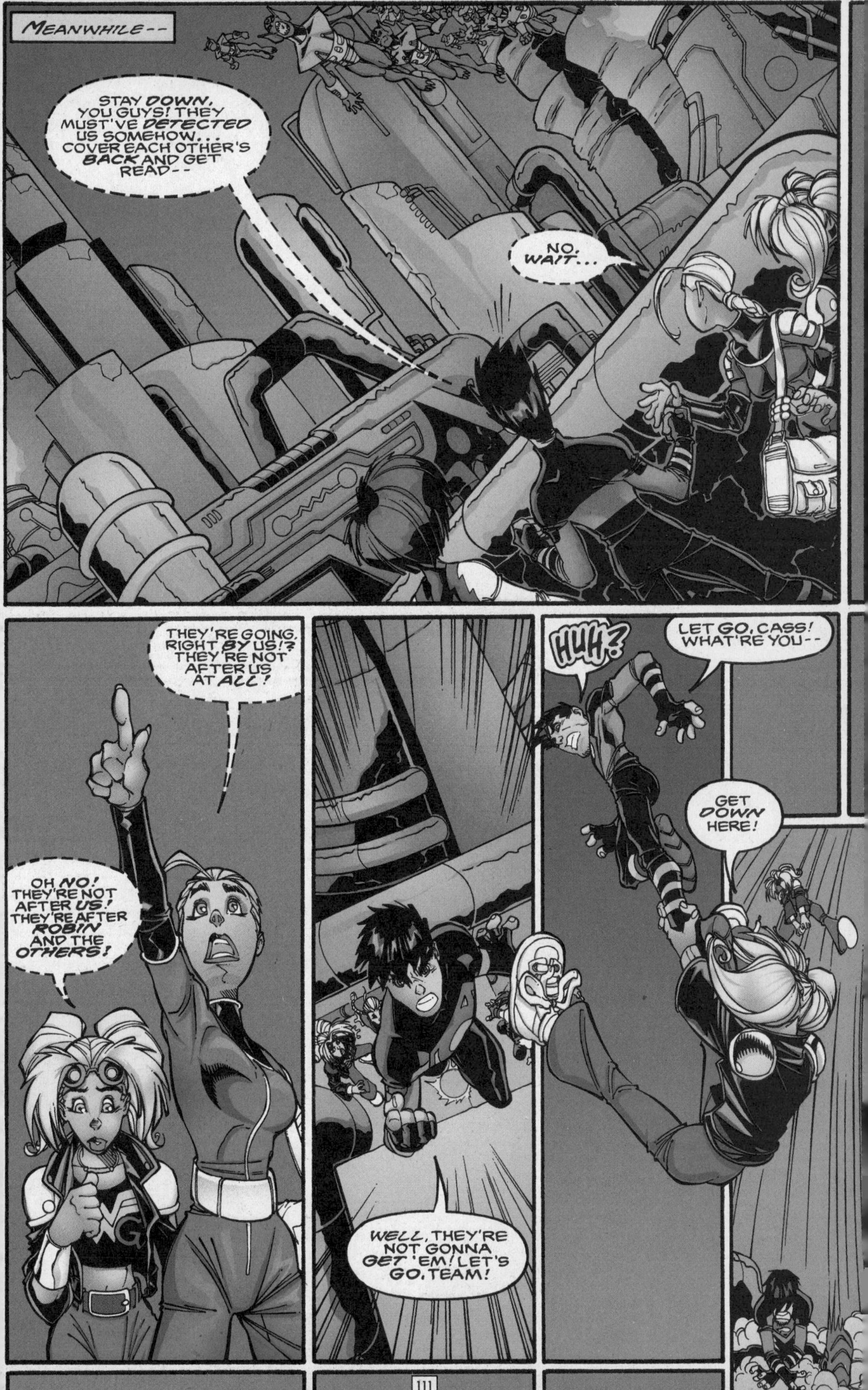
MEANWHILE--
STAY DOWN, YOU GUYS! THEY MUST'VE DETECTED US SOMEHOW... COVER EACH OTHER'S BACK AND GET READ--
NO, WAIT...
THEY'RE GOING RIGHT BY US!? THEY'RE NOT AFTER US AT ALL!
OH NO! THEY'RE NOT AFTER US! THEY'RE AFTER ROBIN AND THE OTHERS!
WELL, THEY'RE NOT GONNA GET 'EM! LET'S GO, TEAM!
HUH?
LET GO, CASS! WHAT'RE YOU--
GET DOWN HERE!

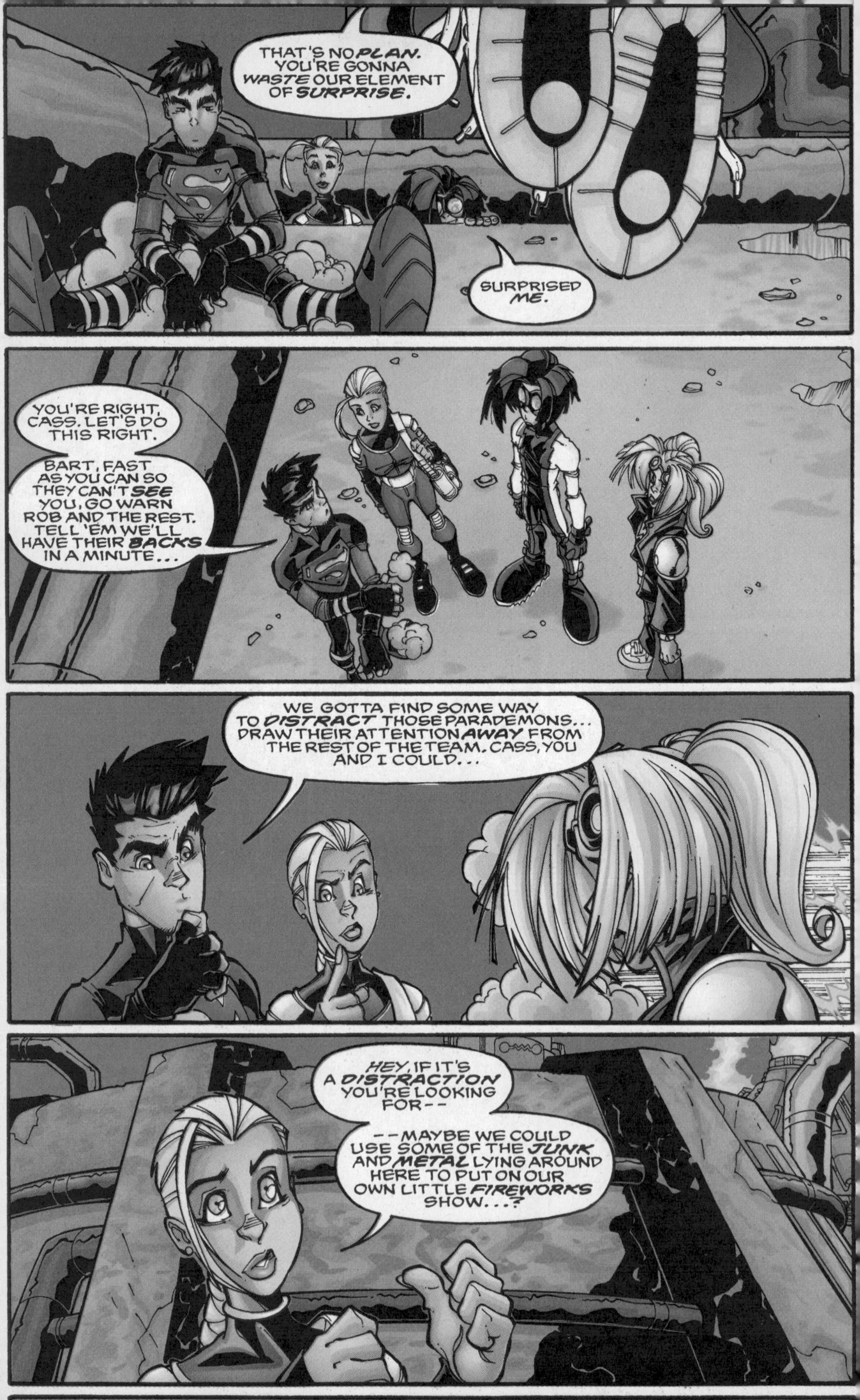
THAT'S NO PLAN. YOU'RE GONNA WASTE OUR ELEMENT OF SURPRISE.
SURPRISED ME.
YOU'RE RIGHT, CASS. LET'S DO THIS RIGHT.
BART, FAST AS YOU CAN SO THEY CAN'T SEE YOU, GO WARN ROB AND THE REST. TELL 'EM WE'LL HAVE THEIR BACKS IN A MINUTE...
WE GOTTA FIND SOME WAY TO DISTRACT THOSE PARADEMONS... DRAW THEIR ATTENTION AWAY FROM THE REST OF THE TEAM. CASS, YOU AND I COULD...
HEY, IF IT'S A DISTRACTION YOU'RE LOOKING FOR--
--MAYBE WE COULD USE SOME OF THE JUNK AND METAL LYING AROUND HERE TO PUT ON OUR OWN LITTLE FIREWORKS SHOW...?

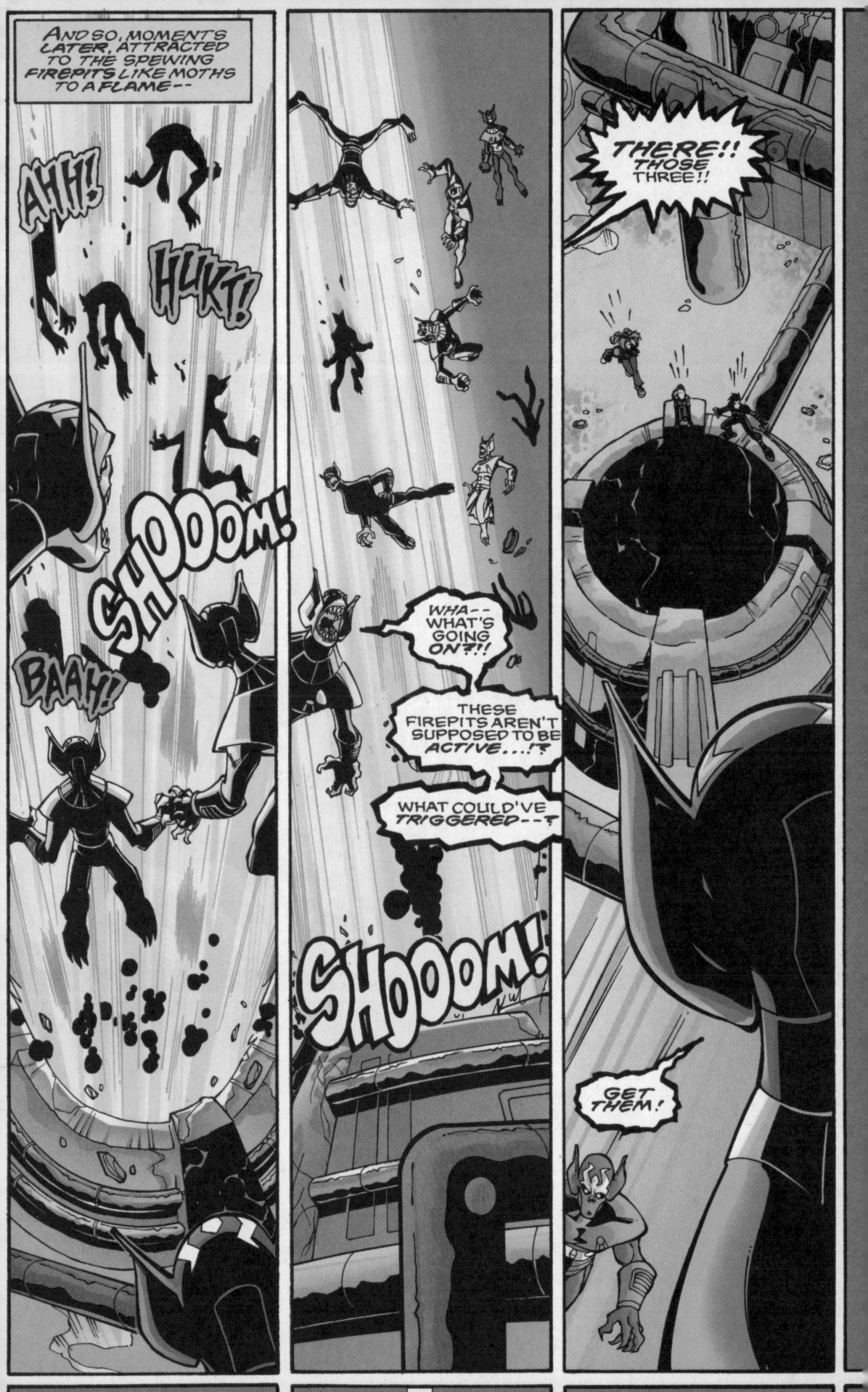

AND SO, MOMENTS LATER, ATTRACTED TO THE SPEWING FIREPITS LIKE MOTHS TO A FLAME--
AHH!
HUK!!
SHOOOM!
BAAH!
WHA--WHAT'S GOING ON?!!
THESE FIREPITS AREN'T SUPPOSED TO BE ACTIVE...!?
WHAT COULD'VE TRIGGERED--?
SHOOOM!
THERE!! THOSE THREE!!
GET THEM!

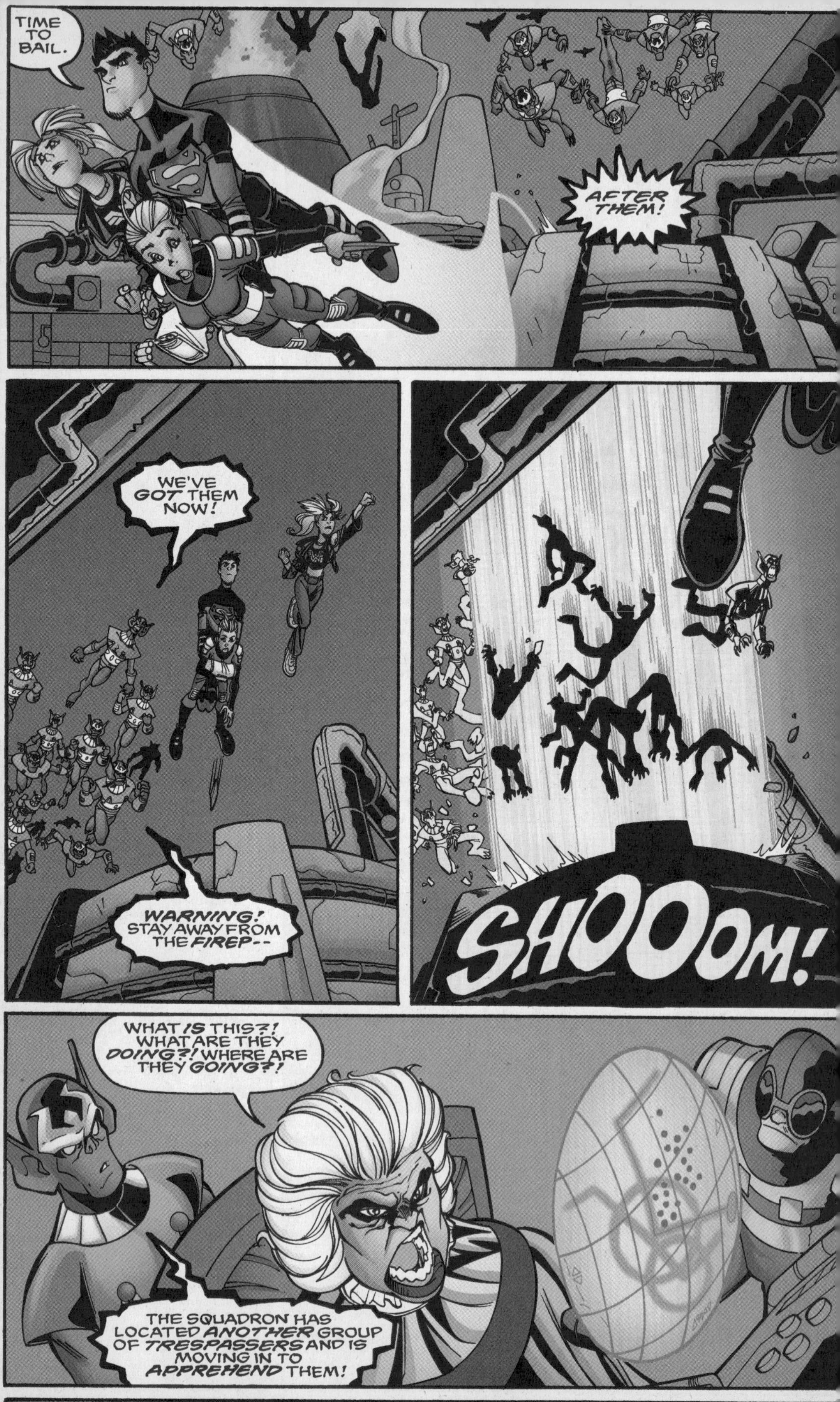
TIME TO BAIL.
AFTER THEM!
WE'VE GOT THEM NOW!
WARNING! STAY AWAY FROM THE FIREP--
SHOOOOM!
WHAT IS THIS?! WHAT ARE THEY DOING?! WHERE ARE THEY GOING?!
THE SQUADRON HAS LOCATED ANOTHER GROUP OF TRESPASSERS AND IS MOVING IN TO APPREHEND THEM!

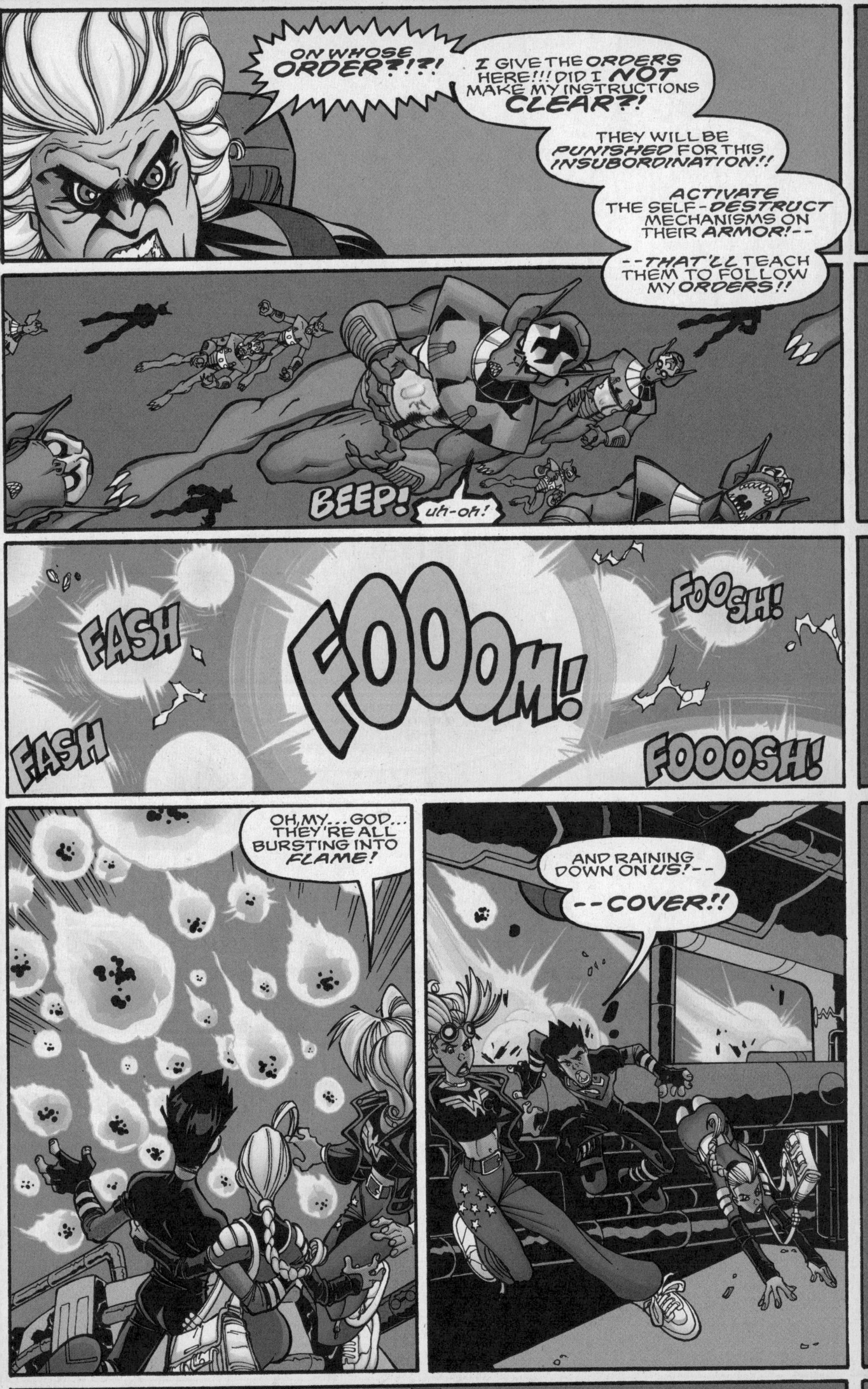
ON WHOSE ORDER?!?!
I GIVE THE ORDERS HERE!!! DID I NOT MAKE MY INSTRUCTIONS CLEAR?!
THEY WILL BE PUNISHED FOR THIS INSUBORDINATION!!
ACTIVATE THE SELF--DESTRUCT MECHANISMS ON THEIR ARMOR!--
--THAT'LL TEACH THEM TO FOLLOW MY ORDERS!!
BEEP!
uh-oh!
FASH
FASH
FOOOM!
FOOSH!
FOOOSH!
OH, MY... GOD... THEY'RE ALL BURSTING INTO FLAME!
AND RAINING DOWN ON US!--
--COVER!!

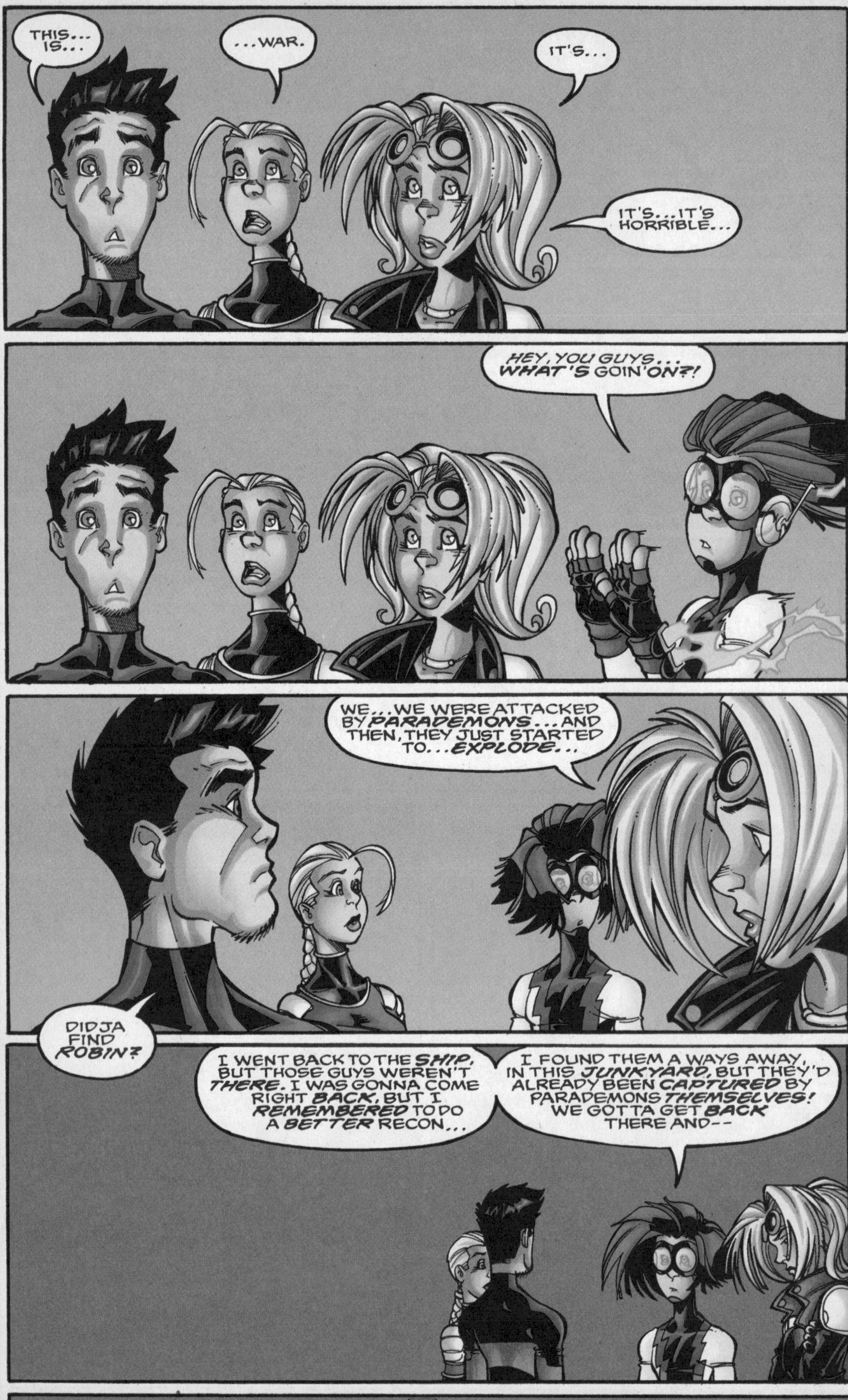
THIS... IS...
...WAR.
IT'S...
IT'S...IT'S HORRIBLE...
HEY, YOU GUYS... WHAT'S GOIN' ON?!
WE...WE WERE ATTACKED BY PARADEMONS...AND THEN, THEY JUST STARTED TO...EXPLODE...
DIDJA FIND ROBIN?
I WENT BACK TO THE SHIP, BUT THOSE GUYS WEREN'T THERE. I WAS GONNA COME RIGHT BACK, BUT I REMEMBERED TO DO A BETTER RECON...
I FOUND THEM A WAYS AWAY, IN THIS JUNKYARD, BUT THEY'D ALREADY BEEN CAPTURED BY PARADEMONS THEMSELVES! WE GOTTA GET BACK THERE AND--

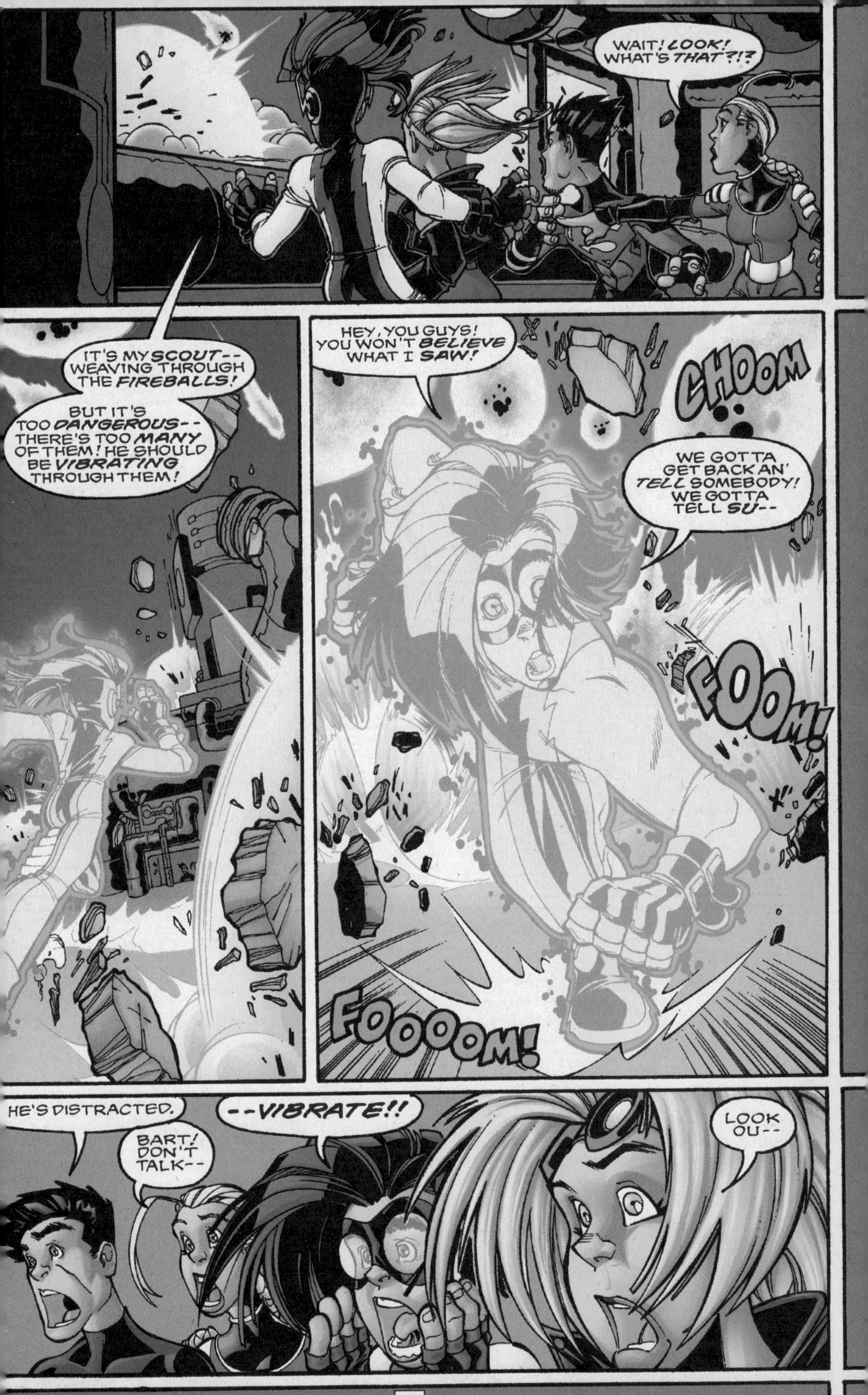
WAIT! LOOK! WHAT'S THAT?!?
IT'S MY SCOUT-- WEAVING THROUGH THE FIREBALLS!
BUT IT'S TOO DANGEROUS-- THERE'S TOO MANY OF THEM! HE SHOULD BE VIBRATING THROUGH THEM!
HEY, YOU GUYS! YOU WON'T BELIEVE WHAT I SAW!
CHOOM
WE GOTTA GET BACK AN' TELL SOMEBODY! WE GOTTA TELL SU--
FOOM!
FOOOOM!
HE'S DISTRACTED.
BART! DON'T TALK--
--VIBRATE!!
LOOK OU--

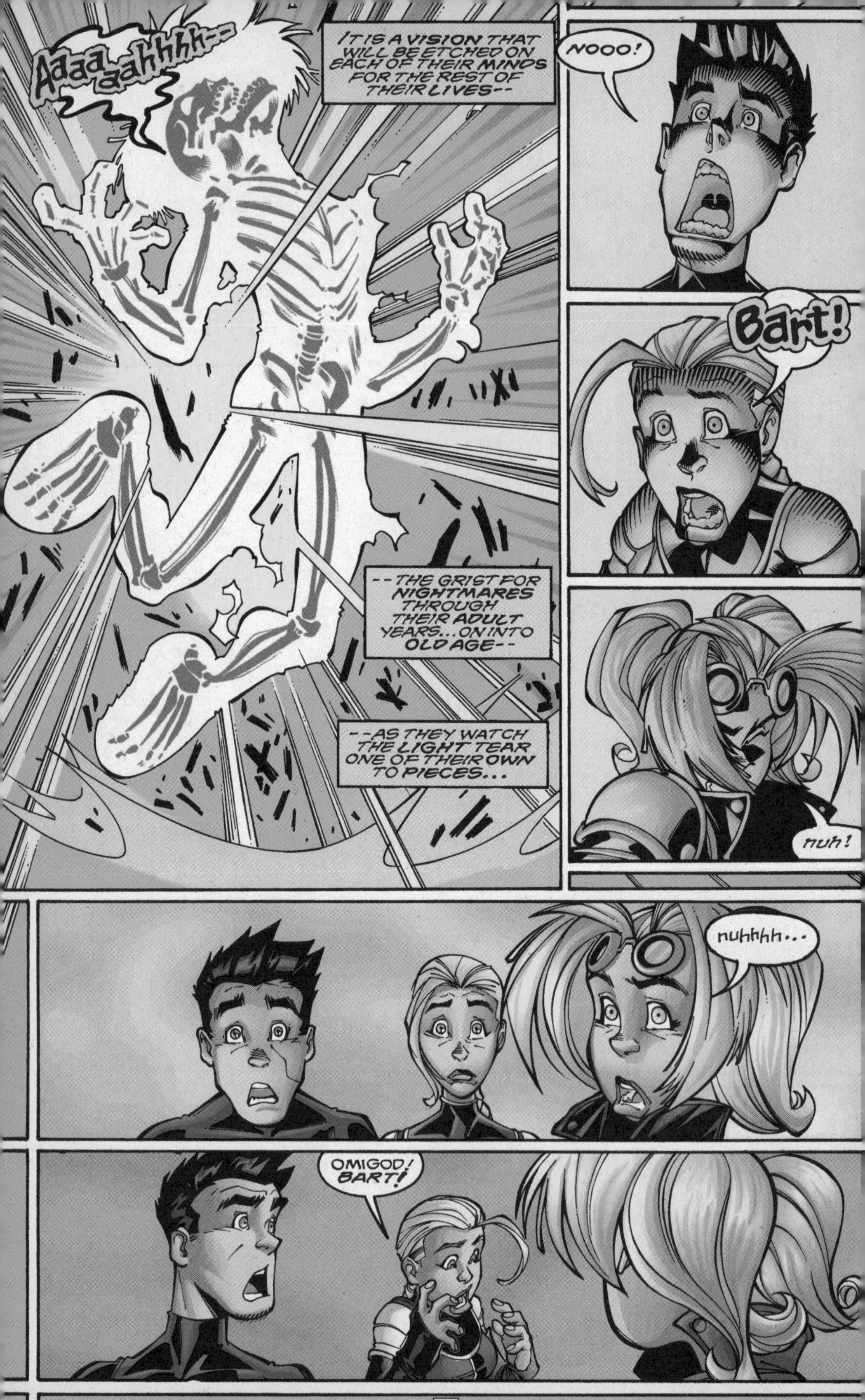

Aaaaaahhhh--
IT IS A VISION THAT WILL BE ETCHED ON EACH OF THEIR MINDS FOR THE REST OF THEIR LIVES--
NOOO!
Bart!
--THE GRIST FOR NIGHTMARES THROUGH THEIR ADULT YEARS...ON INTO OLD AGE--
--AS THEY WATCH THE LIGHT TEAR ONE OF THEIR OWN TO PIECES...
nuh!
nuhhhh...
OMIGOD! BART!

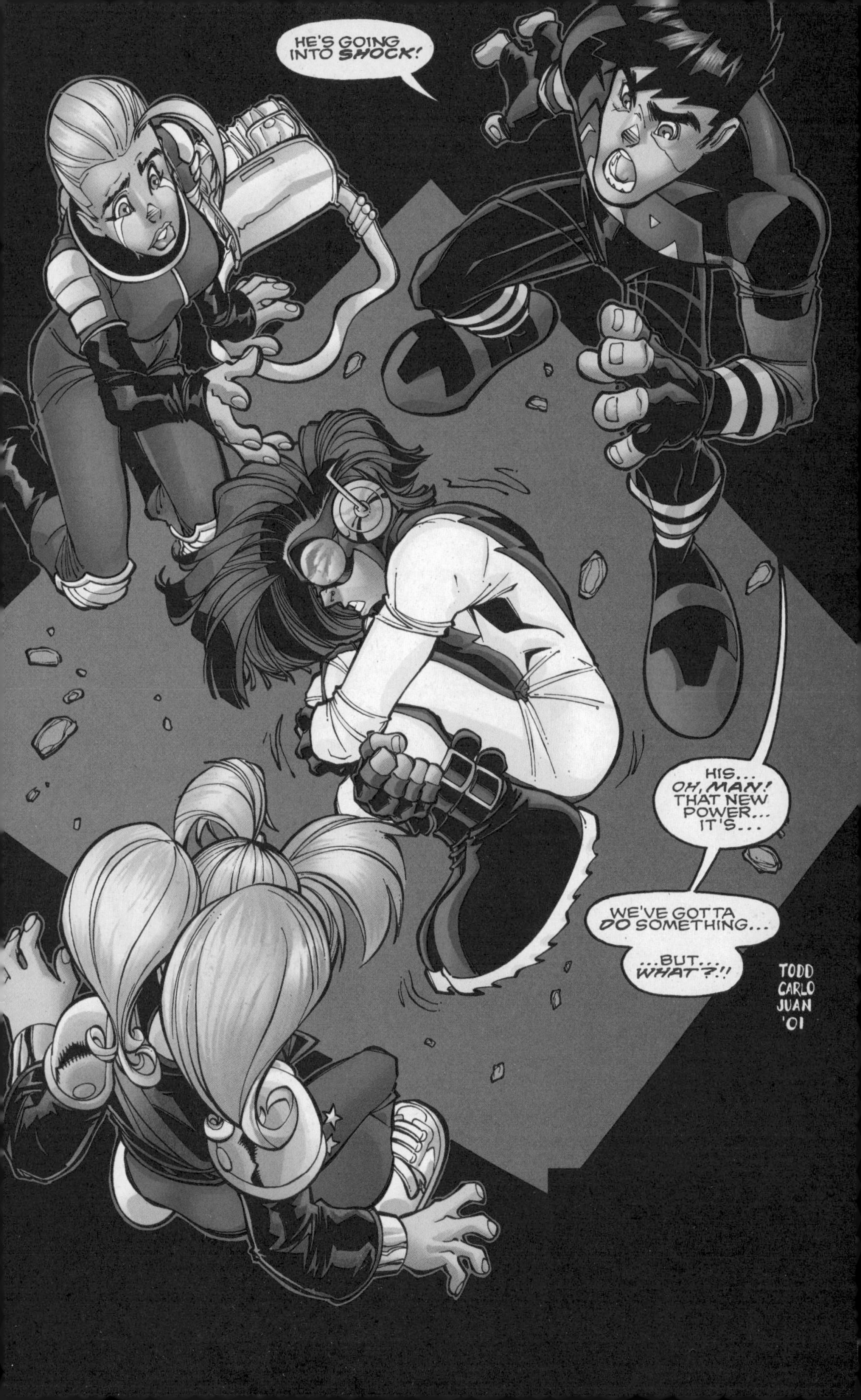
HE'S GOING INTO SHOCK!
HIS... OH, MAN! THAT NEW POWER... IT'S...
WE'VE GOTTA DO SOMETHING...
...BUT... WHAT?!!
TODD CARLO JUAN '01

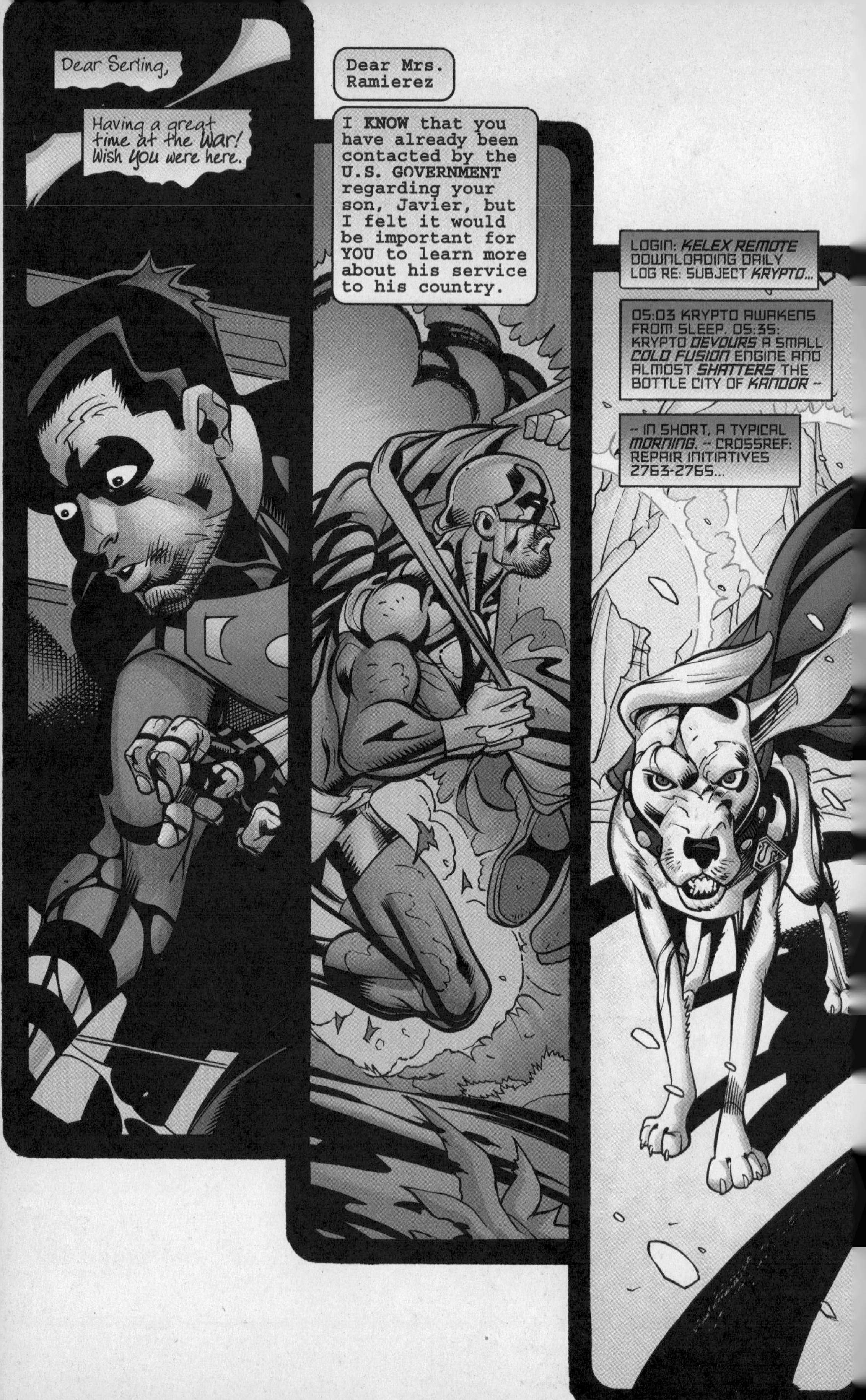
Dear Serling,
Having a great time at the War! Wish you were here.
Dear Mrs. Ramierez
I KNOW that you have already been contacted by the U.S. GOVERNMENT regarding your son, Javier, but I felt it would be important for YOU to learn more about his service to his country.
LOGIN: KELEX REMOTE DOWNLOADING DAILY LOG RE: SUBJECT KRYPTO...
05:03 KRYPTO AWAKENS FROM SLEEP. 05:35: KRYPTO DEVOURS A SMALL COLD FUSION ENGINE AND ALMOST SHATTERS THE BOTTLE CITY OF KANDOR --
-- IN SHORT, A TYPICAL MORNING. -- CROSSREF: REPAIR INITIATIVES 2763-2765...

Of course, I'm DOMINATING. Aliens fear me, ladies love me, metas wanna be me. Florence Nightingale with a FIST!

Seriously though, at first I thought hauling suckers to emergency MED-EVAC for the PARADOCS UNIT was going to be lame. But the volume out in the field is turned WAY past ELEVEN, Seri.

HOT ZONES are full of ALIEN SCAVENGERS -- Gravedigger E.T.S looking to exploit the wounded. So they send ME in, and I buy them a CLUE.

This is WAR. You pick a side, you pitch in, or you get KAKKED. Simple.

Everything in the H.Z. has that adrenaline haze to it, like it isn't REAL half the time --

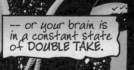

-- or your brain is in a constant state of DOUBLE TAKE.

Even when I'm NOT throwing down, there's some CLOUD over it all. Dreamy...

I've seen things out here... I couldn't believe, no matter HOW long I stared at it.

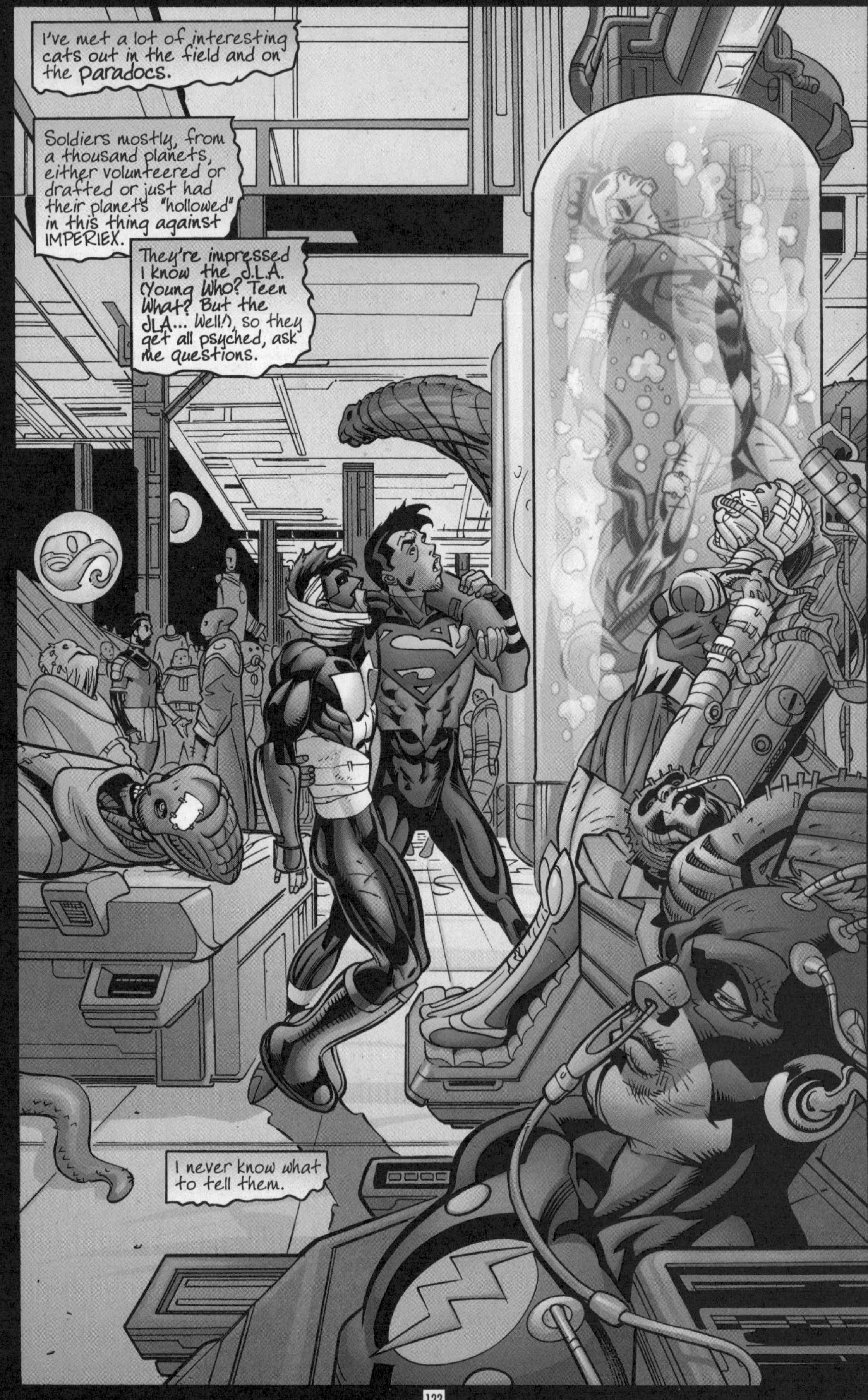
I've met a lot of interesting cats out in the field and on the paradocs.
Soldiers mostly, from a thousand planets, either volunteered or drafted or just had their planet's "hollowed" in this thing against IMPERIEX.
They're impressed I know the J.L.A. (Young Who? Teen What? But the JLA... Well!), so they get all psyched, ask me questions.
I never know what to tell them.

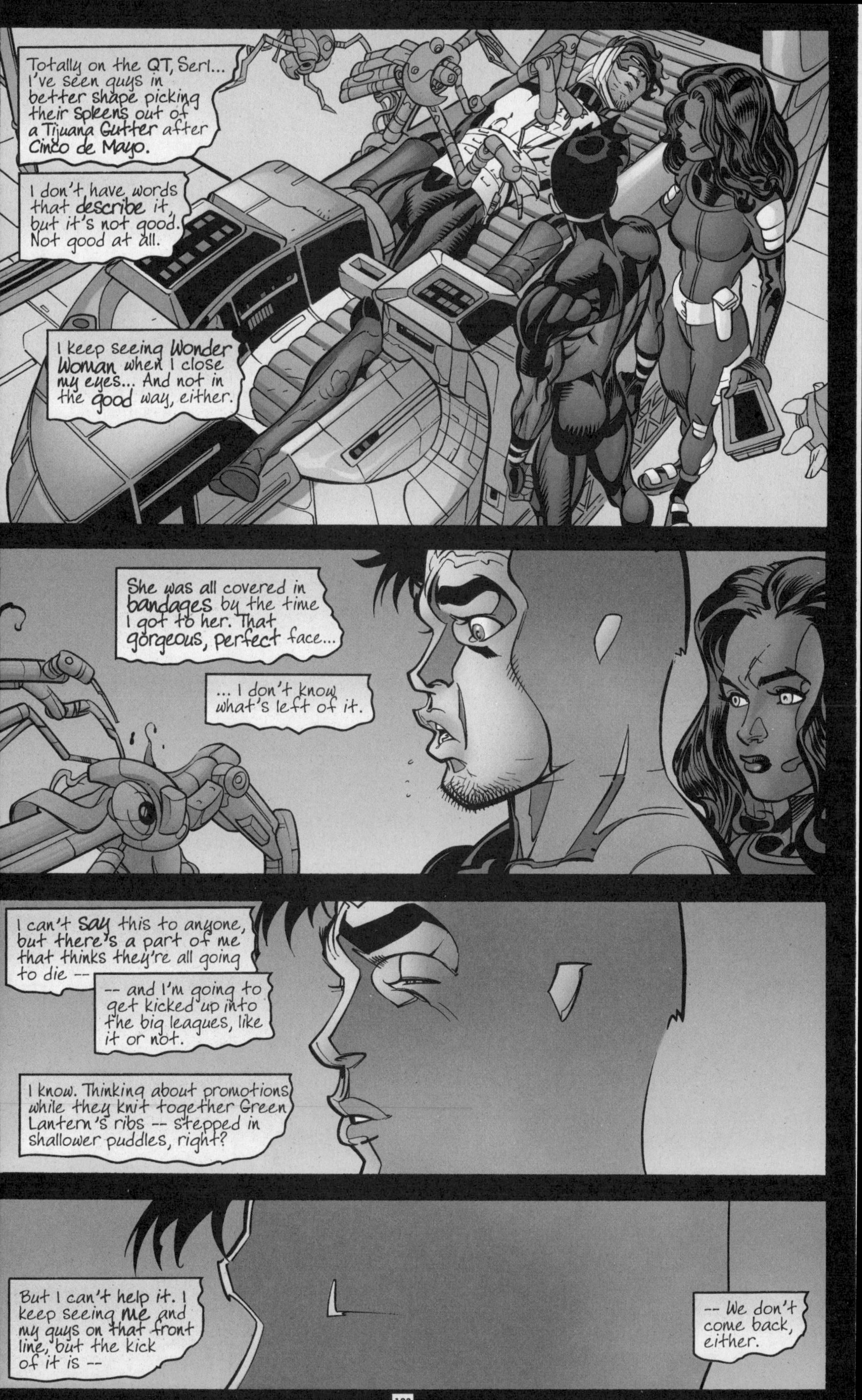

Totally on the QT, Seri... I've seen guys in better shape picking their spleens out of a Tijuana Gutter after Cinco de Mayo.
I don't have words that describe it, but it's not good. Not good at all.
I keep seeing Wonder Woman when I close my eyes... And not in the good way, either.
She was all covered in bandages by the time I got to her. That gorgeous, perfect face...
... I don't know what's left of it.
I can't say this to anyone, but there's a part of me that thinks they're all going to die --
-- and I'm going to get kicked up into the big leagues, like it or not.
I know. Thinking about promotions while they knit together Green Lantern's ribs -- stepped in shallower puddles, right?
But I can't help it. I keep seeing me and my guys on that front line, but the kick of it is --
-- We don't come back, either.

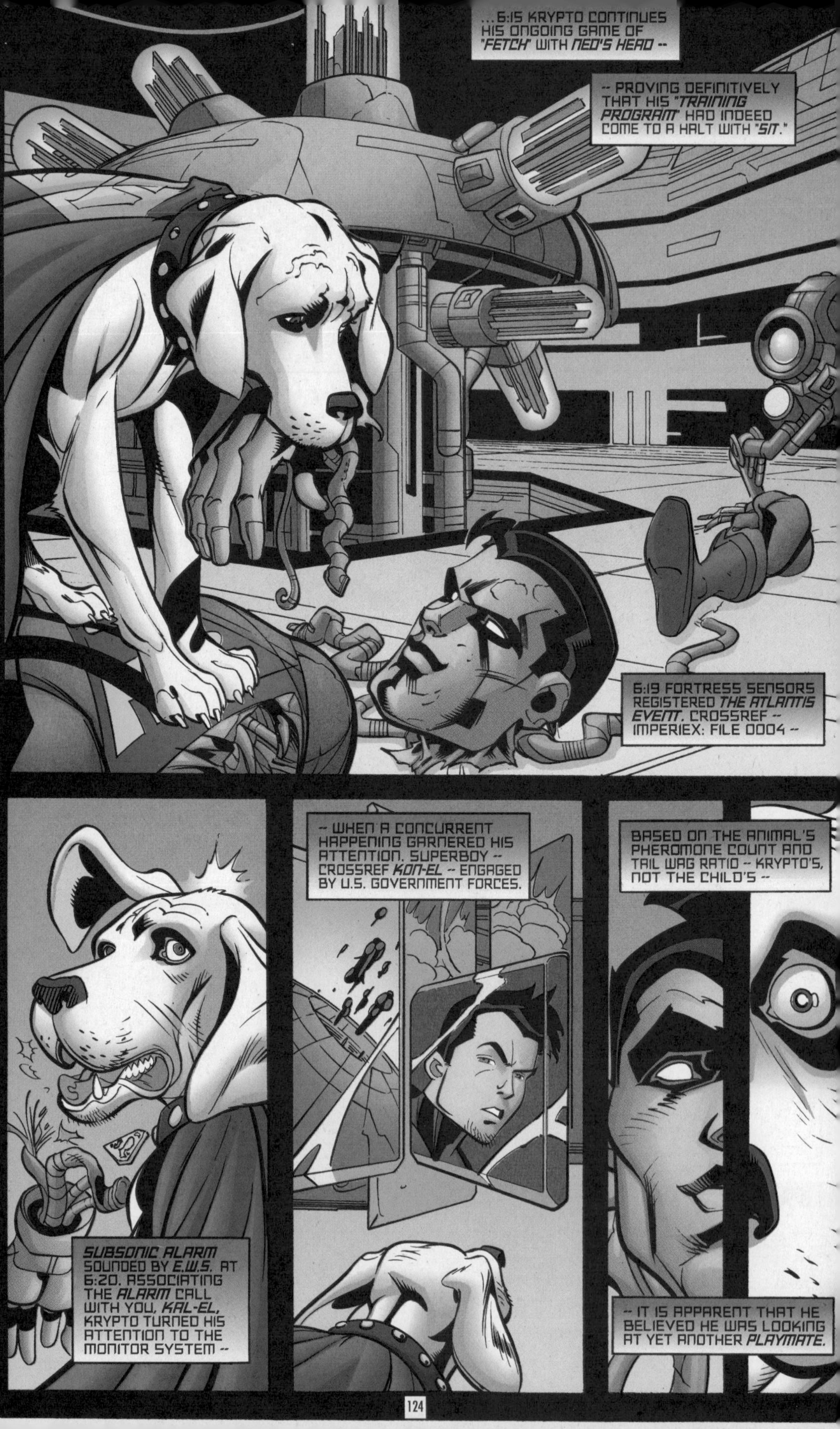

...6:15 KRYPTO CONTINUES HIS ONGOING GAME OF "FETCH" WITH NED'S HEAD --
-- PROVING DEFINITIVELY THAT HIS "TRAINING PROGRAM" HAD INDEED COME TO A HALT WITH "SIT."
6:19 FORTRESS SENSORS REGISTERED THE ATLANTIS EVENT. CROSSREF -- IMPERIEX: FILE 0004 --
SUBSONIC ALARM SOUNDED BY E.W.S. AT 6:20. ASSOCIATING THE ALARM CALL WITH YOU, KAL-EL, KRYPTO TURNED HIS ATTENTION TO THE MONITOR SYSTEM --
-- WHEN A CONCURRENT HAPPENING GARNERED HIS ATTENTION. SUPERBOY -- CROSSREF KON-EL -- ENGAGED BY U.S. GOVERNMENT FORCES.
BASED ON THE ANIMAL'S PHEROMONE COUNT AND TAIL WAG RATIO -- KRYPTO'S, NOT THE CHILD'S --
-- IT IS APPARENT THAT HE BELIEVED HE WAS LOOKING AT YET ANOTHER PLAYMATE.

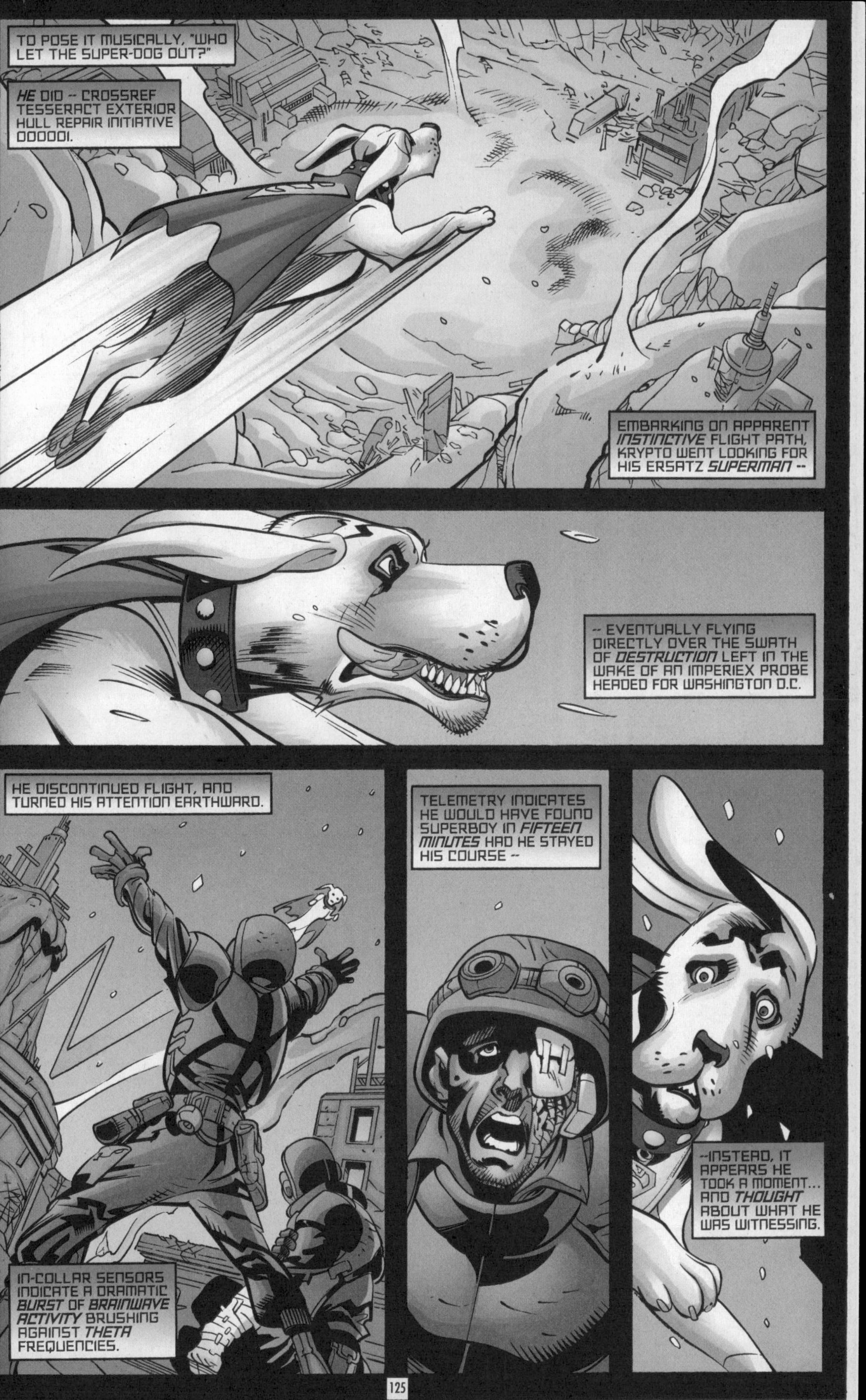
TO POSE IT MUSICALLY, "WHO LET THE SUPER-DOG OUT?"
HE DID -- CROSSREF TESSERACT EXTERIOR HULL REPAIR INITIATIVE 000001.
EMBARKING ON APPARENT INSTINCTIVE FLIGHT PATH, KRYPTO WENT LOOKING FOR HIS ERSATZ SUPERMAN --
-- EVENTUALLY FLYING DIRECTLY OVER THE SWATH OF DESTRUCTION LEFT IN THE WAKE OF AN IMPERIEX PROBE HEADED FOR WASHINGTON D.C.
HE DISCONTINUED FLIGHT, AND TURNED HIS ATTENTION EARTHWARD.
IN-COLLAR SENSORS INDICATE A DRAMATIC BURST OF BRAINWAVE ACTIVITY BRUSHING AGAINST THETA FREQUENCIES.
TELEMETRY INDICATES HE WOULD HAVE FOUND SUPERBOY IN FIFTEEN MINUTES HAD HE STAYED HIS COURSE --
--INSTEAD, IT APPEARS HE TOOK A MOMENT... AND THOUGHT ABOUT WHAT HE WAS WITNESSING.

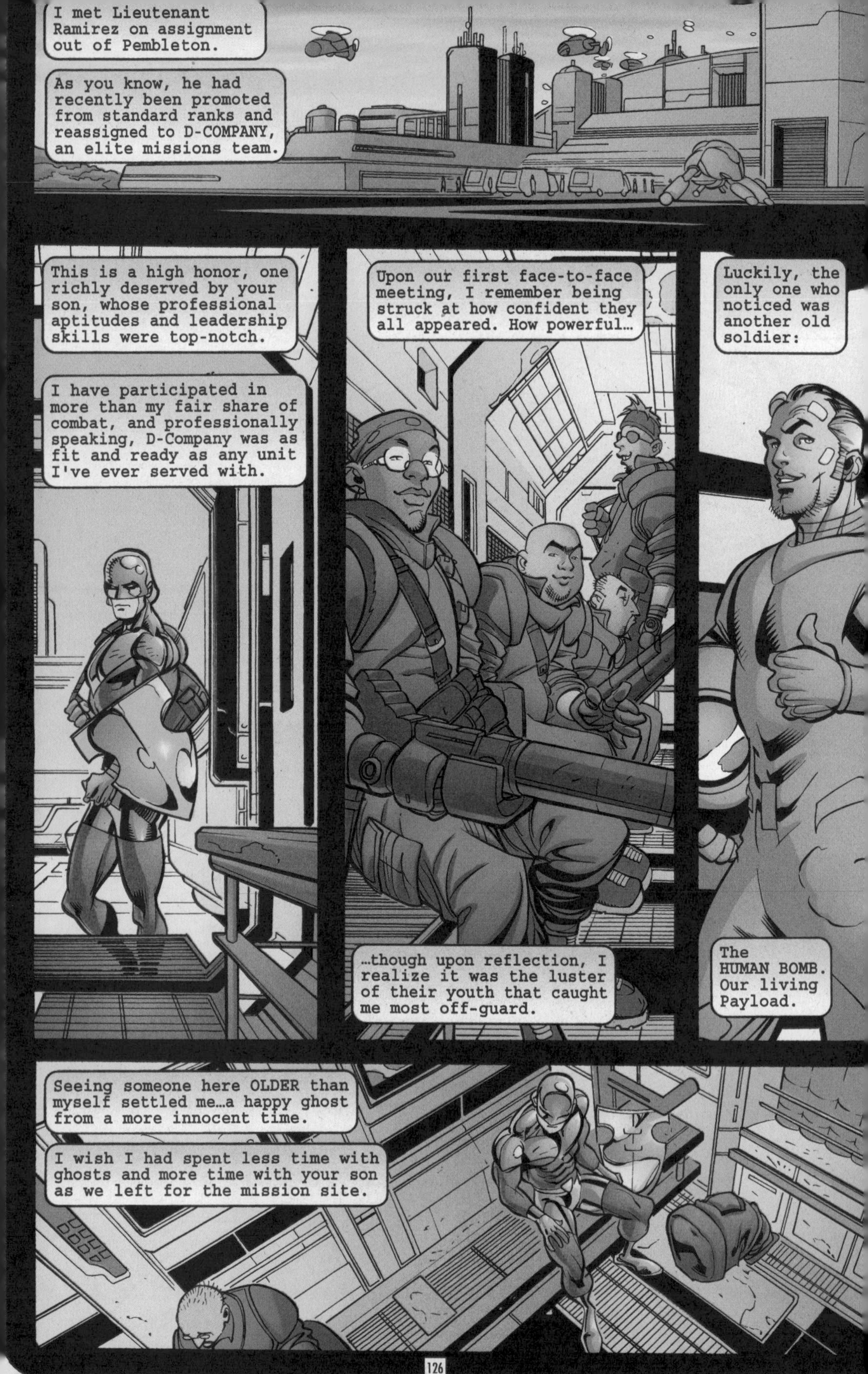

I met Lieutenant Ramirez on assignment out of Pembleton.
As you know, he had recently been promoted from standard ranks and reassigned to D-COMPANY, an elite missions team.
This is a high honor, one richly deserved by your son, whose professional aptitudes and leadership skills were top-notch.
I have participated in more than my fair share of combat, and professionally speaking, D-Company was as fit and ready as any unit I've ever served with.
Upon our first face-to-face meeting, I remember being struck at how confident they all appeared. How powerful…
…though upon reflection, I realize it was the luster of their youth that caught me most off-guard.
Luckily, the only one who noticed was another old soldier:
The HUMAN BOMB. Our living Payload.
Seeing someone here OLDER than myself settled me…a happy ghost from a more innocent time.
I wish I had spent less time with ghosts and more time with your son as we left for the mission site.

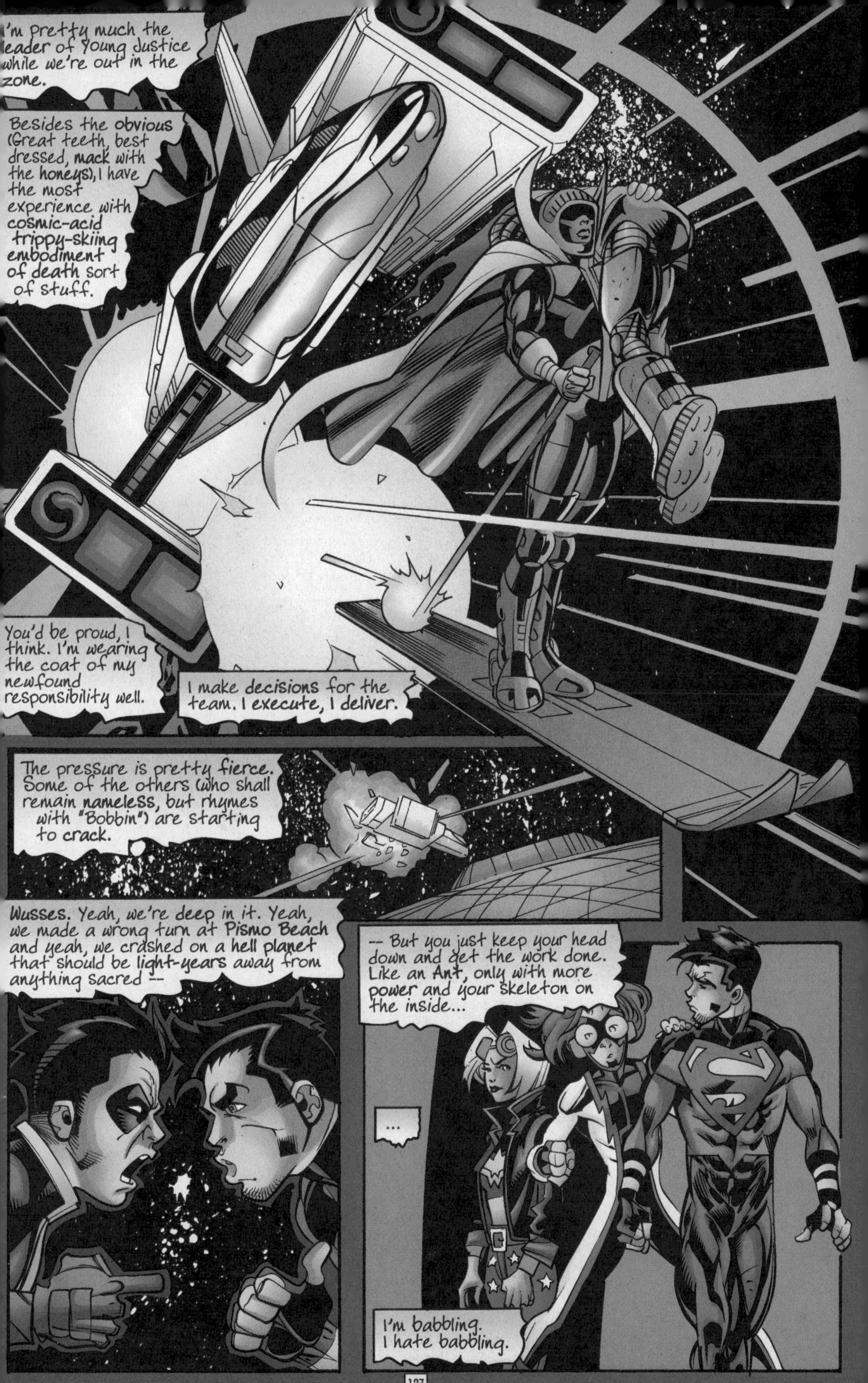
I'm pretty much the leader of Young Justice while we're out in the zone.
Besides the obvious (Great teeth, best dressed, mack with the honeys), I have the most experience with cosmic-acid trippy-skiing embodiment of death sort of stuff.
You'd be proud, I think. I'm wearing the coat of my newfound responsibility well.
I make decisions for the team. I execute, I deliver.
The pressure is pretty fierce. Some of the others (who shall remain nameless, but rhymes with "Bobbin") are starting to crack.
Wusses. Yeah, we're deep in it. Yeah, we made a wrong turn at Pismo Beach and yeah, we crashed on a hell planet that should be light-years away from anything sacred --
-- But you just keep your head down and get the work done. Like an Ant, only with more power and your skeleton on the inside...
...
I'm babbling. I hate babbling.

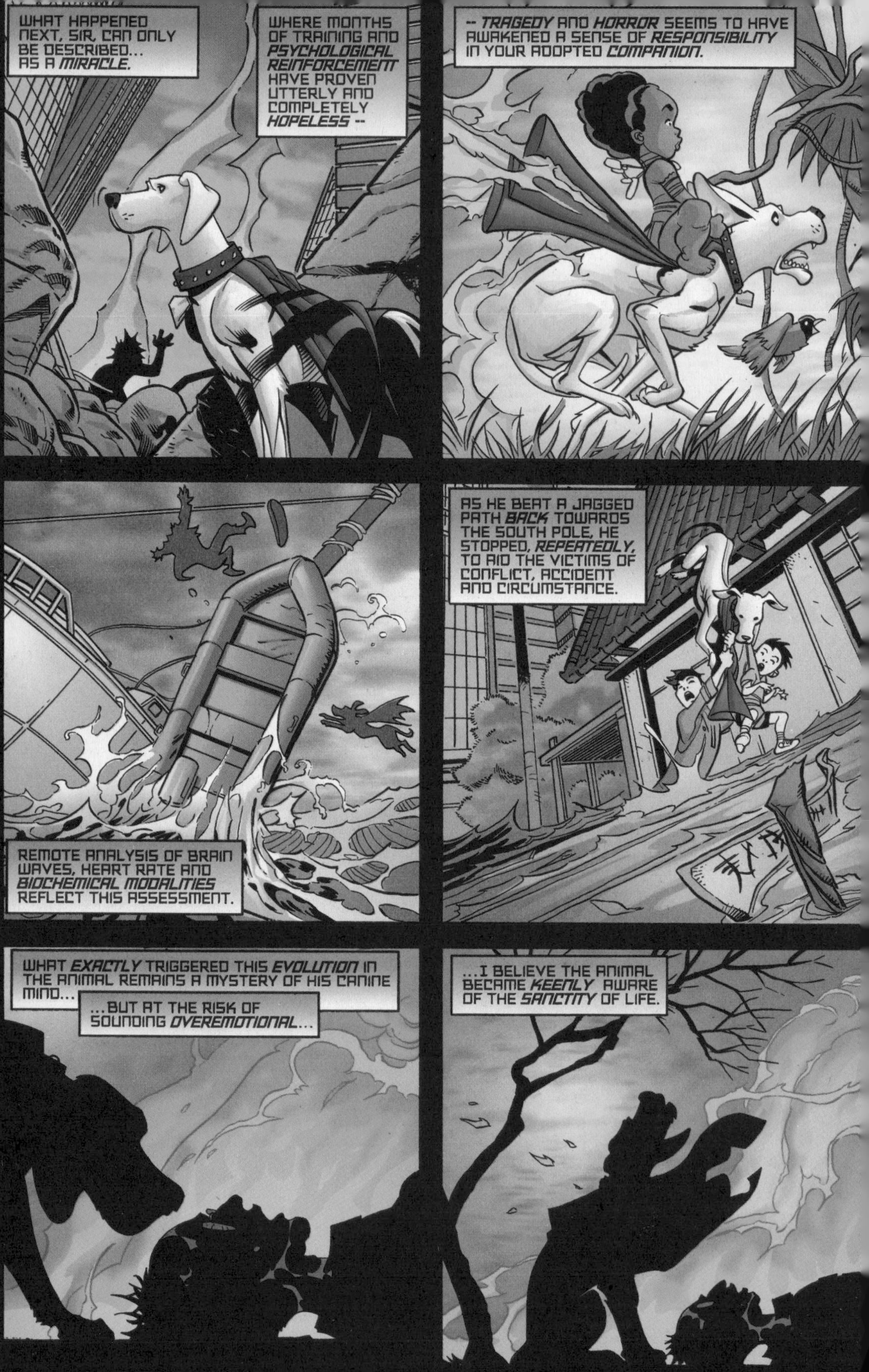
WHAT HAPPENED NEXT, SIR, CAN ONLY BE DESCRIBED... AS A *MIRACLE.*
WHERE MONTHS OF TRAINING AND *PSYCHOLOGICAL REINFORCEMENT* HAVE PROVEN UTTERLY AND COMPLETELY *HOPELESS* --
-- *TRAGEDY* AND *HORROR* SEEMS TO HAVE AWAKENED A SENSE OF *RESPONSIBILITY* IN YOUR ADOPTED *COMPANION.*
REMOTE ANALYSIS OF BRAIN WAVES, HEART RATE AND *BIOCHEMICAL MODALITIES* REFLECT THIS ASSESSMENT.
AS HE BEAT A JAGGED PATH *BACK* TOWARDS THE SOUTH POLE, HE STOPPED, *REPEATEDLY,* TO AID THE VICTIMS OF CONFLICT, ACCIDENT AND CIRCUMSTANCE.
WHAT *EXACTLY* TRIGGERED THIS *EVOLUTION* IN THE ANIMAL REMAINS A MYSTERY OF HIS CANINE MIND...
...BUT AT THE RISK OF SOUNDING *OVEREMOTIONAL*...
...I BELIEVE THE ANIMAL BECAME *KEENLY* AWARE OF THE *SANCTITY* OF LIFE.

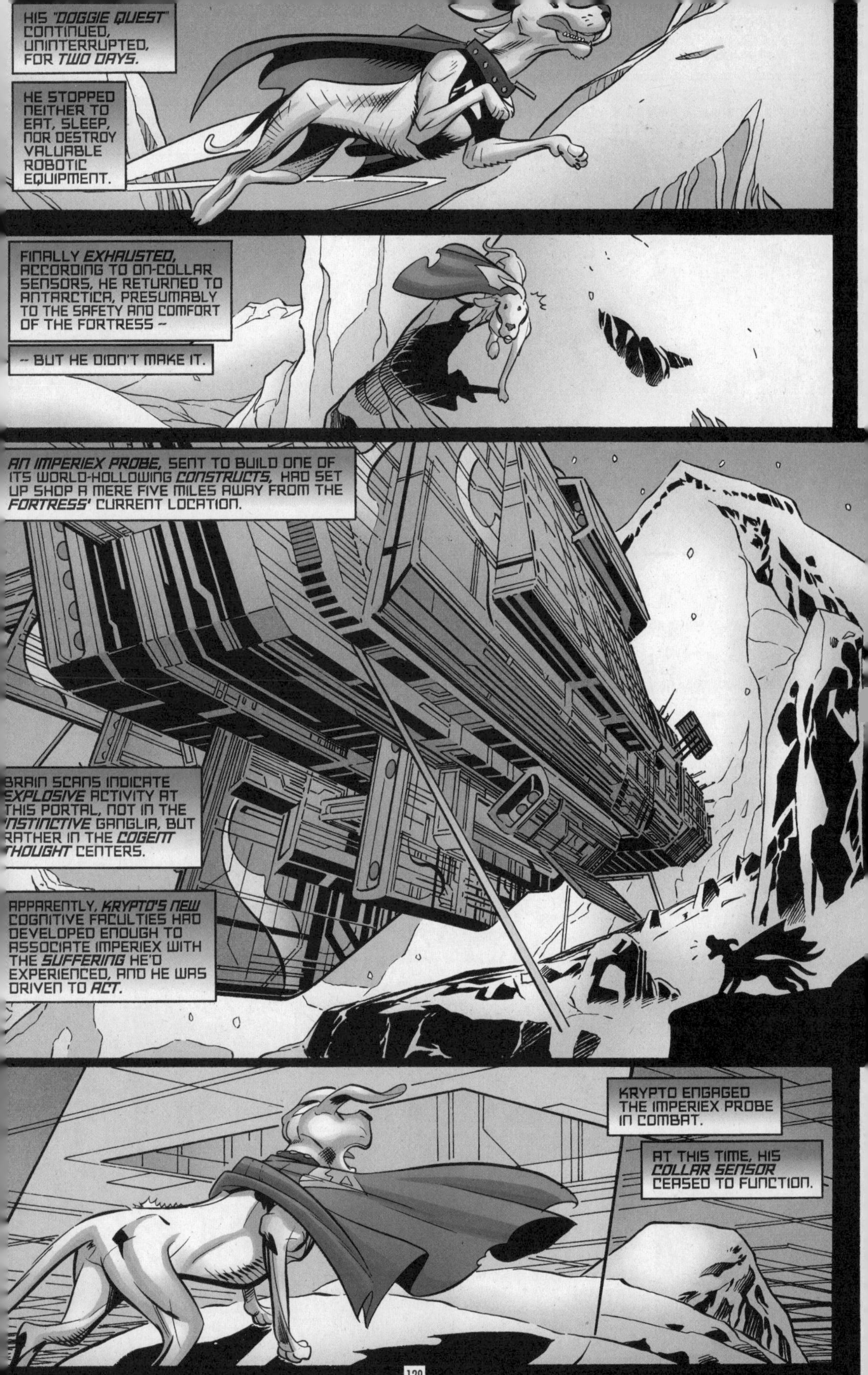
HIS "DOGGIE QUEST" CONTINUED, UNINTERRUPTED, FOR TWO DAYS.
HE STOPPED NEITHER TO EAT, SLEEP, NOR DESTROY VALUABLE ROBOTIC EQUIPMENT.
FINALLY EXHAUSTED, ACCORDING TO ON-COLLAR SENSORS, HE RETURNED TO ANTARCTICA, PRESUMABLY TO THE SAFETY AND COMFORT OF THE FORTRESS --
-- BUT HE DIDN'T MAKE IT.
AN IMPERIEX PROBE, SENT TO BUILD ONE OF ITS WORLD-HOLLOWING CONSTRUCTS, HAD SET UP SHOP A MERE FIVE MILES AWAY FROM THE FORTRESS' CURRENT LOCATION.
BRAIN SCANS INDICATE EXPLOSIVE ACTIVITY AT THIS PORTAL, NOT IN THE INSTINCTIVE GANGLIA, BUT RATHER IN THE COGENT THOUGHT CENTERS.
APPARENTLY, KRYPTO'S NEW COGNITIVE FACULTIES HAD DEVELOPED ENOUGH TO ASSOCIATE IMPERIEX WITH THE SUFFERING HE'D EXPERIENCED, AND HE WAS DRIVEN TO ACT.
KRYPTO ENGAGED THE IMPERIEX PROBE IN COMBAT.
AT THIS TIME, HIS COLLAR SENSOR CEASED TO FUNCTION.

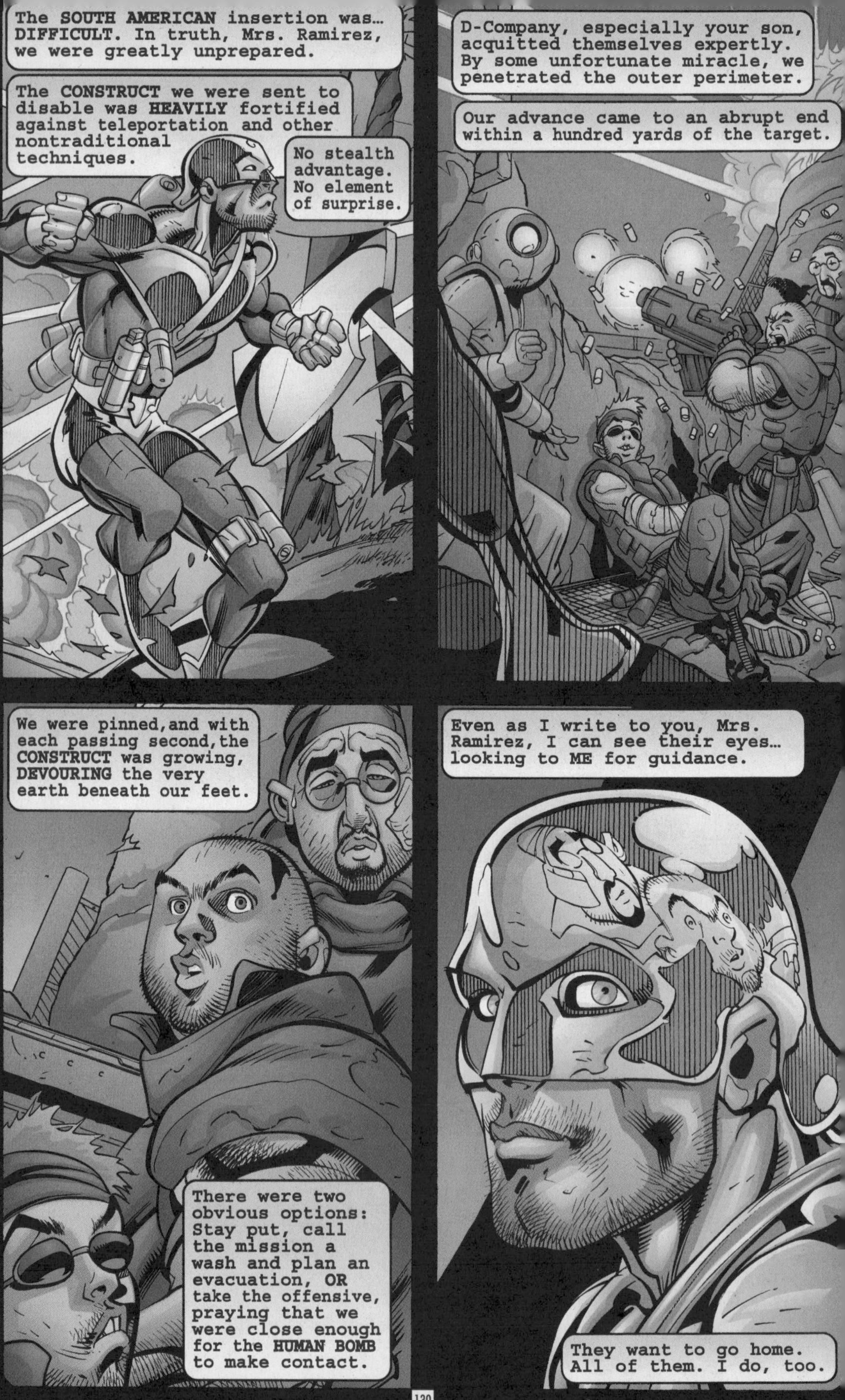
The SOUTH AMERICAN insertion was... DIFFICULT. In truth, Mrs. Ramirez, we were greatly unprepared.
The CONSTRUCT we were sent to disable was HEAVILY fortified against teleportation and other nontraditional techniques.
No stealth advantage. No element of surprise.
D-Company, especially your son, acquitted themselves expertly. By some unfortunate miracle, we penetrated the outer perimeter.
Our advance came to an abrupt end within a hundred yards of the target.
We were pinned, and with each passing second, the CONSTRUCT was growing, DEVOURING the very earth beneath our feet.
There were two obvious options: Stay put, call the mission a wash and plan an evacuation, OR take the offensive, praying that we were close enough for the HUMAN BOMB to make contact.
Even as I write to you, Mrs. Ramirez, I can see their eyes... looking to ME for guidance.
They want to go home. All of them. I do, too.

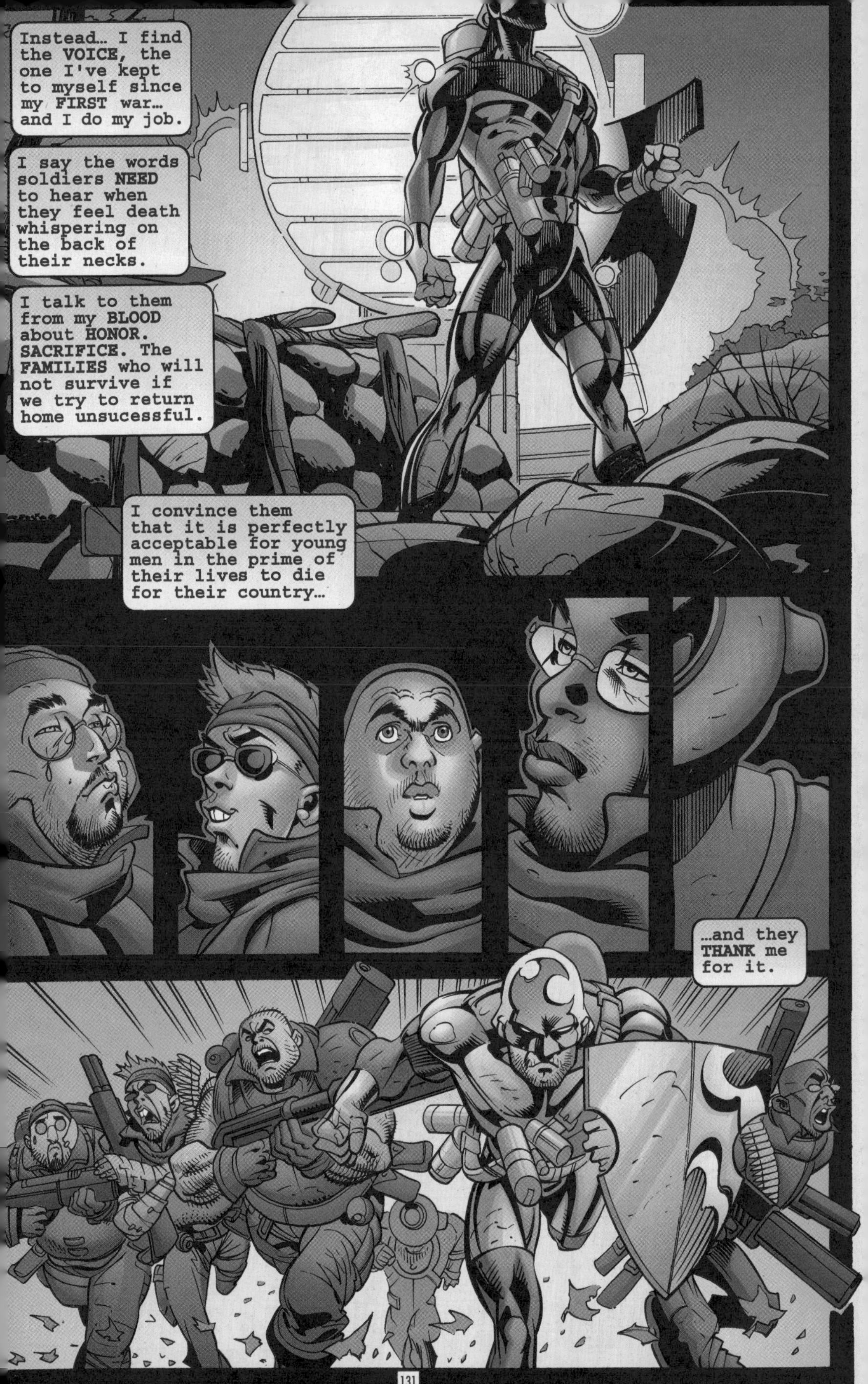
Instead... I find the VOICE, the one I've kept to myself since my FIRST war... and I do my job.
I say the words soldiers NEED to hear when they feel death whispering on the back of their necks.
I talk to them from my BLOOD about HONOR. SACRIFICE. The FAMILIES who will not survive if we try to return home unsucessful.
I convince them that it is perfectly acceptable for young men in the prime of their lives to die for their country...
...and they THANK me for it.

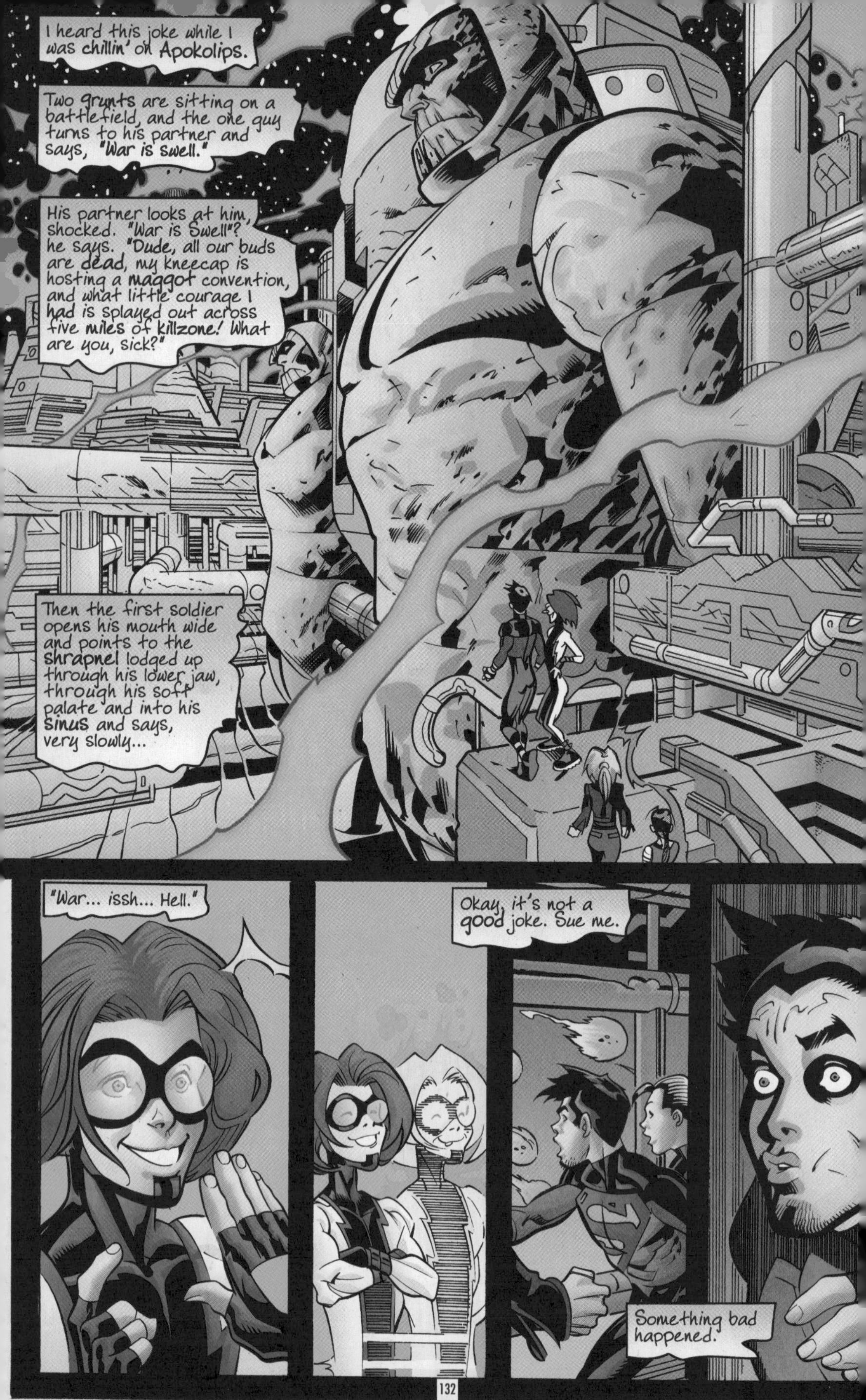

I heard this joke while I was chillin' on Apokolips.
Two grunts are sitting on a battlefield, and the one guy turns to his partner and says, "War is swell."
His partner looks at him, shocked. "War is Swell"? he says. "Dude, all our buds are dead, my kneecap is hosting a maggot convention, and what little courage I had is splayed out across five miles of killzone! What are you, sick?"
Then the first soldier opens his mouth wide and points to the shrapnel lodged up through his lower jaw, through his soft palate and into his sinus and says, very slowly...
"War... issh... Hell."
Okay, it's not a good joke. Sue me.
Something bad happened.

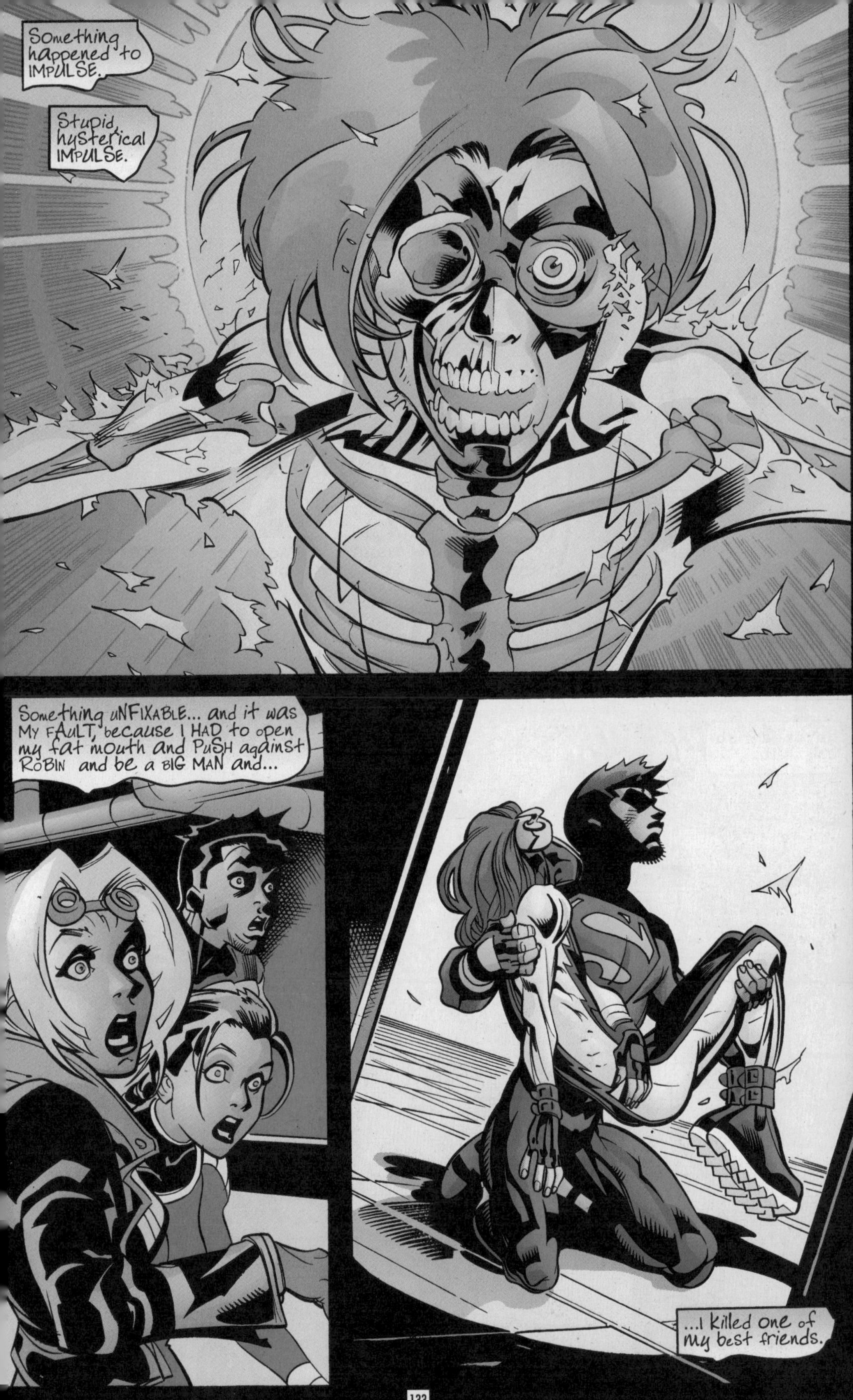
Something happened to IMPULSE.
Stupid, hysterical IMPULSE.
Something UNFIXABLE... and it was MY FAULT, because I HAD to open my fat mouth and PUSH against ROBIN and be a BIG MAN and...
...I killed one of my best friends.

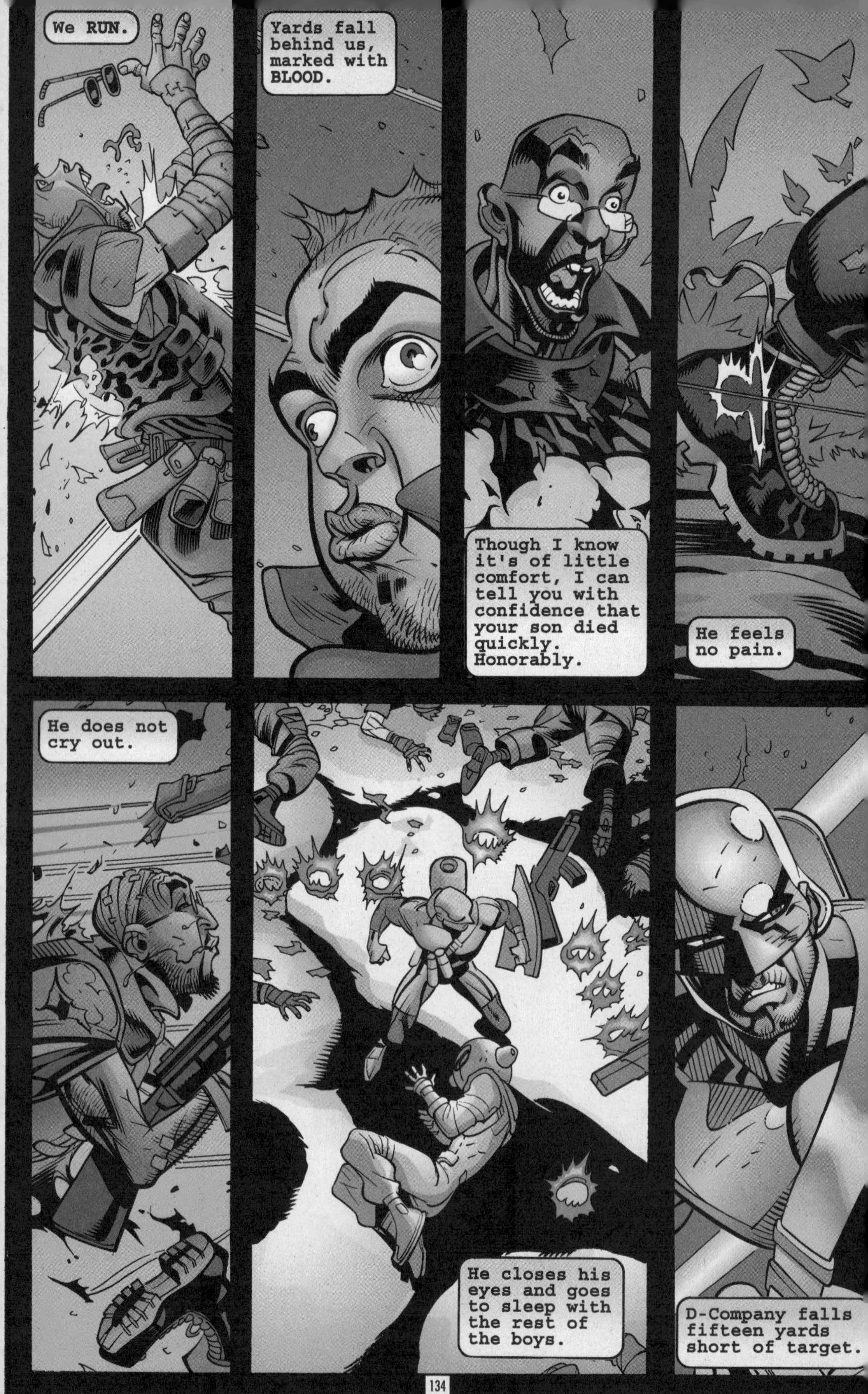
We RUN.
Yards fall behind us, marked with BLOOD.
Though I know it's of little comfort, I can tell you with confidence that your son died quickly. Honorably.
He feels no pain.
He does not cry out.
He closes his eyes and goes to sleep with the rest of the boys.
D-Company falls fifteen yards short of target.

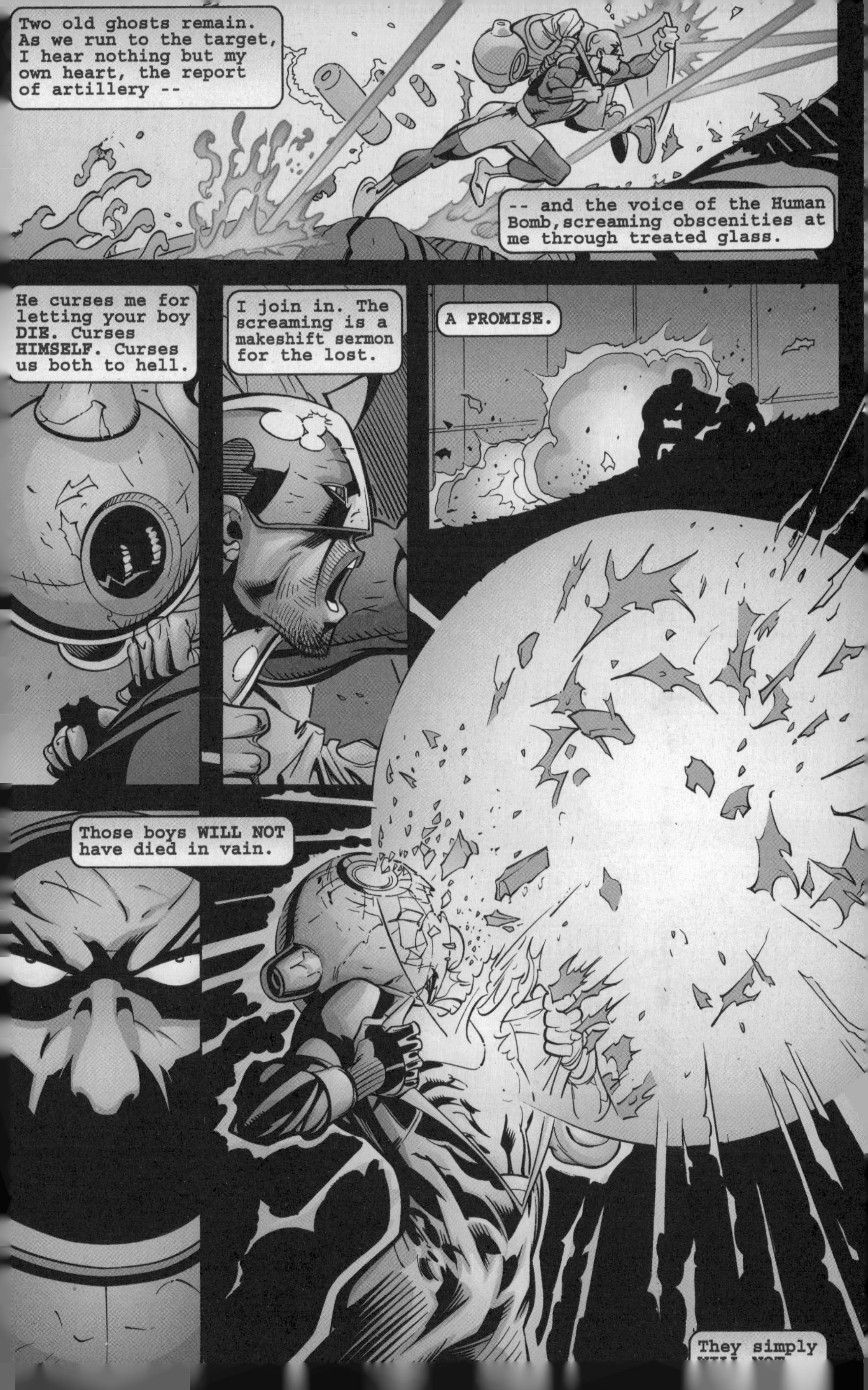
Two old ghosts remain. As we run to the target, I hear nothing but my own heart, the report of artillery --
-- and the voice of the Human Bomb, screaming obscenities at me through treated glass.
He curses me for letting your boy DIE. Curses HIMSELF. Curses us both to hell.
I join in. The screaming is a makeshift sermon for the lost.
A PROMISE.
Those boys WILL NOT have died in vain.
They simply

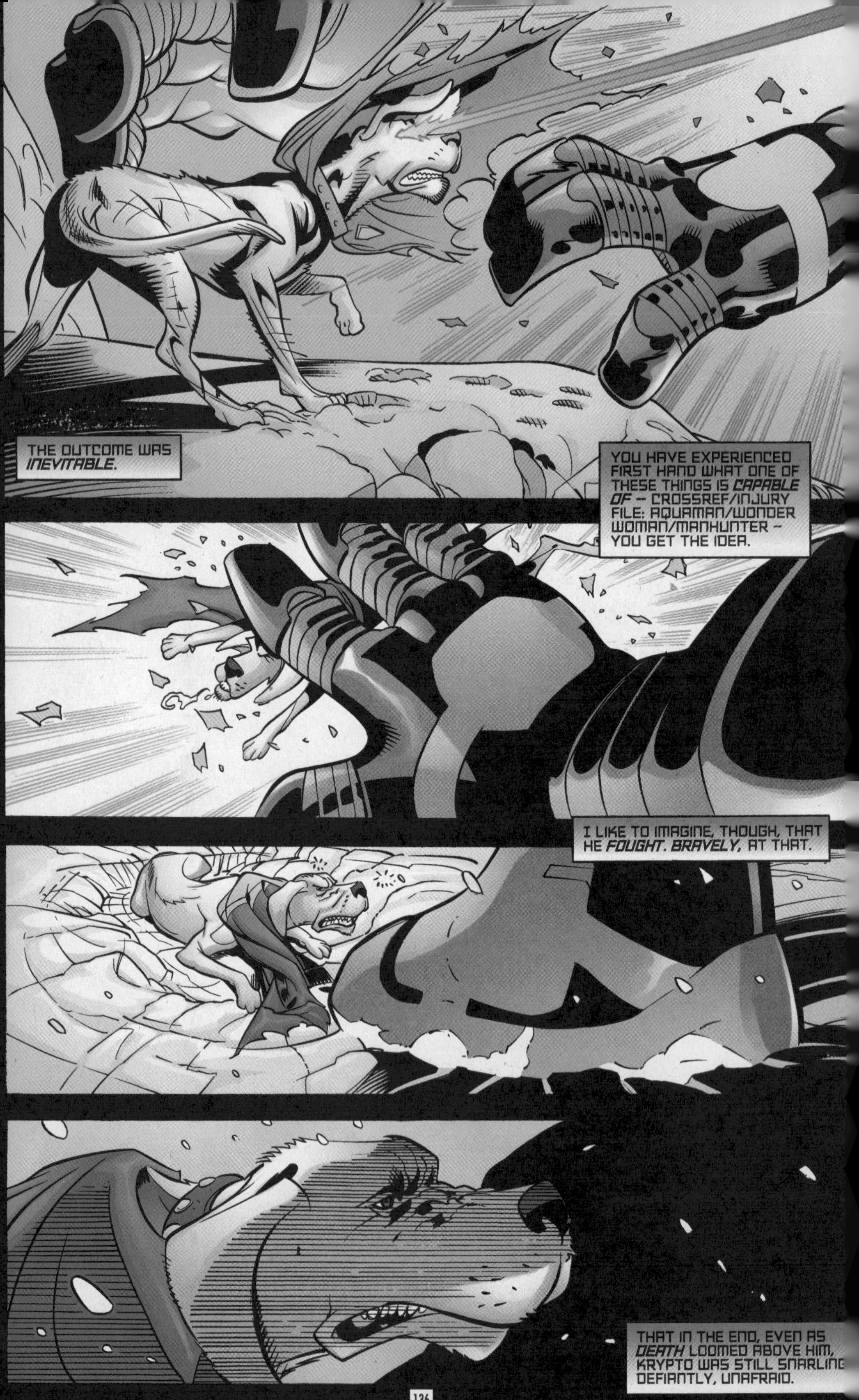
THE OUTCOME WAS *INEVITABLE.*
YOU HAVE EXPERIENCED FIRST HAND WHAT ONE OF THESE THINGS IS *CAPABLE OF* -- CROSSREF/INJURY FILE: AQUAMAN/WONDER WOMAN/MANHUNTER -- YOU GET THE IDEA.
I LIKE TO IMAGINE, THOUGH, THAT HE *FOUGHT. BRAVELY,* AT THAT.
THAT IN THE END, EVEN AS *DEATH* LOOMED ABOVE HIM, KRYPTO WAS STILL SNARLING DEFIANTLY, UNAFRAID.

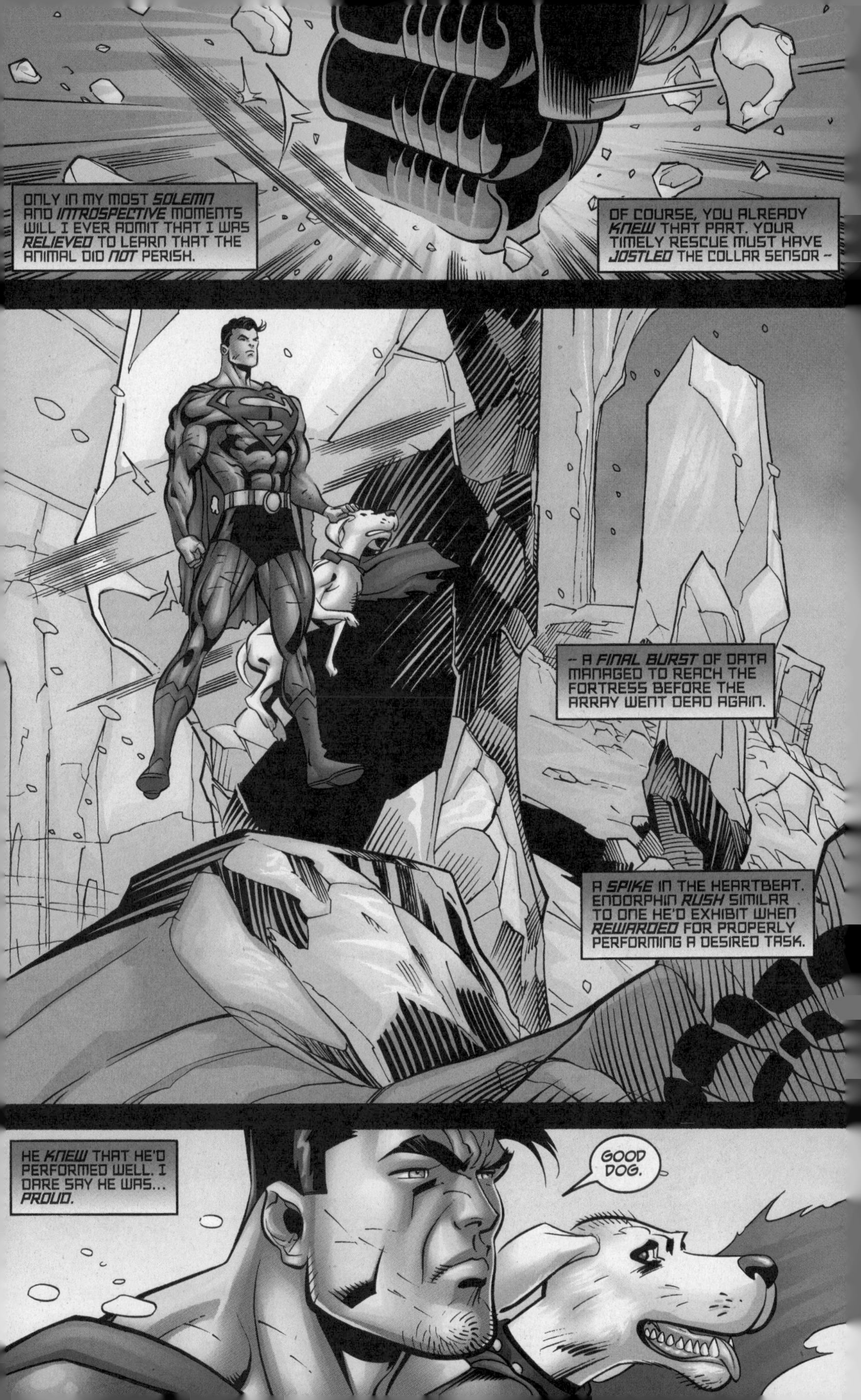

ONLY IN MY MOST SOLEMN AND INTROSPECTIVE MOMENTS WILL I EVER ADMIT THAT I WAS RELIEVED TO LEARN THAT THE ANIMAL DID NOT PERISH.
OF COURSE, YOU ALREADY KNEW THAT PART. YOUR TIMELY RESCUE MUST HAVE JOSTLED THE COLLAR SENSOR --
-- A FINAL BURST OF DATA MANAGED TO REACH THE FORTRESS BEFORE THE ARRAY WENT DEAD AGAIN.
A SPIKE IN THE HEARTBEAT. ENDORPHIN RUSH SIMILAR TO ONE HE'D EXHIBIT WHEN REWARDED FOR PROPERLY PERFORMING A DESIRED TASK.
HE KNEW THAT HE'D PERFORMED WELL. I DARE SAY HE WAS... PROUD.
GOOD DOG.

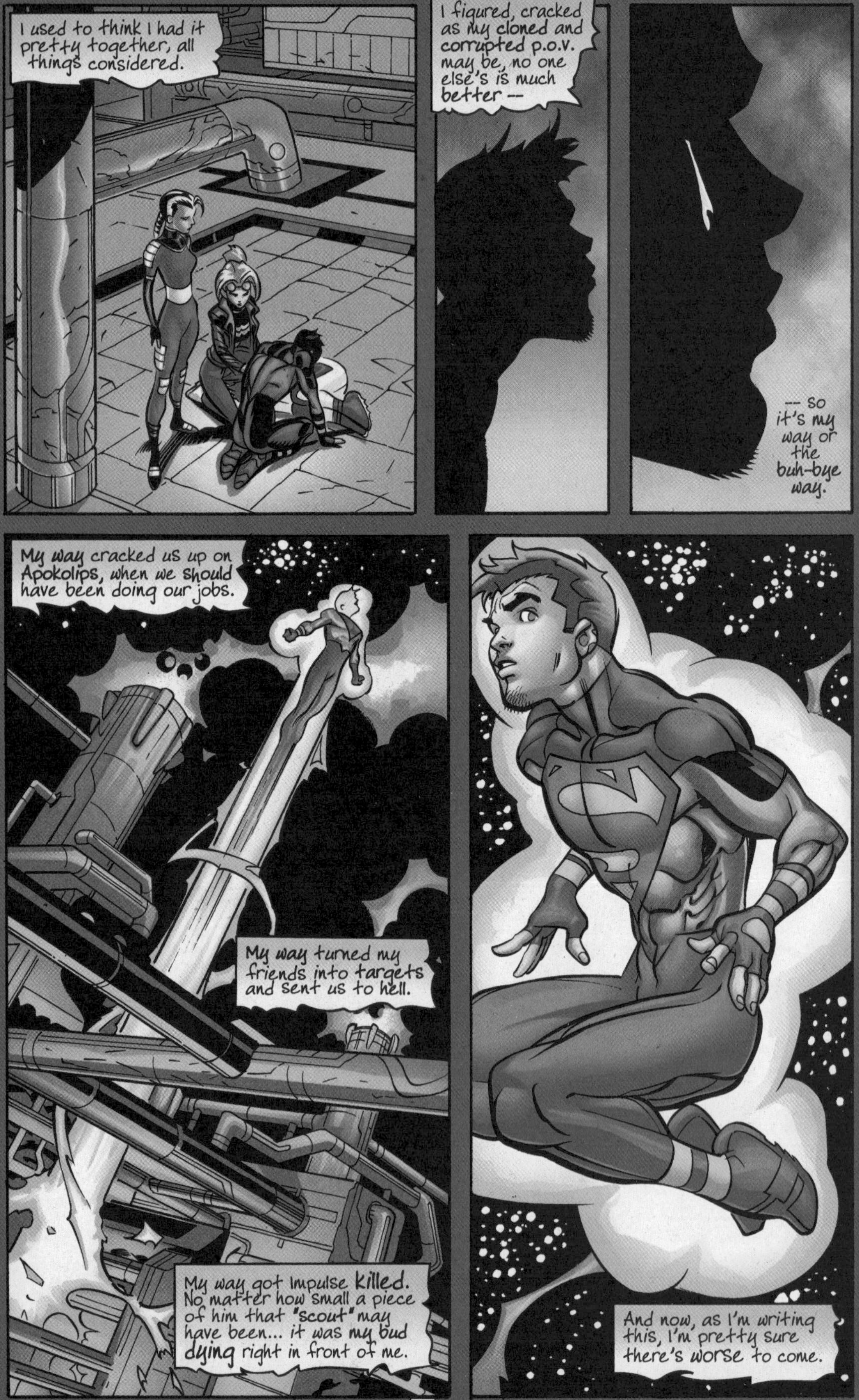
I used to think I had it pretty together, all things considered.
I figured, cracked as my cloned and corrupted p.o.v. may be, no one else's is much better --
-- so it's my way or the buh-bye way.
My way cracked us up on Apokolips, when we should have been doing our jobs.
My way turned my friends into targets and sent us to hell.
My way got Impulse killed. No matter how small a piece of him that "scout" may have been... it was my bud dying right in front of me.
And now, as I'm writing this, I'm pretty sure there's worse to come.

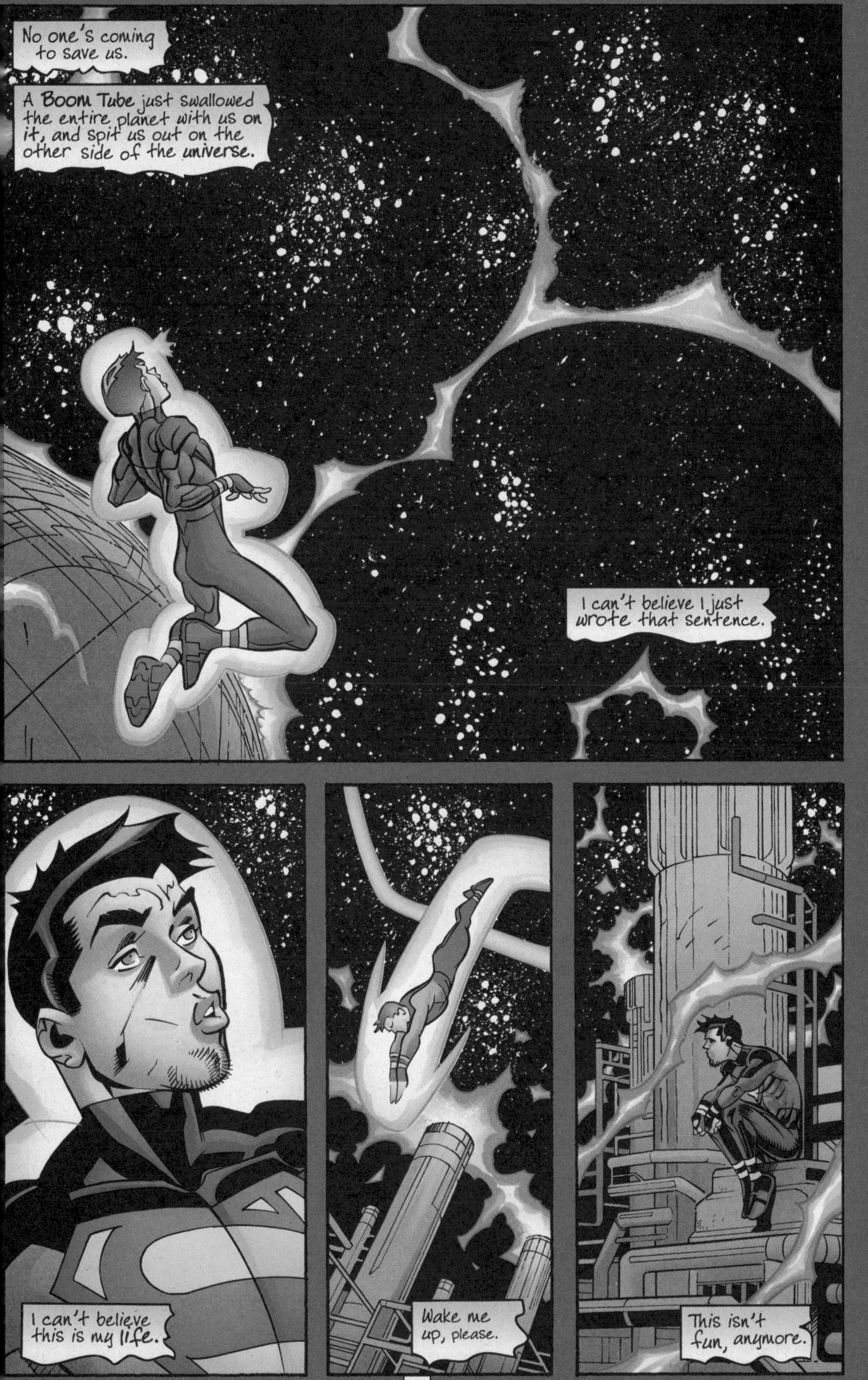
No one's coming to save us.
A Boom Tube just swallowed the entire planet with us on it, and spit us out on the other side of the universe.
I can't believe I just wrote that sentence.
I can't believe this is my life.
Wake me up, please.
This isn't fun, anymore.

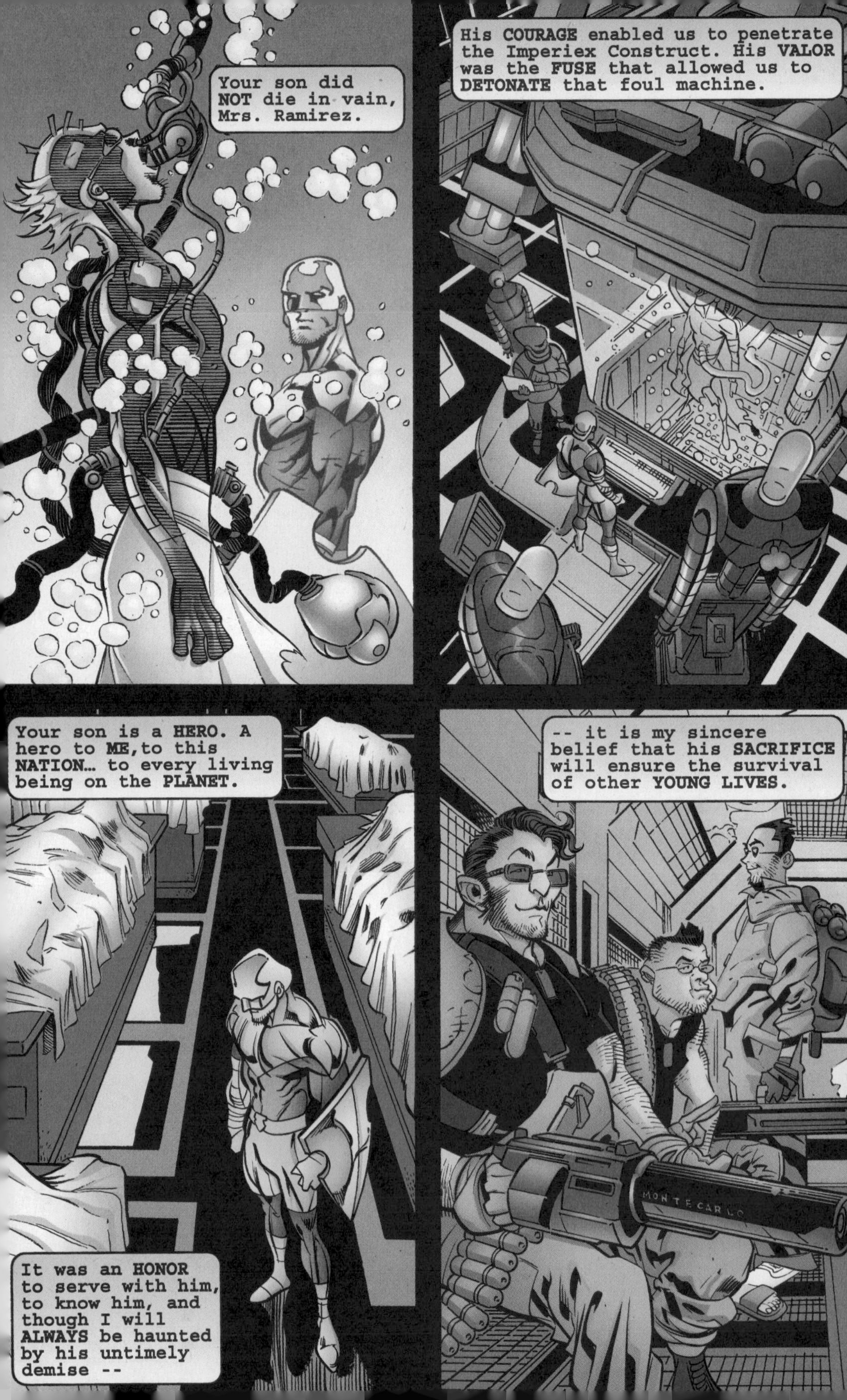
Your son did NOT die in vain, Mrs. Ramirez.
His COURAGE enabled us to penetrate the Imperiex Construct. His VALOR was the FUSE that allowed us to DETONATE that foul machine.
Your son is a HERO. A hero to ME,to this NATION... to every living being on the PLANET.
It was an HONOR to serve with him, to know him, and though I will ALWAYS be haunted by his untimely demise --
-- it is my sincere belief that his SACRIFICE will ensure the survival of other YOUNG LIVES.
MONTECARLO

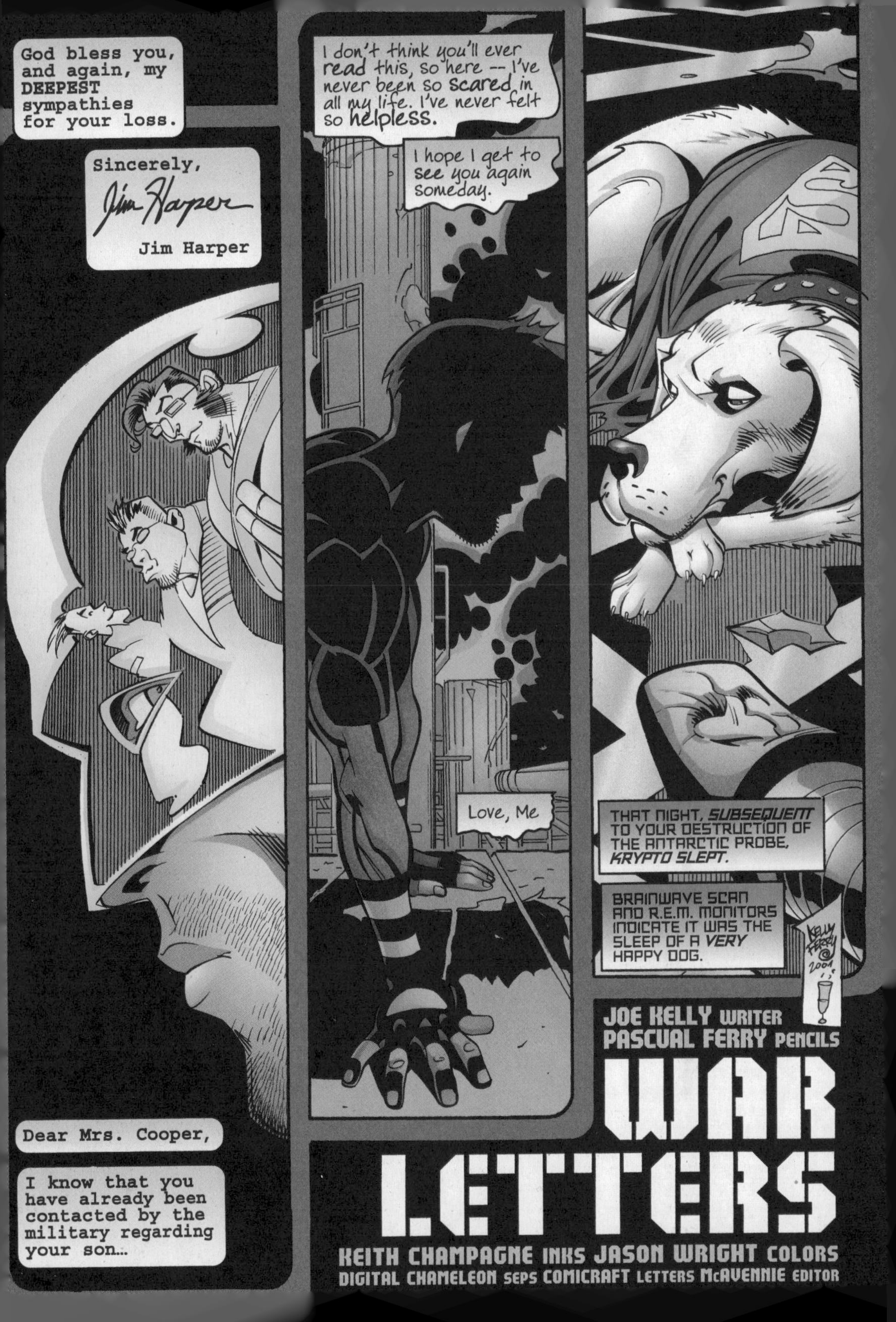

God bless you, and again, my DEEPEST sympathies for your loss.
Sincerely,
Jim Harper
Jim Harper
I don't think you'll ever read this, so here -- I've never been so scared in all my life. I've never felt so helpless.
I hope I get to see you again someday.
Love, Me
THAT NIGHT, SUBSEQUENT TO YOUR DESTRUCTION OF THE ANTARCTIC PROBE, KRYPTO SLEPT.
BRAINWAVE SCAN AND R.E.M. MONITORS INDICATE IT WAS THE SLEEP OF A VERY HAPPY DOG.
JOE KELLY WRITER
PASCUAL FERRY PENCILS
WAR LETTERS
KEITH CHAMPAGNE INKS JASON WRIGHT COLORS
DIGITAL CHAMELEON SEPS COMICRAFT LETTERS McAVENNIE EDITOR
Dear Mrs. Cooper,
I know that you have already been contacted by the military regarding your son...

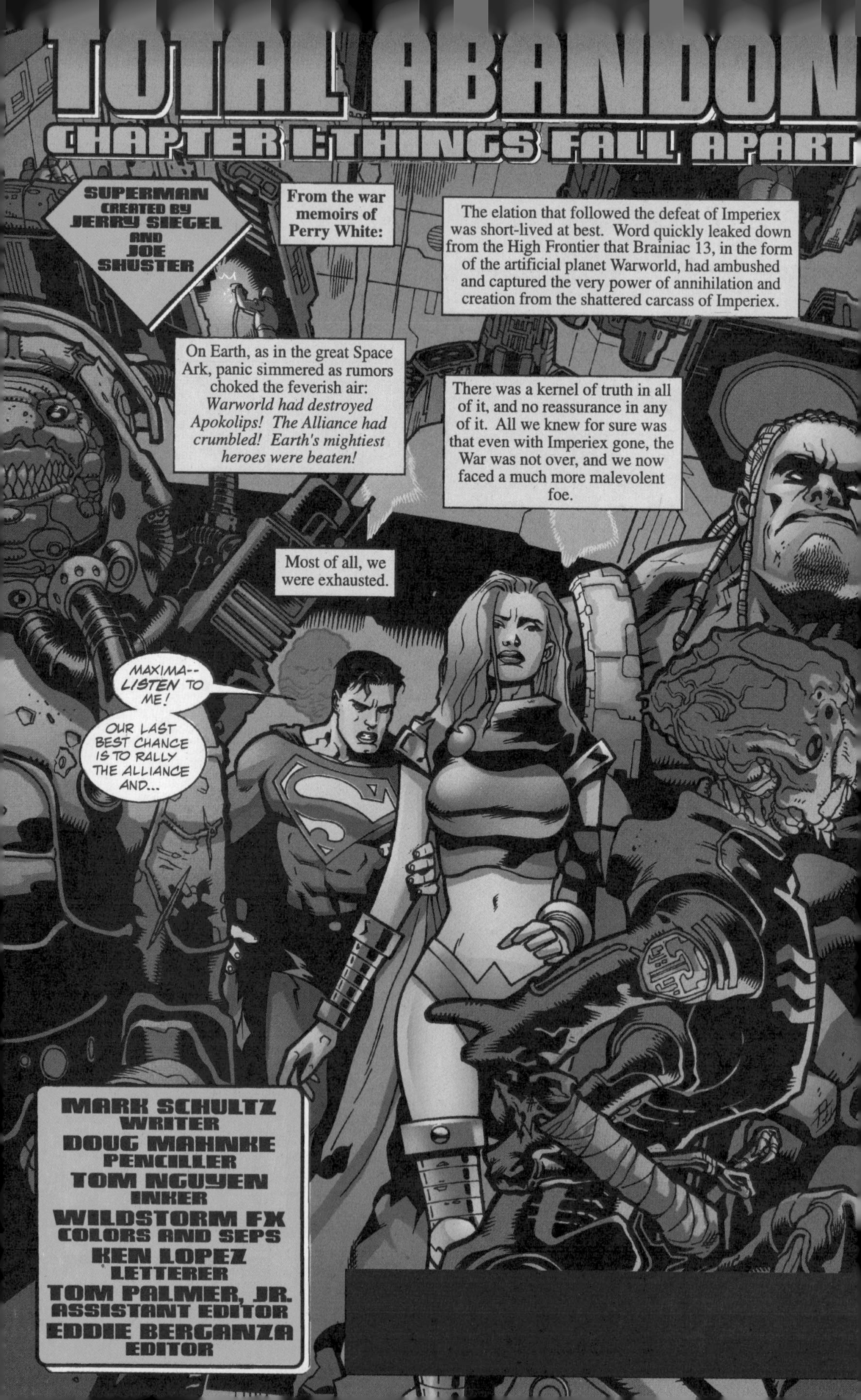
TOTAL ABANDON
CHAPTER I: THINGS FALL APART
SUPERMAN CREATED BY JERRY SIEGEL AND JOE SHUSTER
From the war memoirs of Perry White:
The elation that followed the defeat of Imperiex was short-lived at best. Word quickly leaked down from the High Frontier that Brainiac 13, in the form of the artificial planet Warworld, had ambushed and captured the very power of annihilation and creation from the shattered carcass of Imperiex.
On Earth, as in the great Space Ark, panic simmered as rumors choked the feverish air: *Warworld had destroyed Apokolips! The Alliance had crumbled! Earth's mightiest heroes were beaten!*
There was a kernel of truth in all of it, and no reassurance in any of it. All we knew for sure was that even with Imperiex gone, the War was not over, and we now faced a much more malevolent foe.
Most of all, we were exhausted.
MAXIMA-- LISTEN TO ME!
OUR LAST BEST CHANCE IS TO RALLY THE ALLIANCE AND...
MARK SCHULTZ WRITER
DOUG MAHNKE PENCILLER
TOM NGUYEN INKER
WILDSTORM FX COLORS AND SEPS
KEN LOPEZ LETTERER
TOM PALMER, JR. ASSISTANT EDITOR
EDDIE BERGANZA EDITOR

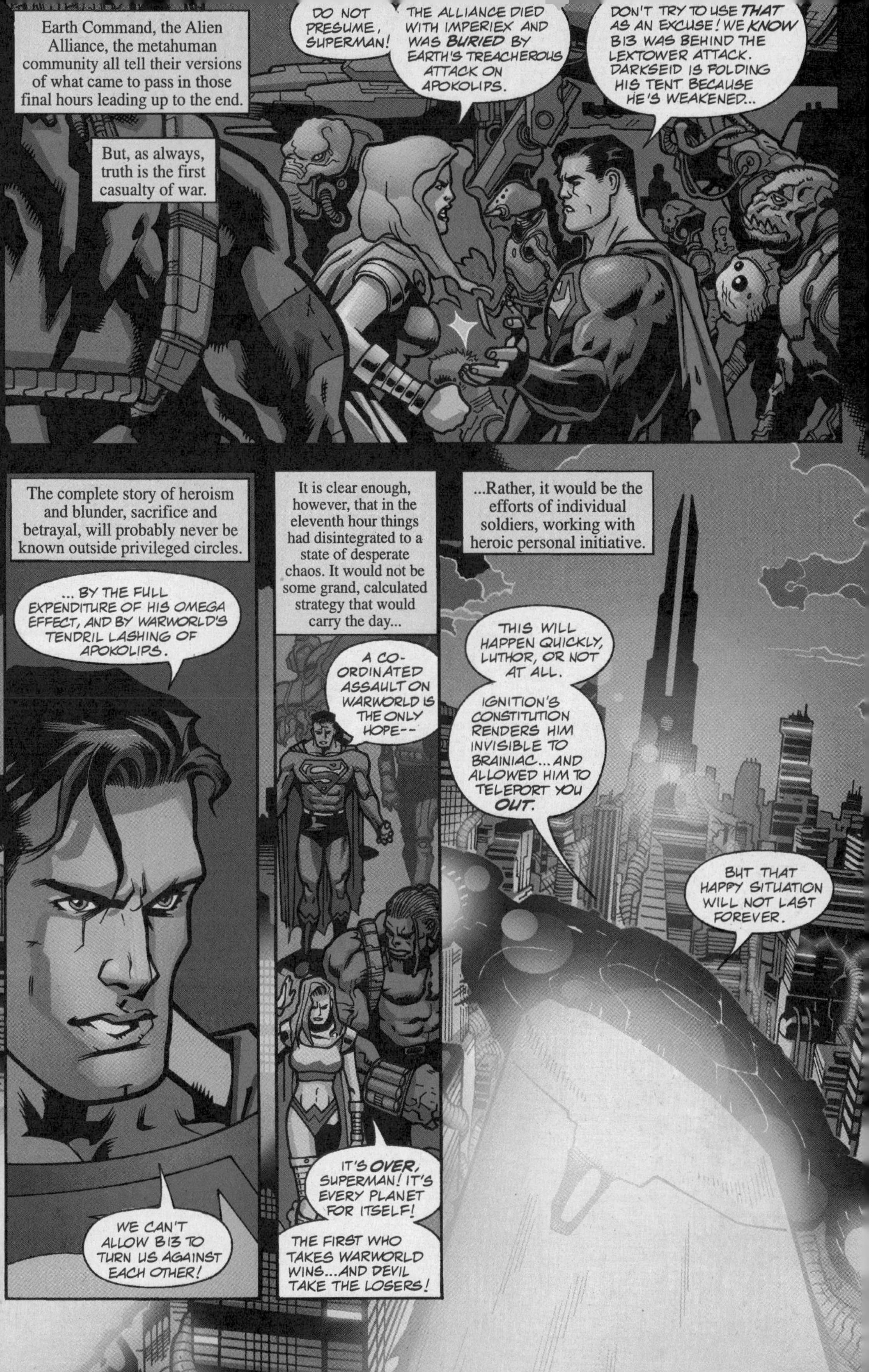
Earth Command, the Alien Alliance, the metahuman community all tell their versions of what came to pass in those final hours leading up to the end.
But, as always, truth is the first casualty of war.
DO NOT PRESUME, SUPERMAN!
THE ALLIANCE DIED WITH IMPERIEX AND WAS BURIED BY EARTH'S TREACHEROUS ATTACK ON APOKOLIPS.
DON'T TRY TO USE THAT AS AN EXCUSE! WE KNOW B13 WAS BEHIND THE LEXTOWER ATTACK. DARKSEID IS FOLDING HIS TENT BECAUSE HE'S WEAKENED...
The complete story of heroism and blunder, sacrifice and betrayal, will probably never be known outside privileged circles.
... BY THE FULL EXPENDITURE OF HIS OMEGA EFFECT, AND BY WARWORLD'S TENDRIL LASHING OF APOKOLIPS.
WE CAN'T ALLOW B13 TO TURN US AGAINST EACH OTHER!
It is clear enough, however, that in the eleventh hour things had disintegrated to a state of desperate chaos. It would not be some grand, calculated strategy that would carry the day...
A CO-ORDINATED ASSAULT ON WARWORLD IS THE ONLY HOPE--
IT'S OVER, SUPERMAN! IT'S EVERY PLANET FOR ITSELF!
THE FIRST WHO TAKES WARWORLD WINS...AND DEVIL TAKE THE LOSERS!
...Rather, it would be the efforts of individual soldiers, working with heroic personal initiative.
THIS WILL HAPPEN QUICKLY, LUTHOR, OR NOT AT ALL.
IGNITION'S CONSTITUTION RENDERS HIM INVISIBLE TO BRAINIAC... AND ALLOWED HIM TO TELEPORT YOU OUT.
BUT THAT HAPPY SITUATION WILL NOT LAST FOREVER.

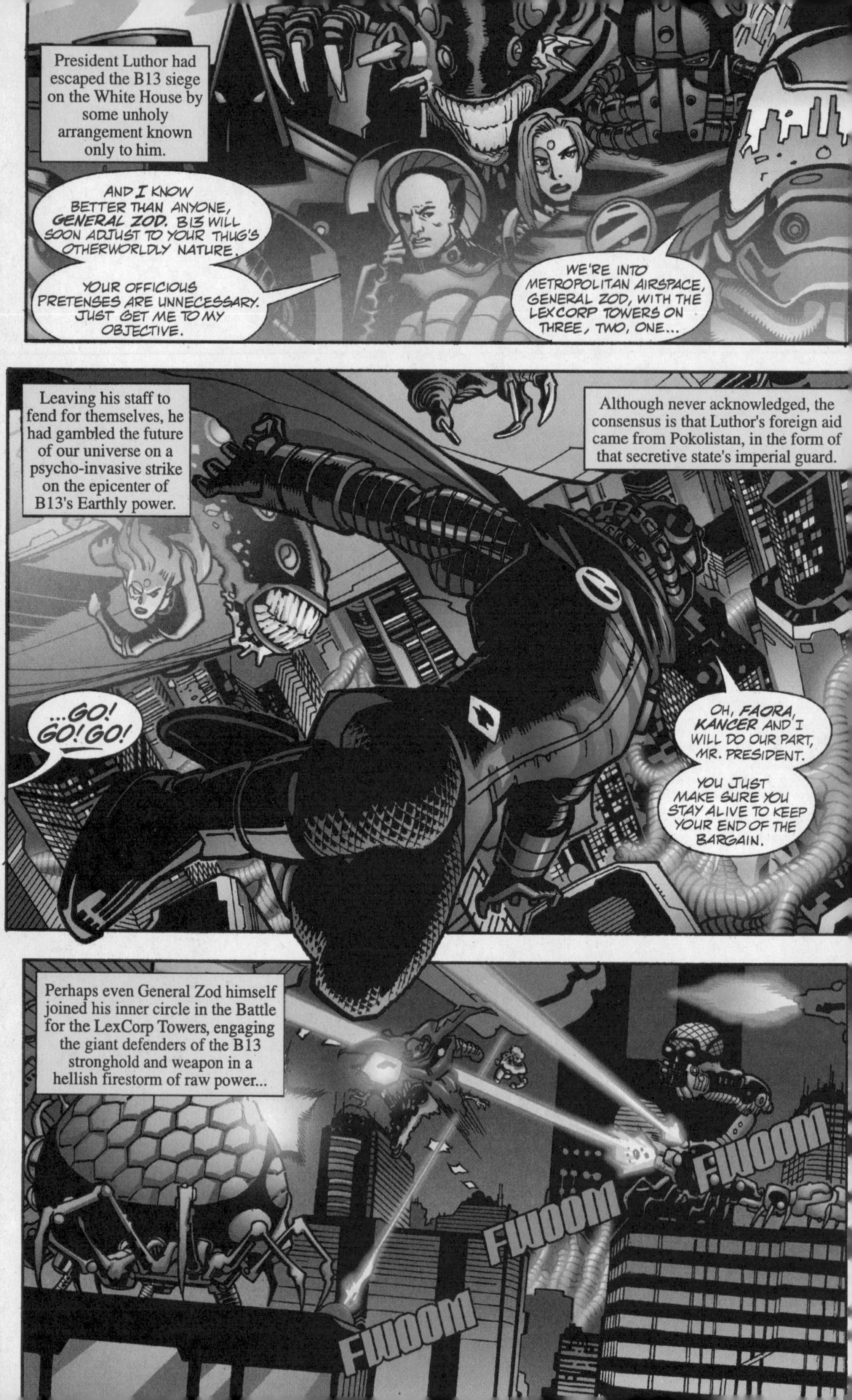
President Luthor had escaped the B13 siege on the White House by some unholy arrangement known only to him.
AND I KNOW BETTER THAN ANYONE, GENERAL ZOD. B13 WILL SOON ADJUST TO YOUR THUG'S OTHERWORLDLY NATURE.
YOUR OFFICIOUS PRETENSES ARE UNNECESSARY. JUST GET ME TO MY OBJECTIVE.
WE'RE INTO METROPOLITAN AIRSPACE, GENERAL ZOD, WITH THE LEXCORP TOWERS ON THREE, TWO, ONE...
Leaving his staff to fend for themselves, he had gambled the future of our universe on a psycho-invasive strike on the epicenter of B13's Earthly power.
Although never acknowledged, the consensus is that Luthor's foreign aid came from Pokolistan, in the form of that secretive state's imperial guard.
...GO! GO! GO!
OH, FAORA, KANCER AND I WILL DO OUR PART, MR. PRESIDENT.
YOU JUST MAKE SURE YOU STAY ALIVE TO KEEP YOUR END OF THE BARGAIN.
Perhaps even General Zod himself joined his inner circle in the Battle for the LexCorp Towers, engaging the giant defenders of the B13 stronghold and weapon in a hellish firestorm of raw power...
FWOOM
FWOOM
FWOOM

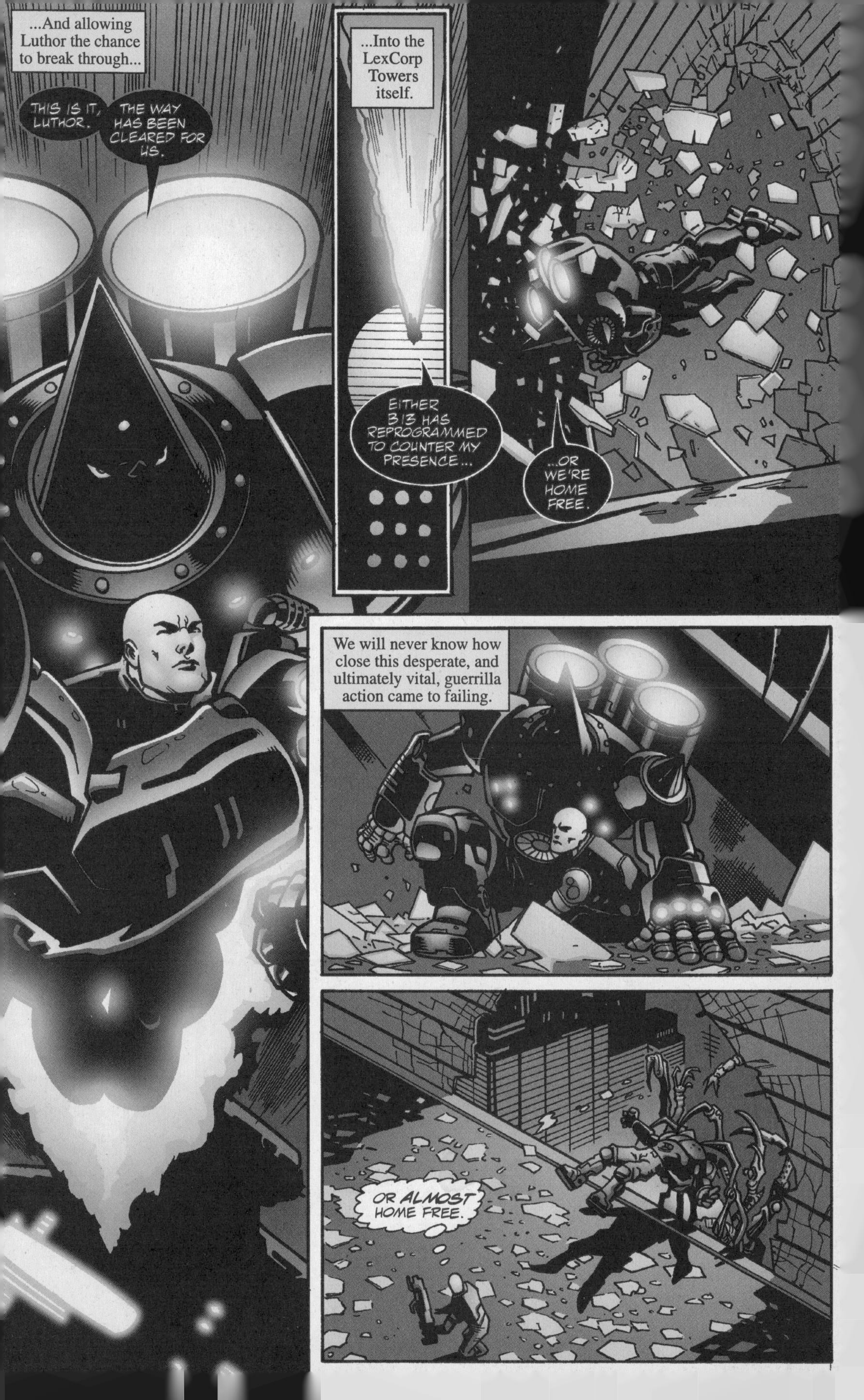
...And allowing Luthor the chance to break through...
THIS IS IT, LUTHOR.
THE WAY HAS BEEN CLEARED FOR US.
...Into the LexCorp Towers itself.
EITHER B13 HAS REPROGRAMMED TO COUNTER MY PRESENCE...
...OR WE'RE HOME FREE.
We will never know how close this desperate, and ultimately vital, guerrilla action came to failing.
OR ALMOST HOME FREE.

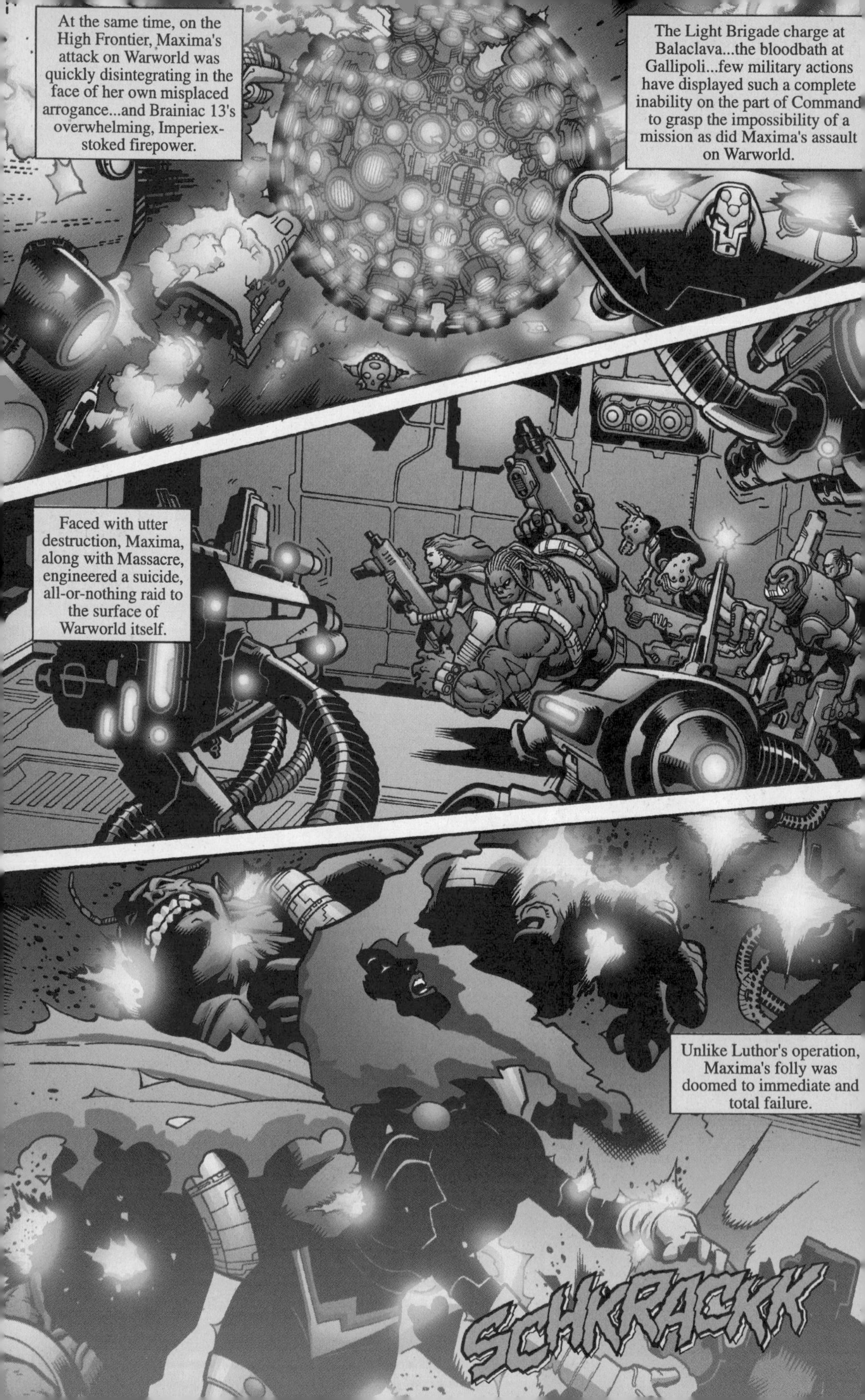
At the same time, on the High Frontier, Maxima's attack on Warworld was quickly disintegrating in the face of her own misplaced arrogance...and Brainiac 13's overwhelming, Imperiex-stoked firepower.
The Light Brigade charge at Balaclava...the bloodbath at Gallipoli...few military actions have displayed such a complete inability on the part of Command to grasp the impossibility of a mission as did Maxima's assault on Warworld.
Faced with utter destruction, Maxima, along with Massacre, engineered a suicide, all-or-nothing raid to the surface of Warworld itself.
Unlike Luthor's operation, Maxima's folly was doomed to immediate and total failure.
SCHKRACKK

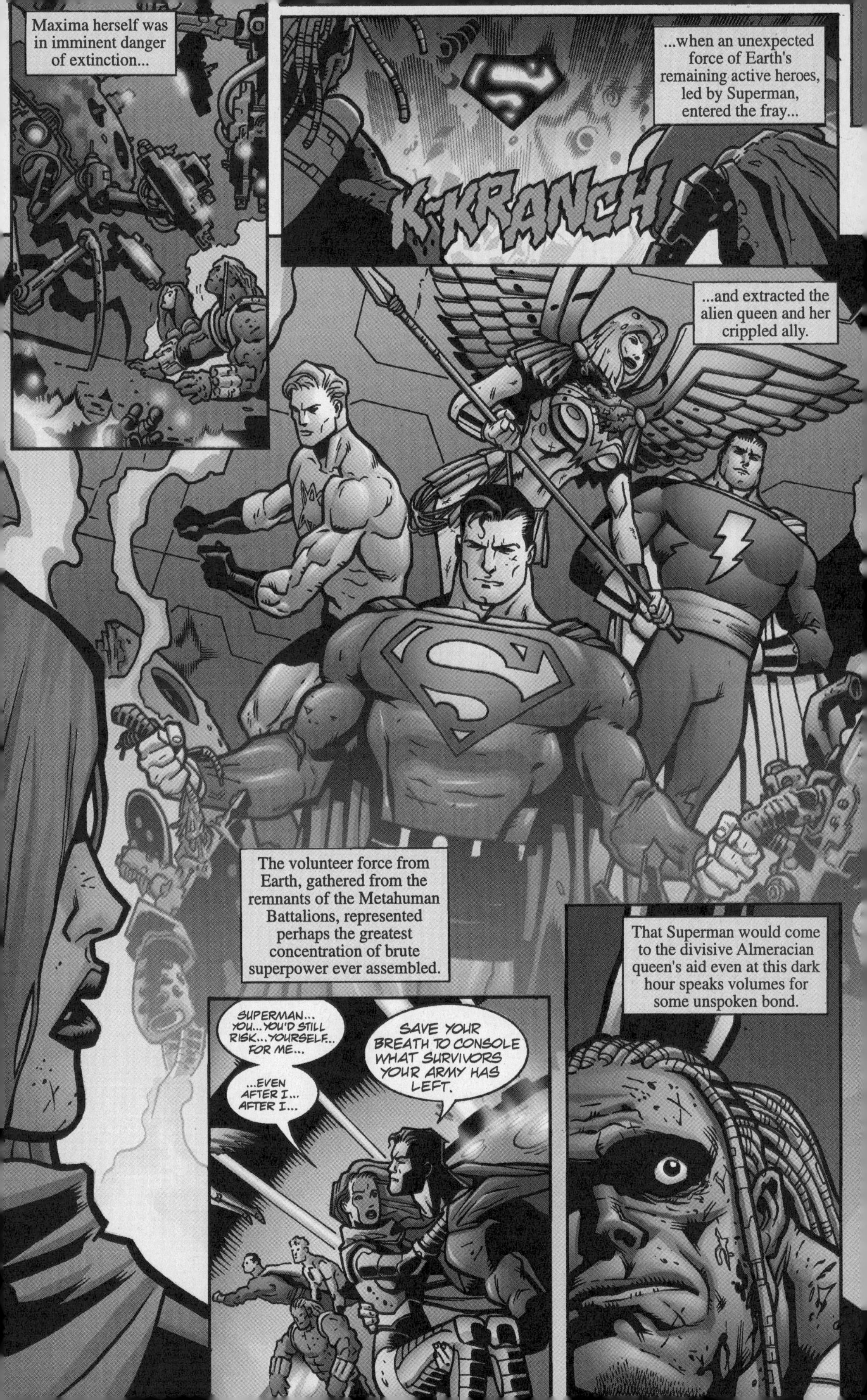
Maxima herself was in imminent danger of extinction...
...when an unexpected force of Earth's remaining active heroes, led by Superman, entered the fray...
K-KRANCH
...and extracted the alien queen and her crippled ally.
The volunteer force from Earth, gathered from the remnants of the Metahuman Battalions, represented perhaps the greatest concentration of brute superpower ever assembled.
That Superman would come to the divisive Almeracian queen's aid even at this dark hour speaks volumes for some unspoken bond.
SUPERMAN... YOU... YOU'D STILL RISK... YOURSELF... FOR ME...
...EVEN AFTER I... AFTER I...
SAVE YOUR BREATH TO CONSOLE WHAT SURVIVORS YOUR ARMY HAS LEFT.

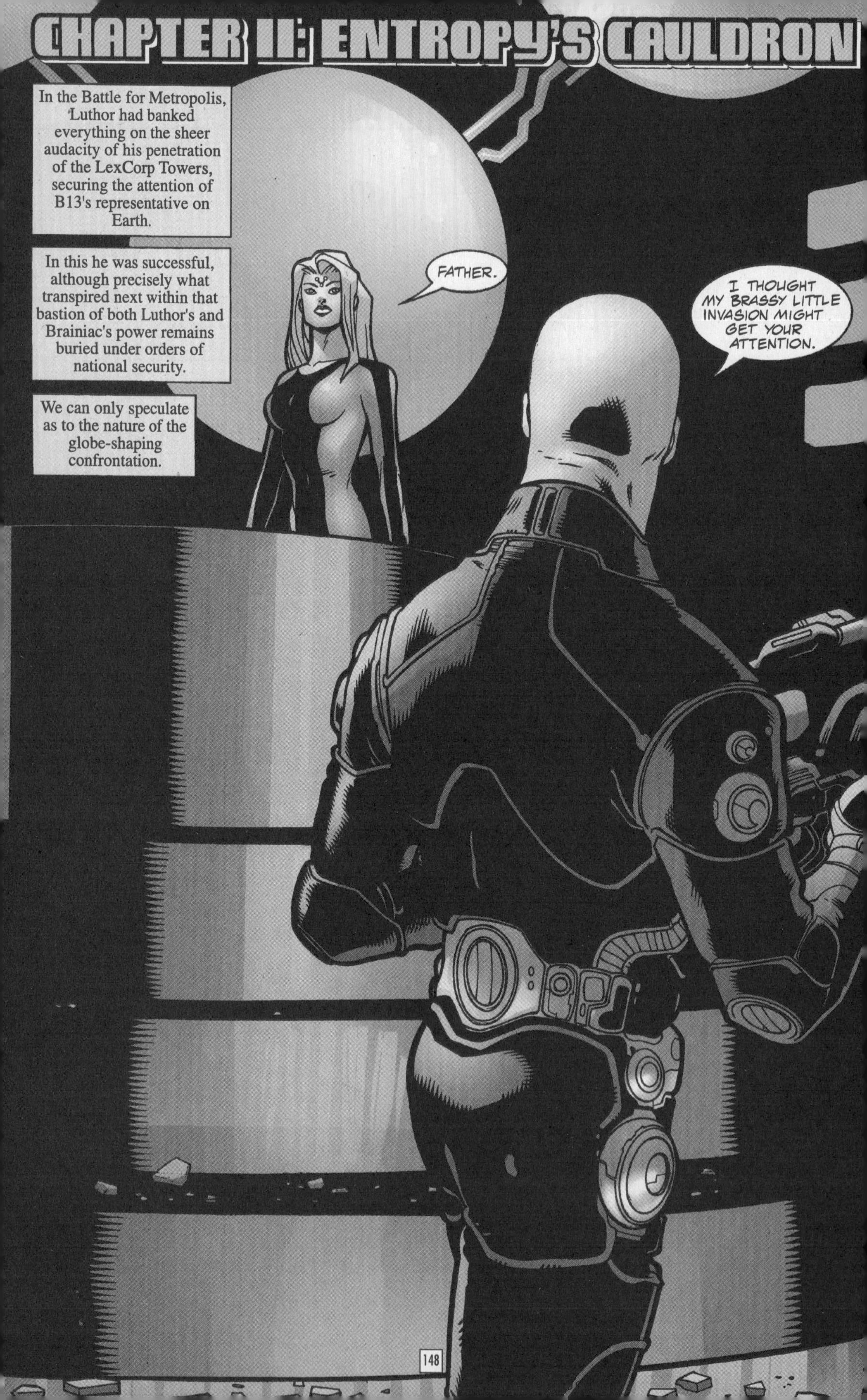
CHAPTER II: ENTROPY'S CAULDRON
In the Battle for Metropolis, Luthor had banked everything on the sheer audacity of his penetration of the LexCorp Towers, securing the attention of B13's representative on Earth.
In this he was successful, although precisely what transpired next within that bastion of both Luthor's and Brainiac's power remains buried under orders of national security.
We can only speculate as to the nature of the globe-shaping confrontation.
FATHER.
I THOUGHT MY BRASSY LITTLE INVASION MIGHT GET YOUR ATTENTION.

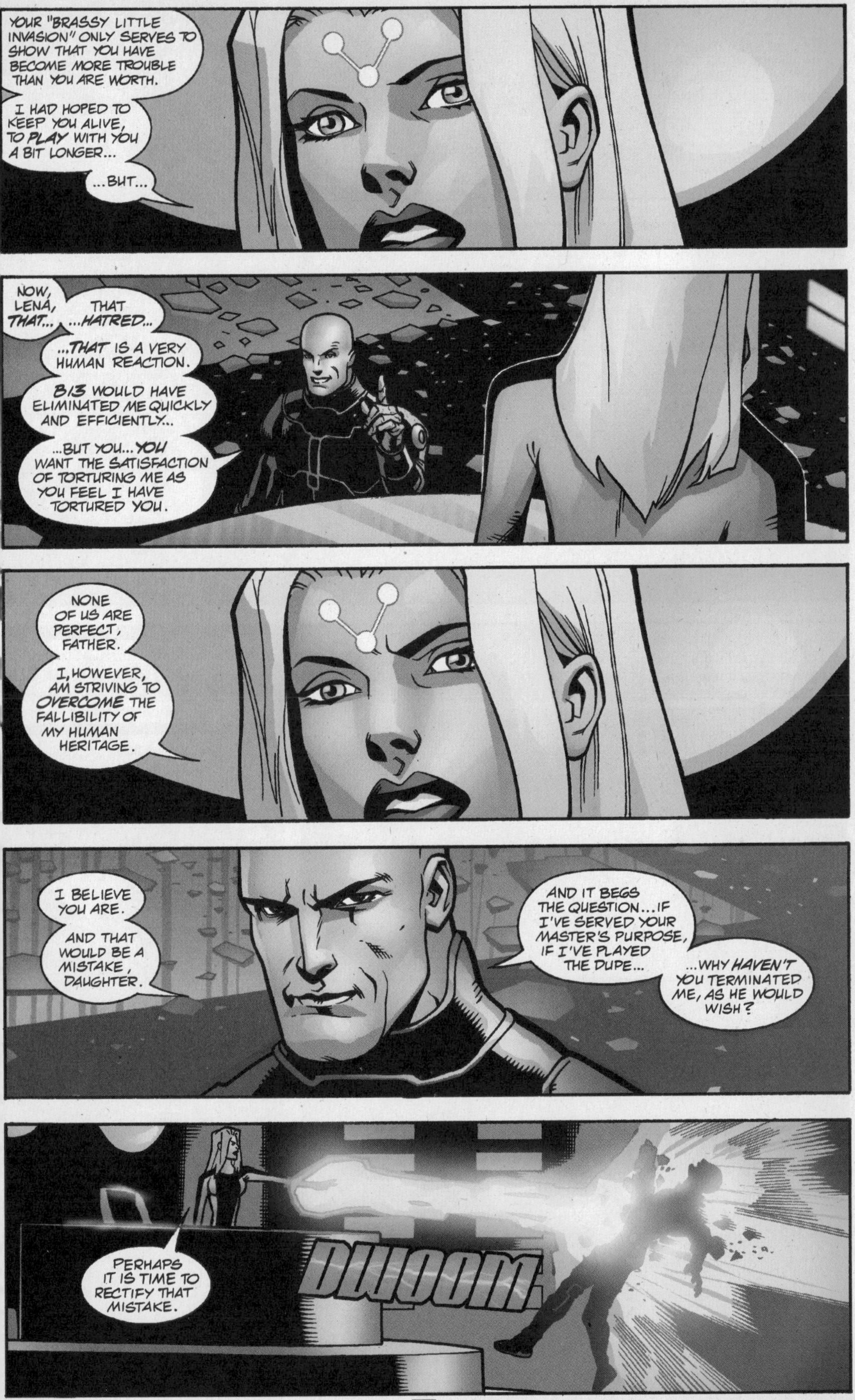
YOUR "BRASSY LITTLE INVASION" ONLY SERVES TO SHOW THAT YOU HAVE BECOME MORE TROUBLE THAN YOU ARE WORTH.
I HAD HOPED TO KEEP YOU ALIVE, TO PLAY WITH YOU A BIT LONGER...
...BUT...
NOW, LENA, THAT...
THAT ...HATRED...
...THAT IS A VERY HUMAN REACTION.
B13 WOULD HAVE ELIMINATED ME QUICKLY AND EFFICIENTLY...
...BUT YOU... YOU WANT THE SATISFACTION OF TORTURING ME AS YOU FEEL I HAVE TORTURED YOU.
NONE OF US ARE PERFECT, FATHER.
I, HOWEVER, AM STRIVING TO OVERCOME THE FALLIBILITY OF MY HUMAN HERITAGE.
I BELIEVE YOU ARE.
AND THAT WOULD BE A MISTAKE, DAUGHTER.
AND IT BEGS THE QUESTION... IF I'VE SERVED YOUR MASTER'S PURPOSE, IF I'VE PLAYED THE DUPE...
...WHY HAVEN'T YOU TERMINATED ME, AS HE WOULD WISH?
PERHAPS IT IS TIME TO RECTIFY THAT MISTAKE.
DUOOM.

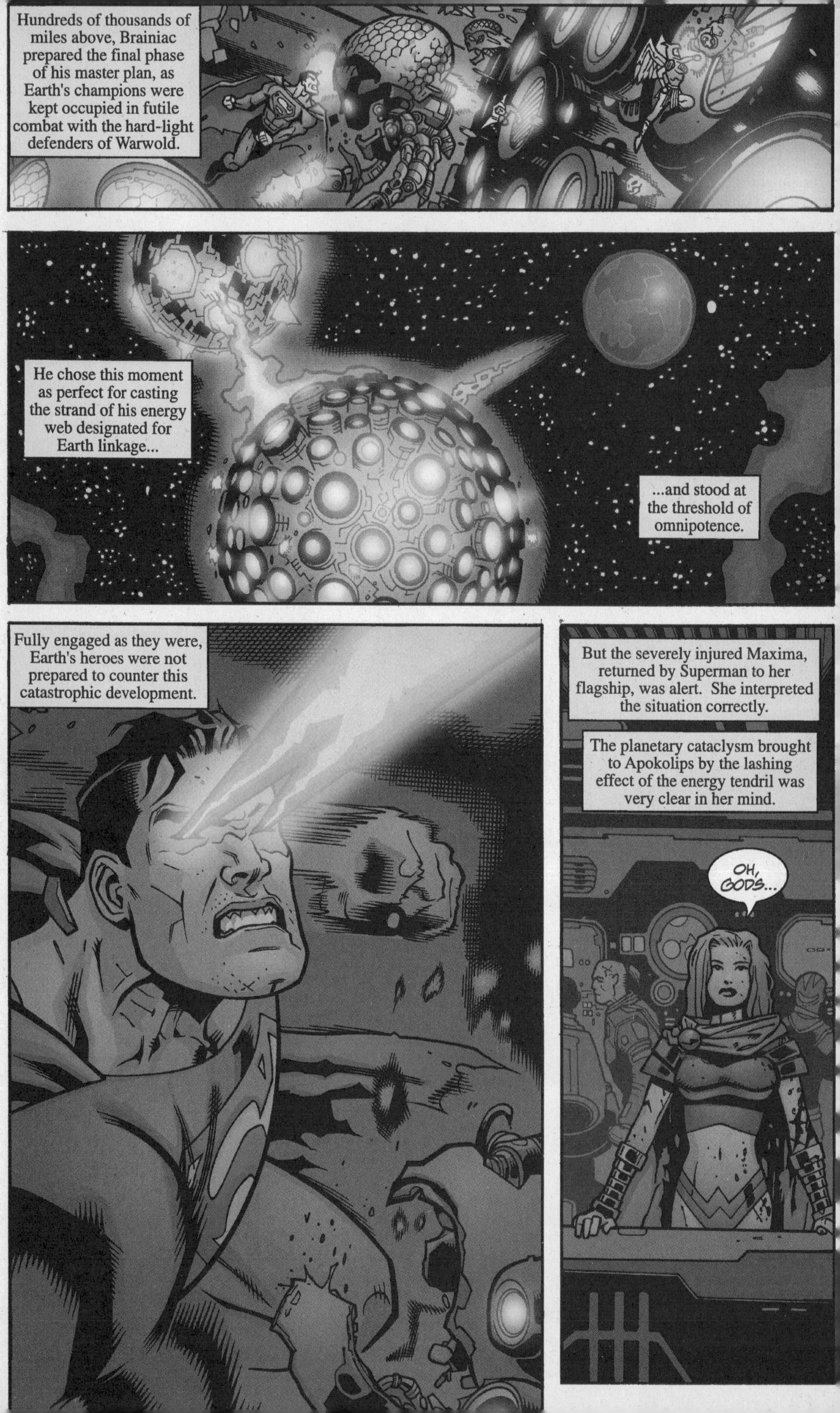
Hundreds of thousands of miles above, Brainiac prepared the final phase of his master plan, as Earth's champions were kept occupied in futile combat with the hard-light defenders of Warwold.
He chose this moment as perfect for casting the strand of his energy web designated for Earth linkage...
...and stood at the threshold of omnipotence.
Fully engaged as they were, Earth's heroes were not prepared to counter this catastrophic development.
But the severely injured Maxima, returned by Superman to her flagship, was alert. She interpreted the situation correctly.
The planetary cataclysm brought to Apokolips by the lashing effect of the energy tendril was very clear in her mind.
OH, GODS...

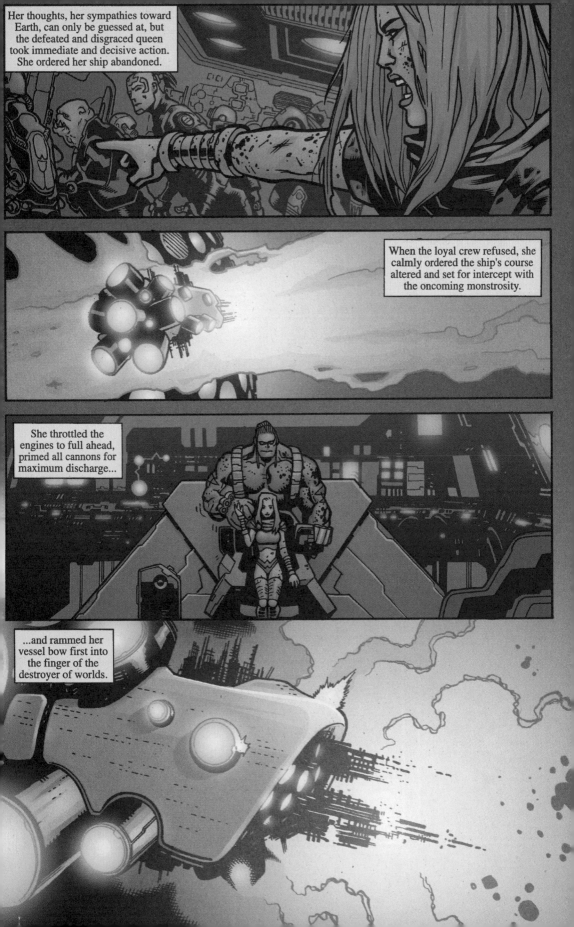

Her thoughts, her sympathies toward Earth, can only be guessed at, but the defeated and disgraced queen took immediate and decisive action. She ordered her ship abandoned.

When the loyal crew refused, she calmly ordered the ship's course altered and set for intercept with the oncoming monstrosity.

She throttled the engines to full ahead, primed all cannons for maximum discharge...

...and rammed her vessel bow first into the finger of the destroyer of worlds.

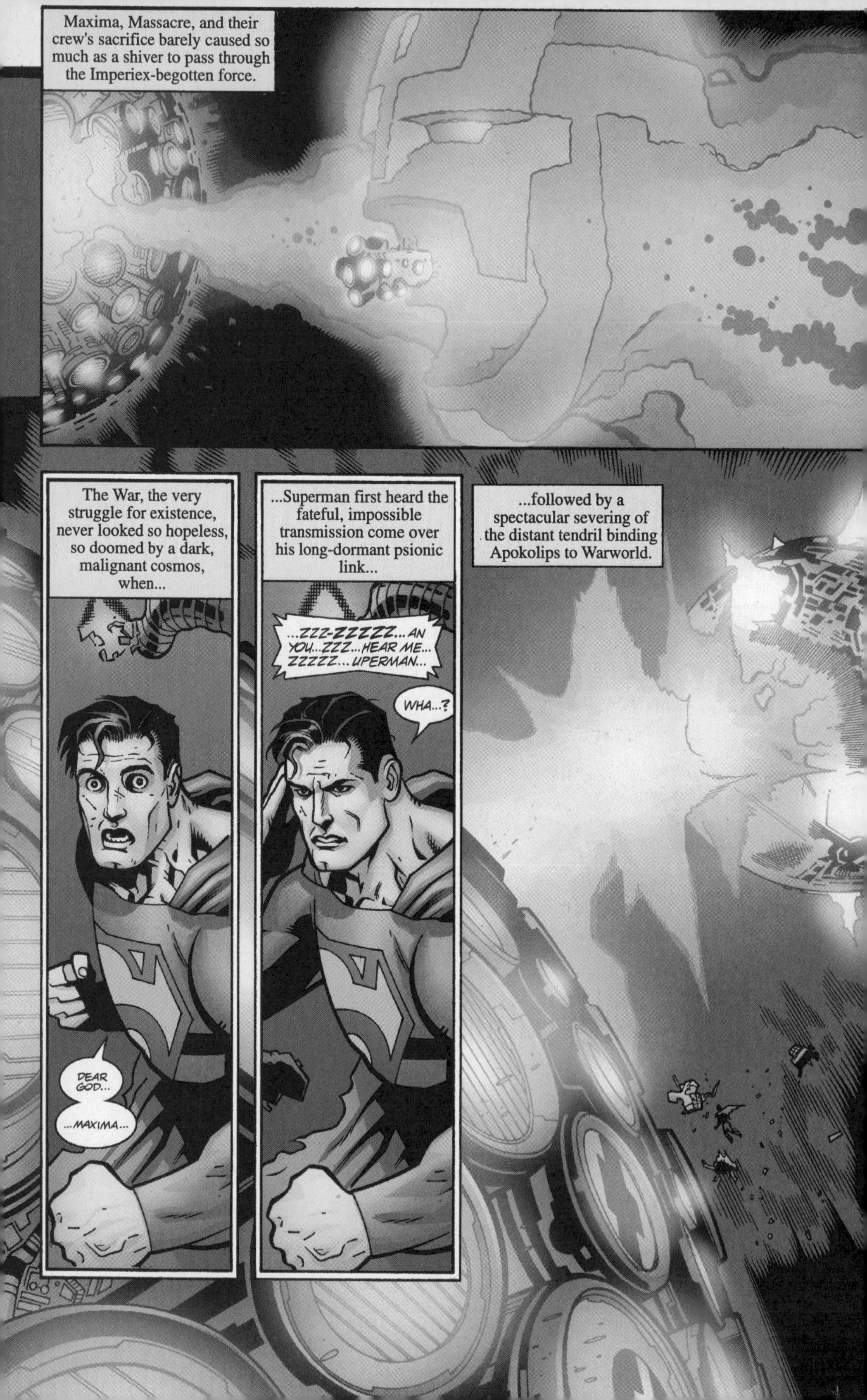

Maxima, Massacre, and their crew's sacrifice barely caused so much as a shiver to pass through the Imperiex-begotten force.
The War, the very struggle for existence, never looked so hopeless, so doomed by a dark, malignant cosmos, when...
DEAR GOD...
...MAXIMA...
...Superman first heard the fateful, impossible transmission come over his long-dormant psionic link...
...ZZZ-ZZZZZ... AN YOU...ZZZ...HEAR ME... ZZZZZ... UPERMAN...
WHA...?
...followed by a spectacular severing of the distant tendril binding Apokolips to Warworld.

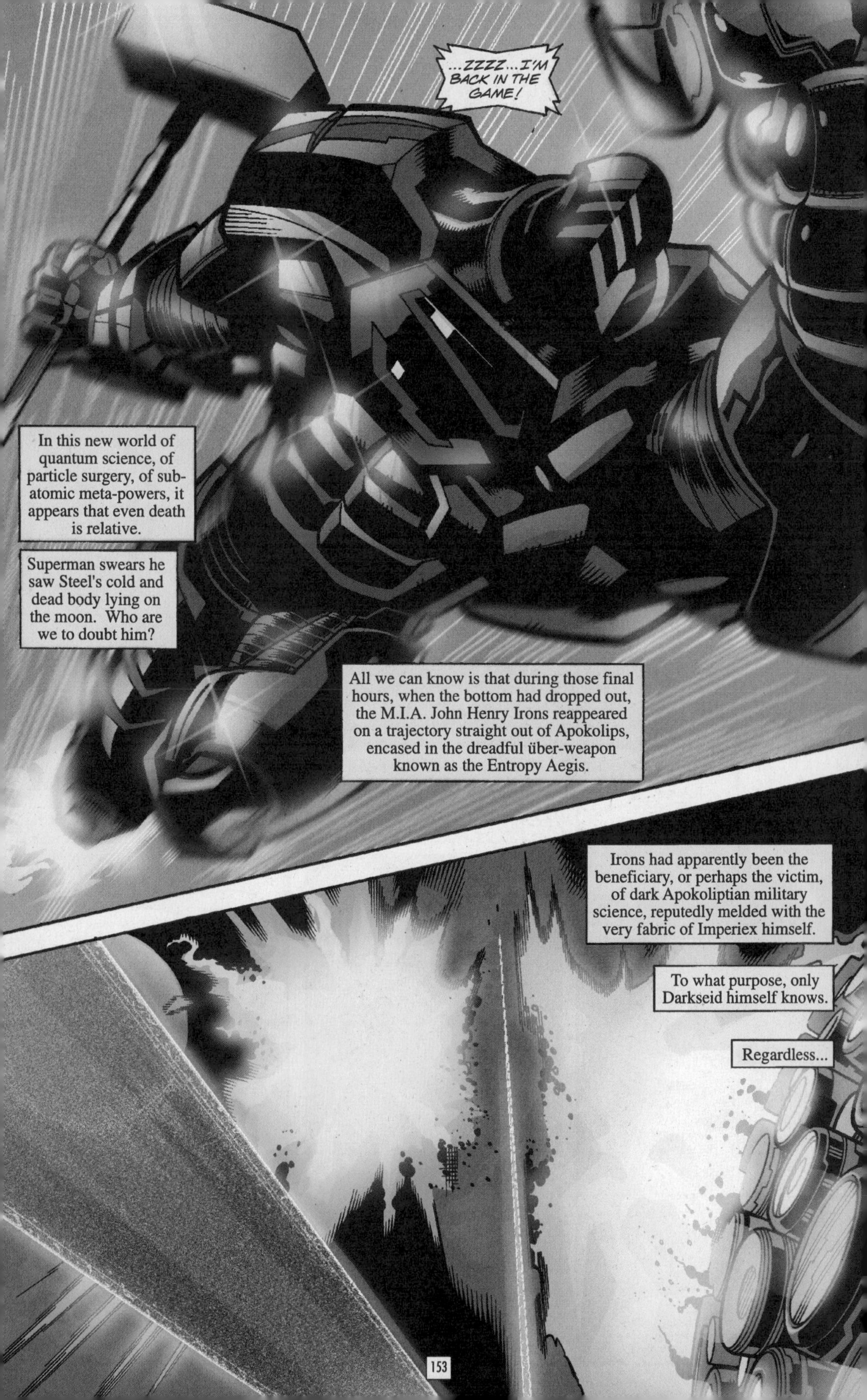
...ZZZZ...I'M BACK IN THE GAME!
In this new world of quantum science, of particle surgery, of sub-atomic meta-powers, it appears that even death is relative.
Superman swears he saw Steel's cold and dead body lying on the moon. Who are we to doubt him?
All we can know is that during those final hours, when the bottom had dropped out, the M.I.A. John Henry Irons reappeared on a trajectory straight out of Apokolips, encased in the dreadful über-weapon known as the Entropy Aegis.
Irons had apparently been the beneficiary, or perhaps the victim, of dark Apokoliptian military science, reputedly melded with the very fabric of Imperiex himself.
To what purpose, only Darkseid himself knows.
Regardless...

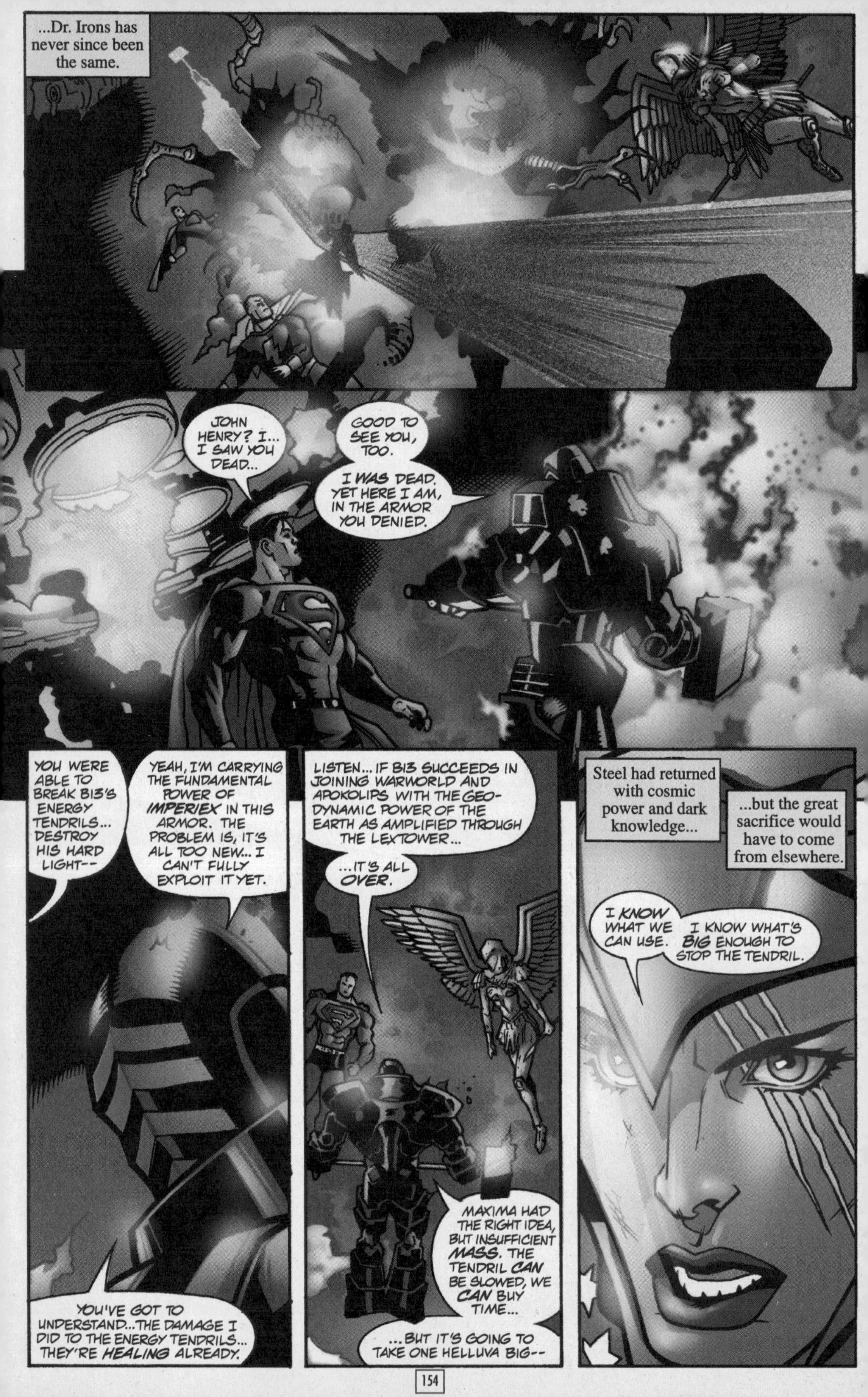

...Dr. Irons has never since been the same.
JOHN HENRY? I... I SAW YOU DEAD...
GOOD TO SEE YOU, TOO.
I WAS DEAD. YET HERE I AM, IN THE ARMOR YOU DENIED.
YOU WERE ABLE TO BREAK B13'S ENERGY TENDRILS... DESTROY HIS HARD LIGHT--
YEAH, I'M CARRYING THE FUNDAMENTAL POWER OF IMPERIEX IN THIS ARMOR. THE PROBLEM IS, IT'S ALL TOO NEW... I CAN'T FULLY EXPLOIT IT YET.
YOU'VE GOT TO UNDERSTAND...THE DAMAGE I DID TO THE ENERGY TENDRILS... THEY'RE HEALING ALREADY.
LISTEN... IF B13 SUCCEEDS IN JOINING WARWORLD AND APOKOLIPS WITH THE GEO-DYNAMIC POWER OF THE EARTH AS AMPLIFIED THROUGH THE LEXTOWER...
...IT'S ALL OVER.
MAXIMA HAD THE RIGHT IDEA, BUT INSUFFICIENT MASS. THE TENDRIL CAN BE SLOWED, WE CAN BUY TIME...
...BUT IT'S GOING TO TAKE ONE HELLUVA BIG--
Steel had returned with cosmic power and dark knowledge...
...but the great sacrifice would have to come from elsewhere.
I KNOW WHAT WE CAN USE.
I KNOW WHAT'S BIG ENOUGH TO STOP THE TENDRIL.

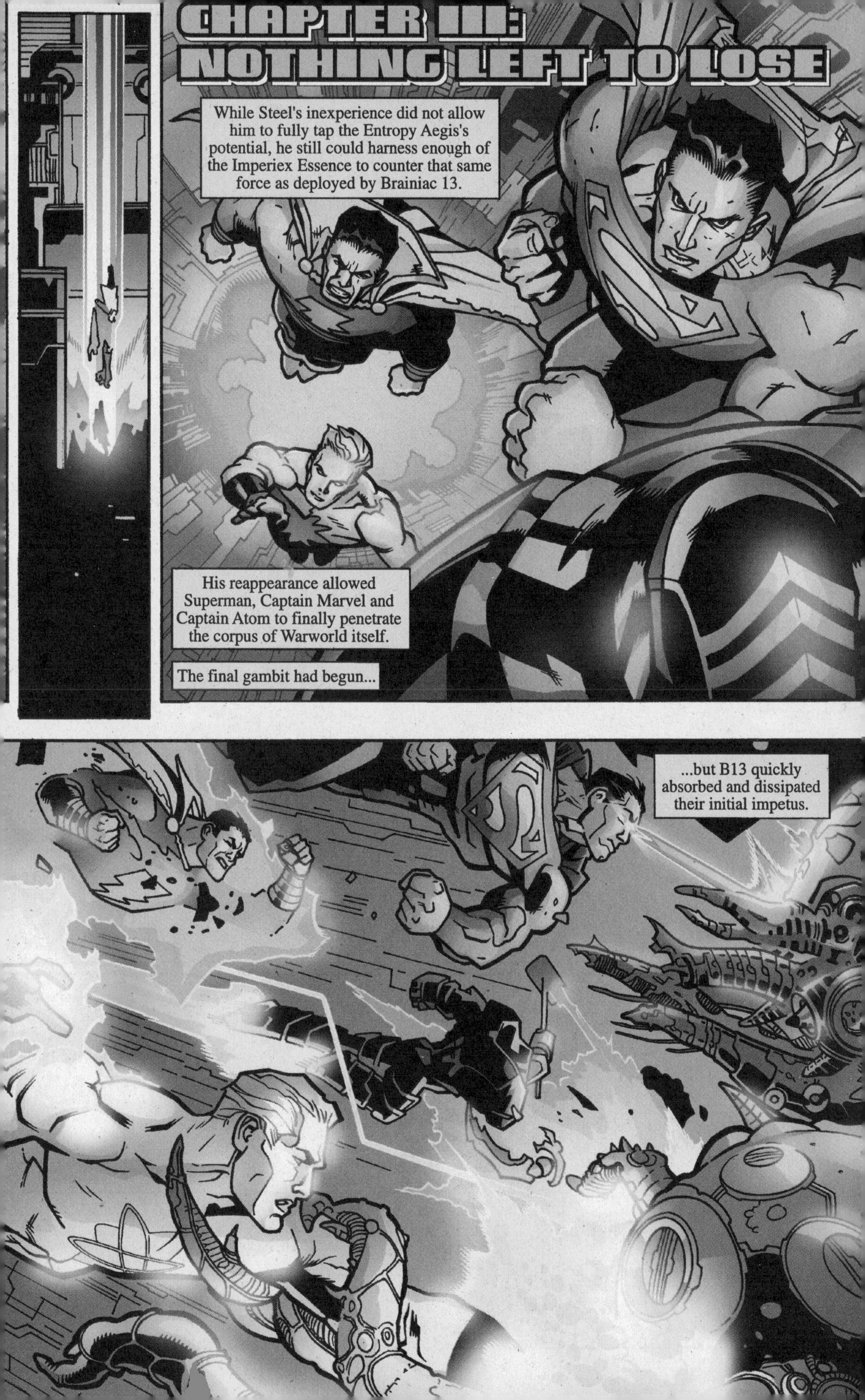
CHAPTER III: NOTHING LEFT TO LOSE
While Steel's inexperience did not allow him to fully tap the Entropy Aegis's potential, he still could harness enough of the Imperiex Essence to counter that same force as deployed by Brainiac 13.
His reappearance allowed Superman, Captain Marvel and Captain Atom to finally penetrate the corpus of Warworld itself.
The final gambit had begun...
...but B13 quickly absorbed and dissipated their initial impetus.

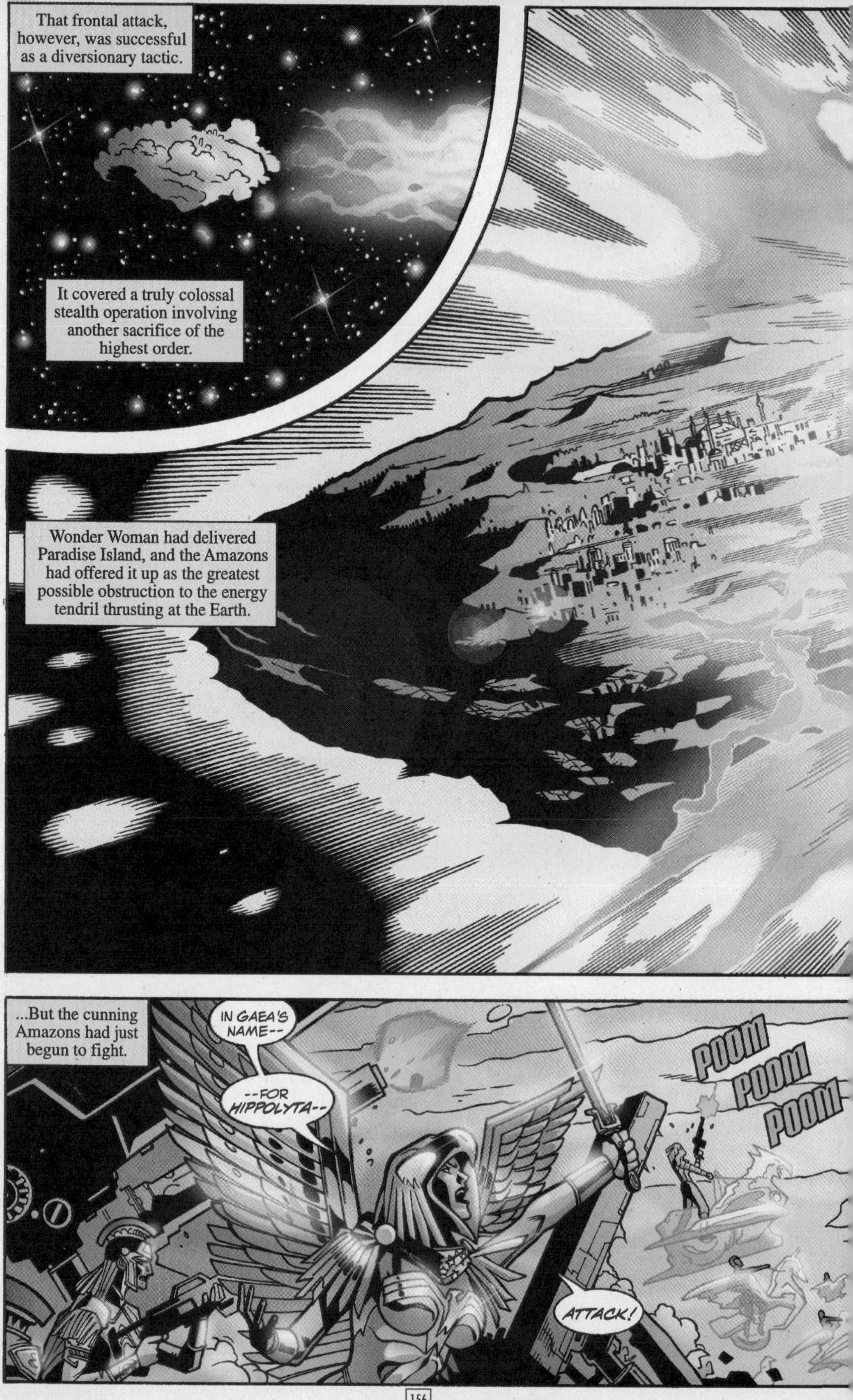
That frontal attack, however, was successful as a diversionary tactic.
It covered a truly colossal stealth operation involving another sacrifice of the highest order.
Wonder Woman had delivered Paradise Island, and the Amazons had offered it up as the greatest possible obstruction to the energy tendril thrusting at the Earth.
...But the cunning Amazons had just begun to fight.
IN GAEA'S NAME--
--FOR HIPPOLYTA--
POOM
POOM
POOM
ATTACK!

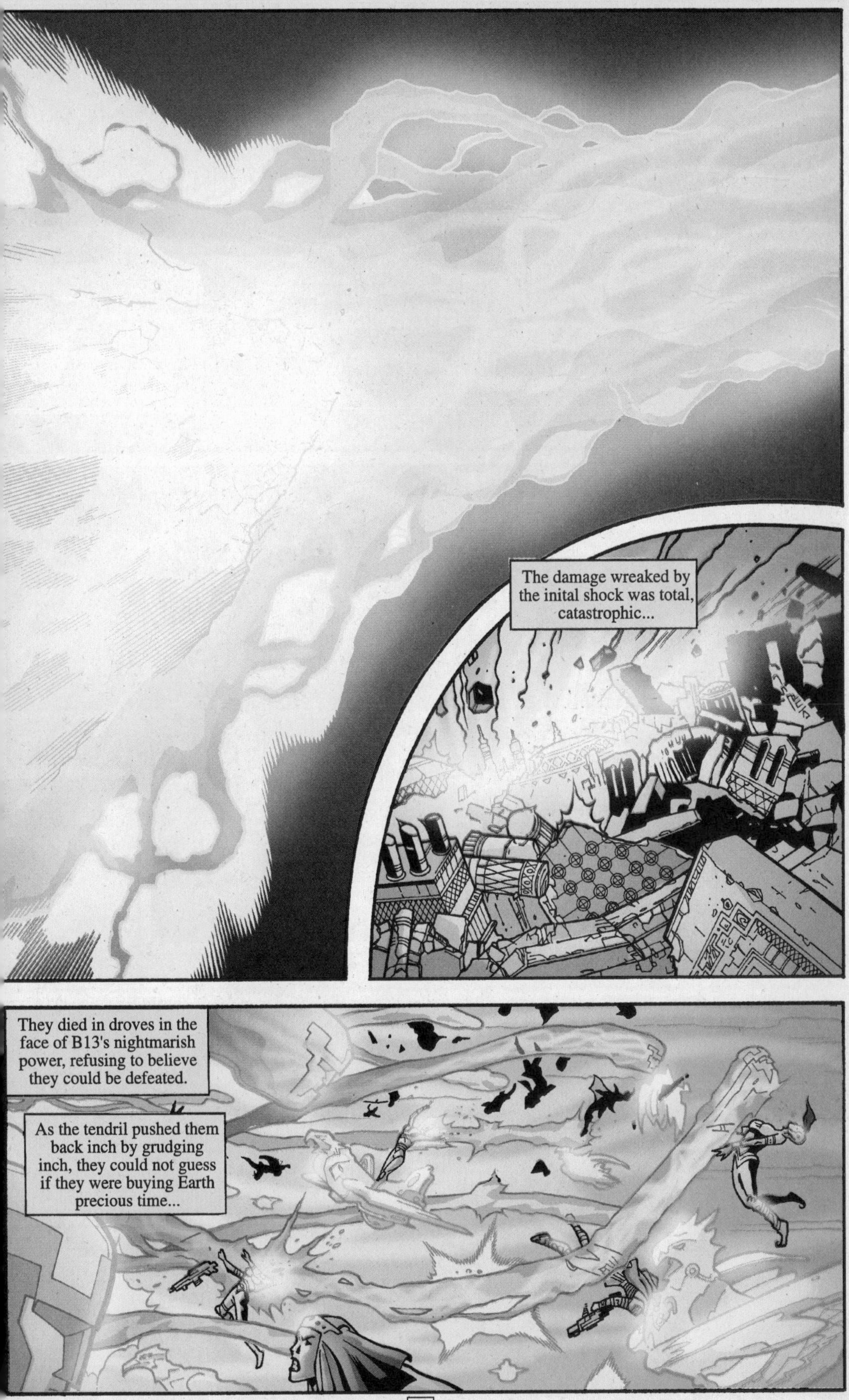
The damage wreaked by the inital shock was total, catastrophic...
They died in droves in the face of B13's nightmarish power, refusing to believe they could be defeated.
As the tendril pushed them back inch by grudging inch, they could not guess if they were buying Earth precious time...

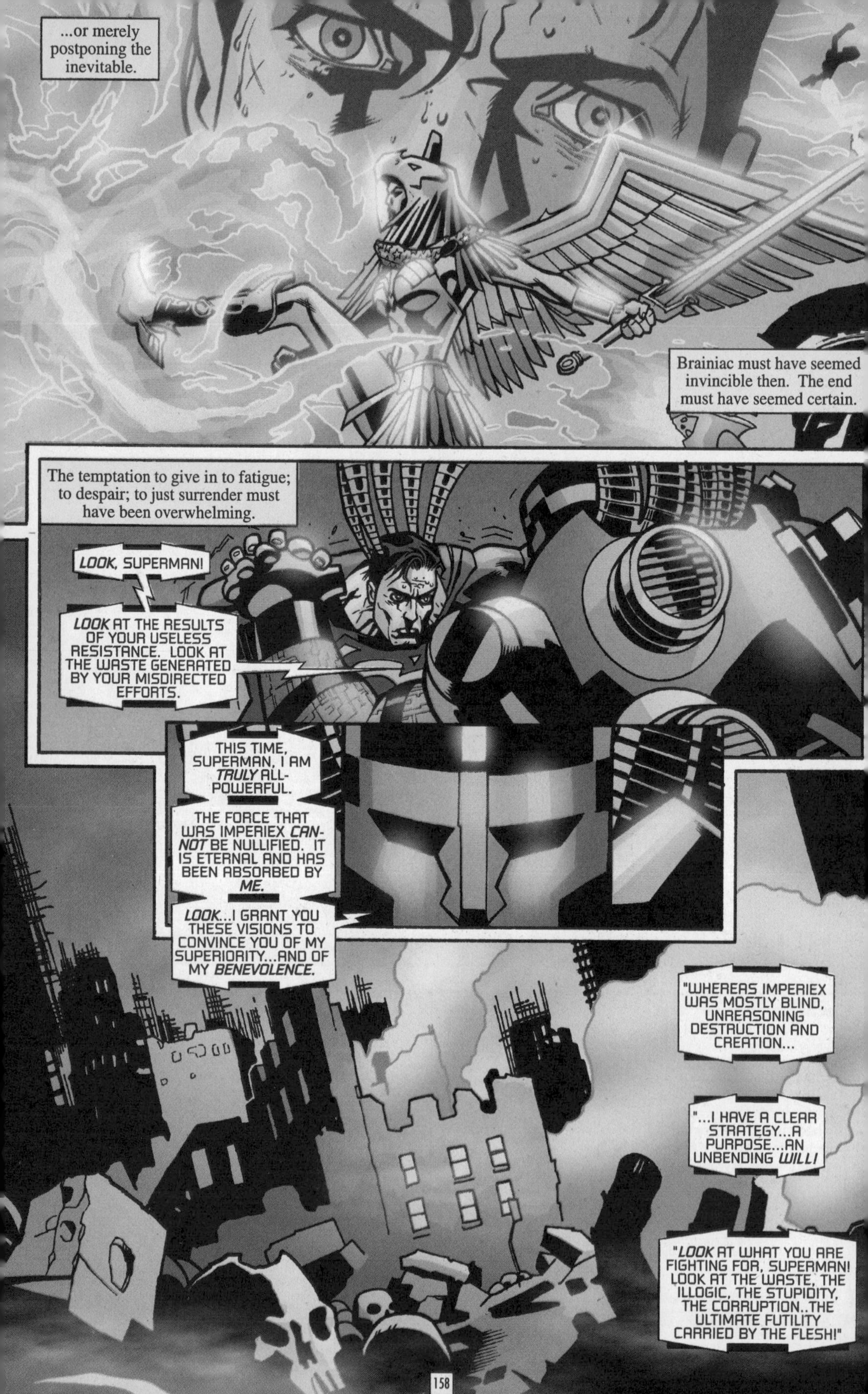
...or merely postponing the inevitable.
Brainiac must have seemed invincible then. The end must have seemed certain.
The temptation to give in to fatigue; to despair; to just surrender must have been overwhelming.
LOOK, SUPERMAN!
LOOK AT THE RESULTS OF YOUR USELESS RESISTANCE. LOOK AT THE WASTE GENERATED BY YOUR MISDIRECTED EFFORTS.
THIS TIME, SUPERMAN, I AM TRULY ALL-POWERFUL.
THE FORCE THAT WAS IMPERIEX CANNOT BE NULLIFIED. IT IS ETERNAL AND HAS BEEN ABSORBED BY ME.
LOOK...I GRANT YOU THESE VISIONS TO CONVINCE YOU OF MY SUPERIORITY...AND OF MY BENEVOLENCE.
"WHEREAS IMPERIEX WAS MOSTLY BLIND, UNREASONING DESTRUCTION AND CREATION...
"...I HAVE A CLEAR STRATEGY...A PURPOSE...AN UNBENDING WILL!
"LOOK AT WHAT YOU ARE FIGHTING FOR, SUPERMAN! LOOK AT THE WASTE, THE ILLOGIC, THE STUPIDITY, THE CORRUPTION..THE ULTIMATE FUTILITY CARRIED BY THE FLESH!"

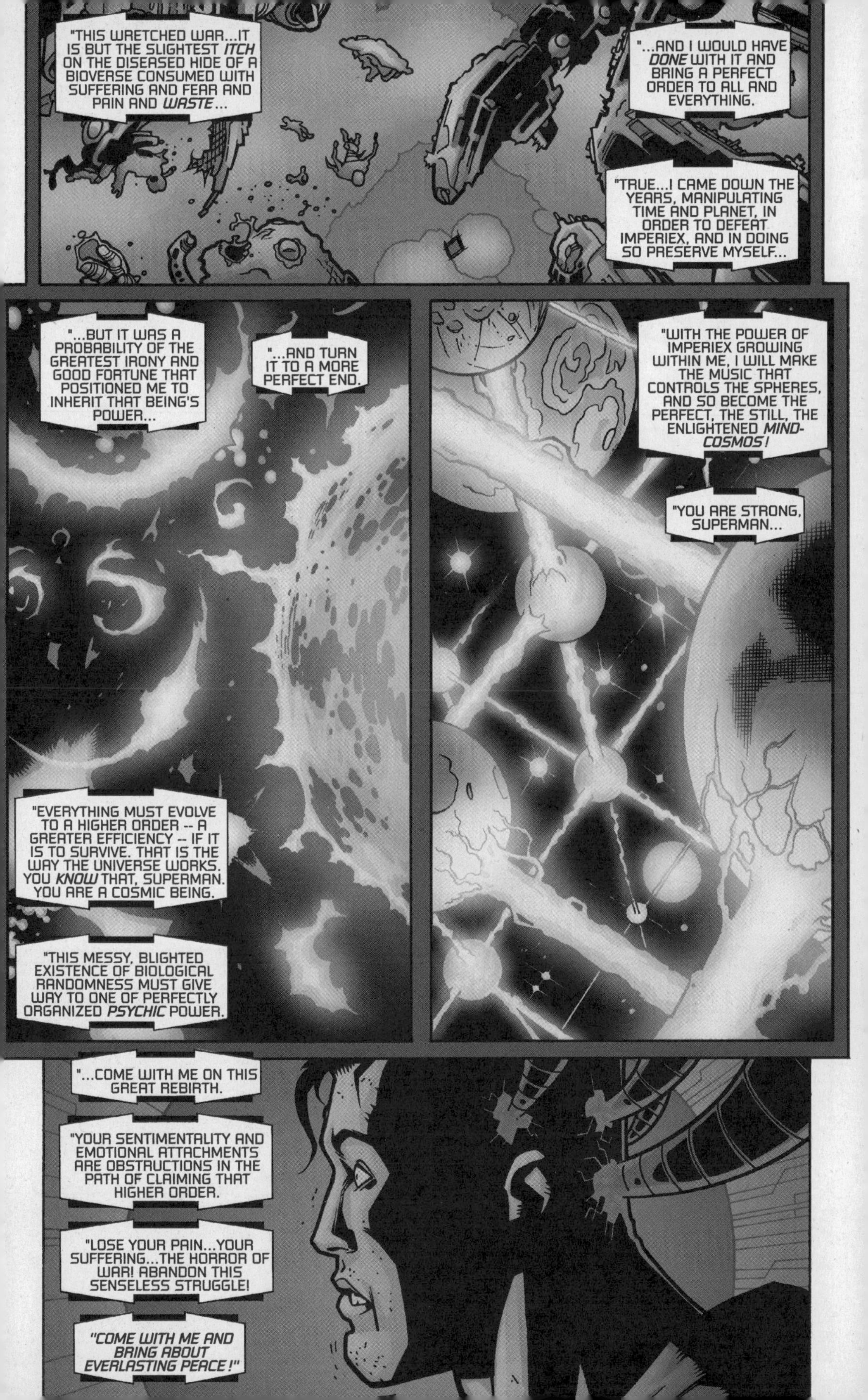
"THIS WRETCHED WAR...IT IS BUT THE SLIGHTEST ITCH ON THE DISEASED HIDE OF A BIOVERSE CONSUMED WITH SUFFERING AND FEAR AND PAIN AND WASTE...
"...AND I WOULD HAVE DONE WITH IT AND BRING A PERFECT ORDER TO ALL AND EVERYTHING.
"TRUE...I CAME DOWN THE YEARS, MANIPULATING TIME AND PLANET, IN ORDER TO DEFEAT IMPERIEX, AND IN DOING SO PRESERVE MYSELF...
"...BUT IT WAS A PROBABILITY OF THE GREATEST IRONY AND GOOD FORTUNE THAT POSITIONED ME TO INHERIT THAT BEING'S POWER...
"...AND TURN IT TO A MORE PERFECT END.
"EVERYTHING MUST EVOLVE TO A HIGHER ORDER -- A GREATER EFFICIENCY -- IF IT IS TO SURVIVE. THAT IS THE WAY THE UNIVERSE WORKS. YOU KNOW THAT, SUPERMAN. YOU ARE A COSMIC BEING.
"THIS MESSY, BLIGHTED EXISTENCE OF BIOLOGICAL RANDOMNESS MUST GIVE WAY TO ONE OF PERFECTLY ORGANIZED PSYCHIC POWER.
"WITH THE POWER OF IMPERIEX GROWING WITHIN ME, I WILL MAKE THE MUSIC THAT CONTROLS THE SPHERES, AND SO BECOME THE PERFECT, THE STILL, THE ENLIGHTENED MIND-COSMOS!
"YOU ARE STRONG, SUPERMAN...
"...COME WITH ME ON THIS GREAT REBIRTH.
"YOUR SENTIMENTALITY AND EMOTIONAL ATTACHMENTS ARE OBSTRUCTIONS IN THE PATH OF CLAIMING THAT HIGHER ORDER.
"LOSE YOUR PAIN...YOUR SUFFERING...THE HORROR OF WAR! ABANDON THIS SENSELESS STRUGGLE!
"COME WITH ME AND BRING ABOUT EVERLASTING PEACE!"

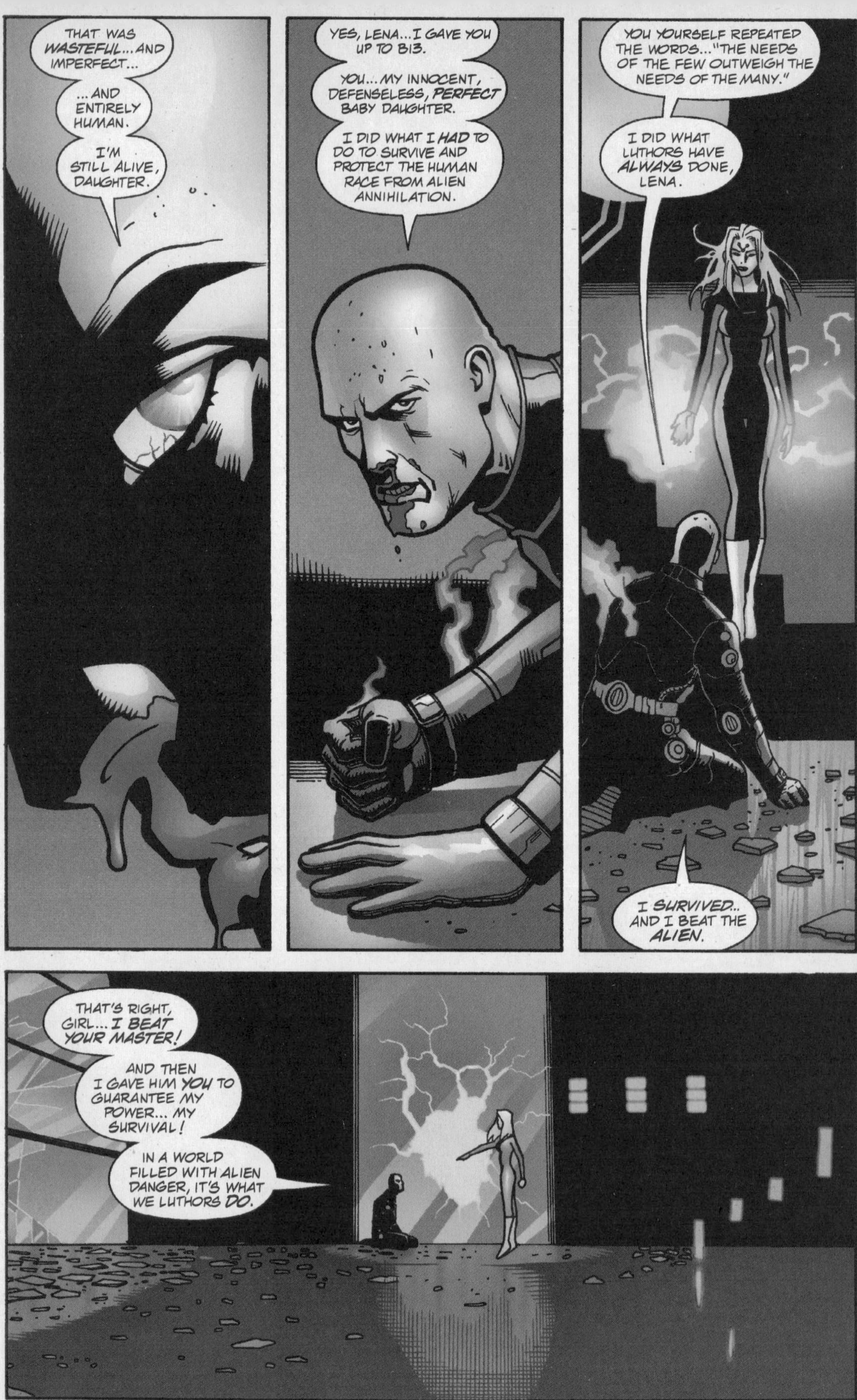
THAT WAS WASTEFUL... AND IMPERFECT...
...AND ENTIRELY HUMAN.
I'M STILL ALIVE, DAUGHTER.
YES, LENA... I GAVE YOU UP TO B13.
YOU... MY INNOCENT, DEFENSELESS, PERFECT BABY DAUGHTER.
I DID WHAT I HAD TO DO TO SURVIVE AND PROTECT THE HUMAN RACE FROM ALIEN ANNIHILATION.
YOU YOURSELF REPEATED THE WORDS... "THE NEEDS OF THE FEW OUTWEIGH THE NEEDS OF THE MANY."
I DID WHAT LUTHORS HAVE ALWAYS DONE, LENA.
I SURVIVED... AND I BEAT THE ALIEN.
THAT'S RIGHT, GIRL... I BEAT YOUR MASTER!
AND THEN I GAVE HIM YOU TO GUARANTEE MY POWER... MY SURVIVAL!
IN A WORLD FILLED WITH ALIEN DANGER, IT'S WHAT WE LUTHORS DO.

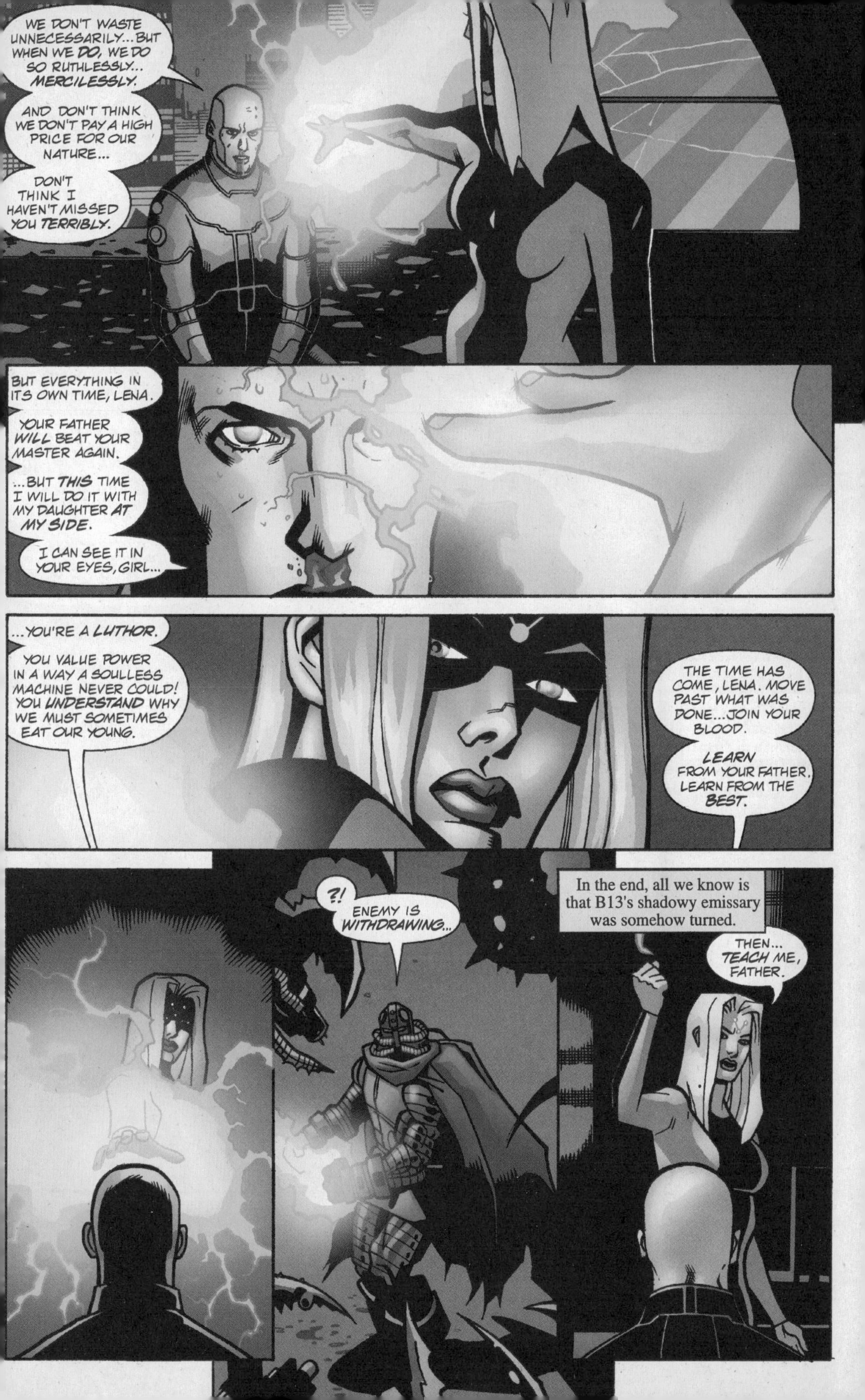
WE DON'T WASTE UNNECESSARILY... BUT WHEN WE DO, WE DO SO RUTHLESSLY... MERCILESSLY.
AND DON'T THINK WE DON'T PAY A HIGH PRICE FOR OUR NATURE...
DON'T THINK I HAVEN'T MISSED YOU TERRIBLY.
BUT EVERYTHING IN ITS OWN TIME, LENA.
YOUR FATHER WILL BEAT YOUR MASTER AGAIN.
...BUT THIS TIME I WILL DO IT WITH MY DAUGHTER AT MY SIDE.
I CAN SEE IT IN YOUR EYES, GIRL...
...YOU'RE A LUTHOR.
YOU VALUE POWER IN A WAY A SOULLESS MACHINE NEVER COULD! YOU UNDERSTAND WHY WE MUST SOMETIMES EAT OUR YOUNG.
THE TIME HAS COME, LENA. MOVE PAST WHAT WAS DONE...JOIN YOUR BLOOD.
LEARN FROM YOUR FATHER. LEARN FROM THE BEST.
?! ENEMY IS WITHDRAWING...
In the end, all we know is that B13's shadowy emissary was somehow turned.
THEN... TEACH ME, FATHER.

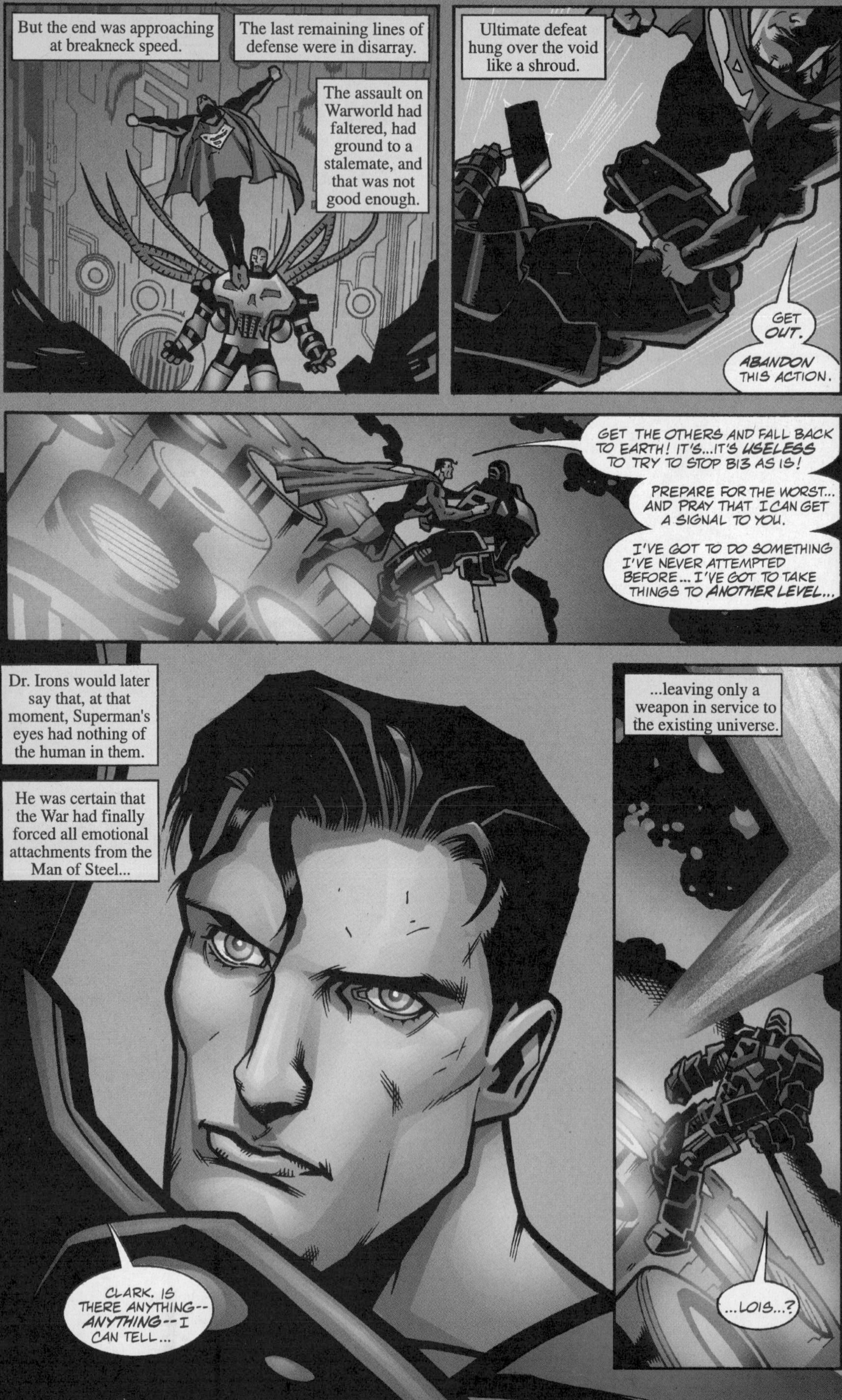
But the end was approaching at breakneck speed.
The last remaining lines of defense were in disarray.
The assault on Warworld had faltered, had ground to a stalemate, and that was not good enough.
Ultimate defeat hung over the void like a shroud.
GET OUT.
ABANDON THIS ACTION.
GET THE OTHERS AND FALL BACK TO EARTH! IT'S...IT'S USELESS TO TRY TO STOP B13 AS IS!
PREPARE FOR THE WORST... AND PRAY THAT I CAN GET A SIGNAL TO YOU.
I'VE GOT TO DO SOMETHING I'VE NEVER ATTEMPTED BEFORE... I'VE GOT TO TAKE THINGS TO ANOTHER LEVEL...
Dr. Irons would later say that, at that moment, Superman's eyes had nothing of the human in them.
He was certain that the War had finally forced all emotional attachments from the Man of Steel...
CLARK. IS THERE ANYTHING-- ANYTHING-- I CAN TELL...
...leaving only a weapon in service to the existing universe.
...LOIS...?

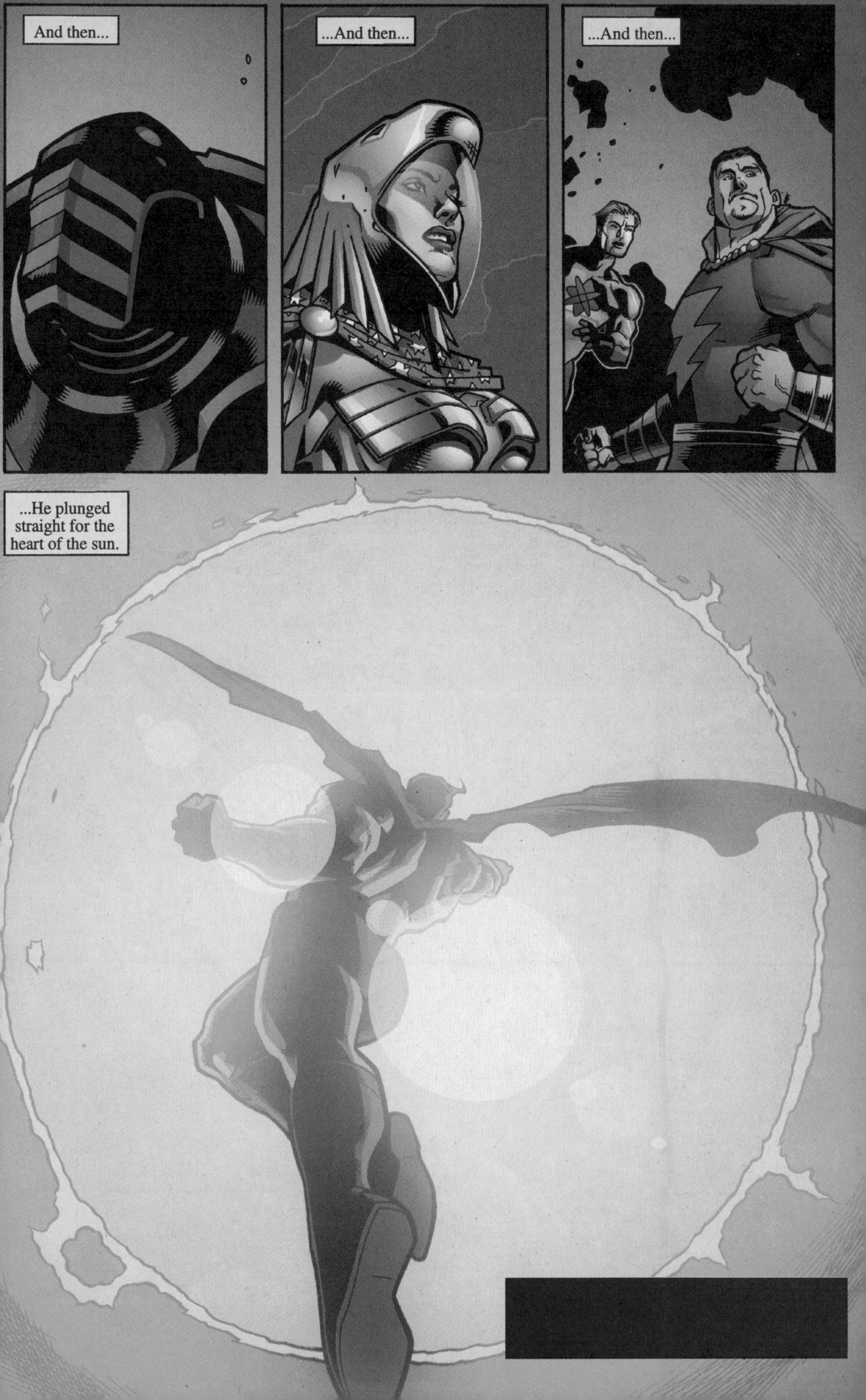
And then...
...And then...
...And then...
...He plunged straight for the heart of the sun.
[redacted]

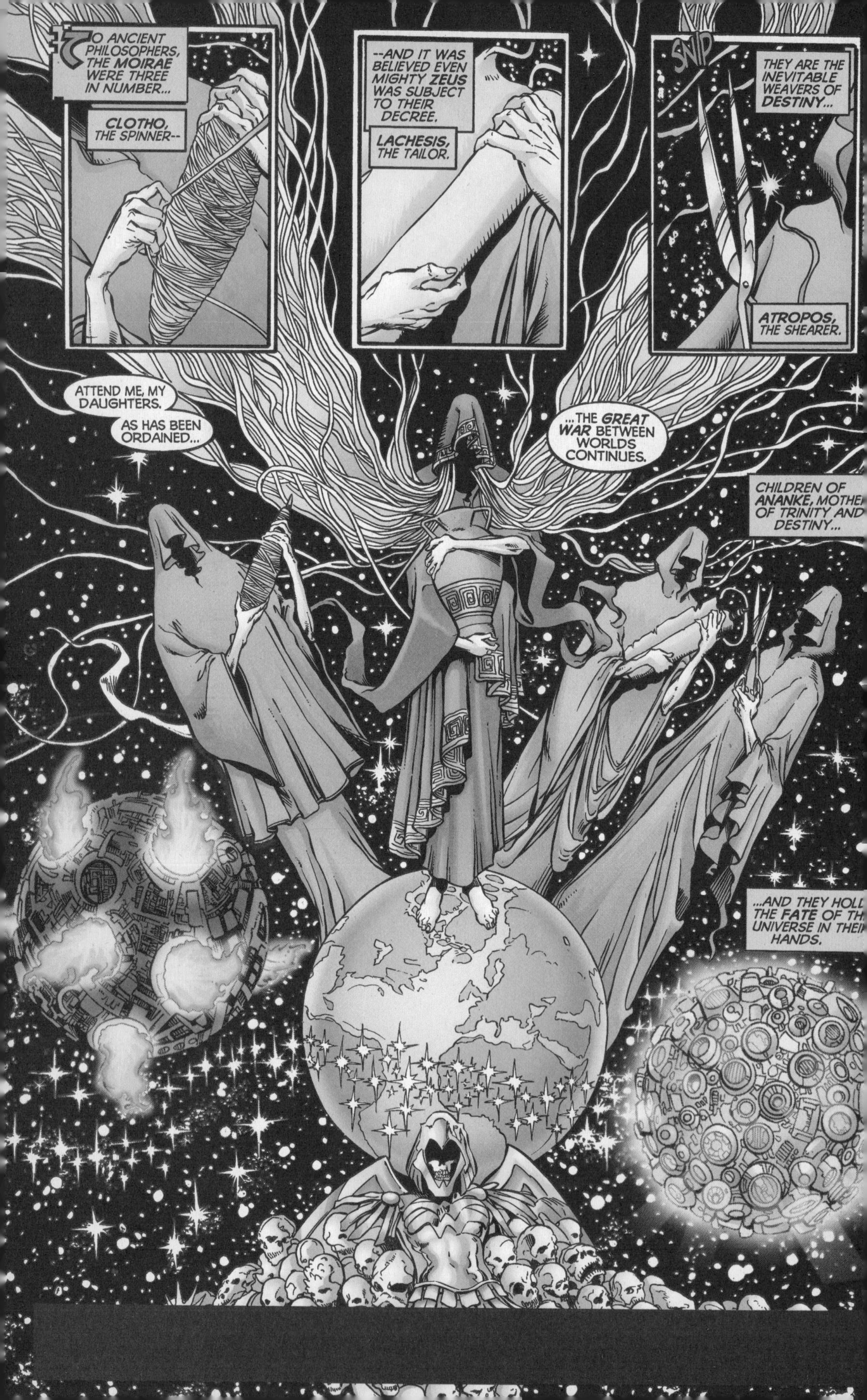
TO ANCIENT PHILOSOPHERS, THE MOIRAE WERE THREE IN NUMBER...
CLOTHO, THE SPINNER--
--AND IT WAS BELIEVED EVEN MIGHTY ZEUS WAS SUBJECT TO THEIR DECREE.
LACHESIS, THE TAILOR.
SNIP
THEY ARE THE INEVITABLE WEAVERS OF DESTINY...
ATROPOS, THE SHEARER.
ATTEND ME, MY DAUGHTERS.
AS HAS BEEN ORDAINED...
...THE GREAT WAR BETWEEN WORLDS CONTINUES.
CHILDREN OF ANANKE, MOTHE OF TRINITY AND DESTINY...
...AND THEY HOLL THE FATE OF TH UNIVERSE IN THEI HANDS.
[redacted]

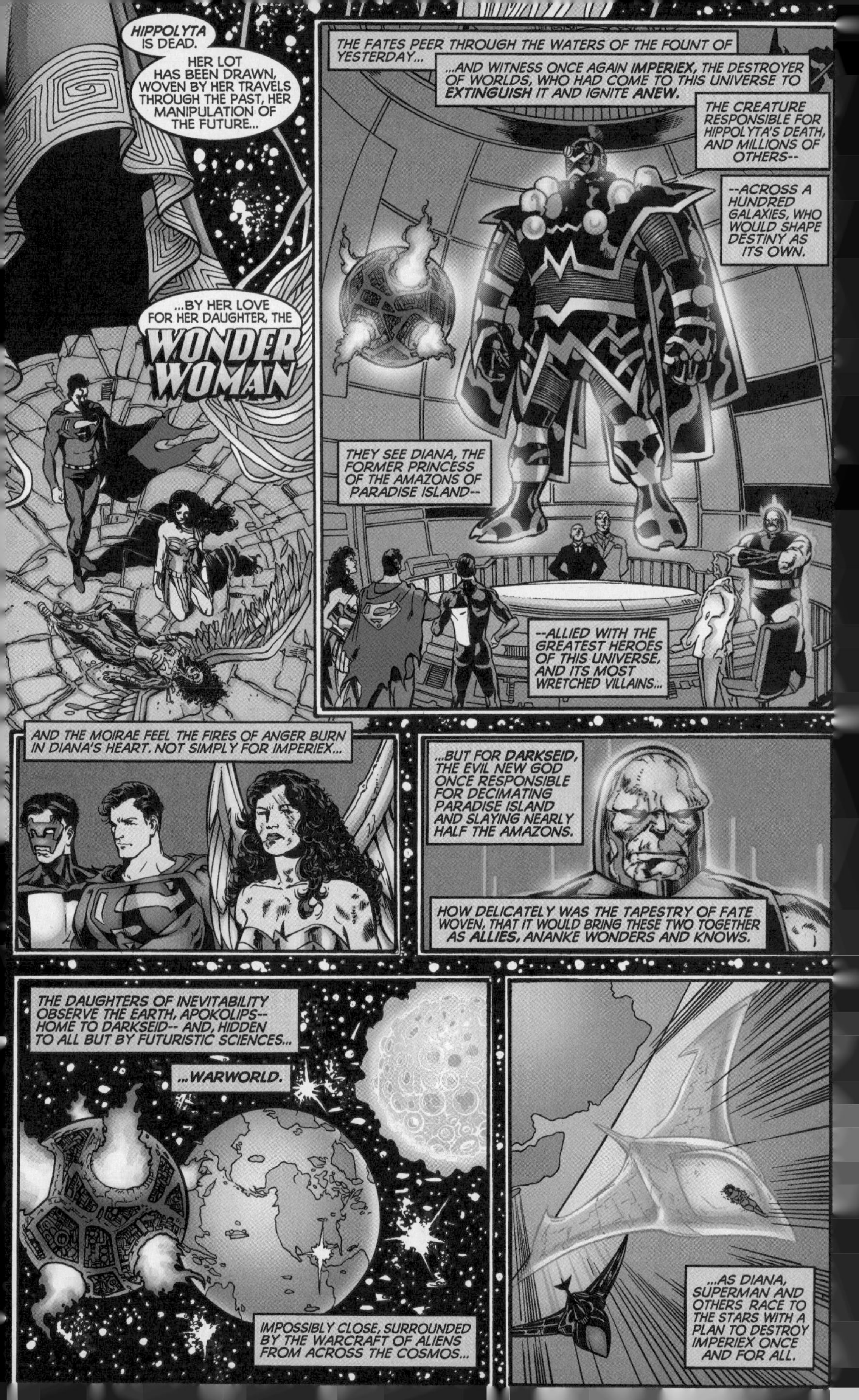
HIPPOLYTA IS DEAD.
HER LOT HAS BEEN DRAWN, WOVEN BY HER TRAVELS THROUGH THE PAST, HER MANIPULATION OF THE FUTURE...
...BY HER LOVE FOR HER DAUGHTER, THE
WONDER WOMAN
THE FATES PEER THROUGH THE WATERS OF THE FOUNT OF YESTERDAY...
...AND WITNESS ONCE AGAIN IMPERIEX, THE DESTROYER OF WORLDS, WHO HAD COME TO THIS UNIVERSE TO EXTINGUISH IT AND IGNITE ANEW.
THE CREATURE RESPONSIBLE FOR HIPPOLYTA'S DEATH, AND MILLIONS OF OTHERS--
--ACROSS A HUNDRED GALAXIES, WHO WOULD SHAPE DESTINY AS ITS OWN.
THEY SEE DIANA, THE FORMER PRINCESS OF THE AMAZONS OF PARADISE ISLAND--
--ALLIED WITH THE GREATEST HEROES OF THIS UNIVERSE, AND ITS MOST WRETCHED VILLAINS...
AND THE MOIRAE FEEL THE FIRES OF ANGER BURN IN DIANA'S HEART. NOT SIMPLY FOR IMPERIEX...
...BUT FOR DARKSEID, THE EVIL NEW GOD ONCE RESPONSIBLE FOR DECIMATING PARADISE ISLAND AND SLAYING NEARLY HALF THE AMAZONS.
HOW DELICATELY WAS THE TAPESTRY OF FATE WOVEN, THAT IT WOULD BRING THESE TWO TOGETHER AS ALLIES, ANANKE WONDERS AND KNOWS.
THE DAUGHTERS OF INEVITABILITY OBSERVE THE EARTH, APOKOLIPS-- HOME TO DARKSEID-- AND, HIDDEN TO ALL BUT BY FUTURISTIC SCIENCES...
...WARWORLD.
IMPOSSIBLY CLOSE, SURROUNDED BY THE WARCRAFT OF ALIENS FROM ACROSS THE COSMOS...
...AS DIANA, SUPERMAN AND OTHERS RACE TO THE STARS WITH A PLAN TO DESTROY IMPERIEX ONCE AND FOR ALL.

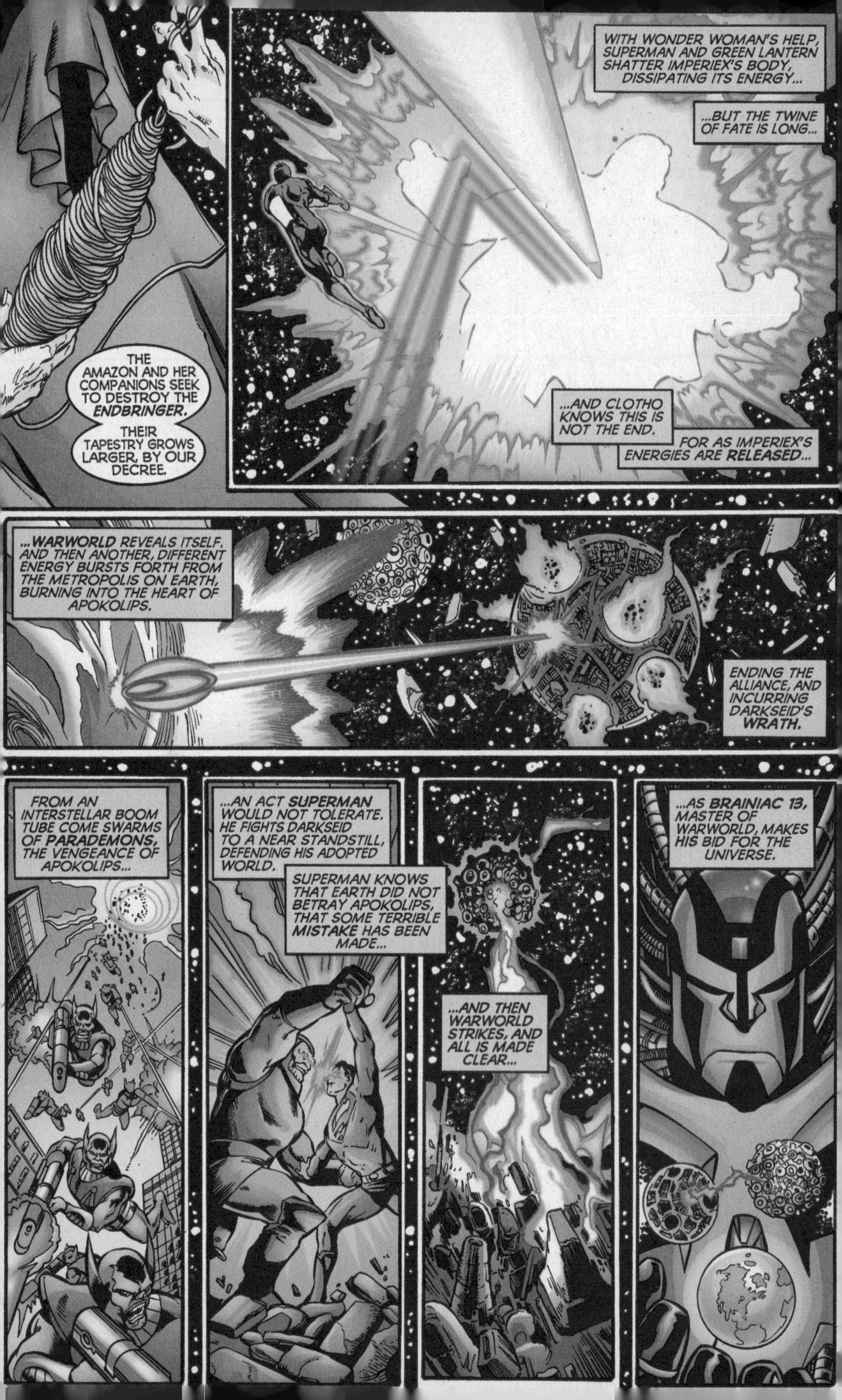
THE AMAZON AND HER COMPANIONS SEEK TO DESTROY THE ENDBRINGER.
THEIR TAPESTRY GROWS LARGER, BY OUR DECREE.
WITH WONDER WOMAN'S HELP, SUPERMAN AND GREEN LANTERN SHATTER IMPERIEX'S BODY, DISSIPATING ITS ENERGY...
...BUT THE TWINE OF FATE IS LONG...
...AND CLOTHO KNOWS THIS IS NOT THE END.
FOR AS IMPERIEX'S ENERGIES ARE RELEASED...
...WARWORLD REVEALS ITSELF, AND THEN ANOTHER, DIFFERENT ENERGY BURSTS FORTH FROM THE METROPOLIS ON EARTH, BURNING INTO THE HEART OF APOKOLIPS.
ENDING THE ALLIANCE, AND INCURRING DARKSEID'S WRATH.
FROM AN INTERSTELLAR BOOM TUBE COME SWARMS OF PARADEMONS, THE VENGEANCE OF APOKOLIPS...
...AN ACT SUPERMAN WOULD NOT TOLERATE. HE FIGHTS DARKSEID TO A NEAR STANDSTILL, DEFENDING HIS ADOPTED WORLD.
SUPERMAN KNOWS THAT EARTH DID NOT BETRAY APOKOLIPS, THAT SOME TERRIBLE MISTAKE HAS BEEN MADE...
...AND THEN WARWORLD STRIKES, AND ALL IS MADE CLEAR...
...AS BRAINIAC 13, MASTER OF WARWORLD, MAKES HIS BID FOR THE UNIVERSE.

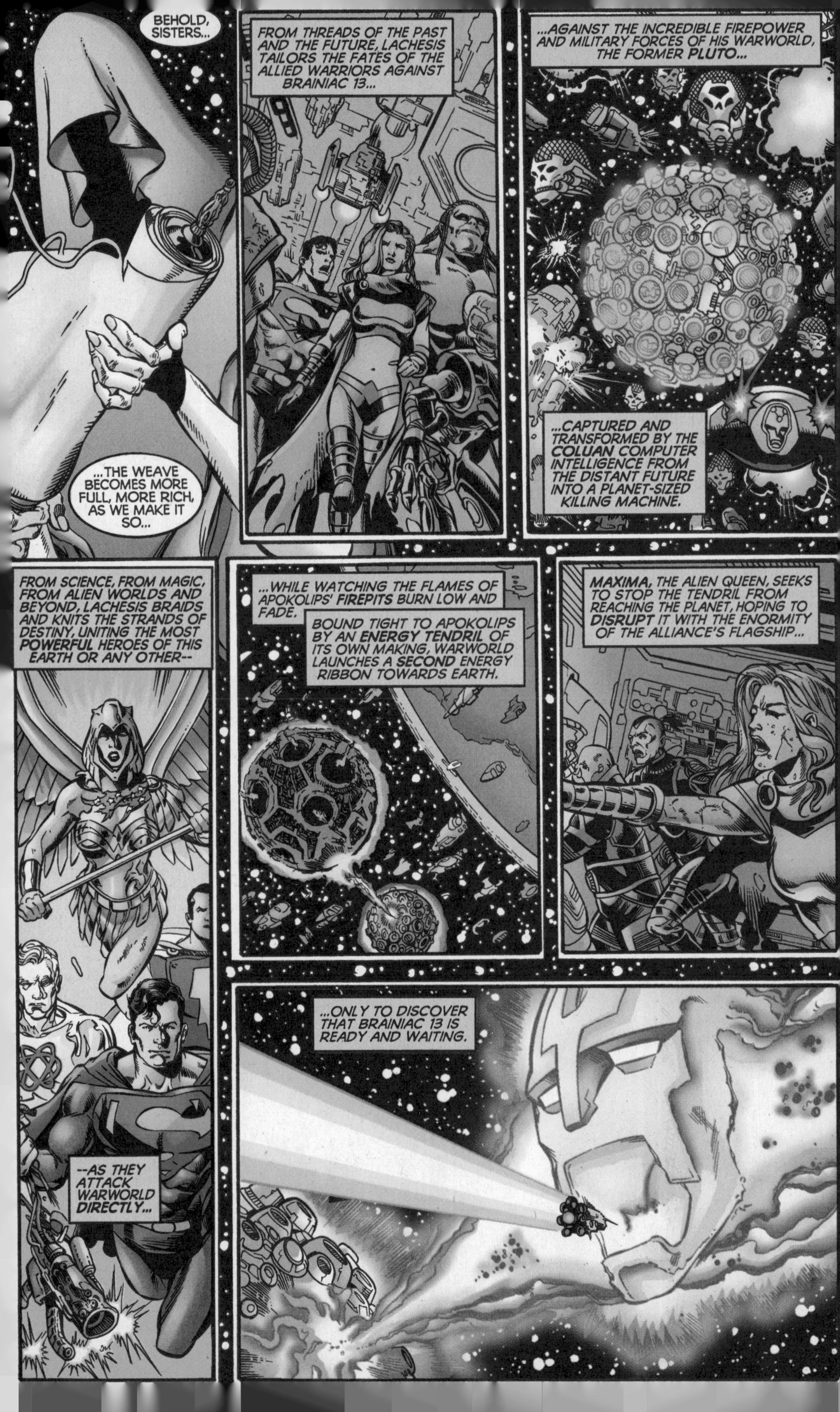
BEHOLD, SISTERS...
...THE WEAVE BECOMES MORE FULL, MORE RICH, AS WE MAKE IT SO...
FROM THREADS OF THE PAST AND THE FUTURE, LACHESIS TAILORS THE FATES OF THE ALLIED WARRIORS AGAINST BRAINIAC 13...
...AGAINST THE INCREDIBLE FIREPOWER AND MILITARY FORCES OF HIS WARWORLD, THE FORMER PLUTO...
...CAPTURED AND TRANSFORMED BY THE COLUAN COMPUTER INTELLIGENCE FROM THE DISTANT FUTURE INTO A PLANET-SIZED KILLING MACHINE.
FROM SCIENCE, FROM MAGIC, FROM ALIEN WORLDS AND BEYOND, LACHESIS BRAIDS AND KNITS THE STRANDS OF DESTINY, UNITING THE MOST POWERFUL HEROES OF THIS EARTH OR ANY OTHER--
--AS THEY ATTACK WARWORLD DIRECTLY...
...WHILE WATCHING THE FLAMES OF APOKOLIPS' FIREPITS BURN LOW AND FADE.
BOUND TIGHT TO APOKOLIPS BY AN ENERGY TENDRIL OF ITS OWN MAKING, WARWORLD LAUNCHES A SECOND ENERGY RIBBON TOWARDS EARTH.
MAXIMA, THE ALIEN QUEEN, SEEKS TO STOP THE TENDRIL FROM REACHING THE PLANET, HOPING TO DISRUPT IT WITH THE ENORMITY OF THE ALLIANCE'S FLAGSHIP...
...ONLY TO DISCOVER THAT BRAINIAC 13 IS READY AND WAITING.

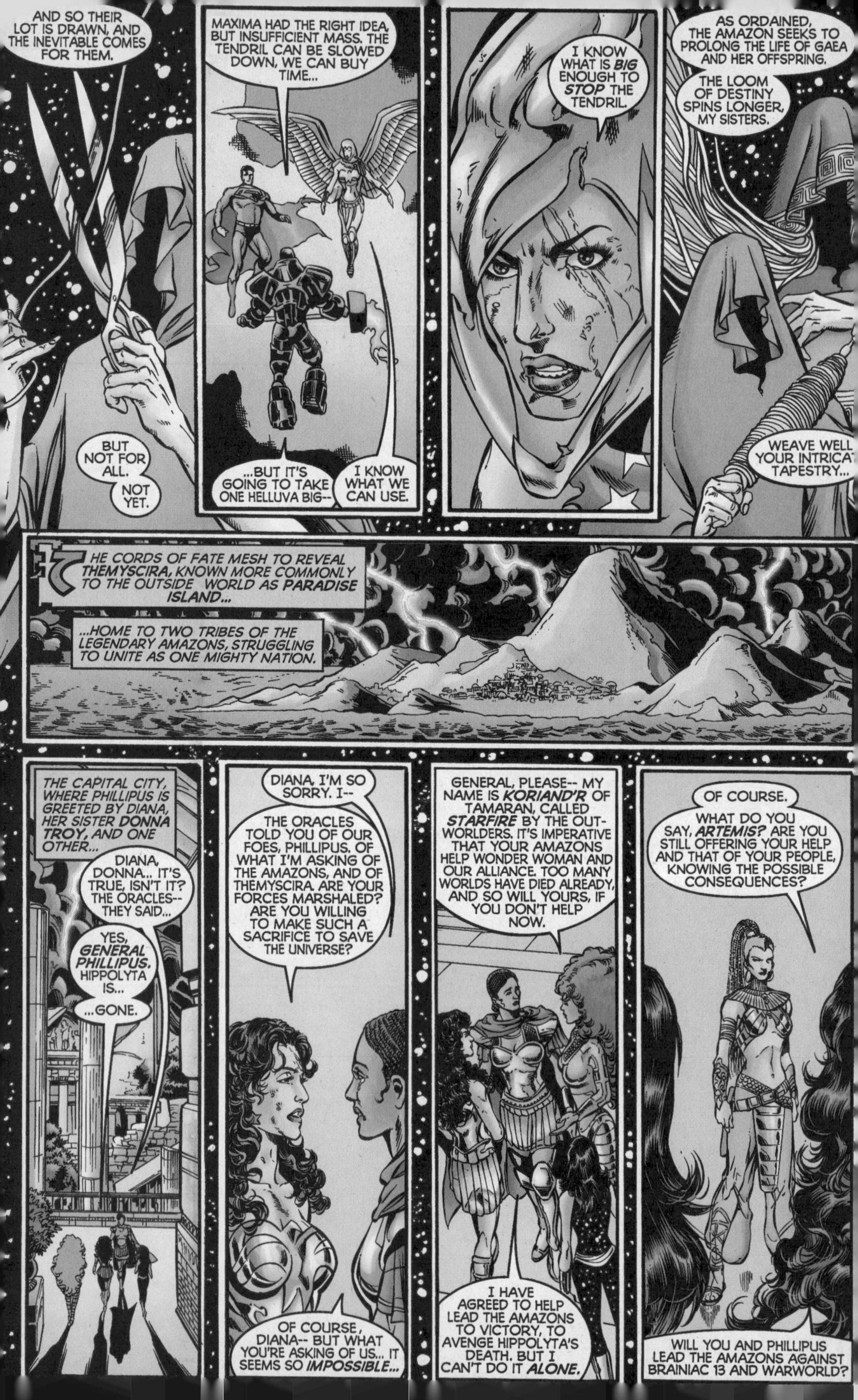
AND SO THEIR LOT IS DRAWN, AND THE INEVITABLE COMES FOR THEM.
BUT NOT FOR ALL.
NOT YET.
MAXIMA HAD THE RIGHT IDEA, BUT INSUFFICIENT MASS. THE TENDRIL CAN BE SLOWED DOWN, WE CAN BUY TIME...
...BUT IT'S GOING TO TAKE ONE HELLUVA BIG--
I KNOW WHAT WE CAN USE.
I KNOW WHAT IS *BIG* ENOUGH TO *STOP* THE TENDRIL.
AS ORDAINED, THE AMAZON SEEKS TO PROLONG THE LIFE OF GAEA AND HER OFFSPRING.
THE LOOM OF DESTINY SPINS LONGER, MY SISTERS.
WEAVE WELL YOUR INTRICAT TAPESTRY...
THE CORDS OF FATE MESH TO REVEAL ***THEMYSCIRA,*** *KNOWN MORE COMMONLY TO THE OUTSIDE WORLD AS* ***PARADISE ISLAND...***
...HOME TO TWO TRIBES OF THE LEGENDARY AMAZONS, STRUGGLING TO UNITE AS ONE MIGHTY NATION.
THE CAPITAL CITY, WHERE PHILLIPUS IS GREETED BY DIANA, HER SISTER ***DONNA TROY,*** *AND ONE OTHER...*
DIANA, DONNA... IT'S TRUE, ISN'T IT? THE ORACLES-- THEY SAID...
YES, ***GENERAL PHILLIPUS.*** HIPPOLYTA IS...
...GONE.
DIANA, I'M SO SORRY. I--
THE ORACLES TOLD YOU OF OUR FOES, PHILLIPUS. OF WHAT I'M ASKING OF THE AMAZONS, AND OF THEMYSCIRA. ARE YOUR FORCES MARSHALED? ARE YOU WILLING TO MAKE SUCH A SACRIFICE TO SAVE THE UNIVERSE?
OF COURSE, DIANA-- BUT WHAT YOU'RE ASKING OF US... IT SEEMS SO ***IMPOSSIBLE...***
GENERAL, PLEASE-- MY NAME IS ***KORIAND'R*** OF TAMARAN, CALLED ***STARFIRE*** BY THE OUT-WORLDERS. IT'S IMPERATIVE THAT YOUR AMAZONS HELP WONDER WOMAN AND OUR ALLIANCE. TOO MANY WORLDS HAVE DIED ALREADY, AND SO WILL YOURS, IF YOU DON'T HELP NOW.
I HAVE AGREED TO HELP LEAD THE AMAZONS TO VICTORY, TO AVENGE HIPPOLYTA'S DEATH. BUT I CAN'T DO IT ***ALONE.***
OF COURSE.
WHAT DO YOU SAY, ***ARTEMIS?*** ARE YOU STILL OFFERING YOUR HELP AND THAT OF YOUR PEOPLE, KNOWING THE POSSIBLE CONSEQUENCES?
WILL YOU AND PHILLIPUS LEAD THE AMAZONS AGAINST BRAINIAC 13 AND WARWORLD?

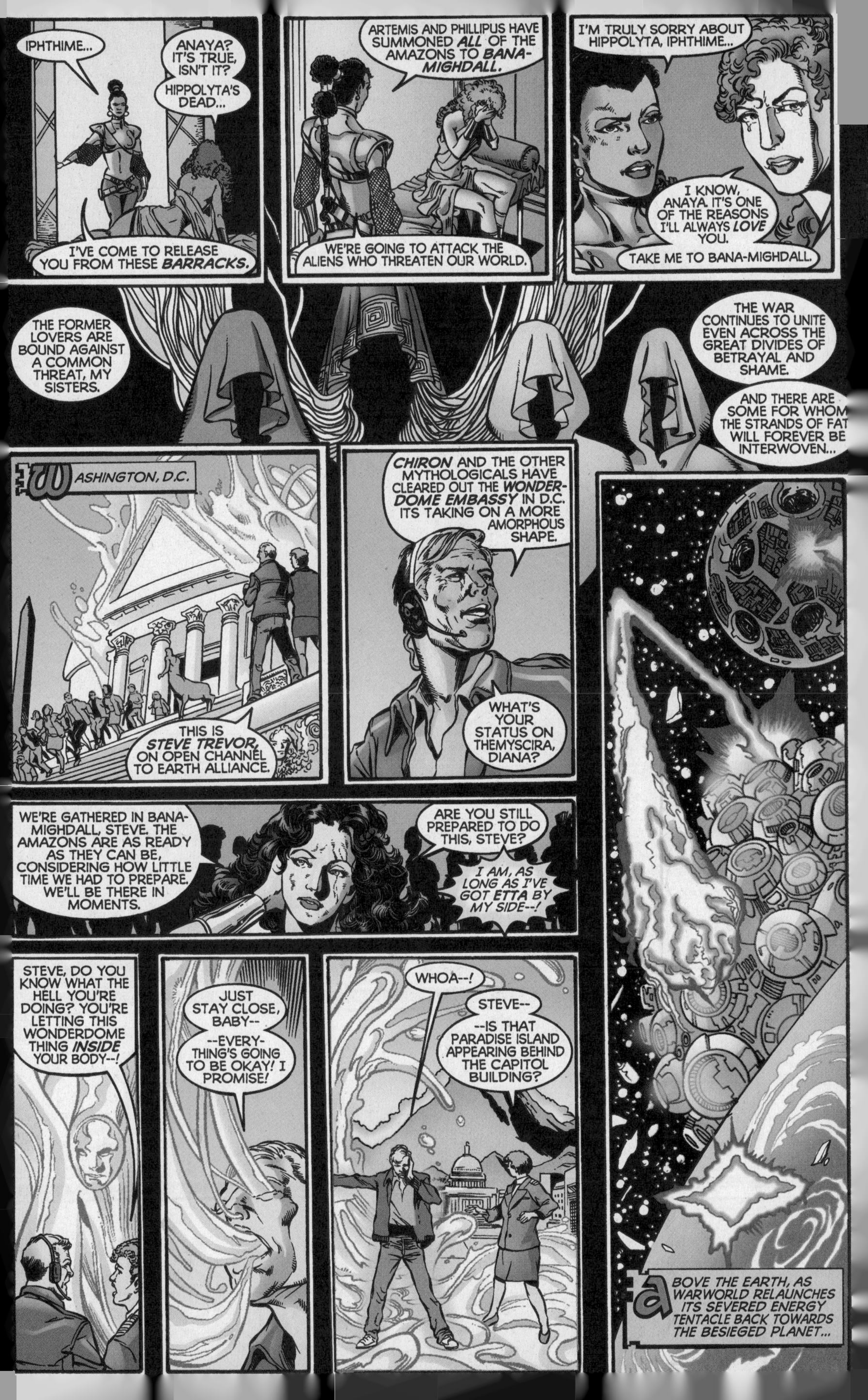

IPHTHIME...
ANAYA? IT'S TRUE, ISN'T IT?
HIPPOLYTA'S DEAD...
I'VE COME TO RELEASE YOU FROM THESE BARRACKS.
ARTEMIS AND PHILLIPUS HAVE SUMMONED ALL OF THE AMAZONS TO BANA-MIGHDALL.
WE'RE GOING TO ATTACK THE ALIENS WHO THREATEN OUR WORLD.
I'M TRULY SORRY ABOUT HIPPOLYTA, IPHTHIME...
I KNOW, ANAYA. IT'S ONE OF THE REASONS I'LL ALWAYS LOVE YOU.
TAKE ME TO BANA-MIGHDALL.
THE FORMER LOVERS ARE BOUND AGAINST A COMMON THREAT, MY SISTERS.
THE WAR CONTINUES TO UNITE EVEN ACROSS THE GREAT DIVIDES OF BETRAYAL AND SHAME.
AND THERE ARE SOME FOR WHOM THE STRANDS OF FAT WILL FOREVER BE INTERWOVEN...
WASHINGTON, D.C.
THIS IS STEVE TREVOR, ON OPEN CHANNEL TO EARTH ALLIANCE.
CHIRON AND THE OTHER MYTHOLOGICALS HAVE CLEARED OUT THE WONDER-DOME EMBASSY IN D.C. ITS TAKING ON A MORE AMORPHOUS SHAPE.
WHAT'S YOUR STATUS ON THEMYSCIRA, DIANA?
WE'RE GATHERED IN BANA-MIGHDALL, STEVE. THE AMAZONS ARE AS READY AS THEY CAN BE, CONSIDERING HOW LITTLE TIME WE HAD TO PREPARE. WE'LL BE THERE IN MOMENTS.
ARE YOU STILL PREPARED TO DO THIS, STEVE?
I AM, AS LONG AS I'VE GOT ETTA BY MY SIDE--!
STEVE, DO YOU KNOW WHAT THE HELL YOU'RE DOING? YOU'RE LETTING THIS WONDERDOME THING INSIDE YOUR BODY--!
JUST STAY CLOSE, BABY--
--EVERY-THING'S GOING TO BE OKAY! I PROMISE!
WHOA--!
STEVE--
--IS THAT PARADISE ISLAND APPEARING BEHIND THE CAPITOL BUILDING?
ABOVE THE EARTH, AS WARWORLD RELAUNCHES ITS SEVERED ENERGY TENTACLE BACK TOWARDS THE BESIEGED PLANET...

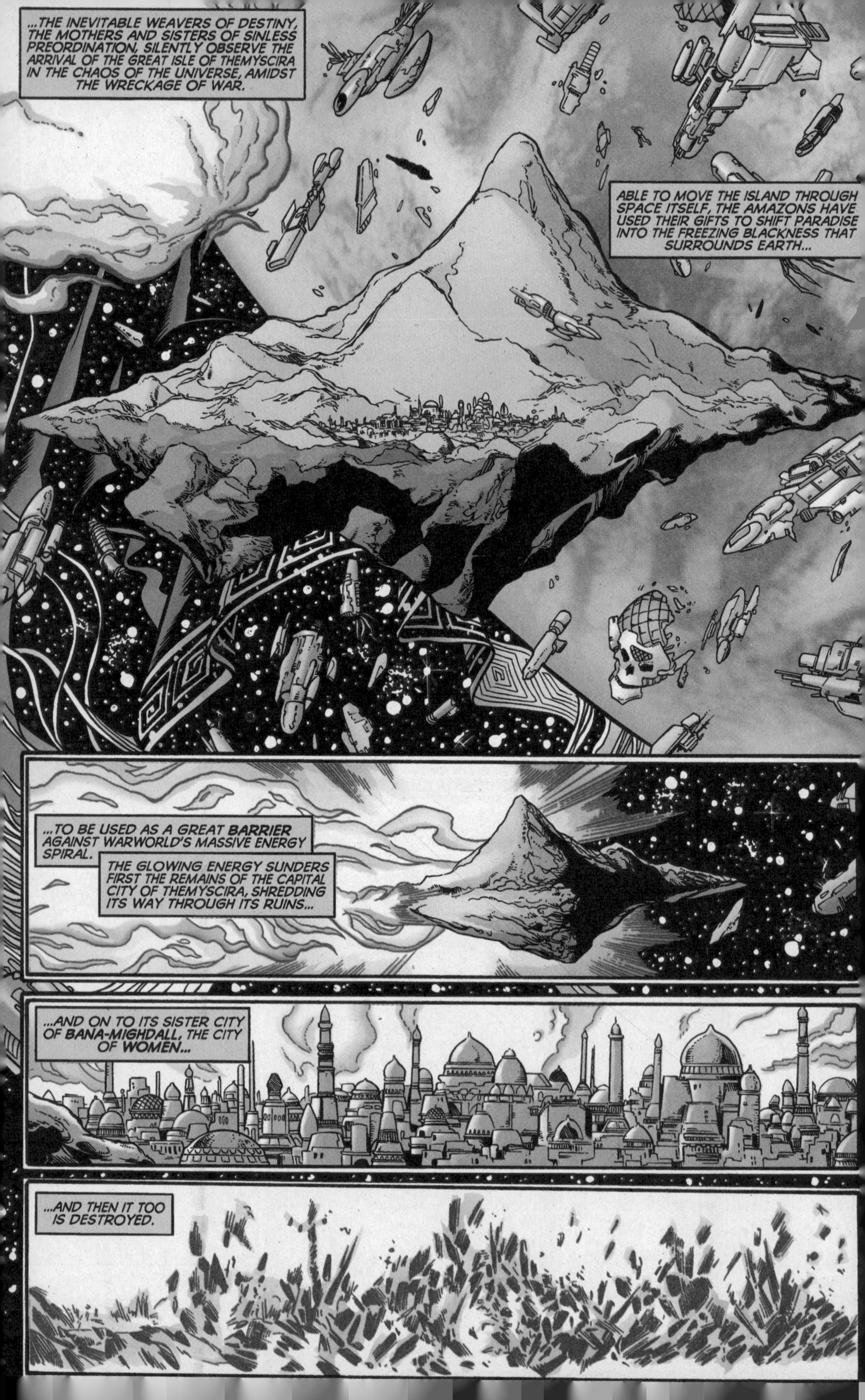
...THE INEVITABLE WEAVERS OF DESTINY, THE MOTHERS AND SISTERS OF SINLESS PREORDINATION, SILENTLY OBSERVE THE ARRIVAL OF THE GREAT ISLE OF THEMYSCIRA IN THE CHAOS OF THE UNIVERSE, AMIDST THE WRECKAGE OF WAR.
ABLE TO MOVE THE ISLAND THROUGH SPACE ITSELF, THE AMAZONS HAVE USED THEIR GIFTS TO SHIFT PARADISE INTO THE FREEZING BLACKNESS THAT SURROUNDS EARTH...
...TO BE USED AS A GREAT BARRIER AGAINST WARWORLD'S MASSIVE ENERGY SPIRAL.
THE GLOWING ENERGY SUNDERS FIRST THE REMAINS OF THE CAPITAL CITY OF THEMYSCIRA, SHREDDING ITS WAY THROUGH ITS RUINS...
...AND ON TO ITS SISTER CITY OF BANA-MIGHDALL, THE CITY OF WOMEN...
...AND THEN IT TOO IS DESTROYED.

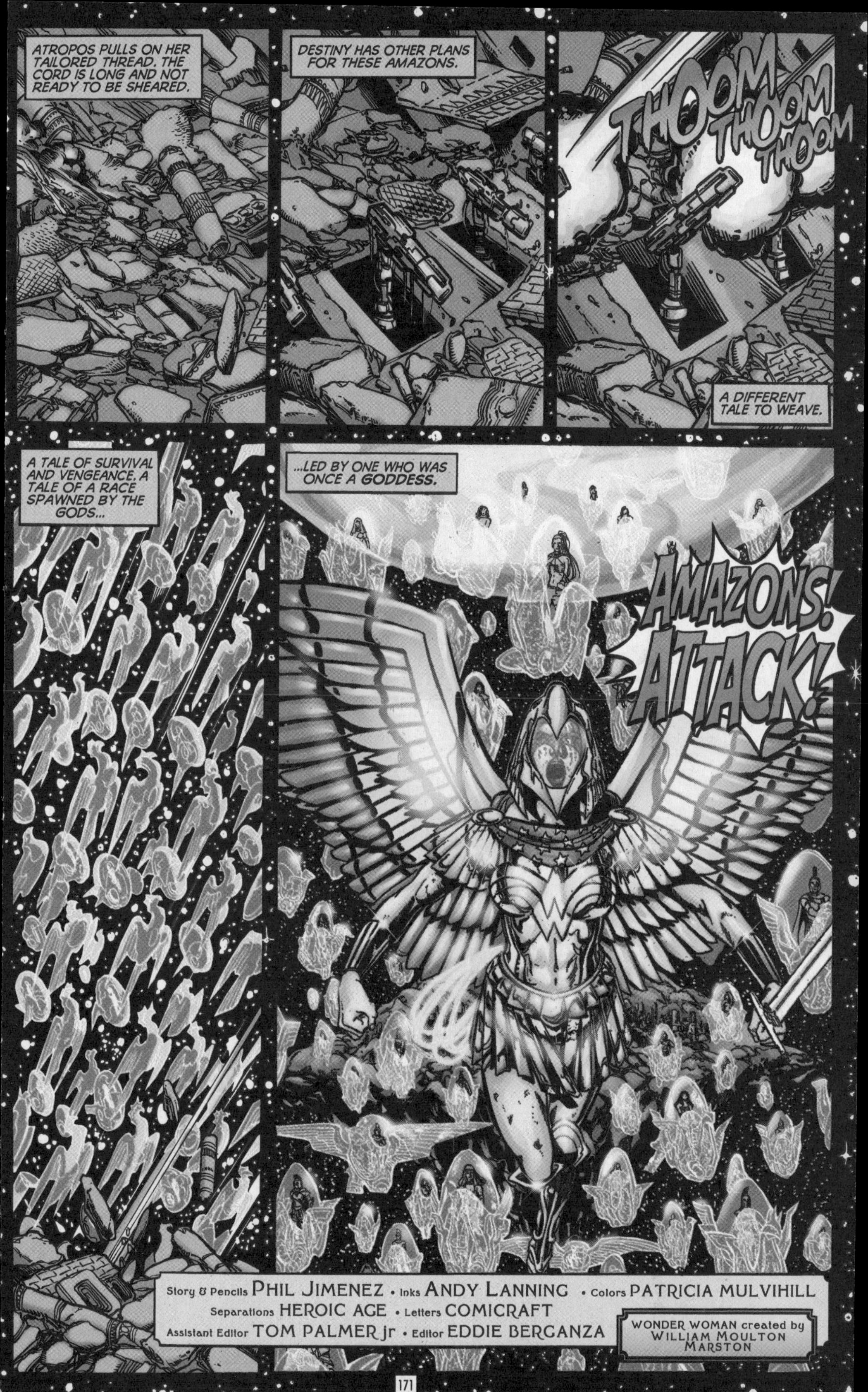
ATROPOS PULLS ON HER TAILORED THREAD. THE CORD IS LONG AND NOT READY TO BE SHEARED.
DESTINY HAS OTHER PLANS FOR THESE AMAZONS.
THOOM THOOM THOOM
A DIFFERENT TALE TO WEAVE.
A TALE OF SURVIVAL AND VENGEANCE. A TALE OF A RACE SPAWNED BY THE GODS...
...LED BY ONE WHO WAS ONCE A GODDESS.
AMAZONS! ATTACK!
Story & Pencils PHIL JIMENEZ • Inks ANDY LANNING • Colors PATRICIA MULVIHILL
Separations HEROIC AGE • Letters COMICRAFT
Assistant Editor TOM PALMER jr • Editor EDDIE BERGANZA
WONDER WOMAN created by WILLIAM MOULTON MARSTON

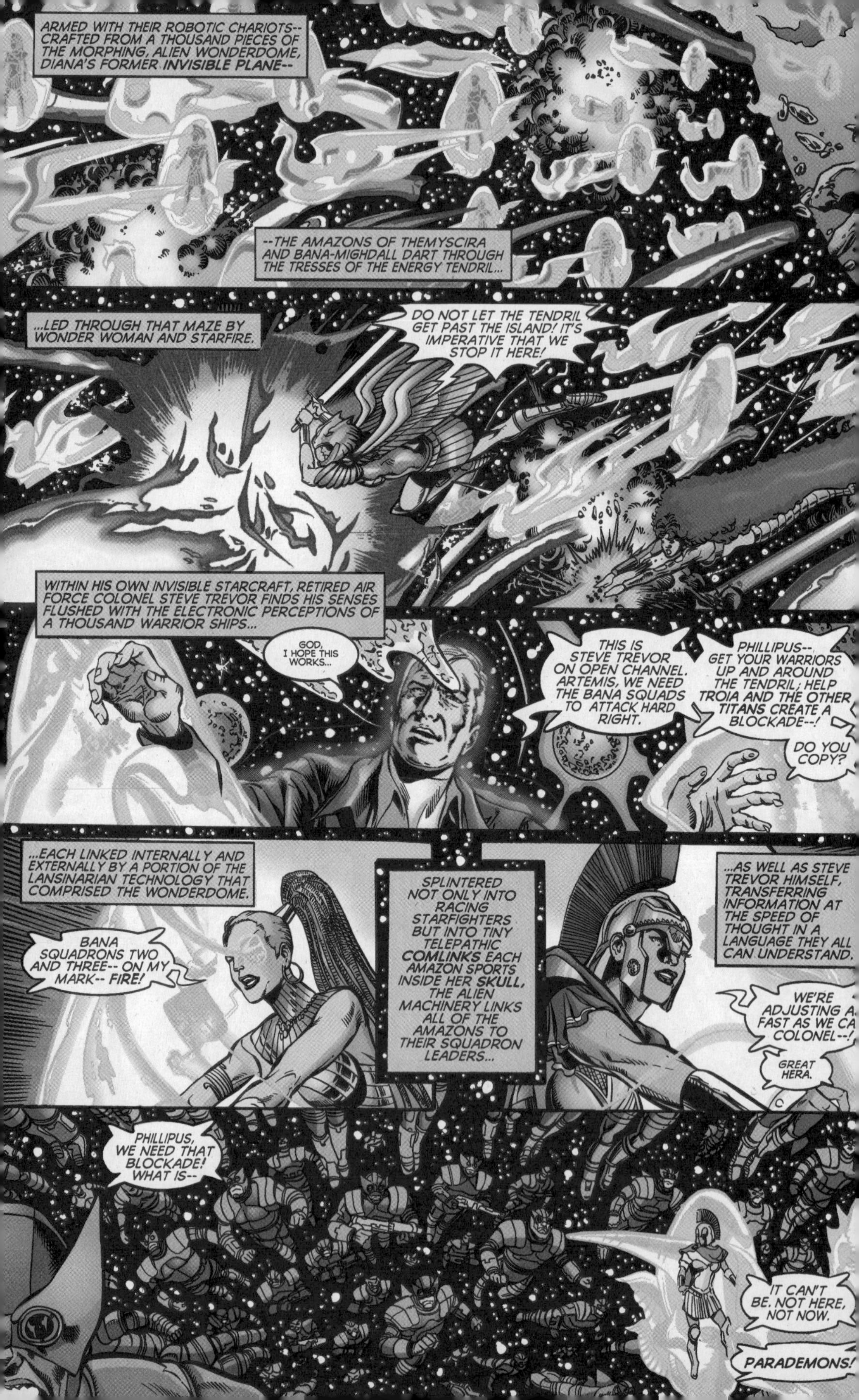
ARMED WITH THEIR ROBOTIC CHARIOTS-- CRAFTED FROM A THOUSAND PIECES OF THE MORPHING, ALIEN WONDERDOME, DIANA'S FORMER INVISIBLE PLANE--
--THE AMAZONS OF THEMYSCIRA AND BANA-MIGHDALL DART THROUGH THE TRESSES OF THE ENERGY TENDRIL...
...LED THROUGH THAT MAZE BY WONDER WOMAN AND STARFIRE.
DO NOT LET THE TENDRIL GET PAST THE ISLAND! IT'S IMPERATIVE THAT WE STOP IT HERE!
WITHIN HIS OWN INVISIBLE STARCRAFT, RETIRED AIR FORCE COLONEL STEVE TREVOR FINDS HIS SENSES FLUSHED WITH THE ELECTRONIC PERCEPTIONS OF A THOUSAND WARRIOR SHIPS...
GOD, I HOPE THIS WORKS...
THIS IS STEVE TREVOR ON OPEN CHANNEL. ARTEMIS, WE NEED THE BANA SQUADS TO ATTACK HARD RIGHT.
PHILLIPUS-- GET YOUR WARRIORS UP AND AROUND THE TENDRIL; HELP TROIA AND THE OTHER TITANS CREATE A BLOCKADE--!
DO YOU COPY?
...EACH LINKED INTERNALLY AND EXTERNALLY BY A PORTION OF THE LANSINARIAN TECHNOLOGY THAT COMPRISED THE WONDERDOME.
BANA SQUADRONS TWO AND THREE-- ON MY MARK-- FIRE!
SPLINTERED NOT ONLY INTO RACING STARFIGHTERS BUT INTO TINY TELEPATHIC COMLINKS EACH AMAZON SPORTS INSIDE HER SKULL, THE ALIEN MACHINERY LINKS ALL OF THE AMAZONS TO THEIR SQUADRON LEADERS...
...AS WELL AS STEVE TREVOR HIMSELF, TRANSFERRING INFORMATION AT THE SPEED OF THOUGHT IN A LANGUAGE THEY ALL CAN UNDERSTAND.
WE'RE ADJUSTING A FAST AS WE CA COLONEL--!
GREAT HERA.
PHILLIPUS, WE NEED THAT BLOCKADE! WHAT IS--
IT CAN'T BE. NOT HERE, NOT NOW.
PARADEMONS!

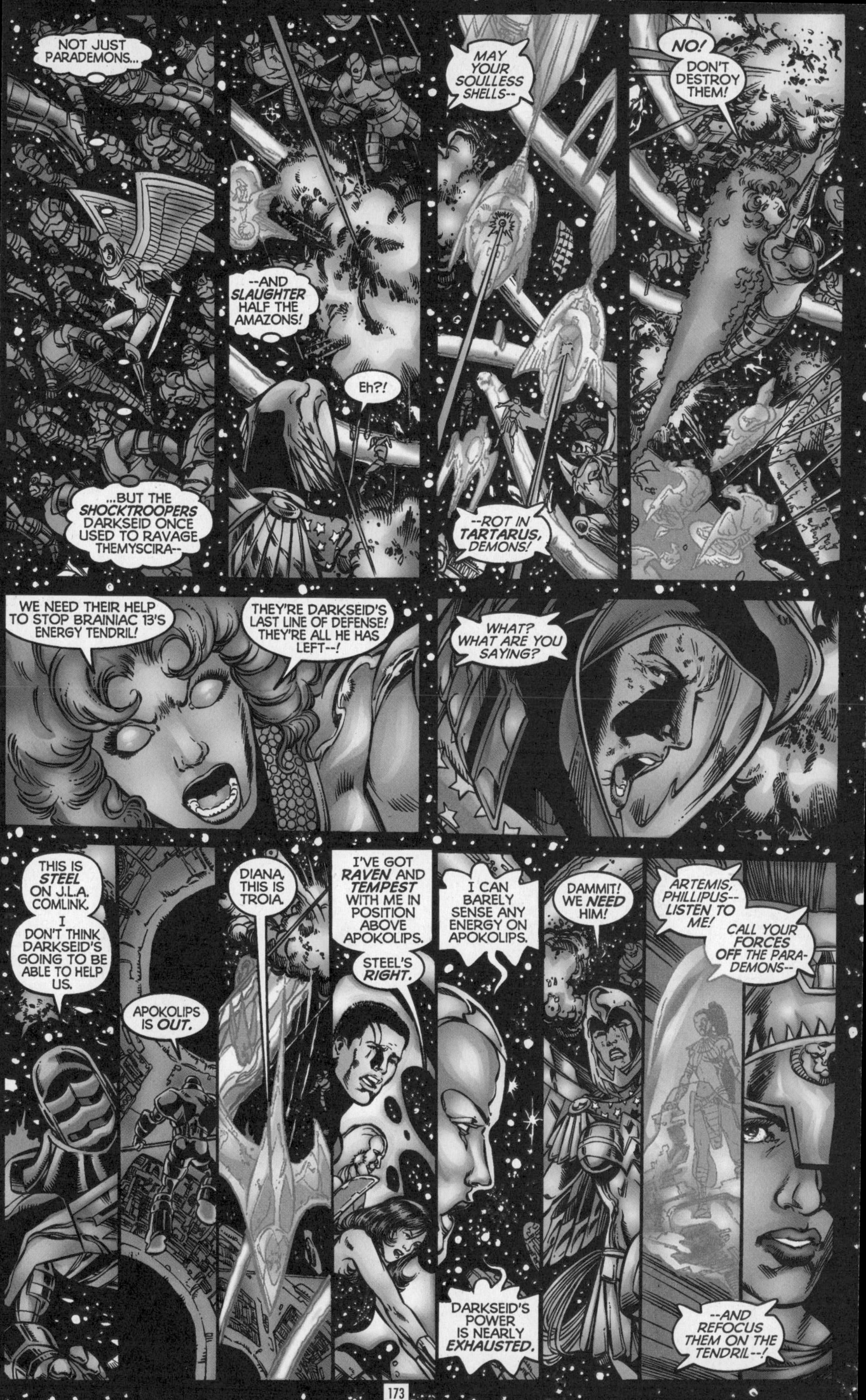
NOT JUST PARADEMONS...
...BUT THE SHOCKTROOPERS DARKSEID ONCE USED TO RAVAGE THEMYSCIRA--
--AND SLAUGHTER HALF THE AMAZONS!
Eh?!
MAY YOUR SOULLESS SHELLS--
--ROT IN TARTARUS, DEMONS!
NO! DON'T DESTROY THEM!
WE NEED THEIR HELP TO STOP BRAINIAC 13'S ENERGY TENDRIL!
THEY'RE DARKSEID'S LAST LINE OF DEFENSE! THEY'RE ALL HE HAS LEFT--!
WHAT? WHAT ARE YOU SAYING?
THIS IS STEEL ON J.L.A. COMLINK. I DON'T THINK DARKSEID'S GOING TO BE ABLE TO HELP US.
APOKOLIPS IS OUT.
DIANA, THIS IS TROIA.
I'VE GOT RAVEN AND TEMPEST WITH ME IN POSITION ABOVE APOKOLIPS.
STEEL'S RIGHT.
I CAN BARELY SENSE ANY ENERGY ON APOKOLIPS.
DARKSEID'S POWER IS NEARLY EXHAUSTED.
DAMMIT! WE NEED HIM!
ARTEMIS, PHILLIPUS-- LISTEN TO ME!
CALL YOUR FORCES OFF THE PARA-DEMONS--
--AND REFOCUS THEM ON THE TENDRIL--!

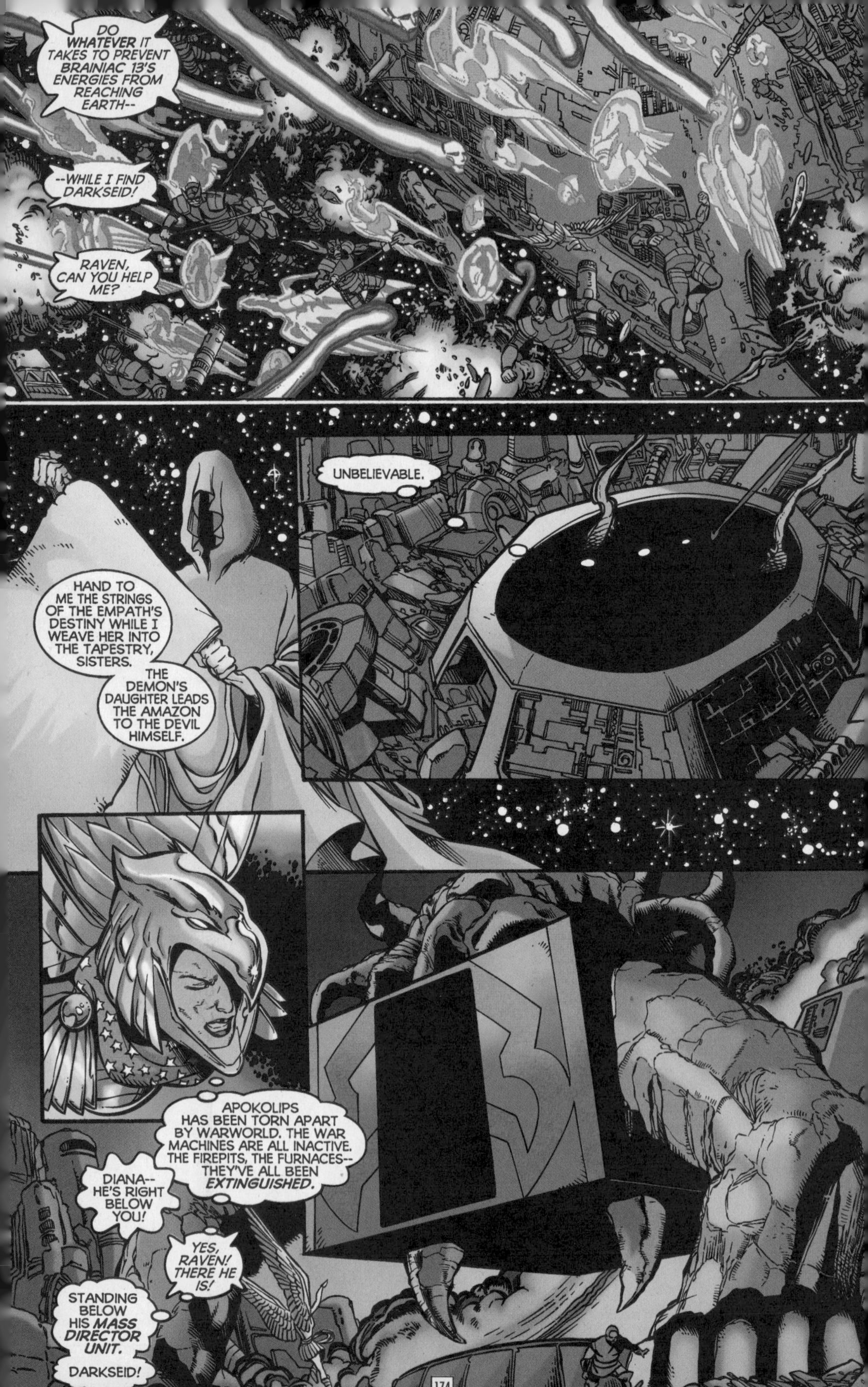
DO WHATEVER IT TAKES TO PREVENT BRAINIAC 13'S ENERGIES FROM REACHING EARTH--
--WHILE I FIND DARKSEID!
RAVEN, CAN YOU HELP ME?
UNBELIEVABLE.
HAND TO ME THE STRINGS OF THE EMPATH'S DESTINY WHILE I WEAVE HER INTO THE TAPESTRY, SISTERS.
THE DEMON'S DAUGHTER LEADS THE AMAZON TO THE DEVIL HIMSELF.
APOKOLIPS HAS BEEN TORN APART BY WARWORLD. THE WAR MACHINES ARE ALL INACTIVE. THE FIREPITS, THE FURNACES-- THEY'VE ALL BEEN EXTINGUISHED.
DIANA-- HE'S RIGHT BELOW YOU!
YES, RAVEN! THERE HE IS!
STANDING BELOW HIS MASS DIRECTOR UNIT.
DARKSEID!

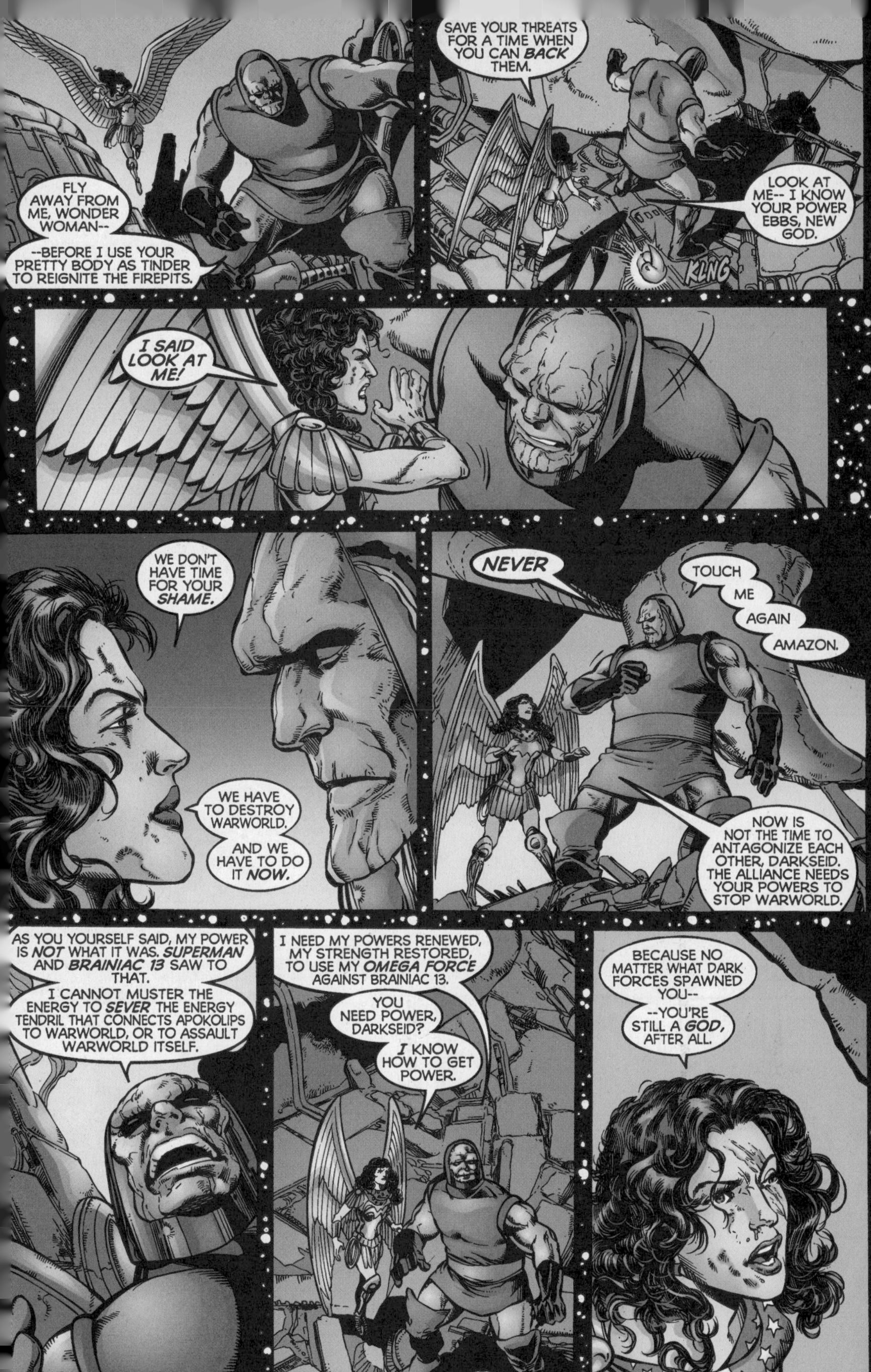
FLY AWAY FROM ME, WONDER WOMAN--
--BEFORE I USE YOUR PRETTY BODY AS TINDER TO REIGNITE THE FIREPITS.
SAVE YOUR THREATS FOR A TIME WHEN YOU CAN BACK THEM.
LOOK AT ME-- I KNOW YOUR POWER EBBS, NEW GOD.
KLNG
I SAID LOOK AT ME!
WE DON'T HAVE TIME FOR YOUR SHAME.
WE HAVE TO DESTROY WARWORLD.
AND WE HAVE TO DO IT NOW.
NEVER
TOUCH
ME
AGAIN
AMAZON.
NOW IS NOT THE TIME TO ANTAGONIZE EACH OTHER, DARKSEID. THE ALLIANCE NEEDS YOUR POWERS TO STOP WARWORLD.
AS YOU YOURSELF SAID, MY POWER IS NOT WHAT IT WAS. SUPERMAN AND BRAINIAC 13 SAW TO THAT.
I CANNOT MUSTER THE ENERGY TO SEVER THE ENERGY TENDRIL THAT CONNECTS APOKOLIPS TO WARWORLD, OR TO ASSAULT WARWORLD ITSELF.
I NEED MY POWERS RENEWED, MY STRENGTH RESTORED, TO USE MY OMEGA FORCE AGAINST BRAINIAC 13.
YOU NEED POWER, DARKSEID?
I KNOW HOW TO GET POWER.
BECAUSE NO MATTER WHAT DARK FORCES SPAWNED YOU--
--YOU'RE STILL A GOD, AFTER ALL.

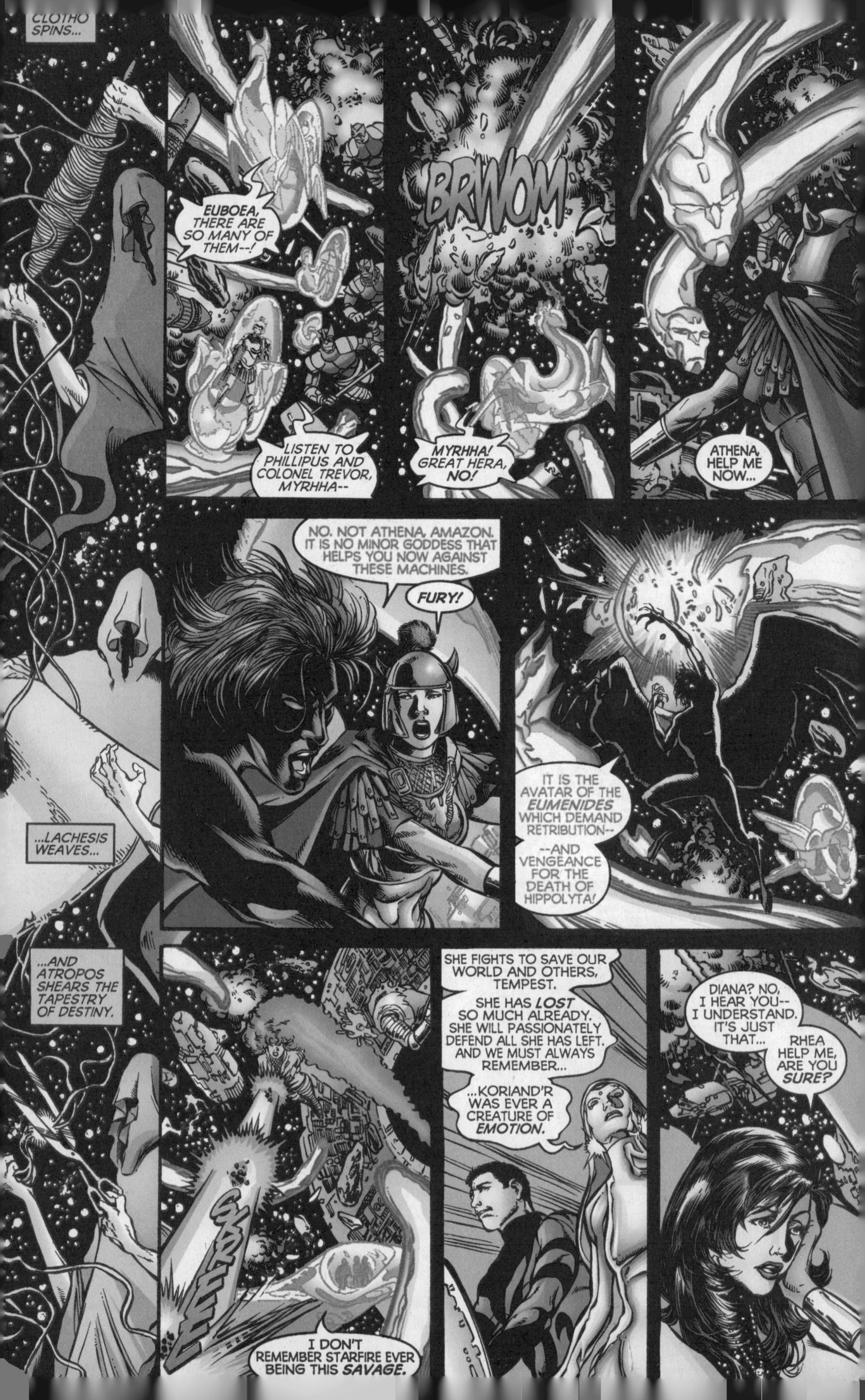
CLOTHO SPINS...
EUBOEA, THERE ARE SO MANY OF THEM--!
LISTEN TO PHILLIPUS AND COLONEL TREVOR, MYRHHA--
BRWOM
MYRHHA! GREAT HERA, NO!
ATHENA, HELP ME NOW...
NO. NOT ATHENA, AMAZON. IT IS NO MINOR GODDESS THAT HELPS YOU NOW AGAINST THESE MACHINES.
FURY!
IT IS THE AVATAR OF THE EUMENIDES WHICH DEMAND RETRIBUTION--
--AND VENGEANCE FOR THE DEATH OF HIPPOLYTA!
...LACHESIS WEAVES...
...AND ATROPOS SHEARS THE TAPESTRY OF DESTINY.
I DON'T REMEMBER STARFIRE EVER BEING THIS SAVAGE.
SHE FIGHTS TO SAVE OUR WORLD AND OTHERS, TEMPEST.
SHE HAS LOST SO MUCH ALREADY. SHE WILL PASSIONATELY DEFEND ALL SHE HAS LEFT. AND WE MUST ALWAYS REMEMBER...
...KORIAND'R WAS EVER A CREATURE OF EMOTION.
DIANA? NO, I HEAR YOU-- I UNDERSTAND. IT'S JUST THAT...
RHEA HELP ME, ARE YOU SURE?

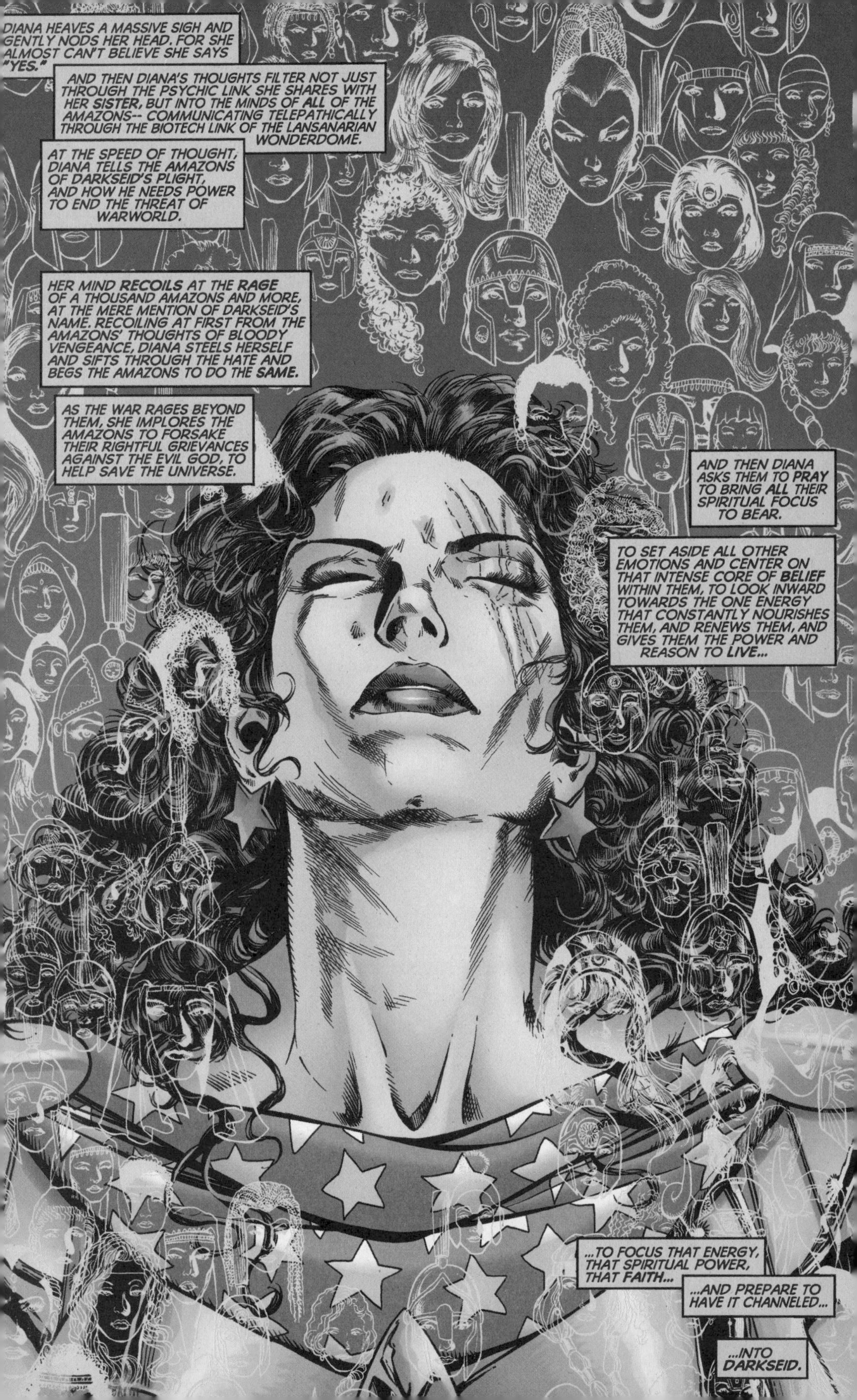
DIANA HEAVES A MASSIVE SIGH AND GENTLY NODS HER HEAD. FOR SHE ALMOST CAN'T BELIEVE SHE SAYS "YES."
AND THEN DIANA'S THOUGHTS FILTER NOT JUST THROUGH THE PSYCHIC LINK SHE SHARES WITH HER SISTER, BUT INTO THE MINDS OF ALL OF THE AMAZONS-- COMMUNICATING TELEPATHICALLY THROUGH THE BIOTECH LINK OF THE LANSANARIAN WONDERDOME.
AT THE SPEED OF THOUGHT, DIANA TELLS THE AMAZONS OF DARKSEID'S PLIGHT, AND HOW HE NEEDS POWER TO END THE THREAT OF WARWORLD.
HER MIND RECOILS AT THE RAGE OF A THOUSAND AMAZONS AND MORE, AT THE MERE MENTION OF DARKSEID'S NAME. RECOILING AT FIRST FROM THE AMAZONS' THOUGHTS OF BLOODY VENGEANCE, DIANA STEELS HERSELF AND SIFTS THROUGH THE HATE AND BEGS THE AMAZONS TO DO THE SAME.
AS THE WAR RAGES BEYOND THEM, SHE IMPLORES THE AMAZONS TO FORSAKE THEIR RIGHTFUL GRIEVANCES AGAINST THE EVIL GOD, TO HELP SAVE THE UNIVERSE.
AND THEN DIANA ASKS THEM TO PRAY TO BRING ALL THEIR SPIRITUAL FOCUS TO BEAR.
TO SET ASIDE ALL OTHER EMOTIONS AND CENTER ON THAT INTENSE CORE OF BELIEF WITHIN THEM, TO LOOK INWARD TOWARDS THE ONE ENERGY THAT CONSTANTLY NOURISHES THEM, AND RENEWS THEM, AND GIVES THEM THE POWER AND REASON TO LIVE...
...TO FOCUS THAT ENERGY, THAT SPIRITUAL POWER, THAT FAITH...
...AND PREPARE TO HAVE IT CHANNELED...
...INTO DARKSEID.

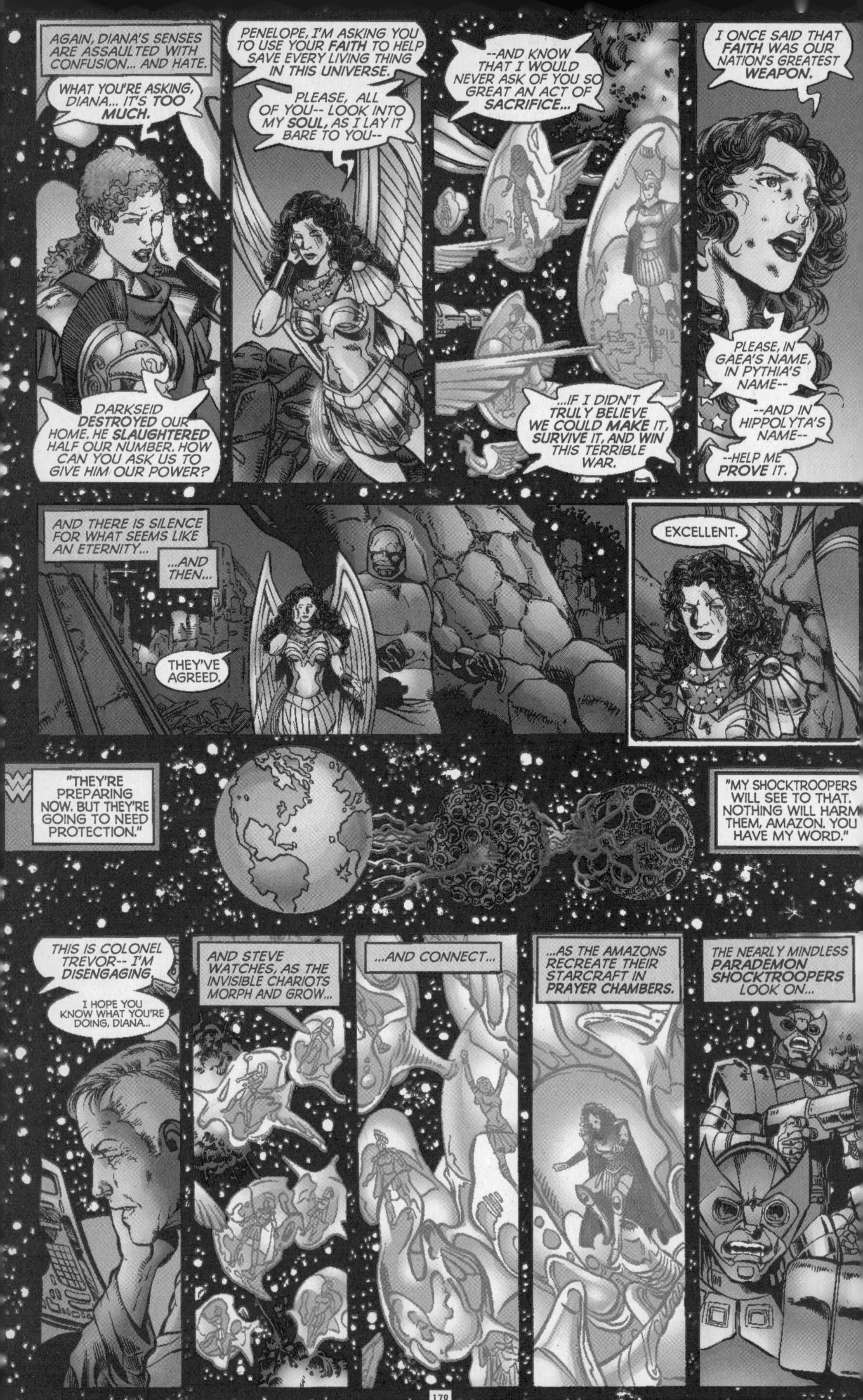
AGAIN, DIANA'S SENSES ARE ASSAULTED WITH CONFUSION... AND HATE.
WHAT YOU'RE ASKING, DIANA... IT'S TOO MUCH.
DARKSEID DESTROYED OUR HOME. HE SLAUGHTERED HALF OUR NUMBER. HOW CAN YOU ASK US TO GIVE HIM OUR POWER?
PENELOPE, I'M ASKING YOU TO USE YOUR FAITH TO HELP SAVE EVERY LIVING THING IN THIS UNIVERSE.
PLEASE, ALL OF YOU-- LOOK INTO MY SOUL, AS I LAY IT BARE TO YOU--
--AND KNOW THAT I WOULD NEVER ASK OF YOU SO GREAT AN ACT OF SACRIFICE...
...IF I DIDN'T TRULY BELIEVE WE COULD MAKE IT, SURVIVE IT, AND WIN THIS TERRIBLE WAR.
I ONCE SAID THAT FAITH WAS OUR NATION'S GREATEST WEAPON.
PLEASE, IN GAEA'S NAME, IN PYTHIA'S NAME--
--AND IN HIPPOLYTA'S NAME--
--HELP ME PROVE IT.
AND THERE IS SILENCE FOR WHAT SEEMS LIKE AN ETERNITY...
...AND THEN...
THEY'VE AGREED.
EXCELLENT.
"THEY'RE PREPARING NOW. BUT THEY'RE GOING TO NEED PROTECTION."
"MY SHOCKTROOPERS WILL SEE TO THAT. NOTHING WILL HARM THEM, AMAZON. YOU HAVE MY WORD."
THIS IS COLONEL TREVOR-- I'M DISENGAGING.
I HOPE YOU KNOW WHAT YOU'RE DOING, DIANA...
AND STEVE WATCHES, AS THE INVISIBLE CHARIOTS MORPH AND GROW...
...AND CONNECT...
...AS THE AMAZONS RECREATE THEIR STARCRAFT IN PRAYER CHAMBERS.
THE NEARLY MINDLESS PARADEMON SHOCKTROOPERS LOOK ON...

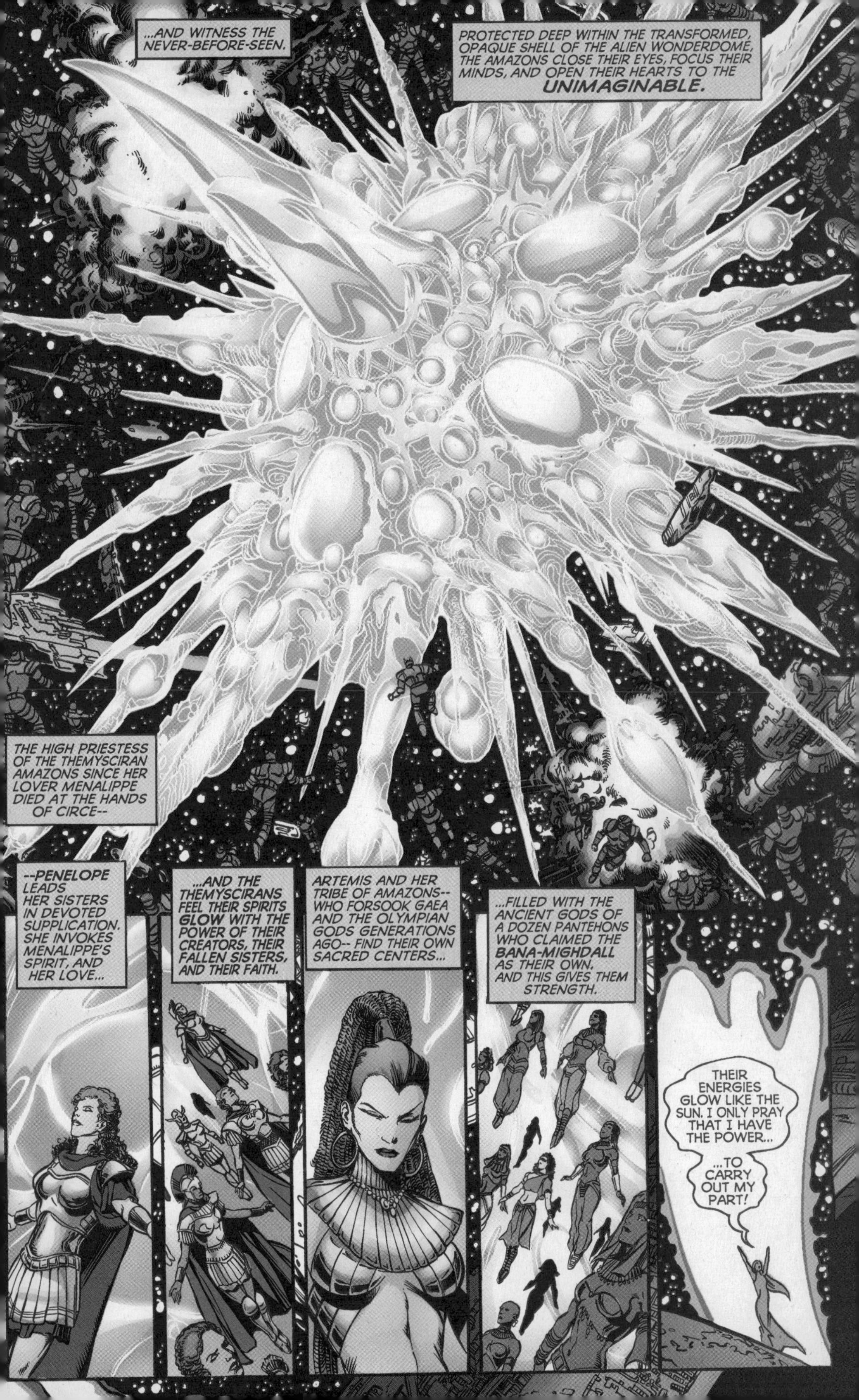

...AND WITNESS THE NEVER-BEFORE-SEEN.
PROTECTED DEEP WITHIN THE TRANSFORMED, OPAQUE SHELL OF THE ALIEN WONDERDOME, THE AMAZONS CLOSE THEIR EYES, FOCUS THEIR MINDS, AND OPEN THEIR HEARTS TO THE UNIMAGINABLE.
THE HIGH PRIESTESS OF THE THEMYSCIRAN AMAZONS SINCE HER LOVER MENALIPPE DIED AT THE HANDS OF CIRCE--
--PENELOPE LEADS HER SISTERS IN DEVOTED SUPPLICATION. SHE INVOKES MENALIPPE'S SPIRIT, AND HER LOVE...
...AND THE THEMYSCIRANS FEEL THEIR SPIRITS GLOW WITH THE POWER OF THEIR CREATORS, THEIR FALLEN SISTERS, AND THEIR FAITH.
ARTEMIS AND HER TRIBE OF AMAZONS-- WHO FORSOOK GAEA AND THE OLYMPIAN GODS GENERATIONS AGO-- FIND THEIR OWN SACRED CENTERS...
...FILLED WITH THE ANCIENT GODS OF A DOZEN PANTEHONS WHO CLAIMED THE BANA-MIGHDALL AS THEIR OWN. AND THIS GIVES THEM STRENGTH.
THEIR ENERGIES GLOW LIKE THE SUN. I ONLY PRAY THAT I HAVE THE POWER...
...TO CARRY OUT MY PART!

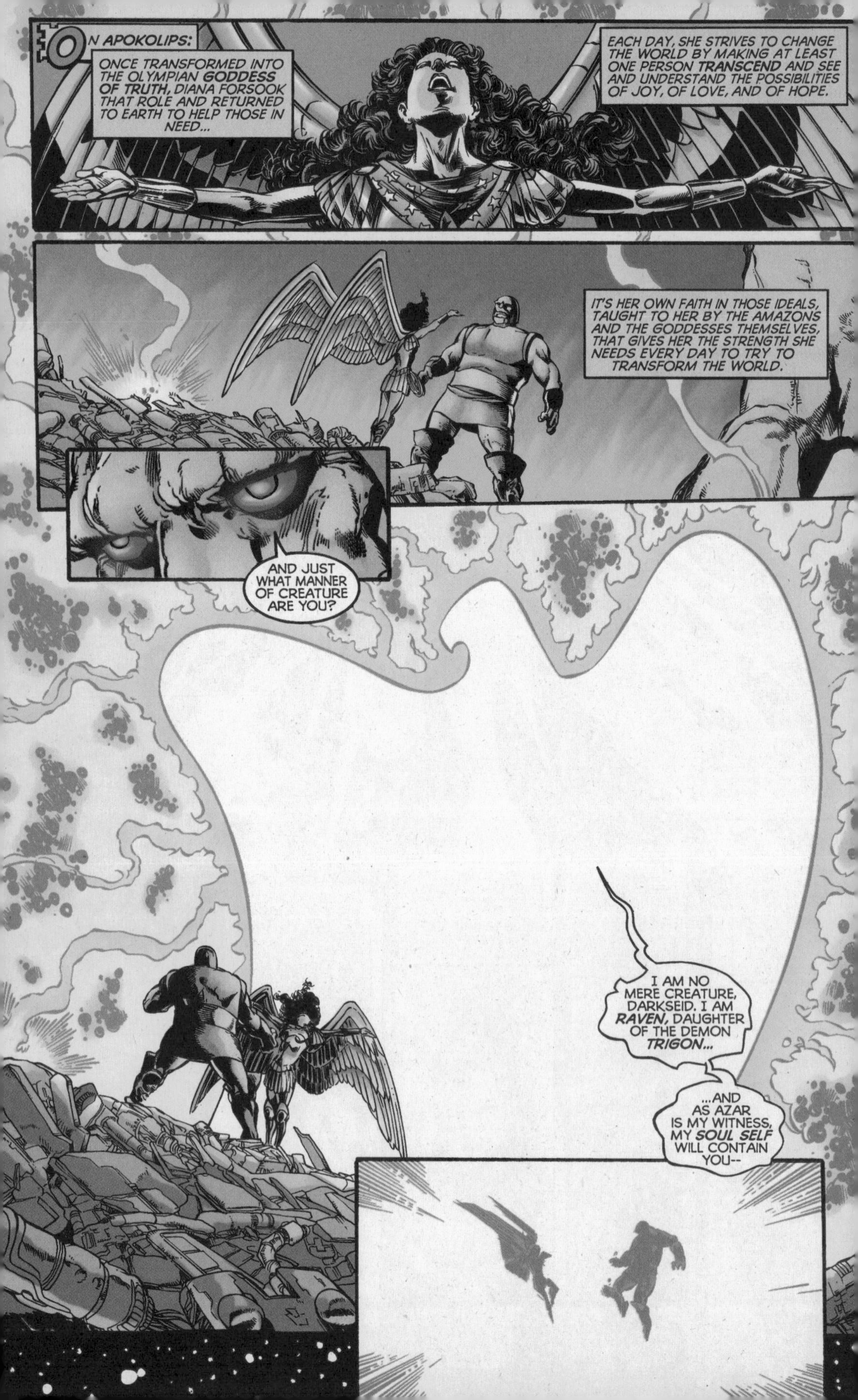
ON APOKOLIPS:
ONCE TRANSFORMED INTO THE OLYMPIAN GODDESS OF TRUTH, DIANA FORSOOK THAT ROLE AND RETURNED TO EARTH TO HELP THOSE IN NEED...
EACH DAY, SHE STRIVES TO CHANGE THE WORLD BY MAKING AT LEAST ONE PERSON TRANSCEND AND SEE AND UNDERSTAND THE POSSIBILITIES OF JOY, OF LOVE, AND OF HOPE.
IT'S HER OWN FAITH IN THOSE IDEALS, TAUGHT TO HER BY THE AMAZONS AND THE GODDESSES THEMSELVES, THAT GIVES HER THE STRENGTH SHE NEEDS EVERY DAY TO TRY TO TRANSFORM THE WORLD.
AND JUST WHAT MANNER OF CREATURE ARE YOU?
I AM NO MERE CREATURE, DARKSEID. I AM RAVEN, DAUGHTER OF THE DEMON TRIGON...
...AND AS AZAR IS MY WITNESS, MY SOUL SELF WILL CONTAIN YOU--

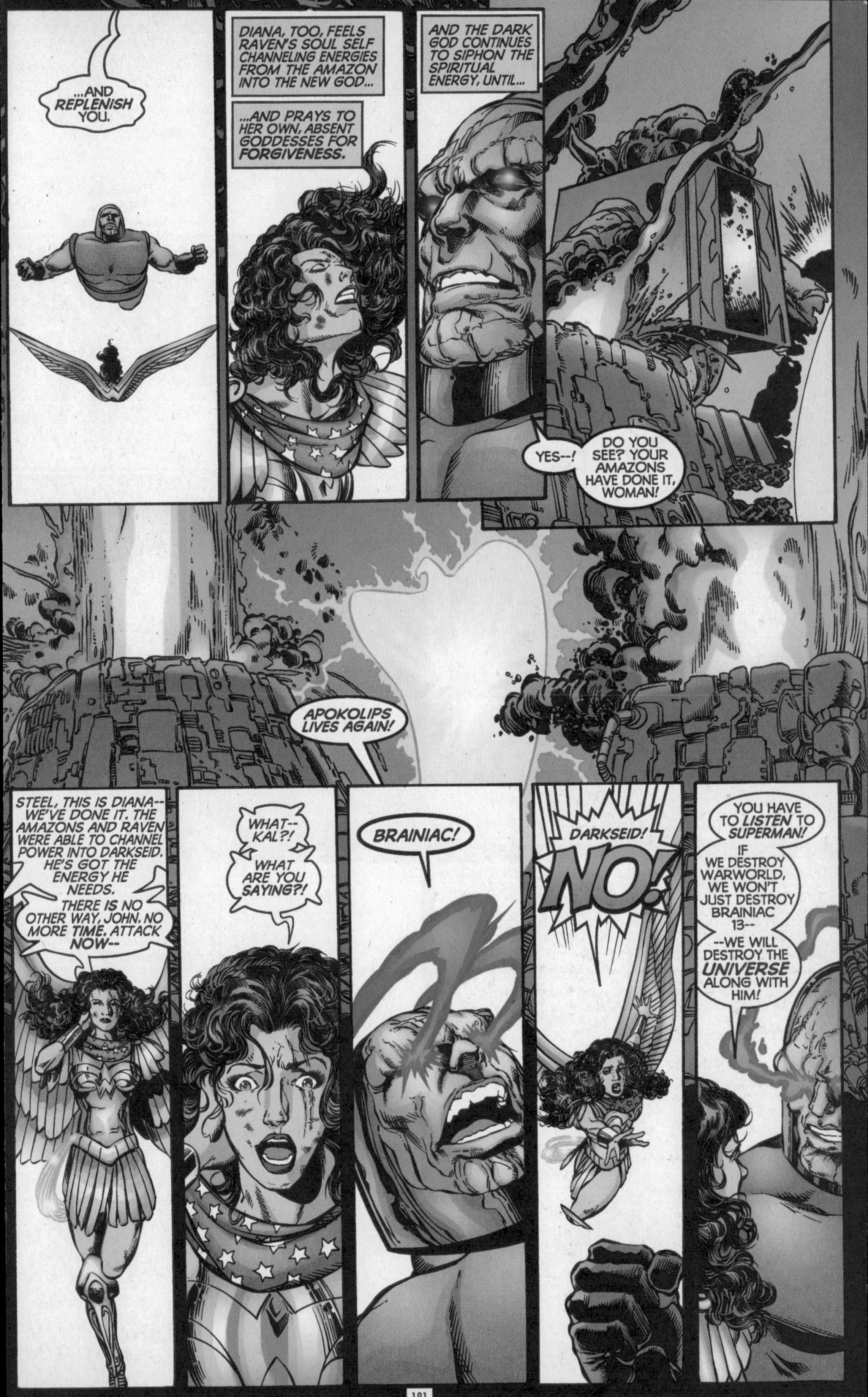
...AND REPLENISH YOU.
DIANA, TOO, FEELS RAVEN'S SOUL SELF CHANNELING ENERGIES FROM THE AMAZON INTO THE NEW GOD...
...AND PRAYS TO HER OWN, ABSENT GODDESSES FOR FORGIVENESS.
AND THE DARK GOD CONTINUES TO SIPHON THE SPIRITUAL ENERGY, UNTIL...
YES--!
DO YOU SEE? YOUR AMAZONS HAVE DONE IT, WOMAN!
APOKOLIPS LIVES AGAIN!
STEEL, THIS IS DIANA-- WE'VE DONE IT. THE AMAZONS AND RAVEN WERE ABLE TO CHANNEL POWER INTO DARKSEID. HE'S GOT THE ENERGY HE NEEDS.
THERE IS NO OTHER WAY, JOHN. NO MORE TIME. ATTACK NOW--
WHAT-- KAL?!
WHAT ARE YOU SAYING?!
BRAINIAC!
DARKSEID!
NO!
YOU HAVE TO LISTEN TO SUPERMAN!
IF WE DESTROY WARWORLD, WE WON'T JUST DESTROY BRAINIAC 13--
--WE WILL DESTROY THE UNIVERSE ALONG WITH HIM!

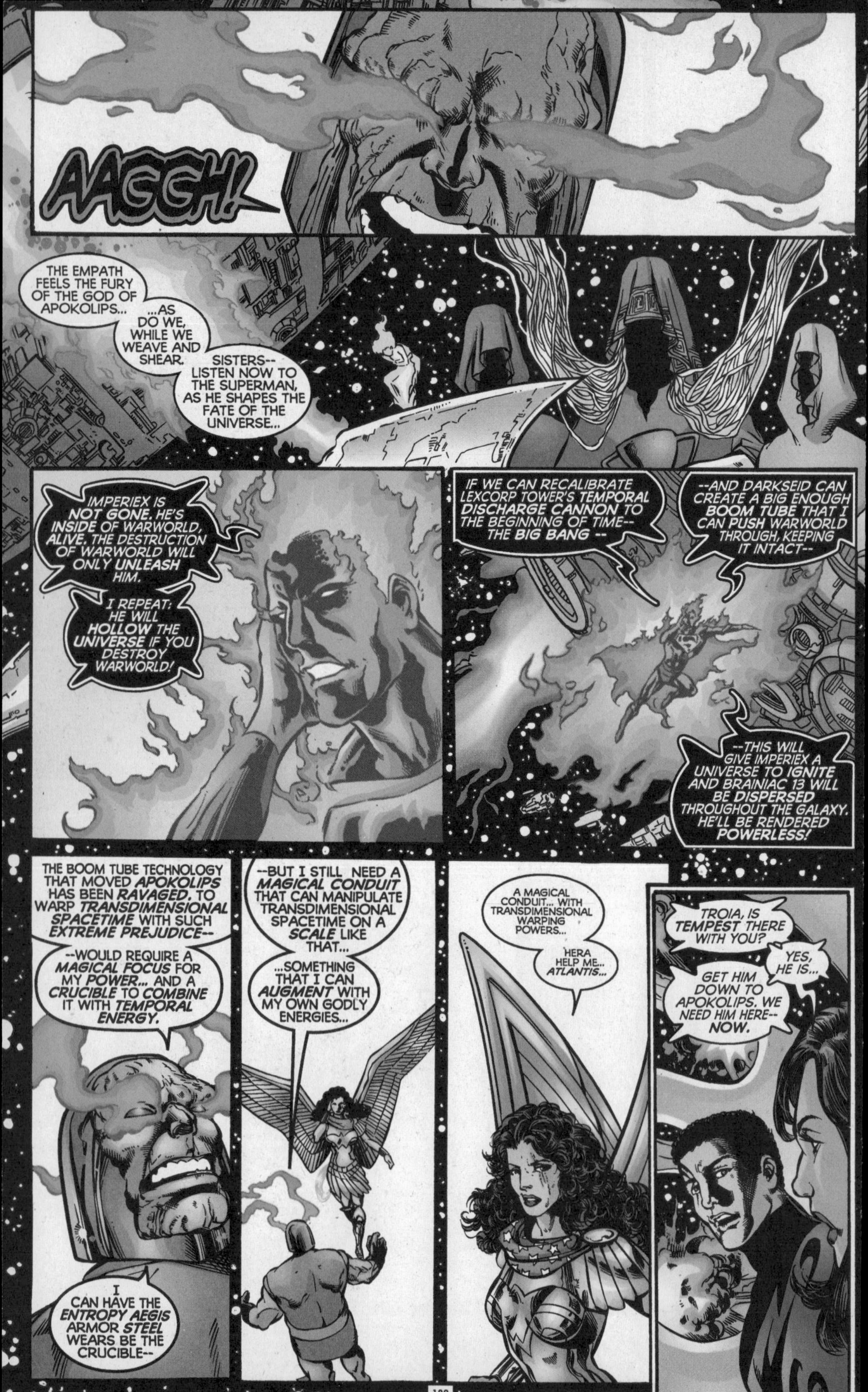
AAGGH!
THE EMPATH FEELS THE FURY OF THE GOD OF APOKOLIPS...
...AS DO WE, WHILE WE WEAVE AND SHEAR.
SISTERS-- LISTEN NOW TO THE SUPERMAN, AS HE SHAPES THE FATE OF THE UNIVERSE...
IMPERIEX IS NOT GONE. HE'S INSIDE OF WARWORLD, ALIVE. THE DESTRUCTION OF WARWORLD WILL ONLY UNLEASH HIM.
I REPEAT: HE WILL HOLLOW THE UNIVERSE IF YOU DESTROY WARWORLD!
IF WE CAN RECALIBRATE LEXCORP TOWER'S TEMPORAL DISCHARGE CANNON TO THE BEGINNING OF TIME-- THE BIG BANG --
--AND DARKSEID CAN CREATE A BIG ENOUGH BOOM TUBE THAT I CAN PUSH WARWORLD THROUGH, KEEPING IT INTACT--
--THIS WILL GIVE IMPERIEX A UNIVERSE TO IGNITE AND BRAINIAC 13 WILL BE DISPERSED THROUGHOUT THE GALAXY. HE'LL BE RENDERED POWERLESS!
THE BOOM TUBE TECHNOLOGY THAT MOVED APOKOLIPS HAS BEEN RAVAGED. TO WARP TRANSDIMENSIONAL SPACETIME WITH SUCH EXTREME PREJUDICE--
--WOULD REQUIRE A MAGICAL FOCUS FOR MY POWER... AND A CRUCIBLE TO COMBINE IT WITH TEMPORAL ENERGY.
I CAN HAVE THE ENTROPY AEGIS ARMOR STEEL WEARS BE THE CRUCIBLE--
--BUT I STILL NEED A MAGICAL CONDUIT THAT CAN MANIPULATE TRANSDIMENSIONAL SPACETIME ON A SCALE LIKE THAT...
...SOMETHING THAT I CAN AUGMENT WITH MY OWN GODLY ENERGIES...
A MAGICAL CONDUIT... WITH TRANSDIMENSIONAL WARPING POWERS...
HERA HELP ME... ATLANTIS...
TROIA, IS TEMPEST THERE WITH YOU?
YES, HE IS...
GET HIM DOWN TO APOKOLIPS. WE NEED HIM HERE-- NOW.

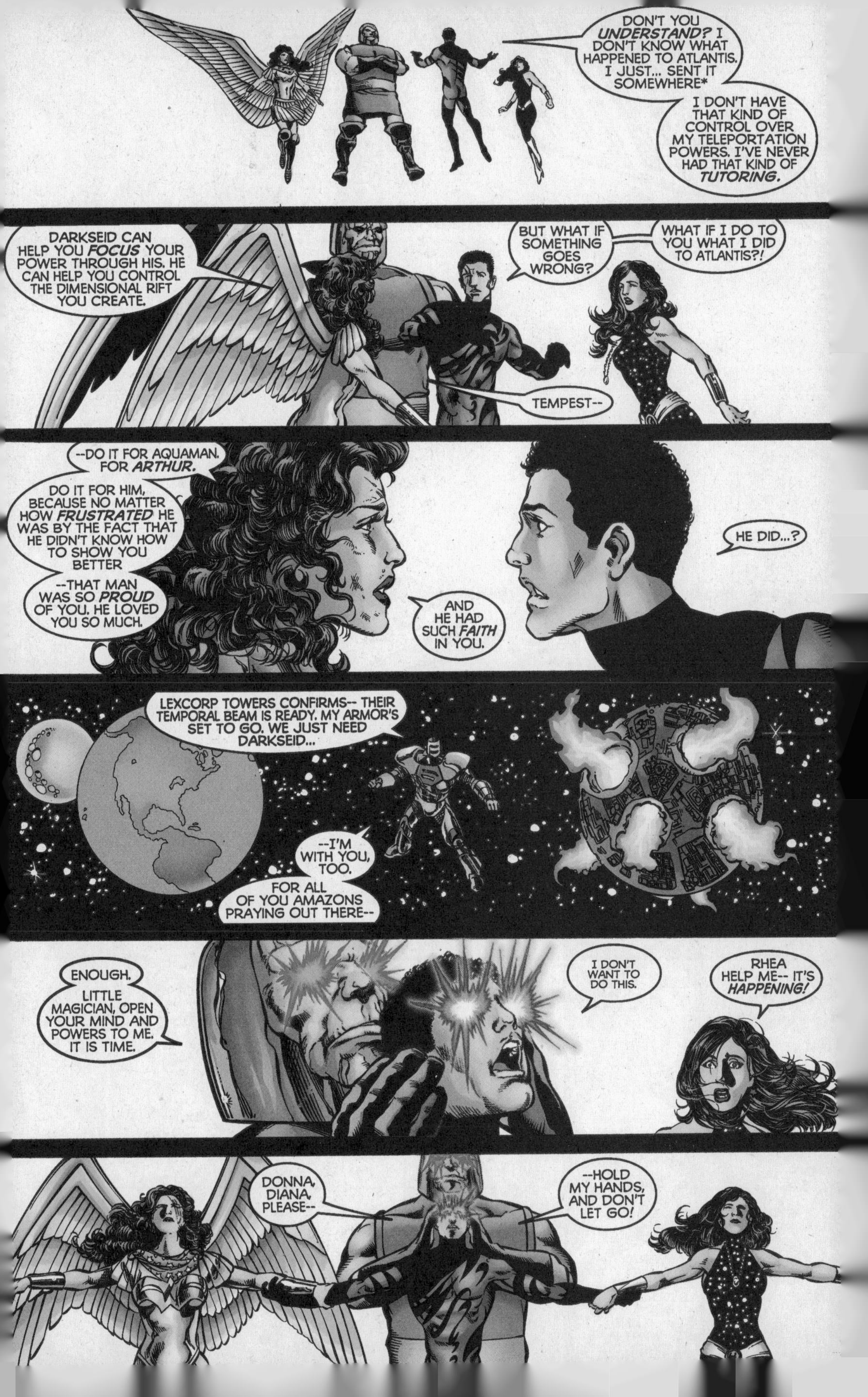
DON'T YOU UNDERSTAND? I DON'T KNOW WHAT HAPPENED TO ATLANTIS. I JUST... SENT IT SOMEWHERE*
I DON'T HAVE THAT KIND OF CONTROL OVER MY TELEPORTATION POWERS. I'VE NEVER HAD THAT KIND OF TUTORING.
DARKSEID CAN HELP YOU FOCUS YOUR POWER THROUGH HIS. HE CAN HELP YOU CONTROL THE DIMENSIONAL RIFT YOU CREATE.
BUT WHAT IF SOMETHING GOES WRONG?
WHAT IF I DO TO YOU WHAT I DID TO ATLANTIS?!
TEMPEST--
--DO IT FOR AQUAMAN. FOR ARTHUR.
DO IT FOR HIM, BECAUSE NO MATTER HOW FRUSTRATED HE WAS BY THE FACT THAT HE DIDN'T KNOW HOW TO SHOW YOU BETTER
--THAT MAN WAS SO PROUD OF YOU. HE LOVED YOU SO MUCH.
AND HE HAD SUCH FAITH IN YOU.
HE DID...?
LEXCORP TOWERS CONFIRMS-- THEIR TEMPORAL BEAM IS READY. MY ARMOR'S SET TO GO. WE JUST NEED DARKSEID...
--I'M WITH YOU, TOO.
FOR ALL OF YOU AMAZONS PRAYING OUT THERE--
ENOUGH.
LITTLE MAGICIAN, OPEN YOUR MIND AND POWERS TO ME. IT IS TIME.
I DON'T WANT TO DO THIS.
RHEA HELP ME-- IT'S HAPPENING!
DONNA, DIANA, PLEASE--
--HOLD MY HANDS, AND DON'T LET GO!

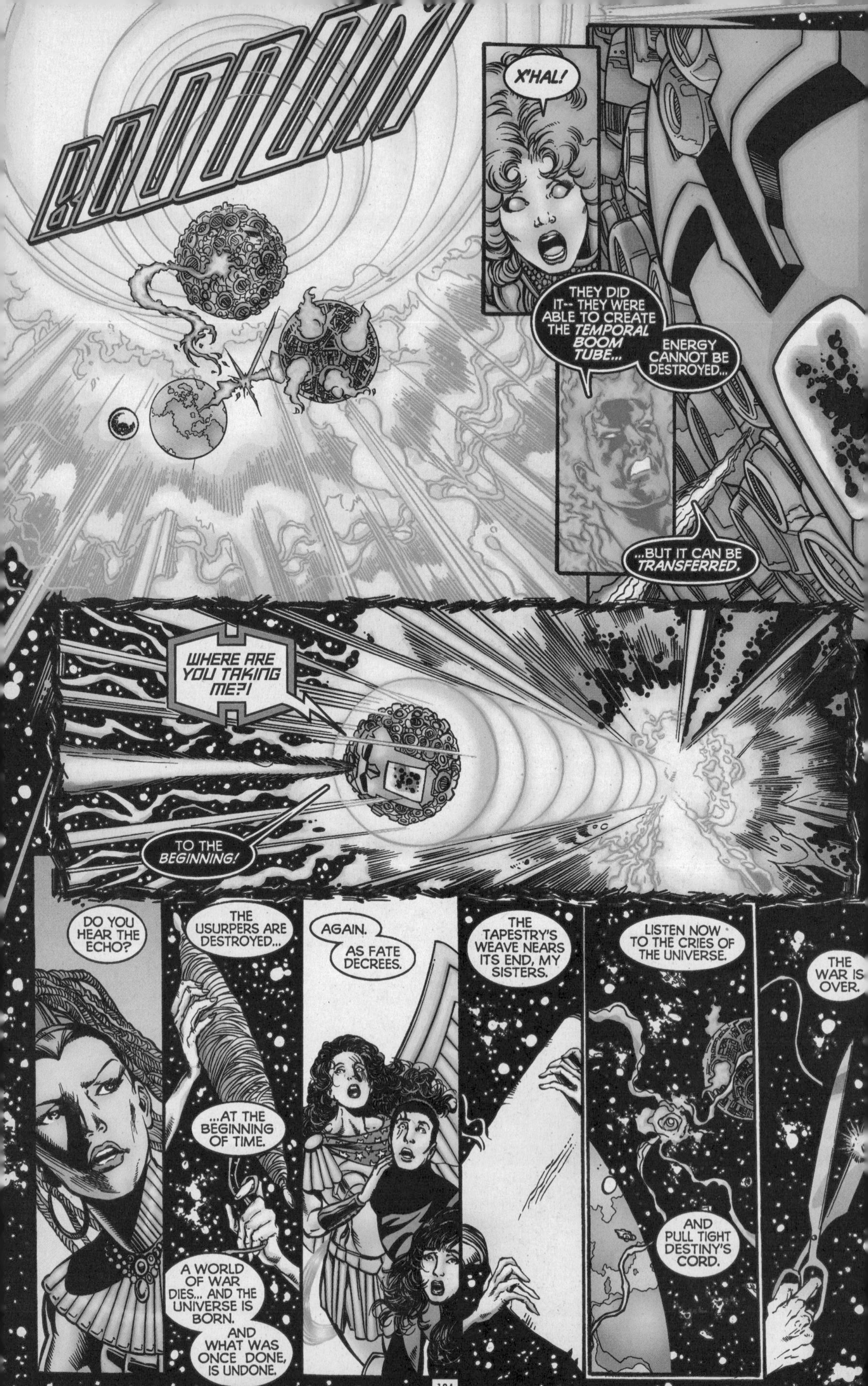
X'HAL!
THEY DID IT-- THEY WERE ABLE TO CREATE THE TEMPORAL BOOM TUBE...
ENERGY CANNOT BE DESTROYED...
...BUT IT CAN BE TRANSFERRED.
WHERE ARE YOU TAKING ME?!
TO THE BEGINNING!
DO YOU HEAR THE ECHO?
THE USURPERS ARE DESTROYED...
...AT THE BEGINNING OF TIME.
A WORLD OF WAR DIES... AND THE UNIVERSE IS BORN.
AND WHAT WAS ONCE DONE, IS UNDONE.
AGAIN.
AS FATE DECREES.
THE TAPESTRY'S WEAVE NEARS ITS END, MY SISTERS.
LISTEN NOW TO THE CRIES OF THE UNIVERSE.
AND PULL TIGHT DESTINY'S CORD.
THE WAR IS OVER.

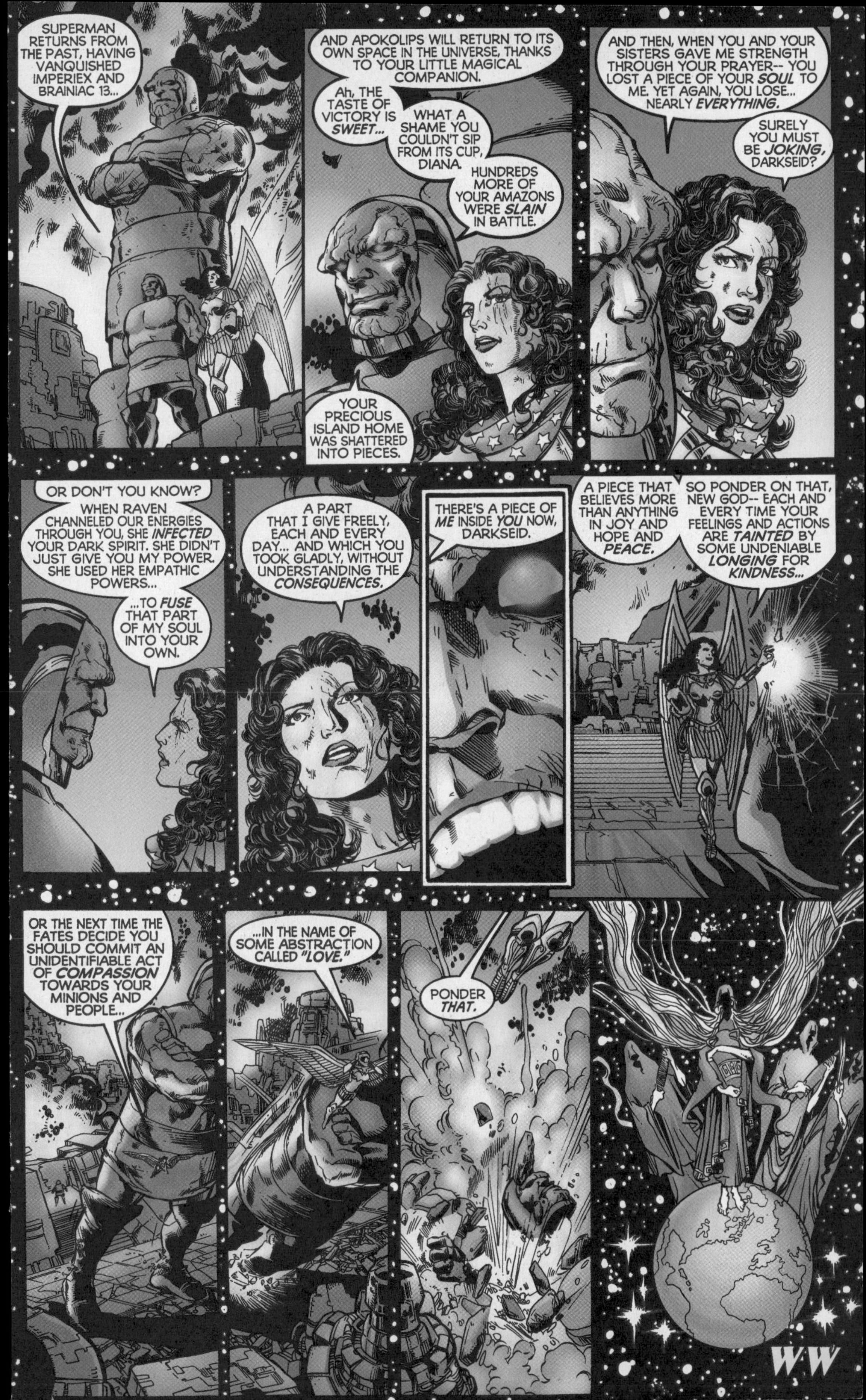
SUPERMAN RETURNS FROM THE PAST, HAVING VANQUISHED IMPERIEX AND BRAINIAC 13...
AND APOKOLIPS WILL RETURN TO ITS OWN SPACE IN THE UNIVERSE, THANKS TO YOUR LITTLE MAGICAL COMPANION.
Ah, THE TASTE OF VICTORY IS SWEET...
WHAT A SHAME YOU COULDN'T SIP FROM ITS CUP, DIANA.
HUNDREDS MORE OF YOUR AMAZONS WERE SLAIN IN BATTLE.
YOUR PRECIOUS ISLAND HOME WAS SHATTERED INTO PIECES.
AND THEN, WHEN YOU AND YOUR SISTERS GAVE ME STRENGTH THROUGH YOUR PRAYER-- YOU LOST A PIECE OF YOUR SOUL TO ME. YET AGAIN, YOU LOSE... NEARLY EVERYTHING.
SURELY YOU MUST BE JOKING, DARKSEID?
OR DON'T YOU KNOW?
WHEN RAVEN CHANNELED OUR ENERGIES THROUGH YOU, SHE INFECTED YOUR DARK SPIRIT. SHE DIDN'T JUST GIVE YOU MY POWER. SHE USED HER EMPATHIC POWERS...
...TO FUSE THAT PART OF MY SOUL INTO YOUR OWN.
A PART THAT I GIVE FREELY, EACH AND EVERY DAY... AND WHICH YOU TOOK GLADLY, WITHOUT UNDERSTANDING THE CONSEQUENCES.
THERE'S A PIECE OF ME INSIDE YOU NOW, DARKSEID.
A PIECE THAT BELIEVES MORE THAN ANYTHING IN JOY AND HOPE AND PEACE.
SO PONDER ON THAT, NEW GOD-- EACH AND EVERY TIME YOUR FEELINGS AND ACTIONS ARE TAINTED BY SOME UNDENIABLE LONGING FOR KINDNESS...
OR THE NEXT TIME THE FATES DECIDE YOU SHOULD COMMIT AN UNIDENTIFIABLE ACT OF COMPASSION TOWARDS YOUR MINIONS AND PEOPLE...
...IN THE NAME OF SOME ABSTRACTION CALLED "LOVE."
PONDER THAT.
W·W

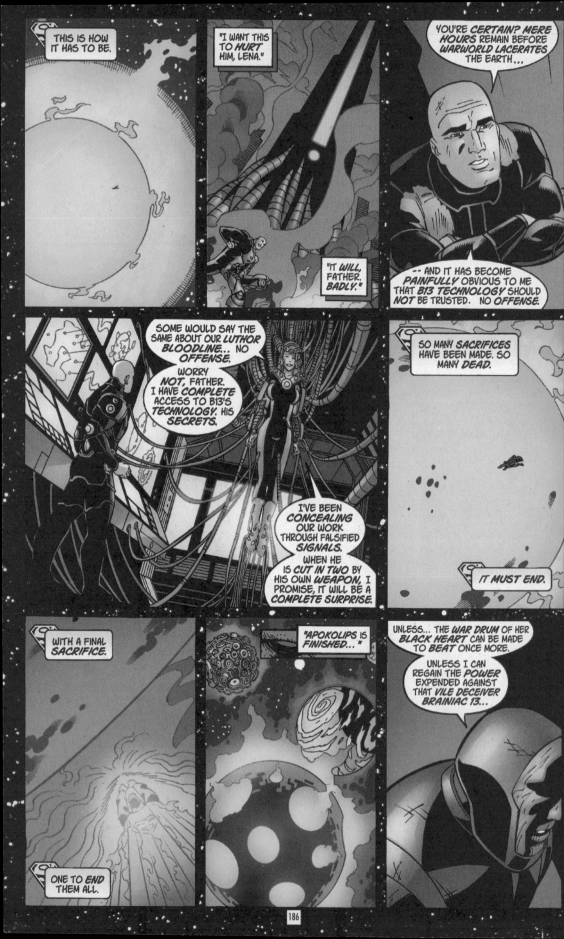

THIS IS HOW IT HAS TO BE.

"I WANT THIS TO *HURT* HIM, LENA."

"IT *WILL*, FATHER. *BADLY*."

YOU'RE *CERTAIN?* MERE *HOURS* REMAIN BEFORE *WARWORLD* LACERATES THE EARTH...

-- AND IT HAS BECOME *PAINFULLY* OBVIOUS TO ME THAT *B13 TECHNOLOGY* SHOULD *NOT* BE TRUSTED. NO *OFFENSE.*

SOME WOULD SAY THE SAME ABOUT OUR *LUTHOR BLOODLINE*... NO *OFFENSE.*

WORRY *NOT*, FATHER. I HAVE *COMPLETE* ACCESS TO B13'S *TECHNOLOGY.* HIS *SECRETS.*

I'VE BEEN *CONCEALING* OUR WORK THROUGH FALSIFIED *SIGNALS.*

WHEN HE IS *CUT IN TWO* BY HIS OWN *WEAPON,* I PROMISE, IT WILL BE A *COMPLETE SURPRISE.*

SO MANY *SACRIFICES* HAVE BEEN MADE. SO MANY *DEAD.*

IT MUST END.

WITH A FINAL *SACRIFICE.*

ONE TO *END* THEM ALL.

"*APOKOLIPS* IS *FINISHED*... "

UNLESS... THE *WAR DRUM* OF HER *BLACK HEART* CAN BE MADE TO BEAT ONCE MORE.

UNLESS I CAN REGAIN THE *POWER* EXPENDED AGAINST THAT *VILE DECEIVER BRAINIAC 13*...

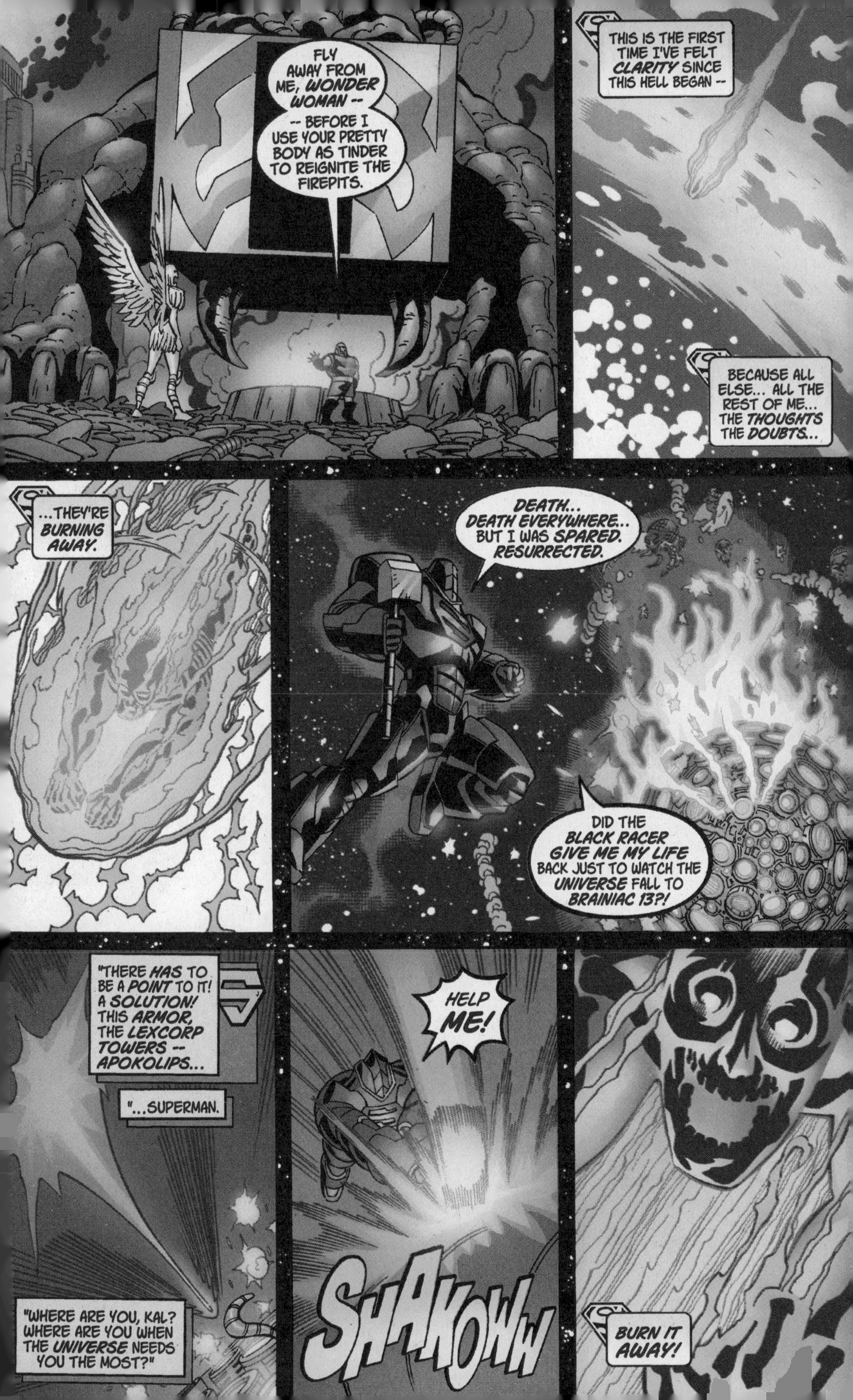
FLY AWAY FROM ME, WONDER WOMAN --
-- BEFORE I USE YOUR PRETTY BODY AS TINDER TO REIGNITE THE FIREPITS.
THIS IS THE FIRST TIME I'VE FELT CLARITY SINCE THIS HELL BEGAN --
BECAUSE ALL ELSE... ALL THE REST OF ME... THE THOUGHTS THE DOUBTS...
...THEY'RE BURNING AWAY.
DEATH... DEATH EVERYWHERE... BUT I WAS SPARED. RESURRECTED.
DID THE BLACK RACER GIVE ME MY LIFE BACK JUST TO WATCH THE UNIVERSE FALL TO BRAINIAC 13?!
"THERE HAS TO BE A POINT TO IT! A SOLUTION! THIS ARMOR, THE LEXCORP TOWERS -- APOKOLIPS...
"...SUPERMAN.
"WHERE ARE YOU, KAL? WHERE ARE YOU WHEN THE UNIVERSE NEEDS YOU THE MOST?"
HELP ME!
SHAKOWW
BURN IT AWAY!

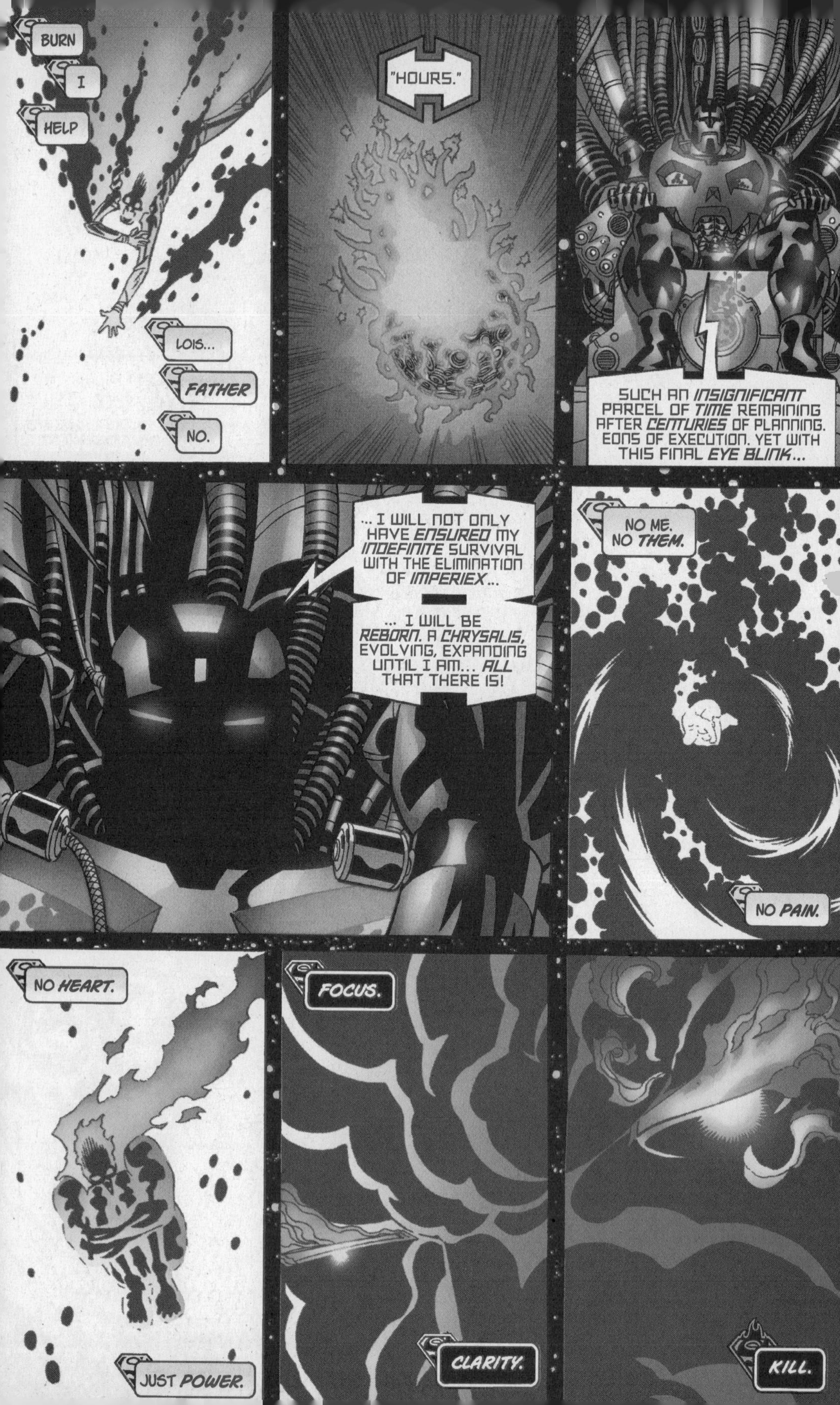
BURN
I
HELP
LOIS...
FATHER
NO.
"HOURS."
SUCH AN INSIGNIFICANT PARCEL OF TIME REMAINING AFTER CENTURIES OF PLANNING. EONS OF EXECUTION. YET WITH THIS FINAL EYE BLINK...
... I WILL NOT ONLY HAVE ENSURED MY INDEFINITE SURVIVAL WITH THE ELIMINATION OF IMPERIEX...
... I WILL BE REBORN. A CHRYSALIS, EVOLVING, EXPANDING UNTIL I AM... ALL THAT THERE IS!
NO ME. NO THEM.
NO PAIN.
NO HEART.
JUST POWER.
FOCUS.
CLARITY.
KILL.

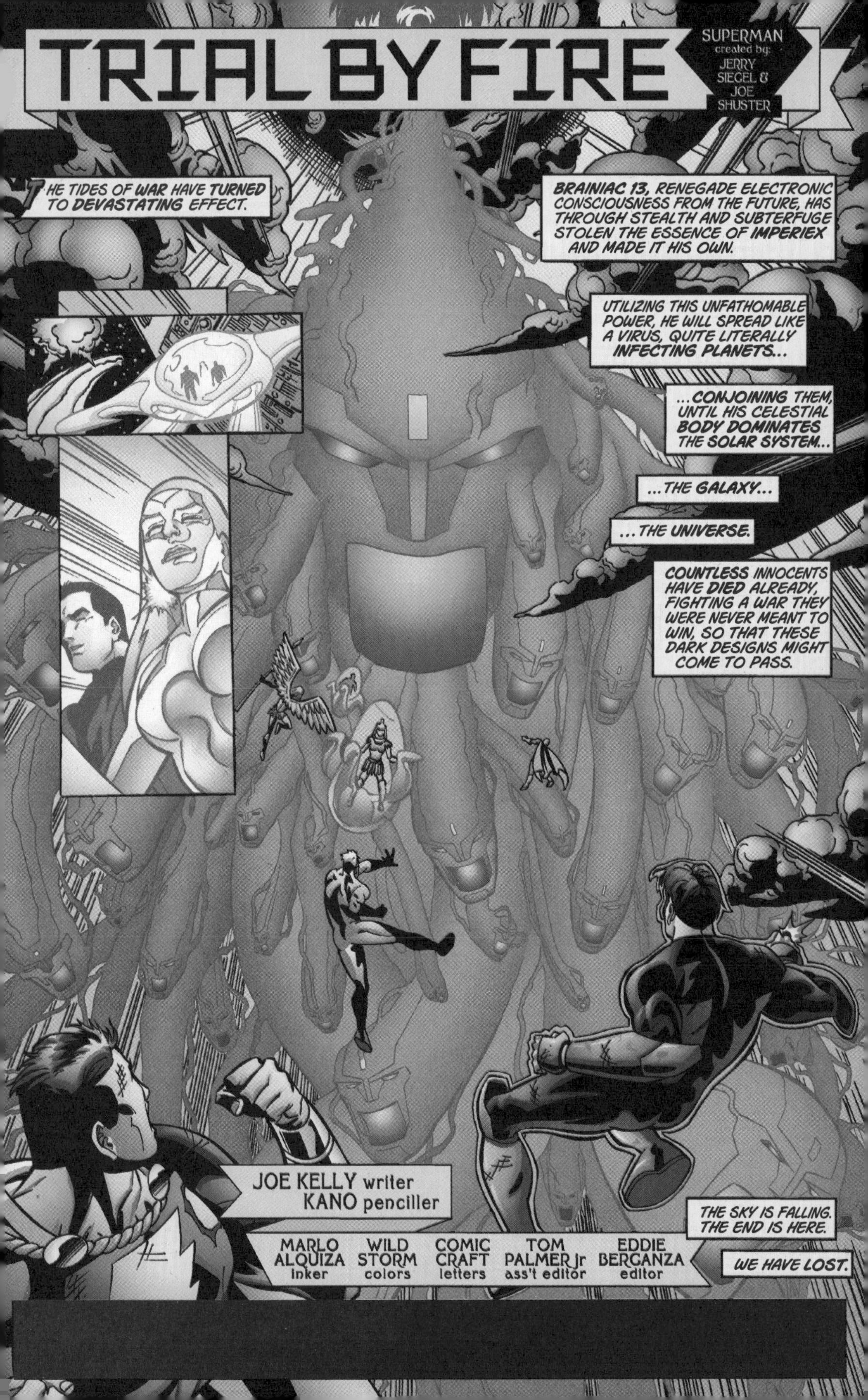
TRIAL BY FIRE
SUPERMAN created by: JERRY SIEGEL & JOE SHUSTER
THE TIDES OF WAR HAVE TURNED TO DEVASTATING EFFECT.
BRAINIAC 13, RENEGADE ELECTRONIC CONSCIOUSNESS FROM THE FUTURE, HAS THROUGH STEALTH AND SUBTERFUGE STOLEN THE ESSENCE OF IMPERIEX AND MADE IT HIS OWN.
UTILIZING THIS UNFATHOMABLE POWER, HE WILL SPREAD LIKE A VIRUS, QUITE LITERALLY INFECTING PLANETS...
...CONJOINING THEM, UNTIL HIS CELESTIAL BODY DOMINATES THE SOLAR SYSTEM...
...THE GALAXY...
...THE UNIVERSE.
COUNTLESS INNOCENTS HAVE DIED ALREADY, FIGHTING A WAR THEY WERE NEVER MEANT TO WIN, SO THAT THESE DARK DESIGNS MIGHT COME TO PASS.
JOE KELLY writer
KANO penciller
MARLO ALQUIZA inker
WILD STORM colors
COMIC CRAFT letters
TOM PALMER jr ass't editor
EDDIE BERGANZA editor
THE SKY IS FALLING. THE END IS HERE.
WE HAVE LOST.

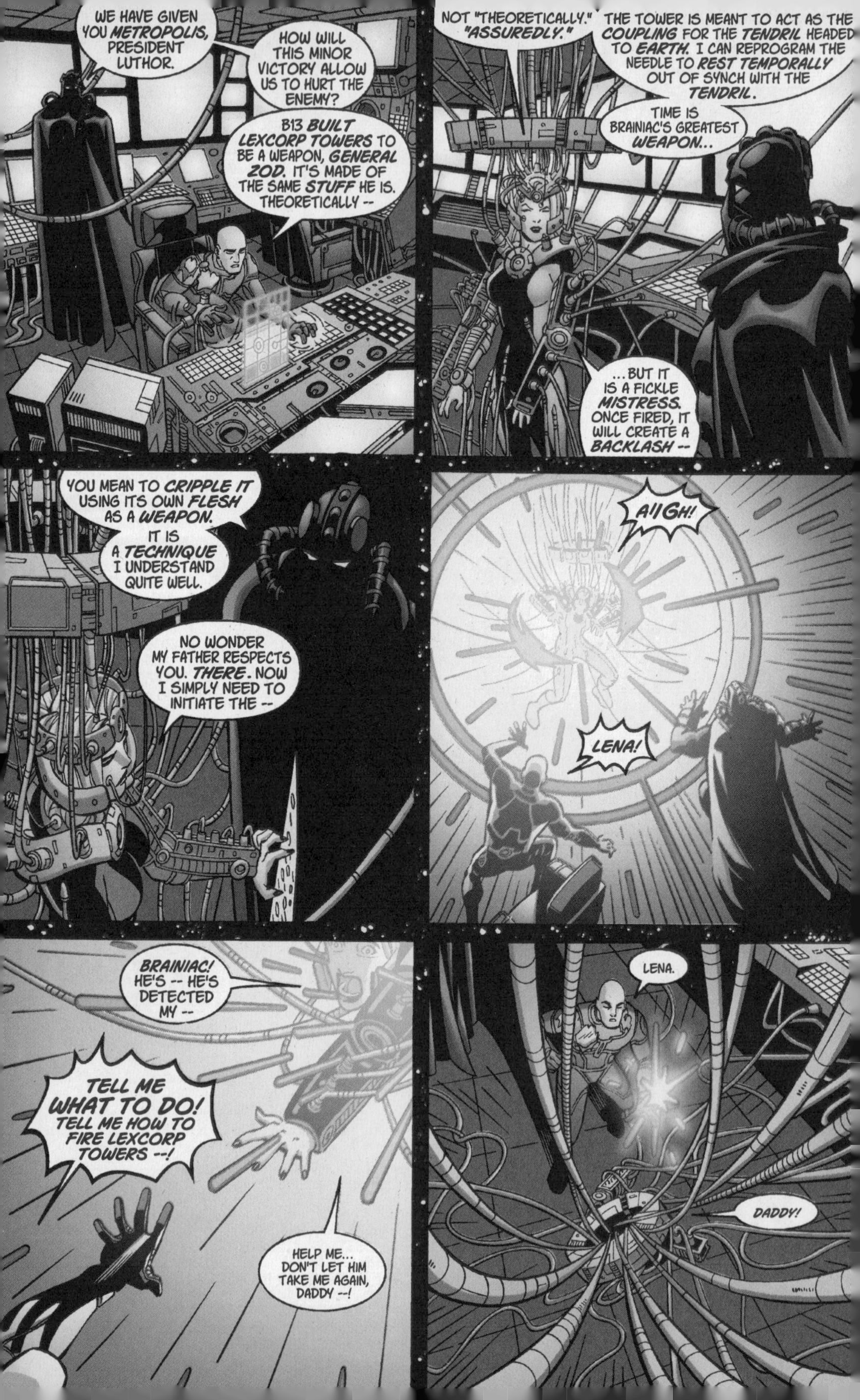
WE HAVE GIVEN YOU METROPOLIS, PRESIDENT LUTHOR.
HOW WILL THIS MINOR VICTORY ALLOW US TO HURT THE ENEMY?
B13 BUILT LEXCORP TOWERS TO BE A WEAPON, GENERAL ZOD. IT'S MADE OF THE SAME STUFF HE IS. THEORETICALLY --
NOT "THEORETICALLY." "ASSUREDLY."
THE TOWER IS MEANT TO ACT AS THE COUPLING FOR THE TENDRIL HEADED TO EARTH. I CAN REPROGRAM THE NEEDLE TO REST TEMPORALLY OUT OF SYNCH WITH THE TENDRIL.
TIME IS BRAINIAC'S GREATEST WEAPON...
...BUT IT IS A FICKLE MISTRESS. ONCE FIRED, IT WILL CREATE A BACKLASH --
YOU MEAN TO CRIPPLE IT USING ITS OWN FLESH AS A WEAPON.
IT IS A TECHNIQUE I UNDERSTAND QUITE WELL.
NO WONDER MY FATHER RESPECTS YOU. THERE. NOW I SIMPLY NEED TO INITIATE THE --
A!!GH!
LENA!
BRAINIAC! HE'S -- HE'S DETECTED MY --
TELL ME WHAT TO DO! TELL ME HOW TO FIRE LEXCORP TOWERS --!
HELP ME... DON'T LET HIM TAKE ME AGAIN, DADDY --!
LENA.
DADDY!

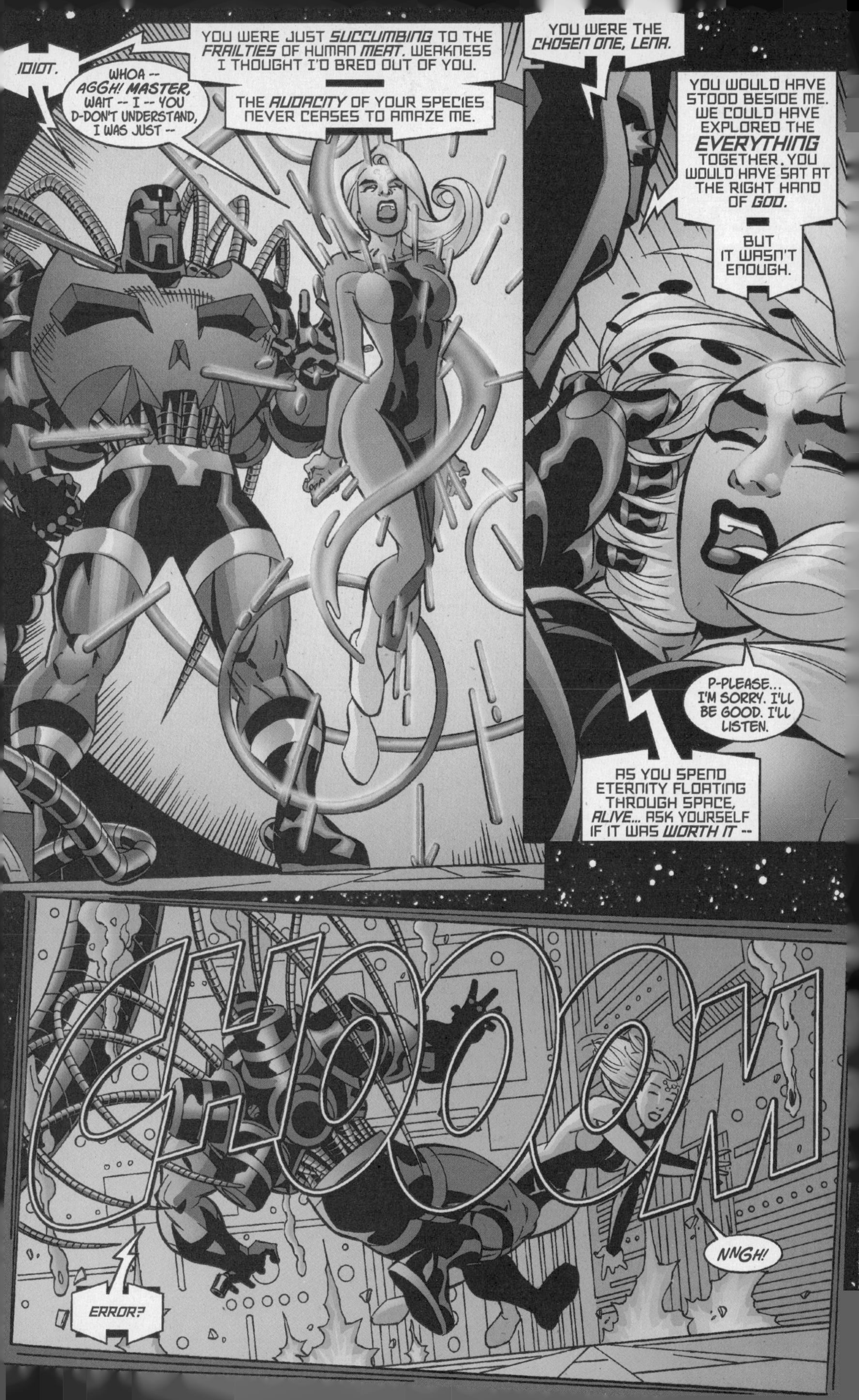
IDIOT.
WHOA -- AGGH! MASTER, WAIT -- I -- YOU D-DON'T UNDERSTAND, I WAS JUST --
YOU WERE JUST SUCCUMBING TO THE FRAILTIES OF HUMAN MEAT. WEAKNESS I THOUGHT I'D BRED OUT OF YOU.
THE AUDACITY OF YOUR SPECIES NEVER CEASES TO AMAZE ME.
YOU WERE THE CHOSEN ONE, LENA.
YOU WOULD HAVE STOOD BESIDE ME. WE COULD HAVE EXPLORED THE EVERYTHING TOGETHER. YOU WOULD HAVE SAT AT THE RIGHT HAND OF GOD.
BUT IT WASN'T ENOUGH.
P-PLEASE... I'M SORRY. I'LL BE GOOD. I'LL LISTEN.
AS YOU SPEND ETERNITY FLOATING THROUGH SPACE, ALIVE... ASK YOURSELF IF IT WAS WORTH IT --
CHOOOM
ERROR?
NNGH!

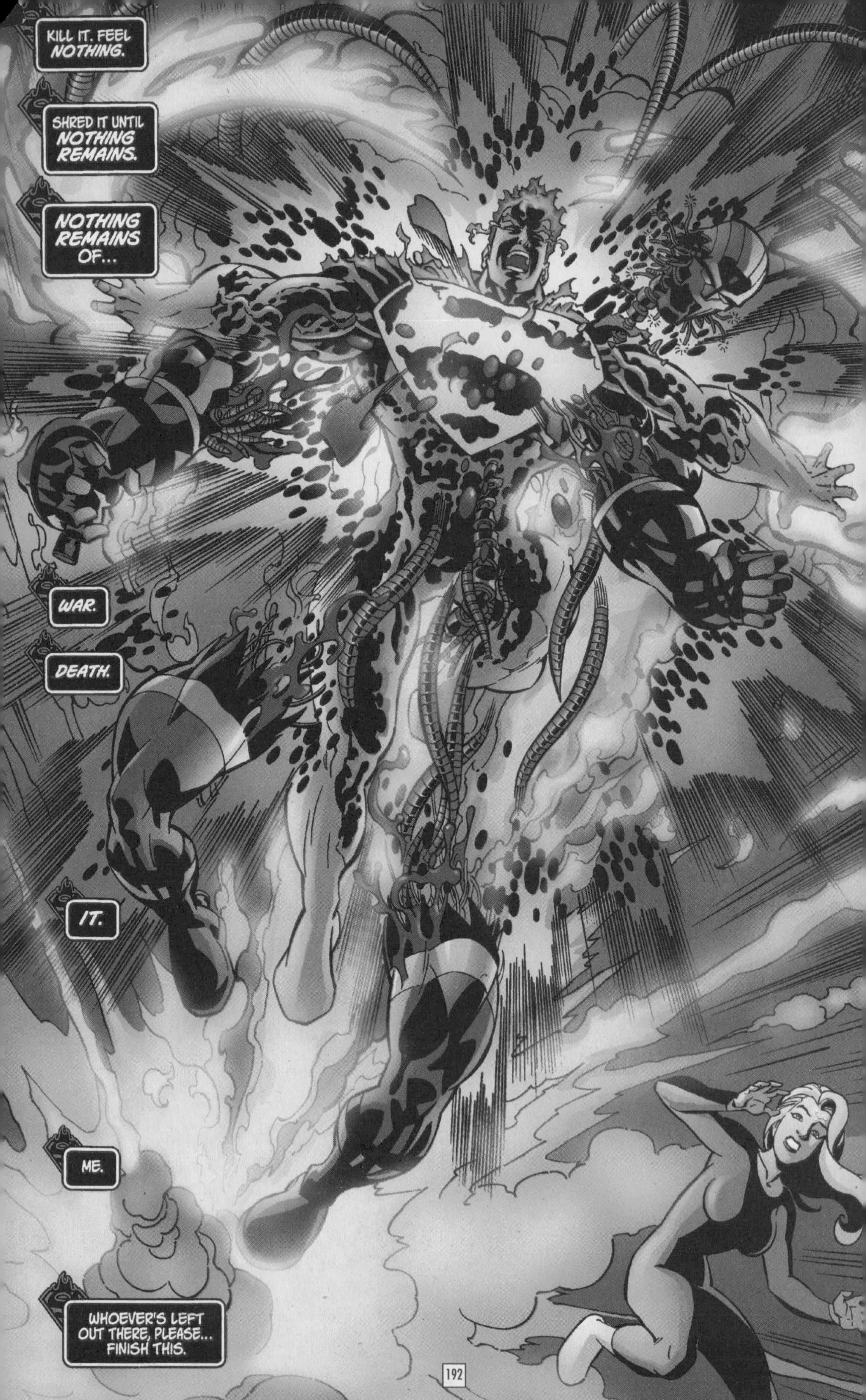
KILL IT. FEEL NOTHING.
SHRED IT UNTIL NOTHING REMAINS.
NOTHING REMAINS OF...
WAR.
DEATH.
IT.
ME.
WHOEVER'S LEFT OUT THERE, PLEASE... FINISH THIS.

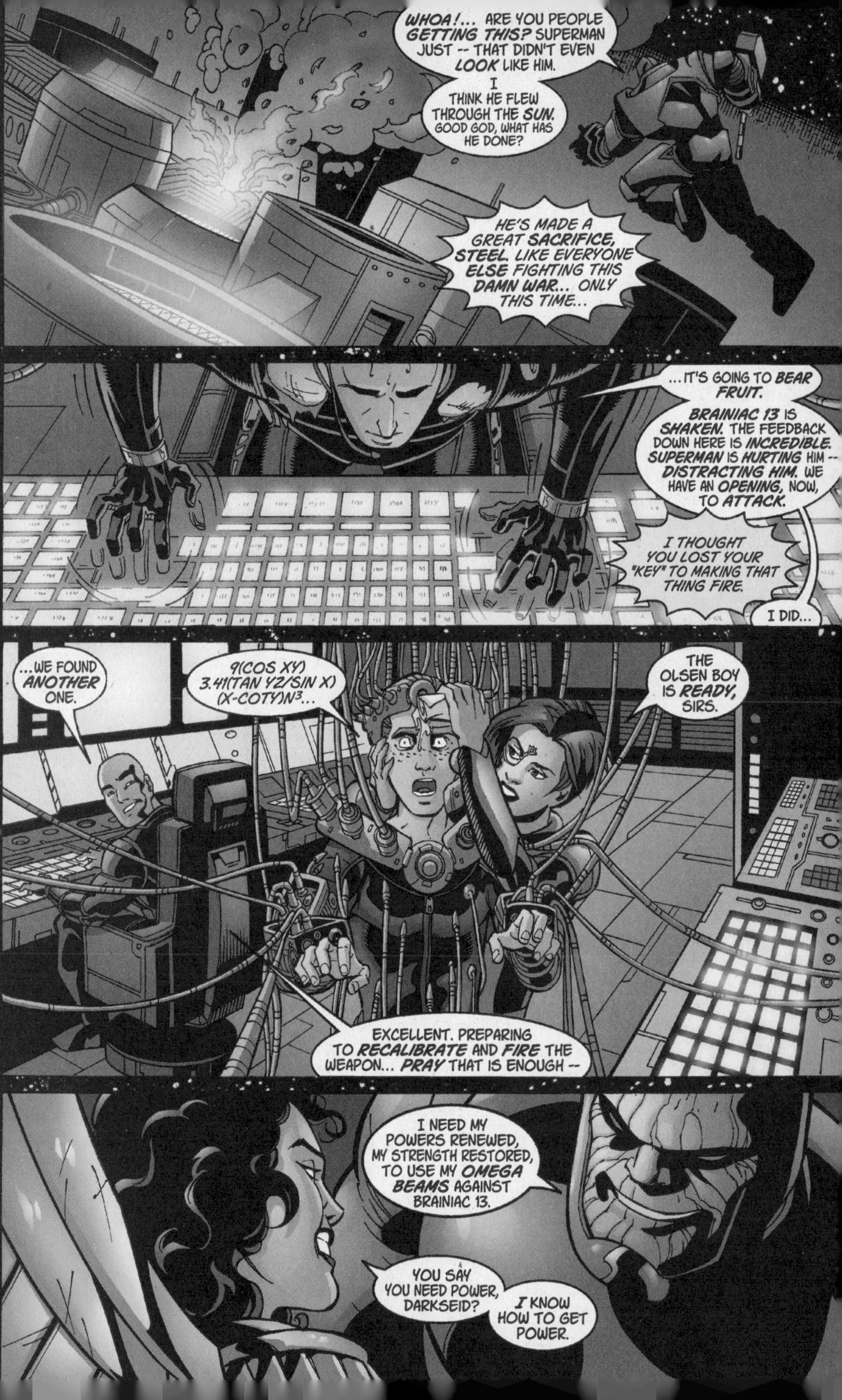
WHOA!... ARE YOU PEOPLE GETTING THIS? SUPERMAN JUST -- THAT DIDN'T EVEN LOOK LIKE HIM.
I THINK HE FLEW THROUGH THE SUN. GOOD GOD, WHAT HAS HE DONE?
HE'S MADE A GREAT SACRIFICE, STEEL. LIKE EVERYONE ELSE FIGHTING THIS DAMN WAR... ONLY THIS TIME...
...IT'S GOING TO BEAR FRUIT.
BRAINIAC 13 IS SHAKEN. THE FEEDBACK DOWN HERE IS INCREDIBLE. SUPERMAN IS HURTING HIM -- DISTRACTING HIM. WE HAVE AN OPENING, NOW, TO ATTACK.
I THOUGHT YOU LOST YOUR "KEY" TO MAKING THAT THING FIRE.
I DID...
...WE FOUND ANOTHER ONE.
9(COS XY) 3.41(TAN Y2/SIN X) (X-COTY)N3...
THE OLSEN BOY IS READY, SIRS.
EXCELLENT. PREPARING TO RECALIBRATE AND FIRE THE WEAPON... PRAY THAT IS ENOUGH --
I NEED MY POWERS RENEWED, MY STRENGTH RESTORED, TO USE MY OMEGA BEAMS AGAINST BRAINIAC 13.
YOU SAY YOU NEED POWER, DARKSEID?
I KNOW HOW TO GET POWER.

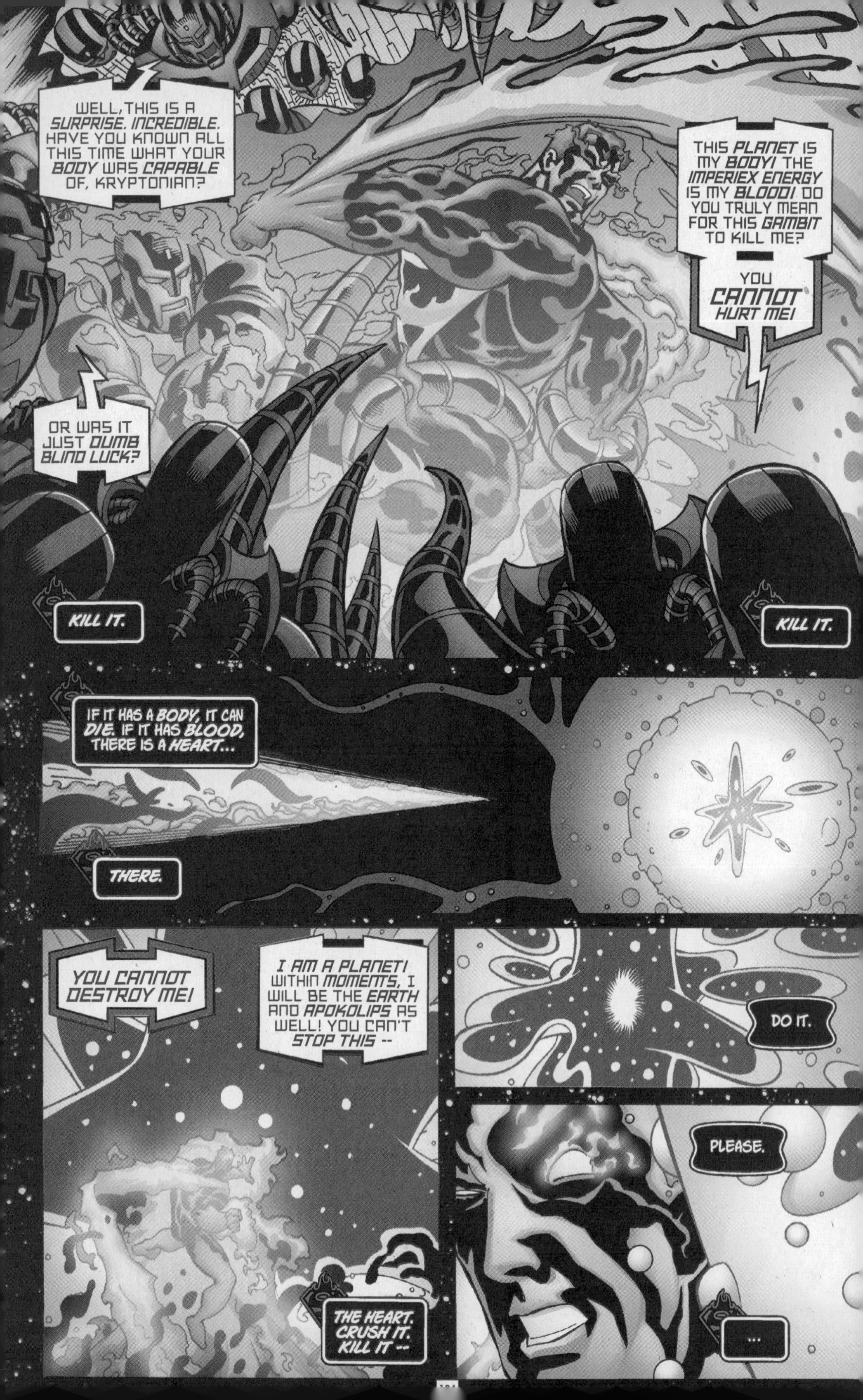

WELL, THIS IS A SURPRISE. INCREDIBLE. HAVE YOU KNOWN ALL THIS TIME WHAT YOUR BODY WAS CAPABLE OF, KRYPTONIAN?
OR WAS IT JUST DUMB BLIND LUCK?
THIS PLANET IS MY BODY! THE IMPERIEX ENERGY IS MY BLOOD! DO YOU TRULY MEAN FOR THIS GAMBIT TO KILL ME?
YOU CANNOT HURT ME!
KILL IT.
KILL IT.
IF IT HAS A BODY, IT CAN DIE. IF IT HAS BLOOD, THERE IS A HEART...
THERE.
YOU CANNOT DESTROY ME!
I AM A PLANET! WITHIN MOMENTS, I WILL BE THE EARTH AND APOKOLIPS AS WELL! YOU CAN'T STOP THIS --
THE HEART. CRUSH IT. KILL IT --
DO IT.
PLEASE.
...

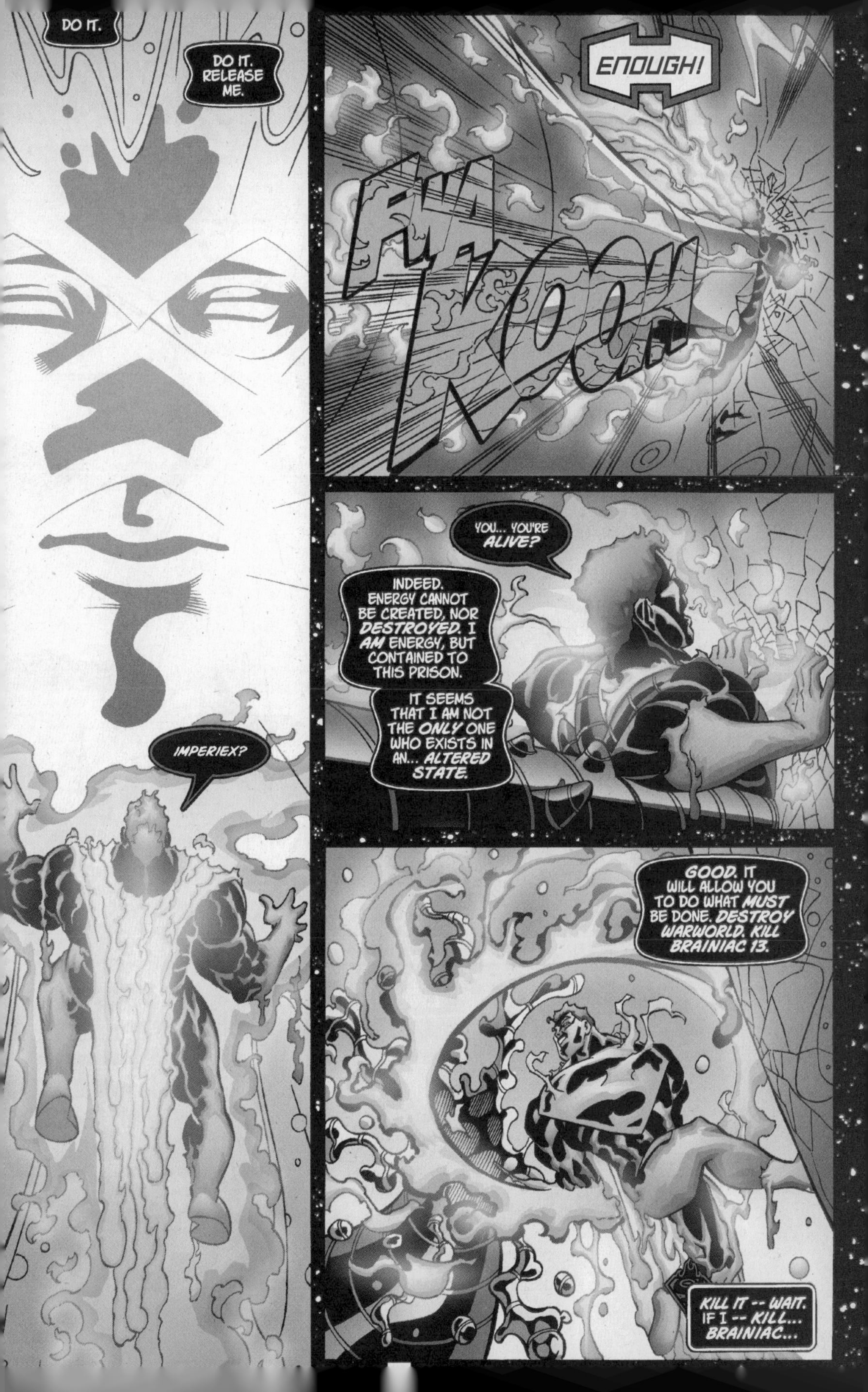
DO IT.
DO IT. RELEASE ME.
IMPERIEX?
ENOUGH!
FWAKOOM
YOU... YOU'RE ALIVE?
INDEED. ENERGY CANNOT BE CREATED, NOR DESTROYED. I AM ENERGY, BUT CONTAINED TO THIS PRISON.
IT SEEMS THAT I AM NOT THE ONLY ONE WHO EXISTS IN AN... ALTERED STATE.
GOOD. IT WILL ALLOW YOU TO DO WHAT MUST BE DONE. DESTROY WARWORLD. KILL BRAINIAC 13.
KILL IT -- WAIT. IF I -- KILL... BRAINIAC...

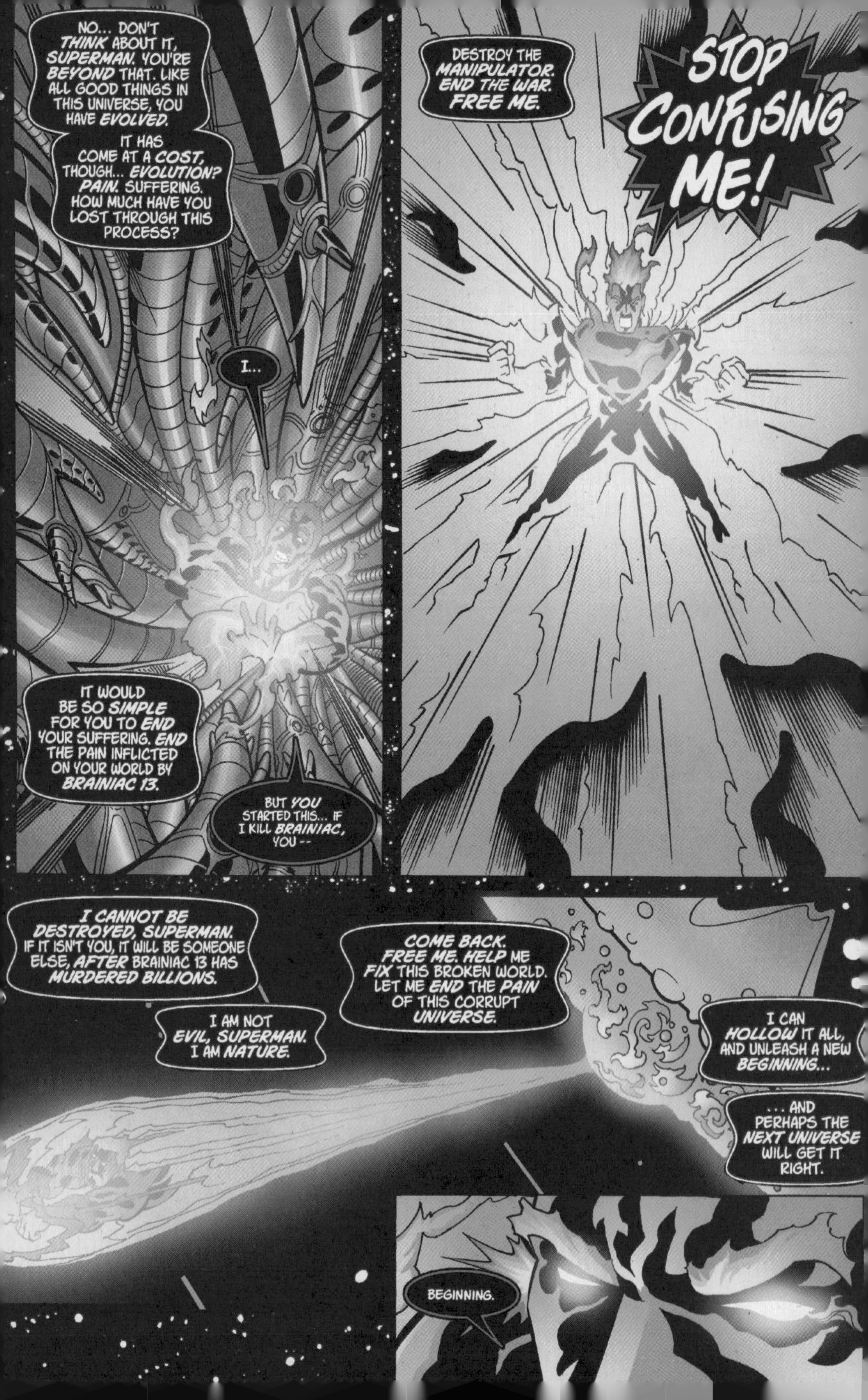
NO... DON'T THINK ABOUT IT, SUPERMAN. YOU'RE BEYOND THAT. LIKE ALL GOOD THINGS IN THIS UNIVERSE, YOU HAVE EVOLVED.
IT HAS COME AT A COST, THOUGH... EVOLUTION? PAIN. SUFFERING. HOW MUCH HAVE YOU LOST THROUGH THIS PROCESS?
I...
IT WOULD BE SO SIMPLE FOR YOU TO END YOUR SUFFERING. END THE PAIN INFLICTED ON YOUR WORLD BY BRAINIAC 13.
BUT YOU STARTED THIS... IF I KILL BRAINIAC, YOU --
DESTROY THE MANIPULATOR. END THE WAR. FREE ME.
STOP CONFUSING ME!
I CANNOT BE DESTROYED, SUPERMAN. IF IT ISN'T YOU, IT WILL BE SOMEONE ELSE, AFTER BRAINIAC 13 HAS MURDERED BILLIONS.
I AM NOT EVIL, SUPERMAN. I AM NATURE.
COME BACK. FREE ME. HELP ME FIX THIS BROKEN WORLD. LET ME END THE PAIN OF THIS CORRUPT UNIVERSE.
I CAN HOLLOW IT ALL, AND UNLEASH A NEW BEGINNING...
... AND PERHAPS THE NEXT UNIVERSE WILL GET IT RIGHT.
BEGINNING.

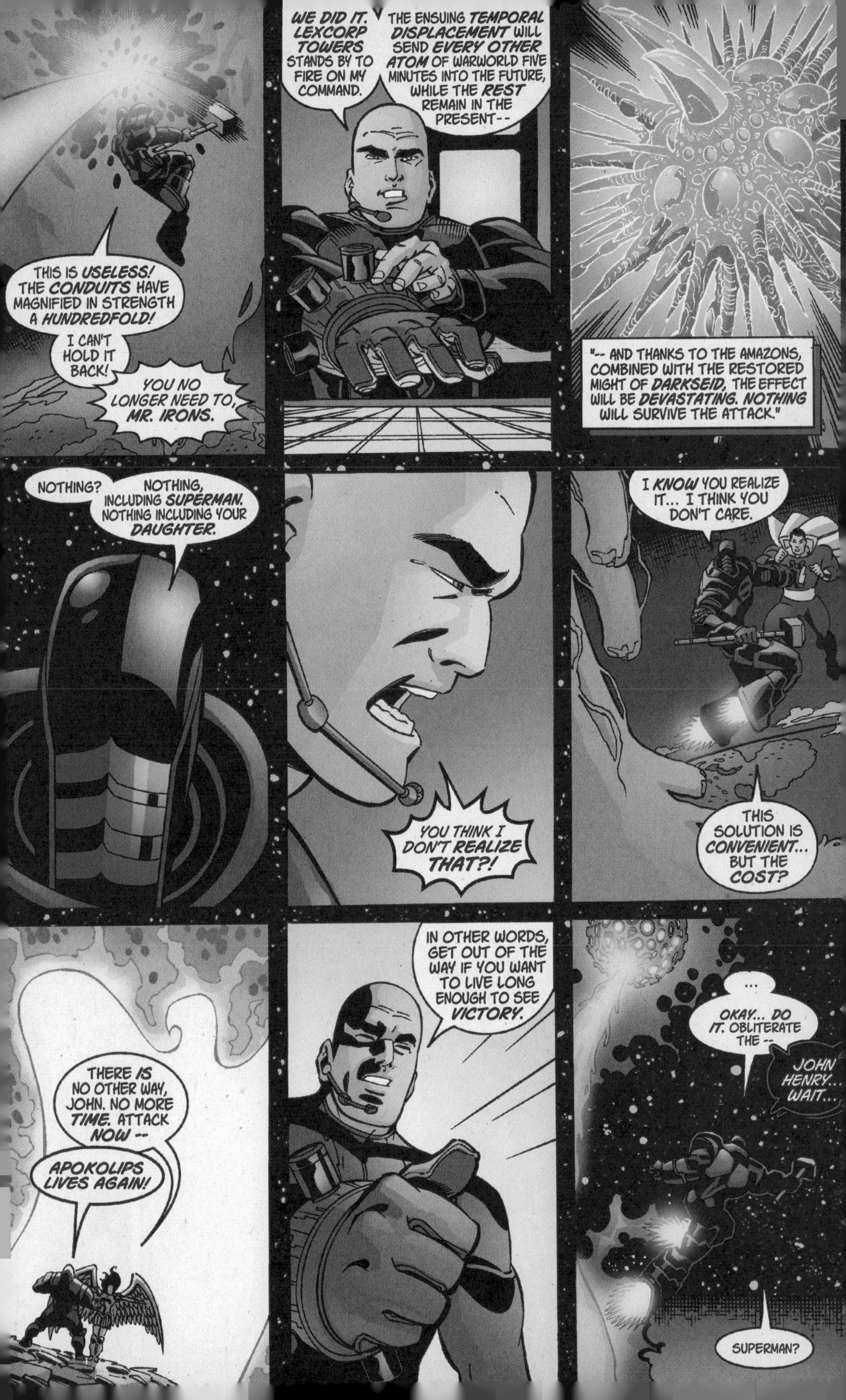

THIS IS USELESS! THE CONDUITS HAVE MAGNIFIED IN STRENGTH A HUNDREDFOLD!
I CAN'T HOLD IT BACK!
YOU NO LONGER NEED TO, MR. IRONS.
WE DID IT. LEXCORP TOWERS STANDS BY TO FIRE ON MY COMMAND.
THE ENSUING TEMPORAL DISPLACEMENT WILL SEND EVERY OTHER ATOM OF WARWORLD FIVE MINUTES INTO THE FUTURE, WHILE THE REST REMAIN IN THE PRESENT--
"-- AND THANKS TO THE AMAZONS, COMBINED WITH THE RESTORED MIGHT OF DARKSEID, THE EFFECT WILL BE DEVASTATING. NOTHING WILL SURVIVE THE ATTACK."
NOTHING?
NOTHING, INCLUDING SUPERMAN. NOTHING INCLUDING YOUR DAUGHTER.
YOU THINK I DON'T REALIZE THAT?!
I KNOW YOU REALIZE IT... I THINK YOU DON'T CARE.
THIS SOLUTION IS CONVENIENT... BUT THE COST?
THERE IS NO OTHER WAY, JOHN. NO MORE TIME. ATTACK NOW --
APOKOLIPS LIVES AGAIN!
IN OTHER WORDS, GET OUT OF THE WAY IF YOU WANT TO LIVE LONG ENOUGH TO SEE VICTORY.
...
OKAY... DO IT. OBLITERATE THE --
JOHN HENRY... WAIT...
SUPERMAN?

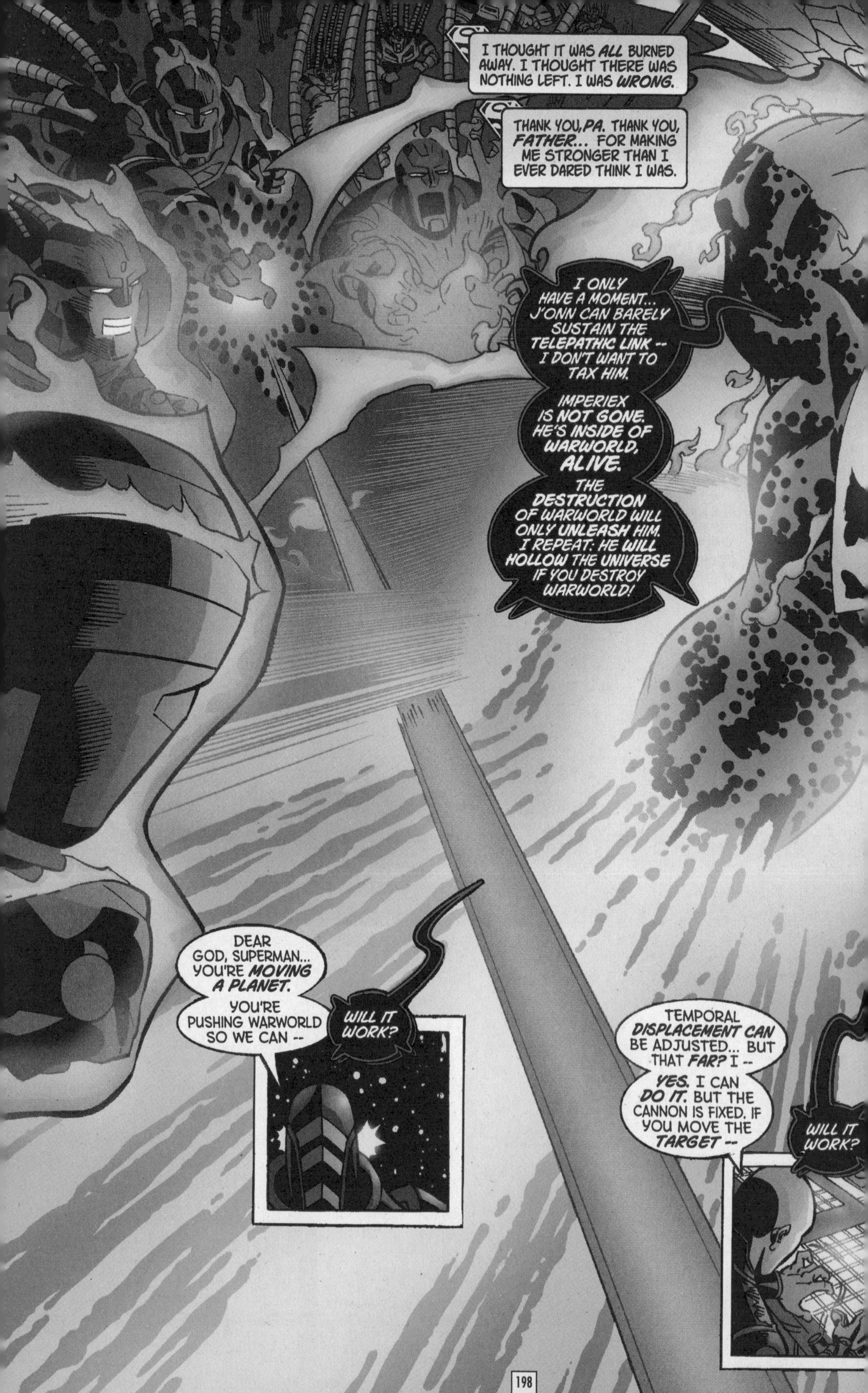

I THOUGHT IT WAS ALL BURNED AWAY. I THOUGHT THERE WAS NOTHING LEFT. I WAS WRONG.
THANK YOU, PA. THANK YOU, FATHER... FOR MAKING ME STRONGER THAN I EVER DARED THINK I WAS.
I ONLY HAVE A MOMENT... J'ONN CAN BARELY SUSTAIN THE TELEPATHIC LINK -- I DON'T WANT TO TAX HIM.
IMPERIEX IS NOT GONE. HE'S INSIDE OF WARWORLD, ALIVE.
THE DESTRUCTION OF WARWORLD WILL ONLY UNLEASH HIM. I REPEAT: HE WILL HOLLOW THE UNIVERSE IF YOU DESTROY WARWORLD!
DEAR GOD, SUPERMAN... YOU'RE MOVING A PLANET.
YOU'RE PUSHING WARWORLD SO WE CAN --
WILL IT WORK?
TEMPORAL DISPLACEMENT CAN BE ADJUSTED... BUT THAT FAR? I --
YES. I CAN DO IT. BUT THE CANNON IS FIXED. IF YOU MOVE THE TARGET --
WILL IT WORK?

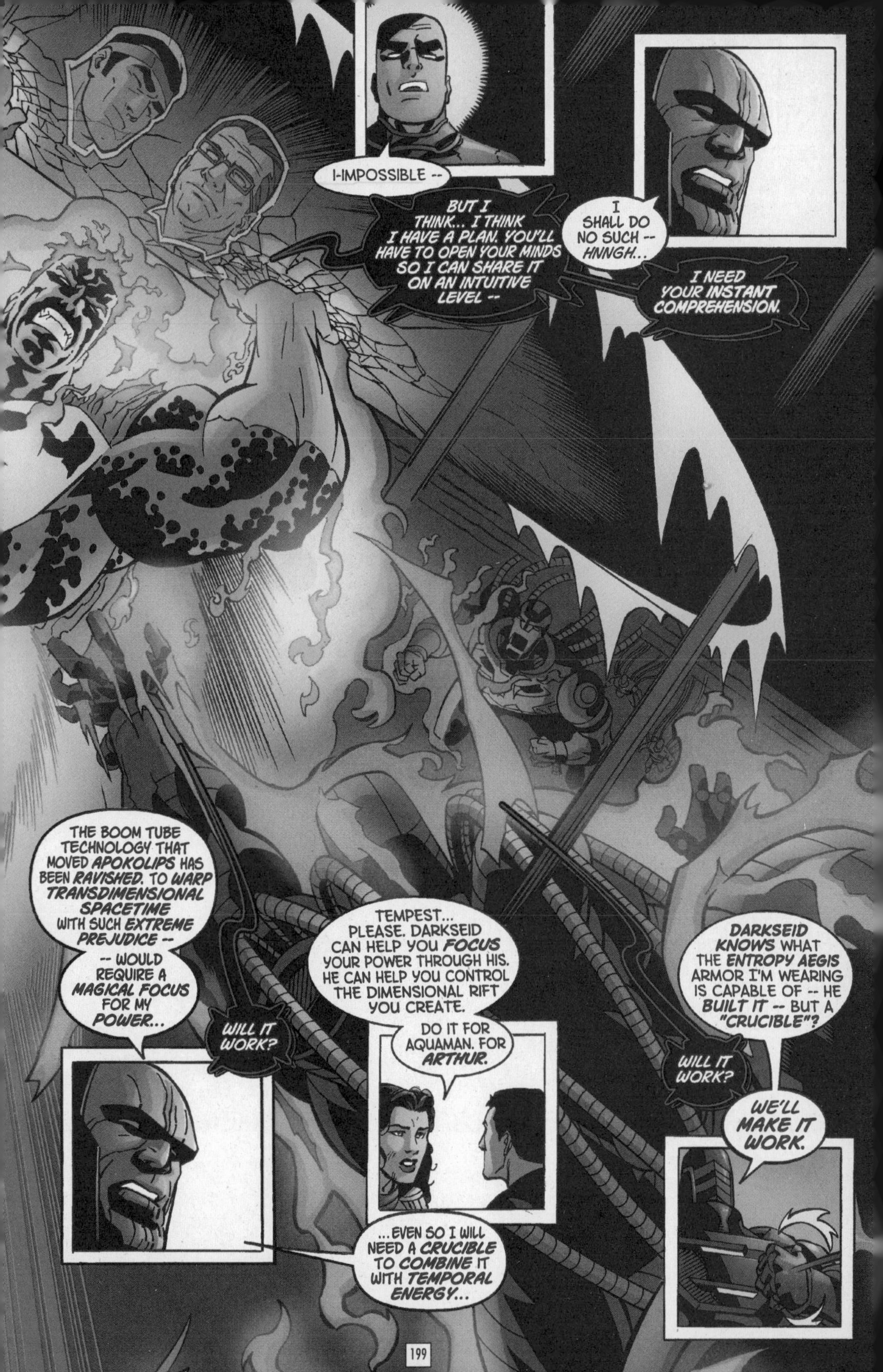
I-IMPOSSIBLE --
BUT I THINK... I THINK I HAVE A PLAN. YOU'LL HAVE TO OPEN YOUR MINDS SO I CAN SHARE IT ON AN INTUITIVE LEVEL --
I SHALL DO NO SUCH -- HNNGH...
I NEED YOUR INSTANT COMPREHENSION.
THE BOOM TUBE TECHNOLOGY THAT MOVED APOKOLIPS HAS BEEN RAVISHED. TO WARP TRANSDIMENSIONAL SPACETIME WITH SUCH EXTREME PREJUDICE --
-- WOULD REQUIRE A MAGICAL FOCUS FOR MY POWER...
WILL IT WORK?
...EVEN SO I WILL NEED A CRUCIBLE TO COMBINE IT WITH TEMPORAL ENERGY...
TEMPEST... PLEASE. DARKSEID CAN HELP YOU FOCUS YOUR POWER THROUGH HIS. HE CAN HELP YOU CONTROL THE DIMENSIONAL RIFT YOU CREATE.
DO IT FOR AQUAMAN. FOR ARTHUR.
DARKSEID KNOWS WHAT THE ENTROPY AEGIS ARMOR I'M WEARING IS CAPABLE OF -- HE BUILT IT -- BUT A "CRUCIBLE"?
WILL IT WORK?
WE'LL MAKE IT WORK.

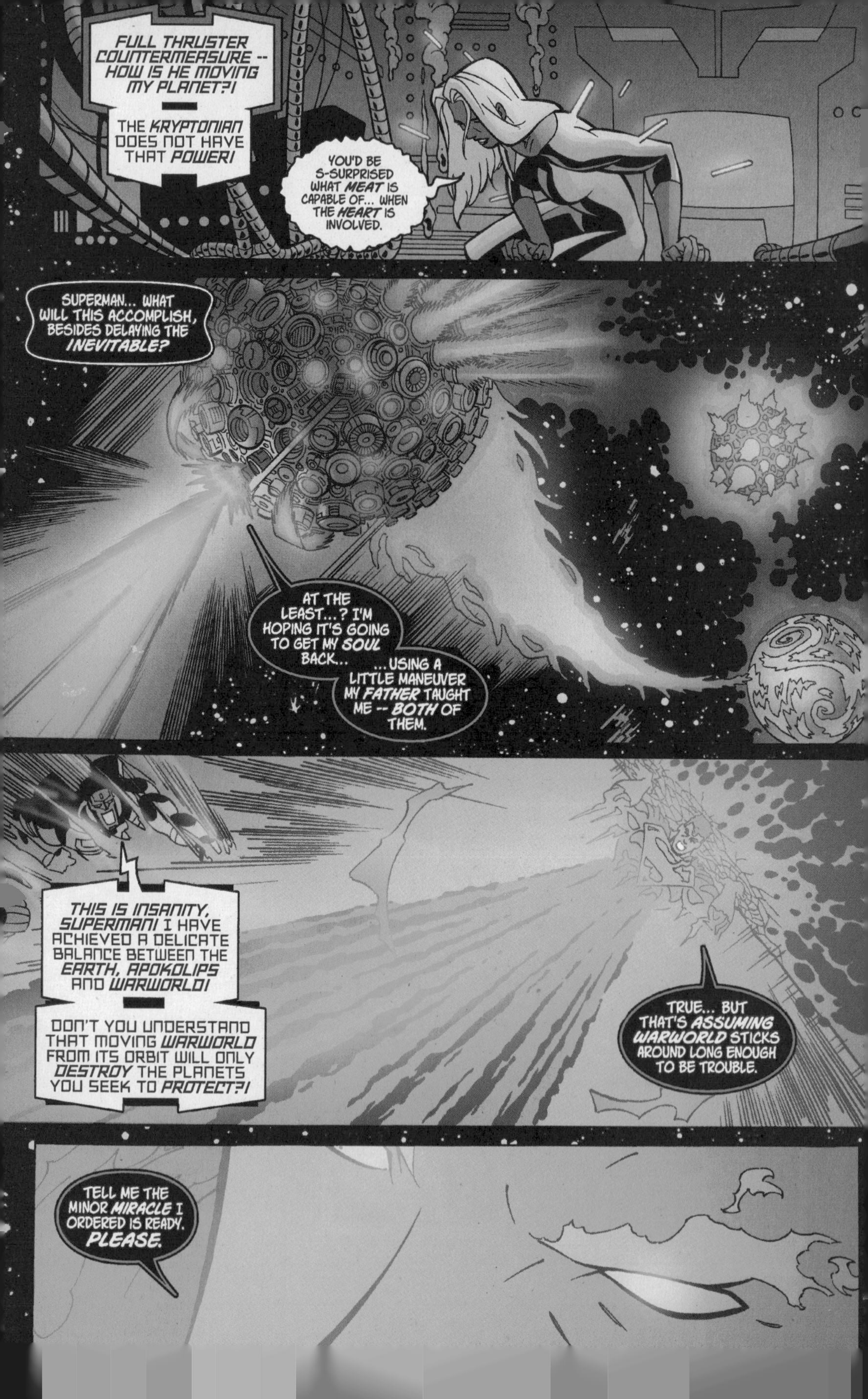
FULL THRUSTER COUNTERMEASURE -- HOW IS HE MOVING MY PLANET?!
THE KRYPTONIAN DOES NOT HAVE THAT POWER!
YOU'D BE S-SURPRISED WHAT MEAT IS CAPABLE OF... WHEN THE HEART IS INVOLVED.
SUPERMAN... WHAT WILL THIS ACCOMPLISH, BESIDES DELAYING THE INEVITABLE?
AT THE LEAST...? I'M HOPING IT'S GOING TO GET MY SOUL BACK...
...USING A LITTLE MANEUVER MY FATHER TAUGHT ME -- BOTH OF THEM.
THIS IS INSANITY, SUPERMAN! I HAVE ACHIEVED A DELICATE BALANCE BETWEEN THE EARTH, APOKOLIPS AND WARWORLD!
DON'T YOU UNDERSTAND THAT MOVING WARWORLD FROM ITS ORBIT WILL ONLY DESTROY THE PLANETS YOU SEEK TO PROTECT?!
TRUE... BUT THAT'S ASSUMING WARWORLD STICKS AROUND LONG ENOUGH TO BE TROUBLE.
TELL ME THE MINOR MIRACLE I ORDERED IS READY. PLEASE.

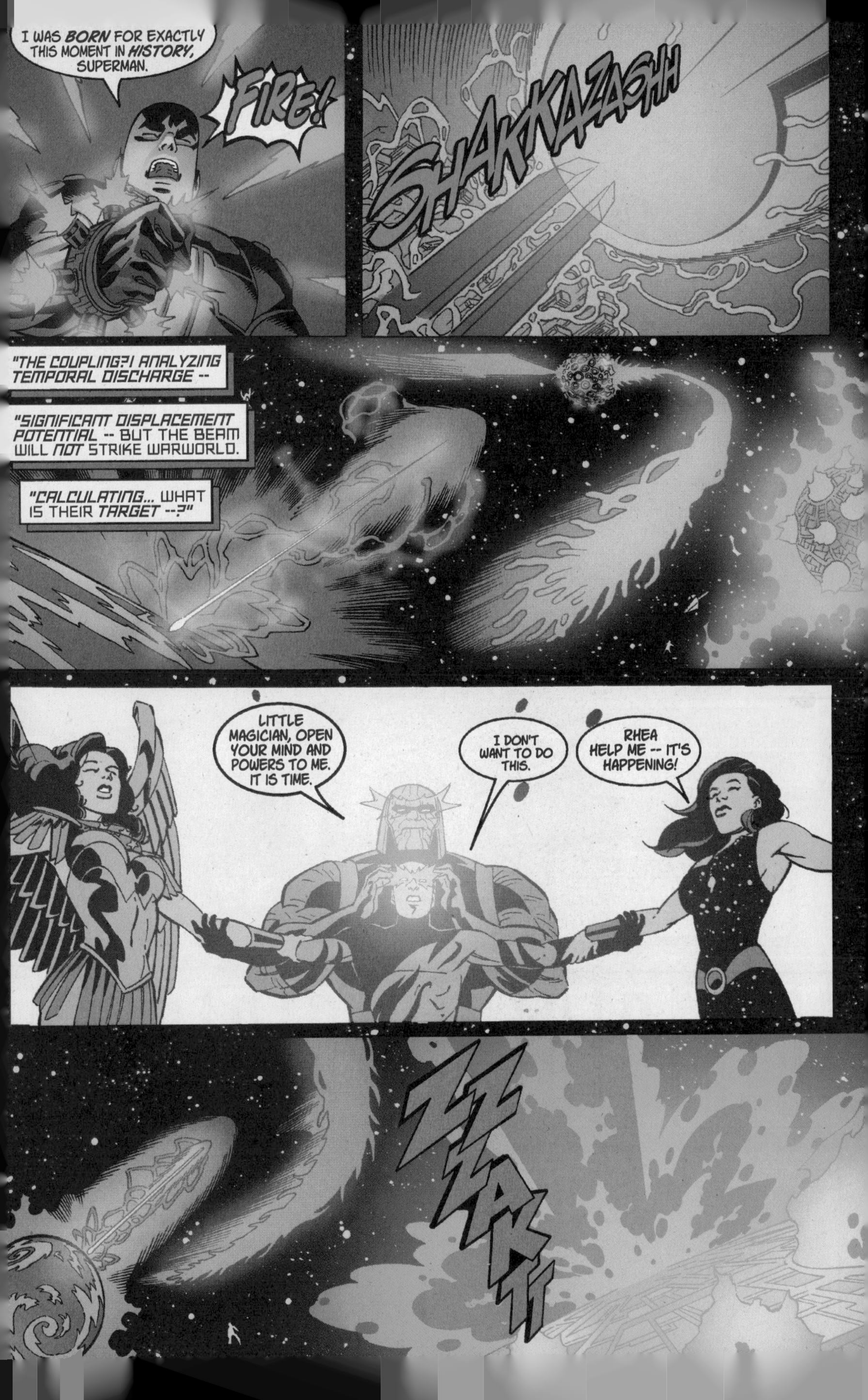
I WAS BORN FOR EXACTLY THIS MOMENT IN HISTORY, SUPERMAN.
FIRE!
SHAKKAZASHH
"THE COUPLING?! ANALYZING TEMPORAL DISCHARGE --
"SIGNIFICANT DISPLACEMENT POTENTIAL -- BUT THE BEAM WILL NOT STRIKE WARWORLD.
"CALCULATING... WHAT IS THEIR TARGET --?"
LITTLE MAGICIAN, OPEN YOUR MIND AND POWERS TO ME. IT IS TIME.
I DON'T WANT TO DO THIS.
RHEA HELP ME -- IT'S HAPPENING!
ZZZAKTT

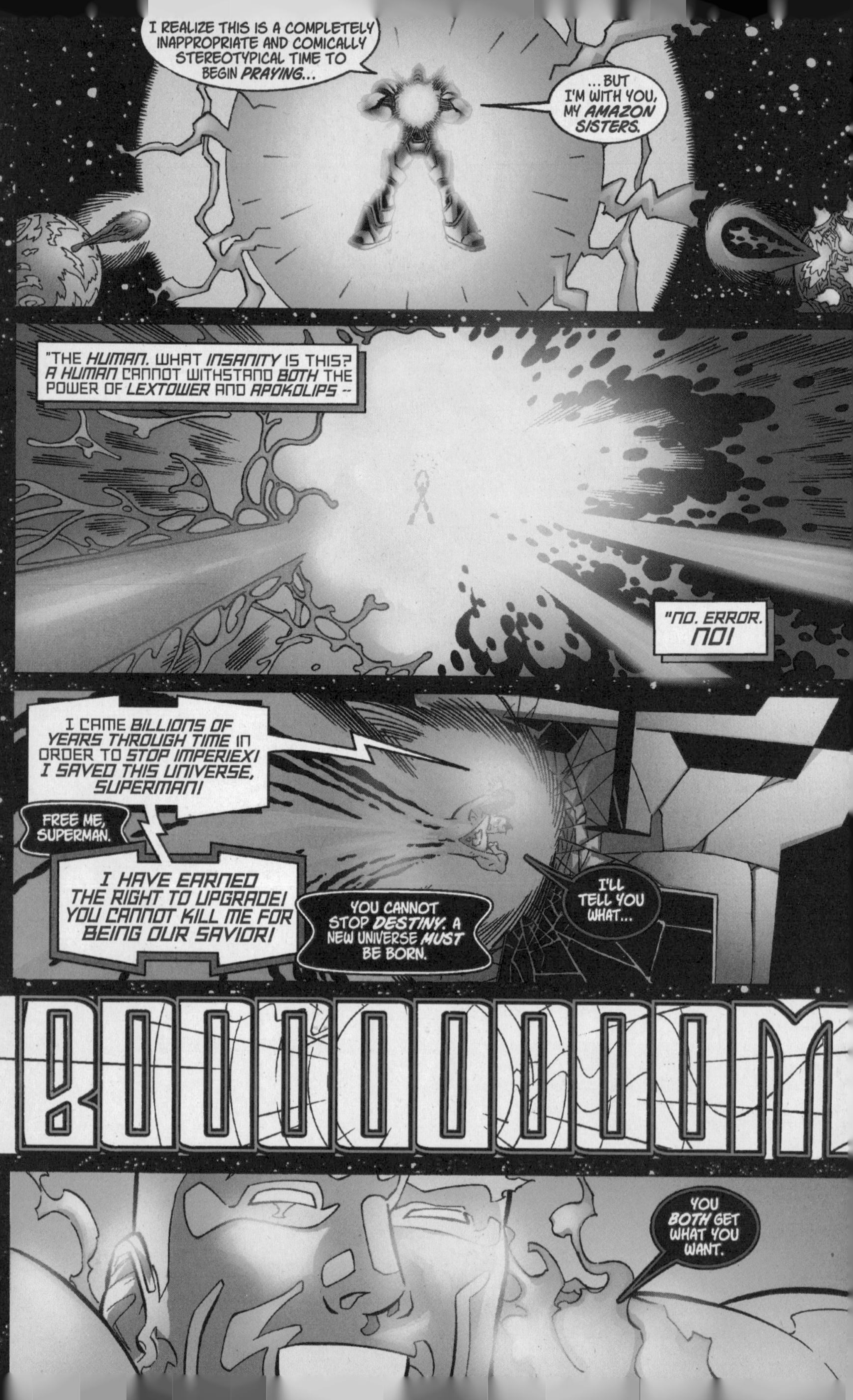
I REALIZE THIS IS A COMPLETELY INAPPROPRIATE AND COMICALLY STEREOTYPICAL TIME TO BEGIN PRAYING...
...BUT I'M WITH YOU, MY AMAZON SISTERS.
"THE HUMAN. WHAT INSANITY IS THIS? A HUMAN CANNOT WITHSTAND BOTH THE POWER OF LEXTOWER AND APOKOLIPS --
"NO. ERROR. NO!
I CAME BILLIONS OF YEARS THROUGH TIME IN ORDER TO STOP IMPERIEX! I SAVED THIS UNIVERSE, SUPERMAN!
FREE ME, SUPERMAN.
I HAVE EARNED THE RIGHT TO UPGRADE! YOU CANNOT KILL ME FOR BEING OUR SAVIOR!
YOU CANNOT STOP DESTINY. A NEW UNIVERSE MUST BE BORN.
I'LL TELL YOU WHAT...
BOOOOOOOOM
YOU BOTH GET WHAT YOU WANT.

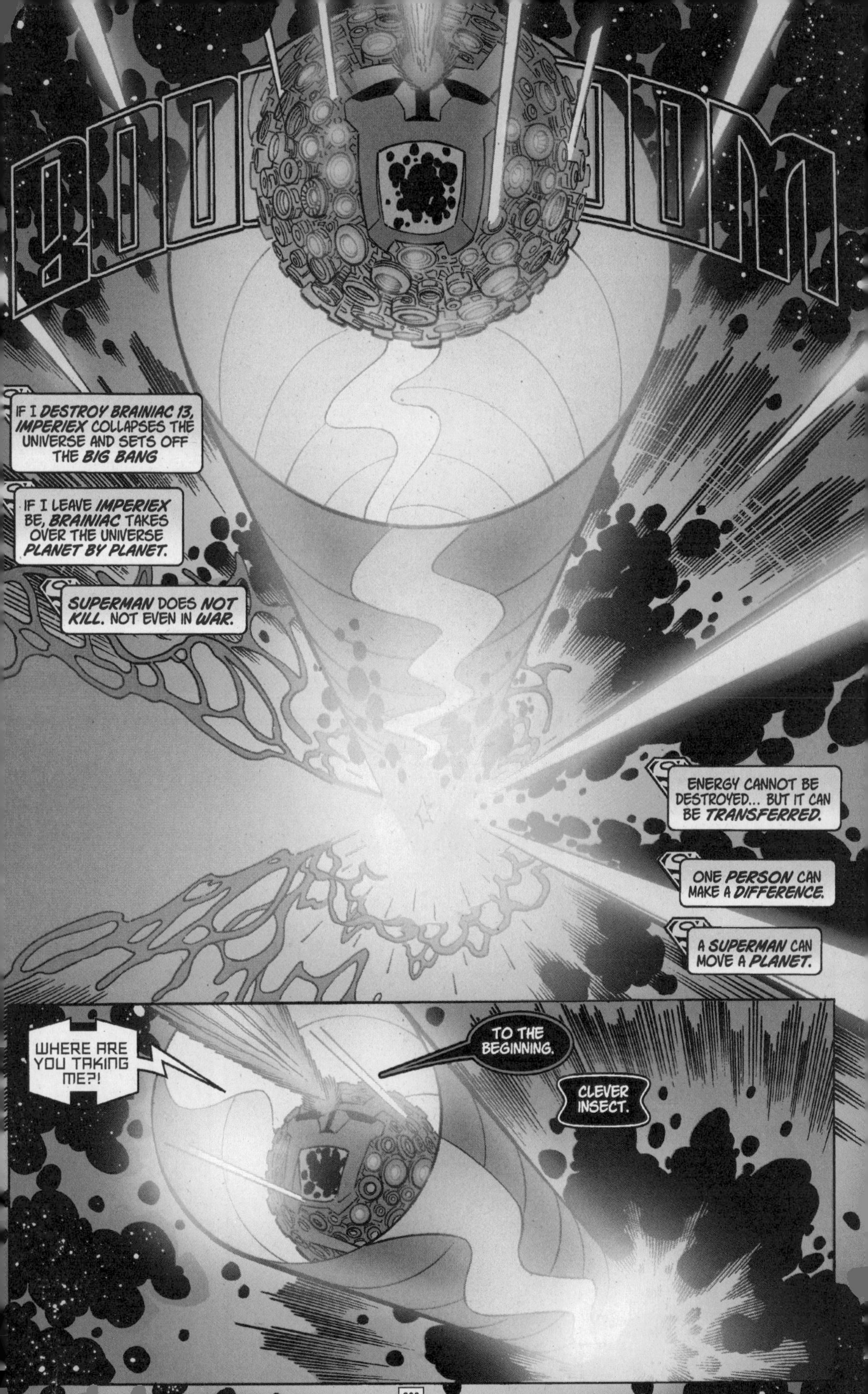
IF I DESTROY BRAINIAC 13, IMPERIEX COLLAPSES THE UNIVERSE AND SETS OFF THE BIG BANG
IF I LEAVE IMPERIEX BE, BRAINIAC TAKES OVER THE UNIVERSE PLANET BY PLANET.
SUPERMAN DOES NOT KILL. NOT EVEN IN WAR.
ENERGY CANNOT BE DESTROYED... BUT IT CAN BE TRANSFERRED.
ONE PERSON CAN MAKE A DIFFERENCE.
A SUPERMAN CAN MOVE A PLANET.
WHERE ARE YOU TAKING ME?!
TO THE BEGINNING.
CLEVER INSECT.

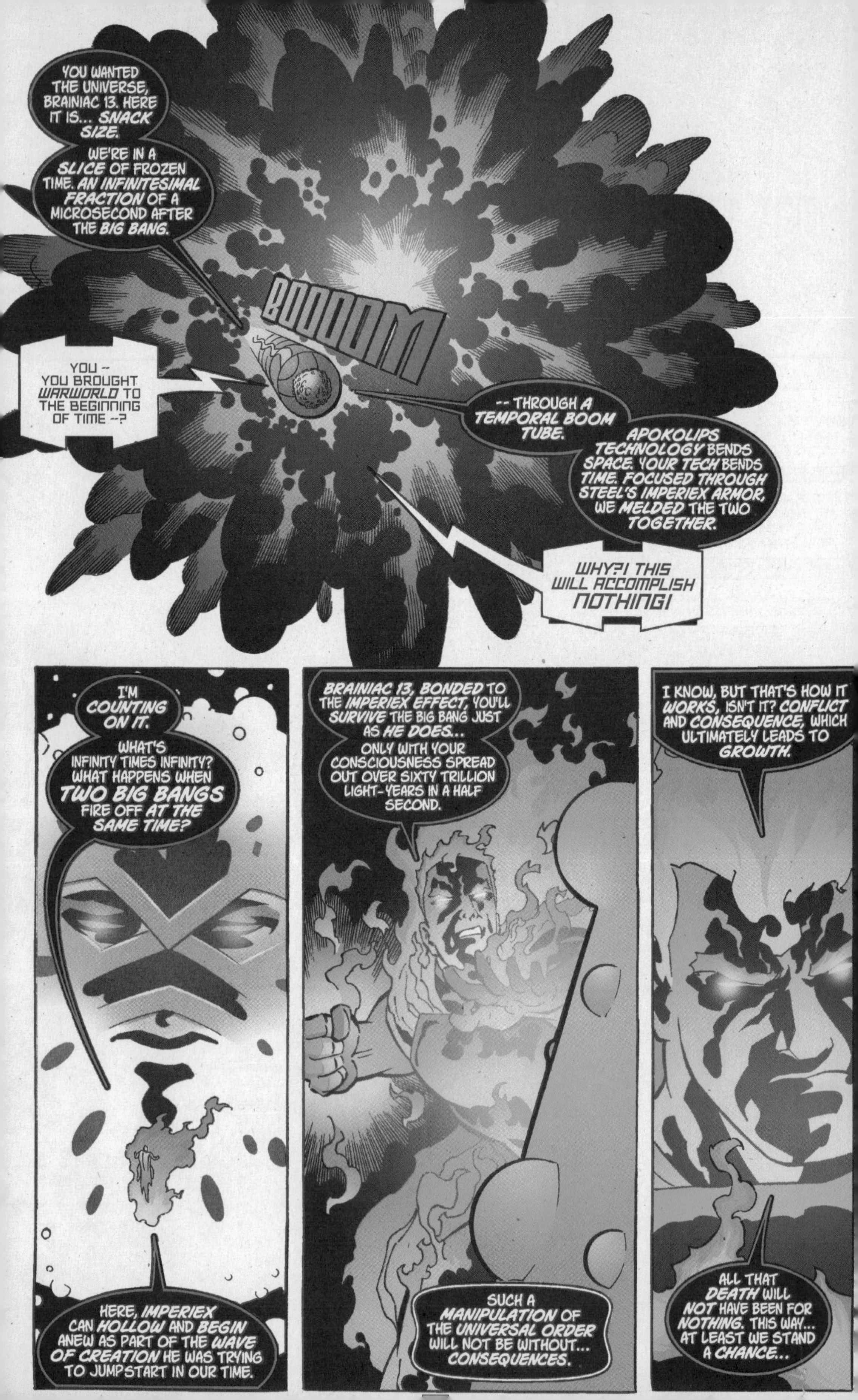
YOU WANTED THE UNIVERSE, BRAINIAC 13. HERE IT IS... SNACK SIZE.
WE'RE IN A SLICE OF FROZEN TIME. AN INFINITESIMAL FRACTION OF A MICROSECOND AFTER THE BIG BANG.
BOOOOM
YOU -- YOU BROUGHT WARWORLD TO THE BEGINNING OF TIME --?
-- THROUGH A TEMPORAL BOOM TUBE.
APOKOLIPS TECHNOLOGY BENDS SPACE. YOUR TECH BENDS TIME. FOCUSED THROUGH STEEL'S IMPERIEX ARMOR, WE MELDED THE TWO TOGETHER.
WHY?! THIS WILL ACCOMPLISH NOTHING!
I'M COUNTING ON IT.
WHAT'S INFINITY TIMES INFINITY? WHAT HAPPENS WHEN TWO BIG BANGS FIRE OFF AT THE SAME TIME?
HERE, IMPERIEX CAN HOLLOW AND BEGIN ANEW AS PART OF THE WAVE OF CREATION HE WAS TRYING TO JUMPSTART IN OUR TIME.
BRAINIAC 13, BONDED TO THE IMPERIEX EFFECT, YOU'LL SURVIVE THE BIG BANG JUST AS HE DOES...
ONLY WITH YOUR CONSCIOUSNESS SPREAD OUT OVER SIXTY TRILLION LIGHT-YEARS IN A HALF SECOND.
SUCH A MANIPULATION OF THE UNIVERSAL ORDER WILL NOT BE WITHOUT... CONSEQUENCES.
I KNOW, BUT THAT'S HOW IT WORKS, ISN'T IT? CONFLICT AND CONSEQUENCE, WHICH ULTIMATELY LEADS TO GROWTH.
ALL THAT DEATH WILL NOT HAVE BEEN FOR NOTHING. THIS WAY... AT LEAST WE STAND A CHANCE...

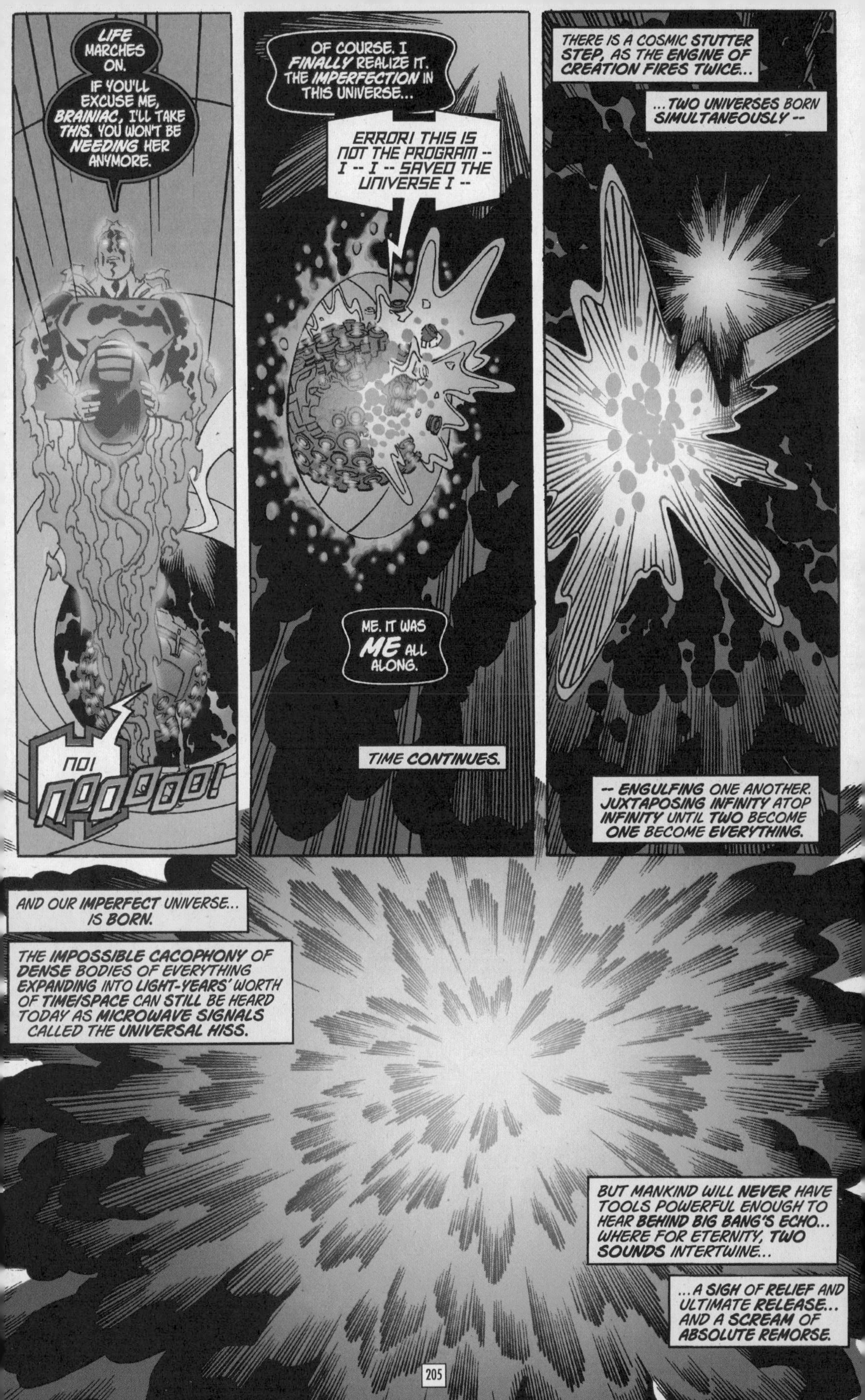

LIFE MARCHES ON.
IF YOU'LL EXCUSE ME, BRAINIAC, I'LL TAKE THIS. YOU WON'T BE NEEDING HER ANYMORE.
NO! NOOOOOO!
OF COURSE. I FINALLY REALIZE IT. THE IMPERFECTION IN THIS UNIVERSE...
ERROR! THIS IS NOT THE PROGRAM -- I -- I -- SAVED THE UNIVERSE I --
ME. IT WAS ME ALL ALONG.
TIME CONTINUES.
THERE IS A COSMIC STUTTER STEP, AS THE ENGINE OF CREATION FIRES TWICE...
...TWO UNIVERSES BORN SIMULTANEOUSLY --
-- ENGULFING ONE ANOTHER. JUXTAPOSING INFINITY ATOP INFINITY UNTIL TWO BECOME ONE BECOME EVERYTHING.
AND OUR IMPERFECT UNIVERSE... IS BORN.
THE IMPOSSIBLE CACOPHONY OF DENSE BODIES OF EVERYTHING EXPANDING INTO LIGHT-YEARS' WORTH OF TIME/SPACE CAN STILL BE HEARD TODAY AS MICROWAVE SIGNALS CALLED THE UNIVERSAL HISS.
BUT MANKIND WILL NEVER HAVE TOOLS POWERFUL ENOUGH TO HEAR BEHIND BIG BANG'S ECHO... WHERE FOR ETERNITY, TWO SOUNDS INTERTWINE...
...A SIGH OF RELIEF AND ULTIMATE RELEASE... AND A SCREAM OF ABSOLUTE REMORSE.

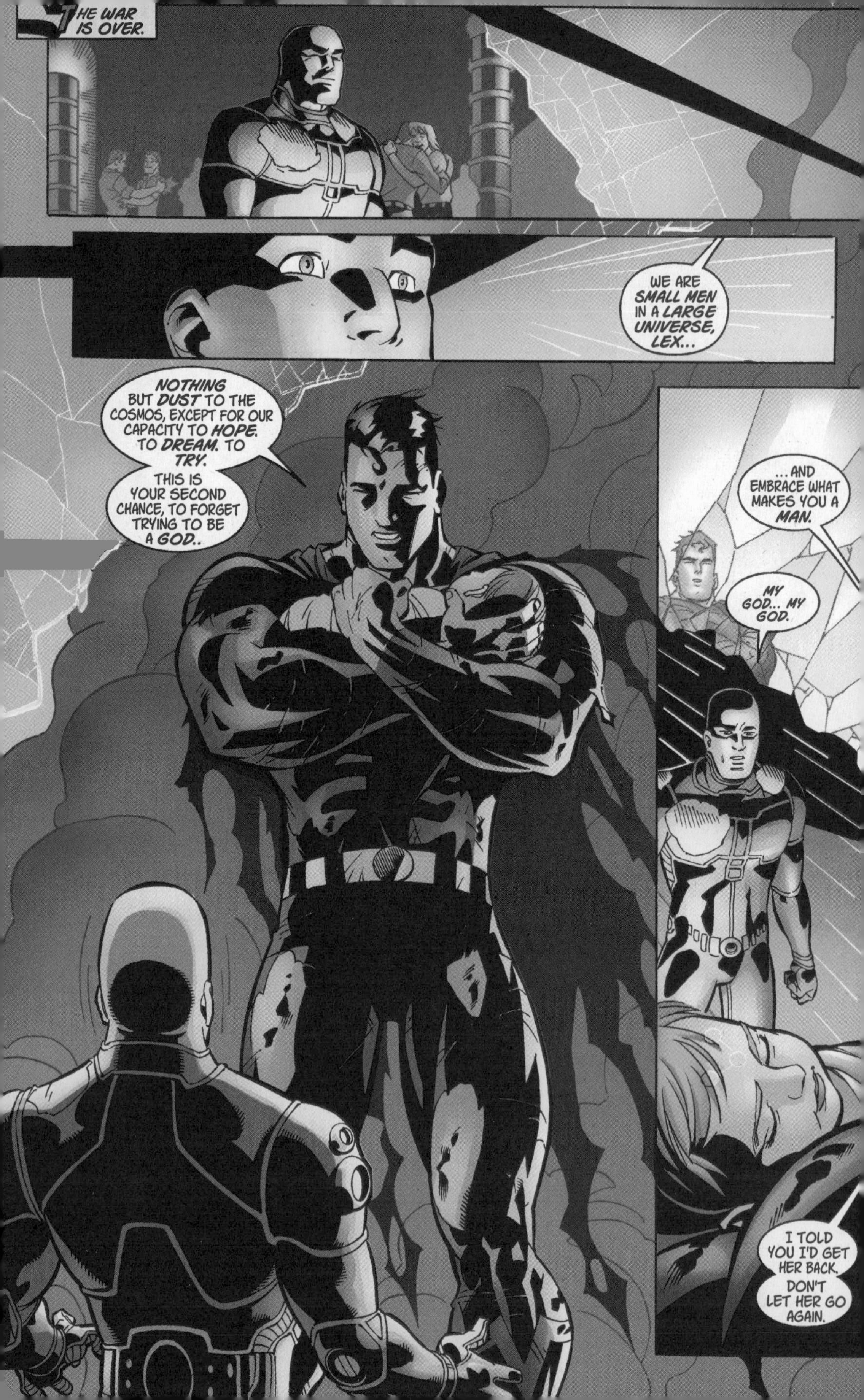
THE WAR IS OVER.
WE ARE SMALL MEN IN A LARGE UNIVERSE, LEX...
NOTHING BUT DUST TO THE COSMOS, EXCEPT FOR OUR CAPACITY TO HOPE. TO DREAM. TO TRY.
THIS IS YOUR SECOND CHANCE, TO FORGET TRYING TO BE A GOD..
...AND EMBRACE WHAT MAKES YOU A MAN.
MY GOD... MY GOD.
I TOLD YOU I'D GET HER BACK.
DON'T LET HER GO AGAIN.

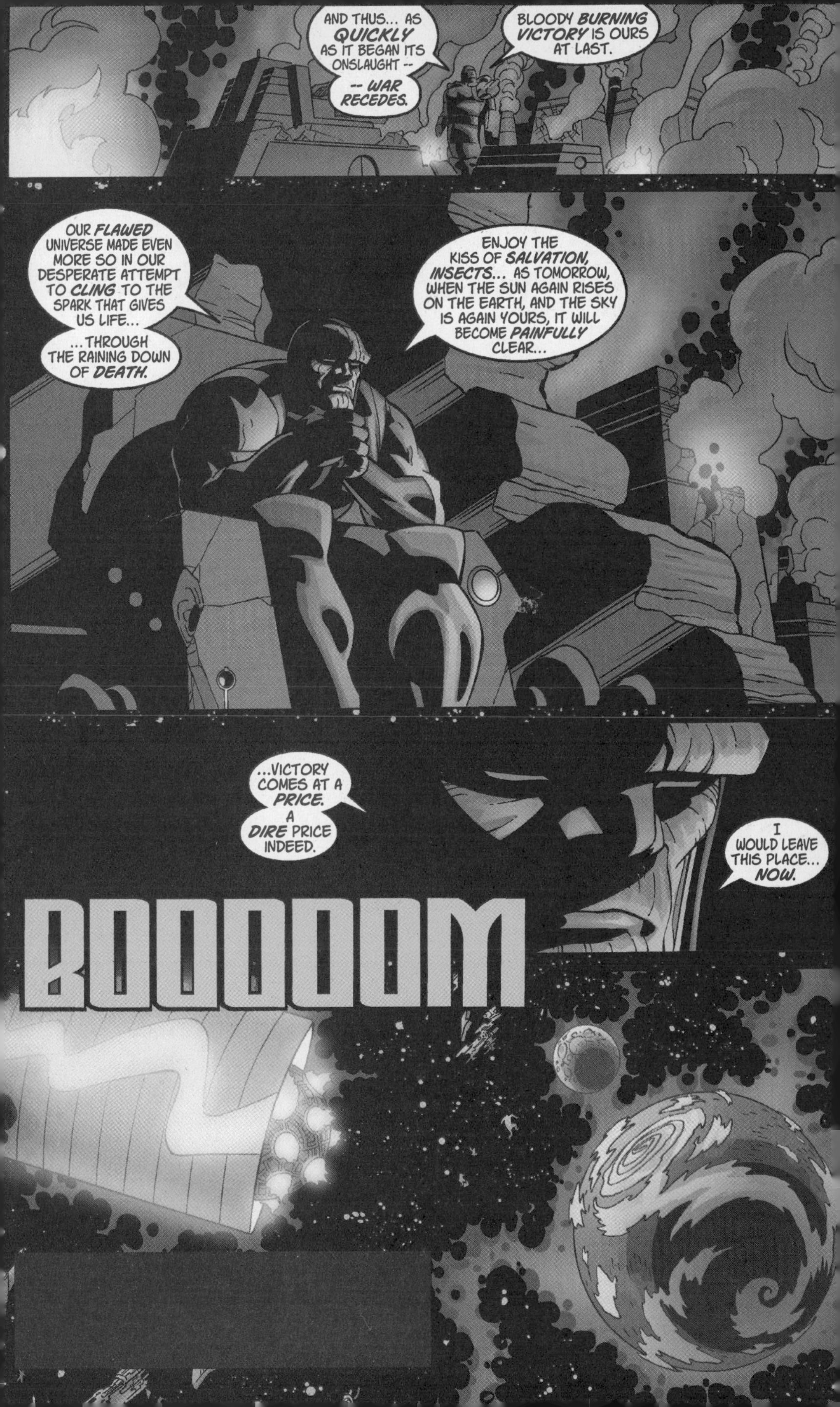

AND THUS... AS QUICKLY AS IT BEGAN ITS ONSLAUGHT --
-- WAR RECEDES.
BLOODY BURNING VICTORY IS OURS AT LAST.
OUR FLAWED UNIVERSE MADE EVEN MORE SO IN OUR DESPERATE ATTEMPT TO CLING TO THE SPARK THAT GIVES US LIFE...
...THROUGH THE RAINING DOWN OF DEATH.
ENJOY THE KISS OF SALVATION, INSECTS... AS TOMORROW, WHEN THE SUN AGAIN RISES ON THE EARTH, AND THE SKY IS AGAIN YOURS, IT WILL BECOME PAINFULLY CLEAR...
...VICTORY COMES AT A PRICE.
A DIRE PRICE INDEED.
I WOULD LEAVE THIS PLACE... NOW.
BOOOOOM

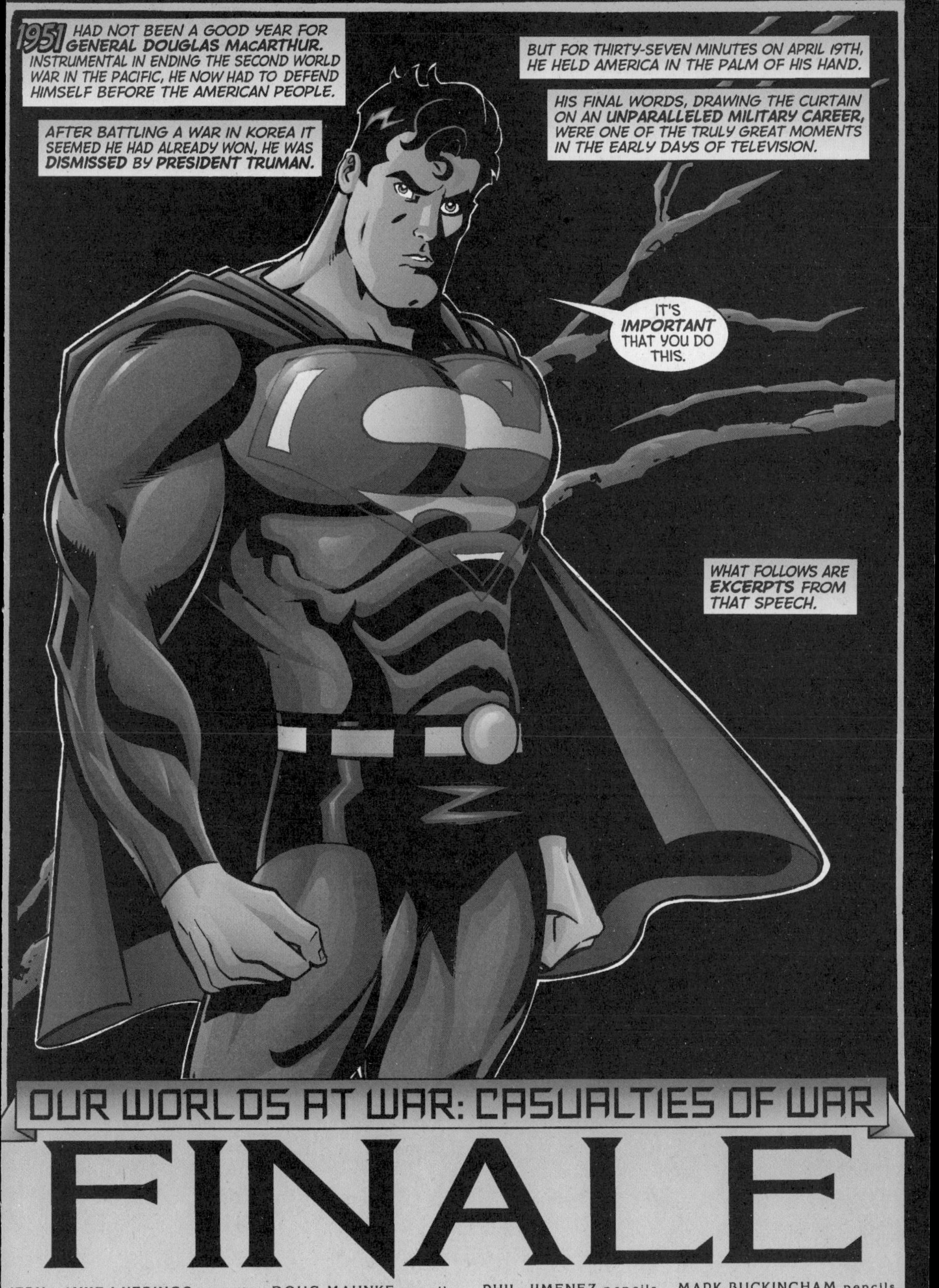
1951 HAD NOT BEEN A GOOD YEAR FOR GENERAL DOUGLAS MacARTHUR. INSTRUMENTAL IN ENDING THE SECOND WORLD WAR IN THE PACIFIC, HE NOW HAD TO DEFEND HIMSELF BEFORE THE AMERICAN PEOPLE.
AFTER BATTLING A WAR IN KOREA IT SEEMED HE HAD ALREADY WON, HE WAS DISMISSED BY PRESIDENT TRUMAN.
BUT FOR THIRTY-SEVEN MINUTES ON APRIL 19TH, HE HELD AMERICA IN THE PALM OF HIS HAND.
HIS FINAL WORDS, DRAWING THE CURTAIN ON AN UNPARALLELED MILITARY CAREER, WERE ONE OF THE TRULY GREAT MOMENTS IN THE EARLY DAYS OF TELEVISION.
IT'S IMPORTANT THAT YOU DO THIS.
WHAT FOLLOWS ARE EXCERPTS FROM THAT SPEECH.

OUR WORLDS AT WAR: CASUALTIES OF WAR

FINALE

JEPH LOEB writer
MIKE WIERINGO pencils JOSE MARZAN jr inks pages 1-5
DOUG MAHNKE pencils WALDEN WONG inks pages 6-10
PHIL JIMENEZ pencils MARK MORALES inks pages 11-13
MARK BUCKINGHAM pencils WAYNE FAUCHER inks pages 14-19
BILL SIENKIEWICZ pencils & inks pages 20-21
YVEL GUICHET pencils DEXTER VINES inks pages 22-23
PASCUAL FERRY pencils MARLO ALQUIZA inks pages 24-26
TODD NAUCK pencils LARY STUCKER inks pages 27-29
WIERINGO pencils MARZAN jr inks page 30
DUNCAN ROULEAU pencils & inks pages 31-34
ED McGUINNESS pencils CAM SMITH inks pages 35-38
ZYLONOL STUDIO colors
COMIC CRAFT letters
TOM PALMER jr ass't editor
EDDIE BERGANZA editor

BATMAN created by BOB KANE • SUPERMAN created by JERRY SIEGEL & JOE SHUSTER
WONDER WOMAN created by WILLIAM MOULTON MARSTON

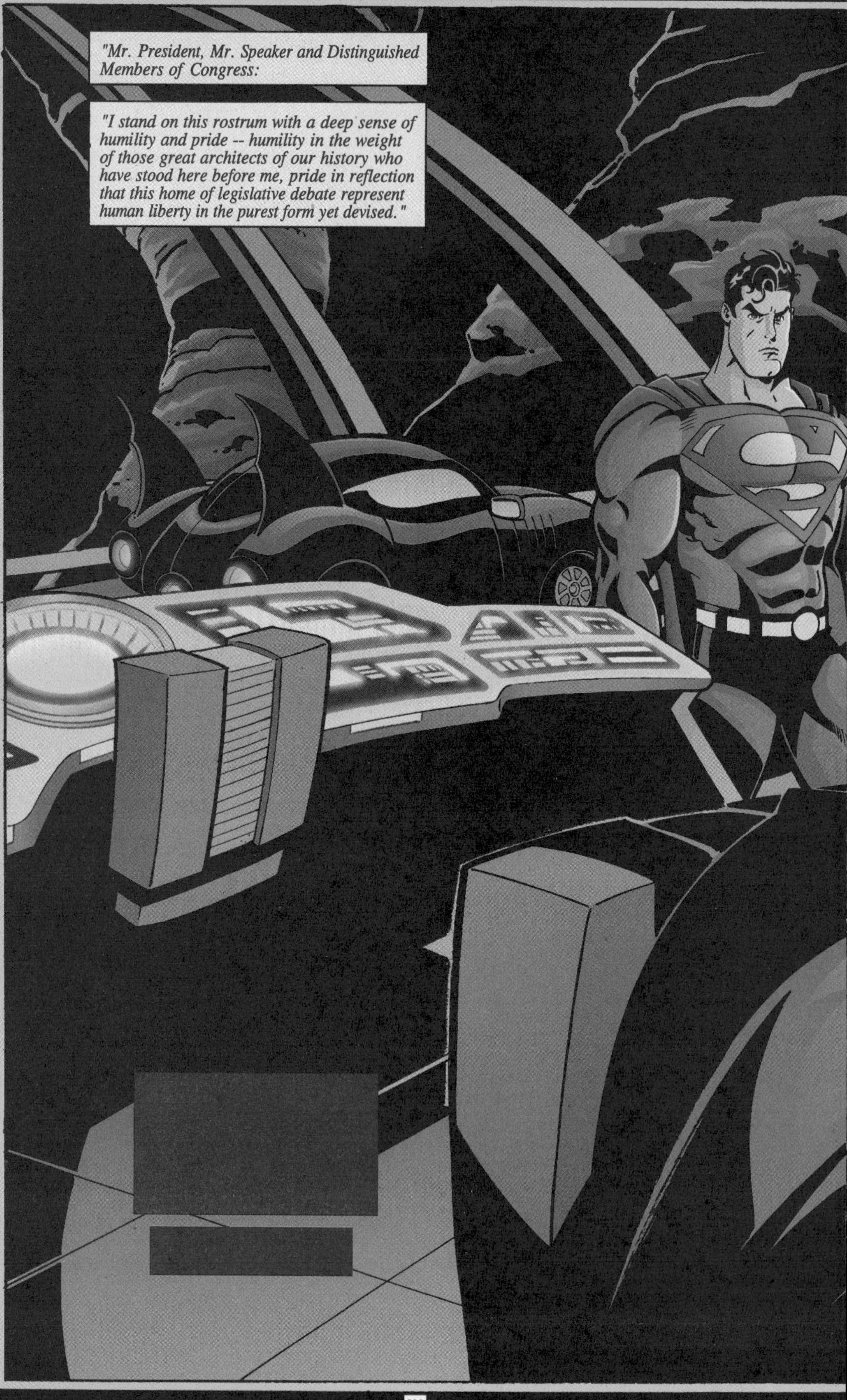
"Mr. President, Mr. Speaker and Distinguished Members of Congress:
"I stand on this rostrum with a deep sense of humility and pride -- humility in the weight of those great architects of our history who have stood here before me, pride in reflection that this home of legislative debate represent human liberty in the purest form yet devised."

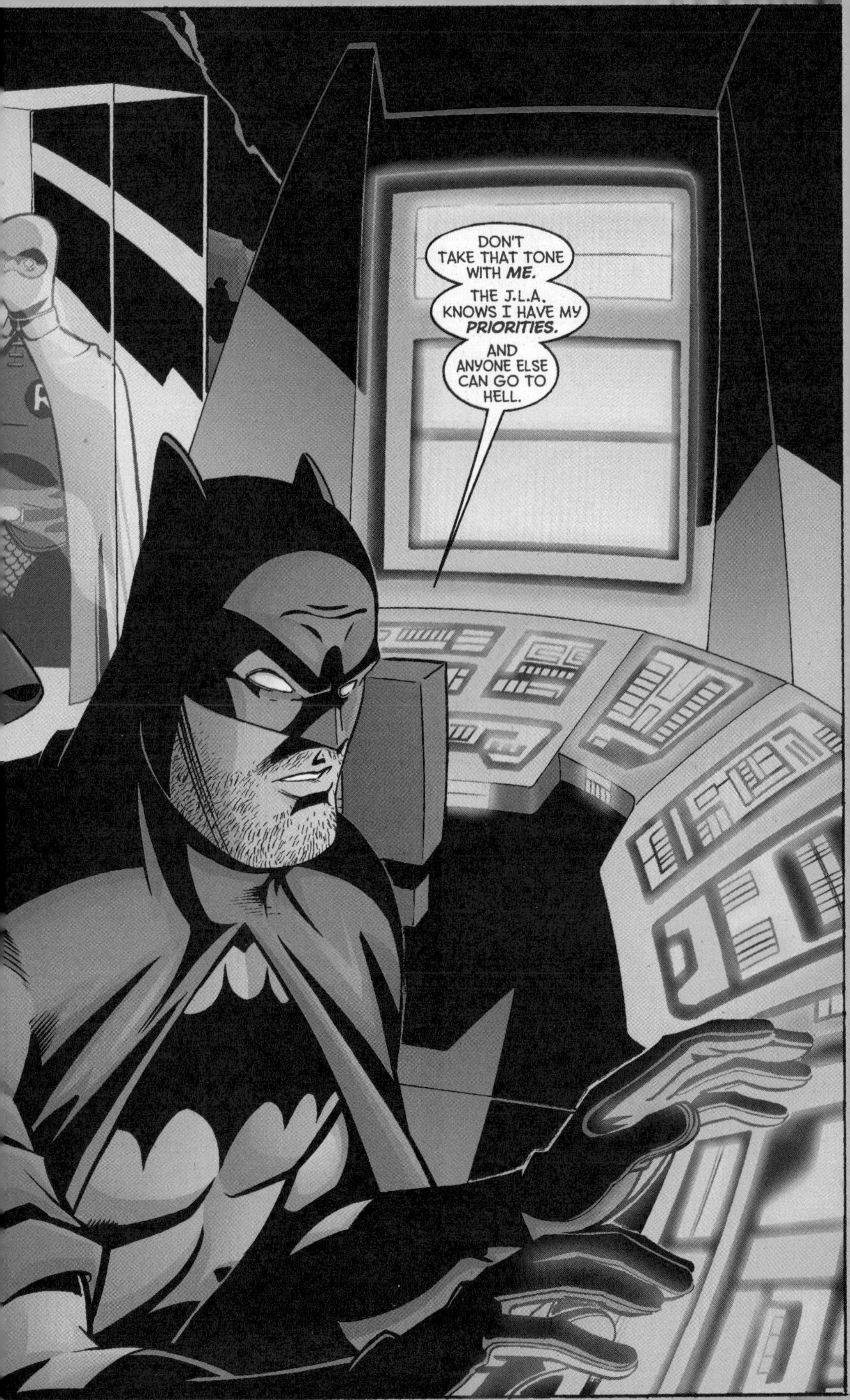
DON'T TAKE THAT TONE WITH ***ME.***
THE J.L.A. KNOWS I HAVE MY ***PRIORITIES.***
AND ANYONE ELSE CAN GO TO HELL.

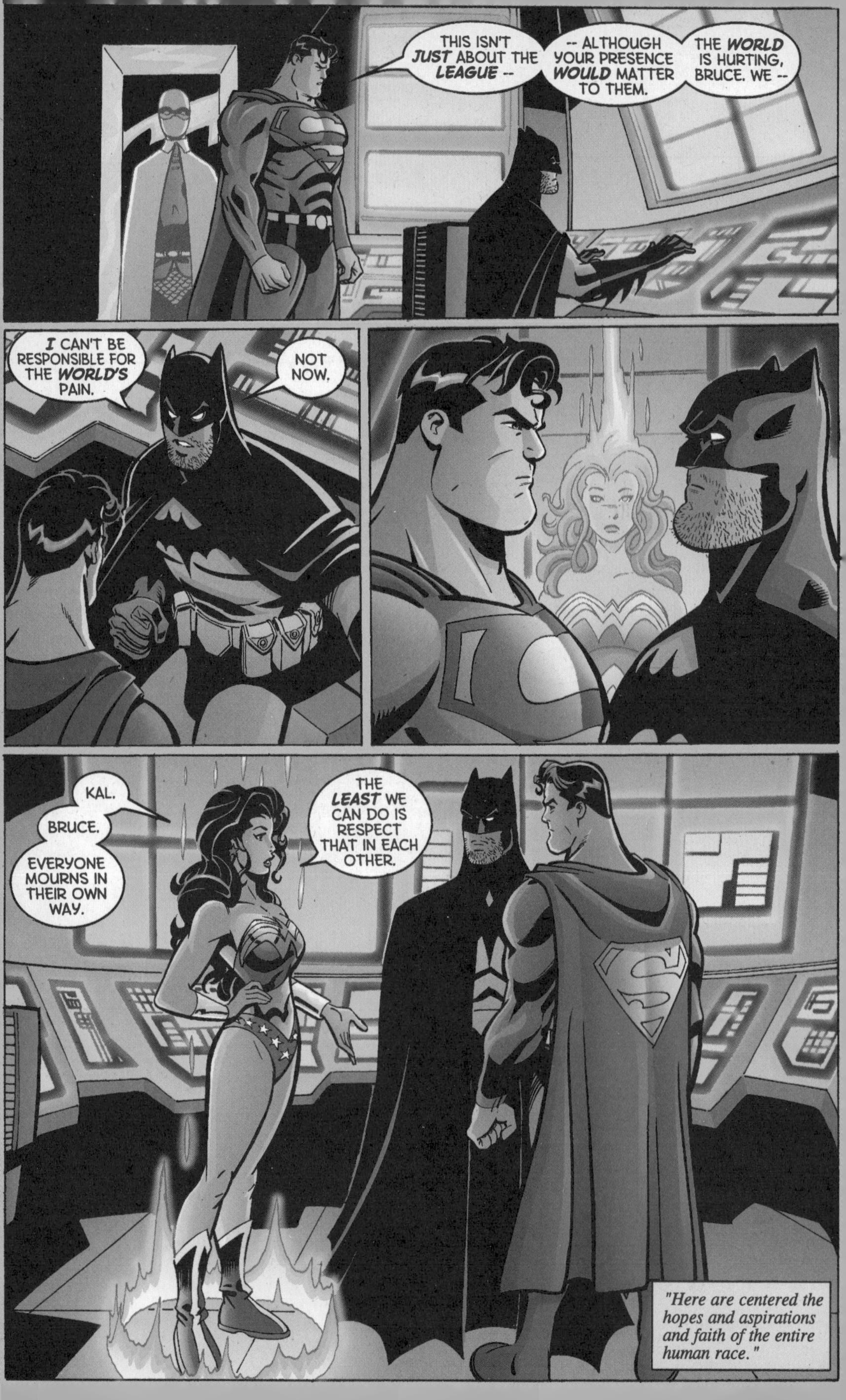
THIS ISN'T *JUST* ABOUT THE *LEAGUE* --
-- ALTHOUGH YOUR PRESENCE *WOULD* MATTER TO THEM.
THE *WORLD* IS HURTING, BRUCE. WE --
I CAN'T BE RESPONSIBLE FOR THE *WORLD'S* PAIN.
NOT NOW.
KAL.
BRUCE.
EVERYONE MOURNS IN THEIR OWN WAY.
THE *LEAST* WE CAN DO IS RESPECT THAT IN EACH OTHER.
"Here are centered the hopes and aspirations and faith of the entire human race."

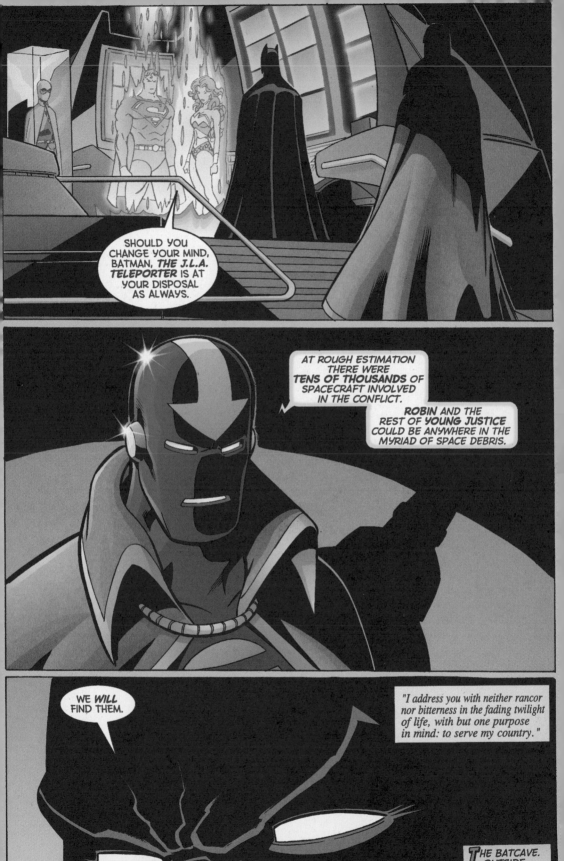

SHOULD YOU CHANGE YOUR MIND, BATMAN, *THE J.L.A. TELEPORTER* IS AT YOUR DISPOSAL AS ALWAYS.

AT ROUGH ESTIMATION THERE WERE *TENS OF THOUSANDS* OF SPACECRAFT INVOLVED IN THE CONFLICT.

ROBIN AND THE REST OF *YOUNG JUSTICE* COULD BE ANYWHERE IN THE MYRIAD OF SPACE DEBRIS.

WE *WILL* FIND THEM.

"I address you with neither rancor nor bitterness in the fading twilight of life, with but one purpose in mind: to serve my country."

THE BATCAVE. OUTSIDE GOTHAM CITY. PAST MIDNIGHT.

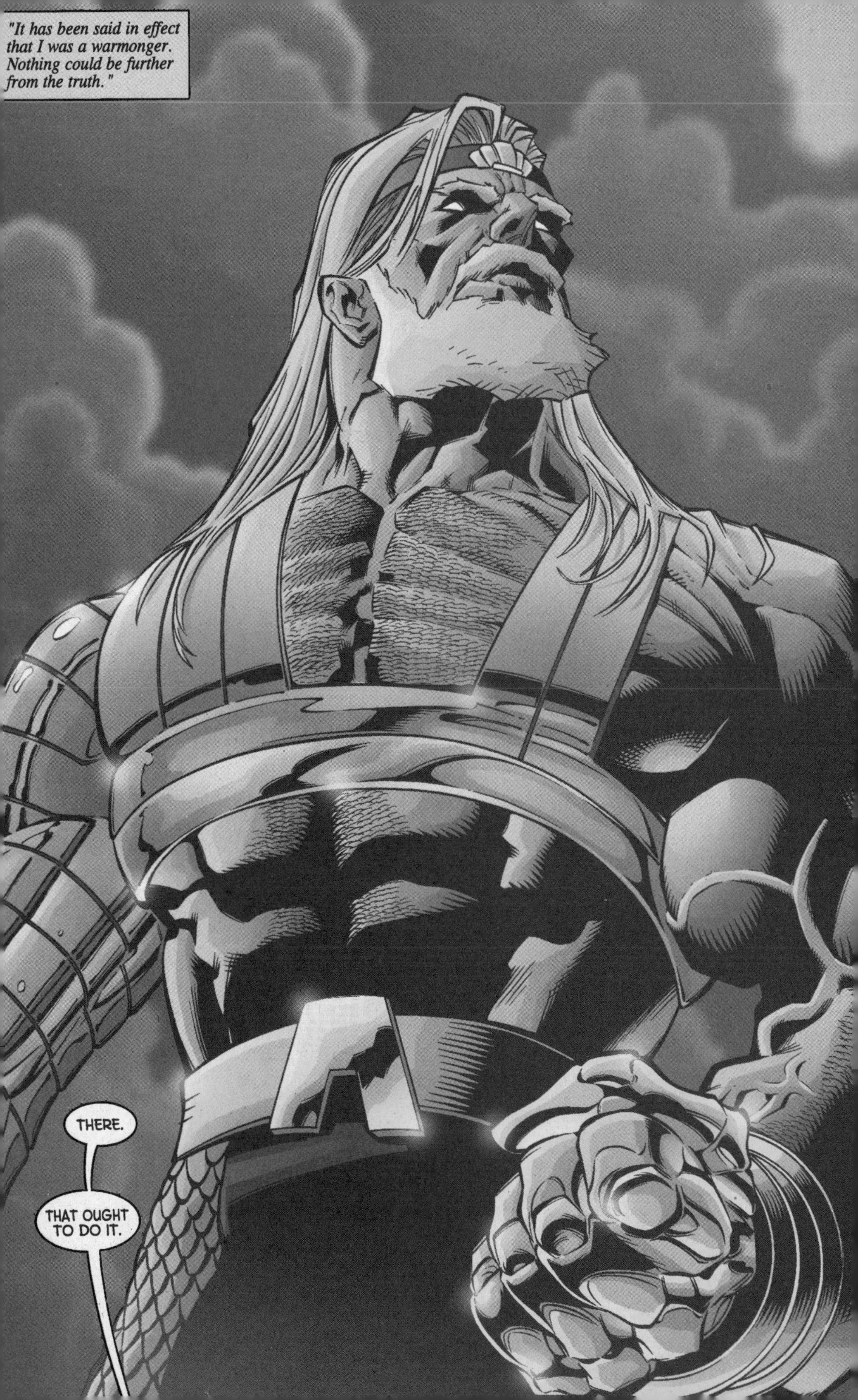
"It has been said in effect that I was a warmonger. Nothing could be further from the truth."
THERE.
THAT OUGHT TO DO IT.

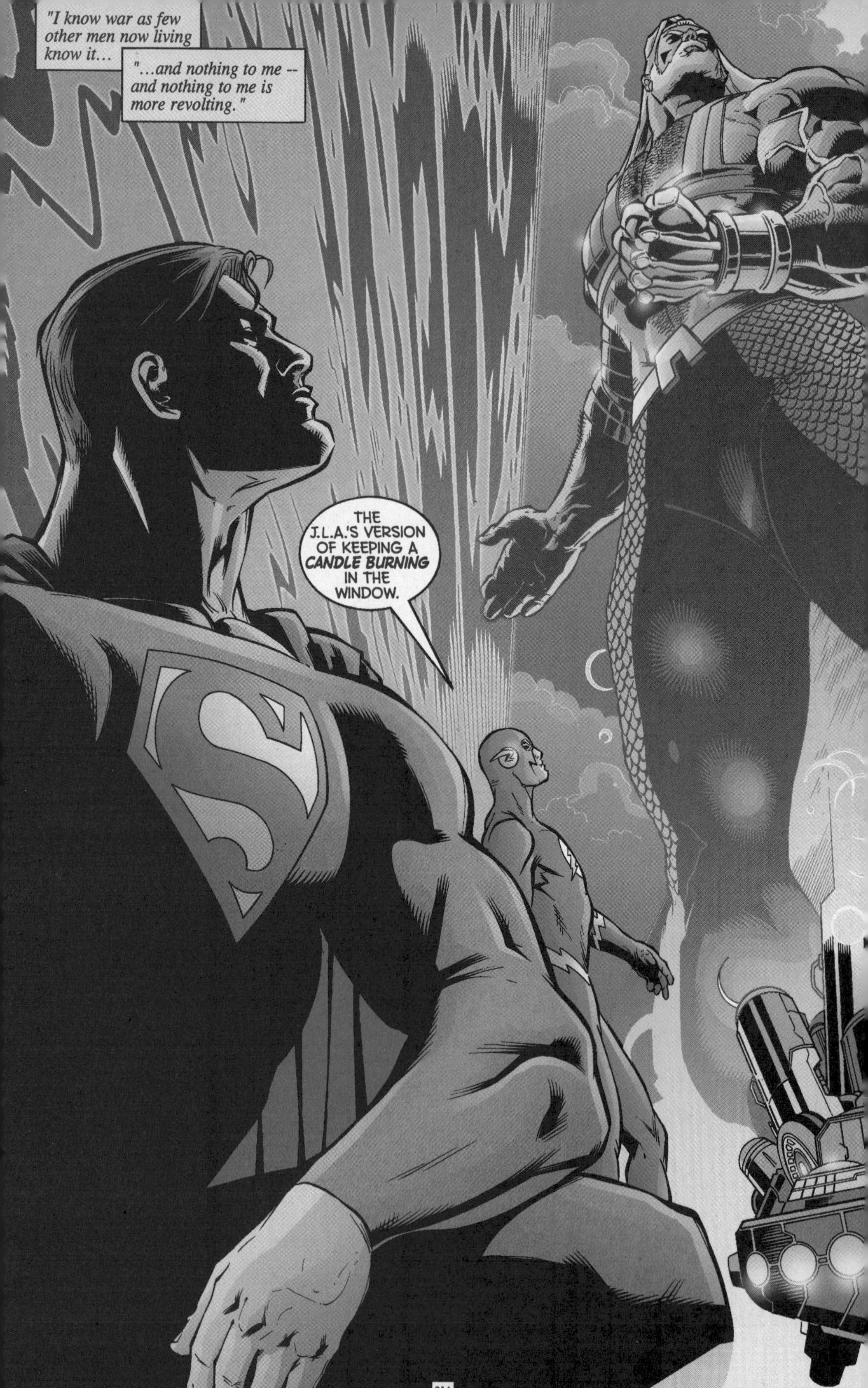
"I know war as few other men now living know it...
"...and nothing to me -- and nothing to me is more revolting."
THE J.L.A.'S VERSION OF KEEPING A CANDLE BURNING IN THE WINDOW.

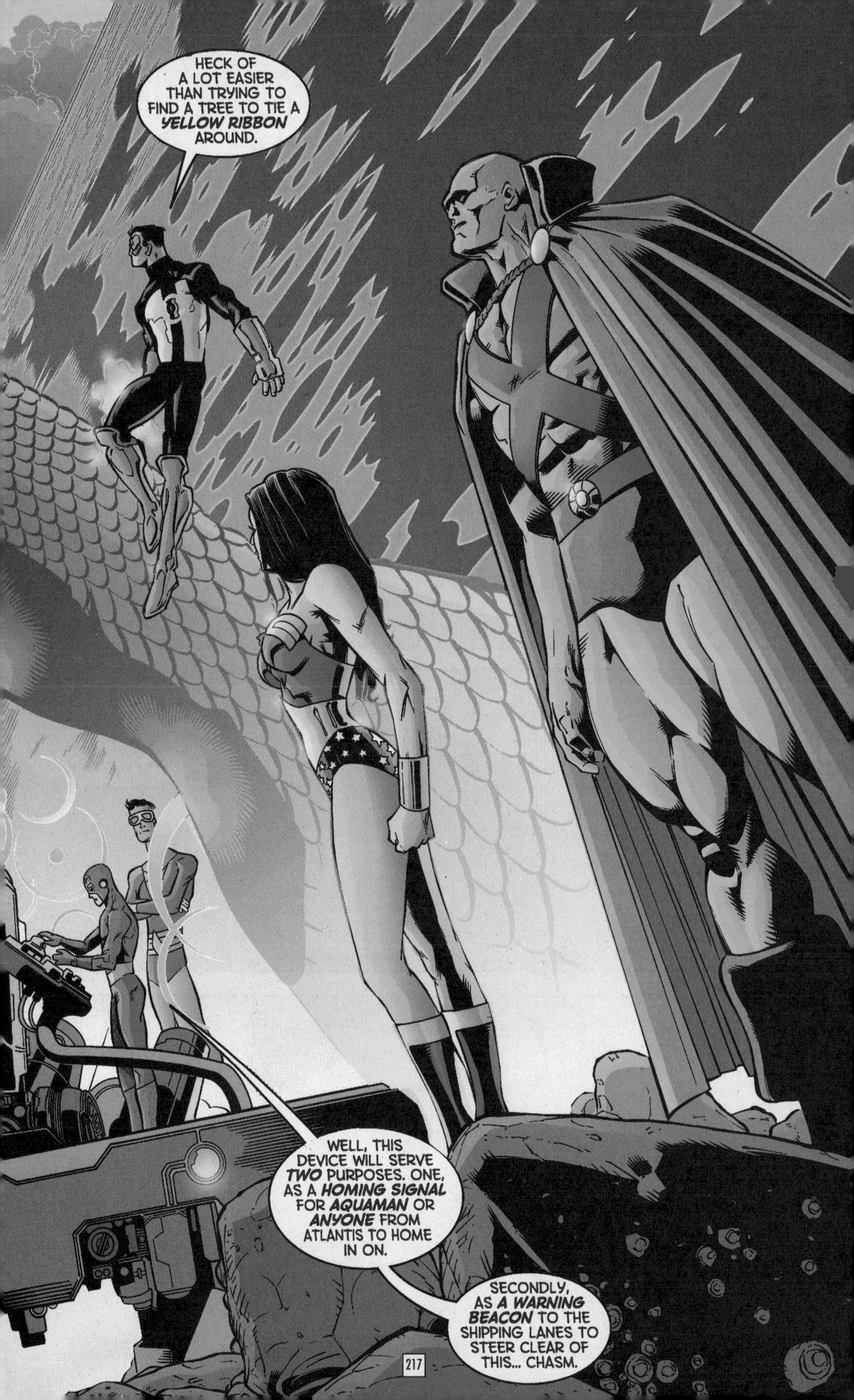
HECK OF A LOT EASIER THAN TRYING TO FIND A TREE TO TIE A YELLOW RIBBON AROUND.
WELL, THIS DEVICE WILL SERVE TWO PURPOSES. ONE, AS A HOMING SIGNAL FOR AQUAMAN OR ANYONE FROM ATLANTIS TO HOME IN ON.
SECONDLY, AS A WARNING BEACON TO THE SHIPPING LANES TO STEER CLEAR OF THIS... CHASM.

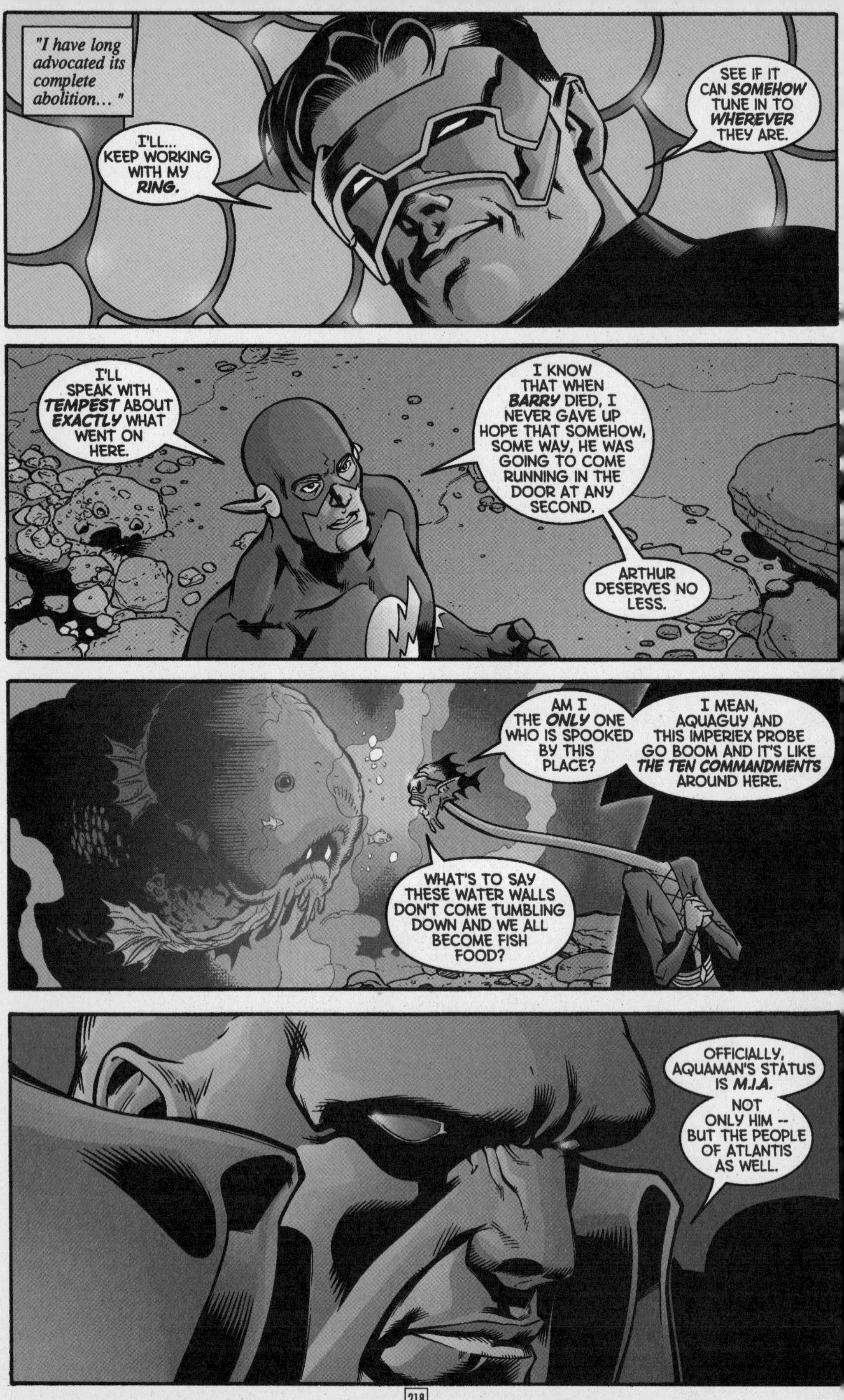
"I have long advocated its complete abolition..."
I'LL... KEEP WORKING WITH MY RING.
SEE IF IT CAN SOMEHOW TUNE IN TO WHEREVER THEY ARE.
I'LL SPEAK WITH TEMPEST ABOUT EXACTLY WHAT WENT ON HERE.
I KNOW THAT WHEN BARRY DIED, I NEVER GAVE UP HOPE THAT SOMEHOW, SOME WAY, HE WAS GOING TO COME RUNNING IN THE DOOR AT ANY SECOND.
ARTHUR DESERVES NO LESS.
AM I THE ONLY ONE WHO IS SPOOKED BY THIS PLACE?
I MEAN, AQUAGUY AND THIS IMPERIEX PROBE GO BOOM AND IT'S LIKE THE TEN COMMANDMENTS AROUND HERE.
WHAT'S TO SAY THESE WATER WALLS DON'T COME TUMBLING DOWN AND WE ALL BECOME FISH FOOD?
OFFICIALLY, AQUAMAN'S STATUS IS M.I.A.
NOT ONLY HIM -- BUT THE PEOPLE OF ATLANTIS AS WELL.

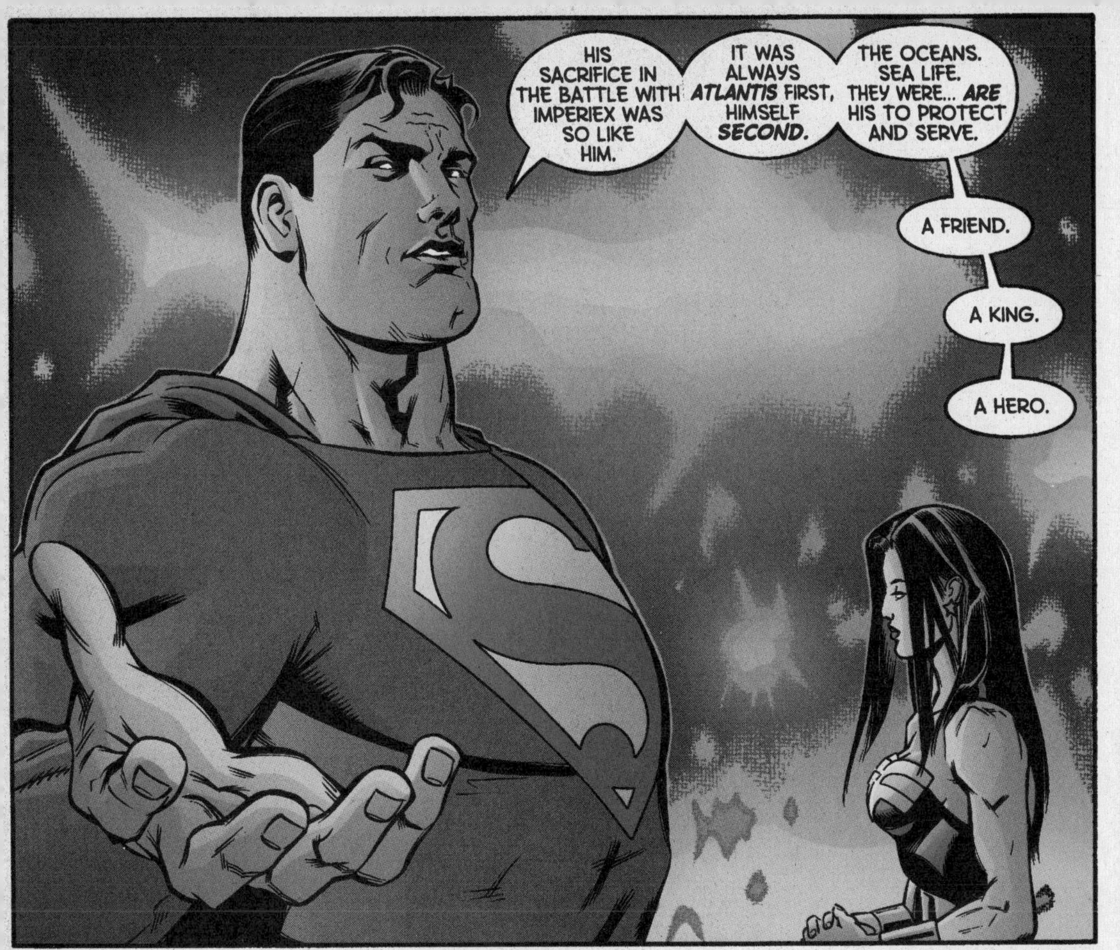
HIS SACRIFICE IN THE BATTLE WITH IMPERIEX WAS SO LIKE HIM.
IT WAS ALWAYS *ATLANTIS* FIRST, HIMSELF ***SECOND.***
THE OCEANS. SEA LIFE. THEY WERE... ***ARE*** HIS TO PROTECT AND SERVE.
A FRIEND.
A KING.
A HERO.

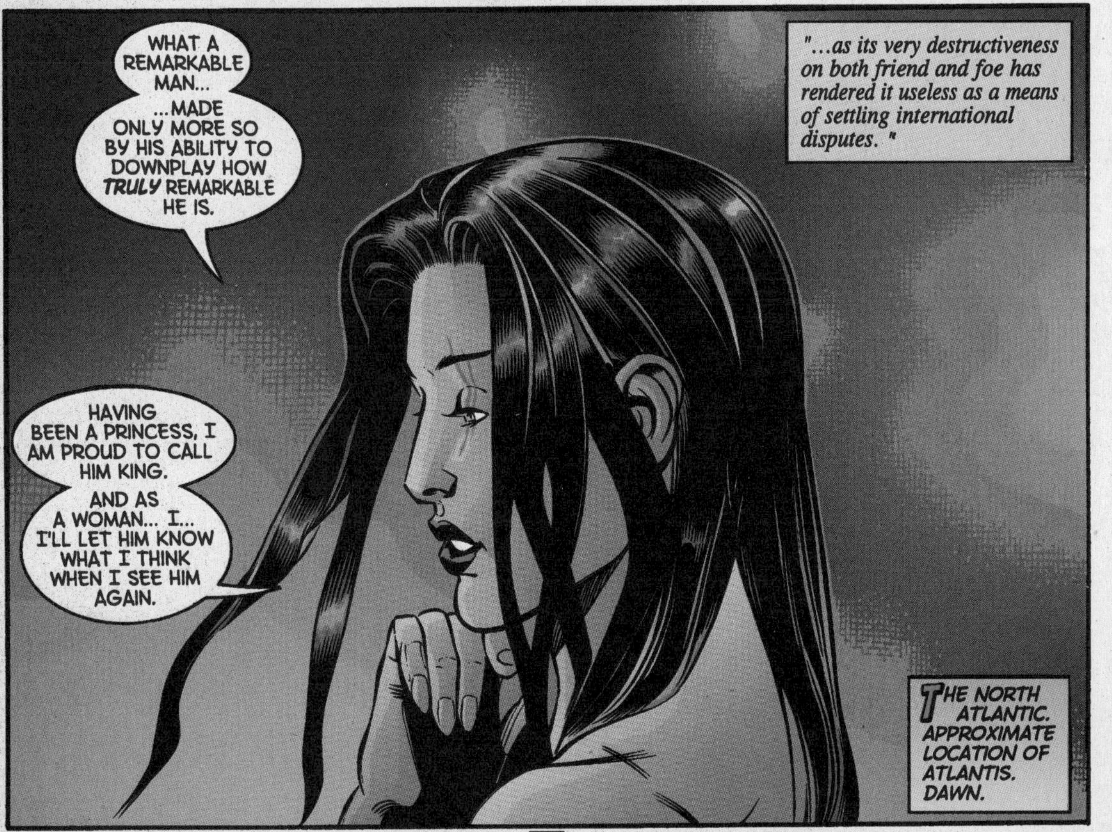
WHAT A REMARKABLE MAN... ...MADE ONLY MORE SO BY HIS ABILITY TO DOWNPLAY HOW ***TRULY*** REMARKABLE HE IS.
"...as its very destructiveness on both friend and foe has rendered it useless as a means of settling international disputes."
HAVING BEEN A PRINCESS, I AM PROUD TO CALL HIM KING.
AND AS A WOMAN... I... I'LL LET HIM KNOW WHAT I THINK WHEN I SEE HIM AGAIN.
THE NORTH ATLANTIC. APPROXIMATE LOCATION OF ATLANTIS. DAWN.

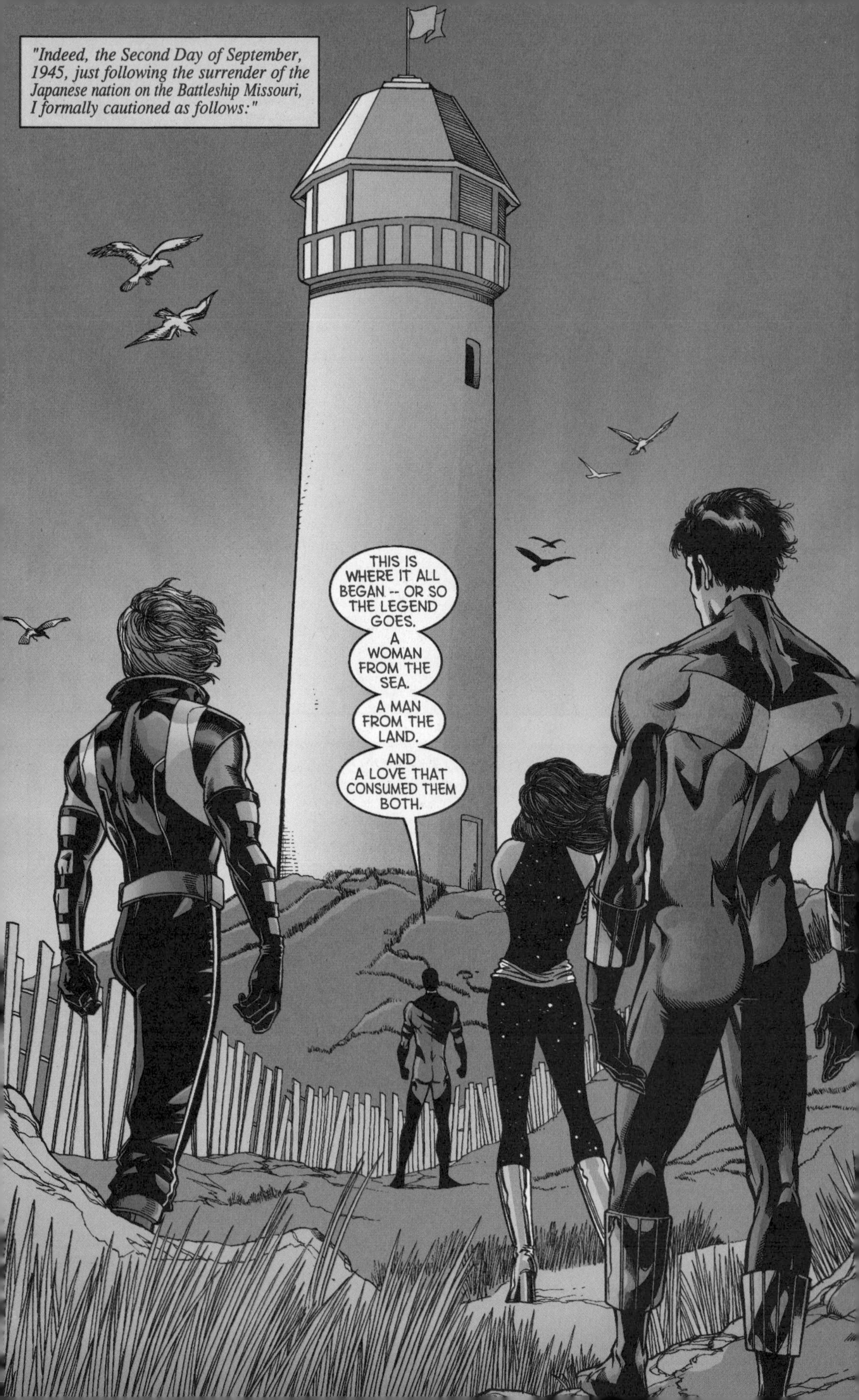
"Indeed, the Second Day of September, 1945, just following the surrender of the Japanese nation on the Battleship Missouri, I formally cautioned as follows:"
THIS IS WHERE IT ALL BEGAN -- OR SO THE LEGEND GOES.
A WOMAN FROM THE SEA.
A MAN FROM THE LAND.
AND A LOVE THAT CONSUMED THEM BOTH.

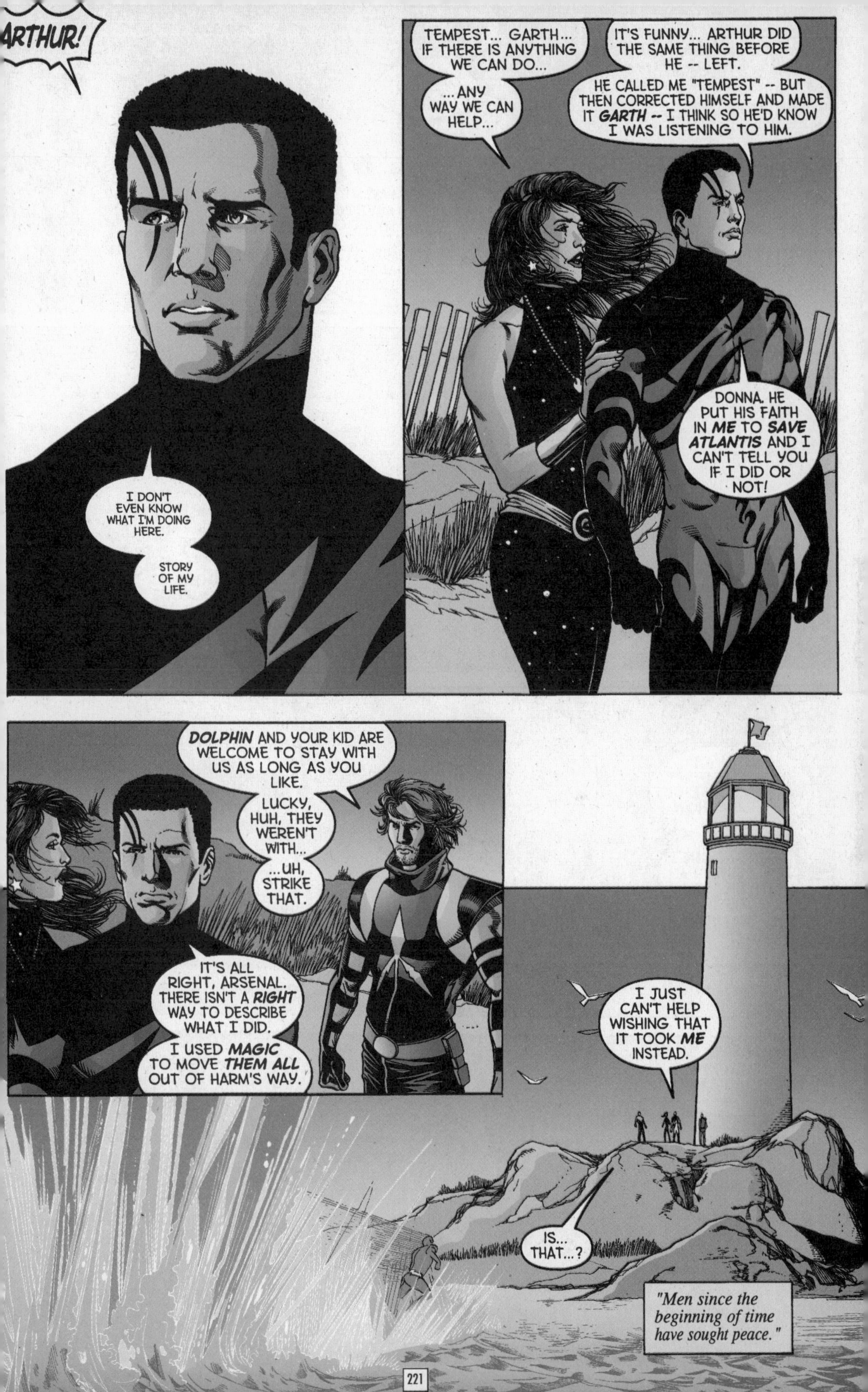
ARTHUR!
I DON'T EVEN KNOW WHAT I'M DOING HERE.
STORY OF MY LIFE.
TEMPEST... GARTH... IF THERE IS ANYTHING WE CAN DO...
...ANY WAY WE CAN HELP...
IT'S FUNNY... ARTHUR DID THE SAME THING BEFORE HE -- LEFT.
HE CALLED ME "TEMPEST" -- BUT THEN CORRECTED HIMSELF AND MADE IT GARTH -- I THINK SO HE'D KNOW I WAS LISTENING TO HIM.
DONNA, HE PUT HIS FAITH IN ME TO SAVE ATLANTIS AND I CAN'T TELL YOU IF I DID OR NOT!
DOLPHIN AND YOUR KID ARE WELCOME TO STAY WITH US AS LONG AS YOU LIKE.
LUCKY, HUH, THEY WEREN'T WITH...
...UH, STRIKE THAT.
IT'S ALL RIGHT, ARSENAL. THERE ISN'T A RIGHT WAY TO DESCRIBE WHAT I DID.
I USED MAGIC TO MOVE THEM ALL OUT OF HARM'S WAY.
I JUST CAN'T HELP WISHING THAT IT TOOK ME INSTEAD.
IS... THAT...?
"Men since the beginning of time have sought peace."

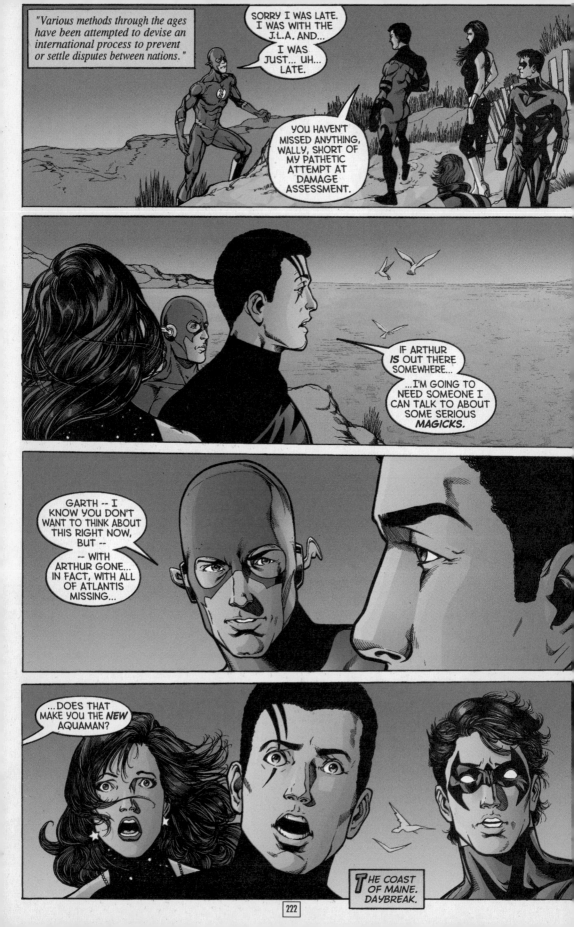

"Various methods through the ages have been attempted to devise an international process to prevent or settle disputes between nations."

SORRY I WAS LATE. I WAS WITH THE J.L.A. AND... I WAS JUST... UH... LATE.

YOU HAVEN'T MISSED ANYTHING, WALLY, SHORT OF MY PATHETIC ATTEMPT AT DAMAGE ASSESSMENT.

IF ARTHUR *IS* OUT THERE SOMEWHERE...

...I'M GOING TO NEED SOMEONE I CAN TALK TO ABOUT SOME SERIOUS *MAGICKS*.

GARTH -- I KNOW YOU DON'T WANT TO THINK ABOUT THIS RIGHT NOW, BUT --

-- WITH ARTHUR GONE... IN FACT, WITH ALL OF ATLANTIS MISSING...

...DOES THAT MAKE YOU THE *NEW* AQUAMAN?

*T*HE COAST OF MAINE. DAYBREAK.

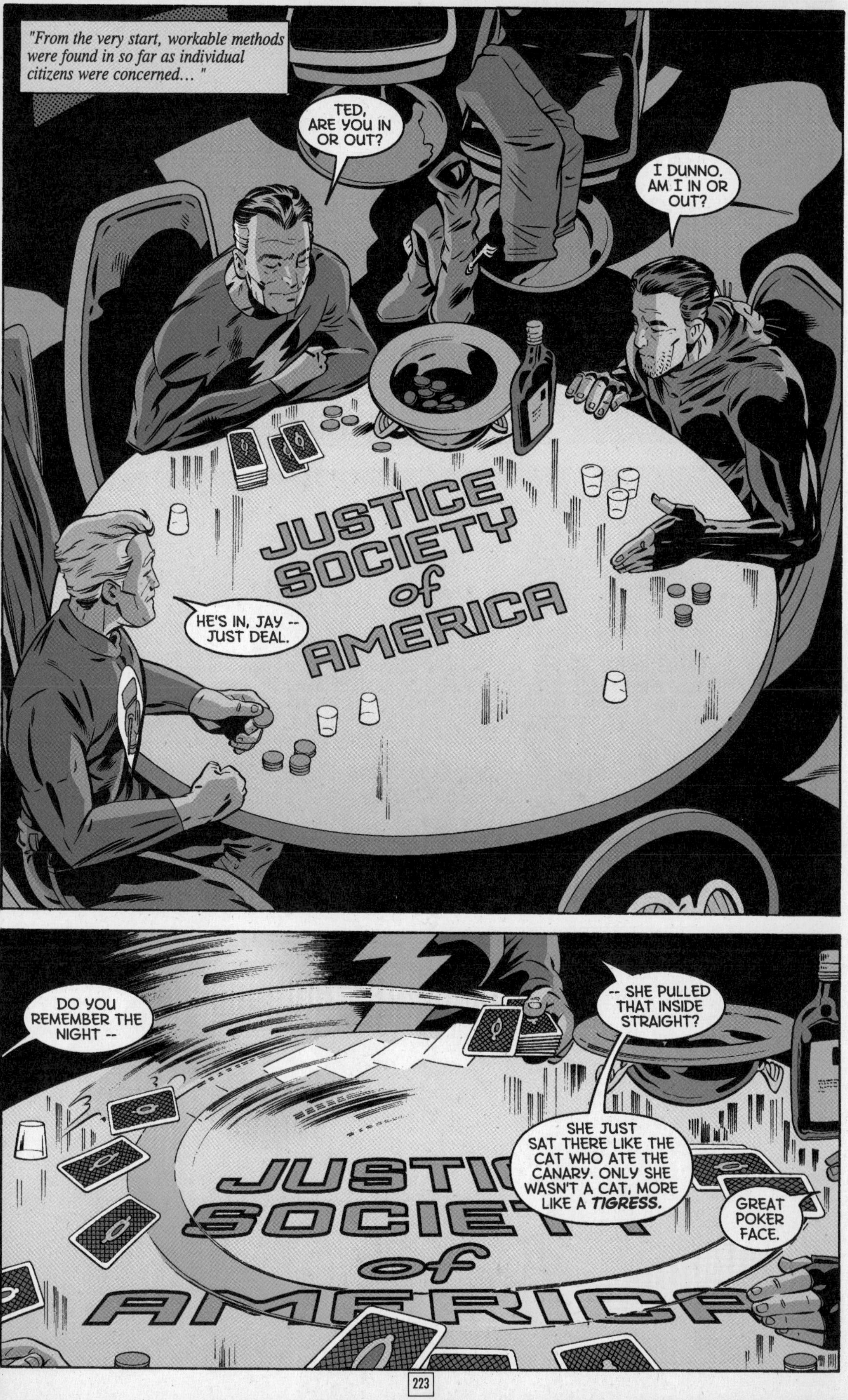
"From the very start, workable methods were found in so far as individual citizens were concerned..."
TED, ARE YOU IN OR OUT?
I DUNNO. AM I IN OR OUT?
JUSTICE SOCIETY of AMERICA
HE'S IN, JAY -- JUST DEAL.
DO YOU REMEMBER THE NIGHT --
-- SHE PULLED THAT INSIDE STRAIGHT?
SHE JUST SAT THERE LIKE THE CAT WHO ATE THE CANARY. ONLY SHE WASN'T A CAT, MORE LIKE A *TIGRESS.*
GREAT POKER FACE.

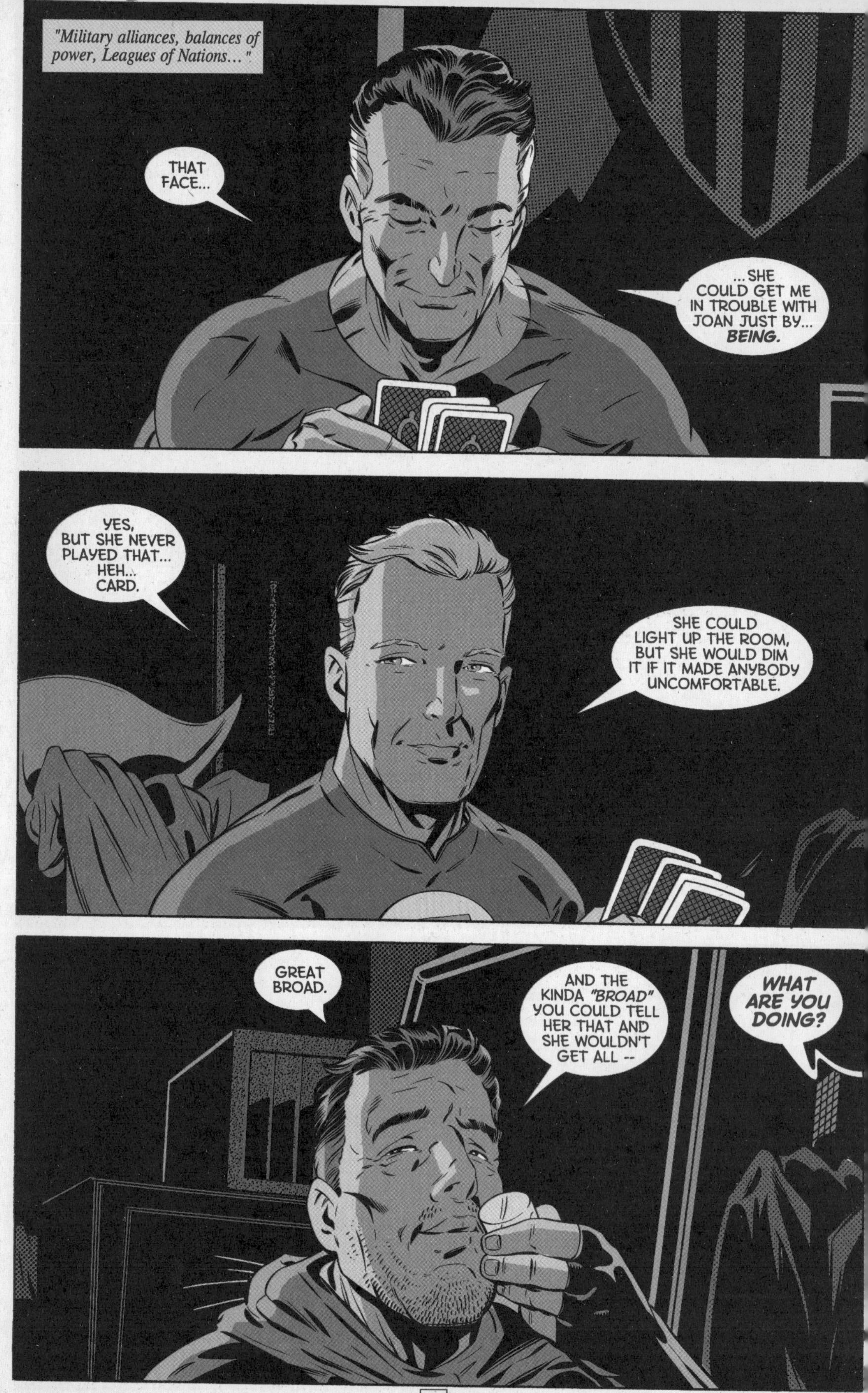
"Military alliances, balances of power, Leagues of Nations..."
THAT FACE...
...SHE COULD GET ME IN TROUBLE WITH JOAN JUST BY... BEING.
YES, BUT SHE NEVER PLAYED THAT... HEH... CARD.
SHE COULD LIGHT UP THE ROOM, BUT SHE WOULD DIM IT IF IT MADE ANYBODY UNCOMFORTABLE.
GREAT BROAD.
AND THE KINDA "BROAD" YOU COULD TELL HER THAT AND SHE WOULDN'T GET ALL --
WHAT ARE YOU DOING?

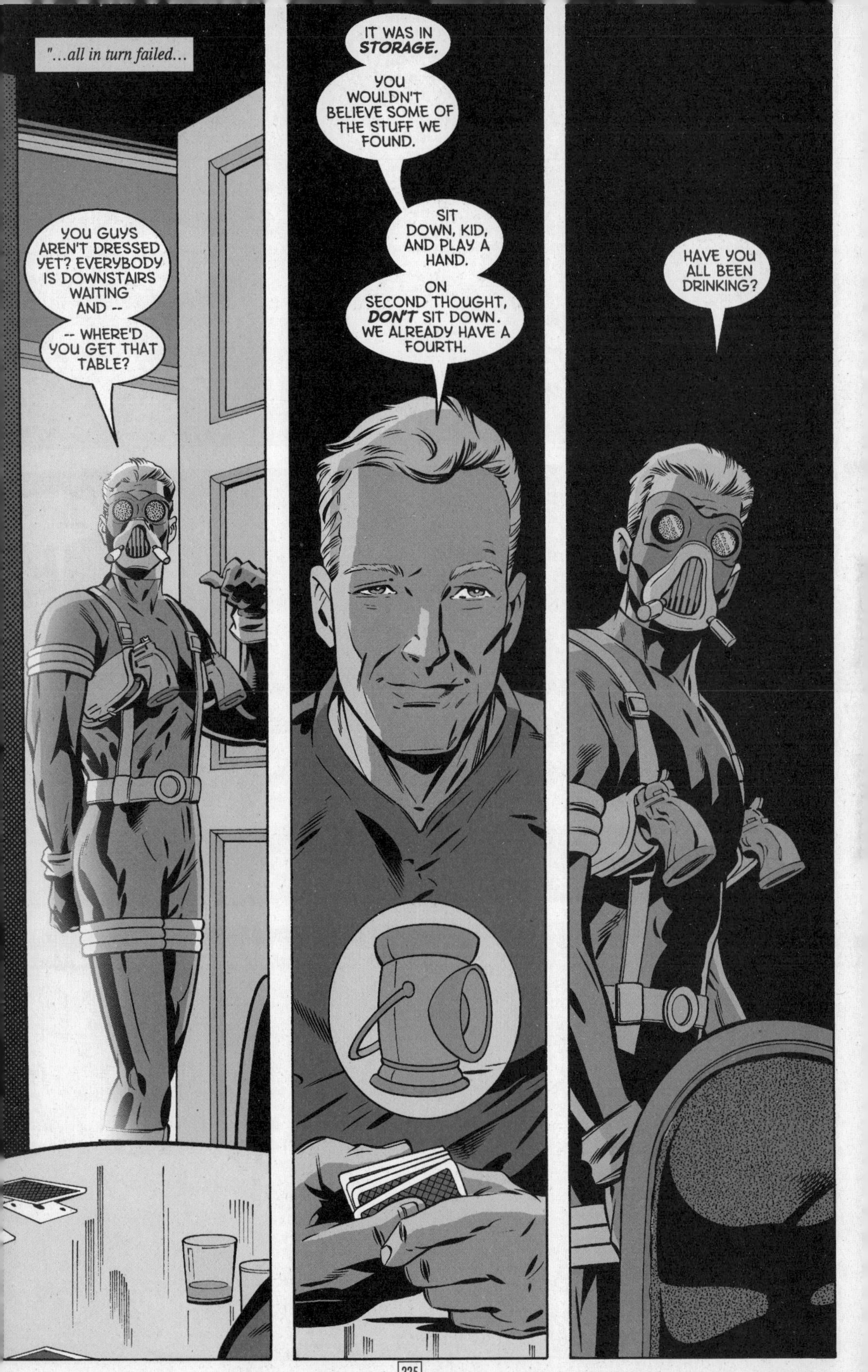
"...all in turn failed...
YOU GUYS AREN'T DRESSED YET? EVERYBODY IS DOWNSTAIRS WAITING AND --
-- WHERE'D YOU GET THAT TABLE?
IT WAS IN STORAGE.
YOU WOULDN'T BELIEVE SOME OF THE STUFF WE FOUND.
SIT DOWN, KID, AND PLAY A HAND.
ON SECOND THOUGHT, DON'T SIT DOWN. WE ALREADY HAVE A FOURTH.
HAVE YOU ALL BEEN DRINKING?

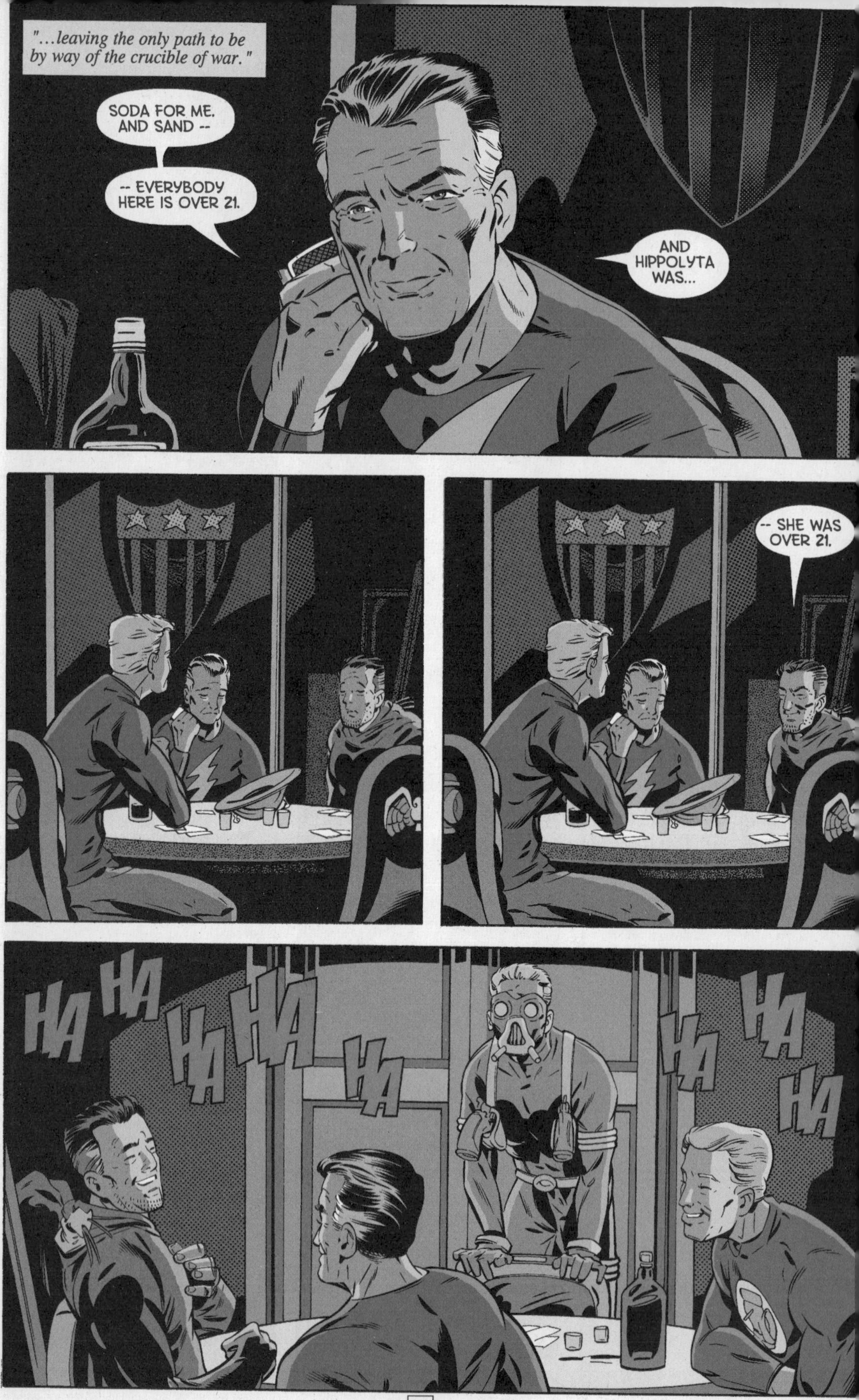
"...leaving the only path to be by way of the crucible of war."
SODA FOR ME. AND SAND --
-- EVERYBODY HERE IS OVER 21.
AND HIPPOLYTA WAS...
-- SHE WAS OVER 21.
HA HA HA HA HA HA HA HA HA

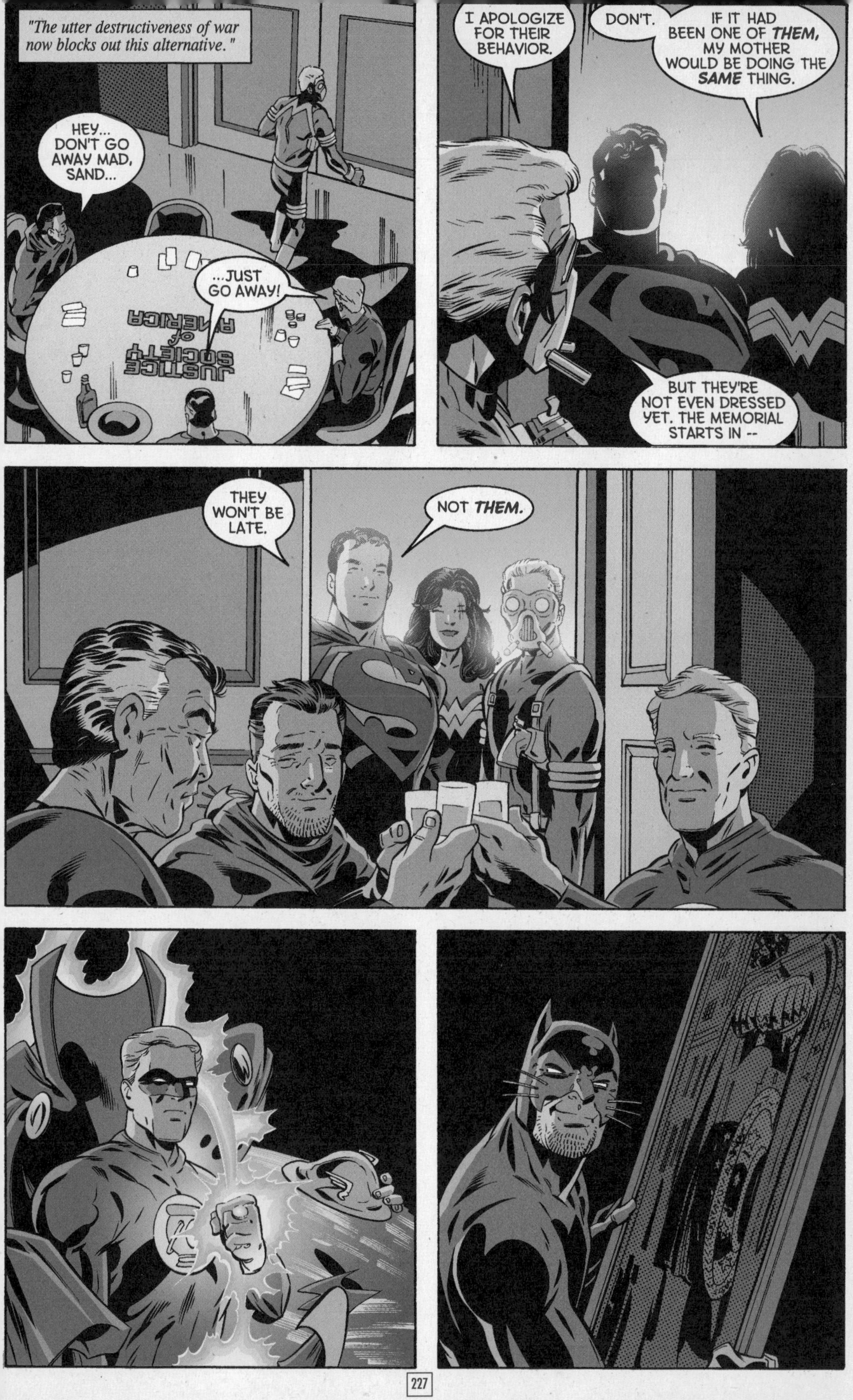
"The utter destructiveness of war now blocks out this alternative."
HEY... DON'T GO AWAY MAD, SAND...
...JUST GO AWAY!
JUSTICE SOCIETY of AMERICA
I APOLOGIZE FOR THEIR BEHAVIOR.
DON'T.
IF IT HAD BEEN ONE OF *THEM,* MY MOTHER WOULD BE DOING THE *SAME* THING.
BUT THEY'RE NOT EVEN DRESSED YET. THE MEMORIAL STARTS IN --
THEY WON'T BE LATE.
NOT *THEM.*

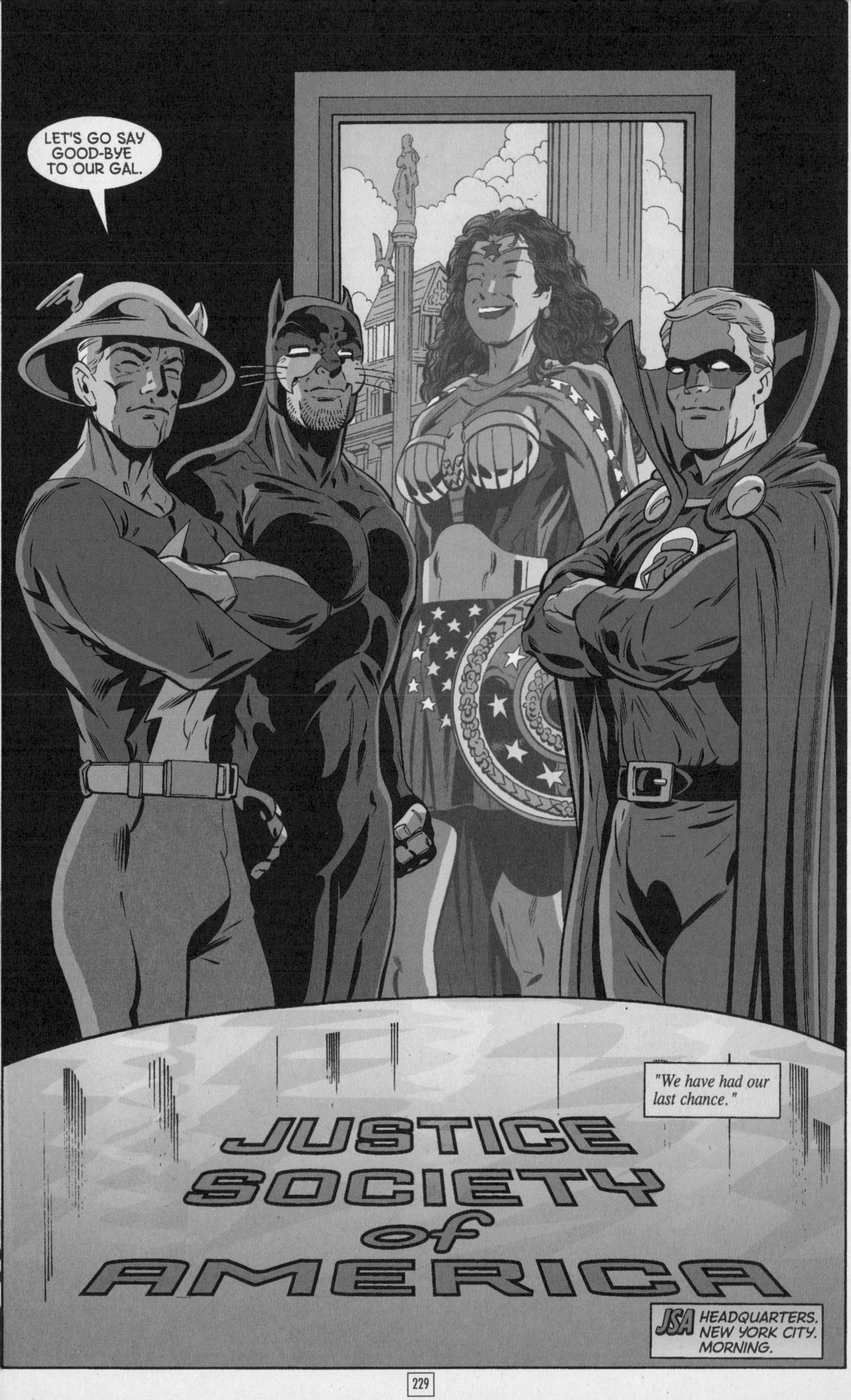

LET'S GO SAY GOOD-BYE TO OUR GAL.
"We have had our last chance."
JUSTICE SOCIETY of AMERICA
JSA HEADQUARTERS. NEW YORK CITY. MORNING.

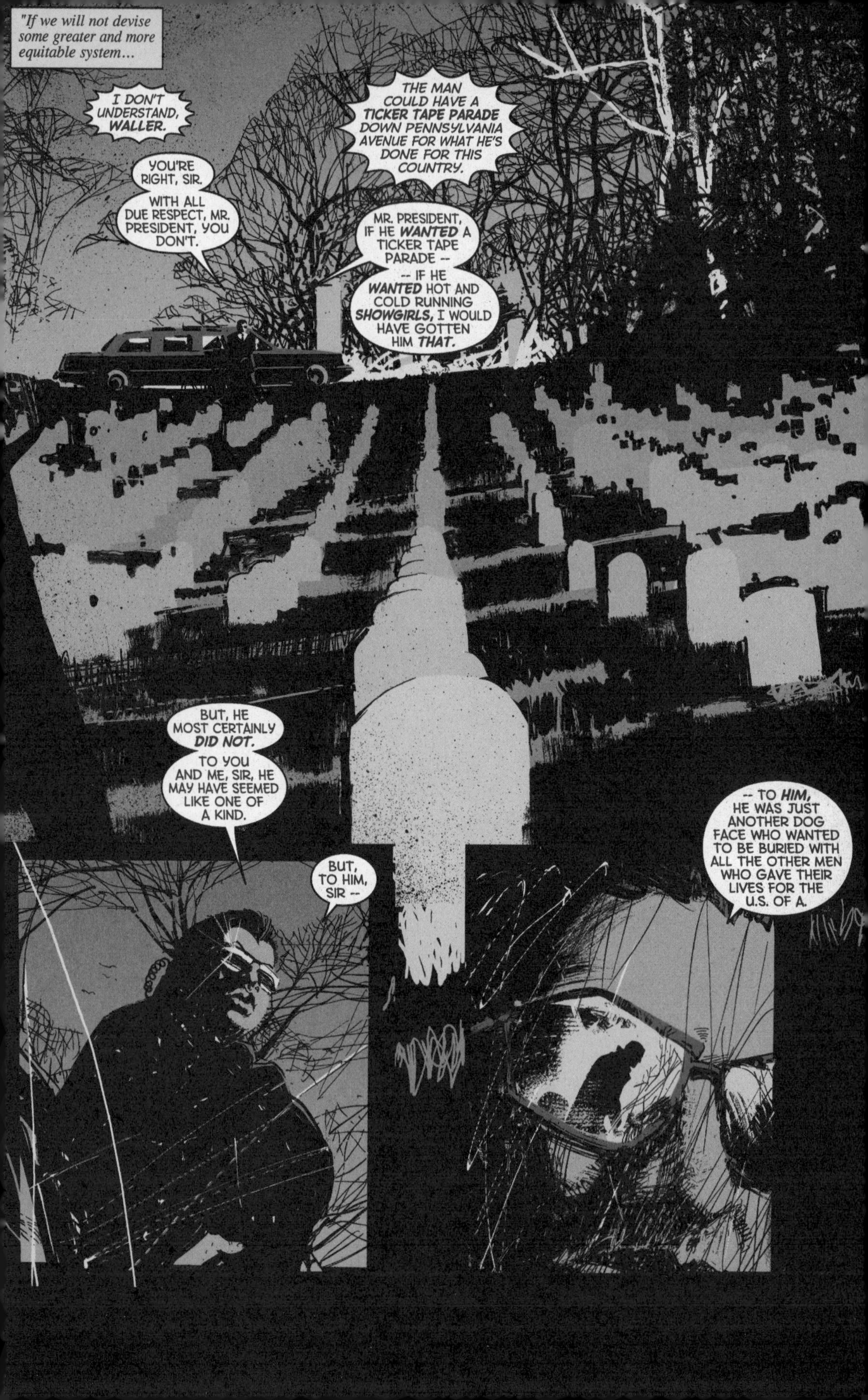
"If we will not devise some greater and more equitable system...
I DON'T UNDERSTAND, WALLER.
THE MAN COULD HAVE A TICKER TAPE PARADE DOWN PENNSYLVANIA AVENUE FOR WHAT HE'S DONE FOR THIS COUNTRY.
YOU'RE RIGHT, SIR.
WITH ALL DUE RESPECT, MR. PRESIDENT, YOU DON'T.
MR. PRESIDENT, IF HE WANTED A TICKER TAPE PARADE --
-- IF HE WANTED HOT AND COLD RUNNING SHOWGIRLS, I WOULD HAVE GOTTEN HIM THAT.
BUT, HE MOST CERTAINLY DID NOT.
TO YOU AND ME, SIR, HE MAY HAVE SEEMED LIKE ONE OF A KIND.
BUT, TO HIM, SIR --
-- TO HIM, HE WAS JUST ANOTHER DOG FACE WHO WANTED TO BE BURIED WITH ALL THE OTHER MEN WHO GAVE THEIR LIVES FOR THE U.S. OF A.

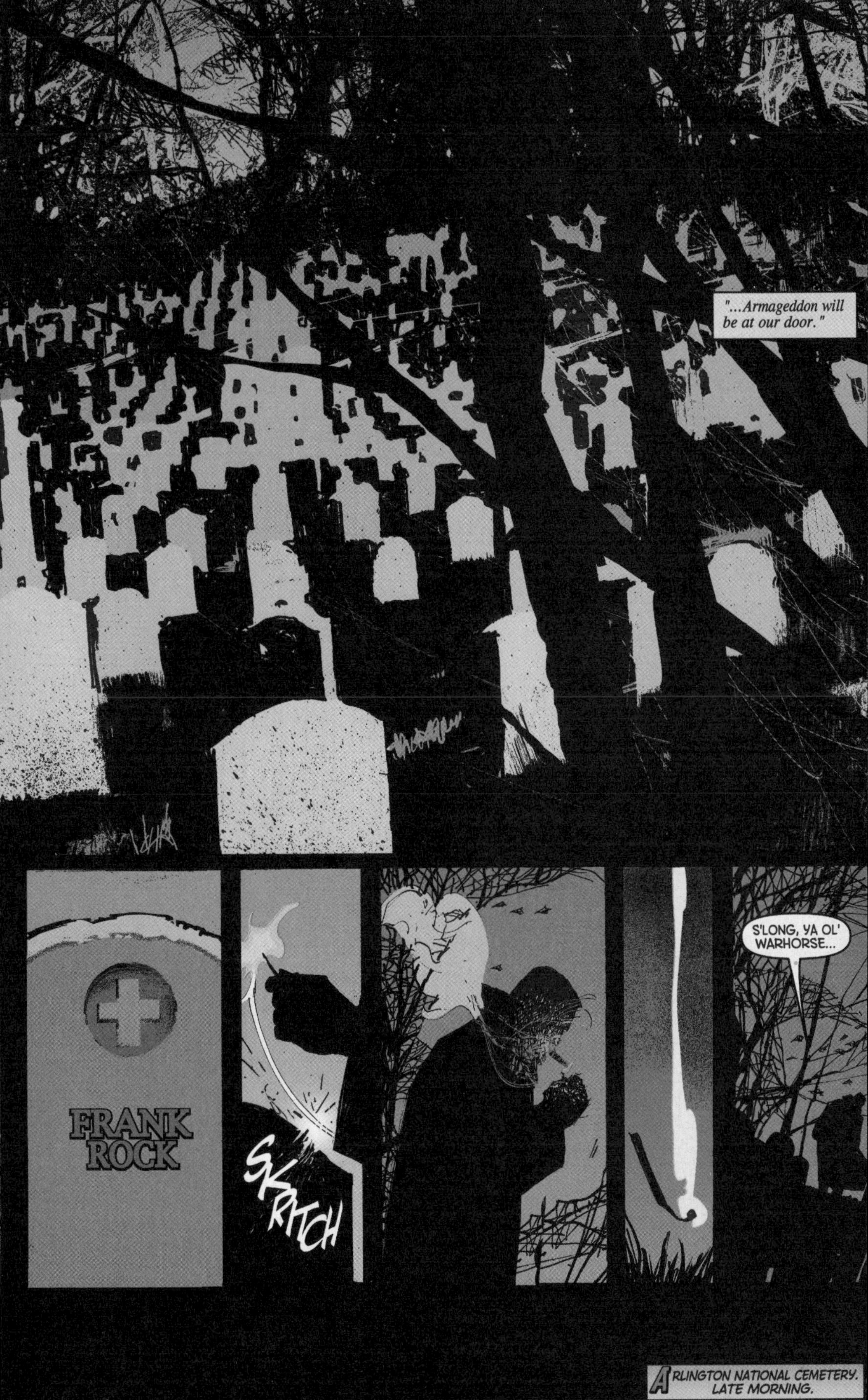
"...Armageddon will be at our door."
FRANK ROCK
SKRITCH
S'LONG, YA OL' WARHORSE...
ARLINGTON NATIONAL CEMETERY. LATE MORNING.

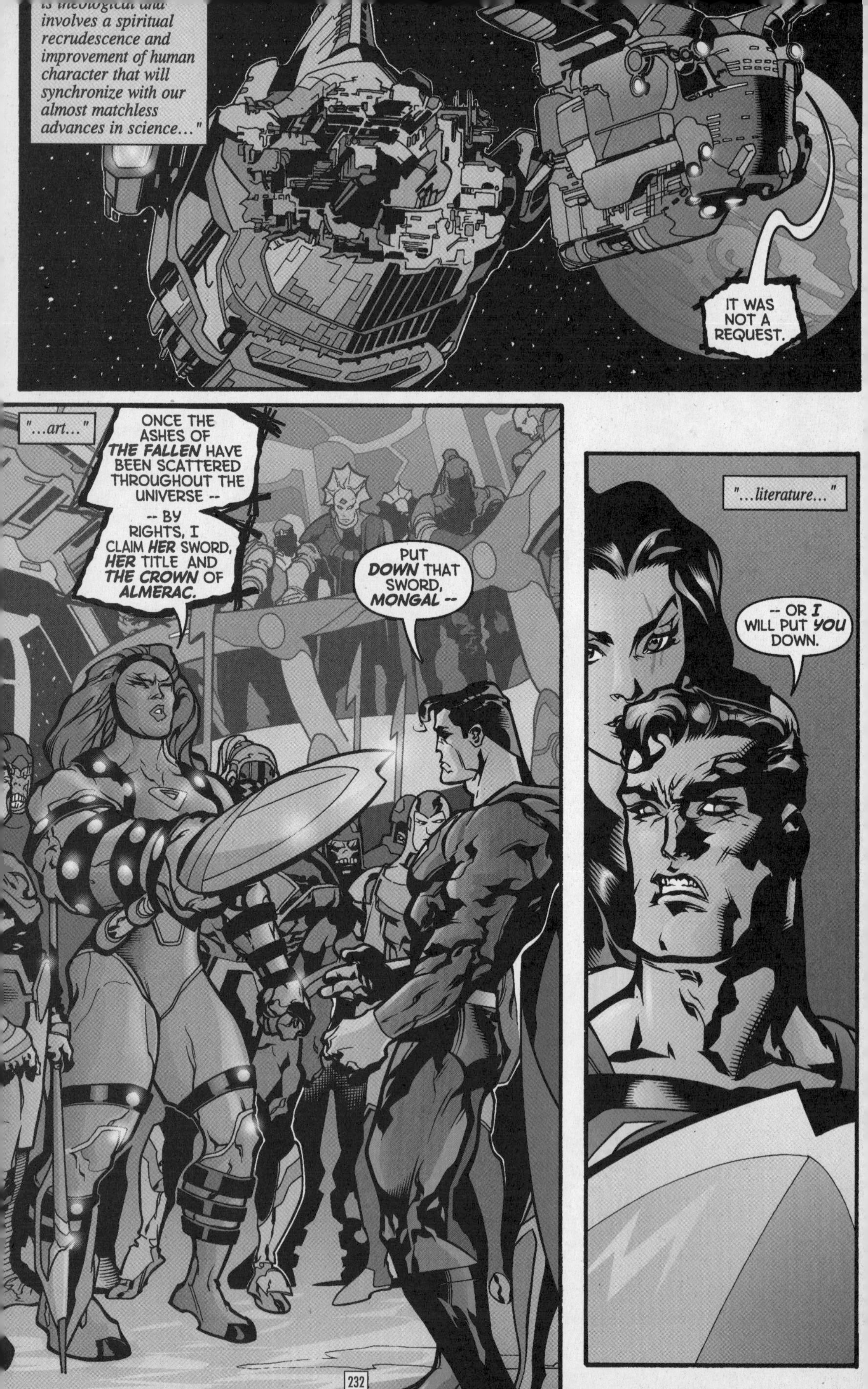
involves a spiritual recrudescence and improvement of human character that will synchronize with our almost matchless advances in science…"
IT WAS NOT A REQUEST.
"…art…"
ONCE THE ASHES OF THE FALLEN HAVE BEEN SCATTERED THROUGHOUT THE UNIVERSE --
-- BY RIGHTS, I CLAIM HER SWORD, HER TITLE AND THE CROWN OF ALMERAC.
PUT DOWN THAT SWORD, MONGAL --
"…literature…"
-- OR I WILL PUT YOU DOWN.

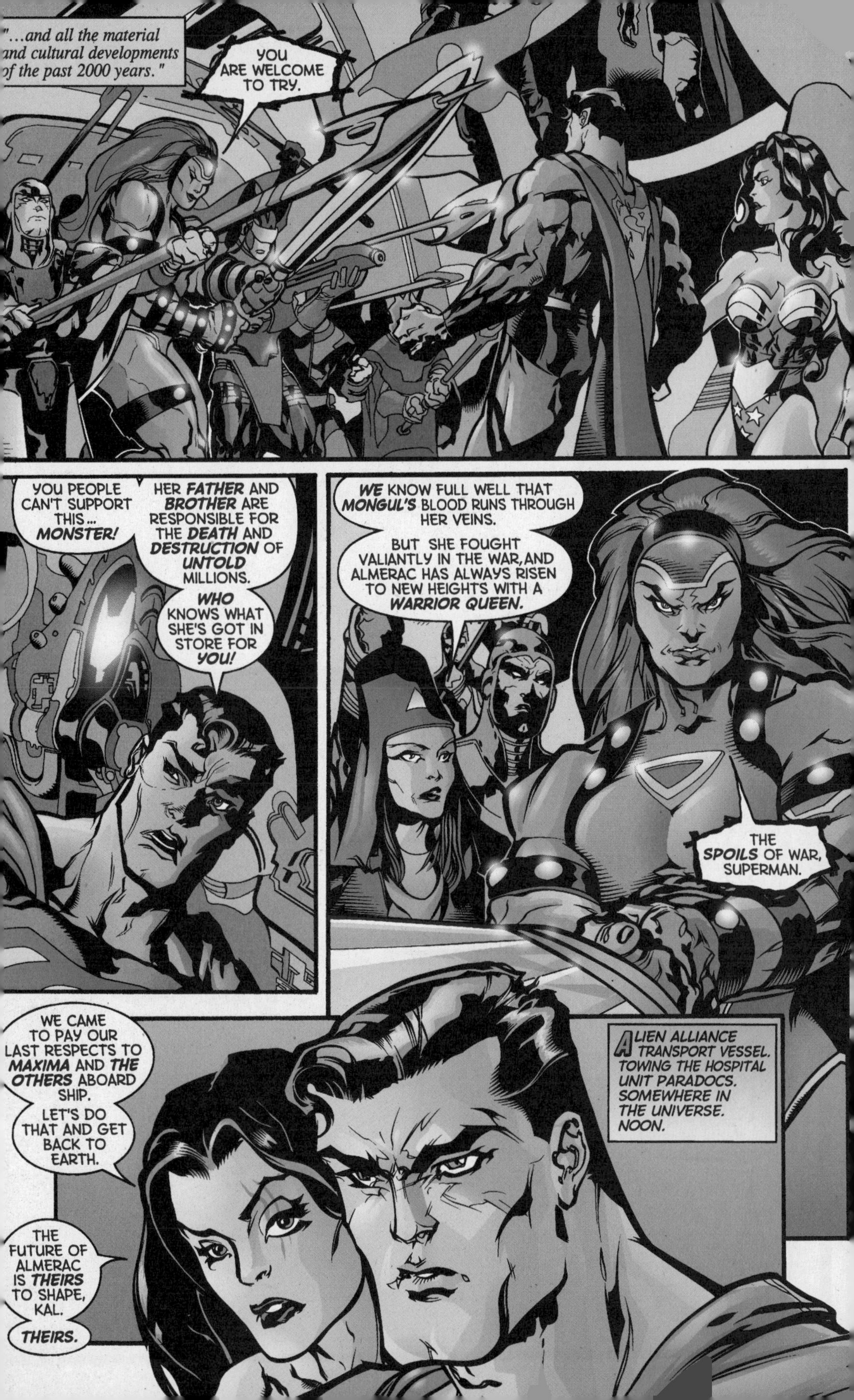
"...and all the material
and cultural developments
of the past 2000 years."
YOU ARE WELCOME TO TRY.
YOU PEOPLE CAN'T SUPPORT THIS... MONSTER!
HER FATHER AND BROTHER ARE RESPONSIBLE FOR THE DEATH AND DESTRUCTION OF UNTOLD MILLIONS.
WHO KNOWS WHAT SHE'S GOT IN STORE FOR YOU!
WE KNOW FULL WELL THAT MONGUL'S BLOOD RUNS THROUGH HER VEINS.
BUT SHE FOUGHT VALIANTLY IN THE WAR, AND ALMERAC HAS ALWAYS RISEN TO NEW HEIGHTS WITH A WARRIOR QUEEN.
THE SPOILS OF WAR, SUPERMAN.
ALIEN ALLIANCE TRANSPORT VESSEL. TOWING THE HOSPITAL UNIT PARADOCS. SOMEWHERE IN THE UNIVERSE. NOON.
WE CAME TO PAY OUR LAST RESPECTS TO MAXIMA AND THE OTHERS ABOARD SHIP.
LET'S DO THAT AND GET BACK TO EARTH.
THE FUTURE OF ALMERAC IS THEIRS TO SHAPE, KAL.
THEIRS.

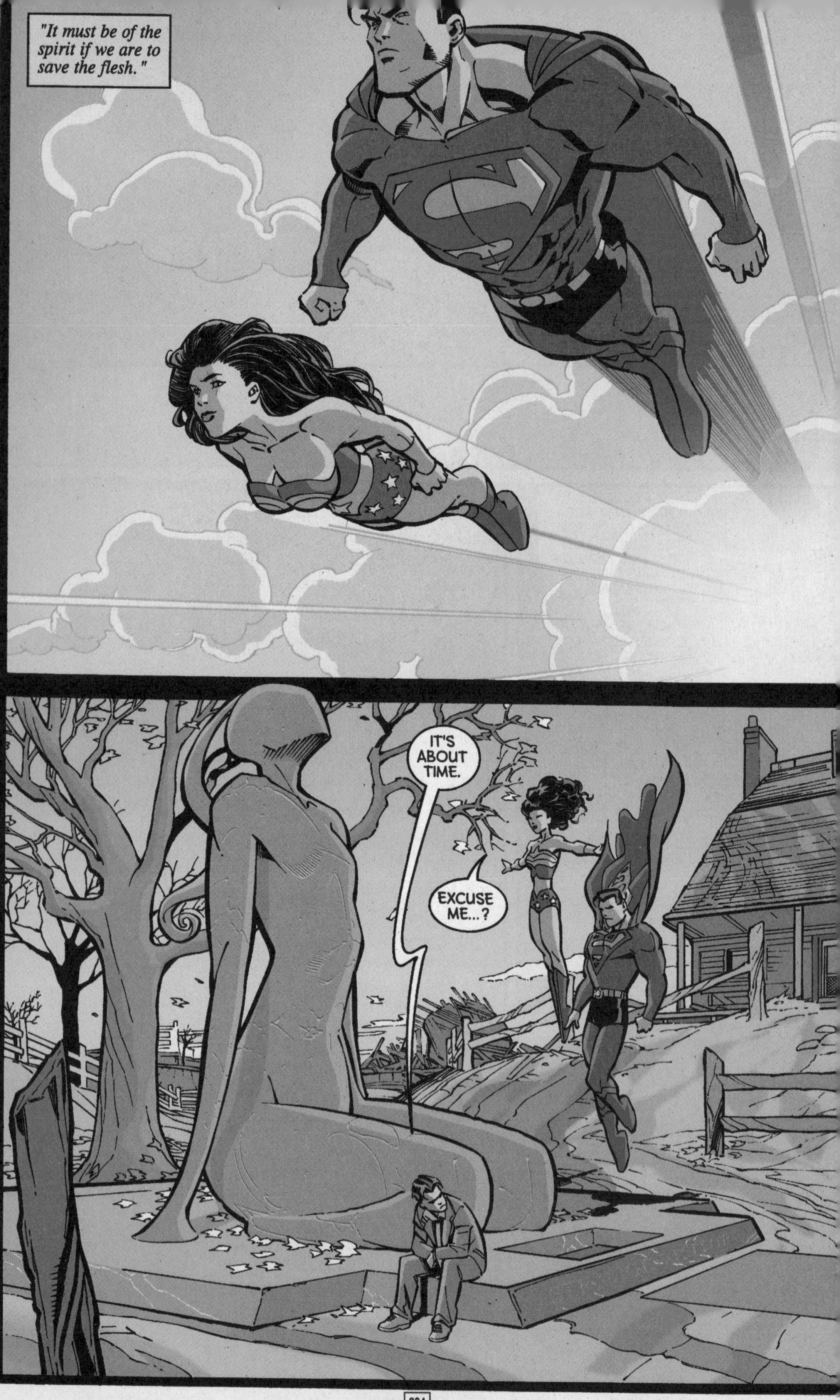
"It must be of the spirit if we are to save the flesh."
IT'S ABOUT TIME.
EXCUSE ME...?

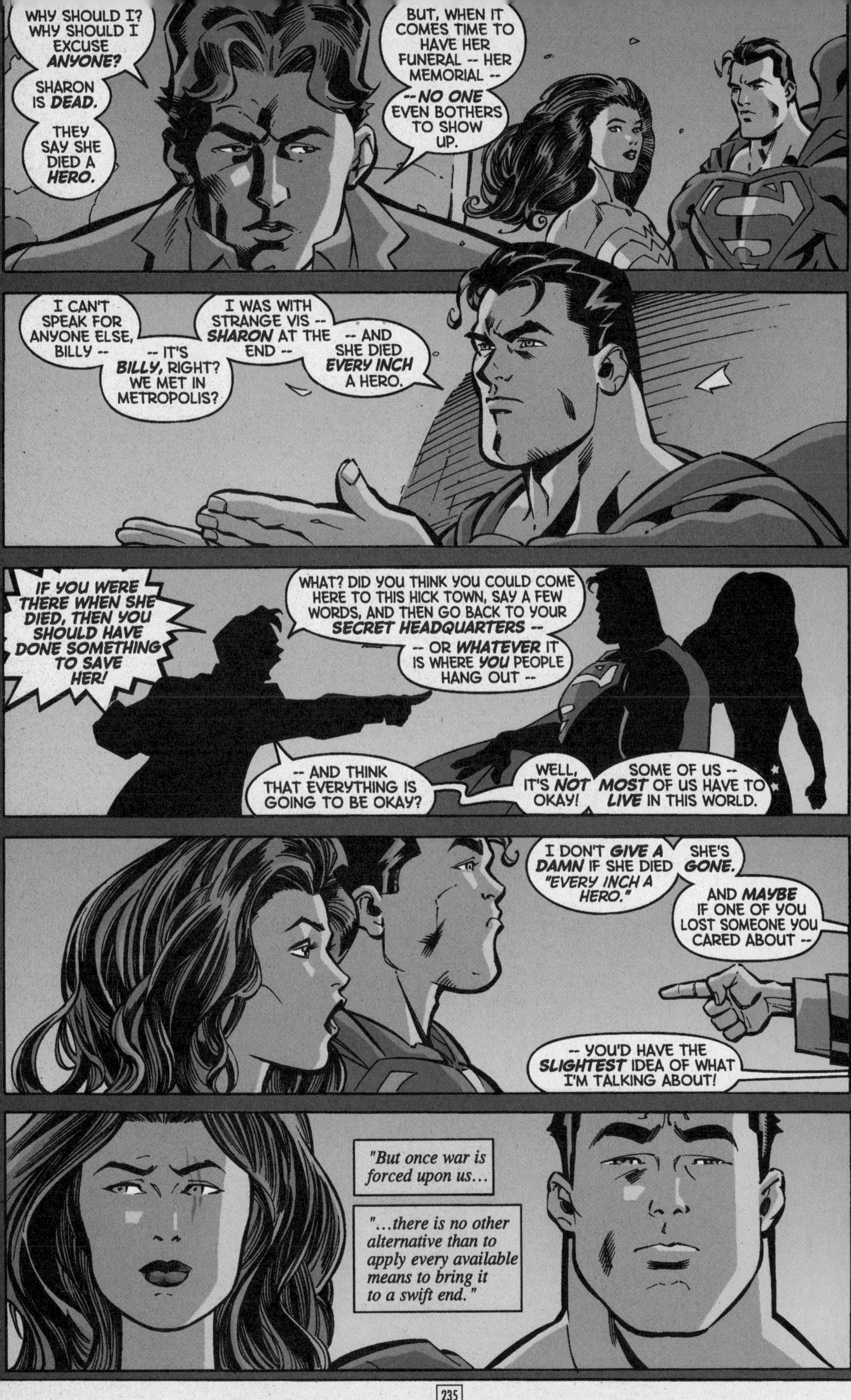

WHY SHOULD I? WHY SHOULD I EXCUSE ANYONE?
SHARON IS DEAD.
THEY SAY SHE DIED A HERO.
BUT, WHEN IT COMES TIME TO HAVE HER FUNERAL -- HER MEMORIAL --
--NO ONE EVEN BOTHERS TO SHOW UP.
I CAN'T SPEAK FOR ANYONE ELSE, BILLY --
-- IT'S BILLY, RIGHT? WE MET IN METROPOLIS?
I WAS WITH STRANGE VIS -- SHARON AT THE END --
-- AND SHE DIED EVERY INCH A HERO.
IF YOU WERE THERE WHEN SHE DIED, THEN YOU SHOULD HAVE DONE SOMETHING TO SAVE HER!
WHAT? DID YOU THINK YOU COULD COME HERE TO THIS HICK TOWN, SAY A FEW WORDS, AND THEN GO BACK TO YOUR SECRET HEADQUARTERS --
-- OR WHATEVER IT IS WHERE YOU PEOPLE HANG OUT --
-- AND THINK THAT EVERYTHING IS GOING TO BE OKAY?
WELL, IT'S NOT OKAY!
SOME OF US -- MOST OF US HAVE TO LIVE IN THIS WORLD.
I DON'T GIVE A DAMN IF SHE DIED "EVERY INCH A HERO."
SHE'S GONE.
AND MAYBE IF ONE OF YOU LOST SOMEONE YOU CARED ABOUT --
-- YOU'D HAVE THE SLIGHTEST IDEA OF WHAT I'M TALKING ABOUT!
"But once war is forced upon us...
"...there is no other alternative than to apply every available means to bring it to a swift end."

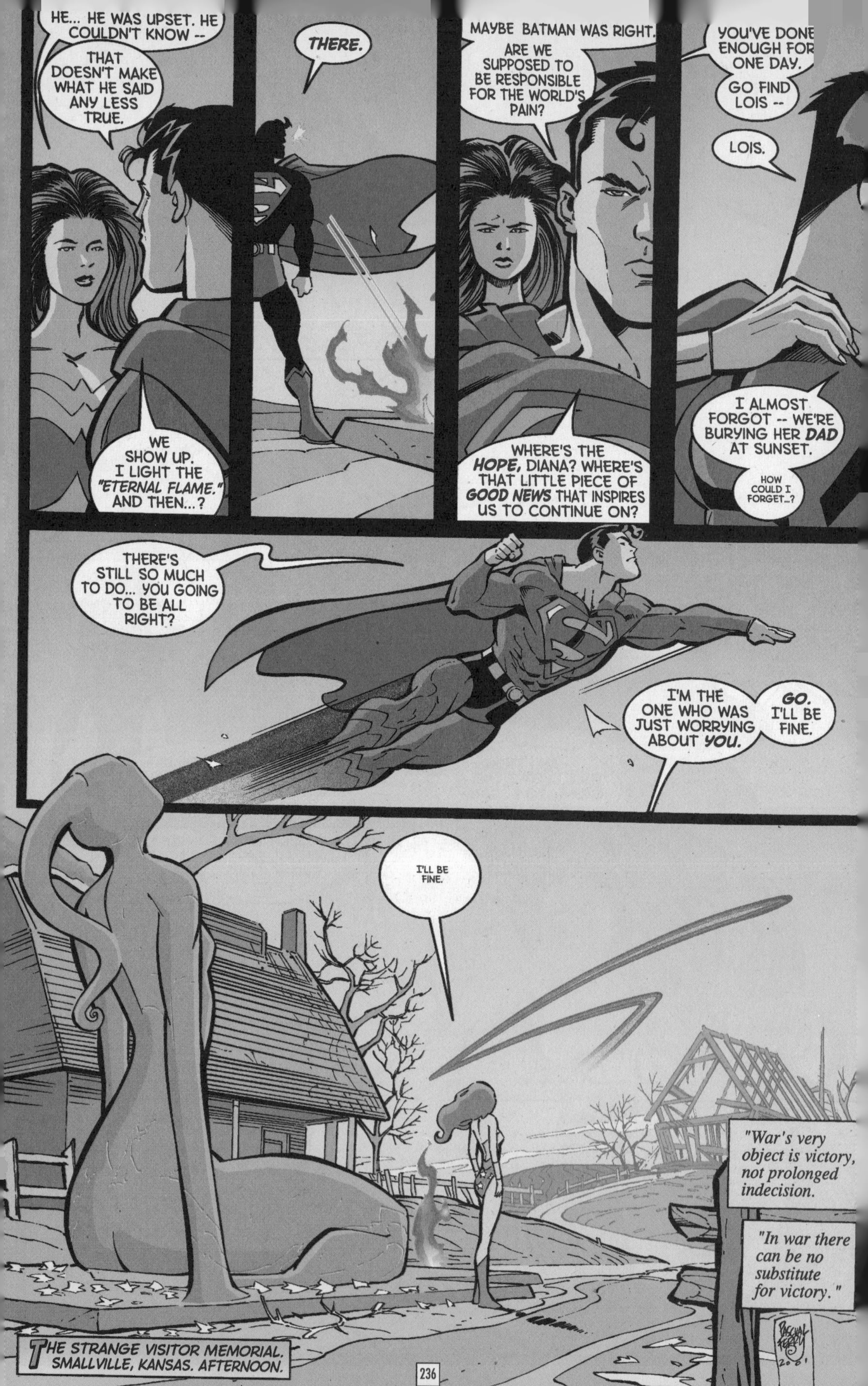
HE... HE WAS UPSET. HE COULDN'T KNOW --
THAT DOESN'T MAKE WHAT HE SAID ANY LESS TRUE.
WE SHOW UP. I LIGHT THE "ETERNAL FLAME." AND THEN...?
THERE.
MAYBE BATMAN WAS RIGHT.
ARE WE SUPPOSED TO BE RESPONSIBLE FOR THE WORLD'S PAIN?
WHERE'S THE HOPE, DIANA? WHERE'S THAT LITTLE PIECE OF GOOD NEWS THAT INSPIRES US TO CONTINUE ON?
YOU'VE DONE ENOUGH FOR ONE DAY.
GO FIND LOIS --
LOIS.
I ALMOST FORGOT -- WE'RE BURYING HER DAD AT SUNSET.
HOW COULD I FORGET...?
THERE'S STILL SO MUCH TO DO... YOU GOING TO BE ALL RIGHT?
I'M THE ONE WHO WAS JUST WORRYING ABOUT YOU.
GO. I'LL BE FINE.
I'LL BE FINE.
"War's very object is victory, not prolonged indecision.
"In war there can be no substitute for victory."
THE STRANGE VISITOR MEMORIAL. SMALLVILLE, KANSAS. AFTERNOON.
PASCUAL FERRY 2001

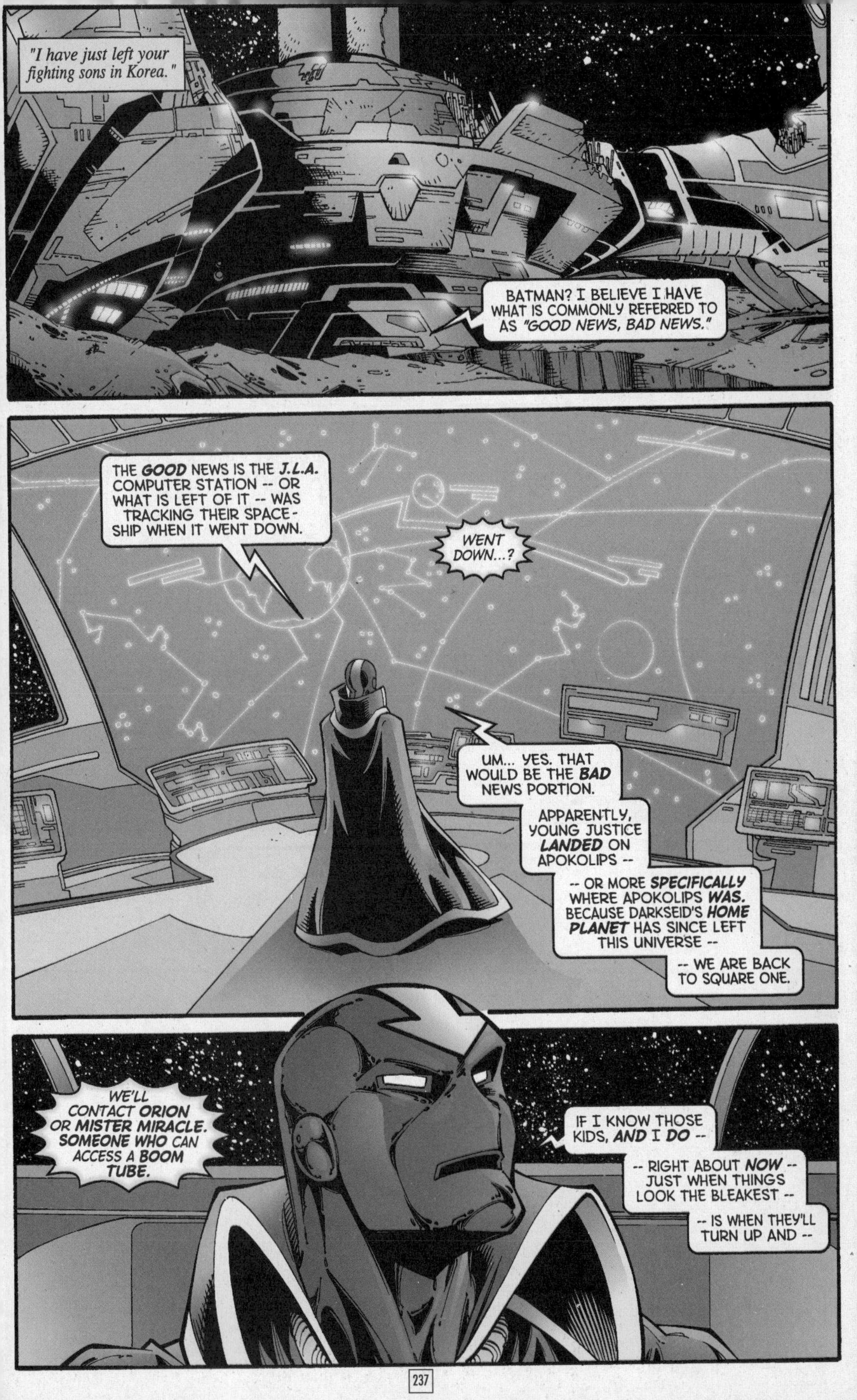
"I have just left your fighting sons in Korea."
BATMAN? I BELIEVE I HAVE WHAT IS COMMONLY REFERRED TO AS "GOOD NEWS, BAD NEWS."
THE GOOD NEWS IS THE J.L.A. COMPUTER STATION -- OR WHAT IS LEFT OF IT -- WAS TRACKING THEIR SPACE-SHIP WHEN IT WENT DOWN.
WENT DOWN...?
UM... YES. THAT WOULD BE THE BAD NEWS PORTION.
APPARENTLY, YOUNG JUSTICE LANDED ON APOKOLIPS --
-- OR MORE SPECIFICALLY WHERE APOKOLIPS WAS. BECAUSE DARKSEID'S HOME PLANET HAS SINCE LEFT THIS UNIVERSE --
-- WE ARE BACK TO SQUARE ONE.
WE'LL CONTACT ORION OR MISTER MIRACLE. SOMEONE WHO CAN ACCESS A BOOM TUBE.
IF I KNOW THOSE KIDS, AND I DO --
-- RIGHT ABOUT NOW -- JUST WHEN THINGS LOOK THE BLEAKEST --
-- IS WHEN THEY'LL TURN UP AND --

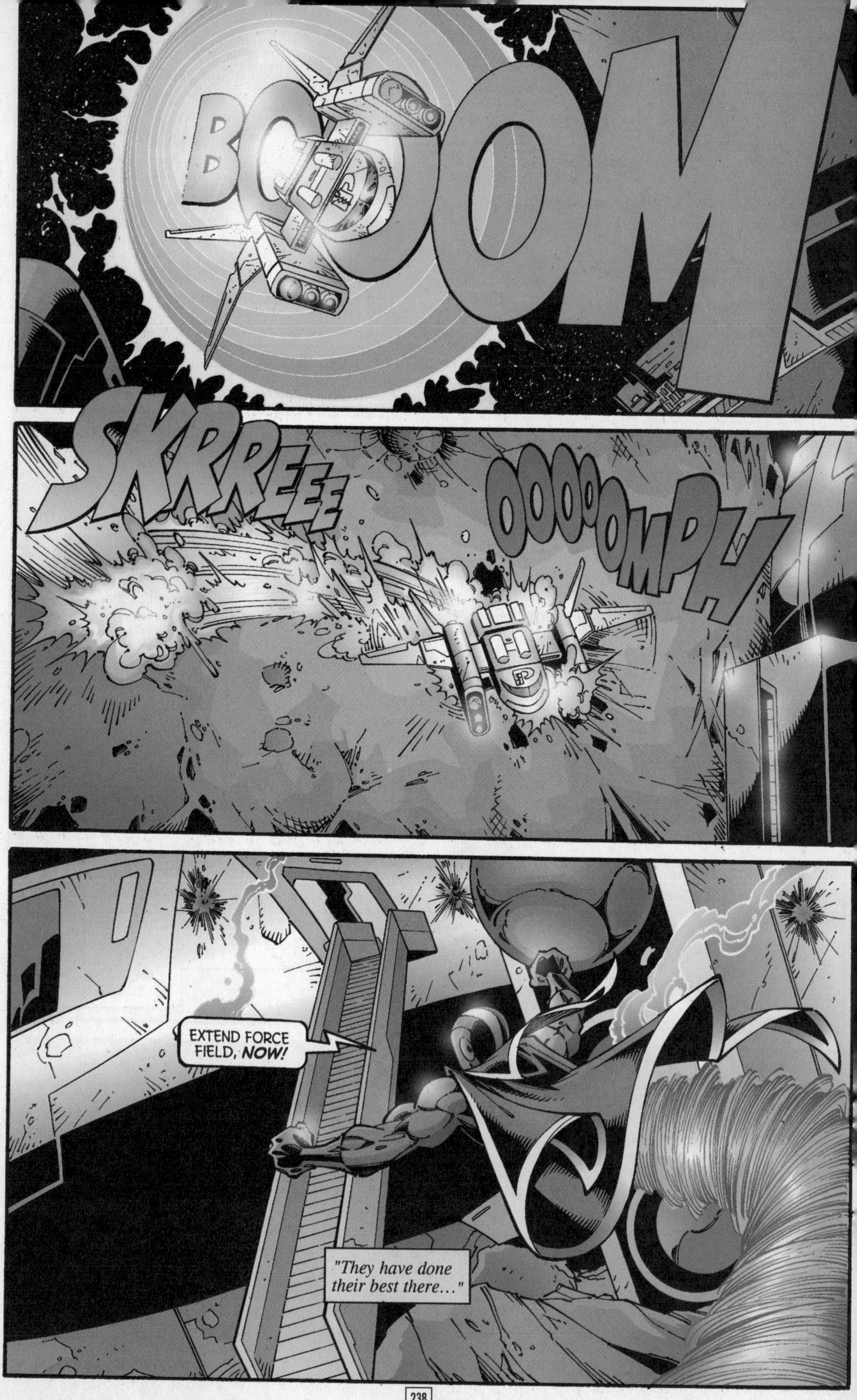
BOOOM
SKRREEE
OOOOOMPH
EXTEND FORCE FIELD, NOW!
"They have done their best there..."

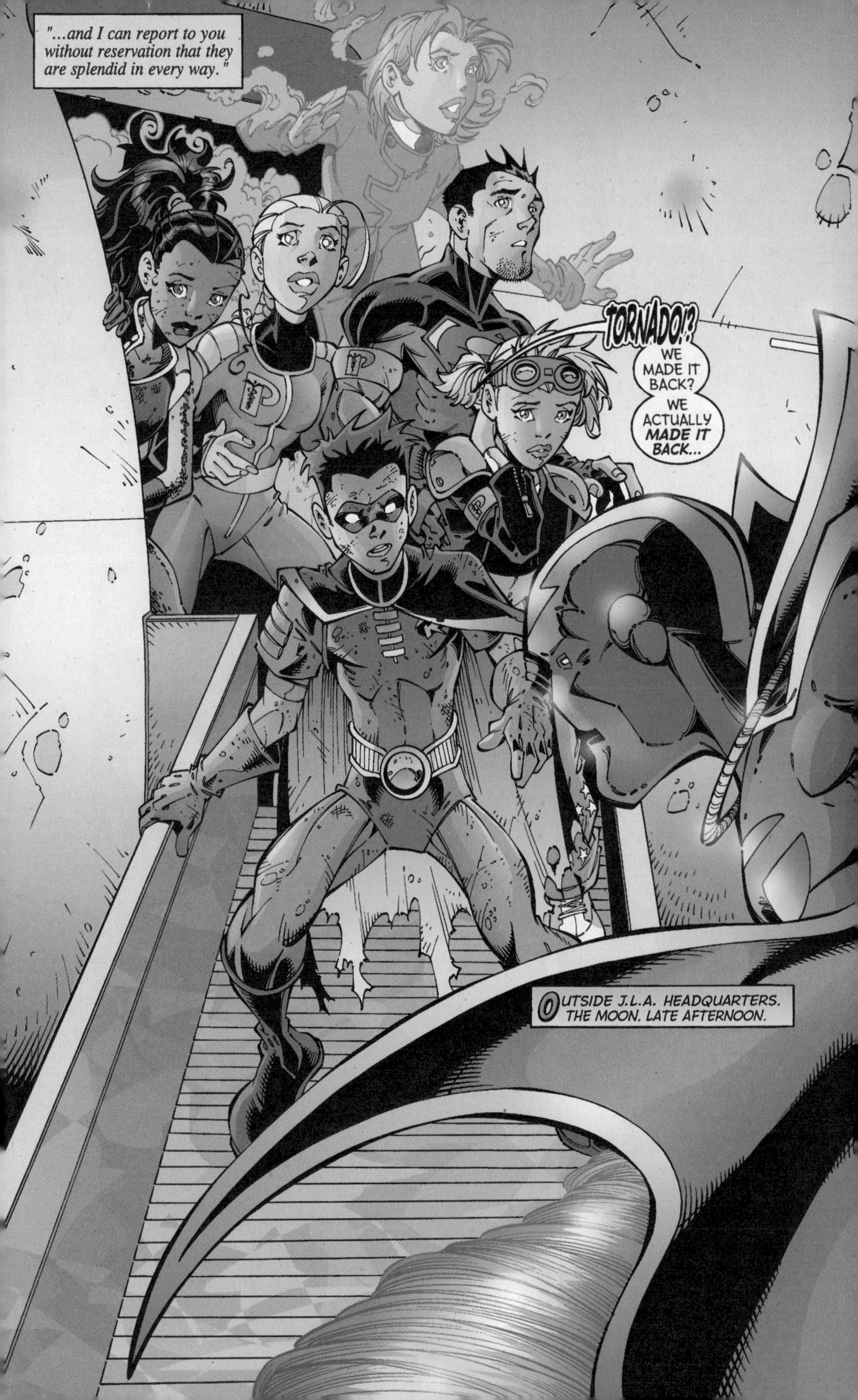
"...and I can report to you without reservation that they are splendid in every way."
TORNADO!?
WE MADE IT BACK?
WE ACTUALLY MADE IT BACK...
OUTSIDE J.L.A. HEADQUARTERS. THE MOON. LATE AFTERNOON.

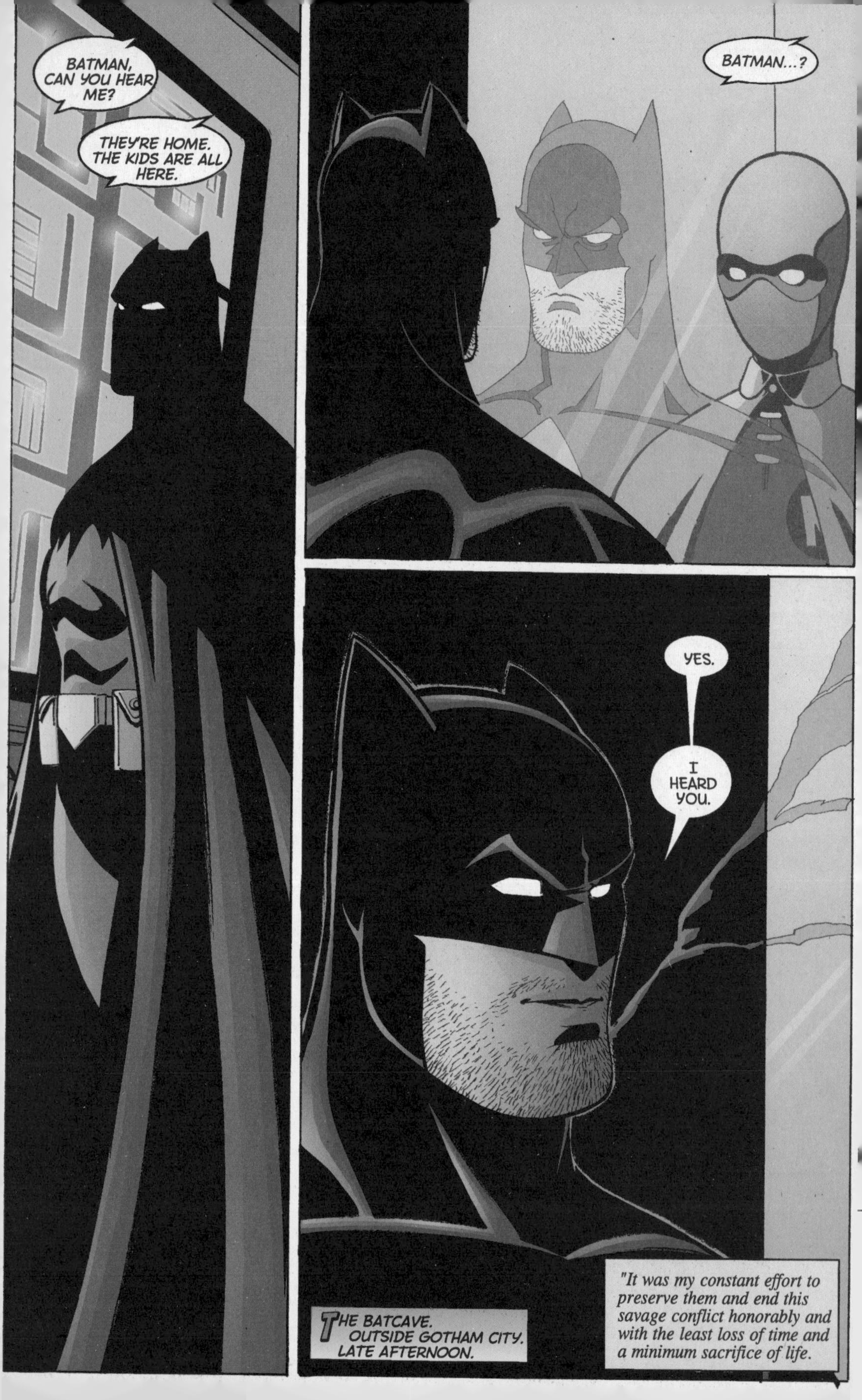
BATMAN, CAN YOU HEAR ME?
THEY'RE HOME. THE KIDS ARE ALL HERE.
BATMAN...?
YES.
I HEARD YOU.
THE BATCAVE. OUTSIDE GOTHAM CITY. LATE AFTERNOON.
"It was my constant effort to preserve them and end this savage conflict honorably and with the least loss of time and a minimum sacrifice of life.

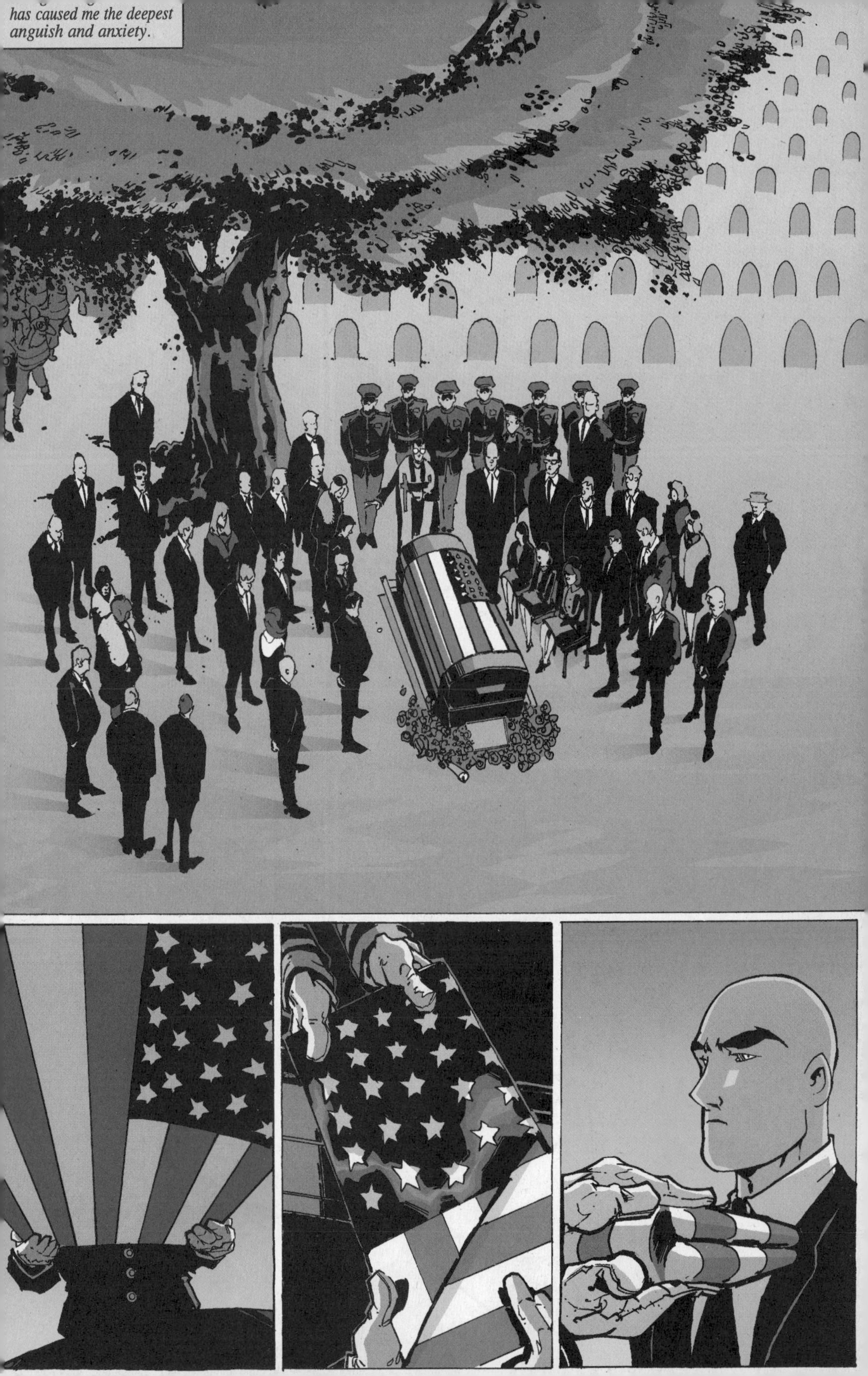
has caused me the deepest anguish and anxiety.

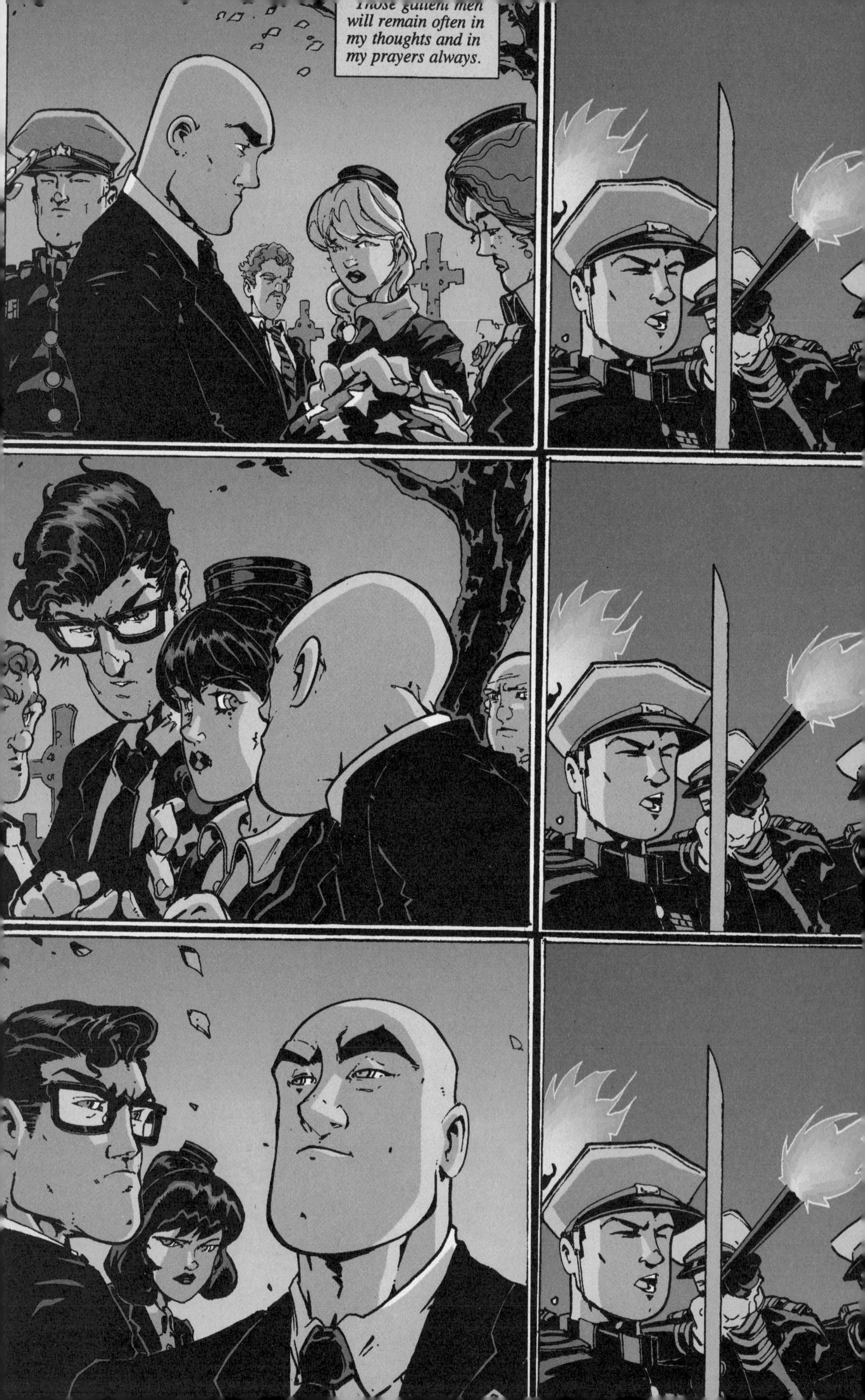
Those gallant men will remain often in my thoughts and in my prayers always.

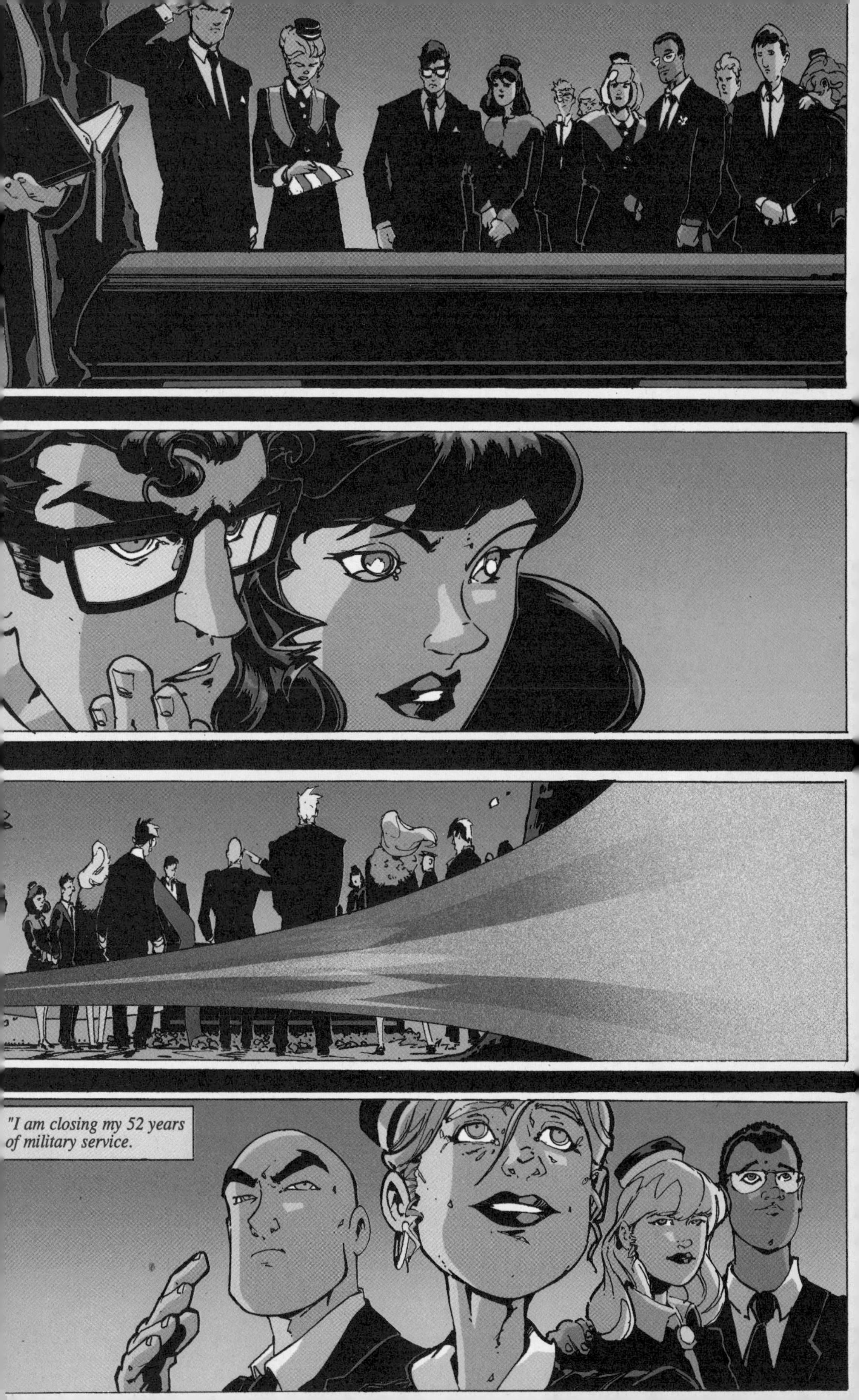
"I am closing my 52 years
of military service.

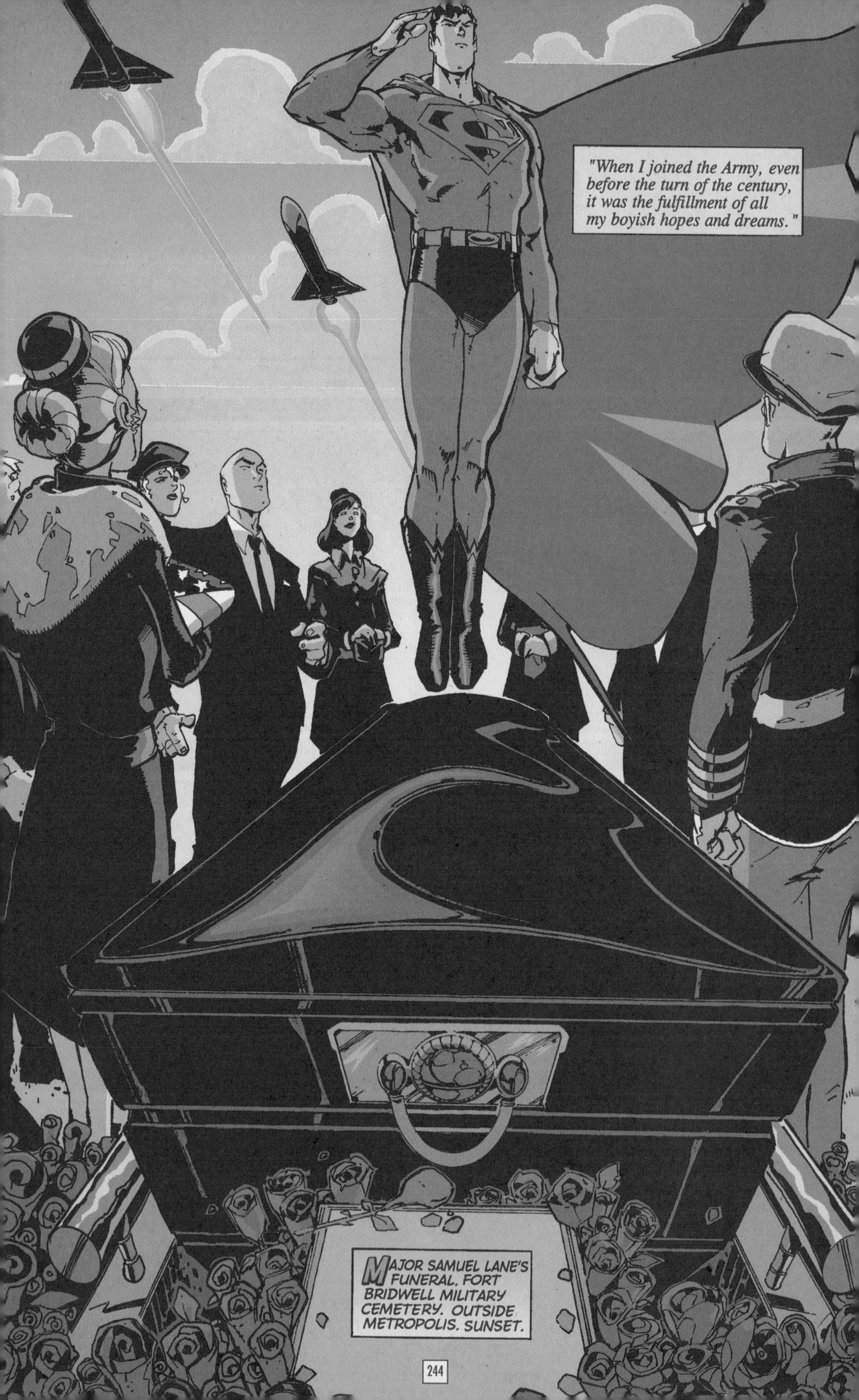
"When I joined the Army, even before the turn of the century, it was the fulfillment of all my boyish hopes and dreams."
MAJOR SAMUEL LANE'S FUNERAL. FORT BRIDWELL MILITARY CEMETERY. OUTSIDE METROPOLIS. SUNSET.

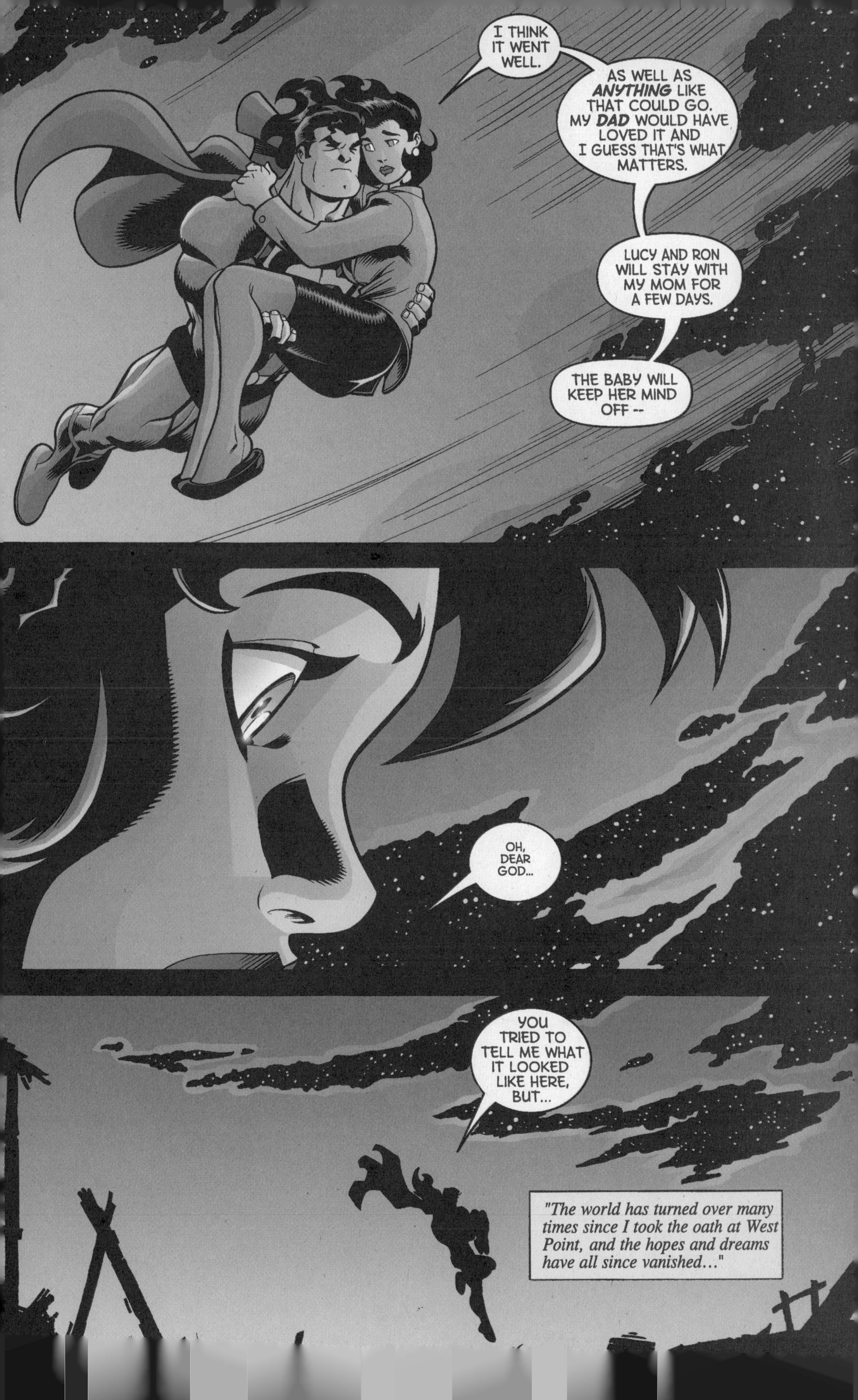
I THINK IT WENT WELL.
AS WELL AS ANYTHING LIKE THAT COULD GO. MY DAD WOULD HAVE LOVED IT AND I GUESS THAT'S WHAT MATTERS.
LUCY AND RON WILL STAY WITH MY MOM FOR A FEW DAYS.
THE BABY WILL KEEP HER MIND OFF --
OH, DEAR GOD...
YOU TRIED TO TELL ME WHAT IT LOOKED LIKE HERE, BUT...
"The world has turned over many times since I took the oath at West Point, and the hopes and dreams have all since vanished..."

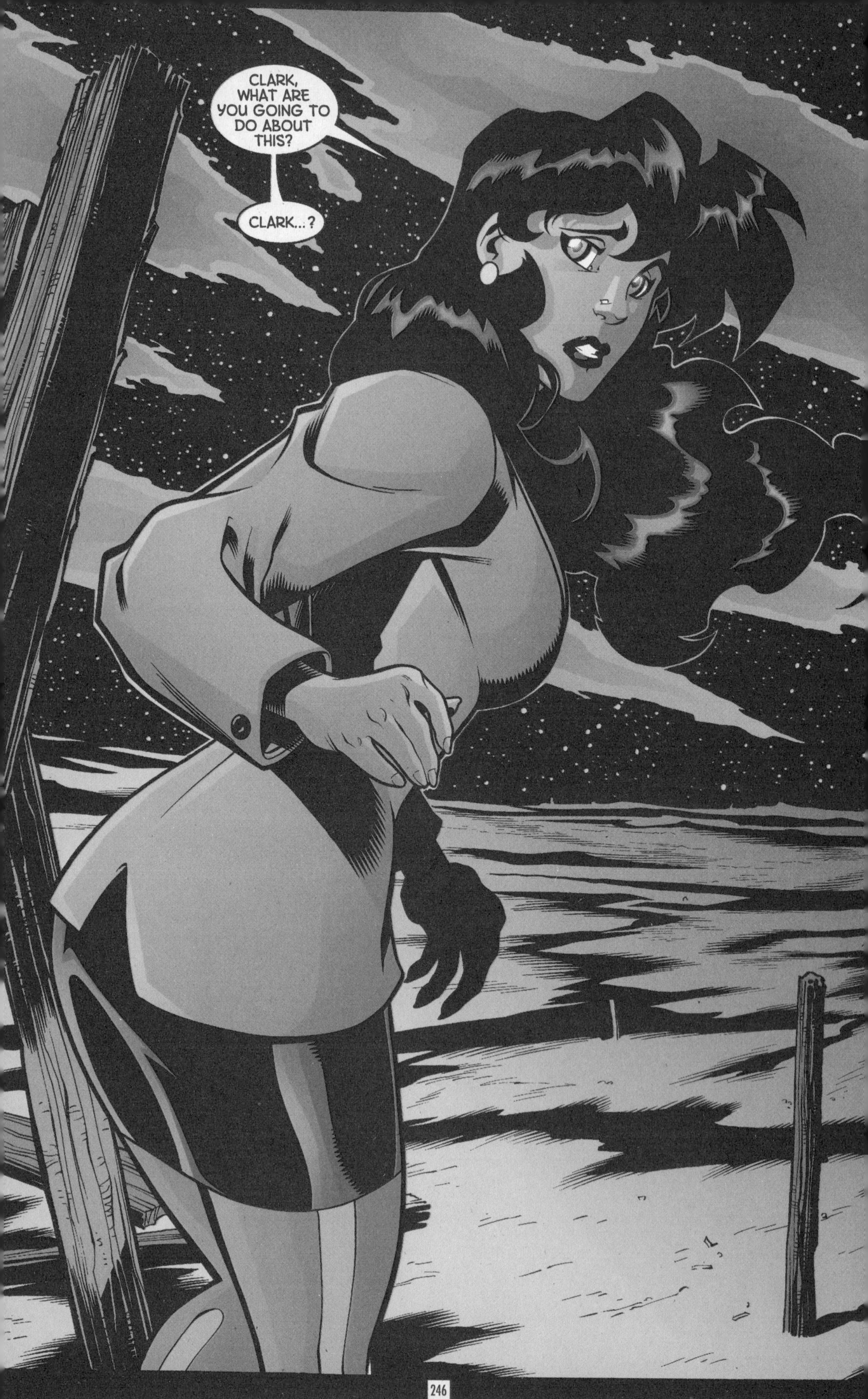
CLARK, WHAT ARE YOU GOING TO DO ABOUT THIS?
CLARK...?

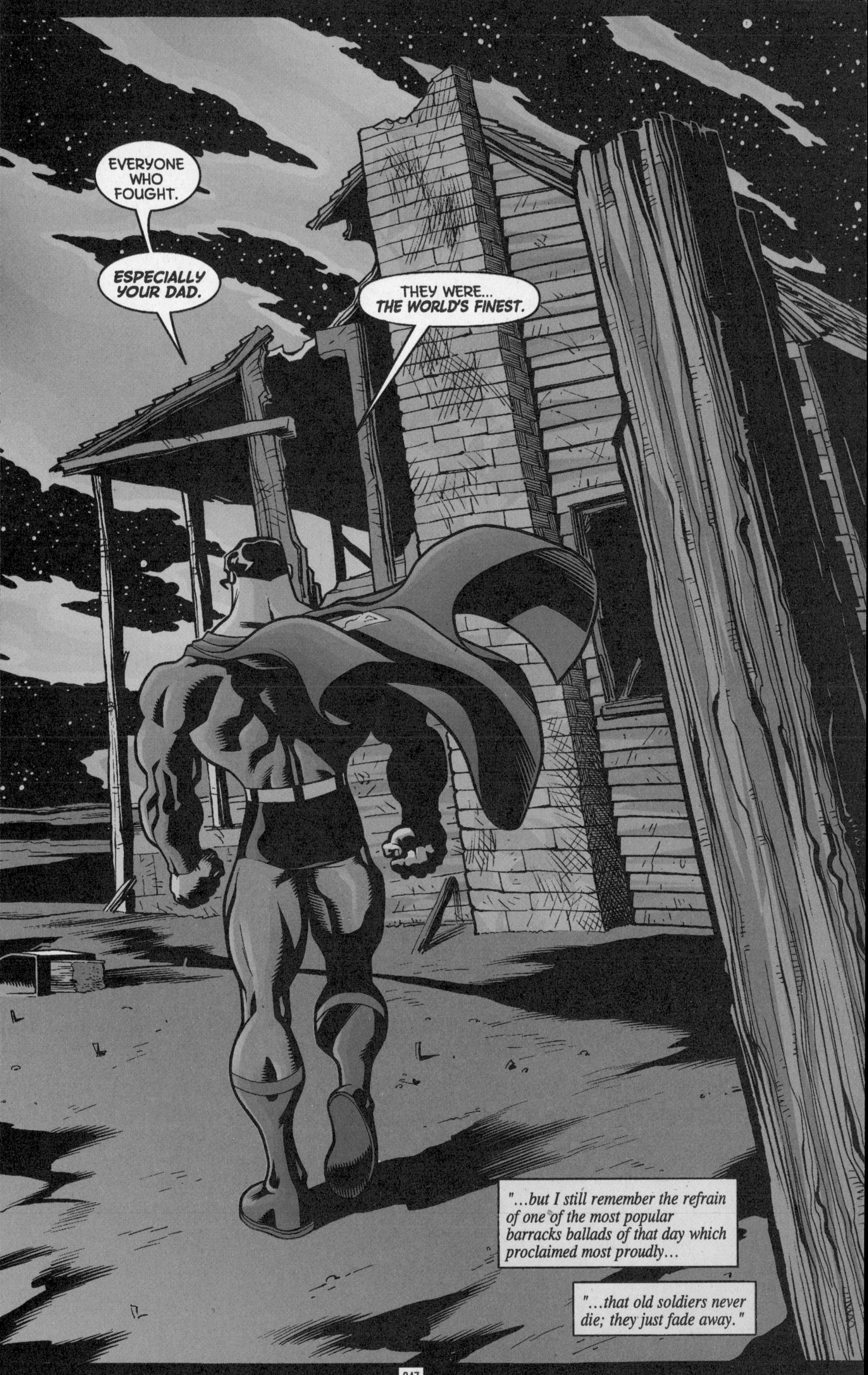
EVERYONE WHO FOUGHT.
ESPECIALLY YOUR DAD.
THEY WERE... THE WORLD'S FINEST.
"...but I still remember the refrain of one of the most popular barracks ballads of that day which proclaimed most proudly...
"...that old soldiers never die; they just fade away."

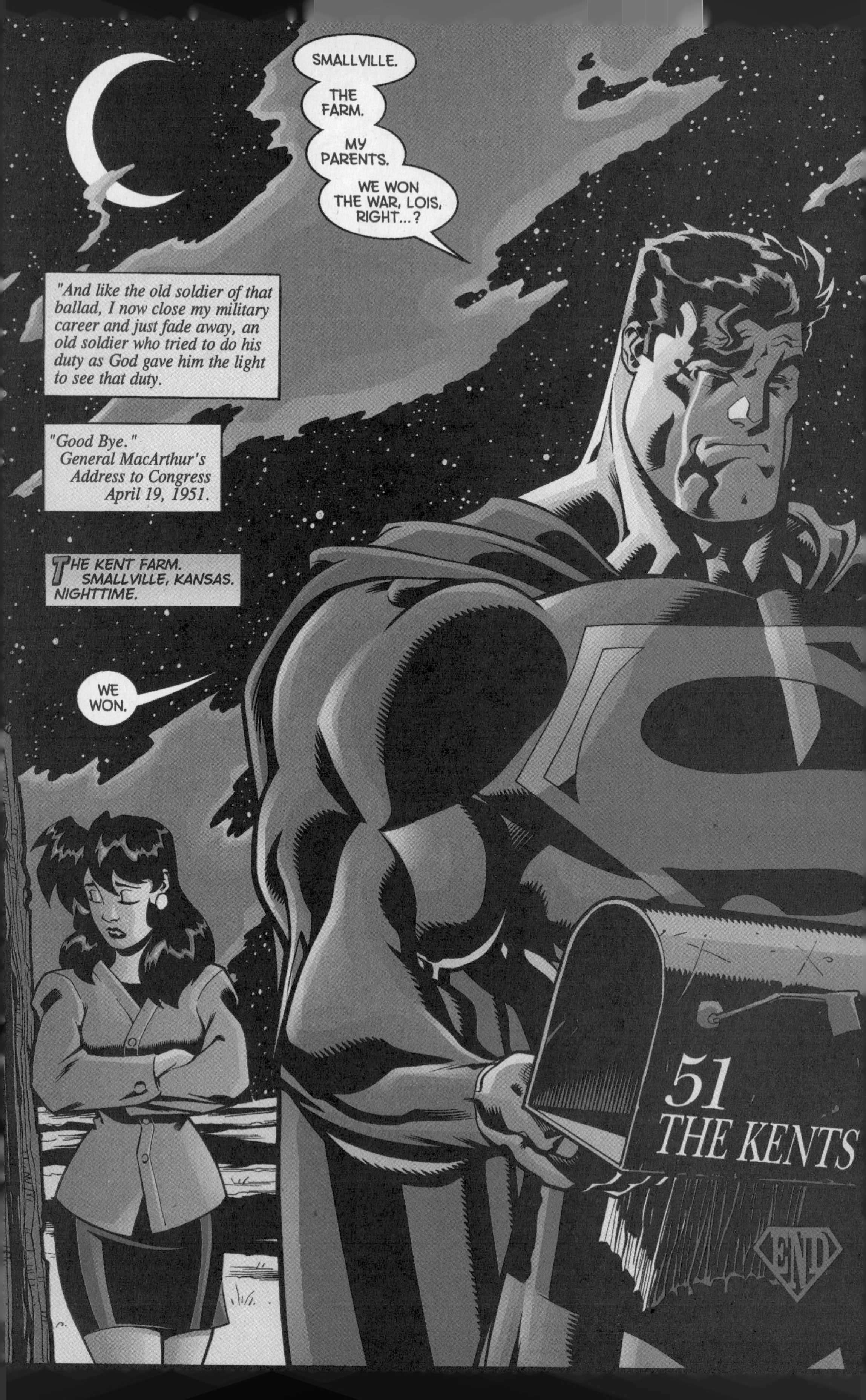
SMALLVILLE.
THE FARM.
MY PARENTS.
WE WON THE WAR, LOIS, RIGHT...?
"And like the old soldier of that ballad, I now close my military career and just fade away, an old soldier who tried to do his duty as God gave him the light to see that duty.
"Good Bye." General MacArthur's Address to Congress April 19, 1951.
THE KENT FARM. SMALLVILLE, KANSAS. NIGHTTIME.
WE WON.
51 THE KENTS
END

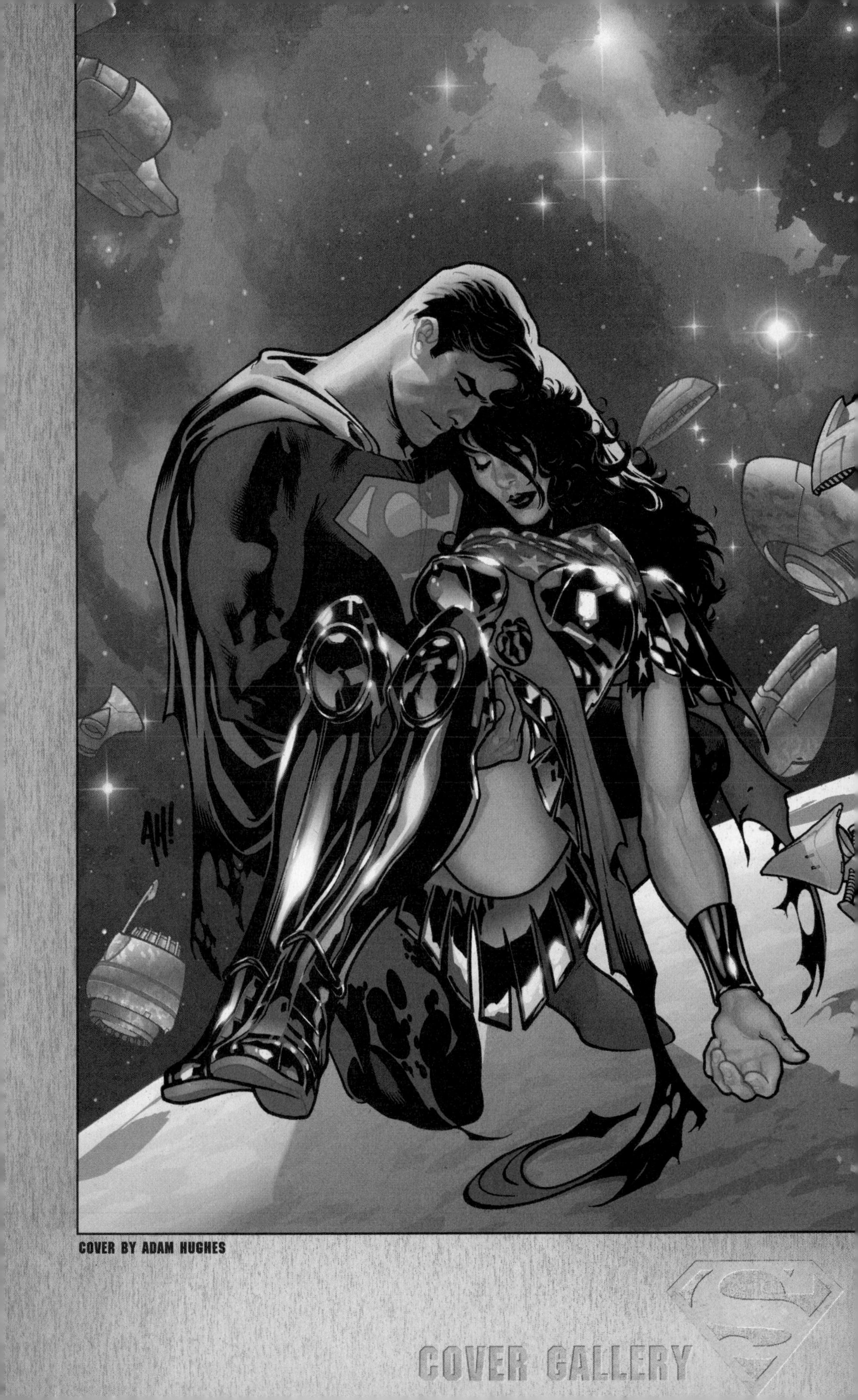

COVER BY ADAM HUGHES

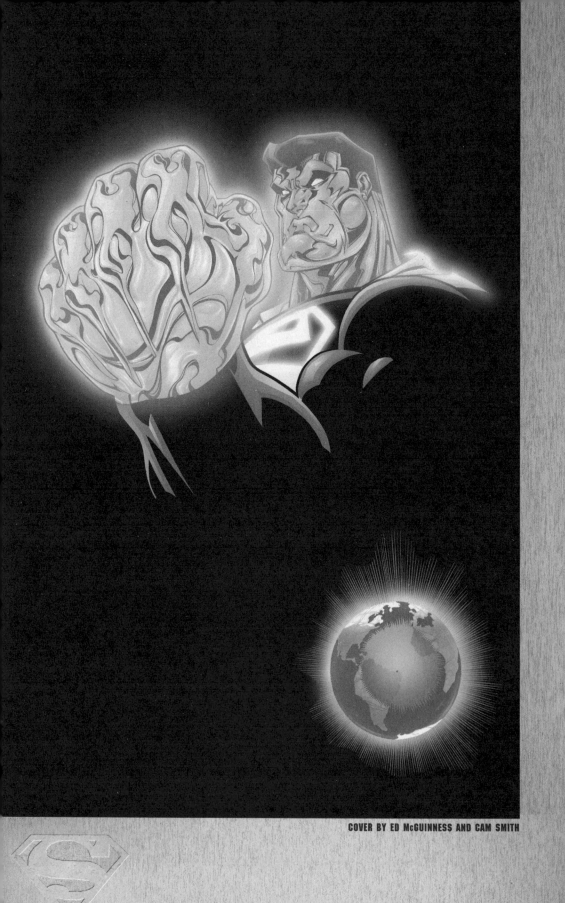

COVER BY ED McGUINNESS AND CAM SMITH

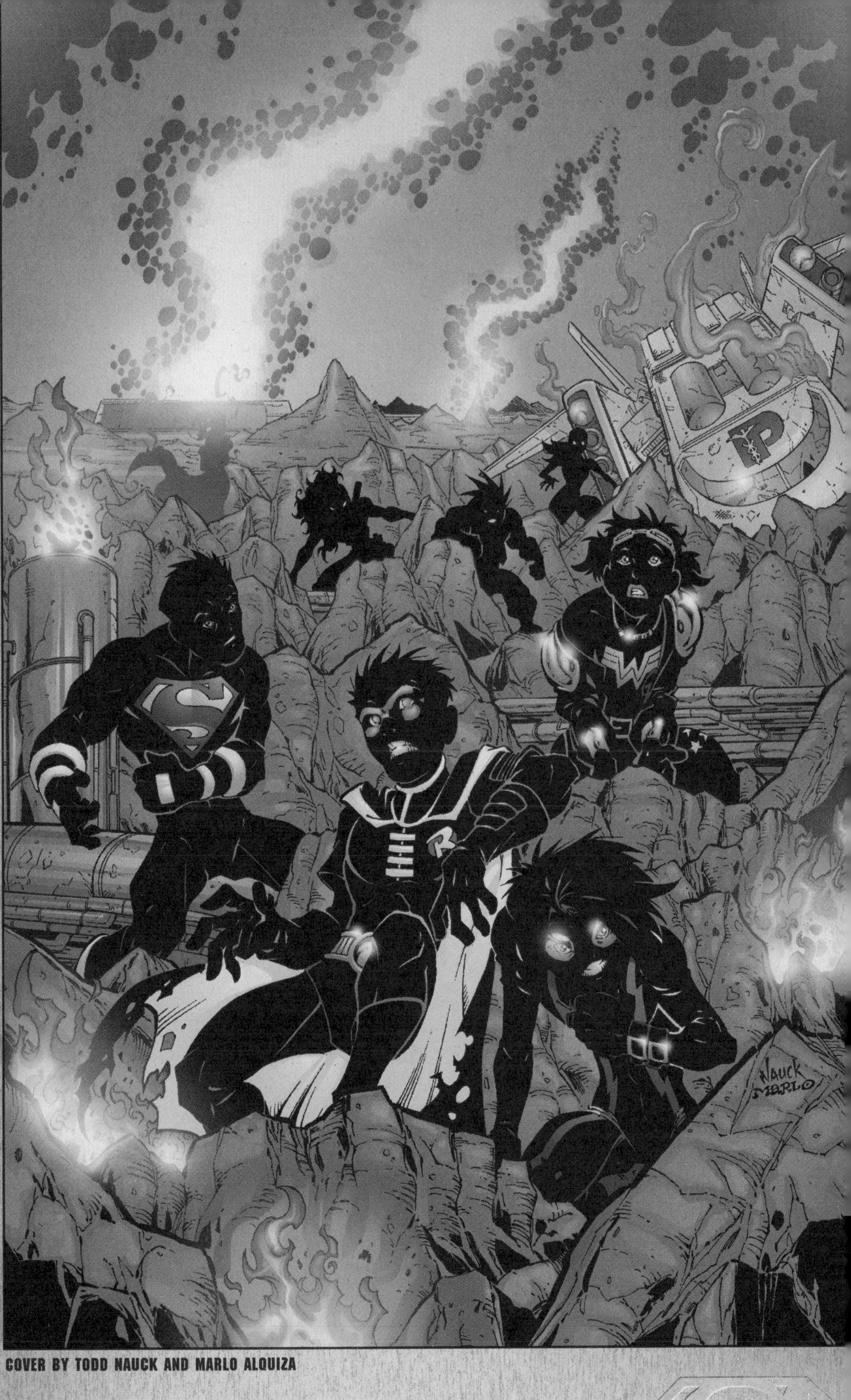
NAUCK
MARLO

COVER BY TODD NAUCK AND MARLO ALQUIZA

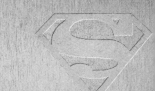

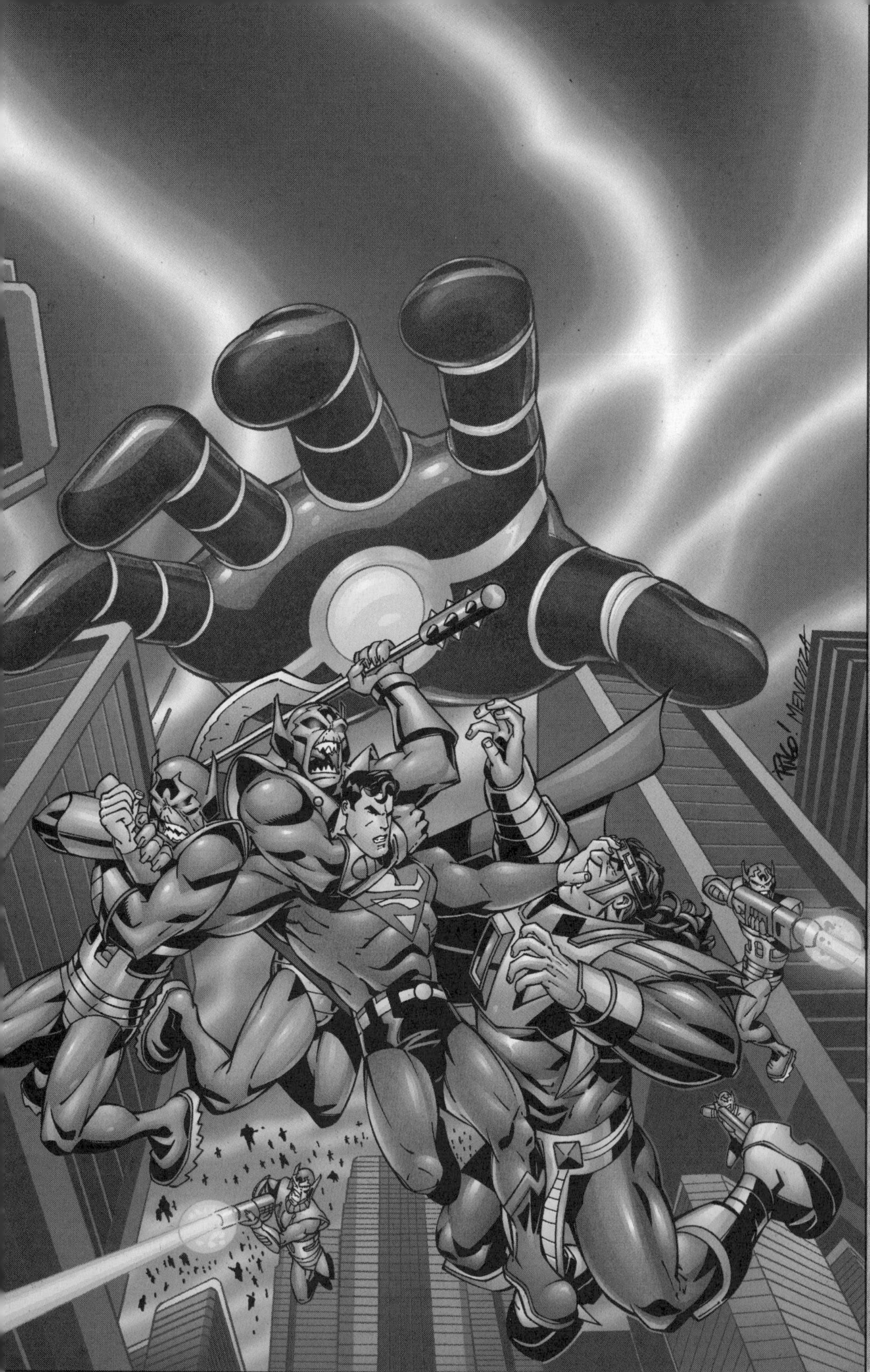

COVER BY MIKE WIERINGO AND JOSÉ MARZÁN, JR.

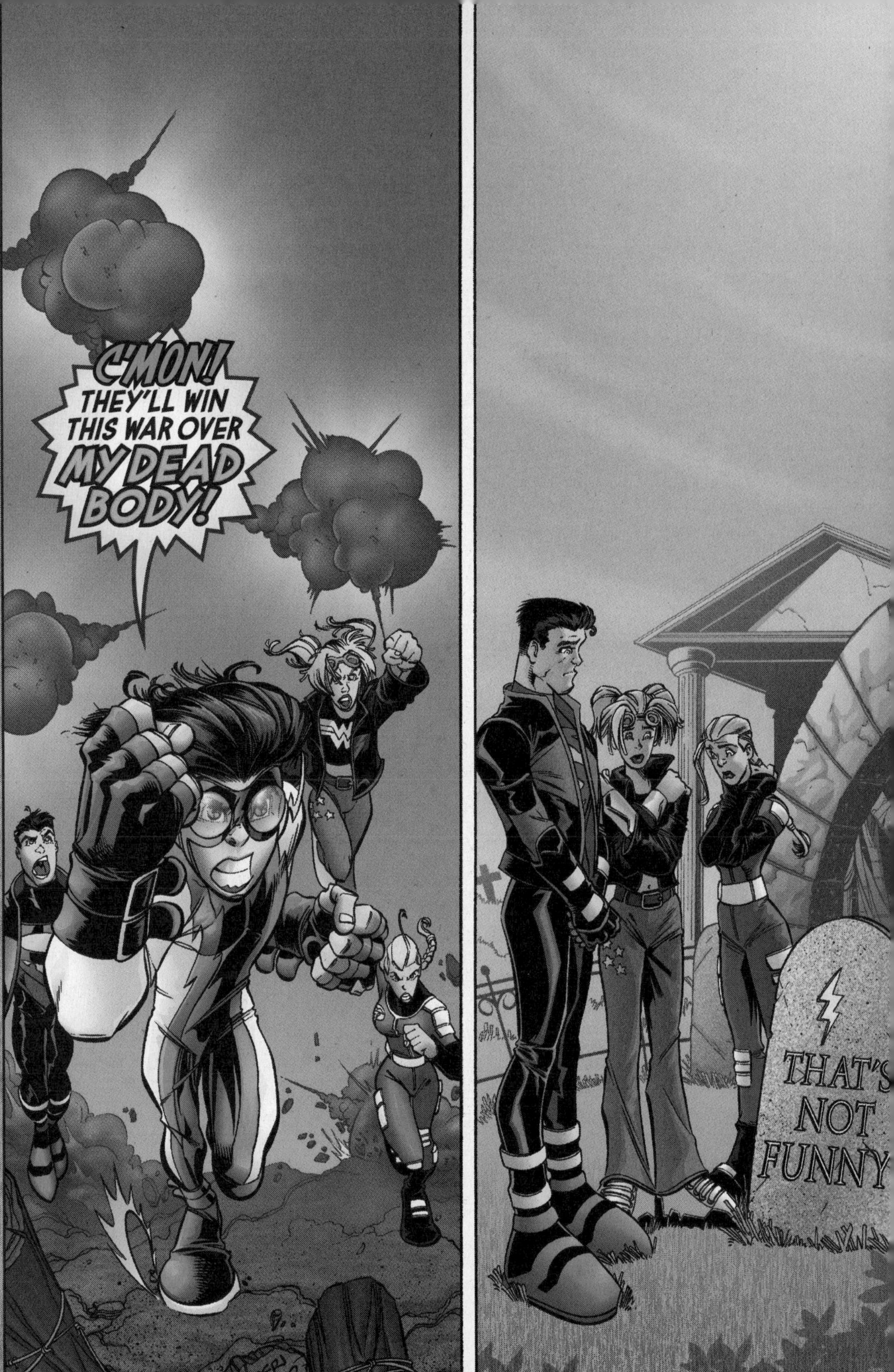
C'MON! THEY'LL WIN THIS WAR OVER MY DEAD BODY!
THAT'S NOT FUNNY

COVER BY CARLO BARBERI & WAYNE FAUCHER

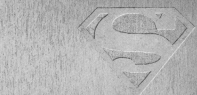

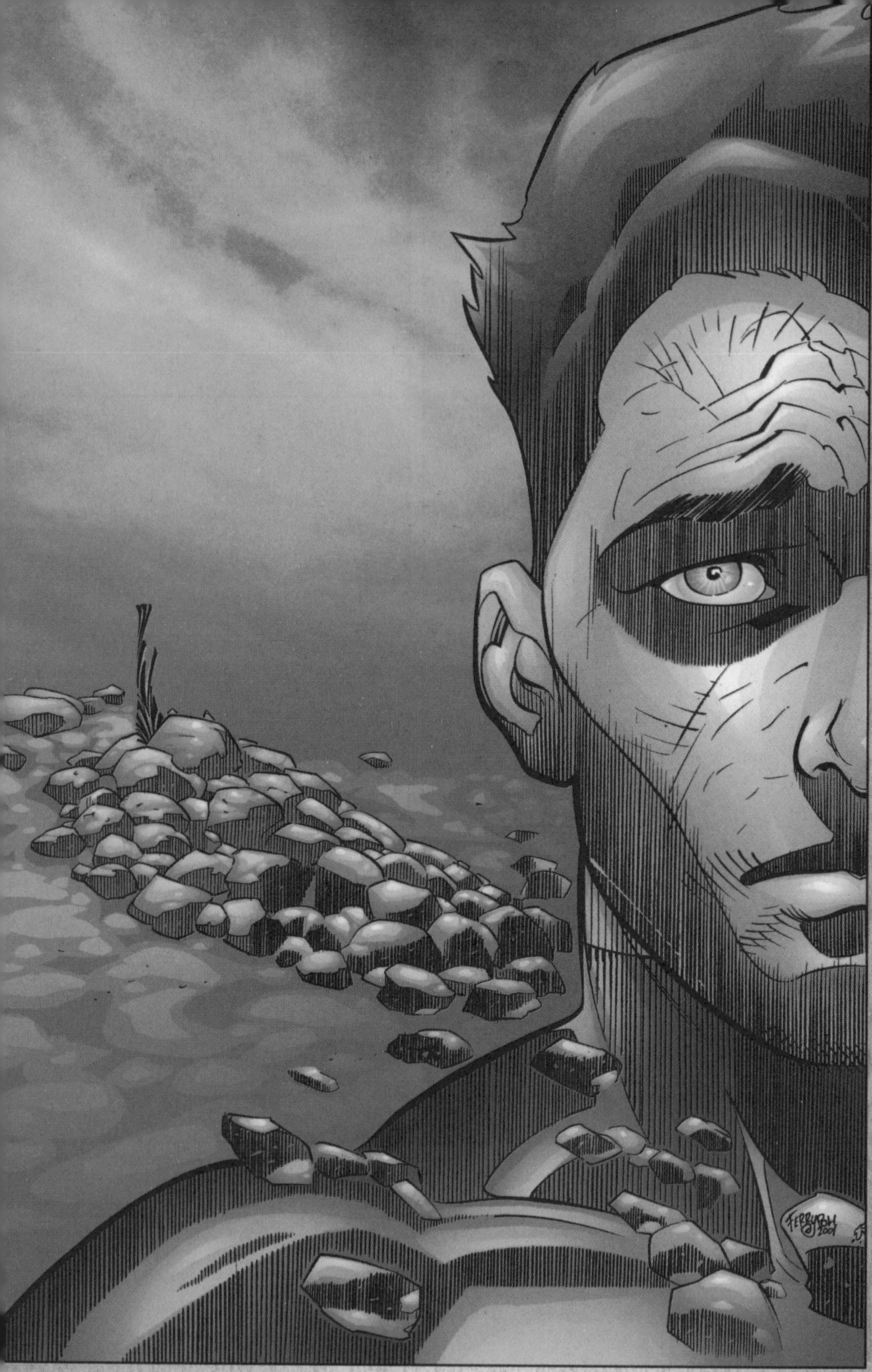

COVER BY PASCUAL FERRY & KEITH CHAMPAGNE

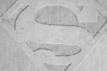

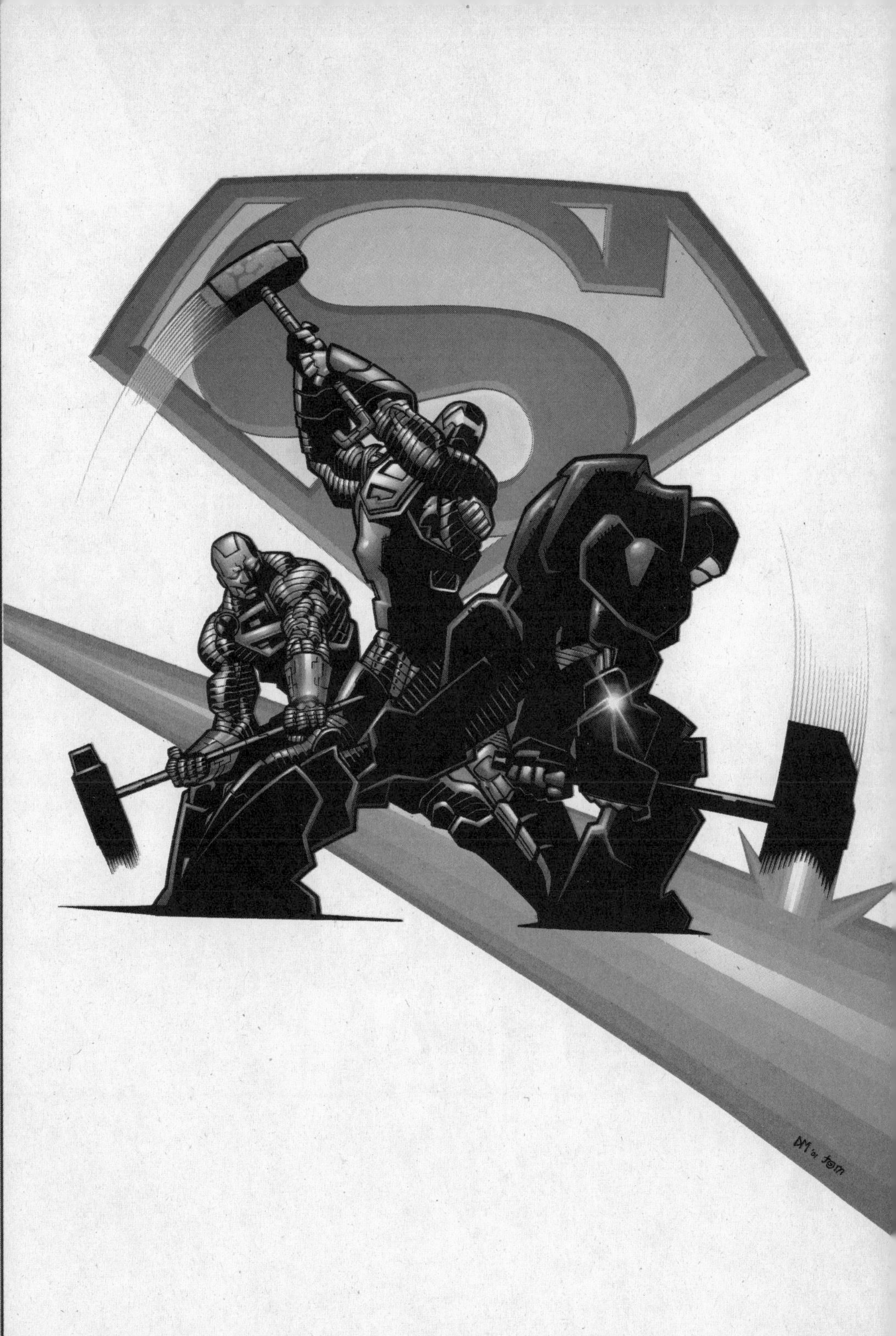

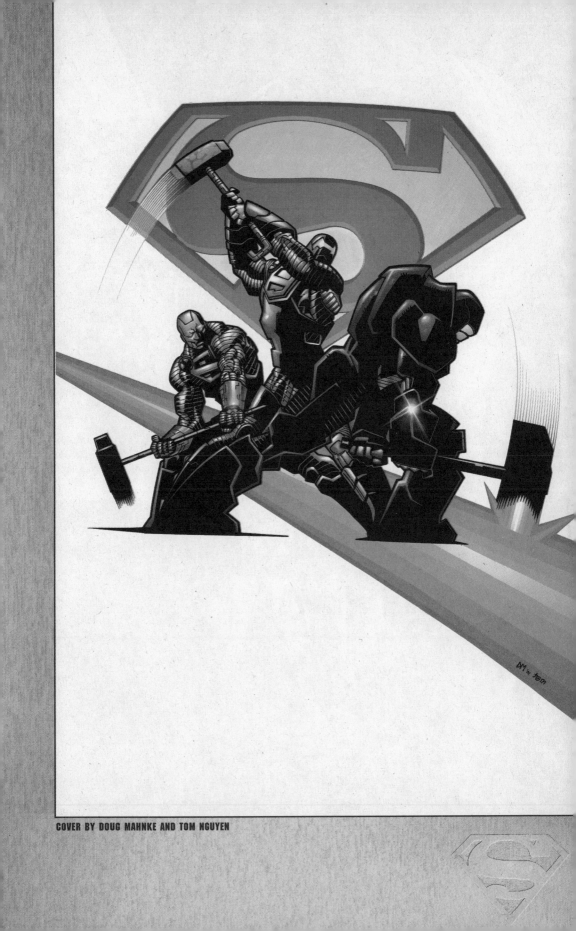

COVER BY DOUG MAHNKE AND TOM NGUYEN

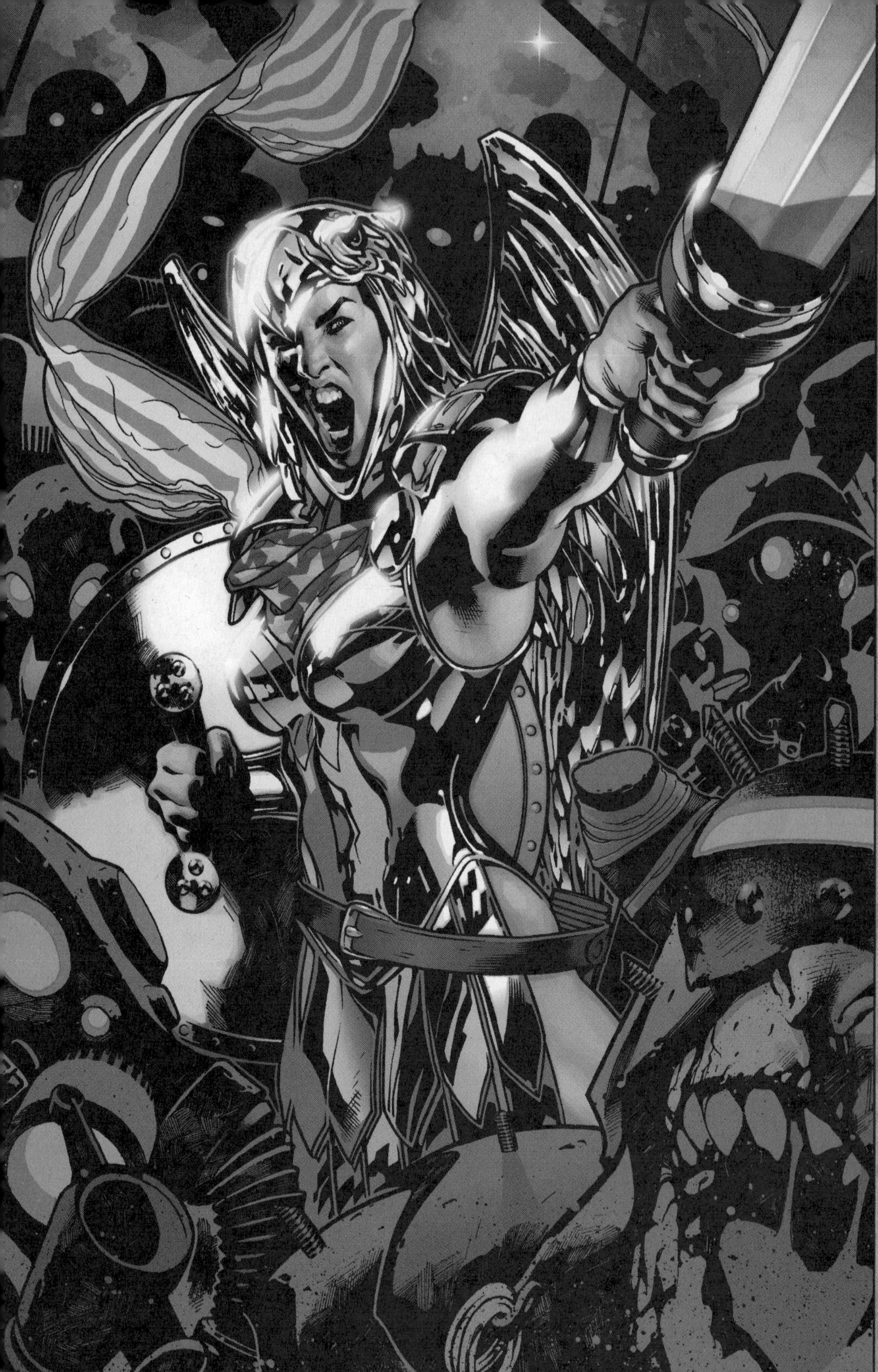
COVER BY ADAM HUGHES

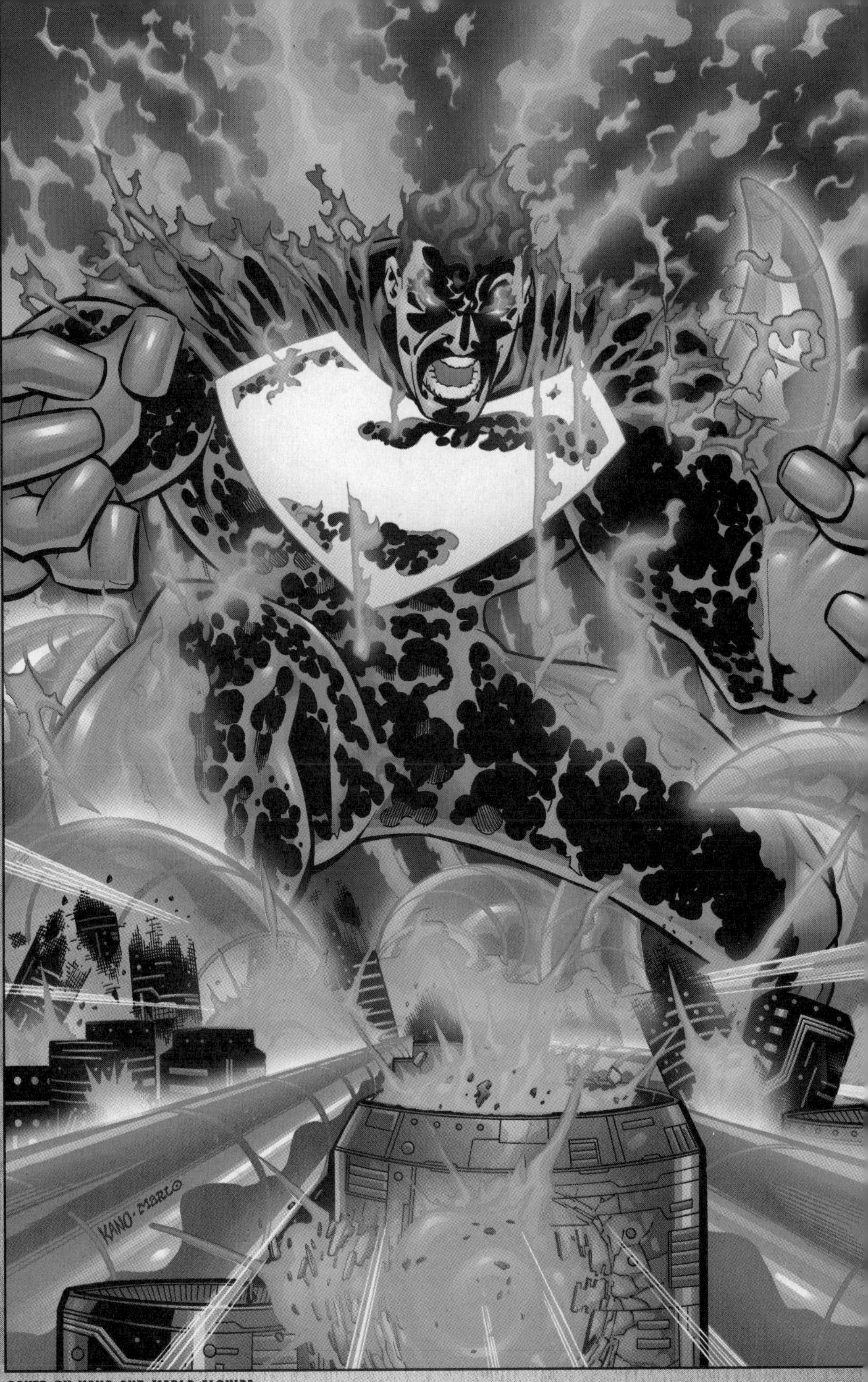
KANO · MARLO

COVER BY KANO AND MARLO ALQUIZA

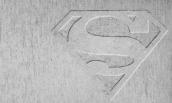

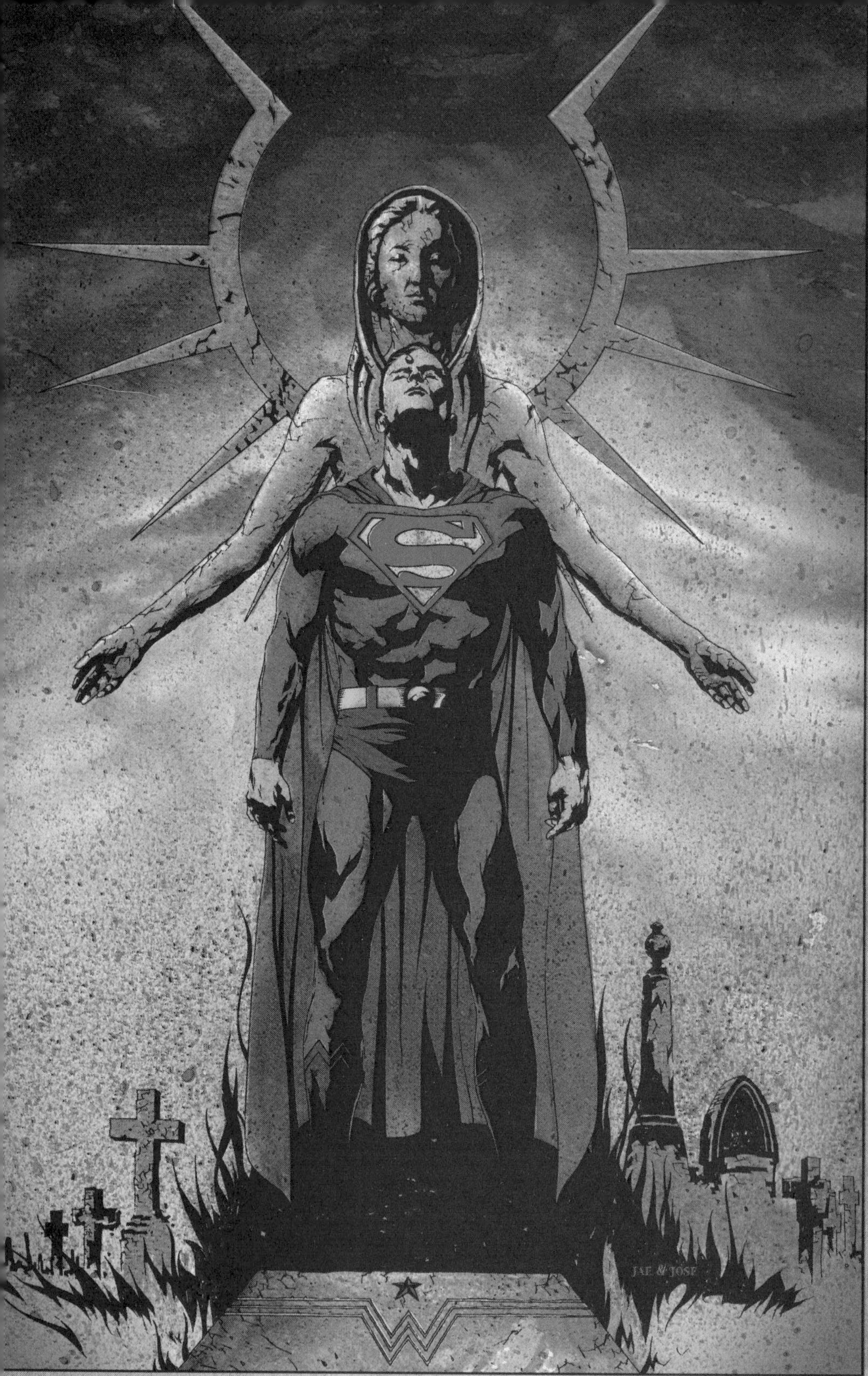
JAE & JOSÉ

COVER BY JAE LEE

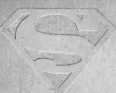

THE ART OF WAR

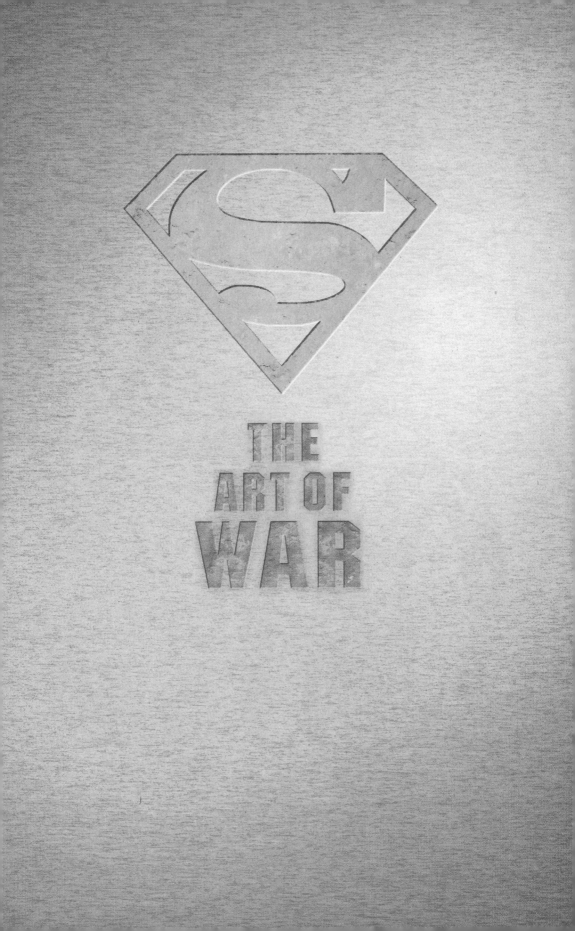

BLACKHAWKS

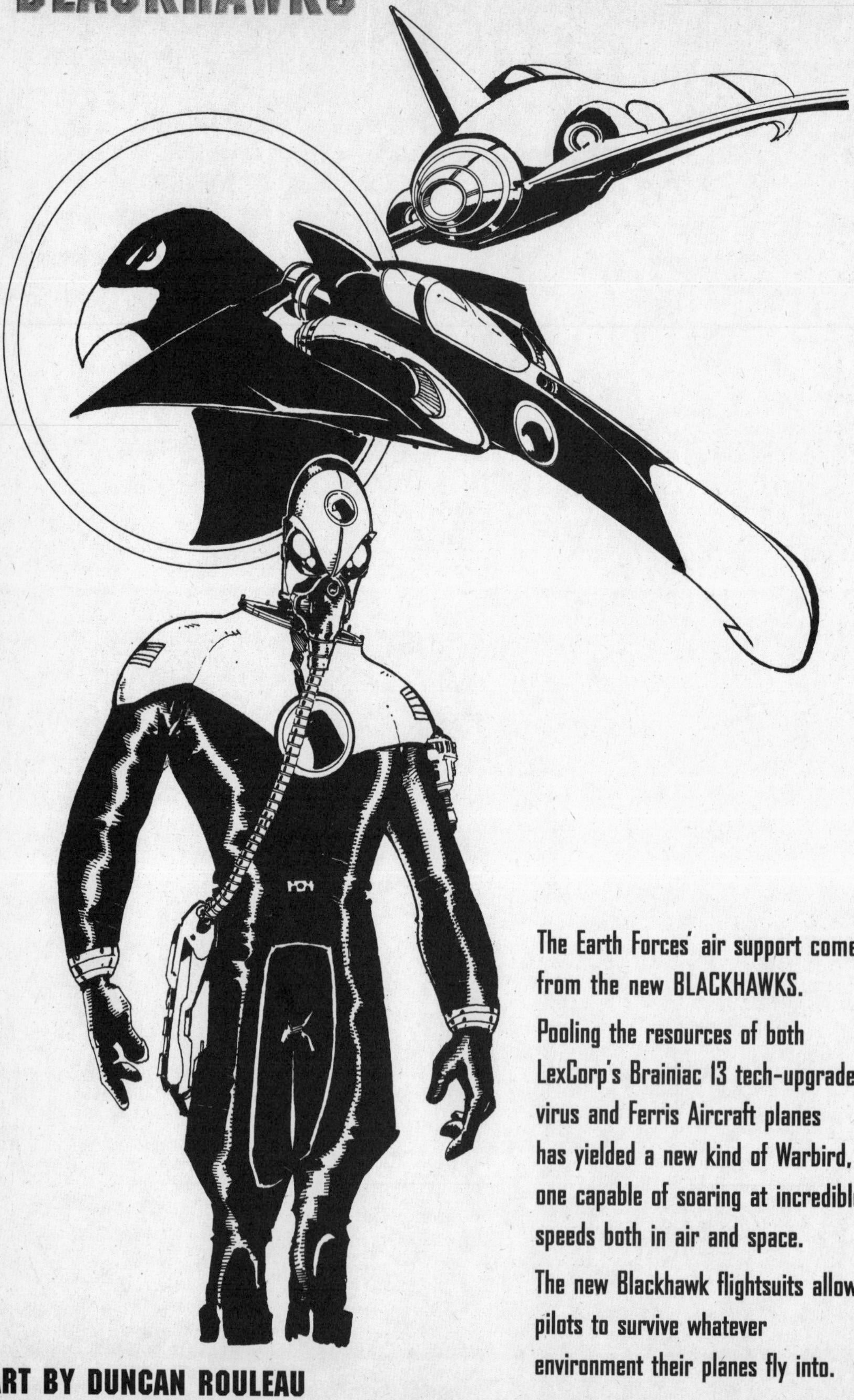

The Earth Forces' air support comes from the new BLACKHAWKS.

Pooling the resources of both LexCorp's Brainiac 13 tech-upgrade virus and Ferris Aircraft planes has yielded a new kind of Warbird, one capable of soaring at incredible speeds both in air and space.

The new Blackhawk flightsuits allow pilots to survive whatever environment their planes fly into.

ART BY DUNCAN ROULEAU

THE NEST

The planes are deployed from "THE NEST," a specially equipped aircraft carrier capable of space travel. It can hold up to five planes.

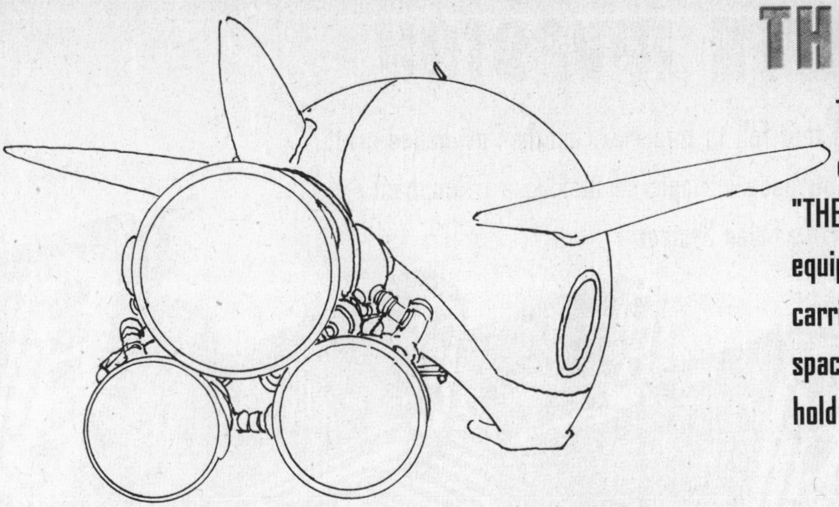

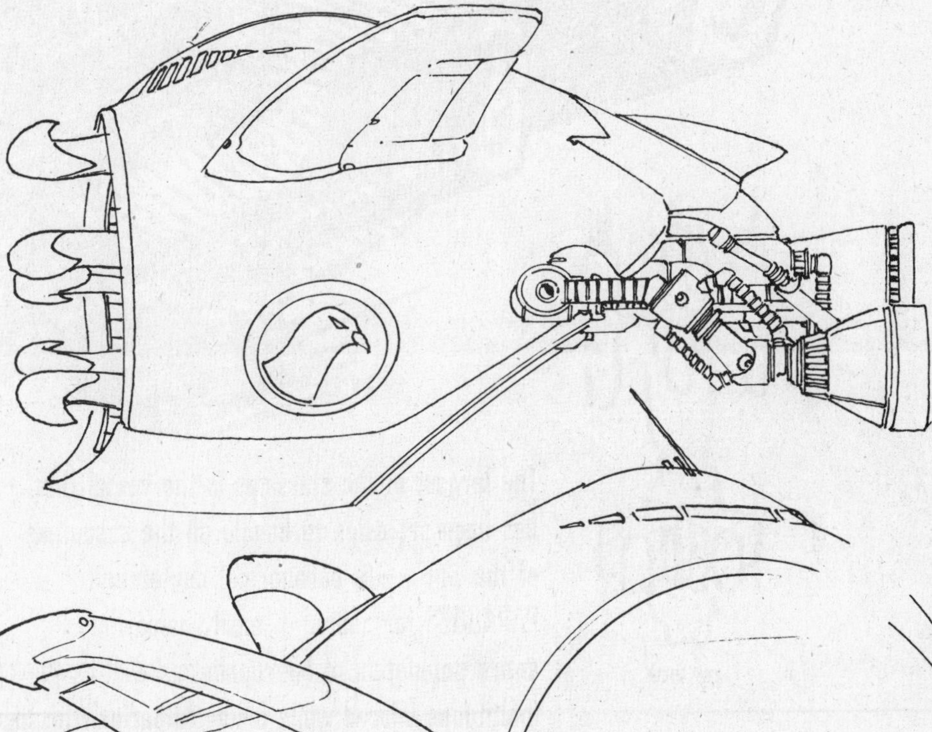

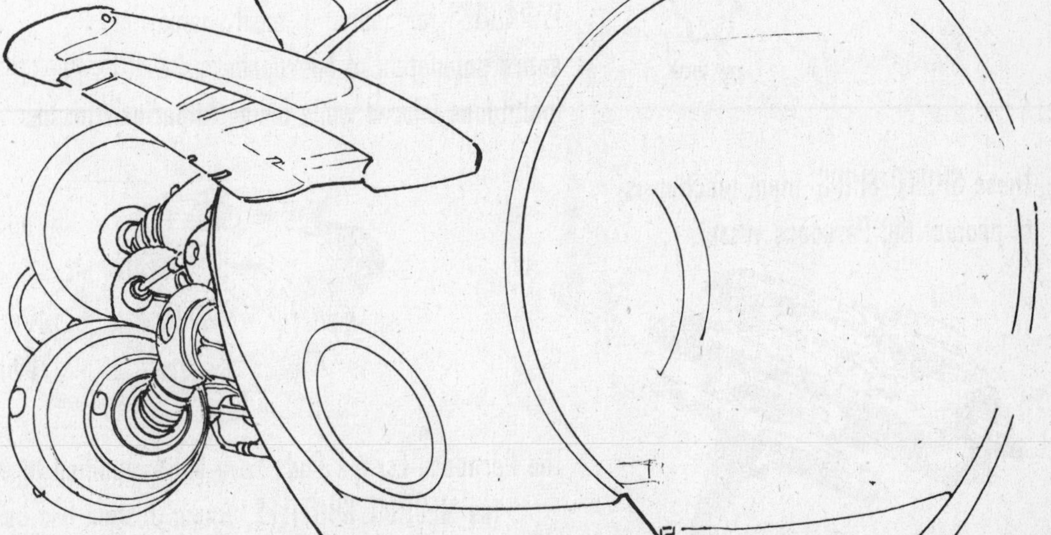

THE ALIEN INVASION

With each world that fell to Imperiex, another orphaned craft joined the Alien Armada in hopes of making a triumphant last stand in Earth's Solar System.

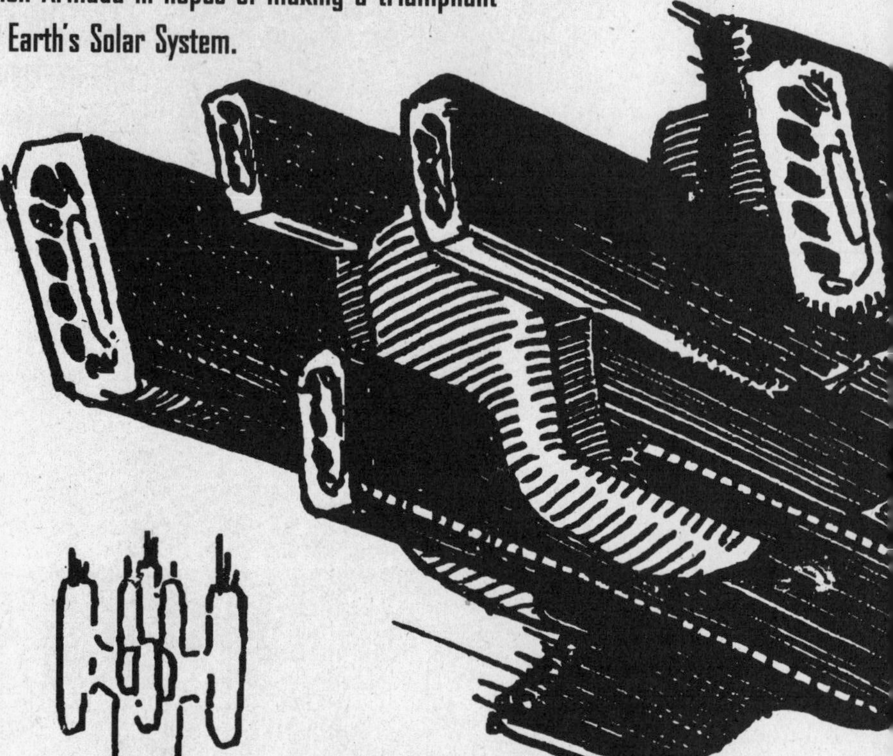

TOP VIEW

The largest of the starships is the vessel that has been set aside to handle all the casualties of the war — a paranormal doctor unit: PARADOCS for short. It easily holds the entire population of Metropolis, as well as the multitudes injured while facing Imperiex's probes.

These SHIELD SHIPS' main function is to protect the Paradocs vessel.

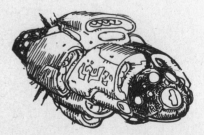

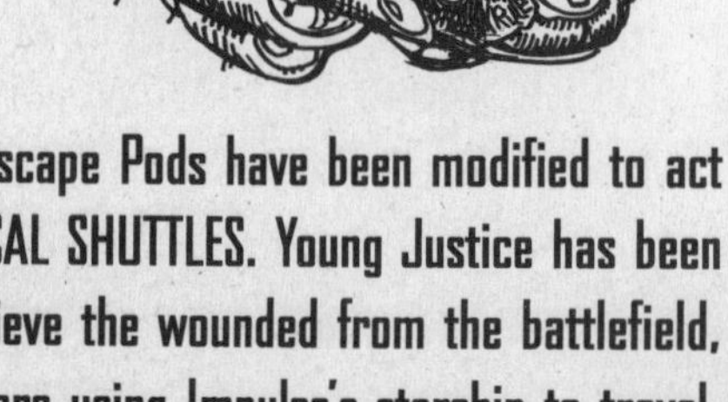

The Paradocs Escape Pods have been modified to act as MEDICAL SHUTTLES. Young Justice has been enlisted to retrieve the wounded from the battlefield, but they are using Impulse's starship to travel.

ART BY DOUG MAHNKE

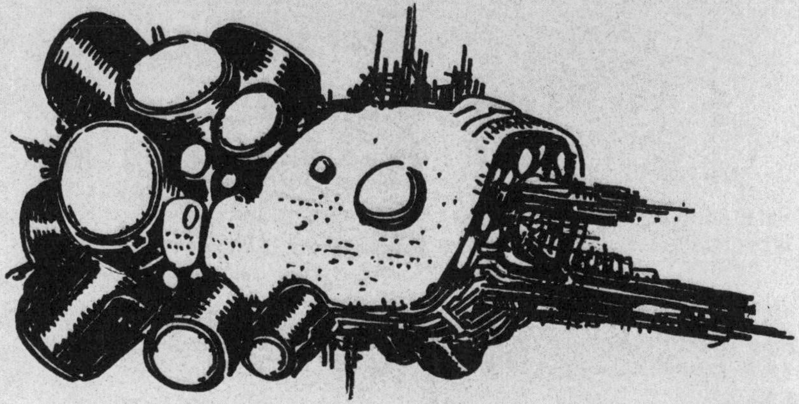

A Khund warship, now modified with Almerac and Rann technology, acts as the FLAGSHIP of the Alien Alliance.

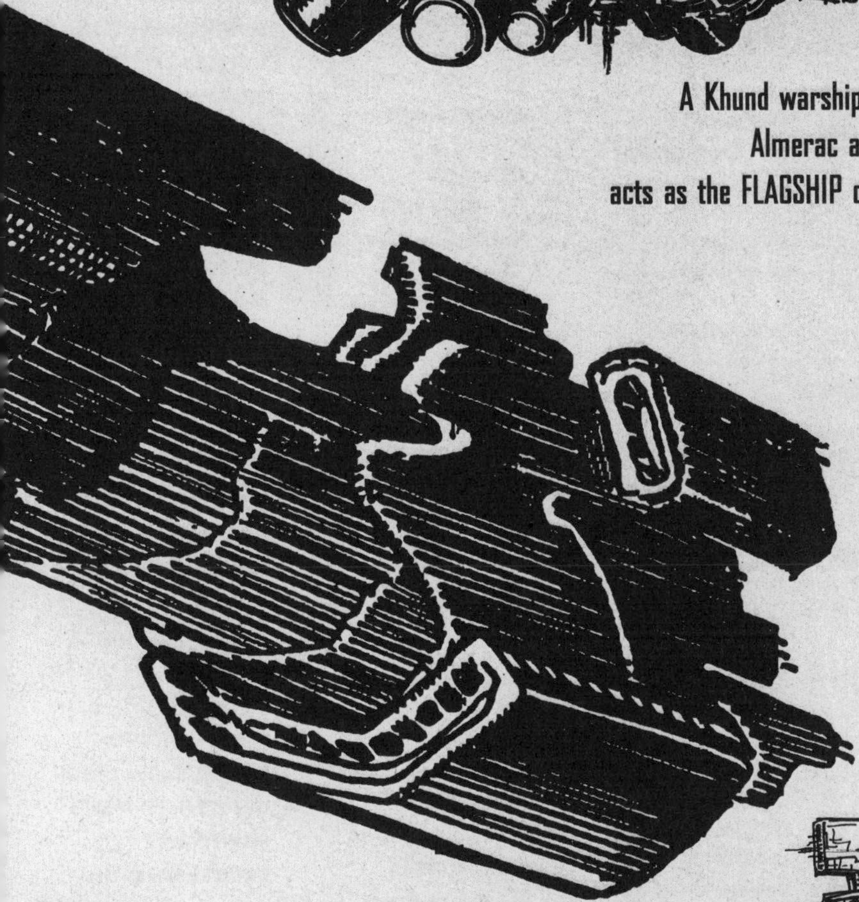

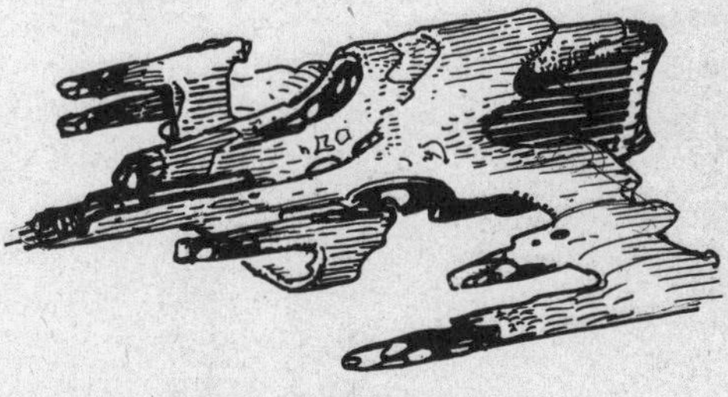

SNUB FIGHTERS are two-passenger attack craft. Ironically, this is a Dominator design that wasn't ready in time for the last invasion of Earth.

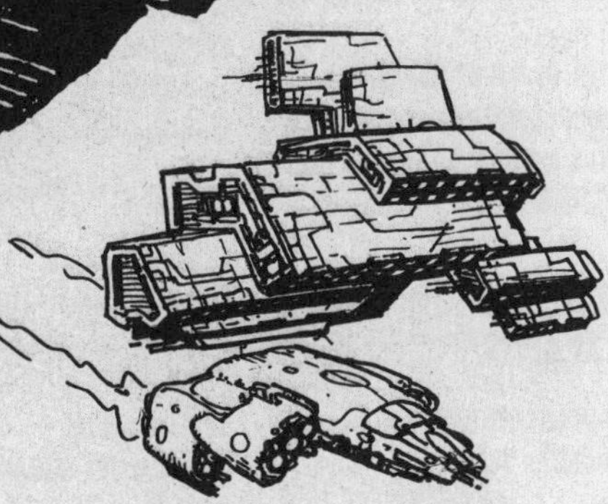

Providing the heavy artillery are these SPACE TANKS of Khundian and Daxamite design. Not only do they carry powerful plasma weaponry, but their heavy plating also allows them to be used to ram into an opponent.

SUPERMAN

THE NEVER-ENDING BATTLE CONTINUES IN THESE BOOKS FROM DC COMICS:

TO FIND MORE COLLECTED EDITIONS AND MONTHLY COMIC BOOKS FROM DC COMICS,
CALL 1-888-COMIC BOOK FOR THE NEAREST COMICS SHOP
OR GO TO YOUR LOCAL BOOK STORE.

9424006

Visit us at www.dccomics.com

SM0011